European Review
of Social Psychology

European Review of Social Psychology

Editorial Board

About the editors

Wolfgang Stroebe has published widely on the topics of attitudes, group processes and health psychology. A former president of the European Association of Experimental Social Psychology and a fellow of the British Psychological Society, the Society for the Psychological Study of Social Issues, and the Society of Personality and Social Psychology, he has recently received an honorary doctorate from the University of Louvain. Having held academic positions in England, USA and Germany he is currently Professor of Social, Organizational and Health Psychology at the University of Utrecht (The Netherlands).

Miles Hewstone has published widely on the topics of social cognition and intergroup relations. He was awarded the British Psychological Society's Spearman Medal in 1987 and its Presidents' Award for Distinguished Contributions to Research in 2001. He was a Fellow at the Center for Advanced Study in the Behavioral Sciences, Stanford, California from 1987–1988 and 1999–2000, and is an Academician of the Academy of Learned Societies in the Social Sciences, and a Fellow of the British Academy. He is Professor of Social Psychology and Fellow of New College, University of Oxford.

European Review
of Social Psychology

Volume 20

Edited by

Wolfgang Stroebe
Utrecht University, The Netherlands

and

Miles Hewstone
Oxford University, UK

Psychology Press
Taylor & Francis Group
HOVE AND NEW YORK

First published in 2009 by Psychology Press
27 Church Road, Hove, East Sussex, BN3 2FA

http://www.psypress.co.uk

Simultaneously published in the USA and Canada
by Psychology Press
270 Madison Avenue, New York, NY 10016

Psychology Press is part of the Taylor & Francis Group, an Informa business

British Library Cataloguing in Publication Data
A catalogue record for this book is available from the British Library

ISBN 13: 978-1-84872-735-9 (hbk)
IBSN 13: 978-1-84872-736-6 (pbk)
ISSN 1046-3283

Cover design by Jim Wilkie
Typeset by KnowledgeWorks Global Limited, Chennai, India
Printed and bound in the UK by TJ International Ltd, Padstow
The publication has been produced with paper manufactured to strict
environmental standards and with pulp derived from sustainable forests.

Contents

List of contributors

Henk Aarts, *Utrecht University, Department of Psychology, PO BOX 80140, Utrecht, TC 3508, The Netherlands*

Mark Alicke, *Department of Psychology, Ohio University, 229 Porter Hall, Athens, OH 45701, USA*

Anthony Bishara, *Department of Psychology, 66 George St, College of Charleston, Charleston, SC 29424, USA*

Pablo Briñol, *Department of Psychology, Universidad Autónoma de Madrid, Campus de Cantoblanco, Carretera de Colmenar, Km. 15, Madrid, 28049, Spain*

Ruud Custers, *Department of Social and Organizational Psychology, Utrecht University, Heidelberglaan 1, 3584 CS Utrecht, The Netherlands*

Mark Dechesne, *Leiden University - Campus The Hague, P.O. Box 13228 2501 EE The Hague, The Netherlands*

Ayelet Fishbach, *The University of Chicago, Booth School of Business, 5807 S. Woodlawn Ave, Chicago, IL 60637, USA*

Lasana Harris, *Department of Psychology, New York University, 6 Washington Place, New York, NY 10003, USA*

Courtney Ignarri, *Department of Psychology, Lehigh University, 17 Memorial Drive East, Bethlehem, PA 18015-3068, USA*

Minjung Koo, *Humanities and Social Sciences Campus, Sungkyunkwan University, 53 Myeongnyun-dong, 3-ga, Jongno-gu, Seoul, 110–745, Korea*

Arie Kruglanski, *Department of Psychology, University of Maryland, College Park, MD 20742, USA*

Gordon Moskowitz, *Department of Psychology, Lehigh University, 17 Memorial Drive East, Bethlehem, PA 18015-3068, USA*

Edward Orehek, *Department of Psychology, University of Maryland, College Park, MD 20742, USA.*

Keith Payne, *Department of Psychology, Campus Box 3270, University of North Carolina, Chapel Hill, Chapel Hill, NC 27599, USA*

Richard Petty, *The Ohio State University, 1835 Neil Avenue, Columbus, Ohio 43210–1222, USA*

Kirsten Ruys, *Department of Psychology, Utrecht University, PO Box 80140, Utrecht, 3508 TC, The Netherlands*

Constantine Sedikides, *Center for Research on Self and Identity, School of Psychology, University of Southampton, Southampton, SO17 1BJ, UK*

Diederik Stapel, *Tilburg University, Department of Social Psychology, PO Box 90153, Tilburg, 5000 LE, The Netherlands*

Martijn Veltkamp, *Faculty of Behavioural Sciences, University of Twente Drienerlolaan 5, 7500 AE Enschede, The Netherlands*

Ying Zhang, *The University of Texas at Austin, 1 University Station C0500, Austin, TX 78712-0233, USA*

Acknowledgments

We would like to thank the following reviewers who helped us, and the authors, to shape these articles into their final versions:

Henk Aarts
Roy Baumeister
Herbert Bless
Ruud Custers
Naomi Ellemers
Klaus Fiedler
Jens Förster
Malte Friese
Bertram Gawronski
Bettina Hannover
Nick Haslam
Wilhelm Hofmann
Ursula Kessels
Jaques-Philippe Leyens
Antony Manstead
Esther Papies
Brian Parkinson
Mike Ross
Maria Ruz
Fritz Strack
Alberto Voci
Henk Aarts
Roy Baumeister
Herbert Bless
Ruud Custers
Naomi Ellemers
Klaus Fiedler
Jens Förster
Malte Friese
Bertram Gawronski
Bettina Hannover
Nick Haslam
Wilhelm Hofmann
Ursula Kessels
Jaques-Philippe Leyens
Antony Manstead

Preface

The *European Review of Social Psychology* (ERSP) is an international journal which aims to further the exchange of ideas by providing an outlet for substantial accounts of theoretical and empirical work. The discipline of social psychology is an international endeavour and this fact underpinned our decision, from the outset, to make the *European Review of Social Psychology* an international review that published outstanding work of authors from all nations rather than restricting it to Europeans. We are 'Europeans', rather, in the nationality of our editors, and that like our sister journal, the *European Journal of Social Psychology*, we are published under the auspices of the European Association of Social Psychology (EASP).

The emphasis of the contributions we publish in ERSP is on substantial individual programmes of research as well as on topics and initiatives of contemporary interest and originality. When articles review individual research programs, it is expected that the primary research on which they are based has resulted in four to five articles which have been published (or accepted for publication) in leading peer-reviewed journals of our discipline.

All articles published by the *European Review*, whether commissioned by the editors or spontaneously submitted by authors, are externally reviewed and publication is subject to a positive outcome of the review process. In making their decisions, the editors are assisted by an international editorial board consisting of senior scholars as well as by *ad hoc* reviewers. Thanks to the quality of the authors as well as of the editorial process the *European Review* has become internationally renowned and widely cited.

Originally an annual series, the *European Review of Social Psychology* was launched in 2003 as an 'e-first journal'. Each chapter is published electronically as soon as the editorial process has been completed; this procedure not only considerably reduces the publication lag, but it also allows libraries to subscribe to the European Review, rather than having to order volume by volume via standing orders. A further advantage of being a journal is that we are now accessed by all important abstracting and indexing services, such as *Current Contents/Social and Behavioral Sciences (CC/S&BS); PsycINFO; Social Sciences Citation Index (SSCI);*

Social Scisearch. However, subscribers (and among them the more than 1000 members and foreign affiliates of the EASP) will not have to do without the familiar blue volumes, because at the end of the year the set of chapters for that year is published as a printed volume, as we have done now for 20 years.

Wolfgang Stroebe
Miles Hewstone

EUROPEAN REVIEW OF SOCIAL PSYCHOLOGY
2009, 20, 1–48

Self-enhancement and self-protection: What they are and what they do

Mark D. Alicke

Ohio University, Athens, OH, USA

Constantine Sedikides

University of Southampton, UK

We define self-enhancement and self-protection as interests that individuals have in advancing one or more self-domains or defending against negative self-views. We review ways in which people pursue self-enhancement and self-protection, discuss the role of these motivational constructs in scientific explanations, argue for their importance in maintaining psychological and physical well-being, and consider the conditions in which they are likely to operate. At various points, we address the perennial "cognition–motivation" debate. We argue that, despite the conceptual and practical difficulties that attend this distinction, the pervasiveness of the self-enhancement and self-protection motives makes it impossible and imprudent to ignore them in explaining self-related findings and theories.

People pursue pleasurable experiences and avoid unpleasant ones. This tenet comes in many flavours, including the law of effect, unconditioned reinforcement, the pleasure principle, biological readiness, minimisation–mobilisation, and minmax decision strategies. Whichever terminology one prefers, it is psychology's most fundamental and immutable behavioural law that people seek to maximise their positive experiences and minimise their negative ones.

This hedonism principle lies at the heart of motivational psychology. Throughout its history, culminating in the behavioural psychology that ruled the roost in the 1950s, psychologists have theorised about the conditions that instigate, maintain, and energise behaviour. Motivational constructs are intervening variables (Reeve, 1997) designed to account for the fact that, with the same stimulus conditions, even animals low on the

Correspondence should be addressed to Mark D. Alicke, Department of Psychology, Ohio University, 229 Porter Hall, Athens, Ohio 45701, USA. E-mail: alicke@ohio.edu

http://www.psypress.com/ersp   DOI: 10.1080/10463280802613866

(increasingly controversial) phylogenetic scale can behave differently. The issue of response variability in the face of identical environmental conditions reaches its apex in accounting for the behaviour of humans, which is driven by diverse motives such as the needs for achievement (Atkinson & Raynor, 1974), social approval (Marlowe & Crowne, 1961), and stimulation (Sales, 1971).

The focus of this chapter is on a particular brand of motivated behaviour, namely the tendency for people to exaggerate their virtues and to minimise their shortcomings, as well as to construe or remember events in a way that places their attributes in the most favourable light that is credible to oneself and others (Alicke & Govorun, 2005; Sedikides & Gregg, 2003, 2008). We refer to these motives as self-enhancement and self-protection. Although many non-motivational factors contribute to the tendency to view oneself more positively, or less negatively, than objective circumstances warrant, we concentrate on the purposive strategies that people pursue to explain or remember their decisions, actions, and characteristics in a way that maintains or advances their desired self-views.

Despite the ubiquity of the self-enhancement and self-protection constructs, these terms have been treated loosely in the literature. Although demonstrations of self-enhancement and self-protection abound, it is unclear what the various behaviours and judgements that reflect these motives have in common, what they aim to accomplish, how and when they are deployed, and how they influence identity and psychological or physical health, as well as social relations. In this chapter we define self-enhancement and self-protection as interests that people have in advancing one or more self-components or defending themselves against negative self-views. We explore the ways in which people pursue self-enhancement and self-protection, discuss the role of these motivational constructs in scientific explanations, argue for their importance, and consider their scope and functionality. At various points, we weigh in on the perennial "cognition–motivation" debate. We argue that, despite the practical difficulties that attend this distinction and notwithstanding some of the unfortunate ways in which it has been construed, the prevalence and importance of motivational phenomena makes it impossible and imprudent to legislate the distinction out of existence and to underestimate the role of self-enhancement and self-protection.

We begin with a short introduction to the emergence of self-enhancement and self-protection themes in social psychology. We then describe self-enhancement and self-protection as instrumental in maintaining, promoting, or safeguarding pivotal interests, and consider the relation between these interests and the ways in which they are regulated. We next discuss the relation between self-enhancement and self-protection, and examine their standing as scientific constructs. We conclude by considering the relevance of self-enhancement and self-protection to psychological theories.

A BRIEF HISTORY OF SELF-ENHANCEMENT AND SELF-PROTECTION MOTIVES IN SOCIAL PSYCHOLOGY

The emergence

Motivational constructs hark back to social psychology's inception, beginning with Triplett's (1897) groundbreaking study, which demonstrated the motivational advantages of riding bicycles in the presence of other people as opposed to solitary time trials. Although the importance of self-enhancement and self-protection motives was widely recognised—by William James (1890), for example, in his discussion of "self-seeking" which promoted vanity and pride, and later by Gordon Allport's (1937) in his view of ego-protection as "nature's eldest law"—the empirical study of these motives awaited a greater emphasis on theory development in social psychology.

The impetus for such theory was provided by Kurt Lewin and his students at the Massachusetts Institute of Technology following the Second World War. Lewin's field theory (1935, 1936), from which many prominent social-psychological research programmes derived, was avowedly dynamic in nature. Lewin's example was the forerunner of influential motivational formulations such as Festinger's cognitive dissonance theory (1957) and Heider's (1958) balance theory. In the late 1950s the needs to maintain cognitive consistency or balance were the foundation for the central motivational theories in social psychology.

By the late 1960s dynamic motivational explanations, primarily in the guise of cognitive dissonance theory, were so ingrained in social psychology that they were virtually unchallenged. Cognitive dissonance theory assumed that post-decisional attitude change reduced the cognitive tension that attitude-discrepant behaviour evoked. The first volley in what came to be known as the "cognition–motivation" debate was fired by Bem (1967) in his self-perception reinterpretation of cognitive dissonance phenomena. Bem argued that people evaluate their internal states (e.g., beliefs, attitudes, traits, intentions) by reviewing their behaviour and the reinforcement conditions that control their actions. When the incentives for behaviour are insufficient to explain it, people assume that it must have issued from a positive attitude or intention. Thus, when a participant in a cognitive dissonance experiment performs a behaviour for a paltry reward, the participant assumes that he or she endorses the behaviour. No motivational assumptions about the need to reduce cognitive tension are required.

After almost four decades of relevant research it is fair to assert that the motivational assumptions of cognitive dissonance theory have been vindicated (Aronson, 1992; Cooper, 2007; Elliot & Devine, 1994). For its part, self-perception theory (Bem, 1972) became an integral component of the burgeoning attributional movement of the 1960s and 1970s. Bem's non-motivational perspective was consistent with earlier and later formulations, which modelled social perception on a "person as scientist" metaphor (Heider, 1958; Kelley, 1967). The aptness of this metaphor was soon questioned, however, when initial tests of Kelley's attributional model by McArthur (1972) showed that people deviated substantially from the model's normative expectations, especially in their neglect of consensus information. More importantly, the dozens of studies that Weiner's (1972) attributional analysis of achievement motivation inspired revealed a tendency for actors to attribute their successful outcomes to internal factors such as ability and effort, and their unsuccessful outcomes to external factors such as bad luck and task difficulty. Despite thorny conceptual problems (e.g., ability, effort, task difficulty, and luck are neither independent nor easily classified as "internal" or "external"), as well as mixed empirical findings (Zuckerman, 1979), this research programme, referred to as "attributional egotism" or the "self-serving bias," became the first major instalment of self-enhancement/self-protection theories in social psychology.

The counterpoint

But no sooner was attributional egotism introduced than it was subjected to a full-frontal assault by Miller and Ross (1975). These authors proposed various non-motivational explanations for the self-serving bias, the most compelling being that people expect success more frequently than failure and make internal attributions for expected outcomes. Although this view was immediately challenged (Weary, 1979; Weary Bradley, 1978), and the weight of the subsequent evidence strongly supported a motivational interpretation of the self-serving bias (Campbell & Sedikides, 1999; Mezulis, Abramson, Hyde, & Hankin, 2004; Roese & Olson, 2007; Sedikides, Campbell, Reeder, & Elliot, 2002a), expectancies provide an alternative to several self-enhancement and self-protection phenomena. We will return to the role of expectancies in self-enhancement and self-protection motives in subsequent sections.

Motivational constructs were briefly submerged with the ascendance of social cognition as the dominant perspective in social psychology in the late 1970s. The initial wave of social cognition research emphasised person memory. Many of the early studies in this area were based on associative network models and computer metaphors, and made no reference to goal-directed behaviour of any sort, whether motivational or non-motivational (Sedikides, Campbell, Reeder, Elliot, & Gregg, 2002b). Given the prevalence of motivational assumptions and explanations throughout social psychology's history, it was only a matter of time until motivational processes insinuated their way back into the fold. Social cognition researchers began to distinguish between "cold" and "hot" cognitive processes, the latter referring to thoughts and judgements that were influenced by "affect". Interestingly, and perhaps ironically, the interplay between affective and cognitive responses has been one of the most researched topics in the whole social cognition enterprise (Forgas, 2001, 2006; Sedikides, 1995).

A resolution

Miller and Ross's (1975) landmark analysis of the self-serving bias, including their non-motivational interpretations of these effects, ignited a wave of attempts to re-establish motivational explanations on a more solid footing. As we noted above, these efforts were largely successful but only after extensive evidence was amassed and considerable controversy had ensued. Frustration with distinguishing between motivational and non-motivational explanations led to questioning whether it was even possible to make this distinction effectively (Tetlock & Levi, 1982).

Insightful and influential work on lay epistemology (Kruglanski, 1989) and on the interplay between motivational biases and cognitive processes (Kunda, 1990; Pyszczynski & Greenberg, 1987) showed how motivational and non-motivational processes could coexist in explaining various psychological phenomena and helped to overcome the tendency to treat cognitive and motivational processes as mutually exclusive. These articles elucidated motivated biases of various types by describing the cognitive processes by which they exerted their influence, and made clear that complete explanations of social behaviour required both of these elements.

In short, self-enhancement and self-protection motives are so fundamental to the way researchers view identity and social relations that it was, and is, virtually impossible to dispense with explanations that incorporate these motives. In fact, such explanations have waxed rather than waned since the days of the self-serving bias controversies. Although the caricatures that once prevailed of people as either coldly rational information processors or self-aggrandising fools have been laid to rest, conceptual confusion about the meaning of self-enhancement and self-protection motives, and their proper sphere of explanation, abounds. Our goal is to provide a framework for these motives that will help to elucidate their meaning and highlight areas in which further empirical clarification is needed.

SELF-ENHANCEMENT AND SELF-PROTECTION IN REGULATING INTERESTS

Primary and secondary control

We preface our analysis of self-enhancement and self-protection with reference to the distinction between primary and secondary control

(Rothbaum, Weisz, & Snyder, 1982). Primary control refers to changing an objective state of affairs by taking effective or instrumental action, whereas secondary control substitutes psychological mechanisms that control events by altering how one perceives or interprets them. Self-enhancement and self-protection are straightforward and non-controversial when considered from the standpoint of primary control. In this capacity, self-enhancement entails instrumental action designed to promote oneself and one's prospects, whereas successful self-protective measures obviate falling below one's standards.

It is with regard to secondary control that issues become more exciting and contentious. When people cannot promote themselves objectively, they have recourse to construal mechanisms such as reinterpreting the meaning of social or task feedback, misremembering or reconstructing events in a self-serving way, and making excuses for poor behaviour or performance. Primary and secondary control efforts are often related, such as when a person relies on the amount of effort he has exerted towards a goal (primary control) as a means to exaggerate how close he has come to accomplishing it (secondary control). We concentrate in this article primarily on such secondary control processes, although we contrast secondary with primary control at various junctures.

Psychological needs as interests

Our analysis of self-enhancement and self-protection relies on the concept of interests as they have been discussed in jurisprudence (Feinberg, 1984) and social and political philosophy (Nozick, 1974; Rawls, 1971). Whereas the law is perforce concerned with ways in which interests can be harmed, we extend the analysis of interests to include benefits (i.e., ways in which interests can be advanced) as well as harms (i.e., ways in which interests can be regressed or thwarted). We focus exclusively on psychological interests to explicate the varieties and complexities of self-enhancement and self-protection strivings.

Psychological interests include security/love, social status, and popularity, as well as the possession of high skill levels and capacities (e.g., intelligence, athleticism, musicality). To say that people have interests is to assume that they will exert primary or secondary control to advance or protect them. A person with an interest in being popular, for example, will either work to increase her or his popularity (primary control) or engage in mental machinations such as misperceiving or misremembering events, or construing comparisons with other people, in a way that achieves the same goal (secondary control). We assume that people resort to secondary control when primary control efforts fail, when they lack confidence that such efforts will succeed, or when such efforts are too onerous to sustain.

Interests can be relatively specific (e.g., to perform well on a test) or general (e.g., to be a good student). Interests entail purely private concerns (e.g., to meet one's personal standards) as well as concerns with public perceptions. Interests also extend to close others and to ingroups, whose life circumstances or outcomes influence one's psychological or physical health. Finally, interests can be either positive or negative. The former include things that people wish to possess or attain (corresponding to approach motives), whereas the latter include things that people wish to circumvent or shun (corresponding to avoidance motives). The same interest can be cast in either a positive frame (e.g., a desire to be viewed as assertive) or a negative frame (e.g., a desire to avoid being seen as unassertive).

Hierarchical network of interests

Interests can be classified in terms of five levels. Each level from the bottom up represents an increasing degree of abstraction or generality. Global self-esteem resides at the top of the hierarchy: All self-enhancement and self-protection processes are geared towards maintaining the most favourable conception of self and positive affect that reality constraints will comfortably allow.

The next highest level includes such interests as security/love, social status, power/effectance, and psychological or physical health. These are "ulterior" interests that virtually all people share to some degree. Thus, global self-esteem, and ulterior interests, are relevant to virtually all experiences that bear on the well-being of the self.

The mid-level features such interests as being popular, respected, affluent, possessing high skill levels, and having successful relationships. These subordinate interests are activated in specific domains of experience. An interest in being popular is evoked, for example, in social situations, whereas an interest in financial gain is activated in situations that are relevant to wealth accumulation. The lower level entails event-specific interests. These subserve one or more superordinate interests and are aroused by individual events or experiences. Criticism from a friend, for example, is relevant to immediate interests such as avoiding a misunderstanding or resolving a dispute. Explaining oneself to the friend may serve higher-order interests such as maintaining one's relationships and reputation, which in turn serves the ulterior interest of psychological health.

Interests comprise a hierarchical network. For example, a low-level interest (e.g., to perform well on a class presentation) might subserve higher-level interests (e.g., to impress a dating partner, to be competitive for a PhD application, to please one's parents). Figure 1 depicts a hypothetical network of interests. Interest networks are connected both horizontally and vertically. At the lowest level of the vertical hierarchy are specific

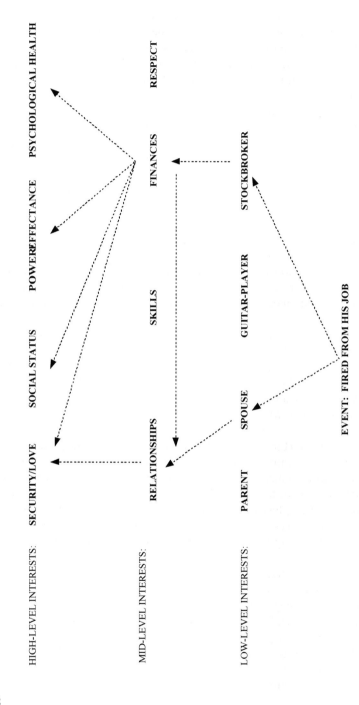

Figure 1. A hypothetical network of interests.

behavioural events or outcomes such as receiving praise from a colleague, purchasing a new car, or obtaining a salary increase. These are the ordinary or everyday concerns about which people spend most of their time thinking and towards which they direct primary control efforts. In the example of Figure 1, the behavioural event is a person being fired from his job.

The first level of abstraction in this example pertains to interests in self-views, only some of which are relevant to the event of being fired. The man's perception of himself as a good spouse and a successful stockbroker are both affected by the loss of his job, whereas his views of himself as a good parent and a competent guitar player are unaffected. At the next level, both his interest in maintaining successful relationships and in being financially secure are threatened. In this example, each of his ulterior interests (security, social status, effectance, and physical health) is influenced by the loss of his job.

Vertical and horizontal connections can be either facilitative or inhibitory. In the case of a facilitative connection, an event that serves one interest simultaneously benefits another, such as when the receipt of a prestigious award serves the interests of public recognition and financial gain. Facilitative connections among interests aid self-enhancement by conferring benefits in multiple self-concept domains. Inhibitory connections, on the other hand, hinder self-enhancement because the value conferred by satisfying one interest impedes the progress of a competing one. For example, receiving a desired promotion, which fulfils one's financial interests, might interfere with an interest in a harmonious family life.

A diversified interest network aids in the pursuit of self-enhancement and self-protection. People whose interests are grouped into a small number of categories have fewer options when events conspire to threaten their cherished self-views (Linville, 1985). For example, a person whose self-concept is predominantly based on an interest in material wealth might possess insufficient resources to combat an extreme financial setback. When interests are diversified, however, a setback in one category can be at least partially offset by emphasising or altering a self-view in another. Thus, a person who experiences a severe financial setback may compensate by highlighting or elevating his perceptions of himself as a good husband and father.

The strength of associations among horizontally oriented and vertically oriented interests in the hierarchy can foster or impede self-enhancement and self-protection, depending on whether an experience is positive or negative and the associations are facilitative or inhibitory. When an event reflects favourably on a particular interest, facilitative vertical connections translate the event into positive, higher-level characteristics. For example, successfully learning to play a piece of music on the guitar may lead to feelings of musical competence, and then to more general conceptions of being a competent person. Inhibitory connections primarily serve self-protection functions; in particular, to avoid the spread of negative events throughout the self-system. However, when strong inhibitory connections are formed, they can have the unwanted effect of preventing the spread of positive experiences. For example, a person who habitually and assiduously avoids translating negative social feedback from peers into higher-level personality characteristics may become so practised at inhibiting these behaviour–trait connections that she or he fails to do so for positive feedback.

Continuing the previous example for horizontal connections, the same feelings of musical competence may lead to feeling skilled at other artistic endeavours and thereby advance interests in those related areas. We refer to such facilitative connections as "horizontal spread". Again, inhibitory connections prevent the spread of positive experiences. People with highly compartmentalised self-systems (McConnell & Strain, 2007; Showers, 1992) may routinely confine their experiences to one interest area and therefore fail to experience the benefits of relating positive experiences to other interest categories.

When it comes to negative events, facilitative vertical and horizontal connections are detrimental. Failing an important exam may make a person feel bad at the material the course covers and then spill over into more general feelings of incompetence (vertical direction). Similarly, feeling incompetent in the material a course covers can lead to feelings of incompetence in other areas (horizontal direction). One of the main functions of self-protection processes is to prevent these negative consequences of vertical and horizontal connections in interest networks. As noted above, inhibitory connections are enlisted in this service such that a negative event in one interest area shuts down related areas to which the implications of the negative event might apply. For example, receiving negative feedback about one's loyalty from a friend could easily affect interests in related social categories such as trustworthiness or kindness (horizontal connections) as well as higher-level interests in being a popular or even a good person (vertical connections). Inhibitory connections are an important aspect of mental health in that they confine negative experiences to the interest categories to which they most directly pertain.

Interest levels

As Figure 2 depicts, we conceive each subordinate interest to contain an *aspiration level*, which represents an individual's ideal level of functioning, a *perceived level*, which represents where the person believes that he or she currently stands with respect to that interest, an *objective level*, which represents where the person actually stands, and a *tolerance level*, below

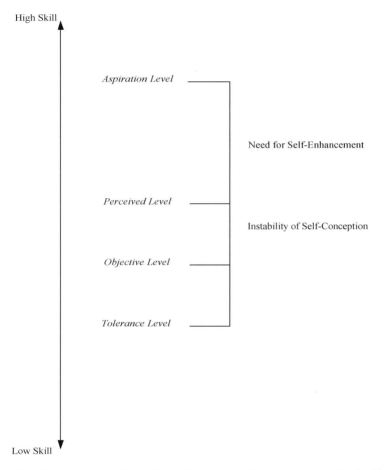

Figure 2. An example of basketball skill with aspiration level, perceived level, objective level, and tolerance.

which the person is motivated to engage primary or secondary control mechanisms to advance back toward the aspiration point.

Interests can be advanced, regressed, reversed, or maintained at their current level by specific events and outcomes (Alicke, LoSchiavo, Zerbst, & Zhang, 1997). For example, a person with an interest in viewing herself as a chess expert can have this interest advanced by winning a chess tournament (primary control). Alternatively, the same person might advance her interest by playing an inferior opponent and exaggerating the opponent's ability (secondary control). Examples of declining interests abound: in essence, any form of task or social feedback that threatens to move a perceived characteristic away from the aspiration point represents a regression in an interest level.

An example of an interest reversal is represented by a husband who, while advancing his interest in being a good parent, receives criticism from his wife. In this example, the husband experiences a reversal of an interest that had been advancing. Going in the opposite direction, a student whose interest in seeing herself as a good mathematician had been declining due to poor course performance may have this interest level reversed by a high maths score on a national standardised examination. Interests can also change in their rate of acceleration towards or away from the aspiration point. However, if interests advance too slowly, or in a way that suggests that the aspiration level is unattainable, secondary control may be engaged even when primary control efforts are ostensibly successful. A student who falls behind his peers due to failure on several medical school exams may conclude that the medical profession is rather dull and tedious and thus not worth pursuing (the *sour grapes effect*; Kay, Jimenez, & Jost, 2002; Wilson, Wheatley, Kurtz, Dunn, & Gilbert, 2004).

The distance between the perceived level of a characteristic and the aspiration level, along with the centrality of the characteristic, determines the need for self-enhancement. In general, primary and secondary control are engaged more vigorously for characteristics that are farther from the aspiration point. The strength of such processes is increased for central (as opposed to peripheral) characteristics; that is, for characteristics on which people stake their self-esteem (Crocker & Wolfe, 2001).

The distance between the perceived level and the objective level defines the instability of self-conceptions. A moral hypocrite, for example, who proclaims exemplary behavioural standards but whose actual behaviour contradicts these proclamations, faces an uphill battle to maintain her illusions. Whereas discrepancies between perceived and aspired levels pose quandaries about how to attain one's goals, large discrepancies between perceived and objective levels threaten one's ability to test reality. Maintaining a desired belief in the face of objective disconfirmation taxes self-enhancement or self-protection efforts, perhaps because it impairs resources used for self-control (Vohs, Baumeister, & Ciarocco, 2005).

Self-enhancement, self-protection, and interest networks

Within this framework of increasing and declining interests, self-enhancement can be viewed as a self-maintenance mechanism that strives to preserve one's perceived level of functioning or to move it closer to the aspiration level. This function can be achieved either through primary or secondary control processes. With all other things being equal, primary control is preferable to secondary control. However, the need for secondary control arises when people cannot approximate their aspiration levels by primary control alone. Nevertheless, reasonable progress towards the aspiration level via primary control makes secondary control processes easier to engage and defend. A person who is actually becoming more considerate, for example, can exaggerate his or her standing on this trait more easily than one who is making no discernible progress towards the aspired level. Secondary control includes construal and memory mechanisms that are designed to exaggerate the favourability of an event or characteristic, or to minimise its negativity. When these mechanisms fail, another possibility is to reduce the aspiration level so that a lower level of functioning on the characteristic becomes tolerable.

The constructs in which people are chronically invested (i.e., in which they have important interests) typically represent compromises between their objective level of functioning and their aspirations. The primary way in which self-enhancement maintains these superordinate interests is by defining self-constructs at an abstract level (Liberman, Trope, & Stephan, 2007). In this way, self-enhancement strivings are protected against objectively poor behavioural outcomes by the difficulty of contradicting abstract self-conceptions. Even if a student performs poorly in her university degree, her perception of herself as an "intelligent" person remains unaffected due to the absence of critical tests for the trait "intelligent". When behavioural adjustments occur, they represent relatively minor tweaks to the data such as according undue weight to positive outcomes that are non-diagnostic of intelligence and according too little weight to highly diagnostic information. Even lowering the aspiration level is often a subtle adjustment rather than blatant self-deception.

Self-enhancement is also served by factoring projected selves (Markus & Nurius, 1986) into self-definitional equations. In this way people may reason that, while they do not presently exhibit much ambition, they will undoubtedly be prodigious in the future. Along these same lines, people harbour fantasies and aspirations that are hidden from others and that may also contribute to their elevated self-conceptions (Klinger, 1990; Oettingen, 1996; Sedikides, Rudich, Gregg, Kumashiro, & Rusbult, 2004b). Finally, selecting situations that encourage success and discourage failure (e.g., the "hometown hero" who never ventures into more competitive waters), or selecting peers who provide predominantly positive feedback, are other common ways of satisfying superordinate or subordinate interests and furthering self-enhancement. In general, therefore, the work that self-enhancement does on experiential data is routine and undramatic. Furthermore, when interests are objectively advanced or maintained at an acceptable level, there is very little need to invoke secondary control processes.

Self-protection is, by contrast, an emergency system that operates when interests are threatened by a possible decline in a self-component below the tolerance point. Put simply, self-protection is a form of damage control. The difference between self-enhancement and self-protection can be likened to the difference between the parasympathetic and sympathetic functions of the autonomic nervous system. The parasympathetic system is responsible for regulating ordinary processes of respiration and digestion. Analogously, self-enhancement regulates the superordinate needs to feel good and to view oneself positively by making slight adjustments in response to environmental disturbances. The sympathetic component of the autonomic system, on the other hand, is an arousal system that marshals the body's defences to counteract environmental challenges or threats. Likewise, self-protective processes are evoked when environmental feedback threatens to reduce an interest below the tolerance point.

Self-protection can also be evoked by a failure of interests to advance sufficiently. A common self-protective mechanism is to assume that unacceptable present circumstances will improve in the future. People who are in financial difficulty, for example, might dream of winning the lottery and deflect current difficulties with the vague assumption of future riches. Mid-life identity crises occur, in part, due to the recognition that the "tomorrow" so long awaited has arrived with no discernible advancement in interests. Self-protective mechanisms, therefore, are more elaborate, dramatic, and difficult to maintain than self-enhancing ones. Consistent with this assumption, the tendency to view one's traits more favourably than others' (representing high-level interests) is greater when considering negative characteristics than when considering positive ones (Alicke & Govorun, 2005).

Whereas self-enhancement strategies typically represent only a minor discrepancy between perceived and objective self-components, self-protective processes sometimes require considerable distortion in order to raise the self back towards the aspiration point, or to prevent further slippage. When an aspiring poet, for example, is rejected by virtually every publication outlet, his continued belief in his superior skill may require extreme measures such as denigrating the whole enterprise of modern poetry. Reality constraints make such self-protective processes difficult to maintain. The success of other poets, the relative transparency of the system, and the continued rejection of one's own works necessitates unusual creativity to maintain the desired self-conception.

Relation between self-enhancement and self-protection

Although self-enhancement and self-protection are sometimes treated as polar ends of a single dimension, our analysis of interests, and empirical evidence as well, suggests that they should be treated separately (Elliot &

Mapes, 2005; Sedikides & Gregg, 2008). In our account, self-enhancement is a routine function that operates to maintain interests in reasonable and defensible proximity to their aspiration levels. Self-protective mechanisms are evoked when an event, or series of events, threatens to decline an interest below the tolerance level, or when high-level interests fail to advance as anticipated.

Explicating the relation between self-enhancement and self-protection is complicated by the fact that some psychological theories and phenomena primarily involve one of these motives, some entail both, and in some instances, self-protective efforts further self-enhancement goals (Sedikides & Green, in press; Sedikides & Luke, 2007; Sedikides & Strube, 1997). For example, individuals are relatively open to negative feedback (Kumashiro & Sedikides, 2005) or remember it well (Green, Sedikides, Pinter, & Van Tongeren, in press) when such openness or efficient memory enables future task performance or good interpersonal relationships. In this case, immediate self-protection concerns relax to make room for long-term self-enhancement gains. In practice it is sometimes difficult to distinguish unequivocally among these possibilities due to the absence of baseline measures to indicate perceived and objective levels of functioning with regard to an interest, or to indicate assessments of aspiration and tolerance levels. It is possible, however, to characterise approximately the relevant literature according to whether a phenomenon is most likely to involve self-enhancement, self-protection, or both.

Examples of self-enhancement primarily entail mid-level or high-level interests such as thinking about oneself in positive global trait terms (e.g., power/effectance). A prominent case is the better-than-average effect: people rate themselves more favourably than an average peer on most trait dimensions (Alicke, 1985; Alicke, Klotz, Breitenbecher, Yurak, & Vredenburg, 1995; Sedikides, Gaertner, & Toguchi, 2003). Although various non-motivational mechanisms contribute to the better-than-average effect (Chambers & Windschitl, 2004; Heine & Hamamura, 2007), the effect is at least partly due to the desire to maintain a favourable self-view (Alicke & Govorun, 2005; Alicke, Vredenburg, Hiatt, & Govorun, 2001; Gaertner, Sedikides, & Chang, 2008). Indeed, people do truly believe they are above average (Williams & Gilovich, 2008).

Self-protection has been aroused in legions of social-psychological studies in which important interests (such as to be intelligent) are threatened in order to assess the effects on various aspects of behaviour or judgement (Beauregard & Dunning, 1998; Buckingham & Alicke, 2002; Green & Sedikides, 2004; Guenther & Alicke, 2008). For the most part, the behavioural and attributional strategies that emerge serve to avoid decrements in self-views rather than to promote one's standing on a dimension (Baumeister, Bratslavsky, Finkenauer, & Vohs, 2001). Students who are told that they are in the 20th percentile on a novel intelligence test, for example, are more likely to find ways to avoid reducing their beliefs in their intelligence than they are to find ways of increasing them.

The self-serving bias (Campbell & Sedikides, 1999; Mezulis et al., 2004) reflects both self-enhancement and self-protection. This phenomenon entails taking more credit than one deserves for positive outcomes (i.e., self-enhancement), as well as failing to accept adequate responsibility for negative outcomes (i.e., self-protection). Striving to enhance the value of positive outcomes serves self-enhancement, whereas striving to deflect blame for negative outcomes serves self-protection, assuming that the negative outcome or feedback threatens to reduce an interest below tolerance.

Instances in which self-protective mechanisms end up serving self-enhancement have long been recognised by psychologists, most notably in the guise of the Freudian defence mechanisms (A. Freud, 1936/1946; S. Freud, 1926/1961c). In current social psychology, terror-management theory (TMT) provides a cogent example. According to TMT, people marshal various resources to deflect anxiety-arousing thoughts about their mortality. In this respect, TMT falls squarely into the self-protection camp. However, many of the terror management strategies that people deploy have self-enhancing consequences, such as bolstering self-esteem, fostering interpersonal relationships, promoting ingroup solidarity, supporting cultural institutions, and even motivating the creation of enduring artworks (Arndt, Routledge, Greenberg, & Sheldon, 2005; Castano, Yzerbyt, & Paladino, 2004; Mikulincer, Florian, & Hirschberger, 2003). In fact, in its most recent incarnations (Landau, Greenberg, Solomon, Pyszczynski, & Martens, 2006; Pyszczynski, Greenberg, & Goldenberg, 2003; Pyszczynski, Greenberg, Solomon, Arndt, & Schimel, 2004), TMT focuses as much on the positive or self-enhancing implications of existential anxiety as on its harmful or destructive consequences.

In this regard, protection against existential anxiety is similar to many of the Freudian defence mechanisms, which are also purported to have self-enhancing consequences. Reaction formation, for example, presumably enables people with moral shortcomings to view themselves as paragons of morality (Baumeister, Dale, & Sommer, 1998). Similarly, projection can create an illusion of superiority by transferring a person's own negative qualities onto others (Schimel, Greenberg, & Martens, 2003).

Just as defence mechanisms against anxiety and unfavourable self-views can transmute self-protection into positive high-level interests, so self-enhancement can serve self-protection interests. Narcissism is a case in point. When threatened with negative performance feedback, narcissists defend themselves through such self-enhancing strategies as displaying the self-serving bias even when the slighted co-worker is a friend (Campbell, Reeder, Sedikides, & Elliot, 2000), or derogating and punishing critics

(Bushman & Baumeister, 1998) in a presumed effort to regain control (DeWall, Baumeister, Stillman, & Gailliot, 2007).

Practical difficulties sometimes obfuscate the distinction between self-enhancement and self-protection. A person who exaggerates her contribution to a group effort may do so protectively (e.g., to avoid looking bad) or enhancingly (e.g., to convince herself and others that she has been underestimated). Furthermore, people are often unaware of which goals they are pursuing. Similarly, people may engage in wishful or fanciful thinking (e.g., imagining inherited wealth) in order to pull themselves out of their financial doldrums (self-protection) or to elevate their standing on the relevant self-domain (e.g., prosperity) (self-enhancement).

What kind of explanations do self-enhancement/self-protection interpretations provide?

In this section we clarify four specific points about self-enhancement and self-protection as explanatory mechanisms that have sometimes been obscured in the literature. First, virtually all interesting psychological phenomena are multiply determined. Self-enhancement and self-protection, therefore, never provide complete accounts of behaviour or judgement. To include self-enhancement and self-protection in explanations is to argue that these motives are necessary components of a behaviour or judgement. For example, it may be impossible to understand why a man who is continually rejected by women persists in viewing himself as a Lothario without recognising the importance of this identity-image in his self-concept. In this case, self-enhancement and self-protection are necessary components of the explanation.

Second, it is critical to reiterate that self-enhancement and self-protection are very specific types of motives. To say that a behaviour was motivated is not necessarily to claim that self-enhancement or self-protection was involved. Self-enhancement and self-protection motives are invoked when investigators wish to claim that behaviour was impelled by the desire to elevate self-regard or to avoid reducing it. In this sense, the "cognition versus motivation" distinction that has pervaded the psychological literature can be misleading. All purposive behaviour is motivated or else people would do nothing at all. Similarly, all non-reflexive behaviour involves cognitive processes. The crucial question, therefore, is whether the self-enhancement/self-protection motives increase the predictive and explanatory power of the phenomenon under investigation or whether it is possible to account for an effect without reference to these motives. The primary advantage of non-motivational explanations is parsimony: If a phenomenon can be explained solely in terms of cognitive processes, then that is one less set of variables to account for.

The parsimony claim can be deceiving, however. Explanations that suffice outside the social realm are often inadequate when applied to social behaviour and judgement. Stereotyping provides a prominent example. As a form of categorisation, stereotyping is a natural outgrowth of the non-motivated tendency to distinguish among classes of objects. In fact, early social-cognitive treatments of stereotyping emphasised this categorisation explanation (Brewer, 1988; Hamilton & Trolier, 1986; Rothbart & John, 1985). However, while it is important to recognise that the natural tendency to categorise makes some form of stereotyping inevitable, it is probably true that relatively few instances of placing people in pernicious social categories can be explained purely by this propensity, and current views recognise that stereotyping can also reflect motives such as defensive projection (Govorun, Fuegen, & Payne, 2006). Again, in our view, the most complete explanations for social behaviour and judgement are likely to involve both the reasons that spurred the event (although these reasons will not always entail self-enhancement or self-protection) and the cognitive processes involved.

Third, self-enhancement and self-protection can be achieved without any motive to enhance or maintain self-views. As Miller and Ross (1975) noted, expectancies provide one non-motivational explanation for such effects: People simply expect to do well and align their perceptions with these expectancies. Even when expectancies suffice, however, they may inadvertently serve self-enhancement. A person who blames others for his misfortunes rather than himself because he (non-motivationally) expects that others are more likely to be at fault, winds up accruing the same self-benefits as one whose implicit or explicit motive is to feel better about herself. Biased memories are an even more potent source of non-motivational self-enhancement and self-protection. When people work on collaborative tasks, for example, their own inputs are naturally more salient (Harris, 2007). Thus it is important to distinguish between self-enhancement and self-protection as processes that are motivated by the desire to promote or protect a self-image, and between self-enhancement and self-protection that are achieved as offshoots of non-motivated processes (Gramzow & Willard, 2006). The former are purposeful, whereas the latter are inadvertent.

Fourth, invoking self-enhancement or self-protection explanations for an event does not imply that these motives are universally linked to such events. For example, the claim that a person denied responsibility for a bad decision in order to avoid self-blame does not entail that all such denials reflect motivated processes. Similarly, claims for motivated self-enhancement and self-protection do not exclude the possibility that other motivational and non-motivational mechanisms operate simultaneously.

WHAT KINDS OF MOTIVES ARE
SELF-ENHANCEMENT AND SELF-PROTECTION?

Although we view the cognition–motivation distinction as a useful heuristic for highlighting different aspects of psychological explanation, the distinction is sometimes obscured by a failure to analyse carefully the properties of self-enhancement and self-protection motives. We therefore begin this section by examining the sense in which judgements and actions reflecting self-enhancement and self-protection can be said to be biased or in error, and clarify the distinction between bias and error. Subsequently we examine the conscious or unconscious nature of these motives and consider the aims towards which they are directed. This is followed by a consideration of whether and to what extent people engage in self-deception when their actions and judgements are characterised by self-enhancement or self-protection.

Relation to error and bias

Researchers who study self-enhancement and self-protection from a motivational perspective generally imply that such judgements are biased or erroneous, but the nature of the presumed bias or error is not always obvious. To assess the relation between self-enhancement and self-protection on the one hand, and error and bias on the other, it is important to be clear about the distinction between error and bias (Funder, 1987; Krizan & Windschitl, 2007; Kruglanski, 1989). An error is a mistake made in relation to a well-established criterion. For example, a person who thinks that it is Tuesday when it is actually Wednesday has made an error by the universally accepted standards of the calendar.

By contrast, a bias is a systematic propensity to reach a certain conclusion. Whereas error refers to the outcome of a judgement, in particular whether the judgement is correct or incorrect, bias refers to its derivation. Biases and errors are not necessarily related. On any particular occasion, a person can be biased but error-free, or erroneous and unbiased. An example of the former is a person with a biased view of his golfing abilities (consistently overestimating) who manages to outplay a far superior opponent. Similarly, a racially biased juror may assume, correctly as it turns out, that a Black defendant is guilty of a crime. Example of erroneous and unbiased judgements abound: Essentially, all random errors fall into this category. Thus, a person who simply guesses, incorrectly, that she will lose a competition that she actually wins is erroneous but not necessarily biased.

Biases and errors can represent purely perceptual or cognitive distortions, or they can serve one or more of an actor's interests. For example, a person who is nearsighted or farsighted has a purely perceptual bias of the visual field, one that is erroneous as well. On the other hand, biased views of one's own traits and abilities, or stereotyped expectations for certain minority groups, can be purposive to the extent that they represent self-promotion, either by exaggerating one's own virtues or by derogating those of another person or group. Biased judges may ignore evidence that contradicts a desired conclusion or distort evidence to support that conclusion.

Viewed in this context, self-enhancement and self-protection motives yield judgements that are biased by the wish to raise a specific or global self-component beyond its current level (i.e., closer to the aspiration level), or to avoid falling below the tolerance level. Such judgements can be correct or incorrect, although biased judgements will likely yield more erroneous judgements than unbiased ones in the long run. Judgements that are both biased and erroneous require the most arduous self-enhancement and self-protection efforts to overcome the reality constraints that contradict them. People who consistently adhere to manifestly erroneous judgements are sometimes said to be "in denial".

Implicit versus explicit aspect

A notable feature of self-enhancement and self-protection motives is that they can be unconscious or implicit. Furthermore, their inaccessibility is different from that of biological motives such as maintaining an optimal balance of blood nutrients. When people self-enhance or self-protect, researchers typically assume that they have reasons for their actions that they are unable or unwilling to explicate (Peters, 1958). For example, a racially prejudiced person might deny that the reason he dislikes minorities is that he is motivated to maintain a positive view of himself by derogating others. Similarly, someone who believes that she is above average on virtually all desirable characteristics might fail to recognise that this view serves to maintain positive, self-related affect as well as an interest in self-perceptions of competence and all-around goodness.

The implicit aspect of self-enhancement and self-protection is tied to the Freudian legacy of unconscious motives whose purpose is to protect the self (i.e., the "ego"). However, the social-psychological use of these terms is much broader than the Freudian one. Whereas Sigmund Freud (1915/1961a, 1923/1961b, 1926/1961c) and Anna Freud (1936/1946) believed that the ego defences were invoked to repress sexual and aggressive urges, the social-psychological use of self-protection and self-enhancement motives applies to any self-related interest, including perceptions of own faces, abilities, social and physical traits, moral standing, beliefs, and values (Dunning, 1999; Epley & Whitchurch, 2008; Sedikides & Gregg, 2008). Social and personality psychologists have therefore expanded considerably the scope of interests to which the self-enhancement and self-protection motives apply. In the modern scheme virtually any self-aspect that is a source of interest or value, or is capable of producing significant psychic pleasure or pain, is a candidate for strategic manoeuvring.

Demonstrations of implicit self-enhancement in the research literature are plentiful. The name-letter effect is one of the most compelling (Nuttin, 1985). In a typical study, when presented with pairs of letters, one from their name and one that is not from their name, research participants reliably prefer the letter that is included in their name. Furthermore, participants are unaware that the basis of their preference is inherent in the association of the letter with their names. Other examples of implicit self-enhancement phenomena include viewing others stereo-typically after receiving negative feedback (Gilbert & Hixon, 1991), or counter-stereotypically after being praised by a minority group member (Sinclair & Kunda, 1999).

Role of self-deception

An important conceptual issue regarding self-enhancement and self-protection is whether self-deception is a necessary component of these motives. In other words, do people know what they are "up to" when they engage in self-enhancement or self-protection? If so, at what level of awareness are such strategies registered?

Consider the example of a student who blames everyone but her own poor study habits for a low test grade. Penetrating these excuses is sometimes as simple as raising an eyebrow or, if that does not work, asking the student to reflect on her test preparation. Rather than representing deeply buried unconscious needs, self-serving tendencies can be motivational ploys of which people are vaguely aware but refuse to "spell out" (Fingarette, 2000). This might be called a light versus a deep form of self-deception, one that is akin to failing to open mail that contains unwanted bills (Greenwald, 1980). In fact, many of the self-protective or self-enhancing tendencies that social psychologists study, in contrast to the unconscious motives that the Freuds postulated, are probably of this preconscious variety. For example, people defend themselves by reinterpret-ing negative attributes or minimising their impact by placing them in a broader context (Dunning, Meyerowitz, & Holzberg, 1989; Murray, 1999).

When extreme self-deceptions occur they are more likely to be enlisted for self-protection than self-enhancement. Whereas self-enhancement is a luxury, self-protection is a necessity. Except for psychotic delusions and extreme personality disorders, self-enhancement includes mundane tenden-cies such as thinking that one is slightly better than others, choosing to compare with worse-off others, and construing events in a way that frames one's actions and attributes in a positive light. These tendencies can sometimes be subverted simply by pointing out the facts to the self-enhancer.

The self-deception involved in self-protection, on the other hand, can be far more potent and hence much more difficult to overcome. Examples abound. Parents refuse to believe the misdeeds of their children even when the facts are obvious; patients go to great lengths to ignore serious health conditions; people make excuses for poor or improper social behaviour that stretch credulity; individuals are convinced they are morally motivated, and they resort to moral superiority judgements when their rationality and agency are questioned; and a large proportion of the civilised world believes that they will lead many, and perhaps infinitely many, lives (Batson, Thompson, & Chen, 2002; Hoorens, 1993; Jordan & Monin, 2008; Sedikides & Gregg, 2008).

However, because self-analysis is frequently a complex and obscure task (Sedikides, Horton, & Gregg, 2007d), dramatic processes such as repression and denial rarely need to be invoked. To take a mundane example, analysing one's traits and abilities requires assessing how one fares in the general distribution of these characteristics. If I were to assess my general intelligence, for example, I should locate where I stand on this trait in a relevant population: It matters little whether I have become smarter over time, particularly if others have become smarter at an even faster rate. In a rational sense, therefore, large-sample social comparison information trumps temporal comparison for analysing general characteristics. Nevertheless, recent research has shown that people use temporal comparison information selectively to further self-enhancement and self-protection purposes. In one study (Zell & Alicke, 2009), actors took different parts of a social sensitivity test biweekly for a 10-week period, and received feedback about their increasing or decreasing performance over that period (temporal comparison information), as well as information about whether they generally performed better or worse than a large sample of other students who took the same test (social comparison information). Yoked observers simply learned of the actors' performance over time and were exposed to the same social comparison information. Results showed that observers paid no attention to temporal comparison information, basing their evaluations of the actors' social sensitivity skills purely on whether they performed better or worse than others. Actors, on the other hand, eschewed temporal comparison information when it suggested that their performance declined, but used it to their advantage when it suggested that they were getting better. Consequently, actors evaluated themselves more favourably than did observers regardless of whether social comparison information indicated that they were better or worse than others. In such nuanced feedback environments, elaborate self-deceptions are not required; rather, simple and chronic biases suffice to enhance and protect the self.

ON MOTIVE ACTIVATION AND MODERATING CONDITIONS

Situationally elicited self-enhancement/self-protection can be understood in terms of the traditional motivational language of Dollard and Miller (1950). Self-enhancement encompasses various approach motives that guide people towards selecting situations in which they are likely to excel, and towards promoting their virtues when there is no fear of contradiction. Self-protection, on the other hand, comprises an assortment of avoidance tendencies, and involves retreating from threatening situations, making excuses designed to deflect negative self-implications, misremembering unfavourable information about the self, avoiding situations that threaten failure, and evaluating other people and groups unfavourably to maintain relatively positive self-views.

We have described self-enhancement as a largely routine regulatory system that operates to maintain interests in acceptable proximity to their aspired levels. However, self-enhancement processes are also activated by situational opportunities. Small gains, such as minor recognitions and faint praise, can be exaggerated; situations in which the deck is stacked in one's favour can be approached (e.g., a student taking an easy class); and peers can be selected with whom comparisons are likely to be favourable (e.g., an older child entering into competitions with younger ones).

Affect plays a relatively minor role in self-enhancement. Events that arouse positive affect may fuel self-enhancement efforts, such as when the positive emotional impact of a successful event boosts related self-constructs—what we have referred to as horizontal spread (Sedikides, 1992). On the other hand, negative affect is a necessary concomitant of self-protection (Leary, Springer, Negel, Ansell, & Evans, 1998). Self-protection, as described earlier, occurs when events threaten to reduce an interest below tolerance. However, if the interest in one's standing with regard to a self-construct is only tepid, self-protective efforts will be minimal or absent. For example, a person who has no desire to be perceived as rude, but does not care a great deal about this characteristic anyway, will have little motivation for self-protection, even when events conspire to make her appear more rude than her tolerance level permits. The context in which self-enhancement and self-protection motives are potentiated, therefore, largely determines their strength. These motives are at their fullest strength when a characteristic is central to the individual's identity, and when an evaluative audience is an important source of social or material reward (Kelly, 2000; Leary, 1995).

Given that self-enhancement and self-protection are but two of the many motives that drive self-evaluation and social-evaluation, their initiation depends on the standing of other motivational conditions. When the stakes are high, and the penalties for bias and error are substantial, accuracy needs may trump self-enhancement/self-protection motives (Dauenheimer, Stahlberg, Spreeman, & Sedikides, 2002; Sedikides & Strube, 2007). People will process carefully and remember negative feedback that is diagnostic of their limitations (Green, Pinter, & Sedikides, 2005 As much as an adolescent music aficionado might like to imagine himself performing to the adulation of millions, a complete lack of musical ability will usually reel in these ambitions. (However, observation of the tryouts for the popular "American Idol" and "Britain's Got Talent" television shows suggests that the latitude for such fantasies is fairly wide.)

The objective determinability of the judgement dimension also constrains the operation of self-enhancement and self-protection: After losing a tennis match without winning a game, it would be pathetic to claim that one's opponent had a lucky day. Furthermore, as Swann and his colleagues (Swann, Rentrow, & Guinn, 2003) have demonstrated in numerous studies, the self-system tends to be conservative, and so fluctuations in current self-conceptions are unlikely to vary dramatically as the result of self-enhancement and self-protection forces. Primarily these motives serve to maintain specific and global self-concepts at a point that is slightly-to-moderately above the veridical level. Note, however, that objectivity and reality can be stretched to accommodate self-protective responding (i.e., social comparisons) as a response to self-threat (Stapel & Johnson, 2007, Study 1).

Cultural specificity versus universality of motives

Self-enhancement and self-protection motives are also manifested differently across cultures. At the explicit level, Easterners (e.g., Japanese) self-enhance less than Westerners (e.g., Americans); that is, the former are less likely to self-aggrandise openly than the latter (Heine & Hamamura, 2007). However, Easterners self-enhance strategically and selectively. In particular, they privately rate themselves as better-than-average on domains that are personally important to them (i.e., collectivistic attributes such as loyal or respectful). Westerners also manifest the same strategic self-enhancement pattern by privately rating themselves as better-than-average on personally important domains (i.e., individualistic attributes such as self-reliant or leader; Sedikides, Gaertner, & Vevea, 2005, 2007a, 2007b). Crucially, an Eastern public preference for collectivistic attributes (e.g., conformity) can also be a strategic, self-protective attempt to avoid a negative reputation (Yamagichi, Hashimoto, & Schug, 2008).

Indeed, although manifestations of self-enhancement and self-protection differ depending on cultural context (Matsumoto, 2007), the motives appear to be equally powerful across cultures. At the implicit level (e.g., response latencies, name-letter preferences, birthday-number preferences, semantic priming), Easterners love the self as much as Westerners do (Hetts, Sakuma, & Pelham, 1999; Kitayama & Karasawa, 1997; Yamaguchi et al., 2007). Also, Easterners do manifest the self-serving bias (Mezulis et al., 2004). In addition, average levels of self-esteem lie above theoretical scale midpoints, while trait self-enhancement (e.g., self-esteem) shows the same structure (i.e., same pattern of correlations with other personality traits) across both Eastern and Western cultures (Cai, Wu, & Brown, in press; Schmitt & Allik, 2005; Sheldon, Elliot, Kasser, & Kim, 2001). Finally, self-enhancement tendencies are positively related to psychological health in both the West (Taylor, Lerner, Sherman, Sage, & McDowell, 2003a) and the East (Cai et al., in press; Gaertner et al., 2008), a topic to which we will return.

What the motives accomplish

The purpose of the Freudian defence mechanisms is to counteract debilitating anxiety. However, anxiety is neither a necessary nor perhaps even a prevalent component of the social-psychological analysis of self-enhancement and self-protection motives. For example, self-enhancement can reflect a quest for self-improvement in a particular domain (Sedikides, 1999, in press) or the illusion of self-improvement (Ross & Wilson, 2003). Likewise, self-protection occurs for purposes such as to avoid losing confidence in a goal-pursuit (Paulhus, Fridhandler, & Hayes, 1997; Sedikides, Green, & Pinter, 2004a; Tesser, 2003). Chronic strategies such as defensive pessimism (Norem & Cantor, 1986) are concocted to avoid disappointments, or to palliate their effects, and, if successful, protect the self by lowering tolerance.

What, then, is the object of a self-protective motive such as taking less responsibility than one deserves for failure? In keeping with our depiction of hierarchically related interests, we argue that such motives serve both lower-level and higher-level interests in the vertical hierarchy. For Freud, the first level of self-protection is to avoid threatening sexual and aggressive thoughts, with the ulterior goal of controlling or limiting anxiety. In our view the immediate interest of self-serving motives and actions is to enhance or defend a specific self-aspect, whereas the broader interest is to maintain the highest feasible level of positive self-evaluations and psychological health. For example, making excuses for poor performance on a math test ameliorates unfavourable evaluations of one's math ability and ultimately serves to prevent negative affect associated with the performance, as well as the spread of negative affect into other self-aspects (Snyder & Higgins, 1988).

BENEFITS AND COSTS

Self-enhancement and self-protection entail physical health benefits (Creswell et al., 2005; Taylor, Lerner, Sherman, Sage, & McDowell, 2003b). In particular, as a response to stress, high (compared to low) self-enhancers have lower cardiovascular responses, more rapid cardiovascular recovery, and lower baseline cortisol levels. Self-enhancement appears to serve a stress-buffering function.

In addition, self-enhancement and self-protection entail psychological health benefits. For example, self-enhancement (multiply operationalised) linearly predicts psychological health (Sedikides et al., 2004b; Taylor et al., 2003a; see also Gramzow, Sedikides, Panter, & Insko, 2000). Specifically, self-enhancement is positively related to psychological resources (e.g., extraversion, positive reframing, optimism, mastery, planning, active coping), social resources (e.g., positive relations, family support), and psychological adjustment (e.g., purpose in life, personal growth, subjective well-being); on the other hand, self-enhancement is negatively related to psychological distress (e.g., anxiety, depression, neuroticism, hostility). Furthermore, self-enhancement is positively related to the psychological health (e.g., positive affect, resilience) of high-exposure survivors of the September 11 terrorist attack (Bonanno, Rennicke, & Dekel, 2005). Finally, self-enhancement is positively related to psychological health (e.g., subjective well-being, self-esteem) and is negatively related to psychological distress (e.g., depression) not only in individualistic cultures but also in collectivistic cultures such as China (Anderson, 1999; Cai et al., in press), Hong Kong (Stewart et al., 2003), Japan (Kobayashi & Brown, 2003), Korea (Chang, Sanna, & Yang, 2003), Taiwan (Gaertner et al., 2008), and Singapore (Kurman & Sriram, 1997). As another case in point, self-enhancement is positively related to the psychological health of civilians exposed to urban combat in wartime and also predicts the psychological health of widows 2 years later in Bosnia (Bonanno, Field, Kovacevic, & Kaltman, 2002). More generally, high self-esteem confers vital benefits to the individual (Swann, Chang-Schneider, & McClarty, 2007), such as psychological health (Trzesniewski et al., 2006), social acceptance (Leary, Cottrell, & Phillips, 2001), and existential safety (Pyszczynski et al., 2004).

Does self-enhancement entail social costs? Individuals (e.g., narcissists) who present themselves to others in an overly grandiose or arrogant manner invite dislike and derision (Robins & Beer, 2001; Sedikides et al., 2002b; Sedikides, Gregg, & Hart, 2007c), and this is no surprise given that the norm of modesty is valued in the West (Gregg, Hart, Sedikides, & Kumashiro, 2008; Sedikides et al., 2007). Such boasters may cope with disapproval by being unaware of it (Kenny & DePaulo, 1993) or immune to it (Robins &

Beer, 2001). Regardless, most people engage in a slightly or moderately positive self-presentation, a tactic that safeguards considerably against disapproval. Indeed, positive self-presentation predicts success in social groups and exchange relationships (Baumeister, 1982; Hogan, 1982). For example, observers perceive actors who claim superior problem-solving skills as honest (Vonk, 1999), and perceive actors who express self-superiority beliefs as open, assertive, and extraverted (Bond, Kwan, & Li, 2000). Moreover, moderate self-enhancers do not appear to endure long-term relational liabilities. For example, high self-esteem facilitates, and low self-esteem constrains, relationship development and satisfaction (Murray, Holmes, & Griffin, 2000; Murray, Rose, Bellavia, Holmes, & Kusche, 2002). In all, slight-to-moderate (i.e., non-narcissistic) self-enhancement appears to entail more social benefits than social costs.

SUPPORTING SELF-ENHANCEMENT/SELF-PROTECTION INTERPRETATIONS

Common ways to support self-enhancement/self-protection explanations

The most compelling way to support self-enhancement/self-protection explanations empirically is to introduce manipulations that potentially affect a self-aspect and then assess their consequences on self- or social-evaluation. Manipulations used in this capacity include providing low versus high performance feedback, furnishing negative versus positive personality feedback, reminding people of their mortality versus a different negative stimulus (e.g., dental pain), supplying objective data to indicate that people's behaviours or characteristics are either worse versus better than others', conveying social criticism versus praise, or introducing superior versus inferior comparison others (Alicke et al., 1997; Campbell & Sedikides, 1999; Pyszczynski et al., 2004; Sedikides & Gregg, 2003).

A second way to support self-enhancement/self-protection explanations is by constructing manipulations that are intended to influence the self or another person differentially (e.g., acquaintance, average peer). Motivational explanations are bolstered when the manipulation influences the self but not others. As a case in point, participants in one study were led to believe (on the basis of an ostensibly valid personality inventory), or were asked to imagine, identical and negative social/performance feedback. Participants remembered the feedback more poorly when it pertained to the self (e.g., "I would often lie to my parents", "I would make fun of others because of their looks") than another person ("Chris would often lie to his parents", "Chris would make fun of others because of their looks"; Green, Sedikides, & Gregg, 2008; Sedikides & Green, 2000, 2004).

A third strategy refers to directing the manipulation at self-aspects that are either high or low in personal relevance (i.e., central vs peripheral). Motivational explanations are supported when the manipulation influences central but not peripheral self-aspects. For example, negative social/ performance feedback is remembered more poorly when it pertains to central self-aspects (e.g., untrustworthy, unkind) rather than peripheral self-aspects (e.g., unpredictable, complaining; Green et al., 2008; Sedikides & Green, 2000, 2004). So, feedback of the form "An employer would not rely on you to have an important project completed by the deadline" and "You would purposely hurt someone to benefit yourself" is remembered poorly compared to feedback of the form "People cannot tell whether you are joking" and "You would get irritated and comment loudly if the weather was bad".

A fourth way to support self-enhancement/self-protection explanations is to demonstrate differences between groups of people whose personal characteristics suggest that they should have varying motivations for self-enhancement or protection. The most prominent studies of this type involve differences between people who score relatively high or low on global self-esteem measures. Research has shown, for example, that low-self-esteem people self-handicap in order to reduce the implications of failure, whereas high-self-esteem people self-handicap in order to enhance the implications of success (Tice, 1991). In addition, compared to their high-self-esteem counterparts, low-self-esteem people are less prone to define their traits self-servingly (Beauregard & Dunning, 2001) and less likely to use their own attributes as a basis for evaluating others (Dunning & Beauregard, 2000).

Various forms of logic provide a fifth means of supporting self-enhancement/self-protection interpretations. For example, if workers on a collaborative project each claim to do more than their share, then it is safe to assume that one of them has miscalculated, although legwork would still be required to tie this misperception to self-enhancement or self-protection motives (Ross & Sicoly, 1979). The better-than-average effect demonstrates similar logic in that investigators can safely assume that, for a given trait, 90% of a population is not really in the top 10% of that population, barring a severely skewed distribution.

Finally, the most direct way to demonstrate a self-enhancement or self-protection bias is to refer a person's actions or attributions to an objective standard. A recent study illustrates this tack (Preuss & Alicke, 2008). In one experiment, actors were led to believe that they were making dating videotapes that would be viewed and evaluated by their peers. On these tapes they described their goals and aspirations, hobbies, and attitudes. After making the videotape, actors watched the tapes that six others had made. Actors then ranked themselves and the six other persons both in terms of their overall dating attractiveness and on a series of personality characteristics. At the same time observers (i.e., people who did not make any video presentations) watched and ranked the same block of seven presentations. Actors and observers also predicted where they thought the actor would be ranked among the six other persons by a group of opposite-sex peers who viewed the presentations (metaperceptions). To assess accuracy, actors' self-rankings and metaperceptions were compared to the ranks given to them by observers. The results were clear: Participants were consistently overly optimistic not only in their self-rankings but also in their projections of how they would be viewed by others. In general, actors overestimated their dating popularity by about one full rank both in terms of their self-rankings and their metaperceptions (i.e., their estimate of the rank that others would give them). Descriptive analysis showed that, on both self-rankings and metaperceptions, 60% of the actors were self-enhancers (i.e., ranked themselves higher than did yoked observers), 25% were self-diminishers, and 15% provided rankings that were identical to those provided by observers. These findings show, therefore, that actors are generally miscalibrated (compared to observers' opinions) in the direction of self-enhancement when it comes evaluating an important characteristic (dating popularity), and that they self-enhance even when strong reality constraints are present—that is, when they run the risk of their self-evaluations being directly contradicted by objective data.

ADDRESSING ALTERNATIVE EXPLANATIONS

Each of the aforementioned methods for supporting self-enhancement/self-protection explanations can, of course, be counterposed by non-motivational alternatives. Four types of alternatives loom most prominently: expectancies, self-presentational concerns, differential memory, and egocentrism.

Expectancies

All experimentally manipulated feedback occurs against the background of existing self-knowledge. This self-knowledge varies in the directness with which it relates to the experimental manipulation. For example, participants who are informed that they are physically weak or unattractive, slow-witted, or socially inept, may have prior evidence to support or contradict this feedback. Researchers therefore often explain to participants that the task measures a novel characteristic in order to minimise the influence of prior knowledge. Nevertheless, participants may still view the feedback in terms of their perceived global standing on the evaluative dimension. In other words, while they may harbour only weak expectations regarding how socially sensitive they are as measured by this specific test, they still have a general sense of their standing on this trait—a standing that is incorporated into their self-evaluation.

Given that there is no way to eliminate global expectations, it is impossible to circumvent this potential quandary completely. However, expectancies only occasionally pose significant problems. In fact, given that most people have comparatively positive self-views, the fact that negative feedback manipulations are so frequently successful suggests that expectancies are usually surmountable. And of course, evidence for self-enhancement and self-protection have been obtained in numerous studies that do not provide task-related feedback and, therefore, that do not entail expectancy issues. Finally, expectancies do not account for the data (but self-enhancement/self-protection explanations do), when expectancies are experimentally controlled or manipulated (Alicke et al., 2001; Sedikides & Green, 2004).

Self-presentation

The possibility sometimes arises that self-enhancement and self-protection efforts are geared primarily to save face in public situations. Self-presentational alternatives first rose to prominence in the early phases of self-serving bias research. According to these views, the tendencies to take undue credit for positive events and to minimise one's role in negative events occur primarily to impress or save face before evaluative audiences. Such machinations reflect a different type of self-enhancement or self-protection, namely a concern with regulating public impressions rather than enhancing or protecting self-images. In response, self-enhancement/self-protection proponents were able to show that these effects persevere in highly private response conditions (Greenberg, Pyszczynski, & Solomon, 1982), thereby establishing that self-presentation could not completely explain the self-serving bias. Demonstrating effects in private response conditions has become a common feature of self-enhancement/self-protection experiments that wish to minimise self-presentational concerns (Sedikides, 1993).

Memory

Differential memory accounts of self-enhancement/self-protection phenomena are usually applied to comparative judgements in which participants compare their characteristics or prospects with those of other peers or groups, or with hypothetical entities such as an average peer. For example, Weinstein's (1980, 1984) original explanation for the optimistic bias—the tendency to view one's life prospects more favourably than those of others—was that people selectively recall their own strengths or others' weaknesses. Similar accounts have been applied to self-serving attributional tendencies.

When people accord themselves more credit than they deserve for positive outcomes, or overestimate their contributions to collaborative efforts, a compelling explanation for these attributions is that their own positive actions, attributes, and efforts are more easily brought to mind.

Of course, this immediately raises the question to a self-enhancement adherent as to why positively biased memories are so readily available; indeed, as diary studies have demonstrated, people remember positive life events better than negative life events (Skowronski, Betz, Thompson, & Shannon, 1991; Walker, Skowronski, & Thompson, 2003) and, relatedly, affect associated with positive life events dissipates at a slower rate than affect associated with negative life events (Skowronski, Gibbons, Vogl, & Walker, 2004; Walker et al., 2003) . It seems plausible to assume that the desire to view oneself favourably could result in positive information receiving a privileged place in memory. This is precisely the type of thorny issue that sometimes makes it difficult to choose between motivational and non-motivational explanations of specific experimental findings (Greenwald, 1975; Tetlock & Levi, 1982). We will return to this issue in a moment. For now, however, it is important to note two points. First, research on self-enhancement and self-protection has moved far beyond its roots in the self-serving bias; our previous discussion of the role of expectancies speaks to this issue. Second, differential memory fails to provide a plausible alternative for many instances of self-protection; we have presented research, for example, showing that self-protection is observed even when controlling for information or feedback availability (Sedikides & Green, 2000, 2004).

Egocentrism

Piaget (1929) introduced egocentrism into the psychology vernacular to refer to children's inability during the preoperational stage of development to adopt the perspective of others, a tendency that is not completely relinquished in adulthood (Epley, Keysar, Van Boven, & Gilovich, 2004). Egocentrism should not be confused with egoism: Whereas egoism refers to self-enhancement that purposefully fosters positive self-feelings or self-beliefs, egocentrism is the tendency to use one's own experiences, attributes, or expectations as a basis for evaluating others (Gilovich, Medvec, & Savitsky, 2000; Kruger, Epley, Parker, & Ng, 2005). Thus, whereas egoism is clearly motivational, egocentrism results from the fact that one's own experiences are hyper-accessible.

Egocentrism has been a frequent explanation for social comparison effects that require people to evaluate their characteristics and outcomes versus those of their peers. Among the findings to which egocentrism explanations have been applied are that self judgements account for more of the variance in self versus average peer comparative judgements than do judgements of the average peer (Klar & Giladi, 1999), that people rate themselves below average in behavioural domains in which they know they fare poorly (presumably because they ruminate disproportionately about their own shortcomings; Kruger, 1999), and that people are unduly pessimistic about their chances in competitions when obstacles are introduced (such as task difficulty) that would impede everyone's performance (again, because they concentrate disproportionately on how the adversity would affect them; Moore & Kim, 2003; Windshitl, Kruger, & Simms, 2003).

Egocentrism is undoubtedly a critical component of many social judgement phenomena, as is focalism (the tendency to over-weight information that is in focal attention rather than the background; Pahl & Eiser, 2006, 2007). However, in most of the studies in which egocentrism and focalism are posed as alternatives to motivational phenomena, the manipulations reduce self-enhancement effects but do not eliminate them. And, while it is demonstrably true that people place undue emphasis on their own experiences, values, and attributes in comparative judgements, it is entirely possible that they sometimes do this to promote their own positive characteristics (Dunning, 2002; Sedikides, 2003). Nevertheless, self-enhancement and self-protection are minimised (but often not eliminated) when the judgement domain is highly objective and verifiable, very difficult, or very rare (Alicke & Govorun, 2005; Burson, Larrick, & Klayman, 2006; Dauenheimer et al., 2002; Kruger & Burrus, 2004), when people are induced to think carefully about their own shortcomings or the obstacles that may obviate success (Sedikides, & Herbst, 2002; Sedikides, Herbst, Hardin, & Dardis, 2002c; Sedikides et al., 2007c), and when people work jointly with close others on interdependent-outcome task (Sedikides, Campbell, Reeder, & Elliot, 1998).

HOPELESS AMBIGUITY?

In 1919 a team of English scientists led by Arthur Eddington of the Cambridge Observatory went on an expedition to observe an eclipse that would provide a critical test of Albert Einstein's general relativity theory and perhaps supplant the long-held cosmology of their own beloved Isaac Newton. In response to Einstein's casual receipt of the information that his theory had been corroborated, a graduate student asked what he would have done if the data had contradicted his theory. Einstein calmly replied, "Then I would have been sorry for the dear Lord; the theory is correct" (Isaacson, 2007, p. 259).

Einstein's comment bespeaks the less dramatic truth that single experiments rarely establish or overturn prevailing theoretical perspectives (Lakatos, 1970). How could one, for example, design an experiment to show unequivocally that high self-esteem protects against existential anxiety, that people evaluate themselves more favourably than others in order to maintain positive self-views, or that making excuses for poor performance forestalls self-concept decline? Support for broad theoretical assumptions, such as whether self-enhancement and self-protection motives contribute significantly to personal identity, social judgement, and intergroup behaviour, depends on the outcomes of whole research programmes rather than individual experiments.

The self-perception versus cognitive dissonance debate that launched the motivation–cognition distinction exemplifies the difficulty of providing conclusive evidence from a single or a small set of studies. Bem's self-perception theory is capable of explaining the acquisition of many self-knowledge components, including knowledge of intentions, goals, inter-personal characteristics, and behavioural traits (Alicke, 1987). On the other hand, even some of cognitive dissonance theory's strongest adherents have advocated delimiting its scope (Cooper & Fazio, 1984). So here's the rub: All motivational accounts are accompanied by cognitive mechanisms that explain how these motives are realised in action and judgement (Kruglanski, 1996; Kunda, 1990), and these cognitive mechanisms, which include expectancies, selective memory, and a host of judgement biases, are often well-established phenomena with wide applicability. Thus, virtually every self-enhancement or self-protection explanation coexists with one or more pervasive non-motivational mechanisms, and it is incumbent on self-theorists to show what self-enhancement/self-protection assumptions can add to these already powerful and compelling explanatory factors.

The illusion of control provides another example of the difficulties that researchers confront in carving out a self-enhancement/self-protection niche against the background of a robust non-motivational phenomenon. The general tendency to exaggerate control is well established and is often exhibited in circumstances that seem unrelated to self-enhancement or self-protection. For example, it is difficult to imagine how self-enhancement is served by paying four times as much money to repurchase a personally chosen lottery ticket versus one that someone else selected (Langer & Roth, 1975). On the other hand, it seems reasonable to assume that overestimating one's control over random events serves sometimes to enhance self-efficacy beliefs (i.e., self-enhancement) or to deflect thoughts of being victimised by such events (i.e., self-protection). The just-world hypothesis, for example, assumes that holding faultless victims responsible for their fates maintains the illusion that the world is an equitable place where rewards and costs are distributed in proportion to good and bad deeds. Although many studies support the just-world hypothesis, the specific motive it posits—the desire to view the world as just—is difficult to pinpoint empirically. Most studies on this topic are consistent with the non-motivational assumption that certain conditions exacerbate the tendency to overestimate how much control victims exerted (Lerner & Miller, 1978; Miller, 2001).

Ultimately, the strength of any scientific hypothesis derives from the weight of evidence from studies designed to demonstrate the validity of its assumptions, and by the diversity of findings that support it. With regard to individual studies, the trick is to hold constant other motives or other non-motivational variables while varying factors designed to increase or decrease self-enhancement/self-protection tendencies. The health and vigour of self-enhancement/self-protection hypotheses derives in part from the numerous studies that have convincingly isolated these motives from alternative interpretations (Alicke & Govorun, 2005; Alicke et al., 2001; Sedikides, 1993; Sedikides & Green, 2004). No single one of these studies provides evidence that a determined and clever naysayer cannot contradict. At this point, however, a preponderance of the evidence clearly establishes self-enhancement and self-protection as vital to explaining how people construct their identities, maintain them, and evaluate other people.

Integrative explanations

In concluding this section we want to emphasise again that either/or explanations are not the answer to the hoary cognition–motivation debate. Self-enhancement and self-protection processes, especially the type that can be manipulated ethically in a laboratory setting, generally occur against the background of powerful perceptual and information-processing forces that can account for many aspects of the phenomenon under investigation. As we have noted previously, for example, egocentrism—a non-motivational factor—is an important contributor to frequently demonstrated phenomena such as the better-than-average effect and the optimistic bias. Self-enhancement is only one explanatory mechanism that contributes to such effects. To take another research example, consider the phenomenon of belief perseverance—the tendency to adhere to beliefs that have been objectively invalidated (Ross, Lepper, & Hubbard, 1975). Belief persever-ance is a robust phenomenon, having been demonstrated in a variety of settings. However, almost all of these studies examine the perseverance of beliefs that are largely irrelevant to the judges' self-concepts. From a self-enhancement or self-protection standpoint, it seems odd that a person would perseverate on a negative self-belief, especially one that was objectively invalidated. Accordingly, recent research (Guenther & Alicke, 2008) has shown that, when participants receive negative feedback about their performance on a task that is said to measure an important intellectual trait, and are subsequently told that this feedback was mistaken, they perseverate on it significantly less than do observers who are simply aware of the feedback. Nevertheless, some degree of perseverance on the negative characteristic remains, showing that perseverance is indeed a viable phenomenon, and that self-protection interests are only partially able to surmount this tendency.

Does it really matter?

Even when the weight of the evidence supports a purposive self-enhancement/self-protection interpretation, the question remains as to what such explanations afford. In other words, is it really worth all the trouble to establish this type of motivational explanation? In our view, there are four related reasons why such explanations are important.

The first reason is an obvious one: to advance effective covering laws that govern a wide range of cases. To illustrate, we return to the example of self-serving attributional biases. In essence these biases involve exaggerating the favourable dispositional implications of positive outcomes and minimising the impact of negative ones. If this occurs because people wish to feel good about themselves, then researchers can anticipate the instigation of these motives and predict their effects. Simply put, these biases should emerge when conditions favour the need for self-enhancement or self-protection and should recede when these needs are diminished (Campbell & Sedikides, 1999). Thus, it should be possible to predict the types of actions and self-evaluations that occur under various conditions, and many studies have been designed for precisely these purposes (Mezulis et al., 2004; Shepperd, Malone, & Sweeny, 2008).

Another reason for pursuing self-enhancement/self-protection explanations is to supplement other explanatory factors that do not provide a complete account of self-related phenomena. The reinterpretation of cognitive dissonance effects by Aronson and colleagues (Aronson et al., 1991) is an illustrative example. These investigators have transported cognitive dissonance into the self-enhancement/self-protection arena by assuming that dissonance reduction is a type of rationalisation that helps people to avoid perceiving themselves as hypocritical. Festinger (1957), of course, conceptualised dissonance in terms of the drive reduction theories that were prevalent in the 1950s, particularly that of Hull (1943). For Festinger, aligning attitudes with behaviours served simply to reduce a tension state, analogous to the reduction of physiological tension. But the perspective of Aronson and colleagues has the advantage of redressing a question that Festinger's formulation ignores: Why would inconsistency produce tension in the first place? Aronson and colleagues make the reasonable assumption that inconsistency, especially between values and behaviours, has potentially negative consequences for the self. The point, then, is to show that attitude change occurs when these negative consequences are present, and is reduced or eradicated when they are absent—an effect that Aronson and his colleagues have demonstrated in a series of studies (Aronson et al., 1991; Fried & Aronson, 1995; Stone, Aronson, Crain, Winslow, & Fried, 1994).

The third reason for invoking self-enhancement/self-protection explanations is that such explanations elucidate behaviours that would otherwise appear puzzling and paradoxical. Such behaviours include setting out to perform badly (Baumeister, Cooper, & Skib, 1979), creating impediments to one's success (Berglas & Jones, 1978), procrastination (Tice & Baumeister, 1997), failure to comply with medical advice (Sacket & Snow, 1979), misguided perseverance (Brockner, Rubin, & Lang, 1981), revenge that is costly to the self (Brown, 1968), and various health risks such as substance abuse, engaging in unprotected sex, sunbathing excessively, failing to exercise, and dieting (Leary, Tchividjian, & Kraxberger, 1994). In all of these cases the motives to enhance or protect the self provide cogent explanations.

The final, more encompassing, reason for pursing motivational self-enhancement/self-protection explanations is that psychology, as the science of thought, behaviour, and emotion, naturally desires to convey an accurate and comprehensive depiction of its subject matter. Although non-human behaviour can be explained without reference to self-enhancement/self-protection, such concepts are indispensable for explaining the antecedents of human functioning and the psychological processes that underlie behavioural decisions and explanations. Human brains not only permit advanced problem solving, verbal representation, and projection into the future, but they also confer the capacity for self-evaluation (Sedikides & Skowronski, 1997, 2003; Sedikides, Skowronski, & Dunbar, 2006). Whereas good and bad feelings in other animals pertain to appetitive needs and freedom from harm, humans have a fundamental need for belongingness and social acceptance (Ellemers, Spears, & Doosje, 2002; Knowles & Gardner, 2008; Leary & Cox, 2007) that leads them to assess whether the impressions they convey are likely to lead to social acceptance or rejection. Furthermore, as terror management theorists have emphasised, humans are aware that their lives are finite, and this recognition spurs many of their actions and judgements, including self- and social evaluations (Pyszczynski et al., 2004).

EPILOGUE

In his best-selling compendium on the works of Shakespeare, the literary critic Harold Bloom (1998) makes the sweeping claim that Shakespeare invented the human being. Bloom does not mean to say that Shakespeare was the first to note that people have expectancies or memories, or that they contrast and assimilate information from a standard. What he means is that Shakespeare, more than any writer before and perhaps since, depicted the ego strivings, self-delusions, passions, and illusions that engender the great tragedies and joys of human experience. In fact the Western literary canon, from Homer to the present, is a long description of these common themes that pervade the human condition.

Social and personality psychologists, following an academic tradition from the pre-Socratics to the existentialists of the late 19th and early 20th centuries, have also pursued these themes throughout their history. And now research on the self-enhancement and self-protection motives stands exactly where Aristippus, Epicurus, Hobbes, and Bentham would like it to stand—at the centre of psychological explanations of self-identity and social attribution. These motives have been invoked as key factors in accounting for the ways in which people view and appraise themselves, their social world, their close others, and their groups. Self-definition and social attribution are complex, multiply-determined processes, and the motives to view oneself favourably, or to avoid viewing oneself unfavourably, are central to a thorough understanding of their operation.

In this article we have defined the motives, delineated their scope, discussed their interrelation, and elaborated on their functionality. In addition, we raised epistemic issues such as what qualifies as a motivational explanation and whether such an explanation matters. We hope that our treatment of the self-enhancement and self-protection motives will clarify their use and interpretation and will further invigorate an already thriving area of research.

REFERENCES

Alicke, M. D. (1985). Global self-evaluation as determined by the desirability and controllability of trait adjectives. *Journal of Personality and Social Psychology, 49*, 1621–1630.

Alicke, M. D. (1987). Public explanation and private ratiocination: Communication between the public and private selves. In R. H. Hogan & W. H. Jones (Eds.), *Perspectives in personality: Theory, measurement, and interpersonal dynamics* (Vol. 2, pp. 143–180). Greenwich, CT: JAI Press.

Alicke, M. D., & Govorun, O. (2005). The better-than-average effect. In M. D. Alicke, D. A. Dunning, & J. I. Krueger (Eds.), *The self in social judgment* (pp. 85–106). Philadelphia, PA: Psychology Press.

Alicke, M. D., Klotz, M. L., Breitenbecher, D. L., Yurak, T. J., & Vredenburg, D. S. (1995). Personal contact, individuation, and the better-than-average effect. *Journal of Personality and Social Psychology, 68*, 804–825.

Alicke, M. D., LoSchiavo, F. M., Zerbst, J. I., & Zhang, S. (1997). The person who outperforms me is a genius: Esteem maintenance in upward social comparison. *Journal of Personality and Social Psychology, 73*, 781–789.

Alicke, M. D., Vredenburg, D. S., Hiatt, M., & Govorun, O. (2001). The "better than myself effect". *Motivation and Emotion, 25*, 7–22.

Allport, G. W. (1937). *Personality: A psychological interpretation*. New York: Holt.

Anderson, C. A. (1999). Attributional style, depression, and loneliness: A cross-cultural comparison of American and Chinese students. *Personality and Social Psychology Bulletin, 25*, 482–499.

Arndt, J., Routledge, C., Greenberg, J., & Sheldon, K. M. (2005). Illuminating the dark side of creative expression: Assimilation needs and the consequences of creative action following mortality salience. *Personality and Social Psychology Bulletin, 31*, 1327–1339.

Aronson, E. (1992). The return of the repressed: Dissonance theory makes a comeback. *Psychological Inquiry, 3*, 303–311.

Aronson, E., Fried, C. B., & Stone, J. (1991). Overcoming denial and increasing the intention to use condoms through the induction of hypocrisy. *American Journal of Public Health, 81*, 1636–1638.

Atkinson, J. W., & Raynor, J. O. (1974). *Motivation and achievement.* Washington, DC: Winston.

Batson, C. D., Thompson, E. R., & Chen, H. (2002). Moral hypocrisy: Addressing some alternatives. *Journal of Personality and Social Psychology, 83*, 330–339.

Baumeister, R. F. (1982). A self-presentational view of social phenomena. *Psychological Bulletin, 91*, 3–26.

Baumeister, R. F., Bratslavsky, E., Finkenauer, C., & Vohs, K. D. (2001). Bad is stronger than good. *Review of General Psychology, 5*, 323–370.

Baumeister, R. F., Cooper, J., & Skib, B. A. (1979). Inferior performance as a selective response to expectancy: Taking a dive to make a point. *Journal of Personality and Social Psychology, 37*, 424–432.

Baumeister, R. F., Dale, K., & Sommer, K. L. (1998). Freudian defense mechanisms and empirical findings in modern social psychology: Reaction formation, projection, displacement, undoing, isolation, sublimation, and denial. *Journal of Personality, 66*, 1081–1124.

Beauregard, K. S., & Dunning, D. (1998). Turning up the contrast: Self-enhancement motives prompt egocentric contrast effects in social judgement. *Journal of Personality and Social Psychology, 74*, 606–621.

Beauregard, K. S., & Dunning, D. (2001). Defining self worth: Trait self-esteem moderates the use of self-serving trait definitions in social judgement. *Motivation and Emotion, 25*, 135–162.

Bem, D. J. (1967). Self-perception: An alternative interpretation of cognitive dissonance phenomena. *Psychological Review, 74*, 183–200.

Bem, D. J. (1972). Self-perception theory. *Advances in Experimental Social Psychology, 6*, 1–62.

Berglas, S., & Jones, E. E. (1978). Drug choice as a self-handicapping strategy in response to noncontingent success. *Journal of Personality and Social Psychology, 36*, 405–417.

Bloom, H. (1998). *Shakespeare: The invention of the human.* New York: Riverhead Books.

Bonanno, G. A., Field, N. P., Kovacevic, A., & Kaltman, S. (2002). Self-enhancement as a buffer against extreme adversity: Civil war in Bosnia and traumatic loss in the United States. *Personality and Social Psychology Bulletin, 28*, 184–196.

Bonanno, G. A., Rennicke, C., & Dekel, S. (2005). Self-enhancement among high-exposure survivors of the September 11th terrorist attack: Resilience or social maladjustment? *Journal of Personality and Social Psychology, 88*, 984–998.

Bond, M. H., Kwan, S. Y., & Li, C. (2000). Decomposing a sense of superiority: The differential social impact of self-regard and regard for others. *Journal of Research in Personality, 34*, 537–553.

Brewer, M. B. (1988). A dual process model of impression formation. In T. K. Srull & R. S. Wyer (Eds.), *Advances in social cognition* (Vol. 1, pp. 1–36). Hillsdale, NJ: Lawrence Erlbaum Associated Inc.

Brockner, J., Rubin, J. Z., & Lang, E. (1981). Face-saving and entrapment. *Journal of Experimental Social Psychology, 17*, 68–79.

Brown, B. R. (1968). The effects of need to maintain face on interpersonal bargaining. *Journal of Experimental Social Psychology, 17*, 68–79.

Buckingham, J. T., & Alicke, M. D. (2002). The influence of individual versus aggregate social comparison information on self-evaluations. *Journal of Personality and Social Psychology, 83*, 1117–1130.

Burson, K. A., Larrick, R. P., & Klayman, J. (2006). Skilled or unskilled, but still unaware of it: How perceptions of difficulty drive miscalibration in relative comparisons. *Journal of Personality and Social Psychology, 90*, 60–77.

Bushman, B. J., & Baumeister, R. F. (1998). Threatened egotism, narcissism, self-esteem, and direct and displaced aggression: Does self-love or self-hate lead to violence? *Journal of Personality and Social Psychology, 75*, 219–229.

Cai, H., Wu, Q., & Brown, J. D. (in press). Is self-esteem a universal need?: Evidence from The People's Republic of China. *Asian Journal of Social Psychology.*

Campbell, K. W., & Sedikides, C. (1999). Self-threat magnifies the self-serving bias: A meta-analytic integration. *Review of General Psychology, 3*, 23–43.

Campbell, W. K., Reeder, G., Sedikides, C., & Elliot, A. J. (2000). Narcissism and comparative self-enhancement strategies. *Journal of Research in Personality, 34*, 329–347.

Castano, E., Yzerbyt, V., & Paladino, M-P. (2004). Transcending oneself through social identification. In J. Greenberg, S. L. Koole, & T. Pyszczynski (Eds.), *Handbook of experimental existential psychology* (pp. 305–321). New York: Guilford Press.

Chambers, J. R., & Windschitl, P. D. (2004). Biases in social comparative judgments: The role of nonmotivated factors in above-average and comparative-optimism effects. *Psychological Bulletin, 130*, 813–818.

Chang, E. C., Sanna, L. J., & Yang, K. (2003). Optimism, pessimism, affectivity, and psychological adjustment in US and Korea: A test of mediation model. *Personality and Individual Differences, 34*, 1195–1208.

Cooper, J. (2007). *Cognitive dissonance: 50 years of a classic theory*. London: Sage Publications.

Cooper, J., & Fazio, R. (1984). A new look at dissonance. In L. Berkowitz (Ed.), *Advances in experimental social psychology* (Vol. 17, pp. 229–268). New York: Academic Press.

Creswell, J. D., Welch, W. T., Taylor, S. E., Sherman, D. K., Gruenewald, T. L., & Mann, T. (2005). Affirmation of personal values buffers neuroendocrine and psychological stress responses. *Psychological Science, 16*, 846–851.

Crocker, J., & Wolfe, C. T. (2001). Contingencies of self-worth. *Psychological Review, 108*, 593–623.

Dauenheimer, D. G., Stahlberg, D., Spreeman, S., & Sedikides, C. (2002). Self-enhancement, self-assessment, or self-verification?: The intricate role of trait modifiability in the self-evaluation process. *Revue Internationale De Psychologie Sociale, 15*, 89–112.

DeWall, C. N., Baumeister, R. F., Stillman, T. F., & Gailliot, M. T. (2007). Violence restrained: Effects of self-regulation and its depletion on aggression. *Journal of Experimental Social Psychology, 43*, 62–76.

Dollard, J., & Miller, N. (1950). *Personality and psychotherapy: An analysis in terms of learning, thinking and culture*. New York: McGraw-Hill.

Dunning, D. (1999). A newer look: Motivated social cognition and the schematic representation of social concepts. *Psychological Inquiry, 10*, 1–11.

Dunning, D. (2002). The zealous self-affirmer: How and why the self lurks so pervasively behind social judgement. In S. Fein & S. Spencer (Eds.), *Motivated social perception: The Ontario symposium* (Vol. 9, 45–72). Mahwah, NJ: Lawrence Erlbaum Associates Inc.

Dunning, D., & Beauregard, K. S. (2000). Regulating impressions of others to affirm images of the self. *Social Cognition, 18*, 198–222.

Dunning, D., Meyerowitz, J. A., & Holzberg, A. D. (1989). Ambiguity and self-evaluation: The role of idiosyncratic trait definitions in self-serving assessments of ability. *Journal of Personality and Social Psychology, 57*, 1082–1090.

Ellemers, N., Spears, R., & Doosje, B. (2002). Self and social identity. *Annual Review of Psychology, 53*, 161–186.

Elliot, A. J., & Devine, P. G. (1994). On the motivational nature of cognitive dissonance: Dissonance as psychological discomfort. *Journal of Personality and Social Psychology, 67,* 382–394.

Elliot, A. J., & Mapes, R. R. (2005). Approach-avoidance motivation and self-concept evaluation. In A. Tesser, J. V. Wood, & D. A. Stapel (Eds.), *On building, defending and regulating the self: A psychological perspective* (pp. 171–196). New York: Psychology Press.

Epley, N., Keysar, B., Van Boven, L., & Gilovich, T. (2004). Perspective taking as egocentric anchoring and adjustment. *Journal of Personality and Social Psychology, 87,* 327–339.

Epley, N., & Whitchurch, E. (2008). Mirror, mirror on the wall: Enhancement in self-recognition. *Personality and Social Psychology Bulletin, 34,* 1159–1170.

Feinberg, J. (1984). *The moral limits of the criminal law: Harm to others* (Vol. 1). New York: Oxford University Press.

Festinger, L. (1957). *A theory of cognitive dissonance.* Evanston, IL: Row, Peterson.

Fingarette, H. (2000). *Self-deception.* Berkeley, CA: University of California Press.

Forgas, J. P. (Ed.). (2001). *The handbook of affect and social cognition.* Mahwah, NJ: Lawrence Erlbaum Associates Inc.

Forgas, J. P. (Ed.). (2006). *Affect in social thinking and behavior: Frontiers in social psychology.* New York: Psychology Press.

Freud, A. (1946). *The ego and the mechanisms of defense.* New York: International Universities Press. [Original work published in 1936.]

Freud, S. (1961a). Instincts and their vicissitudes. In J. Strachey (Ed. & Trans.), *The standard edition of the complete works of Sigmund Freud* (Vol. 14, pp. 111–142). London: Hogarth Press. [Original work published in 1915.]

Freud, S. (1961b). The ego and the id. In J. Strachey (Ed. & Trans.), *The standard edition of the complete works of Sigmund Freud* (Vol. 19, pp. 12–66). London: Hogarth Press. [Original work published in 1923.]

Freud, S. (1961c). Inhibitions, symptoms, and anxiety. In J. Strachey (Ed. & Trans.), *The standard edition of the complete works of Sigmund Freud* (Vol. 20, pp. 77–178). London: Hogarth Press. [Original work published in 1926.]

Fried, C. B., & Aronson, E. (1995). Hypocrisy, misattribution, and dissonance reduction. *Personality and Social Psychology Bulletin, 21,* 925–933.

Funder, D. C. (1987). Errors and mistakes: Evaluating the accuracy of social judgment. *Psychological Bulletin, 101,* 75–90.

Gaertner, L., Sedikides, C., & Chang, K. (2008). On pancultural self-enhancement: Well-adjusted Taiwanese self-enhance on personally valued traits. *Journal of Cross-Cultural Psychology, 39,* 463–477.

Gilbert, D.T., & Hixon, J.G. (1991). The trouble of thinking: Activation and application of stereotypical beliefs. *Journal of Personality and Social Psychology, 60,* 509–517.

Gilovich, T., Medvec, V. H., & Savitsky, K. (2000). The spotlight effect in social judgment: An egocentric bias in estimates of the salience of one's own actions and appearance. *Journal of Personality and Social Psychology, 78,* 211–222.

Govorun, O., Fuegen, K., & Payne, B. K. (2006). Stereotypes focus defensive projection. *Personality and Social Psychology Bulletin, 32,* 781–793.

Gramzow, R. H., Sedikides, C., Panter, A. T., & Insko, C. A. (2000). Aspects of self-regulation and self-structure as predictors of perceived emotional distress. *Personality and Social Psychology Bulletin, 26,* 188–206.

Gramzow, R. H., & Willard, G. (2006). Exaggerating current and past performance: Motivated self-enhancement versus reconstructive memory. *Personality and Social Psychology Bulletin, 32,* 1114–1125.

Green, J. A., & Sedikides, C. (2004). Retrieval selectivity in the processing of self-referent information: Testing the boundaries of self-protection. *Self and Identity, 3,* 69–80.

Green, J. D., Pinter, B., & Sedikides, C. (2005). Mnemic neglect and self-threat: Trait modifiability moderates self-protection. *European Journal of Social Psychology*, *35*, 225–235.

Green, J. D., Sedikides, C., & Gregg, A. P. (2008). Forgotten but not gone: The recall and recognition of self-threatening memories. *Journal of Experimental Social Psychology*, *44*, 547–561.

Green, J. D., Sedikides, C., Pinter, B., & Van Tongeren, D. R. (in press). Two sides to self-protection: Self-improvement strivings and feedback from close relationships eliminate mnemic neglect. *Self and Identity*.

Greenberg, J., Pyszczynski, T., & Solomon, S. (1982). The self-serving attributional bias: Beyond self-presentation. *Journal of Experimental Social Psychology*, *18*, 56–67.

Greenwald, A. G. (1975). On the inconclusiveness of "crucial" cognitive tests of dissonance versus self-perception theories. *Journal of Experimental Social Psychology*, *11*, 490–499.

Greenwald, A. G. (1980). The totalitarian ego: Fabrication and revision of personal history. *American Psychologist*, *35*, 603–618.

Gregg, A. P., Hart, C. M., Sedikides, C., & Kumashiro, M. (2008). Lay conceptions of modesty: A prototype analysis. *Personality and Social Psychology Bulletin*, *34*, 978–992.

Guenther, C. L., & Alicke, M. D. (2008). Self-enhancement and belief perseverance. *Journal of Experimental Social Psychology*, *44*, 706–712.

Hamilton, D. L., & Trolier, T. K. (1986). Stereotypes and stereotyping: An overview of the cognitive approach. In J. F. Dovidio & S. L. Gaertner (Eds.), *Prejudice, discrimination, and racism* (pp. 127–163). Orlando, FL: Academic Press.

Harris, P. (2007). The impact of perceived experience on likelihood judgements for self and others: An experimental approach. *European Journal of Social Psychology*, *37*, 141–151.

Heider, F. (1958). *The psychology of interpersonal relations*. New York: Wiley.

Heine, S. J., & Hamamura, T. (2007). In search of East Asian self-enhancement. *Personality and Social Psychology Review*, *11*, 4–27.

Hetts, J. J., Sakuma, M., & Pelham, B. W. (1999). Two roads to positive regard: Implicit and explicit self-evaluation and culture. *Journal of Experimental Social Psychology*, *35*, 512–559.

Hogan, R. (1982). A socioanalytic theory of personality. In M. M. Page (Ed.), *Nebraska Symposium on Motivation* (pp. 55–89). Lincoln, NE: University of Nebraska Press.

Hoorens, V. (1993). Self-enhancement and superiority biases in social comparison. In W. Stroebe & M. Hewstone (Eds.), *European review of social psychology* (Vol. 4, pp. 113–139). Chichester, UK: Wiley.

Hull, C. L. (1943). *Principles of behavior*. New York: Appleton-Century-Crofts.

Isaacson, W. (2007). *Einstein: His life and universe*. New York: Simon & Schuster.

James, W. (1890). *Principles of psychology (Vols. 1 & 2)*. New York: Holt.

Jordan, A. H., & Monin, B. (2008). From sucker to saint: Moralization in response to self-threat. *Psychological Science*, *19*, 809–815.

Kay, A. C., Jimenez, M. C., & Jost, J. T. (2002). Sour grapes, sweet lemons, and the anticipatory rationalization of the status quo. *Personality and Social Psychology Bulletin*, *28*, 1300–1312.

Kelley, H. H. (1967). Attribution theory in social psychology. In D. Levine (Ed.), *Nebraska symposium on motivation* (Vol. 15, pp. 129–238). Lincoln, NE: University of Nebraska Press.

Kelly, A. E. (2000). Helping construct desirable identities: A self-presentational view of psychotherapy. *Psychological Bulletin*, *126*, 475–494.

Kenny, D. A., & DePaulo, B. M. (1993). Do people know how others view them?: An empirical and theoretical account. *Psychological Bulletin*, *114*, 145–161.

Kitayama, S., & Karasawa, M. (1997). Implicit self-esteem in Japan: Name letters and birthday numbers. *Personality and Social Psychology Bulletin*, *23*, 736–742.

Klar, Y., & Giladi, E. E. (1999). No one in my group can be below the group's average: A robust positivity bias in favor of anonymous peers. *Journal of Personality and Social Psychology*, *73*, 885–901.

Klinger, E. (1990). *Daydreaming: Using waking fantasy and imagery for self-knowledge and creativity*. Los Angeles: Tarcher.

Knowles, M. L., & Gardner, W.L. (2008). Benefits of membership: The activation and amplification of group identities in response to social rejection. *Personality and Social Psychology Bulletin, 34*, 1200–1213.

Kobayashi, C., & Brown, J. D. (2003). Self-esteem and self-enhancement in Japan and America. *Journal of Cross-Cultural Psychology, 34*, 567–580.

Krizan, Z., & Windschitl, P. D. (2007). The influence of outcome desirability on optimism. *Psychological Bulletin, 133*, 95–121.

Kruger, J. (1999). Lake Woebegone be gone! The "below-average-effect" and the egocentric nature of comparative ability judgments. *Journal of Personality and Social Psychology, 77*, 221–232.

Kruger, J., & Burrus, J. (2004). Egocentrism and focalism in unrealistic optimism (and pessimism). *Journal of Experimental Social Psychology, 40*, 332–340.

Kruger, J., Epley, N., Parker, J., & Ng, Z-W. (2005). Egocentrism over e-mail: Can we communicate as well as we think? *Journal of Personality and Social Psychology, 89*, 925–936.

Kruglanski, A. W. (1989). *Lay epistemics and human knowledge: Cognitive and motivational biases*. New York: Plenum Press.

Kruglanski, A. W. (1996). Motivated social cognition: Principles of the interface. In E. T. Higgins & A. W. Kruglanski (Eds.), *Social psychology: A handbook of basic principles* (pp. 493–522). New York: Guilford.

Kumashiro, M., & Sedikides, C. (2005). Taking on board liability-focused feedback: Close positive relationships as a self-bolstering resource. *Psychological Science, 16*, 732–739.

Kunda, Z. (1990). The case for motivated reasoning. *Psychological Bulletin, 108*, 480–498.

Kurman, J., & Sriram, N. (1997). Self-enhancement, generality of self-evaluation, and affectivity in Israel and Singapore. *Journal of Cross-Cultural Psychology, 28*, 421–441.

Lakatos, I. (1970). *Criticism and the growth of knowledge*. New York: Cambridge University Press.

Landau, M. J., Greenberg, J., Solomon, S., Pyszczynski, T., & Martens, A. (2006). Windows into nothingness: Terror management, meaninglessness, and negative reactions to modern art. *Journal of Personality and Social Psychology, 90*, 879–892.

Langer, E. J., & Roth, J. (1975). Heads I win, tails it's chance: The illusion of control as a function of the sequence of outcomes in a pure chance task. *Journal of Personality and Social Psychology, 32*, 951–955.

Leary, M. R. (1995). *Self-presentation: Impression management and interpersonal behavior*. Madison, WI: Brown & Benchmark.

Leary, M. R., Cottrell, C. A., & Phillips, M. (2001). Deconfounding the effects of dominance and social acceptance on self-esteem. *Journal of Personality and Social Psychology, 81*, 898–909.

Leary, M. R., & Cox, C. (2007). Belongingness motivation: The mainspring of social action. In J. Shah & W. Gardner (Eds.), *Handbook of motivation science* (pp. 27–40). New York: Guilford Press.

Leary, M. R., Springer, C., Negel, L., Ansell, E., & Evans, K. (1998). The causes, phenomenology, and consequences of hurt feelings. *Journal of Personality and Social Psychology, 74*, 1225–1237.

Leary, M. R., Tchividjian, L. R., & Kraxberger, B. E. (1994). Self-presentation can be hazardous to your health: Impression management and health risk. *Health Psychology, 13*, 461–470.

Lerner, M. J., & Miller, D. T. (1978). Just-world research and the attribution process: Looking back and ahead. *Psychological Bulletin, 85*, 1030–1051.

Lewin, K. (1935). *A dynamic theory of personality*. New York: McGraw-Hill.

Lewin, K. (1936). *Principles of topological psychology*. New York: McGraw-Hill.

Liberman, N., Trope, Y., & Stephan, E. (2007). Psychological distance. In A. W. Kruglanski & E. T. Higgins (Eds.), *Social psychology: Handbook of basic principles* (Vol. 2, pp. 353–383). New York: Guilford Press.

Linville, P. W. (1985). Self-complexity and affective extremity: Don't put all of your eggs in one basket. *Social Cognition, 3*, 94–120.

Markus, H., & Nurius, P. (1986). Possible selves. *American Psychologist, 41*, 954–969.

Marlowe, D., & Crowne, D. P. (1961). Social desirability and response to perceived situational demands, *Journal of Consulting Psychology, 25*, 109–115.

Matsumoto, D. (2007). Culture, context, and behavior. *Journal of Personality, 75*, 1285–1320.

McArthur, L. A. (1972). The how of what and why: Some determinants and consequences of causal attributions. *Journal of Personality and Social Psychology, 22*, 171–193.

McConnell, A. R., & Strain, L. M. (2007). Content and structure of the self-concept. In C. Sedikides & S. J. Spencer (Eds.), *The self: Frontiers of social psychology* (pp. 51–73). New York: Psychology Press.

Mezulis, A. H., Abramson, L. Y., Hyde, J. S., & Hankin, B. L. (2004). Is there a universal positive bias in attributions?: A meta-analytic review of individual, developmental, and cultural differences in the self-serving attributional bias. *Psychological Bulletin, 130*, 711–747.

Mikulincer, M., Florian, V., & Hirschberger, G. (2003). The existential function of close relationships: Introducing death into the science of love. *Personality and Social Psychology Review, 7*, 20–40.

Miller, D. T. (2001). Disrespect and the experience of injustice. *Annual Review of Psychology, 52*, 527–53.

Miller, D. T., & Ross, M. (1975). Self-serving biases in the attribution of causality: Fact or fiction? *Psychological Bulletin, 82*, 213–225.

Moore, D. A., & Kim, T. G. (2003). Myopic social prediction and the solo comparison effect. *Journal of Personality and Social Psychology, 85*, 1121–1135.

Murray, S. L. (1999). The quest for conviction: Motivated cognition in romantic relationships. *Psychological Inquiry, 10*, 23–34.

Murray, S. L., Holmes, J. G., & Griffin, D. W. (2000). Self-esteem and the quest for felt security: How perceived regard regulates attachment processes. *Journal of Personality and Social Psychology, 78*, 478–498.

Murray, S. L., Rose, P., Bellavia, G., Holmes, J. G., & Kusche, A. (2002). When rejection stings: How self-esteem constrains relationship-enhancement processes. *Journal of Personality and Social Psychology, 83*, 556–573.

Norem, J. K., & Cantor, N. (1986). Defensive pessimism: Harnessing anxiety as motivation. *Journal of Personality and Social Psychology, 51*, 1208–1217.

Nozick, R. (1974). *Anarchy, state and utopia*. New York: Basic Books, Inc.

Nuttin, J. M., Jr. (1985). Narcissism beyond Gestalt and awareness: The name letter effect. *European Journal of Social Psychology, 15*, 353–361.

Oettingen, G. (1996). Positive fantasy and motivation. In P. M. Gollwitzer & J. A. Bargh (Eds.), *The psychology of action: Linking cognition and motivation to behavior* (pp. 236–259). New York: Guilford Press.

Pahl, S., & Eiser, J. R. (2006). The focus effect and self-positivity in ratings of self–other similarity and difference. *British Journal of Social Psychology, 45*, 107–116.

Pahl, S., & Eiser, J. R. (2007). How malleable is comparative self-positivity?: The effects of manipulating judgemental focus and accessibility. *European Journal of Social Psychology, 37*, 617–627.

Paulhus, D. L., Fridhandler, B., & Hayes, S. (1997). Psychological defense: Contemporary theory and research. In R. Hogan, J. Johnson, & S. Briggs (Eds.), *Handbook of personality* (pp. 544–580). New York: Academic Press.

Peters, R. S. (1958). *The concept of motivation.* New York: Humanities Press.

Piaget, J. (1929). *The child's conception of the world.* New York: Harcourt, Brace Jovanovich.

Preuss, G., & Alicke, M. D. (2008). *Self-perceptions, metaperceptions and self-enhancement.* Unpublished manuscript,Ohio University.

Pyszczynski, T., & Greenberg, J. (1987). Toward an integration of cognitive and motivational perspectives on social inference: A biased hypothesis-testing model. *Advances in Experimental Social Psychology, 20,* 297–340.

Pyszczynski, T., Greenberg, J., & Goldenberg, J. L. (2003). Freedom versus fear: On the defense, growth, and expansion of the self. In M. R. Leary & J. P. Tangney (Eds.), *Handbook of self and identity* (pp. 314–343). New York: Guilford Press.

Pyszczynski, T., Greenberg, J., Solomon, S., Arndt, J., & Schimel, J. (2004). Why do people need self-esteem?: A theoretical and empirical review. *Psychological Bulletin, 130,* 435–468.

Rawls, J. (1971). *A theory of justice.* Cambridge, MA: Harvard University Press.

Reeve, J. M. (1997). *Understanding motivation and emotion.* Fort Worth, TX: Harcourt Brace.

Robins, R. W., & Beer, J. S. (2001). Positive illusions about the self: Short-term benefits and long-term costs. *Journal of Personality and Social Psychology, 80,* 340–352.

Roese, N. J., & Olson, J. M. (2007). Better, stronger, faster: Self-serving judgement, affect regulation, and the optimal vigilance hypothesis. *Perspectives on Psychological Science, 2,* 124–141.

Ross, L., Lepper, M. R., & Hubbard, M. (1975). Perseverance in self-perceptions and social perception: Biased attributional processing in the debriefing paradigm. *Journal of Personality and Social Psychology, 32,* 880–892.

Ross, M., & Sicoly, F. (1979). Egocentric biases in availability and attribution. *Journal of Personality and Social Psychology, 37,* 322–336.

Ross, M., & Wilson, A. E. (2003). Autobiographical memory and conceptions of self: Getting better all the time. *Current Directions in Psychological Science, 12,* 66–69.

Rothbart, M., & John, O. P. (1985). Social categorisation and behavioral episodes: A cognitive analysis of the effects of intergroup contact. *Journal of Social Issues, 41,* 81–104.

Rothbaum, F., Weisz, J. R., & Snyder, S. S. (1982). Changing the world and changing the self: A two-process model of perceived control. *Journal of Personality and Social Psychology, 42,* 5–37.

Sacket, D. L., & Snow, J. C. (1979). The magnitude of compliance and noncompliance. In R. B. Haynes, D. W. Taylor, & D. L. Sackett (Eds.), *Compliance in health care* (pp. 11–22). Baltimore, MD: Johns Hopkins University Press.

Sales, S. M. (1971). Need for stimulation as a factor in social behavior. *Journal of Personality and Social Psychology, 19,* 124–134.

Schimel, J., Greenberg, J., & Martens, A. (2003). Evidence that projection of a feared trait can serve a defensive function. *Personality and Social Psychology Bulletin, 29,* 969–979.

Schmitt, D. P., & Allik, J. (2005). Simultaneous administration of the Rosenberg self-esteem scale in 53 nations: Exploring the universal and culture-specific features of global self-esteem. *Journal of Personality and Social Psychology, 89,* 623–642.

Sedikides, C. (1992). Changes in the valence of the self as a function of mood. *Review of Personality and Social Psychology, 14,* 271–311.

Sedikides, C. (1993). Assessment, enhancement, and verification determinants of the self-evaluation process. *Journal of Personality and Social Psychology, 65,* 317–338.

Sedikides, C. (1995). Central and peripheral self-conceptions are differentially influenced by mood: Tests of the differential sensitivity hypothesis. *Journal of Personality and Social Psychology, 69,* 759–777.

Sedikides, C. (1999). A multiplicity of motives: The case of self-improvement. *Psychological Inquiry, 9*, 64–65.

Sedikides, C. (2003). On the status of self in social prediction: Comment on Karniol (2003). *Psychological Review, 110*, 591–594.

Sedikides, C. (in press). On self-protection and self-enhancement regulation: The role of self-improvement and social norms. In J. P. Forgas, R. F. Baumeister, & D. Tice (Eds.), *The psychology of self-regulation.* New York: Psychology Press.

Sedikides, C., Campbell, W. K., Reeder, G., & Elliot, A. J. (1998). The self-serving bias in relational context. *Journal of Personality and Social Psychology, 74*, 378–386.

Sedikides, C., Campbell, W. K., Reeder, G., & Elliot, A. J. (2002a). The self in relationships: Whether, how, and when close others put the self "in its place". In W. Stroebe & M. Hewstone (Eds.), *European review of social psychology* (Vol. 12, pp. 237–265). Chichester, UK: Wiley.

Sedikides, C., Campbell, W. K., Reeder, G., Elliot, A. J., & Gregg, A. P. (2002b). Do others bring out the worst in narcissists? The "others exist for me" illusion. In Y. Kashima, M. Foddy, & M. Platow (Eds.), *Self and identity: Personal, social, and symbolic* (pp. 103–123). Mahwah, NJ: Lawrence Erlbaum Associates Inc.

Sedikides, C., Gaertner, L., & Toguchi, Y. (2003). Pancultural self-enhancement. *Journal of Personality and Social Psychology, 84*, 60–70.

Sedikides, C., Gaertner, L., & Vevea, J. L. (2005). Pancultural self-enhancement reloaded: A meta-analytic reply to Heine (2005). *Journal of Personality and Social Psychology, 89*, 539–551.

Sedikides, C., Gaertner, L. & Vevea, J. L. (2007a). Inclusion of theory-relevant moderators yield the same conclusions as Sedikides, Gaertner, and Vevea (2005): A meta-analytic reply to Heine, Kitayama, and Hamamura (2007). *Asian Journal of Social Psychology, 10*, 59–67.

Sedikides, C., Gaertner, L. & Vevea, J. L. (2007b). Evaluating the evidence for pancultural self-enhancement. *Asian Journal of Social Psychology, 10*, 201–203.

Sedikides, C., & Green, J. D. (2000). On the self-protective nature of inconsistency/negativity management: Using the person memory paradigm to examine self-referent memory. *Journal of Personality and Social Psychology, 79*, 906–922.

Sedikides, C., & Green, J. D. (2004). What I don't recall can't hurt me: Information negativity versus information inconsistency as determinants of memorial self-defense. *Social Cognition, 22*, 4–29.

Sedikides, C., & Green, J. D. (in press). Memory as a self-protective mechanism. *Social and Personality Psychology Compass.*

Sedikides, C., Green, J. D., & Pinter, B. (2004). Self-protective memory. In D. R. Beike, J. M. Lampinen, & D. A. Behrend (Eds.), *The self and memory* (pp. 161–179). Philadelphia, PA: Psychology Press.

Sedikides, C., & Gregg, A. P. (2003). Portraits of the self. In M. A. Hogg & J. Cooper (Eds.), *Sage handbook of social psychology* (pp. 110–138). London: Sage Publications.

Sedikides, C., & Gregg, A. P. (2008). Self-enhancement: Food for thought. *Perspectives on Psychological Science, 3*, 102–116.

Sedikides, C., Gregg, A. P., & Hart, C. M. (2007c). The importance of being modest. In C. Sedikides & S. Spencer (Eds.), *The self: Frontiers in social psychology* (pp. 163–184). New York: Psychology Press.

Sedikides, C., & Herbst, K. (2002). How does accountability reduce self-enhancement?: The role of self-focus. *Revue Internationale De Psychologie Sociale, 15*, 113–128.

Sedikides, C., Herbst, K. C., Hardin, D. P., & Dardis, G. J. (2002c). Accountability as a deterrent to self-enhancement: The search for mechanisms. *Journal of Personality and Social Psychology, 83*, 592–605.

Sedikides, C., Horton, R. S., & Gregg, A. P. (2007d). The why's the limit: Curtailing self-enhancement with explanatory introspection. *Journal of Personality*, *75*, 783–824.

Sedikides, C., & Luke, M. (2007). On when self-enhancement and self-criticism function adaptively and maladaptively. In E. C. Chang (Ed.), *Self-criticism and self-enhancement: Theory, research, and clinical implications* (pp. 181–198). Washington, DC: APA Books.

Sedikides, C., Rudich, E. A., Gregg, A. P., Kumashiro, M., & Rusbult, C. (2004b). Are normal narcissists psychologically healthy?: Self-esteem matters. *Journal of Personality and Social Psychology*, *87*, 400–416.

Sedikides, C., & Skowronski, J. A. (1997). The symbolic self in evolutionary context. *Personality and Social Psychology Review*, *1*, 80–102.

Sedikides, C., & Skowronski, J. J. (2003). Evolution of the self: Issues and prospects. In M. R. Leary & J. P. Tangney (Eds.), *Handbook of self and identity* (pp. 594–609). New York: Guilford Press.

Sedikides, C., Skowronski, J. J., & Dunbar, R. I. M. (2006). When and why did the human self evolve? In M. Schaller, J. A. Simpson, & D. T. Kenrick (Eds.), *Evolution and social psychology: Frontiers in social psychology* (pp. 55–80). New York: Psychology Press.

Sedikides, C., & Strube, M. J. (1997). Self-evaluation: To thine own self be good, to thine own self be sure, to thine own self be true, and to thine own self be better. *Advances in Experimental Social Psychology*, *29*, 209–269.

Sheldon, K. M., Elliot, A. J., Kim, Y., & Kasser, T. (2001). What's satisfying about satisfying events? Comparing ten candidate psychological needs. *Journal of Personality and Social Psychology*, *80*, 325–339.

Shepperd, J., Malone, W., & Sweeny, K. (2008). Exploring causes of the self-serving bias. *Social and Personality Psychology Compass*, *2*, 895–908.

Showers, C. (1992). Compartmentalization of positive and negative self-knowledge: Keeping bad apples out of the bunch. *Journal of Personality and Social Psychology*, *62*, 1036–1049.

Sinclair, L., & Kunda, Z. (1999). Reactions to a Black professional: Motivated inhibition and activation of conflicting stereotypes. *Journal of Personality and Social Psychology*, *77*, 885–904.

Skowronski, J. J., Betz, A. L., Thompson, C. P., & Shannon, L. (1991). Social memory in everyday life: Recall of self-events and other-events. *Journal of Personality and Social Psychology*, *60*, 831–843.

Skowronski, J. J., Gibbons, J. A., Vogl, R. J., & Walker, W. R. (2004). The effect of social disclosure on the affective intensity provoked by autobiographical memories. *Self and Identity*, *3*, 285–309.

Snyder, C. R., & Higgins, R. L. (1988). Excuses: Their effective role in the negotiation of reality. *Psychological Bulletin*, *104*, 23–35.

Stapel, D. A., & Johnson, C. S. (2007). When nothing compares to me: How defensive motivations and similarity shape social comparison effects. *European Journal of Social Psychology*, *37*, 824–838.

Stewart, S. M., Byrne, B. M., Lee, P. W. H., Ho, L. M., Kennard, B. D., Hughes, C., et al. (2003). Personal versus interpersonal contributors to depressive symptoms among Hong Kong adolescents. *International Journal of Psychology*, *38*, 160–169.

Stone, J., Aronson, E., Crain, A. L., Winslow, M. P., & Fried, C. B. (1994). Inducing hypocrisy as a means of encouraging young adults to use condoms. *Personality and Social Psychology Bulletin*, *20*, 116–128.

Swann, W. B. Jr. Chang-Schneider, C., & McClarty, K. (2007). Do our self-views matter?: Self-concept and self-esteem in everyday life. *American Psychologist*, *62*, 84–94.

Swann, W. B. Jr., Rentfrow, P. J., & Guinn, J. (2003). Self-verification: The search for coherence. In M. Leary & J. Tangney (Eds.), *Handbook of self and identity*. New York: Guilford Press.

Taylor, S. E., Lerner, J. S., Sherman, D. K., Sage, R. M., & McDowell, N. K. (2003a). Portrait of the self-enhancer: Well-adjusted and well-liked or maladjusted and friendless? *Journal of Personality and Social Psychology, 84*, 165–176.

Taylor, S. E., Lerner, J. S., Sherman, D. K., Sage, R. M., & McDowell, N. K. (2003b). Are self-enhancing cognitions associated with healthy or unhealthy biological profiles? *Journal of Personality and Social Psychology, 85*, 605–615.

Tesser, A. (2003). Self-evaluation. In M. Leary & J. Tangney (Eds.), *Handbook of self and identity* (pp. 275–290). New York: Guilford Press.

Tetlock, P. E. & Levi, A. (1982). Attribution bias: On the inconclusiveness of the cognition–motivation debate. *Journal of Experimental Social Psychology, 18*, 68–88.

Tice, D. M. (1991). Esteem protection or enhancement?: Self-handicapping motives and attributions differ by trait self-esteem. *Journal of Personality and Social Psychology, 60*, 711–725.

Tice, D. M., & Baumeister, R. F. (1997). Longitudinal study of procrastination, performance, stress, and health: The costs and benefits of dawdling. *Psychological Science, 8*, 454–458.

Triplett, N. (1897). The dynamogenic factors in pacemaking and competition. *American Journal of Psychology, 9*, 507–533.

Trzesniewski, K. H., Donnellan, M. B., Caspi, A., Moffitt, T. E., Robins, R. W., & Poultin, R. (2006). Adolescent low self-esteem is a risk factor for adult poor health, criminal behavior, and limited economic prospects. *Developmental Psychology, 42*, 381–390.

Vohs, K. D., Baumeister, R. F., & Ciarocco, N. J. (2005). Self-regulation and self-presentation: Regulatory resource depletion impairs impression management and effortful self-presentation depletes regulatory resources. *Journal of Personality and Social Psychology, 88*, 632–657.

Vonk, R. (1999). Impression formation and impression management: Motives, traits, and likeability inferred from self-promoting and self-deprecating behavior. *Social Cognition, 17*, 390–412.

Walker, W. R., Skowronski, J. J., & Thompson, C. P. (2003). Life is pleasant—and memory helps to keep it that way. *Review of General Psychology, 7*, 203–210.

Weary, G. (1979). Self-serving attributional biases: Perceptual or response distortions? *Journal of Personality and Social Psychology, 37*, 1418–1420.

Weary Bradley, G. (1978). Self-serving biases in attribution process: A re-examination of the fact or fiction question. *Journal of Personality and Social Psychology, 36*, 56–71.

Weiner, B. (1972). *Theories of motivation: From mechanism to cognition.* Chicago: Rand McNally.

Weinstein, N. D. (1980). Unrealistic optimism about future life events. *Journal of Personality and Social Psychology, 39*, 806–820.

Weinstein, N. D. (1984). Why it won't happen to me: Perceptions of risk factors and susceptibility. *Health Psychology, 3*, 431–457.

Williams, E. F., & Gilovich, T. (2008). Do people really believe they are above average? *Journal of Experimental Social Psychology, 44*, 1121–1128.

Wilson, T. D., Wheatley, T. P., Kurtz, J. L., Dunn, E. W., & Gilbert, D. T. (2004). When to fire: Anticipatory versus postevent reconstrual of uncontrollable events. *Personality and Social Psychology Bulletin, 30*, 340–351.

Windschitl, P. D., Kruger, J., & Sims, E. N. (2003). The influence of egocentrism and focalism on people's optimism in competition: When what affects us equally affects me more. *Journal of Personality and Social Psychology, 85*, 389–408.

Yamagichi, T., Hashimoto, H., & Schug, J. (2008). Preferences versus strategies as explanations for culture-specific behavior. *Psychological Science, 19,* 579–584.

Yamaguchi, S., Greenwald, A. G., Banaji, M. R., Murakami, F., Chen, D., Shiomura, K., et al. (2007). Apparent universality of positive implicit self-esteem. *Psychological Science, 18,* 498–500.

Zell, E., & Alicke, M.D. (in press). Self-evaluative effects of temporal and social comparison information. *Journal of Experimental Social Psychology, 45,* 223–227.

Zuckerman, M. (1979). Attribution of success and failure revisited, or: The motivational bias is alive and well in attribution theory. *Journal of Personality, 47,* 245–287.

EUROPEAN REVIEW OF SOCIAL PSYCHOLOGY
2009, 20, 49–96

Source factors in persuasion:
A self-validation approach

Pablo Briñol

Universidad Autónoma de Madrid, Spain

Richard E. Petty

Ohio State University, Columbus, OH, USA

The persuasion literature has examined several mechanisms that have contributed to understanding the effectiveness of credible, attractive, similar, and powerful sources. These traditionally studied processes focus on how persuasive sources can affect attitudes by serving as peripheral cues or by influencing the direction or the amount of thoughts generated. After describing these processes that operate at the primary level of cognition, we review research on self-validation that demonstrates how and when source factors can affect a secondary cognition—thought confidence. Thought confidence refers to a metacognitive form of cognition. This recently discovered mechanism can account for some already established persuasion outcomes (e.g., more persuasion with high- than low-credibility or similar sources), but by a completely different process than postulated previously. Moreover, under some circumstances we have also been able to obtain findings opposite to those typically observed (e.g., more persuasion with low- than high-credible or similar sources). Our research reveals that a consideration of self-validation processes provides an integrative mechanism for understanding many other unexplored source variables, such as oneself as a source, source matching and mimicry, and threatening sources.

Social influence through persuasion is the most prevalent as well as the most civil means of social control available to governments as well as to individuals. In contrast to satisfying wants and needs by using force, violence, terror or threats, persuasion provides an option that is more likely to be successful, lasting, satisfying, and rewarding for everyone. Thus, persuasion is likely to be the most frequent and ultimately efficient approach

Correspondence should be addressed to Pablo Briñol, Department of Psychology, Universidad Autónoma de Madrid, Campus de Cantoblanco, Carretera de Colmenar, Km. 15, Madrid, 28049, Spain. E-mail: pablo.brinnol@uam.es

http://www.psypress.com/ersp   DOI: 10.1080/10463280802643640

to social influence. Among many other reasons, understanding persuasion is important because if the attitudes of a large number of individuals change, then societal norms (governments, habits, and ways of life) presumably will change as well.

We all try to persuade others in both professional and personal contexts. Given that people try to persuade and are also targets of persuasion in many of their social interactions, they have learned something about how persuasion works (e.g., persuasive strategies) thorough trial and error. Practitioners like lawyers, politicians, and salespeople have also devoted an incredible amount of time and effort to understanding persuasion, and what they can do to be more persuasive sources of influence. In contrast to this intuitive persuasion knowledge, scholars in disciplines like social psychology, marketing, and communication have systematically studied persuasion for many years through empirical observations and experimental approaches. In this review we describe how these more rigorous approaches have been useful for understanding the psychology of persuasive sources.

We use the term persuasion to refer to any procedure with the potential to change someone's mind. Although many constructs can be targeted for change (e.g., emotions, beliefs, behaviours), we focus on attitudes (people's general evaluations of people, objects, and issues) because attitudes serve a key mediational role (e.g., attitude change mediates the impact of belief change on behaviour change) and have been the focus of most persuasion research. Nevertheless, the same fundamental persuasion processes can operate regardless of the target of change.

In the typical situation in which persuasion might take place, a person or a group of people (i.e., the recipient, or audience) receives a communication (i.e., the message) from another individual or group (i.e., the source) in a particular setting (i.e., the context). The success of a persuasive attempt depends in part on whether the attitudes of the recipients are modified in the desired direction, with special attention to whether these attitudes in turn influence people's subsequent behaviour. In this review, we focus on the study of how different aspects of the source who delivers a persuasive proposal can influence recipient's attitudes towards that proposal.

More specifically, this chapter describes the basic mechanisms by which source factors can influence persuasion highlighting the role of a recently discovered process—called *self-validation* (Petty, Briñol, & Tormala, 2002). Unlike previous mechanisms that focus on primary or first-order cognition, this new process emphasises secondary or metacognition (Petty, Briñol, Tormala, & Wegener, 2007). In particular, we argue that source variables, such as credibility, attractiveness, status, and power can affect attitude change not only by previously studied mechanisms such as serving as a peripheral cue or by affecting the number or valence of thoughts generated

(Petty & Cacioppo, 1986), but by a new mechanism—affecting thought confidence.

We provide a comprehensive review of the primary and secondary processes by which source factors affect attitude change, and describe some research illustrating these processes. In reviewing the basic mechanisms underlying source persuasion we will: (1) provide a brief overview of social psychology's historical contribution to this area of research, outlining a general framework for understanding the key processes of persuasion, (2) use this framework to review classic and contemporary research on source-induced attitude change based on processes involving primary cognitions, (3) highlight *self-validation* as the most recently discovered process underlying source persuasion, (4) describe how the operation of this metacognitive process is moderated by several variables and how it differs from other mechanisms based on secondary cognition, (5) describe research revealing that self-validation can contribute to understanding traditional and new source phenomena in persuasion, (6) examine the impact of source variables on other, additional metacognitive dimensions, and (7) discuss how the self can also be interpreted as a persuasive source in attitude change.

SOURCE FACTORS IN PERSUASION: A BRIEF HISTORY

The first intuitive and empirical approaches to source factors in persuasion were guided by relatively simple questions that focused on main effects (e.g., are experts more or less persuasive than non-experts?). These early ideas about persuasion also tended to focus on just one process by which sources would have their impact (e.g., increased credibility increasing persuasion by enhancing learning of the message arguments; see Petty, 1997).

Although the main-effect and single process assumptions provided a reasonable early start to the field, it was not long before complications arose (see Petty & Briñol, 2008). First, source credibility was sometimes associated with increased attitude change and sometimes with decreased influence. Also, support for any one mechanism by which persuasion worked was not compelling. Finally, a puzzle that researchers have struggled with for decades is that sometimes attitude changes generated by source factors tended to be relatively durable and impactful (e.g., guiding behaviour), but sometimes the attitude changes produced were rather transitory and inconsequential. Thus, theories evolved to account for multiple effects, processes, and consequences of persuasion variables. Contemporary theories of persuasion, such as the elaboration likelihood model (ELM; Petty & Cacioppo, 1986), the heuristic-systematic model (HSM; Chaiken, Liberman,

& Eagly, 1989), and the unimodel (Kruglanski & Thompson, 1999) were generated to articulate multiple ways in which source (and other) variables could affect attitudes in different situations.

For example, the ELM holds that there are a finite set of persuasion processes, and that source factors (like any other communication variable) can influence attitudes by affecting one of these processes (see Petty & Briñol, 2006, for a discussion of other taxonomies of fundamental processes underlying persuasion). That is, any given feature of the persuasive setting (e.g., source attractiveness), can affect attitudes in one of five ways. As illustrated in Figure 1, the variable can (1) serve as a peripheral cue, or (2) serve as an issue-relevant argument, or (3) affect the motivation or ability to think about the message, or (4) bias the nature of the thoughts that come to mind, or (5) affect structural properties of the thoughts, such as how much confidence people have in them. The ELM also identifies the general conditions under which source variables act in each of the different roles, such as the likelihood of extensive or minimal thinking. In addition, because the ELM postulates that people want attitudes that are adaptive, it allows for the possibility that people will correct their initial judgemental tendency when people suspect that a source has biased their judgement (e.g., see Wegener & Petty, 1997).

In line with the ELM's multiple roles postulate, source factors, such as expertise, attractiveness, and power, have been found to affect attitude change through these different processes depending on the situation. Thus, source factors have been found to influence persuasion by serving as a peripheral cue when elaboration is relatively low, and by affecting how much thinking people do about the message when elaboration is not constrained to be high or low. On the other hand, when motivation and ability to think are relatively high, source factors have influenced persuasion by biasing the

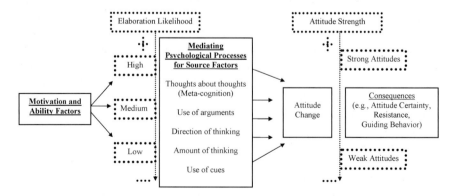

Figure 1. Fundamental processes by which source factors influence attitude change.

direction of the thoughts, serving as persuasive arguments, and affecting thought confidence.

As we describe briefly in the first part of this review, source factors can influence each of the above-mentioned processes depending on the circumstances. In this review we first mention some of the traditionally studied processes by which sources have been shown to influence persuasion and review some illustrative research. Then we focus more extensively on the more recent self-validation mechanism and the evidence for it.

MECHANISMS OF PERSUASION BASED ON PRIMARY COGNITION

Source factors can serve as cues

Early approaches to persuasion gave source factors just one role in the persuasion process, although the particular role varied with the theory. For example, in the original Hovland (Yale) learning framework, source variables (e.g., trustworthy sources) affected persuasion by increasing learning of the message (Hovland, Janis, & Kelley, 1953). In a second version of Hovland's theory, however, sources were proposed to serve as simple augmenting/discounting cues (Kelman & Hovland, 1953), which could increase or decrease persuasion independent of argument learning. In yet another account of source variables proposed by Kelman (1958) some source variables (expert sources) induced persuasion because of internalisa-tion of message arguments, whereas other source variables (attractive sources) induced persuasion because of identification with the source. Thus, in these theories, particular content (e.g., attractive source) mapped onto particular processes (e.g., persuasion by augmenting cue or identification).

As noted in the introduction, a unique feature of contemporary theories of persuasion (e.g., ELM, HSM, unimodel) in contrast to prior approaches is that the new theories do not confound content and process. In these new theories, any one variable (e.g., an expert source) can induce persuasion by multiple processes. Thus, contemporary research has pointed to numerous source variables that can serve as simple cues when motivation and ability to think are relatively low (e.g., Briñol, Petty, & Tormala, 2004, Chaiken, 1980; Petty, Cacioppo, & Goldman, 1981). Furthermore, several specific mechan-isms by which these source cues can affect attitudes when thinking is low have been proposed (e.g., classical conditioning, identification with the source, and use of heuristics). When source factors serve as heuristics or simple cues they produce persuasion in the same direction as their valence. Thus, likable, attractive, similar, or expert sources produce more persuasion than dislikeable, unattractive, dissimilar, or inexpert sources.

For example, in one study illustrating a cue role for sources, Petty et al. (1981) presented undergraduate students with a counter-attitudinal advocacy (implementing comprehensive exams) containing either strong or weak arguments that emanated from a source of either high (a professor of education) or low expertise (a local high school student). For some participants, the policy was high in personal relevance (they were told that the policy would begin the following year so that they would be affected by it) whereas for others the policy was low in relevance (the changes would take place in 10 years so it would not affect them personally). Attitudes towards the proposal were influenced primarily by the quality of the arguments in the message under high relevance, whereas under low relevance attitudes were influenced primarily by the expertise of the source. Thus, under low thinking conditions, rather than diligently considering the issue-relevant arguments, a person may accept an advocacy simply because it was presented by an expert (e.g., "if an expert says it, it must be true"; see also Chaiken, 1980).

Source factors can affect the amount of thinking

When thinking is not constrained to be high or low by other variables, one of the most fundamental things that source variables can do to influence attitudes is to affect the amount of thinking people do about a persuasive communication. Increasing the amount of thinking can get people to carefully process the relevant information presented and therefore be influenced by it. Getting people to process information carefully magnifies the impact of the quality of the arguments in the message. Thus, enhancing thinking about strong arguments tends to produce more persuasion, but enhancing thinking about weak arguments tends to reduce persuasion. For example, several studies have shown that when a person is not normally motivated to think about the message arguments, more thinking can be provoked by having the individual arguments presented by multiple sources rather than just one (Harkins & Petty, 1981). When the arguments are strong, having multiple sources thereby increases persuasion, but when the arguments are weak, having multiple sources present the arguments reduces persuasion.

It is also important to note that individuals vary in what type of source information serves as a motivator of thought. For example, DeBono and Harnish (1988) found that individuals low in self-monitoring (Snyder, 1974) processed messages to a greater extent when they were presented by an expert rather than an attractive source (see also Petty & Cacioppo, 1983; Puckett, Petty, Cacioppo, & Fisher, 1983). High self-monitors did the opposite. This is because source factors can be associated with the type of information of most interest to high and low self-monitors respectively (i.e., image versus quality information). Source factors can also influence persuasion by affecting the ability (rather than the motivation) to process carefully. For example, if the speaker talks too quickly (Briñol & Petty, 2003), thinking about the message has been found to be disrupted (resulting in reduced argument quality effects on attitudes).[1]

People not only think more carefully when they have the resources to do so, and when the message stems from several sources rather than just one, but also when they perceive the source to be similar to themselves in one way or another. This is presumably because linking a message to a similar source increases its self-relevance (Petty & Cacioppo, 1979). For example, people tend to think more about a persuasive message when it is presented by a source who shares the message recipient's group membership than when it is delivered by a source who does not share this membership (e.g., Mackie, Worth, & Asuncion, 1990). This increase in message elaboration as a function of similarity based on belonging to the same group is more likely to occur when the topic of the message is group-related (Mackie, Gastardo-Conaco, & Skelly, 1992; van Knippenberg & Wilke, 1992) and when the message is delivered by a prototypical or representative group member (van Knippenberg, Lossie, & Wilke, 1994). These effects on extent of thinking based on group membership are also more likely to occur when background levels of elaboration likelihood are relatively moderate. As is the case with other source factors, social identity can also influence persuasion by other, different processes under other circumstances (for an extensive review of social identity and persuasion, see, e.g., Fleming & Petty, 2000).[2]

In addition to affecting the perceived self-relevance of a message, message sources can sometimes induce a general sense of certainty or doubt. In general people will think more about messages from sources who make them feel doubt rather than certainty. Sources can induce doubt or uncertainty when the source of the message is seen as untrustworthy (Priester & Petty,

---

[1] Of course, as noted earlier, when motivation to think is already set at a high or low level, these same source factors can serve in other roles. For example, when motivation to think is relatively low, a fast-talking speaker can be more persuasive, presumably because the fast-talking speaker is assumed to be more knowledgeable (e.g., see Smith & Shaffer, 1995).

[2] Identifying with the source of a message can (a) serve as a peripheral cue to decide about the proposal under low elaboration conditions, (b) bias the direction of the thoughts that come to mind under high thinking conditions, and (c) increase thinking under moderate elaboration likelihood. In general, a match of any kind (e.g., similarity) between the message source and the recipient, not just identity, can lead to persuasion through different processes in different situations. Thus, in addition to the mechanisms already described, similarity with the source or a matching in any dimension between source and recipient can presumably operate through self-validation processes as well. For example, if a woman who is highly identified with her gender learns that the speaker is a woman after thinking about the message, a feeling of confidence in her thoughts should be enhanced relative to conditions in which the recipient learns that the source is a male.

1995) or surprising (Ziegler, Diehl, & Ruther, 2002). Related to this possibility, people can also be ambivalent towards the source of a message. Thus, a recipient can feel doubt by having both positive and negative evaluative reactions towards the source (i.e., explicit attitudinal ambivalence) or by feeling any other form of discrepancy with regard to the source (e.g., when the source has conflicting expertise and attractiveness information).

The literature has documented that such explicit conflicts are typically experienced as aversive and dysfunctional (e.g., Abelson & Ronsenberg, 1958; Higgins, 1987; Newcomb, 1968; Osgood & Tannenbaum, 1955). As a consequence people attempt to deal with their ambivalence in one way or another. Perhaps the most common approach to dealing with ambivalence is enhanced thinking or information processing (e.g., Abelson et al., 1968; Aronson, 1969; Festinger, 1957; Hass, Katz, Rizzo, Bailey, & Moore, 1992; Heider, 1958; Nordgren, van Harreveld, & van der Pligt 2006). By considering additional information, individuals can hope to gain enough information for one or the other side of the discrepancy in order to resolve or minimise the inconsistency, or at least the subjective discomfort that results from it (e.g., Hänze, 2001; Hodson, Maio, & Esses, 2001; Jonas, Diehl, & Bromer, 1997). For example, Maio, Bell, and Esses (1996) measured participants' attitudinal ambivalence regarding immigration to Canada, and then exposed them to a discrepancy-relevant message favouring immigration from Hong Kong to Canada that contained either strong or weak arguments. The extent to which participants processed the message information was assessed by examining the extent to which the quality of the arguments made a difference in post-message immigration attitudes. As noted earlier, for people to be differently affected by strong and weak persuasive messages they have to carefully attend to and think about the content of the information. As expected, Maio et al. (1996) found that individuals who had ambivalent attitudes towards immigration were more influenced by argument quality than were unambivalent individuals, suggesting that they engaged in enhanced scrutiny of the issue-relevant information presented.

Although research has focused extensively on explicit discrepancies, relatively little work has examined the potential existence of and consequences of discrepancies in which one cognitive element may not be easily accessible (i.e., implicit ambivalence; see Petty & Briñol, 2009). That is, people can also be ambivalent towards the source of a message, both at the explicit level and the implicit level (e.g., when some information about the source is not consciously endorsed, but still influences automatic measures, creating implicit–explicit discrepancies; see Briñol, Petty, & Wheeler, 2006; Petty, Tormala, Briñol, & Jarvis, 2006).

Relevant to this issue is work on the persuasiveness of stigmatised sources. For example, there are now a number of studies suggesting that

Whites will sometimes engage in greater processing of a persuasive message from a Black than a White source. In the first research on this topic White and Harkins (1994) presented White participants with a persuasive message from a White or a Black source on the topic of senior comprehensive exams. The message contained either strong or weak arguments. Across several replications, they consistently found that the impact of argument quality on attitudes was greater when the source was Black rather than White.

In series of follow-up studies Petty, Fleming, and White (1999) suggested that this enhanced scrutiny might stem from a "watchdog motivation". That is, Whites might be processing messages from Blacks more than Whites in order to guard against possible prejudice towards Black sources. Petty et al. reasoned that if this were true, it should only be Whites low in prejudice who would show the enhanced scrutiny effect. To examine this, prejudice was assessed with several explicit measures (Katz & Hass, 1988; McConahay, Hardee, & Batts, 1981), and reactions to persuasive messages from Black and White sources were assessed. In several studies it was found that only Whites who were low in explicit prejudice processed messages more for Black than White sources. This enhanced scrutiny of Black sources by low-prejudiced individuals was replicated when the message was about a Black versus a White target individual rather than from a Black versus a White source (Fleming, Petty, & White, 2005; see alsoLivingston & Sinclair, 2008).

In a recent series of studies we tested a variation of the watchdog hypothesis based on the idea of implicit ambivalence (see Petty & Briñol, 2009). Specifically, our conceptualisation of implicit ambivalence suggests that among individuals low in explicit (i.e., deliberative) prejudice it is those who are also high in implicit (i.e., automatic) prejudice who will do the most processing. If people are also low in implicit prejudice, there is nothing internal to watch out for. Also, our framework suggests that individuals who are high in explicit prejudice and low in implicit prejudice will also engage in enhanced message processing. The reason is that these individuals would also experience some implicit ambivalence because their deliberative attitudes do not match their automatic evaluations.

To examine this possibility, in an initial study (Petty, Briñol, See, & Fleming, 2008), we assessed Ohio State University students' attitudes towards African-Americans using both automatic and deliberative measures. The automatic measure was an implicit association test (IAT) in which stereotypically Black names (e.g., Tyrone, LaToya) and White names (e.g., Andrew, Katie) were paired with good (e.g., freedom, love) and bad (e.g., poison, disease) terms (see Greenwald et al., 1998, for the scoring procedure and rationale). The explicit measure consisted of a series of pro and anti Black statements to which participants were to rate their extent of agreement (see Katz & Hass, 1988, for the scoring procedure and rationale).

The explicit and implicit measures of attitudes were unrelated to each other. Following previous research on explicit–implicit discrepancies (Briñol et al., 2006), an index of explicit–implicit discrepancy was formed as the absolute value of the difference between the standardised explicit and implicit measures of racial attitudes. We also coded for the direction of discrepancy (i.e., implicit score more prejudiced than explicit or vice versa) to see if this mattered.

After completing the implicit and explicit measures of racial attitudes, all of the students were exposed to a message advocating a new programme to hire African-American faculty at their university that was supported with either strong or weak arguments. As in past research, the strong arguments were designed to elicit favourable thoughts if people thought about them, whereas the weak arguments were designed to elicit mostly unfavourable thoughts (see Petty & Cacioppo, 1986). The strong arguments, among other things, mentioned that the new programme would allow class sizes to be reduced and would allow a greater percentage of classes to be taught by faculty rather than graduate students. In contrast, the message with weak arguments argued that the new proposal was desirable because it would allow current professors to have more free time and that several parents wrote letters in support of the proposal.

Consistent with the idea that people with automatic–deliberative discrepancies would act as if they were ambivalent, discrepancy interacted with argument quality to predict attitudes towards the programme. That is, as illustrated in Figure 2, as the discrepancy between attitudes assessed with implicit and explicit measures increased, attitudes were more affected by argument quality. Notably, the direction of the discrepancy did not further qualify the results, although there were relatively few individuals who on an absolute basis were high in explicit prejudice and low in implicit prejudice. Nevertheless, these results clearly demonstrated that among those who were low in their explicit prejudice, it was primarily those high in implicit prejudice who engaged in greater scrutiny of a message about a programme favouring Blacks.

In summary, source factors can influence persuasion by affecting the extent to which the recipient of a proposal thinks carefully about it. In this section we have reviewed how several aspects of the source can affect the ability (e.g., when sources speak too quickly) and the motivation (e.g., when sources make the recipient doubtful) of the recipient to think. Special attention was dedicated to the cases in which the message was presented by stigmatised sources, and when the recipient of the persuasive message was ambivalent towards those sources, both at the explicit and implicit levels. In the next section we describe how these and other source factors can influence persuasion not only by affecting the amount but also the direction of the thoughts generated by the recipient.

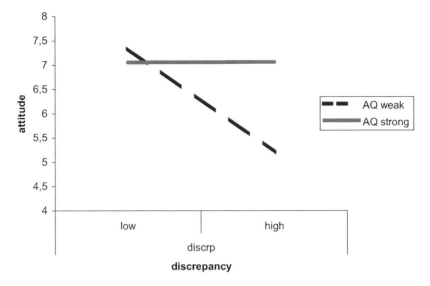

Figure 2. Attitudes as a function of argument quality and automatic–deliberative discrepancies regarding the group of the source. Adapted from Petty, Briñol, See, and Fleming (2008). As implicit ambivalence increases, elaboration also increases, and attitudes are more affected by argument quality.

Source factors can affect the direction of thinking

When motivation and ability to think are high, such as when the topic is one of high personal relevance (Petty & Cacioppo, 1979) and there are few distractions present (Petty, Wells, & Brock, 1976), people will be engaged in careful thought about a proposal, but that thinking can be biased by source variables. Most importantly, source variables can motivate or enable people to either support or derogate the content of the information provided. Some features of the source increase the likelihood of favourable thoughts being elicited, but others increase the likelihood of unfavourable thoughts coming to mind. For example, Chaiken and Maheswaran (1994) demonstrated that an expert (vs non-expert) source had a greater impact on attitudes by affecting the direction of the thoughts generated in response to a proposal, but only when the message was ambiguous (vs unambiguous), and when personal importance of the message topic was high (vs low). Under similar conditions, Tormala, Briñol, and Petty (2006) found that persuasion was mediated by the biased thoughts generated towards the proposal. Importantly, other research has also shown if people believe that their thoughts have been biased by the source, they can adjust their judgements in a direction opposite to the implication of the thoughts (correction processes; Petty, Wegener, & White, 1998; Wegener & Petty, 1995, 1997).

Source factors serving as arguments

According to the ELM, when the amount of thinking is high people assess the relevance of *all* of the information in the context and that comes to mind in order to determine the merits of the attitude object under consideration (Petty & Cacioppo, 1986). That is, people examine source factors (in addition to other information from the message, recipient, context, and internally generated information) as possible arguments or reasons for favouring or disfavouring the attitude object (see also Kruglanski et al., 2005). For example, source attractiveness has been found to influence persuasion by serving as an argument when it related to the central merits of the proposal (e.g., public image of a restaurant, beauty products; Petty & Cacioppo, 1983). Just as individual differences such as self-monitoring can affect what type of source information serves as persuasive evidence for any given attitude object, so too can features of the situation (e.g., dimensions of judgement that have recently been primed; e.g., Sherman, Mackie, & Driscoll, 1990).

Summary of the influence of source factors on thinking processes

One of the earliest and most well-known findings in the persuasion literature is that high-credibility sources often produce more attitude change than sources of low credibility. Similar findings have been found for high (vs low) attractive sources, as well as for sources with relative differences in social status and power. In this section we have outlined four ways in which these source effects (and the opposite) could come about according to the ELM. That is, depending on the message recipient's extent of thinking, source factors such as source credibility, attractiveness, and status have been found to influence persuasion by serving as a simple cue, biasing the thoughts message recipients have, serving as a piece of evidence relevant to the central merits of the issue, and determining the amount of information processing that occurs. In the next section we will describe how these and other source factors can also influence persuasion by affecting a recently discovered process. Understanding process by which source variables can produce persuasion is important because it informs us of both the immediate and long-term consequences for persuasion.

A NEW PROCESS FOR SOURCE PERSUASION: SELF-VALIDATION

Having provided a brief description and some illustrations of the more traditionally studied persuasion processes (which focused on primary cognition), we turn to the core of this review, which is on how and when source factors affect persuasion by influencing thought confidence (which focuses on secondary cognition). Primary thoughts are those that occur at a direct level of cognition and involve our initial associations of some object with some attribute or feeling (e.g., this proposal is stupid). Following a primary thought, people can also generate other thoughts that occur at a second level, which involve reflections on the first-level thoughts (am I sure that the proposal is stupid?). *Metacognition* refers to these second-order thoughts, or our thoughts about our thoughts or thought processes (Petty et al., 2007; Jost, Kruglanski & Nelson, 1998). In other words, metacognition refers to thinking about thinking.

In recent years metacognition has assumed a prominent role not only in the domain of social psychology (Jost et al., 1998: Petty et al., 2007), but also in memory research (Koriat & Goldsmith, 1996), clinical practice (Beck & Greenberg, 1994), and advertising (Friestad & Wright, 1995). Indeed, metacognition has been touted as one of the top 100 topics in psychological research (Nelson, 1992).

According to most metacognitive views (including self-validation), secondary metacognitive processes are consequential in guiding further thinking, judgement, and action. For example, other research on metacognition has found that the stronger one's *feeling of knowing* about a piece of information, the more time one is willing to spend searching for it (e.g., Costermans, Lories, & Ansay 1992), particularly when one has the subjective experience that the information is on the *tip of the tongue* (Yzerbyt, Lories, & Dardenne, 1998). Instead of examining the feeling of knowing, the self-validation approach focuses on a sense of confidence in one's thoughts. We argue that metacognitive confidence is consequential because the extent of thought confidence affects whether people use their thoughts. That is, the extent of confidence determines whether people translate their individual thoughts into more general judgements or evaluations that in turn guide behaviour. Thus, two people might have the *same* thought but one person might have considerably greater confidence in that thought than the other, and the greater confidence in the thought, the greater its impact on judgement. This idea is referred to as the *self-validation hypothesis* (Petty et al., 2002). The key notion is that generating thoughts is not sufficient for them to have an impact on judgements. Rather, one must also have confidence in them.

Importantly for the present review, source factors can influence attitude change by affecting thought confidence, which is the key component of the *self-validation* mechanism of persuasion. According to the self-validation logic, when people are thinking, it is not only the number and nature of thoughts (i.e., the two dimensions of thoughts relevant to mechanisms based on primary cognition) people have that determines the extent of influence, but also the confidence with which people hold their thoughts. Increasing confidence in positive thoughts should increase persuasion, but increasing confidence in negative thoughts should reduce persuasion. The opposite holds for increasing doubt. When doubt in favourable thoughts is increased, persuasion declines, but when doubt in unfavourable thoughts is increased, resistance is undermined and persuasion is enhanced.

In an initial study to examine whether the key idea of the self-validation hypothesis had any merit, thought confidence was assessed following a persuasive message along with the traditionally measured variables of thought valence and thought number. In this study Petty et al. (2002) asked participants to read a persuasive message about a campus issue, to think carefully about the proposal, and to list what they thought about the proposal. Following the thought-listing task, participants reported the confidence they had in the thoughts they listed as well as their attitudes towards the proposal. In accord with the self-validation hypothesis, the relationship between thoughts and attitudes was significantly greater to the extent that confidence was relatively high rather than low. In other words, to the extent that people had confidence in their thoughts, persuasion depended on the valence of those thoughts. On the other hand, to the extent that people lacked confidence in their thoughts, persuasion was less dependent on thought valence. This study showed that thought confidence could play an important role in persuasion and thus understanding the origins of thought confidence was important. Again, this is important because previous mechanisms of persuasion were based exclusively on the valence and number of thoughts.

For practical purposes it was very informative to know that measuring thought confidence can lead to increased predictability in attitudes. Nevertheless, because confidence was measured rather than manipulated in this study, some question could be raised concerning the interpretation of the results. For example, although we found no differences in the number or quality of the thoughts generated across levels of thought confidence, it remains a possibility that our measures of these constructs were ineffective. Thus, it was important to manipulate thought confidence to isolate the causal role of this variable. Furthermore, if it could be shown that direct manipulations of thought confidence were effective in modifying the impact of thoughts on attitudes, this would provide a new and unexplored way to produce persuasion.

In one study demonstrating this, college students were exposed to a message containing strong or weak arguments in favour of a new university exam policy (Petty et al., 2002). Examples of the gist of strong arguments include that students' grades would improve if the exams were adopted and that the average starting salary of graduates would increase. Examples of the gist of weak arguments, on the other hand, include that implementing the exams would allow the university to take part in a national trend and that the exams would give students the opportunity to compare their scores with those of students at other universities. After thinking about the message and listing their thoughts towards the proposal, participants were asked to think about personal experiences in which they experienced confidence or doubt. Those who articulated past instances of confidence became more certain of the validity of their recently generated thoughts to the message compared to those who reflected on instances of doubt. That is, the feeling of confidence stemming from the memory exercise was overgeneralised (or misattributed) to the thoughts recently generated to the persuasive message. Furthermore, this confidence led to greater persuasion when recipients' thoughts were largely favourable (i.e., to the strong arguments), but more confidence led to less persuasion when recipients' thoughts were largely unfavourable (i.e., to the weak arguments). Thus, as shown in Figure 3, confidence (vs doubt) increased the impact of thought valence (and argument quality) on attitudes.

This study indicates that in addition to considering the number and valence of thoughts elicited by a message, confidence in thoughts can play a causal role in persuasion. That is, manipulating confidence after generating thoughts ruled out the possibility that there were unmeasured differences in the quality or the cogency or the number of thoughts listed by high- and low-confidence individuals that might have contributed to the effects observed in the initial study. Taken together, these studies reveal that persuasion attempts can be unsuccessful not because a message has failed to elicit many favourable thoughts, but because people lack confidence in the thoughts they generated. Similarly, people might fail to resist influence not because they have not generated counterarguments to the message but because they fail to have confidence in those thoughts.

Figure 3. Attitudes as a function of argument quality and confidence. Adapted from Petty et al. (2002, exp. 3).

Summary of self-validation

The initial studies on self-validation indicated that the relationship between thoughts and attitudes was significantly greater to the extent that confidence was relatively high rather than low. When individuals wrote favourable thoughts, increased confidence was associated with more persuasion, but when individuals wrote negative thoughts, increased confidence was associated with reduced persuasion. It is important to note that in studies described in the above section, the self-validation hypothesis was supported whether thought confidence was measured or manipulated. We also used two different kinds of measures of thought confidence: assessing confidence in each individual thought or in all of one's thoughts together. Furthermore, as we will emphasise in the next section, we measured confidence both before and after attitude expression in different studies. We also used different ways to vary the valence of thinking (e.g., argument quality and instructed thinking). None of these differences changed the self-validation effects observed. Finally, across the studies in this original series we were able to demonstrate that the effects of thought confidence on attitudes are not accounted for by related constructs, such as belief likelihood or desirability.

Moderating factors of self-validation

In addition to proposing thought confidence as a general mediator of the impact of diverse variables on judgement, self-validation research also points to unique moderators that have either been ignored or viewed in different ways by other theories. Thus, another contribution of our initial research has been to specify the circumstances in which thought confidence is likely to influence judgements. Petty et al. (2002) demonstrated that self-validation is more likely to take place when people have the motivation and ability to attend to and interpret their own cognitive experience (e.g., participants are high in need for cognition; Cacioppo & Petty, 1982; when there is high personal relevance of the persuasion topic; Petty & Cacioppo, 1979). There are at least two reasons for this. First, for validation processes to matter, people need to have some thoughts to validate. Second, people need some motivation and ability not only to think at the primary level of cognition but also to think and care about their thoughts.

Thus the self-validation processes we documented have some boundary conditions, such as requiring relatively high levels of thinking. However, it is important to note that this does not mean it is necessary to ask people explicitly to evaluate their thought confidence in order to observe self-validation effects. In fact, our research has revealed that for thought confidence to be consequential it is not necessary to measure it at any point, making it unlikely that such a dimension needed to be primed explicitly for the effect to occur. Thus, self-validation effects hold for situations in which thought confidence is assessed or not (e.g., Petty et al., 2002; for another example, see Briñol, Petty, & Barden, 2007a). As mentioned earlier, our research has clearly shown that self-validation processes occur regardless of *whether* (or not), *when* (before or after reporting attitudes), and *how* (individually or globally) thought confidence is assessed (for a review, see Briñol & Petty, 2004). In other words, the notion that people might not be constantly aware of their confidence in their thoughts does not make it less impactful or any less metacognitive in nature. Indeed, metacognition (like regular, primary cognition) can sometimes have implicit bases and implicit effects. People might not even be able to consciously verbalise or explain the basis of their metacognition when asked to do so (just as they cannot verbalise the basis of their primary cognition). Yet such cognition could still have an impact. We have found that, when asked to do so, people are capable of reporting their confidence in their thoughts, and that this confidence maps onto predictable and potentially important outcomes. However, people are unlikely to have much conscious recognition of the *origins* of this confidence.[3]

Subsequent research has identified another limiting condition on the self-validation effect. That is, confidence should be salient *following* thought generation rather than prior to it. For example, as we will describe in detail in subsequent sections, Tormala, Briñol, and Petty (2007a) demonstrated that when the validating information (source credibility) preceded the message, it biased the generation of thoughts, consistent with past research (Chaiken & Maheswaran, 1994), but it affected thought confidence when it followed the message. As illustrated in Figure 4, our findings on self-validation argue that research on persuasion can benefit from considering the timing of the key manipulations as placement of the independent variable in the sequence of persuasion stimuli can have an impact on the mechanism by which it operates. In line with this notion, timing will play an essential role in the studies of this review.

Finally, in addition to source factors reviewed here, and other situational determinants of thought confidence (from the message, context, and recipient), it is important to note that there might also be dispositional determinants of the use of mental contents. In a preliminary test of this idea, DeMarree, Petty, and Briñol (2008b) found that attitudes were more in line with participants' thoughts when participants were high rather than low in general self-confidence. Across several studies, self-confidence was measured in a variety of different ways (e.g., certainty in a diversity of attitudes or self

---

[3] We have also measured confidence and doubt using an implicit measure (IAT) in the context of studying the implicit ambivalence that can emerge from automatic–deliberative discrepancies (see Petty & Briñol, 2009).

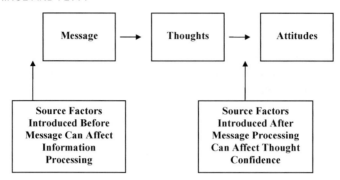

Figure 4. Impact of source variables on psychological processes underlying attitude change as a function of timing.

traits, perceived self-confidence, and judgemental self-confidence) and regardless of the measurement, individuals who were high in self-confidence relied more on their thoughts in forming their attitudes than those who were low in self-confidence. These results held across different thought inductions, and after controlling for self-esteem and other related constructs. Furthermore, as expected from a self-validation approach, these findings were moderated by amount of elaboration. That is, the individual difference in self-confidence only mattered under high thinking conditions. This line of research suggests that the self-validation approach provides an integrative mechanism for understanding how many diverse variables can operate, and suggests that many additional variables are also likely to benefit by considering self-validation processes.

THE UNIQUENESS OF THE SELF-VALIDATION APPROACH

Now that the self-validation approach has been described, it is important to note that the self-validation framework shares features with some other metacognitive theories in social psychology, but also has notable differences.[4] Most obviously, the self-validation approach agrees with other

---

[4] We use the term self-validation in order to emphasise that what people validate are their own thoughts. In a persuasion paradigm, the objects of validation are the cognitive responses that the person generates in response to the persuasive proposal received. However, as we describe later in this review, our self-validation view argues that metacognitive confidence can magnify the effect of not just attitude-relevant thoughts, but any content that is currently available in people's minds. It is important to note that the term self-validation has been used slightly differently in other domains of social psychology. For example, Crocker and Park (2004) use the term self-validation to refer to situations in which people want (mostly through others) to validate their abilities and qualities, and ultimately their self-worth. In this case, self-validation

recent theories on the importance of secondary cognition. However, previous approaches have generally examined and attempted to explain one single source of metacognitive influence. For example, Kruglanski's (1989) lay epistemic theory (LET) has been applied to causal attributions and argues that validation processes are affected by the number of causal explanations generated—the more alternative explanations generated for any given event, the less confidence a person has in any one given causal explanation. Generating few explanations, then, leads to greater confidence.

Perhaps the most well-known metacognitive theory in social psychology is that of Schwarz and colleagues (1991) on ease of retrieval effects. In this work the focus is on the ease with which primary cognitions come to mind and the key finding is that cognitions that come to mind easily are more impactful than those that are difficult to access. In a separate line of work, Clore and colleagues (Clore, Gaspar, & Garvin, 2001; Clore & Huntsinger, 2007) have focused on emotions, and have proposed that cognitions accompanied by positive emotions are more likely to be used than cognitions accompanied by negative emotions because of the promotive nature of positive emotions.

Interestingly, by focusing on particular variables (e.g., number of cognitions, ease, emotion), these theorists have developed rather specific rationales for why and when their particular variable of interest would matter. In contrast, and as will be evident in the studies that we review, the self-validation framework is designed to be a general metacognitive approach that can explain the effects of a wide array of variables that have been examined separately under the rubric of different theories. We also aim to explain the impact of variables that have not been considered to have a metacognitive impact by any prior theory.

To help understand how the self-validation approach differs from other theories focused on single variables, consider the ease of retrieval phenomena just mentioned. Schwarz et al. (1991) argue that when thoughts are easy to generate (e.g., generate two reasons to buy a BMW), people infer (mistakenly) that there are more reasons available than when they are difficult to generate (e.g., generate eight reasons). Because of this availability heuristic, generating two reasons in favour of something can lead to more persuasion than generating eight reasons. Furthermore, because the ease effect is presumed to be mediated by use of a heuristic, the ease effect is argued to be more likely when people are not thinking very much (e.g., for a low-importance topic; see Rothman & Schwarz, 1998). In contrast, the

---

is a goal that motivates people to seek and pursue self-esteem. This use of the term self-validation is similar to the meaning of that exact term within clinical psychology where self-validation is often seen as the process of restoring and reinforcing the sense of self-worth, meaning of life, and personal identity.

self-validation approach assumes that easily generated thoughts have greater impact because people infer greater validity of thoughts that are generated easily. This would be true independent of the actual number of thoughts that are generated. Second, the self-validation approach assumes that because a metacognitive inference of validity is involved, the ease effect should be magnified under high rather than low levels of thinking. Thus, the self-validation approach postulates a different mediator and different moderation from classic ease of retrieval theory.

In a series of studies examining both mediation and moderation of ease of retrieval effects we found that the ease effect was mediated by thought confidence rather than the availability heuristic, and occurred to a greater extent when thinking was high rather than low. In these studies Tormala, Petty, and Briñol (2002) asked participants to generate many (10) or few (2) thoughts in favour of a given proposal (e.g., instituting comprehensive exams for college seniors). Consistent with prior work on ease effects (e.g., Schwarz et al., 1991), participants who were asked to generate only 2 positive thoughts were more favourable towards the proposal than those asked to generate 10 favourable thoughts. Importantly, participants were more confident in their favourable thoughts when few rather than many were generated, and this thought confidence mediated the effects of ease of generation on attitudes. Furthermore, the ease effect was greater under high than low thinking conditions (e.g., high versus low need for cognition participants).

Subsequent research has replicated these findings using different paradigms (Tormala, Falces, Briñol, & Petty, 2007b).[5] As in prior research on self-validation effects, the impact of ease on confidence occurred only under high thinking conditions. This is notable given that the ease of retrieval effect had largely been assumed to be a phenomenon only of low cognitive effort based on the availability heuristic (e.g., Rothman & Schwarz, 1998). However, according to the ELM ease, like other variables, should be capable of affecting judgements by different mechanisms in different situations.

Finally, although self-validation focuses on confidence as the main metacognitive dimension, it is important to note that other metacognitive aspects can also be explored in relation to thoughts. For example, it is well established that thoughts and mental constructs that are highly accessible

---

[5] In addition to self-validation, Tormala et al. (2007b) uncovered another mechanism relevant to understanding ease of retrieval effects in the most common paradigm in which people are asked to generate a high (difficult) or low (easy) number of cognitions in a given direction. Specifically, it was predicted and found that when it is difficult for people to generate the specific type of cognition requested, they are more likely to spontaneously generate unrequested cognitions, and the presence of these opposite-direction cognitions can play a mediating role in ease of retrieval effects.

are more consequential in terms of durability and subsequent impact than less accessible thoughts (e.g., DeMarree, Petty, & Briñol, 2007). Although accessibility and other features of thoughts (e.g., importance) are often related to confidence, they are relatively independent features of cognition (for a review, see Petty et al., 2007). Our research on self-validation has also differentiated on both conceptual and operational levels between confidence and other previously studied dimensions, such as desirability and likelihood (Briñol et al., 2004). We have distinguished thought confidence not only from other dimensions at the primary level of cognition, but also from other approaches to confidence that have focused exclusively on one aspect of confidence such as confidence in the *likelihood* component of a belief (e.g., Smith, 1993). Thought confidence is a broader concept that incorporates this as well as other sources of confidence (e.g., confidence in desirability, confidence that stems from ease of retrieval of the thought, etc.).

In sum, the self-validation notion seems to be relevant for understanding how source and other variables (e.g., such as ease) can affect attitude change not only by affecting the number or valence of thoughts generated, but also by affecting thought confidence. That is, the self-validation hypothesis provides a completely new mechanism by which a large number of traditionally studied source variables can have an impact on attitudes in persuasion situations. Next we describe how this new mechanism can be useful in accounting for the effects of numerous source variables in persuasion, such as credibility, similarity, status, and power, including also a section on the effects of the non-verbal behaviour of the source, and another one on the self as a source.

SOURCE CREDIBILITY

As outlined earlier, source credibility can influence persuasion through different underlying processes that rely on primary cognition. That is, depending on the message recipient's extent of thinking, source credibility has been found to work by different mechanisms. In particular, source credibility has been shown to affect persuasion by serving as a simple cue, biasing the thoughts that message recipients have, serving as a piece of evidence relevant to the central merits of the issue, and determining the amount of thinking that occurs.

Recently we have argued that source credibility can also influence persuasion by affecting the confidence people have in the thoughts they generated in response to a message. This hypothesis relies on the assumption that source credibility can influence the perceived validity of the information in a persuasive proposal. When one has already thought about information in a proposal and then discovers that it came from a high- or low-credibility source, one's thoughts can also be validated or invalidated by this source information. For example, if people learn that a source is high in credibility they might think that, because the information is presumably valid, their thoughts in response to the message can be trusted. If they learn that the source has low credibility, however, they might think the information itself is invalid and thus have less confidence in the thoughts generated to the information. That is, if the credibility of the information in a message is undermined, confidence in one's thoughts that were based on that information is likely to be undermined as well.

In an initial demonstration of this possibility, Briñol et al. (2004) exposed participants to arguments in favour of the benefits of phosphate detergents. The ad was presented on a computer and contained either strong or mixed (i.e., both strong and weak) arguments in favour of phosphate-based laundry detergents. For example, in the strong argument condition, participants were told that in comparison with non-phosphate detergents, phosphate detergents were considerably less expensive, safer, and superior in cleaning power, which helps clothes last longer. In the mixed argument condition, participants were told that the packaging of most phosphate detergents was more attractive and colourful, which enhanced their appearance for shoppers. After reading the persuasive message, all participants listed their thoughts. We expected and found participants to generate a clear pattern of favourable thoughts towards the product only in the condition in which the ad contained convincing arguments. When the ad was mixed, thoughts were found to be mixed as well (i.e., both favourable and unfavourable).

Importantly, after receiving the ad and listing thoughts, but before reporting attitudes, source credibility was manipulated. That is, following receipt of the message, participants learned that the source of the information was either a government consumer agency (high credibility) or a major phosphate manufacturer (low credibility). This order was used to ensure that participants in the high- and low-credibility conditions would have generated basically the same thoughts overall, which could then be validated or invalidated by the source information. Following the source information, participants were asked to rated the confidence they had in the thoughts listed when they read the persuasive message (using a composite measure of several items assessing how confident they felt about the thoughts) and reported their attitudes towards the product (using a series of semantic differential scales). Finally, at the end of the experiment all participants completed the Need for Cognition (NC) Scale. NC refers to the tendency to engage in and enjoy effortful thought (for reviews, see Cacioppo et al., 1996: Petty, Briñol, Loersch, & McCaslin, in press). The self-validation reasoning is that when thoughts are generated in response to credible information people can be relatively confident in their thoughts, but when people learn that their thoughts were generated to a source of low credibility, doubt is instilled. The results showed that, although participants in both high- and low-credibility conditions generated equally favourable thoughts to the strong arguments, participants exposed to the high- (vs low-) credibility source had more confidence in their thoughts, relied on them more, and were therefore more persuaded by the proposal (see top panel of Figure 5).

In addition to highlighting the role of thought confidence in source credibility effects, this research identified one of the limiting conditions on the self-validation process. Briñol et al. (2004) argued that the thought confidence mechanism for source effects is confined to high elaboration, or high thought, instances. As noted when describing the moderating factors relevant to self-validation, the metacognitive activity involved in this process is more likely to take place when people have the motivation and ability to

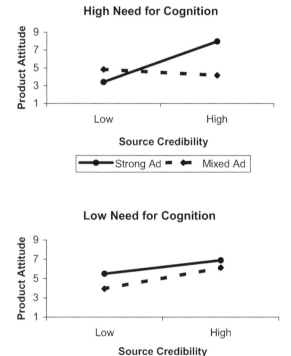

Figure 5. Attitudes as a function of argument quality, need for cognition, and source credibility. Adapted from Briñol et al. (2004, exp. 2). Source credibility validating thoughts (top panel) for high-thinking participants, and source credibility acting as a cue (bottom panel) for low-thinking participants.

attend to and interpret their own cognitive experience (e.g., Petty et al., 2002, 2007). Indeed, people need to have some thoughts to validate, and also need some motivation and ability to think about the validity of their thoughts.

Consistent with this idea, Briñol et al. (2004) found that thought confidence explained source credibility effects among high but not low need for cognition (NC; Cacioppo & Petty, 1982) individuals. Source credibility effects were only guided by thought confidence when people have the motivation and ability to think about their thoughts and gauge their confidence in them. That is, the effects of the source on attitudes was mediated by the confidence people placed in their thoughts, with individuals exposed to the high-credibility source expressing more thought confidence than those who were exposed to the low-credibility source (see figure 6). For individuals low in NC, confidence in thoughts did not mediate the attitude effects, which is consistent with prior research suggesting that low-elaboration individuals rely on source information as a cue to whether or not they should be persuaded (e.g., Petty et al., 1981; see bottom panel of Figure 5). This research extended the ELM notion that source variables can play a number of different roles in persuasion depending on the elaboration conditions. When elaboration was low, credibility served as a peripheral cue. However, when elaboration was relatively high, credibility influenced the confidence with which participants held their thoughts in response to the message.

One of the most intriguing implications of the self-validation hypothesis for source credibility is that increasing the credibility of the source of a persuasive message might sometimes undermine the persuasive potential of that message. Specifically, if credibility can influence thought confidence, high credibility might lead to less persuasion than low credibility when message recipients' thoughts are predominantly negative—for example, when the message contains weak arguments (see Petty & Cacioppo, 1986). Indeed, as thought confidence increases people rely more on their thoughts in forming their attitudes, so more confidence in negative thoughts would lead to more negative attitudes.

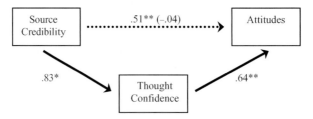

Figure 6. Mediation of the impact of source credibility on attitudes for individuals high in need for cognition. Adapted from Briñol et al. (2004, exp. 2).

In a follow-up study Tormala et al. (2006) explored this counterintuitive prediction that under some conditions high source credibility backfires and results in *less* persuasion than does low source credibility. Specifically, we predicted that because of the self-validation role for sources, a high-credibility source can lead to either more or less persuasion than a low-credibility source depending on the nature of people's thoughts in response to the persuasive message. In particular, when arguments are weak and thoughts were unfavourable, high source credibility following message processing should reduce persuasion, because people would develop greater confidence in their negative thoughts than when the same information was presented by a source of low credibility.

In one of the studies of this series, participants received strong or weak arguments promoting a new brand of pain reliever. This manipulation was designed to influence the overall valence, or direction, of participants' thoughts. In the strong arguments condition the message stated that the new product works 50% faster than other aspirins, lasts 3 hours longer than other aspirins, has no harmful side effects, and recently received a perfect score of 10 in quality and efficiency testing. In the weak arguments condition the message stated that the new product lasts about as long as other aspirins, has very few harmful side effects, contains only small amounts of caffeine and sodium, and recently received a score of 6 out of 10 in quality and efficiency testing. Following the message and thought-listing task, participants received source credibility information. In the high-credibility condition participants were told that the information about the product was taken from a pamphlet from a federal agency that conducts research on medical products. In the low-credibility condition participants were led to believe that the information was taken from a class report written by Jonathon Bower (age 14), a local high school freshman. This manipulation was designed to influence perceived source expertise. Immediately following the source information, participants reported their attitudes towards the product. Then, after reporting their attitudes, participants were asked to think back to the thoughts they listed about the product and rate their overall confidence in them.

Consistent with the self-validation hypothesis, this study demonstrated that source credibility information following a message can affect thought confidence, and that increasing source credibility can lead to relatively favourable or unfavourable attitudes, depending on the valence of thoughts elicited by the message. As shown in Figure 7 (top panel), when the message was strong and produced primarily favourable thoughts, high source credibility was more persuasive than low source credibility. When the message was weak and produced primarily unfavourable thoughts, high source credibility actually backfired and resulted in *less* persuasion than low source credibility.

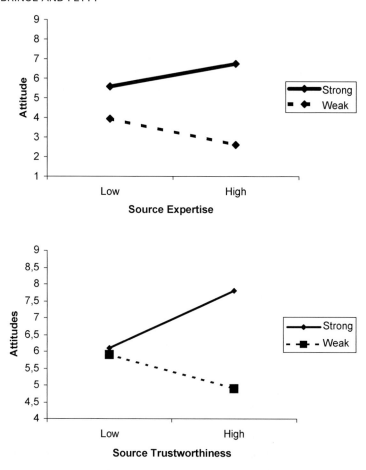

Figure 7. Attitudes as a function of argument quality and source expertise (top panel) and source trustworthiness (bottom panel). Adapted from Tormala et al. (2006).

A second study replicated these findings using a different manipulation of source credibility, focusing on trustworthiness rather than expertise. In particular, in this study participants first received a persuasive message in favour of phosphate detergents that contained strong or weak arguments. The message was designed to argue unambiguously in favour of phosphate detergents in both the strong and weak argument conditions. In the strong arguments condition the message contained rather compelling reasons to buy phosphate detergents (e.g., they are cheaper and more effective), whereas in the weak arguments condition the message contained less compelling reasons to buy phosphate detergents (e.g., they are useful in cleaning a wide range of materials and they have no scent). After the message, participants were instructed to list the thoughts they had as they read the message. Participants then received source credibility information. In the high-credibility (trustworthy) condition participants were told that the information in the message was taken from a pamphlet from a consumer advocacy group that investigates consumer products with the express purpose of helping consumers make sound decisions. In the low-credibility (untrustworthy) condition participants were led to believe that the information in the message was taken from a pamphlet from a major soap and detergent manufacturer that sells phosphate detergents and thus encourages people to use them. Given its clear vested interest in the product, the latter source was expected to be viewed skeptically. Finally, after receiving the source information, participants were asked to report attitudes and thought confidence and complete a number of additional measures. As illustrated in the bottom panel of Figure 7, this study provided more evidence for the reverse effect of credibility on attitudes under weak arguments conditions. Thus, this research revealed that a high-credibility source can yield either more or less persuasion than a low-credibility source depending on the circumstances.

These two studies reveal that high source credibility can backfire relative to low source credibility. Other researchers have also suggested that high source credibility can backfire when weak arguments are presented, but do so for a different reason. For example, we have already seen that when a high-credible source is presented before a message and elaboration is unconstrained, greater credibility is associated with more processing of the weak arguments and this can reduce persuasion. However, because we presented the source after the message, it is unlikely to affect processing. Another possibility is that reduced persuasion might emerge because weak arguments violate people's expectancies for expert sources, leading to less persuasion (Bohner, Ruder, & Erb, 2002). If the mechanism is one of expectancy violation, then participants would be more likely to generate negative thoughts in that condition, which we did not find to be the case. Alternatively, one might argue that people reason that there must only be weak arguments out there, since a credible source would have proposed better arguments if these existed. This reasoning is consistent with the idea that low credibility leads to doubt, but it implies that doubt emerges from the incompleteness of the information provided.

Thus, although the reversed credibility effect for weak arguments conditions is not unique to our metacognitive approach, the specific mediating and moderating predictions are only derived from the self-validation approach. Furthermore, under high thinking conditions the processes based on primary cognition described earlier would always have predicted more persuasion for high- than low-credible sources regardless of the quality of the arguments included. Thus, we argue that the reversed finding obtained for source credibility under high thinking conditions adds to a growing body of evidence suggesting that the self-validation framework can enhance our understanding of paradoxical effects in persuasion—e.g., generating few arguments yielding more persuasion than generating many arguments (Tormala et al., 2002); head shaking yielding more persuasion than head nodding (Briñol & Petty, 2003).

In a subsequent line of research, Tormala et al. (2007a) confirmed that source credibility affected thought confidence only when the source information followed, rather than preceded, the persuasive message, and when thinking was high rather than low or moderate. In this line of research participants were presented with a persuasive message from a high- or low-credibility source under high elaboration conditions. We varied whether the credibility manipulation came before or after the message. Because all participants received arguments that were somewhat ambiguous but that led to mostly favourable thoughts in pilot testing, we predicted that, regardless of source timing, attitudes would be more favourable in the high- compared to low-credibility condition. However, we expected the mechanism for this effect to vary with timing. When the source preceded the message, we predicted that source credibility would affect attitudes by influencing thought favourability, making thoughts more favourable than they would otherwise be. When the source followed the message, however, we predicted that source credibility would affect attitudes by influencing thought confidence, leading people to rely on the favourable thoughts they have generated. In the experiments of this series we measured attitudes, thought favourability, and thought confidence.

As shown in Figure 8 (top panel), this research showed that when credibility preceded message processing under high thinking conditions it biased the thoughts generated, consistent with past research (Chaiken & Maheswaran, 1994). Only when the source information followed the message did it affect thought confidence (see Figure 8, bottom panel). As noted earlier, these findings argue that research on persuasion can benefit from considering the timing of the source information, since placement of the source and other independent variables in the sequence of persuasion stimuli can have an impact on the mechanism by which the variable operates.

In sum, this research clearly showed that the self-validation process should be added to the other mechanisms previously identified for explaining the impact of source credibility on attitudes, and it indicated the importance of considering the order of presentation of persuasion stimuli. In closing this section it is important to note that our work on self-validation has demonstrated that credible sources can validate thoughts regardless of the content and valence of the thoughts generated. In all of these studies the content of the thoughts did not matter for validation

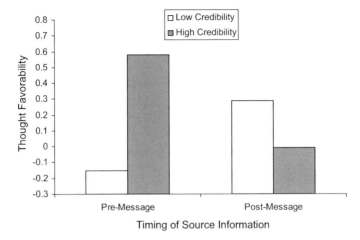

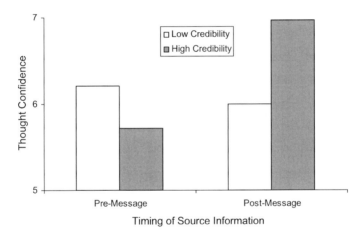

Figure 8. Thought favourability (top panel) and thought confidence (bottom panel) as a function of source credibility and timing. Adapted from Tormala et al. (2007a). Source credibility only affected the direction of the thoughts when it preceded the persuasive message (top panel), but only affected thought confidence when it followed the processing of the message (bottom panel).

purposes because the thoughts generated were unrelated to the source of the information (i.e., they were about the source's *proposal* rather than the source). However, it might be different when the target of the persuasion attempt is thinking about the source (Clark, Wegener, Briñol, & Petty, in press). For example, a credible source might validate thoughts in response to strong arguments if the judgement is about the source's intelligence, since in this case the person would be thinking that the source was intelligent based on the strong arguments and then the expertise information would provide convergent validity for this judgement. Similarly, a non-expert source would validate judgements about the lack of intelligence when weak arguments are offered. This suggests that sources with low (vs high) credibility can affect judgements by validating thoughts under some circumstances such as when the source is the object of the thoughts, and when thoughts are stereotypical or match the nature of the source.

SOURCE SIMILARITY

Source attractiveness effects have not been as well studied in the literature as source credibility, but we have collected some initial evidence for self-validation effects of source similarity. It is important to begin by noting that the similarity of the source delivering the message was not directly manipulated in this research. Instead, we manipulated whether participants thought that other people had similar or dissimilar thoughts (i.e., thought similarity). In one study, for example, Petty et al. (2002, exp. 4) examined how telling people that others had similar versus dissimilar thoughts can affect the perceived validity of those thoughts and thereby modify their impact on attitudes. Participants in this study first received a message advocating the implementation of a new comprehensive exam policy at their university. In order to manipulate the direction of the thoughts towards the proposal, the message they received contained adaptations of either the strong or weak arguments on this now familiar topic in the persuasion literature. After listing their thoughts, participants were told that those thoughts were going to be analysed by the computer and compared with a pool of thoughts of many other students from their own university. After 10 seconds a new computer screen appeared with the ostensible outcome of this comparison. Half of the participants were told that their thoughts had been rejected for future research because they were very different from the rest of the members of their group. The other half of the participants were told their thoughts had been accepted into the pool for future research because they were quite similar to the thoughts listed by other members of their group. This induction was designed to influence the perceived similarity of their thoughts to others, and thus the confidence they had in their thoughts. After receiving this fictitious information, participants were asked to think back to the thoughts they listed about the exam topic and were asked several questions about the confidence they had in the thoughts. Finally, participants reported their attitudes and then completed the NC scale.

As anticipated by Festinger's (1950) notion of consensual validation, this study found that social consensus information affected persuasion by influencing thought confidence (see also Orive, 1988a, 1988b; Stroebe & Diehl, 1988). People reported more confidence in their thoughts when these thoughts were said to be similar to those generated by others than when they were not. When thoughts were favourable towards the proposal, sharing thoughts with others increased persuasion, but when thoughts were not favourable, sharing thoughts with others reduced persuasion. In other words, as shown in Figure 9, the interaction between argument quality and consensus showed that the effect of argument quality on attitudes was greater when high rather than low thought similarity (confidence) was induced. With high levels of confidence in their own cognitive responses, participants viewed their positive and negative thoughts to the arguments as valid and relied on them in forming attitudes. However, when low confidence in their cognitive responses was induced (by leading participants to believe that had dissimilar thoughts), they viewed their positive and negative thoughts as less valid and relied on them less in forming attitudes.

Importantly, the results in support of the self-validation hypothesis were apparent particularly for participants high in need for cognition, who are more chronically motivated to engage in extensive thinking. This finding is similar to the one described above for source credibility, and is also consistent with the notion that metacognitive processes tend to be more pronounced to the extent that people have the motivation and ability to engage in considerable thinking. The effects of this study are especially interesting to compare with prior work on need for cognition and persuasion. Past studies have been reasonably consistent in their finding that individuals high in need for cognition are more responsive to the quality of the arguments in a persuasive message than are individuals low in need for cognition (for reviews, see Cacioppo, Petty, Feinstein, & Jarvis, 1996; Petty et al., in press). In line with the studies described earlier, the current

Figure 9. Attitudes of high need for cognition participants as a function of argument quality and confidence. Confidence was induced by others producing similar thoughts or not. Adapted from Petty et al. (2002, exp. 4).

study shows that the impact of argument quality on attitudes for high-NC individuals can be eliminated when these people lose confidence in the thoughts that they have generated. That is, generating appropriate thoughts to strong and weak messages is only one factor in producing argument quality effects on attitudes. People also need to have confidence in the validity of the thoughts that they generate.

In this research, having thoughts similar to those generated by others increased perceived validity compared to having dissimilar thoughts, This suggests that if source similarity were manipulated directly, similar sources would induce more thought confidence than dissimilar sources. However, this implication might only hold when the message is on a matter of opinion rather than fact. Following prior work by Goethals and Nelson (1973), it could be that agreement with *dissimilar* others would increase thought confidence if the message was on a topic considered to be a matter of fact rather than opinion. Thus, agreement by similar (vs dissimilar) others might increase or decrease perceived validity depending on the circumstances, such as the nature of the topic being considered.

SOURCE MAJORITY/MINORITY STATUS

The work described in the above section on source similarity compared the effects of a majority of others who shared or did not share a participant's thoughts. Other work has compared the influence of acceptance from a majority or a minority of others. Both the conformity and persuasion literatures have accumulated considerable evidence suggesting that endorsement from numerical majorities often exerts greater influence than do numerical minorities (e.g., Wood, Lundgren, Quellette, Busceme, & Blackstone, 1994) although sometimes minorities can be more effective, e.g., Crano & Chen, 1998; Moscovici, 1980; Mugny & Perez, 1991). Several traditional mechanisms have been shown for minority sources. Thus, endorsement of an issue by a numerical minority (vs majority) has led to resistance to attitude change by a low-effort rejection process when thinking was likely to be low, and by a more thoughtful but negatively biased processing mechanism under high thinking conditions. However, when elaboration is not constrained by other variables to be high or low, minorities can influence attitude change by influencing the amount of thinking (e.g., Baker & Petty, 1994; for a review of these mechanisms, see Martin & Hewstone, 2008; Tormala, Petty, & DeSensi, in press).

We have recently conducted a line of research in which we proposed that minorities can affect persuasion not only by serving as cues or affecting the direction and the amount of thinking, but also by influencing the confidence with which people hold their thoughts in response to the persuasive message (Horcajo, Petty, & Briñol, 2008a). That is, we propose that at least under some circumstances, such as when the source information follows the message and the extent of thinking is high, minority influence can operate through self-validation processes.

In one of the studies of this series participants were presented with a message introducing a new company. The message was composed of either strong or weak arguments about the firm. The gist of one strong argument in favour of the company was that workers reported high satisfaction because of the flexibility in their work schedule. In contrast, the gist of one weak argument in favour of this firm was that they used recycled paper in one of the departments during an entire year. After reading and thinking about this information, participants listed their thoughts in response to the proposal. Next we manipulated source status by attributing the message to a source in the numerical minority or majority (e.g., 88% versus 18% of their fellow students support the company; see Baker & Petty, 1994). Consistent with the self-validation hypothesis, we predicted and found that the status of the source (minority vs majority) influenced the confidence with which participants held their thoughts about the company. Specifically, participants tended to have higher thought confidence when the message was endorsed by a majority rather than a minority. As a consequence, majority (vs minority) increased argument quality effects in persuasion.

Among other things these findings are important because in virtually all of the prior studies manipulating source status and argument quality the manipulation of source status has *preceded* presentation of the persuasive message. As explained earlier for source credibility, in this order any variable (e.g., source status) can affect the amount of information processing that takes place as long as it is not already constrained to be high or low by other variables. In contrast, in the study just described the status of the source was introduced when processing of the message proposal was already done, and operated through thought confidence. Thus, the effects of source status on attitude change and the mechanisms underlying those effects vary as a function of the timing in which the source information is introduced in the persuasion process.

SOURCE POWER

Power has been recognised as a central motivating force in human relationships and action, being considered as one of the most fundamental concepts in social science. Although prior research on source power has emphasised its role in producing compliance rather than internalised change (e.g., Kelman, 1958), the self-validation mechanism holds open the possibility of internalised change for powerful sources. In a line of research inspired by the self-validation hypothesis we examined the effect of the message *recipients'* power on attitude change (Briñol, Petty, Valle, Rucker,

& Becerra, 2007c). It is important to highlight that this research did not manipulate the power of the source delivering a message, but the power of the recipient of the proposal. It is also true that power often involves a relative relationship between two or more individuals. Although not studied directly, the more powerful the message recipient feels, the less powerful the message source would seem in comparison. Or, stated differently, in studies where the message source is powerful, the message recipient feels relatively powerless. Because of the interpersonal nature of power, research and theory on the power of message recipients might be useful to make inferences about the power of message sources (and vice versa). Thus, although in the research described in this section we did not manipulate the power of the message source directly, we still think that it can illustrate how self-validation processes can be relevant to this aspect of the source.

In one study on power, for example, participants were first led to generate either positive or negative thoughts about a mandatory flu vaccination policy for students on campus. Following this induction participants were told that they were going to take part in another study related to memory. As part of that unrelated study, participants were instructed to recall either two incidents in their lives in which they had power over another person (high-power condition), or in which someone else had power over them (low-power condition). Thus, participants had to write about situations in which they controlled the ability of another person to get something they wanted and were in a position to evaluate those individuals (high power), or about situations in which someone had control over their ability to get something they wanted and were in a position to evaluate them (low power). This experimental procedure has been used successfully to manipulate feelings of power in previous research (e.g., Galinsky, Gruenfeld, & Magee, 2003). Following this manipulation, participants' attitudes towards the proposal were measured. Finally participants were asked to return to the thoughts they listed about the vaccination policy and report how confident and valid their thoughts were.

Relative to powerless individuals, those induced to have power following message processing reported greater confidence in their thoughts about the campus policy. As a consequence, the effect of the direction of the thoughts generated on attitudes was greater when power was high rather than low. Furthermore, thought confidence mediated the observed effects of power on persuasion. As in the prior self-validation studies, these effects were only present under high elaboration conditions and when power followed thought generation.

As suggested above, research on recipient power might shed light on previous findings in the literature on a *source*'s power and persuasion because power typically involves a relative relationship between two or more individuals. For example, prior theorists have suggested that if the high power of a message source is made salient prior to a message, it should enhance the information processing of recipients (Fiske, 1993). Notably, this prediction implies that powerless message recipients would engage in greater message processing than powerful ones. Indeed we have found precisely this pattern when feelings of recipient power or powerlessness were induced *prior* to a persuasive message (e.g., Study 2, Briñol et al., 2007c). In this study participants were informed that they were going to participate in a study about non-verbal behaviour associated with different roles. In an interpersonal situation, each participant was randomly assigned to either a boss role (high-power condition) or an employee role (low-power condition), and asked to engage in a role-playing task in which they had to role-play one meeting they might have at work. That is, the role-playing task required one person to be the manager and the other to be the subordinate. Previous research (e.g., Kipnis, 1972; Overbeck & Park, 2001) has demonstrated the effectiveness of this kind of role-playing in inducing high and low power states. Also, in order to fit with the cover story, the person assigned to play the role of the manager was sitting down in a higher and better-looking chair than the one playing the role of the subordinate.

After the power induction we assessed the extent to which participants processed information by varying the quality of the arguments contained within a persuasive message, and by measuring the impact of these arguments on attitudes. Specifically, participants received a persuasive message consisting of an advertisement for a new mobile phone. Examples of the gist of the strong arguments in favour of the mobile phone included that the battery could be recharged in 5 minutes and that the material with which it was made was ecologically safe and completely unbreakable. Examples of the gist of the weak arguments in favour of the mobile phone included that it had a broad currency converter and that the PIN code was just two digits long.

Importantly, if power reduces processing of the message arguments, as it should if it induces a feeling of certainty prior to message reception, it should reduce the effects of argument quality on subsequent attitudes. That is, if people are thinking less about the arguments when they have power, they should be less influenced by the quality of the arguments presented. Thus, whereas power was found to increase the impact of an argument quality manipulation on attitudes when power was induced following message processing (because power increased reliance on thoughts to the message), in this study we expected that power would decrease the impact of an argument quality manipulation on attitudes when power was induced before message processing (because power would reduce processing of the message). The results of this study were consistent with our hypothesis that power can influence attitude change by affecting the extent to which people think about a message when it is induced before receiving the message, and also with previous research showing that confident individuals are less attentive to argument quality differences (e.g., Briñol et al., 2006; Petty et al., 2006; Tiedens & Linton, 2001; Weary & Jacobson, 1997).

Thus, as was the case for other variables, whether the (source) induction comes before or after the message can have a profound impact on the effects obtained. When people feel powerless prior to a message (e.g., because the source is powerful), they process the message more and attitudes are affected by the thoughts generated. When people feel powerless after a message, they lose confidence in their thoughts and rely on them less. Interestingly, although the mechanism of attitude change is different when power precedes or comes after a message, in both cases power appears to work by affecting confidence. When people feel a lack of confidence prior to a message (e.g., due to low power), they come to doubt their initial opinions and thus process a message more carefully to obtain certainty. However, when people feel a lack of confidence after already processing a message, then they come to doubt the thoughts they have recently generated.

NON-VERBAL BEHAVIOUR OF THE SOURCE

Although source information is sometimes provided explicitly, sometimes a source's credibility, similarity, and many other qualities (e.g., status, power) can be inferred from the non-verbal behaviour of the source. Thus, the non-verbal behaviour of the message source can change the attitudes of the recipient by affecting the perception of these dimensions. As any other variable, a smiling source can produce more persuasion than a frowning source by acting as a simple valence cue (under low thinking conditions) or by biasing the thoughts generated by the recipient (under high thinking conditions). When thinking is not constrained to be high or low, a source smiling (vs frowning) can influence attitudes by affecting the amount of thinking the audience does about the persuasive communication. Consistent with this later possibility, Ottati, Terkildsen, and Hubbard (1997) found that happy faces reduced information processing in a television impression-formation task, as revealed by less discrimination between strong and weak arguments when delivered by a source with a happy (vs a control) face.

As is the case with any source factors, different aspects of the source's behaviour (e.g., happy facial expression) can also influence persuasion by affecting the confidence the recipients have in the thoughts they generated in response to a message. In order to examine this possibility, DeMarree, Briñol, and Petty (2008a) conducted research in which participants were presented with different facial expressions of emotion on a computer screen after thinking about a persuasive message. As expected if the source's facial expression influences thought confidence, people relied on their thoughts more when exposed to facial expressions depicting emotions associated with confidence (e.g., happiness, anger) than when exposed to facial expressions depicting emotions associated with doubt (e.g., sadness, surprise). Thus we might validate or invalidate the thoughts of others by smiling or frowning following their comments because of the cognitive appraisals associated with these emotional expressions (see e.g., Smith & Ellsworth, 1985; Tiedens & Linton, 2001).

After describing research revealing that the non-verbal behaviour of the source can influence persuasion by validating the thoughts of the recipient, we consider research on behavioural mimicry—where recipients match a source's behaviour. Numerous studies have now documented that others' behaviour can function as a prime to automatically activate our behaviour (e.g., Chartrand & Bargh, 1999). Thus the behaviour of the source can prime similar behaviours in the recipient.[6] The behaviour generated by the recipient in response to the behaviour of the source, like any other variable described so far, can lead to persuasion through multiple roles (for a review, see Briñol & Petty, 2008). For example, the behaviour of the person can influence attitudes by serving as simple cues and by affecting either the amount or direction of thinking. Importantly, the behaviour of others (and our own behaviour) can influence not only the amount and direction of thoughts, but also what people think about their thoughts—especially thought confidence. As was the case with source credibility and power, the confidence (or doubt) that emerges from the non-verbal behaviour of the source and the recipient can magnify (or attenuate) the effect of anything that is currently available in people's minds.[7]

THE SELF AS A SOURCE

Although this review has focused on external sources, sometimes people try to persuade themselves (i.e., serve as the source of the message). In fact,

---

[6] In this section we briefly mention cases when recipients of persuasion imitate what they observe in the source of a communication. If the source of a persuasive message smiles or nods their head at you, you are likely to smile and nod back. Alternatively, however, people sometimes respond to others' behaviour in contrasting, complementary ways (e.g., Tiedens & Fragale, 2003). The self-validation effect would follow the impact of the recipient's own behaviour.

[7] A final case of mimicry comes from research in which the source adapts his or her behaviour to match the non-verbal behaviour of the recipient. Recent research has suggested that even behaviours performed by a computer-controlled digital representation of the person in a virtual environment can induce subsequent changes in judgement. In one illustration, Bailenson and Yee (2005) found that digital agents who were high in behavioural realism by mimicking the head movements of participants were more persuasive than agents who did not mimic and merely displayed other realistic movements. Of course there are multiple mechanisms by which these effects can come about (e.g., mimicking a persona's behaviour might enhance thought confidence).

there is a very long tradition in the study of attitude change involving self-persuasion through role-playing (e.g., Janis & King, 1954). In a recent line of research, Briñol, Petty, and Gasco (2008) compared the self as a source to another person as the source. In one of the studies participants were first asked to generate positive or negative thoughts regarding their bodies. Then participants were led to believe that their thoughts originated externally or internally (by the self). Specifically, thoughts about the body were said to emerge from the particular views of their culture through socialisation (external origin) or to emerge from deep down inside the self. Because participants had more confidence in their thoughts in the latter than in the former condition, the direction of their thoughts generated had a greater impact on how satisfied they felt with their bodies when the origin of the those thoughts was perceived to be the self. As a result, perceiving positive thoughts to come from the self (vs externally) made people feel better about their body image, but produced the opposite effect for those with negative thoughts. In another study in this line of research we replicated these findings for attitudes towards fast food. Specifically, after thinking about the benefits or costs of eating fast food, participants were led to believe that food-related thoughts were learned from others (external source) or were innate (internal source). As expected, the direction of the thoughts (positive or negative) had a greater impact on the attitudes and behavioural intentions regarding eating fast food when people perceived the self (vs others) as the source of the thoughts.[8]

VALIDATION OF THOUGHTS VERSUS OTHER MENTAL CONTENTS

The research covered so far in this review has focused on how source factors can influence persuasion by affecting thought confidence. As described, when source features influence the confidence with which people hold their thoughts, sources affect attitude change. The self-validation view argues that metacognitive confidence can magnify the effect of not just attitude-relevant thoughts but any content that is currently available in people's minds. This can include other mental contents ranging from attitudes to emotions and goals. That is, confidence can be applied to whatever the salient or available mental contents are. Following a persuasive message, for example, what is most salient are the thoughts that just came to mind. However, in other circumstances the content and nature of available cognitions will be

---

[8]These findings were restricted to participants who considered the self to be a valuable source (i.e., high self-esteem). For those with low self-esteem the opposite interaction emerged, revealing that external sources had more impact on the reliance on their thoughts than internal sources.

different. Our reasoning is similar to the argument made in work on priming where an activated concept (e.g., "hostile") can be applied to whatever the person is thinking about, whether it is the self (e.g., DeMarree, Wheeler, & Petty, 2005) or another person (e.g., Higgins, Rholes, & Jones, 1977).

Given that metacognitive confidence can be applied to any cognition, an interesting case to examine would be when source factors influence the confidence (or doubt) that people have in their attitudes (rather than in their thoughts). Indeed, other metacognitive lines of research have found that different variables in the persuasion context are capable of influencing attitude confidence directly (even in the absence of changes in attitudes). Affecting attitude confidence is important because confidence is generally understood as a core component of attitude strength (e.g., Barden & Petty, 2008). That is, to the extent that attitudes are held with confidence they are likely to persist over time, resist change, and influence thinking and behaviour (see Petty & Krosnick, 1995). For example, we have already noted that power induced prior to a message can affect confidence in a person's initial attitude and thereby reduce the perceived need for information processing.

A number of research findings converge on the notion that individuals are more certain of an attitude when that attitude stems from a credible (i.e., trustworthy and expert) source than from one that is not credible. For example, Clarkson, Tormala, and Rucker (2008) exposed participants to a message for a department store that came from a source low or high in credibility. They found that individuals were more certain of their attitude when the source was high as opposed to low in credibility. Credible sources can increase confidence because they are likely to be viewed as possessing both the ability (i.e., expertise) and the motivation (i.e., trustworthiness) to provide valid information to recipients.

In the self-validation framework described earlier in this review the confidence that emerges from credible sources is often applied to thoughts, whereas the research just described by Clarkson et al. (2008) showed that the confidence produced by the source had an impact on confidence in attitudes. That is, the object of confidence that emerges from source factors can be thoughts or attitudes. As noted, this difference is important because the impact of thought confidence is often reflected in subsequent attitude extremity, whereas the impact of attitude confidence influences subsequent behaviours and thinking activities. In both cases conviction increases the reliance and use of the mental construct to which it is attached. Thus, thought confidence increases the use of those thoughts in affecting attitudes, whereas attitude certainty increases the reliance on those attitudes in guiding further information processing and behaviour.

Given that some of the same variables (e.g., source credibility) have been shown to influence the confidence attached to both thoughts and attitudes, and given that the consequences are different in those two cases (i.e., changes in attitude extremity or changes in subsequent thoughts and behaviours, respectively), it is important to specify under what conditions a given variable will influence thought confidence versus attitude certainty. Although this is an important area for future research, initial research suggests that the sequence of persuasion stimuli affects to what construct confidence is attached.

As introduced earlier, a variable appears to be more inclined to operate by affecting attitude certainty (therefore influencing the extent or direction of thinking) when it is induced prior to the reception of persuasive information, and by affecting thought certainty (therefore influencing attitude extremity) when it is induced after the presentation of a message. Consistent with this notion, the same source variable can have opposite interactions with argument quality depending on its placement before or after a message. As described earlier, Briñol et al. (2007c) proposed that power can validate whatever mental constructs are activated in the power-holder. As a result, when power *preceded* message processing, power validated one's initial attitudes and therefore affected the amount of information processing (high-power participants showed a smaller differentiation between weak and strong arguments). In contrast, when power was induced *after* information processing, high-power participants were more likely to rely on their recently generated thoughts (showing a larger argument quality effect). This research builds on the idea that the timing of the induction is one critical factor in producing different outcomes depending on whether the variable is induced prior to message processing (thus affecting attitude certainty) or after message processing (thus affecting thought certainty).

SUMMARY AND CONCLUSION

Source factors are one of the most studied variables in persuasion research and several mechanisms have contributed to the effectiveness of credible, attractive, and powerful sources. The key mechanisms by which source variables in a persuasion setting can influence attitude change are: (a) by serving as simple cues and heuristics; (b) by affecting the amount of information processing; (c) by biasing the thoughts that are generated; or (d) by serving as persuasive arguments or evidence. By grouping the persuasion processes into meaningful categories specified by the elaboration likelihood model (ELM) of persuasion, we aimed to provide a useful guide to organise and facilitate access to key findings in the literature on source factors in persuasion.

After briefly describing these traditionally studied processes (focused on primary cognition), we reviewed research on how and when source factors can affect thought confidence (a secondary, metacognitive form of cognition). The former processes were covered illustratively, whereas the relatively new evidence regarding source factors and metacognition was treated more comprehensively. The self-validation research reviewed has shown that this new mechanism can account for some already established persuasion outcomes (e.g., more persuasion with high- than low-credibility sources), but by a completely different process than postulated previously. Moreover, we have also been able to obtain findings opposite to those typically observed (e.g., when thoughts are mostly unfavourable there is more persuasion to low- than high-credible sources).

Given that different processes are associated with different consequences (e.g., with high thought attitude change processes leading to greater attitude strength than low thought attitude change processes; see Petty, Haugtvedt, & Smith, 1995) even for the same outcome, it is essential to distinguish among the different processes underlying source persuasion. This aspect is crucial because it shows that the same source variable (e.g., a source smiling) can lead to the same outcome (more persuasion) by serving as a simple cue (for conditions of low elaboration) or by biasing the generation of positive thoughts (for conditions of high elaboration) or by validating those thoughts (for conditions in which people think about their thoughts; see Petty, Schumann, Richman, & Strathman, 1993). Although those effects might seem similar on the surface, the underlying mechanism that produces them is different, leading to differences in the strength of the judgements formed.

Importantly, we described a theoretical framework to understand the circumstances under which the different (primary and secondary) cognitive processes are more likely to influence our judgements, such as when variables precede or follow thought generation, and when the extent of thinking is relatively low, medium, or high. Although we have covered some source factors (e.g., speed of speech, stigmatised origin of the source) mostly as relevant to one of the key processes (e.g., amount of thinking), each of the source factors (ranging from expertise to similarity) is amenable to operating through different processes depending on the circumstances.

In closing, we have seen how self-validation not only relates to some classic topics in the psychology of the source of persuasion (e.g., credibility, attractiveness, status, and power), but also to more recent or relatively novel phenomena (e.g., one's self as a source). A consideration of self-validation processes might expand our understanding of the dynamics of other unexplored source variables that could influence persuasion either by increasing (e.g., source mimicry, source personalisation) or decreasing (e.g., threatening sources) thought confidence (e.g., Horcajo, See, Briñol, & Petty, 2008b).

It is also worth noting that research conducted on self-validation has examined the effect of thought confidence with regard to a variety of attitude objects and measures increasing the potential applicability of these results in the real world. Indeed, there might be many practical applications of the self-validation findings for sources to be more persuasive. For example, we might validate or invalidate the thoughts of others by smiling or frowning following their comments. Consider a situation in which, after having discussed a given proposal in a meeting, someone makes a funny joke and everybody laughs; or consider a situation in which, following the expression of some ideas, you relate them to a recent sad event or you make a sad facial expression. In these circumstances the source variable (expressions of emotions) will follow thought generation and, according to the present research, its effects on judgement can be understood in terms of self-validation process. Indeed, there may be many life circumstances in which some thinking takes place only to be followed in short order by a confident or doubtful expression of the source. The current research suggests that these irrelevant life events could affect the use of one's thoughts.

Although the source of a persuasive message has been the focus of the present review, an advantage of establishing a new basic mechanism such as self-validation is that it can provide scholars with a novel framework to examine other variables in the persuasion domain. For example, in addition to the analysis of source persuasion, the self-validation framework can also be applied to the study of numerous message, context, and recipient factors, such as bodily responses (Briñol & Petty, 2003), emotional states (Briñol et al., 2007a), self-affirmation (Briñol, Petty, Gallardo, & DeMarree, 2007b), and ease of retrieval (Tormala et al., 2002, 2007b). In each case our research has shown that the self-validation framework provides a novel way to understand the effects of the variable, pointing to new effects and a new view of established effects.

REFERENCES

Abelson, R. P., Aronson, E., McGuire, W. J., Newcomb, T. M., Rosenberg, M. J., & Tannenbaum, P. H. (1968). *Theories of cognitive consistency: A sourcebook*. Chicago: Rand McNally.

Abelson, R. P., & Rosenberg, M. J. (1958). Symbolic psycho-logic: A model of attitudinal cognition. *Behavioural Science, 3*, 1–13.

Aronson, E. (1969). Cognitive dissonance: A current perspective. In L. Berkowitz (Ed.), *Advances in experimental social psychology* (Vol. 4, pp. 1–34). New York: Academic Press.

Bailenson, J., & Yee, N. (2005). Digital chameleons: Automatic assimilation of nonverbal gestures in immersive virtual environments. *Psychological Science, 16*, 814–819.

Baker, S. M., & Petty, R. E. (1994). Majority and minority influence: Source-position imbalance as a determinant of message scrutiny. *Journal of Personality and Social Psychology*, *67*, 5–19.

Barden, J., & Petty, R. E. (2008). The mere perception of elaboration creates attitude certainty: Exploring the thoughtfulness heuristic. *Journal of Personality and Social Psychology*, *95*, 489–509.

Beck, A. T., & Greenberg, R. L. (1994). Brief cognitive therapies. In A. E. Bergin & S. L. Garfield (Eds.), *Handbook of psychotherapy and behaviour change* (pp. 230–249). New York: J. Wiley.

Bohner, G., Ruder, M., & Erb, H. P. (2002). When expertise backfires: Contrast and assimilation effects in persuasion. *British Journal of Social Psychology*, *41*, 495–519.

Briñol, P., & Petty, R. E. (2003). Overt head movements and persuasion: A self-validation analysis. *Journal of Personality and Social Psychology*, *84*, 1123–1139.

Briñol, P., & Petty, R. E. (2004). Self-validation processes: The role of thought confidence in persuasion. In G. Haddock & G. Maio (Eds.), *Contemporary perspectives on the psychology of attitudes* (pp. 205–226). Philadelphia, PA: Psychology Press.

Briñol, P., & Petty, R. E. (2008). Embodied persuasion: Fundamental processes by which bodily responses can impact attitudes. In G. R. Semin & E. R. Smith (Eds.), *Embodiment grounding: Social, cognitive, affective, and neuroscientific approaches* (pp. 184–207). Cambridge, UK: Cambridge University Press.

Briñol, P., Petty, R. E., & Barden, J. (2007a). Happiness versus sadness as determinants of thought confidence in persuasion: A self-validation analysis. *Journal of Personality and Social Psychology*, *93*, 711–727.

Briñol, P., Petty, R. E., Gallardo, I., & DeMarree, K. G. (2007b). The effect of self-affirmation in non-threatening persuasion domains: Timing affects the process. *Personality and Social Psychology Bulletin*, *33*, 1533–1546.

Briñol, P., Petty, R. E., & Gasco, M. (2008). *The origin of thoughts in persuasion*. Unpublished manuscript.

Briñol, P., Petty, R. E., & Tormala, Z. L. (2004). The self-validation of cognitive responses to advertisements. *Journal of Consumer Research*, *30*, 559–573.

Briñol, P., Petty, R. E., Valle, C., Rucker, D. D., & Becerra, A. (2007c). The effects of message recipients' power before and after persuasion: A self-validation analysis. *Journal of Personality and Social Psychology*, *93*, 1040–1053.

Briñol, P., Petty, R. E., & Wheeler, S. C. (2006). Discrepancies between explicit and implicit self-concepts: Consequences for information processing. *Journal of Personality and Social Psychology*, *91*, 154–170.

Cacioppo, J. T., & Petty, R. E. (1982). The need for cognition. *Journal of Personality and Social Psychology*, *42*, 116–131.

Cacioppo, J. T., Petty, R. E., Feinstein, J. A., & Jarvis, W. B. G. (1996). Dispositional differences in cognitive motivation: The life and times of individuals varying in need for cognition. *Psychological Bulletin*, *119*, 197–253.

Chaiken, S. (1980). Heuristic versus systematic information processing in the use of source versus message quest in persuasion. *Journal of Personality and Social Psychology*, *39*, 752–766.

Chaiken, S., Liberman, A., & Eagly, A. H. (1989). Heuristic and systematic processing within and beyond the persuasion context. In J. S. Uleman & J. A. Bargh (Eds.), *Unintended thought* (pp. 212–252). New York: Guilford Press.

Chaiken, S., & Maheswaran, D. (1994). Heuristic processing can bias systematic processing: Effects of source credibility, argument ambiguity, and task importance on attitude judgement. *Journal of Personality and Social Psychology*, *66*, 460–473.

Chartrand, T. L., & Bargh, J. A. (1999). The chameleon effect: The perception behaviour link and social interaction. *Journal of Personality and Social Psychology*, *76*, 893–910.

Clark, J. K., Wegener, D. T., Briñol, P., & Petty, R. E. (in press). Discovering that the shoe fits: The self-validating role of stereotypes. *Psychological Science*.

Clarkson, J. J., Tormala, Z. L., & Rucker, D. D. (2008). A new look at the consequences of attitude certainty: The amplification hypothesis. *Journal of Personality and Social Psychology*, *95*, 810–825.

Clore, G. L., Gasper, K., & Garvin, E. (2001). Affect as information. In J. P. Forgas (Ed.), *Handbook of affect and social cognition* (pp. 121–144). Mahwah, NJ: Lawrence Erlbaum Associates Inc.

Clore, G. L., & Huntsinger, J. R. (2007). How emotions inform judgement and regulate thought. *Trends in Cognitive Science*, *11*, 393–399.

Costermans, J., Lories, G., & Ansay, C. (1992). Confidence level and feeling of knowing in question answering: The weight of inferential processes. *Journal of Experimental Psychology: Learning, Memory, and Cognition*, *18*, 142–150.

Crano, W. D., & Chen, X. (1998). The leniency contract and persistence of majority and minority influence. *Journal of Personality and Social Psychology*, *74*, 1437–1450.

Crocker, J., & Park, L. E. (2004). The costly pursuit of self-esteem. *Psychological Bulletin*, *130*, 392–414.

DeBono, K. G., & Harnish, R. J. (1988). Source expertise, source attractiveness, and processing or persuasive information: A functional approach. *Journal of Personality and Social Psychology*, *55*, 541–546.

DeMarree, K. G., Briñol, P., & Petty, R. E. (2008a). *Assimilation and contrast of facial expressions: A self-validation approach*. Unpublished manuscript.

DeMarree, K. G., Petty, R. E., & Briñol, P. (2007). Self and attitude strength parallels: Focus on accessibility. *Social and Personality Psychology Compass*, *1*, 441–468.

DeMarree, K. G., Petty, R. E., & Briñol, P. (2008b). *In search of individual differences in the use of mental contents*. Unpublished manuscript.

DeMarree, K. G., Wheeler, S. C., & Petty, R. E. (2005). Priming a new identity: Self-monitoring moderates the effects of non-self primes on self-judgements and behaviour. *Journal of Personality and Social Psychology*, *89*, 657–671.

Festinger, L. (1950). Informal social communication. *Psychological Review*, *57*, 271–282.

Festinger, L. (1957). *A theory of cognitive dissonance*. Stanford, CA: Stanford University Press.

Fiske, S. T. (1993). Controlling other people: The impact of power in stereotyping. *American Psychologist*, *48*, 621–628.

Fleming, M. A., & Petty, R. E. (2000). Identity and persuasion: An elaboration likelihood approach. In D. J. Terry & M. A. Hogg (Eds.), *Attitudes, behaviour, and social context: The role of norms and group membership* (pp. 171–199). Mahwah, NJ: Lawrence Erlbaum Associates Inc.

Fleming, M. A., Petty, R. E., & White, P. H. (2005). Stigmatized targets and evaluation: Prejudice as a determinant of attribute scrutiny and polarization. *Personality and Social Psychology Bulletin*, *31*, 496–507.

Friestad, M., & Wright, P. (1995). Persuasion knowledge: Lay people's and researchers' beliefs about the psychology of persuasion. *Journal of Consumer Research*, *27*, 123–156.

Galinsky, A. D., Gruenfeld, D. H., & Magee, J. C. (2003). From power to Action. *Journal of Personality and Social Psychology*, *85*, 453–466.

Goethals, G., & Nelson, R. E. (1973). Similarity in the influence process: The belief–value distinction. *Journal of Personality and Social Psychology*, *25*, 117–122.

Greenwald, A. G., McGhee, D. E., & Schwartz, J. L. K. (1998). Measuring individual differences in implicit cognition: The Implicit Association Test. *Journal of Personality and Social Psychology*, *74*, 1464–1480.

Hänze, M. (2001). Ambivalence, conflict, and decision making: Attitudes and feelings in Germany towards NATO's military intervention in the Kosovo war. *European Journal of Social Psychology, 31*, 693–706.

Harkins, S. G., & Petty, R. E. (1981). The effects of source magnification of cognitive effort on attitudes: An information processing view. *Journal of Personality and Social Psychology, 40*, 401–413.

Hass, R. G., Katz, I., Rizzo, N., Bailey, J., & Moore, L. (1992). When racial ambivalence evokes negative affect, using a disguised measure of mood. *Personality and Social Psychology Bulletin, 18*, 786–797.

Heider, F. (1958). *The psychology of interpersonal relations*. New York: Wiley.

Higgins, E. T. (1987). Self-discrepancy: A theory relating self and affect. *Psychological Review, 94*, 319–340.

Higgins, E. T., Rholes, W. S., & Jones, C. R. (1977). Category accessibility and impression formation. *Journal of Experimental Social Psychology, 13*, 141–154.

Hodson, G., Maio, G. R., & Esses, V. M. (2001). The role of attitudinal ambivalence in susceptibility to consensus informative. *Basic and Applied Social Psychology, 23*, 197–205.

Horcajo, J., Petty, R. E., & Briñol, P. (2008a). *Minority influence: A new look from the self-validation perspective*. Unpublished manuscript.

Horcajo, J., See, M., Briñol, P., & Petty, R. E. (2008b). The role of mortality salience in consumer persuasion. *Advances in Consumer Research, 35*, 782–783.

Hovland, C. I., Janis, I. L., & Kelley, H. H. (1953). *Communication and persuasion: Psychological studies of opinion change*. New Haven, CT: Yale University Press.

Janis, I. L., & King, B. T. (1954). The influence of role-playing on opinion change. *Journal of Abnormal and Social Psychology, 49*, 211–218.

Jonas, K., Diehl, M., & Bromer, P. (1997). Effects of attitudinal ambivalence on information processing and attitude–intention consistency. *Journal of Experimental Social Psychology, 33*, 190–210.

Jost, J. T., Kruglanski, A. W., & Nelson, T. O. (1998). Social metacognition: An expansionist review. *Personality and Social Psychology Review, 2*, 137–154.

Katz, I., & Hass, R. G. (1988). Racial ambivalence and American value conflict: Correlational and priming studies of dual cognitive structures. *Journal of Personality and Social Psychology, 55*, 893–905.

Kelman, H. C. (1958). Compliance, identification and internalization: Three processes of attitude change. *Journal of Conflict Resolution, 2*, 51–60.

Kelman, H. C., & Hovland, C. I. (1953). "Reinstatement" of the communicator in delayed measurement of opinion change. *Journal of Abnormal and Social Psychology, 48*, 327–335.

Kipnis, D. (1972). Does power corrupt? *Journal of personality and Social Psychology, 24*, 33–41.

Koriat, A., & Goldsmith, M. (1996). Monitoring and control processes in the strategic regulation of memory accuracy. *Psychological Review, 103*, 490–517.

Kruglanski, A. W. (1989). *Lay epistemics and human knowledge: Cognitive and motivational bases*. New York: Plenum Press.

Kruglanski, A. W., Raviv, A., Bar-Tal, D., Raviv, A., Sharvit, K, Ellis, S., et al. (2005). Says who? Epistemic authority effects in social judgement. In M. P. Zanna (Ed.), *Advances in experimental social psychology* (Vol. 37, pp. 346–392). San Diego, CA: Academic Press.

Kruglanski, A. W., & Thompson, E. P. (1999). Persuasion by a single route: A view from the unimodel. *Psychological Inquiry, 10*, 83–110.

Livingston, S. D., & Sinclair, L. (2008). Taking the watchdog off its leash: Personal prejudices and situational motivations jointly predict derogation of a stigmatized source. *Personality and Social Psychology Bulletin, 34*, 210–223.

Mackie, D. M., Gastardo-Conaco, M. C., & Skelly, J. J. (1992). Knowledge of the advocated position and the processing of in-group and out-group persuasive messages. *Personality and Social Psychology Bulletin*, *18*, 145–151.

Mackie, D. M., Worth, L. T., & Asuncion, A. G. (1990). Processing of persuasive in-group messages. *Journal of Personality and Social Psychology*, *58*, 812–822.

Maio, G. R., Bell, D. E., & Esses, V. M. (1996). Ambivalence and persuasion: The processing of messages about immigrant groups. *Journal of Experimental Social Psychology*, *32*, 513–536.

Martin, R., & Hewstone, M. (2008). Majority versus minority influence, message processing and attitude change: The source-context-elaboration model. In M. Zanna (Ed.), *Advances in experimental social psychology*. San Diego, CA: Academic Press.

McConahay, J. B., Hardee, B. B., & Batts, V. (1981). Has racism declined in America? It depends on who is asking and what is asked. *Journal of Conflict Resolution*, *25*, 563–579.

Moscovici, S. (1980). Toward a theory of conversion behaviour. In L. Berkowitz (Ed.), *Advances in experimental social psychology* (Vol. 13, pp. 209–239). New York: Academic Press.

Mugny, G., & Perez, J. A. (1991). *The social psychology of minority influence*. Cambridge, UK: Cambridge University Press.

Nelson, T. O. (1992). *Metacognition: Core readings*. Boston: Allyn & Bacon.

Newcomb, T. M. (1968). Interpersonal balance. In R. P. Abelson, E. Aronson, W. J. McGuire, T. M. Newcomb, M. J. Rosenberg, & P. H. Tannenbaum (Eds.), *Theories of cognitive consistency: A sourcebook* (pp. 28–51). Chicago: Rand McNally.

Nordgren, L. F., van Harreveld, F., & van der Pligt, J. (2006). Ambivalence, discomfort, and motivated information processing. *Journal of Experimental Social Psychology*, *42*, 252–258.

Orive, R. (1988a). Group consensus, action immediacy, and opinion confidence. *Personality and Social Psychology Bulletin*, *14*, 573–577.

Orive, R. (1988b). Social projection and social comparison of opinions. *Journal of Personality and Social Psychology*, *54*, 953–964.

Osgood, C. E., & Tannenbaum, P. H. (1955). The principle of congruity in the prediction of attitude change. *Psychological Review*, *62*, 42–55.

Ottati, V., Terkildsen, N., & Hubbard, C. (1955). Happy faces elicit heuristic processing in a televised impression formation task: A cognitive tuning account. *Personality and Social Psychology Bulletin*, *23*, 1144–1156.

Overbeck, J. R., & Park, B. (2001). When power does not corrupt: Superior individuation processes among powerful perceivers. *Journal of Personality and Social Psychology*, *81*, 549–565.

Petty, R. E. (1997). The evolution of theory and research in social psychology: From single to multiple effect and process models. In C. McGarty & S. A. Haslam (Eds.), *The message of social psychology: Perspectives on mind in society* (pp. 268–290). Oxford, UK: Blackwell.

Petty, R. E., & Briñol, P. (2006). Understanding social judgement: Multiple systems and processes. *Psychological Inquiry*, *17*, 217–223.

Petty, R. E., & Briñol, P. (2008). Persuasion: From single to multiple to metacognitive processes. *Perspectives on Psychological Science*, *3*, 137–147.

Petty, R. E., & Briñol, P. (2009). Implicit ambivalence: A metacognitive approach. In R. E. Petty, R. H. Fazio, & P. Briñol (Eds.), *Attitudes: Insights from the new implicit measures* (pp. 119–164). New York: Psychology Press.

Petty, R. E., Briñol, P., Loersch, C., & McCaslin, M. J. (in press). The need for cognition. In M. R. Leary & R. H. Hoyle (Eds.), *Handbook of individual differences in social behaviour*. New York: Guilford Press.

Petty, R. E., Briñol, P., See, M., & Fleming, M. A. (2008). *Watchdog: A new look from the implicit ambivalence perspective*. Unpublished manuscript.

Petty, R. E., Briñol, P., & Tormala, Z. L. (2002). Thought confidence as a determinant of persuasion: The self-validation hypothesis. *Journal of Personality and Social Psychology, 82*, 722–741.

Petty, R. E., Briñol, P., Tormala, Z. L., & Wegener, D. T. (2007). The role of metacognition in social judgement. In E. T. Higgins & A. W. Kruglanski (Eds.) *Social psychology: A handbook of basic principles* (2nd ed., pp. 254–284). New York: Guilford Press.

Petty, R. E., & Cacioppo, J. T. (1979). Issue involvement can increase or decrease persuasion by enhancing message-relevant cognitive responses. *Journal of Personality and Social Psychology, 37*, 1915–1926.

Petty, R. E., & Cacioppo, J. T. (1983). Central and peripheral routes to persuasion: Application to advertising. In L. Percy & A. Woodside (Eds.), *Advertising and consumer psychology* (pp. 3–23). Lexington, MA: D. C. Heath.

Petty, R. E., & Cacioppo, J. T. (1986). *Communication and persuasion: Central and peripheral routes to attitude change*. New York: Springer-Verlag.

Petty, R. E., Cacioppo, J. T., & Goldman, R. (1981). Personal involvement as a determinant of argument-based persuasion. *Journal of Personality and Social Psychology, 41*, 847–855.

Petty, R. E., Fleming, M. A., & White, P. (1999). Stigmatized sources and persuasion: Prejudice as a determinant of argument scrutiny. *Journal of Personality and Social Psychology, 76*, 19–34.

Petty, R. E., Haugtvedt, C., & Smith, S. M. (1995). Elaboration as a determinant of attitude strength: Creating attitudes that are persistent, resistant, and predictive of behaviour. In R. E. Petty & J. A. Krosnick (Eds.), *Attitude strength: Antecedents and consequences* (pp. 93–130). Mahwah, NJ: Lawrence Erlbaum Associates Inc.

Petty, R. E., & Krosnick, J. A. (Eds.). (1995). *Attitude strength: Antecedents and consequences*. Mahwah, NJ: Lawrence Erlbaum Associates Inc.

Petty, R. E., Schumann, D. W., Richman, S. A., & Strathman, A. J. (1993). Positive mood and persuasion: Different roles for affect under high and low elaboration conditions. *Journal of Personality and Social Psychology, 64*, 5–20.

Petty, R. E., Tormala, Z. L., Briñol, P., & Jarvis, W.B.G. (2006). Implicit ambivalence from attitude change: An exploration of the PAST Model. *Journal of Personality and Social Psychology, 90*, 21–41.

Petty, R. E., Wegener, D. T., & White, P. (1998). Flexible correction processes in social judgement: Implications for persuasion. *Social Cognition, 16*, 93–113.

Petty, R. E., Wells, G. L., & Brock, T. C. (1976). Distraction can enhance or reduce yielding to propaganda: Thought disruption versus effort justification. *Journal of Personality and Social Psychology, 34*, 874–884.

Priester, J. M., & Petty, R. E. (1995). Source attributions and persuasion: Perceived honesty as a determinant of message scrutiny. *Personality and Social Psychology Bulletin, 21*, 637–654.

Puckett, J. M., Petty, R. E., Cacioppo, J. T., & Fisher, D. L. (1983). The relative impact of age and attractiveness stereotypes on persuasion. *Journal of Gerontology, 38*, 340–343.

Rothman, A. J., & Schwarz, N. (1998). Constructing perceptions of vulnerability: Personal relevance and the use of experiential information in health judgements. *Personality and Social Psychology Bulletin, 24*, 1053–1064.

Schwarz, N., Bless, H., Strack, F., Klumpp, G., Rittenauer-Schatka, H., & Simons, A. (1991). Ease of retrieval as information: Another look at the availability heuristic. *Journal of Personality and Social Psychology, 61*, 195–202.

Sherman, S. J., Mackie, D. M., & Driscoll, D. M. (1990). Priming and the differential use of dimensions in evaluation. *Personality and Social Psychology Bulletin, 16*, 405–418.

Smith, C. A., & Ellsworth, P. C. (1985). Patterns of cognitive appraisal in emotion. *Journal of Personality and Social Psychology, 48*, 813–838.

Smith, R. E. (1993). Integrating information from advertising and trial: Processes and effects on consumer response to product information. *Journal of Marketing Research, 30*, 204–219.

Smith, S. M., & Shaffer, D. R. (1995). Speed of speech and persuasion: Evidence for multiple effects. *Personality and Social Psychology Bulletin, 21*, 1051–1060.

Snyder, M. (1974). Self-monitoring of expressive behaviour. *Journal of Personality and Social Psychology, 30*, 526–537.

Stroebe, W., & Diehl, M., (1988). When social supports fails: Supporter characteristics in compliance-induced attitude change. *Personality and Social Psychology Bulletin, 14*, 136–144.

Tiedens, L. Z., & Fragale, A. R. (2003). Power moves: complementarity in dominant and submissive nonverbal behaviour. *Journal of Personality and Social Psychology, 84*, 558–568.

Tiedens, L. Z., & Linton, S. (2001). Judgement under emotional certainty and uncertainty: The effects of specific emotions on information processing. *Journal of Personality and Social Psychology, 81*, 973–988.

Tormala, Z. L., Briñol, P., & Petty, R. E. (2006). When credibility attacks: The reverse impact of source credibility on persuasion. *Journal of Experimental Social Psychology, 42*, 684–691.

Tormala, Z. L., Briñol, P., & Petty, R. E. (2007a). Multiple roles for source credibility under high elaboration: It's all in the timing. *Social Cognition, 25*, 536–552.

Tormala, Z. L., Falces, C., Briñol, P., & Petty, R. E. (2007b). Ease of retrieval effects in social judgement: The role of unrequested cognitions. *Journal of Personality and Social Psychology, 93*, 143–157.

Tormala, Z. L., Petty, R. E., & Briñol, P. (2002). Ease of retrieval effects in persuasion: A self-validation analysis. *Personality and Social Psychology Bulletin, 28*, 1700–1712.

Tormala, Z. L., Petty, R. E., & DeSensi, V. L. (in press). Multiple roles for minority sources in persuasion and resistance. In R. Martin & M. Hewstone (Eds.), *Minority influence and innovation: Antecedents, processes, and consequences.* Hove, UK: Psychology Press.

van Knippenberg, D., Lossie, N., & Wilke, H. (1994). In-group prototypicality and persuasion: Determinants of heuristic and systematic processing. *British Journal of Social Psychology, 33*, 289–300.

van Knippenberg, D., & Wilke, H. (1992). Prototypicality of arguments and conformity to in-group norms. *European Journal of Social Psychology, 22*, 141–155.

Weary, G., & Jacobson, J. A. (1997). Causal uncertainty beliefs and diagnostic-information seeking. *Journal of Personality and Social Psychology, 73*, 839–848.

Wegener, D. T., & Petty, R. E. (1995). Flexible correction processes in social judgement: The role of naive theories in corrections for perceived bias. *Journal of Personality and Social Psychology, 68*, 36–51.

Wegener, D. T., & Petty, R. E. (1997). The flexible correction model: The role of naive theories of bias in bias correction. In M. P. Zanna (Ed.), *Advances in experimental social psychology* (Vol. 29, pp. 141–208). San Diego, CA: Academic Press.

White, P. H., & Harkins, S. G. (1994). Race of source effects in the elaboration likelihood model. *Journal of Personality and Social Psychology, 67*, 790–807.

Wood, W., Lundgren, S., Quellette, J. A., Busceme, S., & Blackstone, T. (1994). Minority influence: A meta-analytic review of social influence processes. *Psychological Bulletin, 115*, 323–345.

Yzerbyt, V. Y., Lories, G., & Dardenne, B. (1998). *Metacognition: Cognitive and social dimensions.* Thousand Oaks, CA: Sage Publications.

Ziegler, R., Diehl, M., Ruther, A. (2002). Multiple source characteristics and persuasion: Source inconsistency as a determinant of message scrutiny. *Personality and Social Psychology Bulletin, 28*, 496–508.

EUROPEAN REVIEW OF SOCIAL PSYCHOLOGY
2009, 20, 97–145

Implicit volition and stereotype control

Gordon B. Moskowitz and Courtney Ignarri

Lehigh University, Bethlehem, PA, USA

Goals are mental representations that vary in accessibility and operate within goal systems. The implicit nature of goal activation and pursuit is shown here to make goals effective not merely at overturning the influence of an activated stereotype on how people respond to members of stereotyped groups, but effective at implicitly controlling the activation of stereotypes in the first place. In a set of experiments examining chronic egalitarian goals, faces and names of members of stereotyped groups presented as target stimuli led to the inhibition of stereotypes, as well as to the heightened accessibility of egalitarian goals. A separate set of experiments illustrate a similar ability of individuals to control stereotype activation when egalitarian goals are temporarily triggered within a context, rather than being chronically held. Goals that require one to inhibit stereotypic associations to a target can lead to the intended, yet implicit, control of stereotype activation, even when one is not aware the goal is active or being pursued or being regulated.

Keywords: Compensatory cognition; Goal priming; Implicit goals; Inhibition; Stereotyping.

Stereotyping is one example of a cognitive process that can bias human responding. It influences basic processes such as attention and memory, as well as directing judgement and action. Because of this impact, often an undetected one, stereotyping may contribute to social problems and inter-group conflict (e.g., Allport, 1954; Blair, 2001; Correll, Park, Wittenbrink, & Judd, 2002; Macrae, Bodenhausen, Milne, & Jetten, 1994). Given its undesired effects, stereotyping represents a class of human responding that a given individual may want to control. The intended control over unwanted cognition and action, and particularly

Correspondence should be addressed to Dr Gordon B. Moskowitz, Department of Psychology, Lehigh University, 17 Memorial Drive East, Bethlehem, PA 18015-3068, USA. E-mail: gbm4@Lehigh.EDU

DOI: 10.1080/10463280902761896

the automatic elements of such control, has been a topic of increased empirical focus over the past decade (e.g., Shah & Gardner, 2007). This review focuses on one class of responding to be brought under intentional control, and the implicit nature of intentional control—control of stereotype activation.

Traditional approaches to controlling stereotyping have examined (1) how the behaviour of a stereotyped person instigates, in the mind of the perceiver, individuated thinking about that person (e.g., Czopp, Monteith, & Mark, 2006; Hamilton & Trolier, 1986), (2) how a perceiver's consciously selected goals might over-ride already triggered stereotypes, thus replacing biased responding with either goal-consistent or individuated responding (e.g., Brewer, 1988; Fiske & Neuberg, 1990; Macrae et al., 1994), and (3) the incidental interference with stereotyping from cognitive responses that utilise competing resources (e.g., Blair & Banaji, 1996; Gilbert & Hixon, 1991; Kawakami, Dovidio, Moll, Hermsen, & Russin, 2000; Macrae, Bodenhausen, Milne, Thorn, & Castelli, 1997). The first two approaches examine how conscious goals impact one's use of already triggered stereotypes (differing along the dimension of the source of the goals—triggered in the perceiver by another's behaviour versus selected by a perceiver due to a concern with bias). The third approach shifts from explicit to implicit sources of stereotype disruption, and shifts the focus to the disruption of stereotype activation (as opposed to stereotype use following activation). Additionally, however, it shifts the emphasis away from goals and the self-regulatory system as the source of the disruption.

Our approach to this question fuses the concern with the implicit disruption of stereotype activation with self-regulation. Drawing on recent work on the ability of goals to be both primed and regulated automatically (e.g., Bargh, 1990; Chartrand & Bargh, 1996; Förster, Liberman, & Friedman, 2007; Kruglanski et al., 2002; Moskowitz, Li, & Kirk, 2004; Shah, 2005), it asks whether the implicit processes of goal pursuit play a role in helping the individual to control unwanted behaviour/cognition such as stereotyping. Specifically we illustrate that stereotype activation, presumed to have been beyond control (e.g., Bargh, 1999; Devine, 1989), can be controlled and inhibited by implicit goals. The review provides a 2 × 2 framework for thinking about control, both in the domain of stereotyping and beyond. Stereotyping can be controlled via cognitive/behavioural operations used in goal pursuit, with a distinction being made between the explicit versus implicit nature of these operations. In turn, these operations may be a result of the explicit versus implicit activation of goals. This framework thus describes four general categories of control, each with unique implications for stereotyping.

STEREOTYPE ACTIVATION AND BELIEFS ABOUT ITS CONTROL

The pervasive and silent process of stereotype activation

Stereotypes are sets of beliefs about a group of people—a list or picture in our heads of the traits, attributes, and behaviours a social group is likely to possess (e.g., Allport, 1954; Hamilton & Sherman, 1994; Stangor & Lange, 1994; Von Hippel, Sekaquaptewa, & Vargas, 1995). The stereotype can bias responding in many distinct ways. However, what we wish to highlight here is not the myriad forms of bias resulting from a stereotype—detailed reviews exist elsewhere (e.g., Biernat, 2003; Blair, 2001; Hamilton & Trolier, 1986; Von Hippel et al., 1995). Instead our focus is on an important distinction arising from such work between *activation* of a stereotype and the *application/use* of a stereotype. Dissociating these processes is well accepted, with Kunda and Spencer (2003) clearly distinguishing between "stereotype activation, that is, the extent to which a stereotype is accessible in one's mind, and stereotype application, that is, the extent to which one uses a stereotype to judge a member of a stereotyped group" (p. 522).

Stereotype activation has been discussed as central to stereotyping since the time of Allport (1954). Stereotypes have been described as cognitive constructs that may be activated from the presence of a particular cue in the environment: "every event has certain marks that serve as a cue to bring the category of prejudgement into action ..." (Allport, 1954, p. 21). In more recent terminology stereotypes have been discussed as automatically triggered cognitive constructs (e.g., Banaji, Hardin, & Rothman, 1993; Bargh, 1999; Devine, 1989). Devine (1989), along with (at the time radically new) reaction time evidence from Dovidio, Evans, and Tyler (1986), ushered in a wave of experiments illustrating the silent and pervasive nature of stereotype activation. Devine argued that the fact that all people know the social stereotypes for a group leads to that stereotype being automatically activated—inescapably and uncontrollably—upon the mere presence of a group member. Goals, even the chronic goal to be egalitarian and anti-prejudice, appeared to lack the ability in Devine's research to control stereotype activation. The implicit activation of stereotypes makes one ready to be influenced, even though one may not be aware of an influence and even though one has the experience of being "bias-free" (a form of naïve realism arising from the fact that the source of the bias lies in the stereotype's implicit accessibility).

Controlling the use of stereotypes

Devine (1989) linked stereotyping as a process to other dual process models in social psychology (e.g., Chaiken & Trope, 1999) and cognitive psychology

(Logan, 1980; Posner & Snyder, 1975) by asserting a dissociation model of stereotyping where stereotyping is viewed as a process unfolding in stages. The first stage involves the activation of the stereotype, the second the application or use of the stereotype in memory of, judgement of, or behaviour towards, a person.

A dissociation model. The dissociation hypothesis is that stereotype control is exerted over the *use* of, not the activation of, stereotypes. According to this model individuals categorise people automatically, and these categories have associated with them cognitive routines, modes of responding, and affective reactions. This results in "automatic stereotype activation" (as well as automatic prejudice). However, a distinctly different form of processing can over-ride the outputs of such processing, thus altering one's ultimate response. This separate mode of thinking is based in consciousness and the effortful exertion of specific types of cognition that require cognitive resources. The model's key assertion is that while these processes involved in stereotype use may require little attention or effort to be engaged, they require *some amount* of attention and effort and thus are not inevitably engaged. Devine (1989, p. 15) stated: "non-prejudiced responses are, according to the dissociation model, a function of intentional, controlled processes, and require a conscious decision to behave in a nonprejudiced fashion". This is to be contrasted with stereotype activation, which the model views as unavoidable. Thus, stereotypes are said to be triggered inevitably, but control, when desired, is not inevitable. It can be derailed.

What determines, from a dual-process perspective, whether one's response towards a target is biased by (compatible with) the automatically activated stereotype or impacted by effortful (resource-dependent) processing incompatible with the stereotype? The answer is goals. The dual process logic is that the default responses yielded by one mode of processing are supplanted by the responses yielded by a second mode of processing, but a goal must be in place that motivates the cognitive system to shift from the default mode to the more effortful mode.

A goal's incidental incompatibility with stereotyping. One need not have the motivation to be unbiased or fair-minded to produce goals that are incompatible with stereotyping. Goals can have unintended consequences that interfere with implicit cognition such as stereotype activation. Macrae et al. (1997) gave participants the goal of scanning an image (a person's face) for dots. The goal was in no way relevant to stereotype control, yet the goal of focusing on a minute feature of the stimulus (scanning for dots) nonetheless interfered with stereotype activation (likely due to disrupting categorisation of the target).

A goal's intended incompatibility with stereotyping. Perhaps more intuitive when discussing control are examples of an individual having goals that are expected to have an intended effect (and have that effect). For example, goals that explicitly are related to the control of stereotyping, such as the motivation to be unbiased and fair-minded, are known to control the expression of stereotypes. Devine (1989) illustrated that low- and high-prejudiced people differ in both their conscious goals to overturn a stereotypic response they have made (once becoming aware of such bias) and in their implementation of that goal. Participants were first asked to list a set of offensive words and slurs that may be used to describe Blacks. They were later shown to compensate for this response in a subsequent task only if they had the goal to be non-biased.

A variety of goals lead the individual to overturn processing that relies on stereotypes. These include goals leading the individual to desire greater processing effort, or at least to desire processing that is perceived to be more accurate in its outputs than more heuristic/stereotype-based modes of thought (e.g., Chaiken, Liberman, & Eagly, 1989; Petty & Wegener, 1999). Some goals are selected by the individual (such as desires for accuracy, open-mindedness, and fairness), while some goals are imposed on the individual by others who confront the individual about his/her bias (e.g., Czopp et al., 2006; Whitehead, Schmader, & Stone, 2008), or by others with authority over the individual (such as with accountability goals). Some goals are introduced by a situational press (such as new information calling into question one's existing knowledge, creating uncertainty/doubt in such stereotype-based knowledge). Fiske and Neuberg (1990) provide a comprehensive review of how goals intended to reduce stereotyping do so by overturning the more implicit, stereotype-based judgement that the cognitive system initially rendered. Goals "correct for" the stereotype.

Pitfalls to conscious control. "Correction" is an important form of control. Yet Wilson and Brekke (1994) highlight some troubling facts facing this type of control. First the effort, consciousness, and motivation that control is said to require are often not available. For it to be successful one must be (a) aware of a stereotype's biasing influence, (b) in possession of an accurate theory of how one is being influenced and how to accurately correct it (e.g., Moskowitz, Skurnik, & Galinsky, 1999b; Wegener, Dunn, & Tokusato, 2001), (c) motivated to "debias" or remove that unwanted influence, and (d) in possession of the cognitive capacity to exert the required effort that such control mandates. The resources one requires for such control are often not present. Goal pursuit itself is a resource drain, leaving the person ill prepared for subsequent volitional activity (e.g., Baumeister, Bratslavsky, Muraven, & Tice, 1998; Vohs, Kaikati, Kerkhof, & Schmeichel, 2009). The impact of limited resources on increasing stereotyping and decreasing control is well established (e.g., Gilbert & Hixon, 1991; Kruglanski & Freund, 1983).

Even when resources are available, control attempts may not produce the results that the individual intended. For example, the goal to control stereotyping can also have unintended consequences that promote stereotyping, introducing a new contaminant to judgement while attempting to remove another! An illustration of such an ironic failure in one's explicit control of stereotypes is provided by Macrae et al. (1994). Although people who were asked to suppress stereotypes successfully suppressed the stereotype in an initial task, the use and accessibility of the stereotype was later heightened, ironically, for these people relative to people who had not been suppressing stereotypes. Wegner (1994) posits that suppressing a thought, such as a stereotype, activates two concurrent systems: the operating system and the monitoring system. *Monitoring* detects failures of control, looking for references to the unwanted thought. This requires holding in mind (at least below consciousness) the stereotype that is not to enter consciousness. The *operating process* seeks items inconsistent with the unwanted thought to replace it in consciousness. The operating process requires cognitive resources, but monitoring is simpler and relatively free from capacity restrictions. Thus the monitoring process continues to function, but the operating process is disabled, when there are drains on cognitive resources. This differential use of processing resources across two concurrently running processes is what Wegner claims causes the ironic increase in (or "rebound" of) thoughts one intends to suppress. Anything that disables the operating process (cognitive load, a change in explicit goals), but leaving the monitoring process unharmed, will result in the unwanted thought (stereotype) becoming highly accessible (e.g., Galinsky & Moskowitz, 2007; Wegner & Erber, 1992).

An alternative route to stereotype control not subject to such obstacles would be expected of an efficient organism. Indeed, Bargh and Huang (2009) argue that the conscious nature of goals is an evolutionary later development relative to implicit goal pursuit. They argue for implicit goal operations to be a natural state of affairs, with people able to regulate responding without the burden of consciousness. Our research has applied this logic to stereotyping, arguing that implicit goals, such as to be to be egalitarian, can be engaged silently and efficiently, thus directing information processing and resulting in control over stereotype activation.

SIX PRINCIPLES OF IMPLICIT VOLITION

Our argument is that intentional, yet implicit, control of stereotype activation can occur despite the perceiver having categorised the person to a group with which a stereotype is associated. This possibility hinges on the notion that control occurs outside consciousness, directing what associations are triggered and deemed relevant to a given category in a given situation. It assumes goal activation/pursuit need not be effortful and resource dependent. A watershed moment in the examination of motivation occurred when Bargh (1990) introduced the notion of *auto-motives* because it freed control from consciousness. Where do goals come from? They can be triggered by the environment; primed without awareness. How do goals operate? Silently, through cognitive routines associated with the goal. Bargh (1990, p. 100) stated: "the motive-goal-plan structure becomes activated whenever the relevant triggering situational features are present". A growing literature on implicit goals, as well as the principles governing implicit regulation, provides the foundation for our assumptions regarding stereotype control. Reviews of this literature exist elsewhere (e.g., Custers & Aarts, 2005a; Förster et al., 2007; Kruglanski et al., 2002; Moskowitz et al., 2004). The detailing in this section of six principles relating to implicit goals is done in the light of reviews existing elsewhere, and only to frame the underlying logic for stereotype activation as under the control of implicit goals.

The first principle of implicit volition: Goals are mental representations

Bargh (1990) described goals as cognitive structures, similar in many respects to social constructs such as schemas and stereotypes. In order for the environment to trigger goal-relevant behaviour directly, the goal must be stored internally—a mental representation. Bargh was not the first to discuss goals as mental representations. Tolman (1932) posited that environmental cues become associated with need-states of the organism when these external cues have, in the past, satisfied these need-states. This association is internally represented in the mind of the perceiving organism. The representation of the actions, outcomes, and objects associated with a need-state was then described as ready in the mind and able to be brought to bear on a current context, specifying what value stimuli encountered in the new context might have for the organism.

The second principle of implicit volition: Goal representations include affect and tension

The content and structure of goal representations are distinct from other representations. Custers (2009) invites us to take a closer look at goal representations: How do they develop? And most importantly: how can our brain recognise an accessible mental representation as a desired state that is worth pursuing and translate this information in motivational behaviour?

Consensus has formed around several central elements of goal representations. They specify standards/end-states that the individual is committed to, with varying degrees of strength, approach or avoid (Carver & Scheier, 1981). This requires having semantic knowledge of the standard, as well as standard-relevant items. The standard-relevant items contained in the representation include among them knowledge of one's efficacy in the domain, means towards achieving the standard (directions for action), obstacles to attaining it, and expectancies relating to successfully attaining the goal associated given the means and obstacles (Kruglanski, 1996).

However, semantic knowledge alone is not what is associated with the goal structure. In addition, goal representations capture valence (Custers, 2009; Custers & Aarts, 2005b; Ferguson & Porter, 2009). The strength of this affective component can lead the individual to initiate or withdraw from goal-relevant responding (dependent on whether positive or negative valence exists). Finally, goal representations contain, in addition to semantic knowledge and valence, a tension-state. This tension represents the motivational force attached to the discrepancy between one's current standing regarding a desired end-state and that which is specified by one's standard. The psychological tension is akin to a drive (Lewin, 1936) in that it impels the organism to compensate for the state, seeking to reduce the tension and approach the standard. In various literatures this tension has been referred to as a feeling of incompleteness (e.g., Wicklund & Gollwitzer, 1982), a self-discrepancy (e.g., Higgins, 1989), a failure or shortcoming (e.g., Carver & Scheier, 1981), and a lack of affirmation (e.g., Steele, 1988).

The tension state, though traditionally discussed as an explicit/conscious recognition of one's standing regarding the pursuit of a self-relevant goal, need not require consciousness. It is possible that one may implicitly detect such shortcomings, or have the discrepancy implicitly triggered (e.g., Custers & Aarts, 2007). What is required is the ability to monitor both one's current standing in relation to the desired standard as well as one's rate of progress in movement toward that standard (Carver & Scheier, 1998, 1999). Wegner (1994, reviewed above) suggested that such monitoring processes often require little-to-no cognitive resources.

The third principle of implicit volition: Goal representations vary in implicit accessibility

The notion that goals are mentally represented leads naturally to the idea that these representations, just as with other types of representations, can vary in their accessibility. Level of accessibility can be determined not merely by personal factors (history of experience with the construct in question, as with chronic accessibility) but triggered by the situation and relevant cues within that situation (e.g., Higgins, 1996). Goals can be triggered outside awareness by diverse things in the environment such as odours (Holland, Hendricks, & Aarts, 2005), people (Fitzsimons & Bargh, 2003; Shah, 2003), subliminal words (Chartrand & Bargh, 1996), objects such as briefcases (Kay, Wheeler, Bargh, & Ross, 2004), and from inferring intentions in others (Aarts, Gollwitzer, & Hassin, 2004). Our goal here is not to review all of the ways in which researchers have illustrated how a goal attains a heightened state of accessibility. The experimental evidence for the priming of goals is by now overwhelming, and such reviews exist elsewhere (see Dijksterhuis, Aarts, & Chartrand, 2007; Moskowitz & Gesundheit, 2009).

The point to be stressed here is simply that goal priming can occur following explicit attempts to pursue a goal (such as after deliberating among goals and selecting a goal to pursue), which then triggers the representation and increases its accessibility. Yet goal priming can also occur following the implicit triggering of the representation by goal-relevant stimuli in the environment (such as when stimuli are subliminally detected) or by implicit cognition that results in the goal's activation (such as when the intentions of others are implicitly inferred). In some instances the very same cognitive process can make goals accessible either explicitly or implicitly. For example, many models of goal pursuit begin with a goal being consciously triggered by the individual detecting a discrepancy between their desired end-state and their current state (e.g., Carver & Scheier, 1981; Lewin, 1936; Powers, 1973). However, discrepancies between a desired end-state and a current state can also be detected by the individual's implicit monitoring processes. Discrepancy detection is thus one way a goal attains heightened accessibility, yet the discrepancy detection process is at times explicit, at other times implicit.

What does it mean to say that a goal is non-consciously activated? We define such activation as meeting one of two criteria: Either the stimulus that activates the goal is not consciously detected by the perceiver, or the state of heightened activation is not consciously noticed by the perceiver at the time of responding, even if it had been noticed at some prior point in time. This definition allows for the possibility that even a goal that had at one point in time been consciously selected may, at a later point in time, retain heightened accessibility without one's awareness. Thus, even explicitly activated goals can become implicit goals if that goal's heightened accessibility is no longer consciously detected and its impact not known to exist.

The fourth principle of implicit volition: Individual goals exist and operate in a goal system

Kruglanski et al. (2002) build an extensive case for the idea that goals, as representations, exist among a system, or network, of related representations. The idea of a goal system requires coordination among goals within the system. By coordination it is meant that movement towards one goal impacts one's standing on another (e.g., Fishbach & Trope, 2008; Shah & Kruglanski, 2002). Goals may be compatible such that movement towards one may facilitate movement towards other goals. Goals may compete, and movement towards one may require inhibiting competing goals to "shield" the focal goal (e.g., Bargh, Gollwitzer, Lee-Chai, Barndollar, & Trötschel, 2001; Fishbach, Friedman, & Kruglanski, 2003; Shah, Friedman, & Kruglanski, 2002). Additionally, resources for goal pursuit are limited (Vohs et al., 2009), and one must anticipate other goals in the system that may need to be pursued in the near future to efficiently allocate resources among goal pursuits (e.g., Shah, 2005; Shah, Hall, & Leander, 2009).

Goal shielding: (In)Compatibility among goals in the goal system. One consequence of goal systems is goal shielding. Goal shielding describes the general set of processes by which a given goal is promoted through cognitive activity meant to inhibit distractions to the goal and facilitate the detection and processing of goal-relevant stimuli (as well as other goals) that are compatible with and facilitate the focal goal. For example, Shah (2003) illustrated that priming a goal that was related to a focal goal improved task performance on the focal goal. Shah (2003) further illustrated that *incompatible* goals produce an inhibitory effect on the accessibility, commitment, and pursuit of one of the goals. When a goal incompatible with verbal fluency was primed prior to a task assessing verbal fluency, the goal system shielded the primed goal by inhibiting the goal of verbal fluency, evidenced by decreased performance on the fluency task. Aarts, Custers, and Holland (2007) also illustrated inter-goal inhibition in a goal system. Participants were primed with the goal of socialising while simultaneously primed with a goal incompatible with socialising—studying. They then examined accessibility of the goal to socialise and found goal shielding. People with studying goals inhibited the goal to socialise.

Counteractive control. A final example of the goal-systems logic is provided by research on *counteractive control*. Adopting a structural view of goal systems, Fishbach et al. (2003) argue that higher-order goals, lower-order goals, and temptations to lower-order goals are all defined with respect to each other. The model posits that temptations away from a goal trigger that incompatible higher-order goal, setting in motion processes that over-ride the temptation, or counteract the value of the temptation. Thus any goal can constitute an interfering temptation with respect to another higher-order goal, while that same goal could be an overriding goal with respect to another interfering temptation. For example, Fishbach et al. (2003) primed some participants with a temptation to fattening food, others with the goal of dieting. When later asked to choose between a chocolate bar and an apple as a departure gift, both the food-primed and diet-primed participants were more likely than control participants to choose the apple. The fattening food temptation did not trigger eating of fattening food, but instead counteracted this tendency.[1]

The fifth principle of implicit volition: Goal-relevant operations are implicit

Goals once activated are pursued, and goal pursuit is regulated. There exists tremendous variety in the types of responses that are in the service of one's goals, ranging from overt actions one consciously selects to implicit processes that set thresholds for construct accessibility and for selective attention. A well-known example of this fifth principle implicates each of these two classes of responses—research on stereotype suppression reviewed above (e.g., Wegner, 1994).

Implicit operations promote goal attainment.   Literally thousands of examples of implicit operations triggered by one's goals exist in the literature. Indeed, huge swathes of cognitive psychology experiments and social cognition experiments could be used to illustrate this point. Unlike the suppression research, most do not point to unwanted and paradoxical effects of having an efficient regulatory system. Indeed, in many cases the implicit operations promote efficient and successful goal pursuit.[2] In social psychology such illustrations range from the rules people implicitly follow when forming attributions (e.g., Jones & Davis, 1965) to the research of Dijksterhuis, Bos, Nordgren, and van Baaren (2006) on the implicit evaluation of information in decision making. Dijksterhuis et al. gave participants an explicit goal of choosing between several products

---

[1]In another experiment participants were primed with words related to either a known temptation or goal. When primed with a temptation, response times on a lexical decision task were faster to words associated with the relevant (but incompatible) goal relative to an irrelevant goal. When primed with a goal, lexical decision responses to words relevant to the temptation were not faster relative to those irrelevant to the temptation. Thus, temptations (fattening foods, primed words) primed goals with which the temptation was incompatible, whereas those goals did not prime the temptation. These experiments support the goal systems hierarchical logic.

[2]The specific type of implicit operations triggered by a goal may depend on the opportunities that are present. For example, Fein and Spencer (1997) found that failure feedback on a test led to increased stereotyping of others. Koole, Smeets, van Knippenberg, and Dijksterhuis (1999) found that negative feedback following the same test led to different operations—ruminating on the test. Beauregard and Dunning (1998) showed that the threat to self following this failure feedback led to derogating another's intellect.

(from among four cars, as an example). Some participants were allowed to consciously evaluate the qualities of each of the options prior to being asked to make a decision. Other participants were not able to employ conscious operations and routines relating to the focal goal. Responses (choice) varied between the groups, but not in the intuitively obvious direction—those not able to consciously deliberate performed better on the task. Participants all begin with the explicit goal to make a decision, yet some have this goal released from consciousness. The goal, now implicit, continues to direct unconscious deliberation, employing implicit routines and operations that yield a better choice than people with conscious goals and conscious deliberation.

Inhibition as an implicit goal operation. As stated above, the implicit nature of the operations that service a goal is hardly a recent idea (and is exemplified by much of the work in cognitive psychology and social cognition in the last four decades). Both temporary and chronic goals have long been known to trigger implicit processes of inhibition that help the individual in goal pursuit. Tipper (1985) demonstrated that explicitly giving individuals the goal to ignore an object triggers implicit processes of spreading inhibition and negative priming (see also Fox, 1995). Stroop (1935) had participants repeatedly perform a colour-naming task over several weeks. Words were presented in coloured inks, and participants had to name the colour. Stroop found not only that word meaning interfered with colour naming, but also that the goal of colour naming eventually inhibited the ability to name words (Logan, 1980). Bruner (1957) reviewed evidence illustrating that information antagonistic with a chronically accessible goal was preconsciously avoided, making that information less likely to enter consciousness. And we have reviewed one example of implicit inhibition earlier—goal shielding involves one implicitly inhibiting responses to help regulate one's pursuit of a goal (Aarts et al., 2007; Shah, 2003). For example, participants primed with the goal to study implicitly inhibited the incompatible goal to socialise.

The sixth principle of implicit volition: The dissociation of goal activation and application

Theory and research on concept priming as well as stereotyping (e.g., Blair & Banaji, 1996; Devine, 1989; Higgins, 1996; Kunda & Spencer, 2003) has raised a key distinction between concept activation versus application. A similar distinction should be made with goal representations. The activation of the goal is separate from the regulatory processes that are initiated in an attempt to pursue the goal. Compensatory actions, selective attention to goal-relevant cues and objects, detection of opportunities to pursue a goal, the spreading of activation and inhibition across the goal system (from one goal to another) to shield one's activated goals, are all examples of operations that may occur following the activation of a goal.

Dissociating goal operations from activation reveals that goal activation can be implicit or explicit, and goal operations can be implicit or explicit. This creates a minimum of four categories of goal pursuits: the wholly explicit goal pursuit (explicit activation and operations), the wholly implicit goal pursuit (implicit activation and operations), explicitly primed goals with implicit operations, and implicitly primed goals with explicit operations. We briefly review each.

Consciously activated goals with conscious goal operations.   A primary example of this category of goal pursuit is work on achievement motivation, where people are explicitly given goals (such as performance goals versus learning goals) and then explicitly asked to perform a task relevant to the goal (e.g., Barron & Harackiewicz, 2001; Elliott & Dweck, 1988; Grant & Gelety, 2009). A second example is the bulk of the work on correction/control in dual process models. For instance, research on the impact of accountability/ accuracy goals on stereotyping typically has participants explicitly asked to be accurate and then to explicitly form judgements regarding a target person (e.g., Fiske & Neuberg, 1990; Neuberg, 1989; Tetlock, 1985).

Consciously activated goals with implicit goal operations.   The history of social cognition is replete with examples of implicit operations following explicit goals. The research we have previously reviewed on stereotype suppression (e.g., Macrae et al., 1994; Wegner & Erber, 1992) is prototypic of this category of goal pursuit. So too is much of the early research on control over bias, often in cases where one is not aware the bias exists or is being controlled—the implicit operations merely alter processing so that the bias is curtailed. For example, Thompson, Roman, Moskowitz, Chaiken, and Bargh (1994) found accuracy goals eliminated priming effects. Uleman and Moskowitz (1994) showed that explicit goals shape implicit trait inference. Clearly not all implicit operations associated with a conscious goal have unintended effects. The review of the role of goals in information processing provided by Srull and Wyer (1986) is largely a review of experiments where people are provided with goals, often called instructional sets, or tasks, and a desired effect is produced due to implicit processing.[3]

---

[3]One example is Hastie and Kumar's (1979) research in which participants are given either the goal to form impressions of others or to memorise information about others. These goals alter the way people attend to information consistent or inconsistent with a prior impression of a person, determining the manner in which such information is encoded and recalled. Hamilton, Katz, and Leirer (1980), as well as Srull (1983), provide a second example, focusing on how goals impact the manner in which information is integrated and then clustered in memory.

Implicitly activated goals with explicit goal operations. This category of goal pursuit describes people explicitly aware that they are pursuing a cognitive operation, yet unaware they have a goal accessible that these operations are serving. For example, Fitzsimons and Bargh (2003) illustrated that subtly priming "mother" activated an achievement goal associated with mother. People were next explicitly asked to try to achieve at a task and did not realise the implicit goal was impacting those efforts. In Aarts et al.'s (2004) research on *goal contagion* people were asked to perform a series of tasks on a computer, and were told that if time permitted they could earn money on the last task. Participants knew they were working fast to receive money at the last stage. What they did not know was that their goals were being manipulated in the experiment by a *contagion* procedure and that goal accessibility dictated the speed with which they worked.

Implicitly activated goals with implicit goal operations. This category of goal pursuit is wholly implicit: goals unknowingly triggered impact implicit cognitive operations. This category includes experiments in which sub-liminal or subtle primes impact implicit cognition (e.g., Chartrand & Bargh, 1996) and experiments illustrating an impact of chronically accessible goals on implicit cognition (such as the impact of need for structure on spontaneous trait inference, Moskowitz, 1993, and stereotyping, Neuberg & Newsome, 1993).[4]

STEREOTYPE ACTIVATION AND IMPLICIT VOLITION

The principles of implicit volition reviewed above are essential to our model of stereotype control. We argue that goals, including those incompatible with stereotyping, are represented in the mind (principle one). We focus largely, though not exclusively, on the goal of being egalitarian. It is further posited that goals have tension-states that dictate when goals will be accessible versus "shut down" (principle two). When a tension-state exists, or a discrepancy exists between how egalitarian one wishes to be and how egalitarian one currently feels, the egalitarian goal attains heightened accessibility. This goal can be implicit and persist in situations beyond the context in which the discrepancy was detected (principle three). The triggering of the goal is a distinct and separate stage of processing from the

---

[4]If we grant that implementation intentions are implicitly triggered, despite having been consciously set at a prior point in time, then experiments illustrating their influence on implicit operations would fit here as well (e.g., Aarts et al., 1999; Gollwitzer, 1999).

operations used to pursue the goal, and each may be implicit or explicit (principle six). The operations triggered are specific to the goal that is being pursued and the opportunities afforded to the individual in the context. These operations are often implicit, and include basic processes such as directing how a stimulus is categorised, where attention is focused, and what associations are triggered following categorisation (principle five). Finally, following principle four, we believe that goals reside in a cognitive system that allows for management between goals. Thus, goal shielding becomes a crucial element to control over stereotype activation. We posit that natural processes of shielding among goals in a goal system can lead to the inhibition of stereotypes (when such activation serves a goal incompatible with one's focal goal, such as the goal to be egalitarian).

Implicit volition and its implications for stereotype control

The research reviewed next examines stereotype control from a goal systems approach. It asserts that people are relevant to our goals. They both trigger goals and serve as means towards attaining our goals. A given "target person" affords many types of potential responses that will depend on (a) which of a given individual's goals are most accessible upon perceiving the target, and (b) which of a given individual's goals is afforded an opportunity to be seized on by the context in which that target is encountered. The activation of stereotypes associated with categories such as race and gender is one potential response under some goal conditions (perhaps under default goal conditions that operate during many interpersonal interactions—such as understanding/labelling behaviour, predicting what a person will do next, and getting along/having a smooth interaction). But is such a response inevitable for all goals a perceiver may hold?

The goal systems approach argues that goals reside in an associatively linked, hierarchically organised system with facilitative and inhibitory relationships among goals that are either compatible or incompatible. Two points link these ideas to stereotype control. The first point is that because people are relevant to our goals, as either means to those goals or exemplars of the goal (or both), they can prime goals and initiate goal shielding. Thus, people can be seen as a temptation away from a goal, should the goals associated with the person be incompatible with a focal goal; people can also be seen as a means towards attaining a goal, or facilitating goal pursuit. The second point is that person perception is goal based. In some sense the goals associated with person perception are extremely high-order. Heider (1944), for example, described categorising and making sense of people as fundamental, sitting at the top of the goal hierarchy. In another sense the goals associated with person perception are extremely low-order. There are many lower-order goals used for making sense of people, among them (but not an exhaustive list): comparing people (Stapel & Koomen, 2001), interpreting actions (Li & Moskowitz, 2007), searching for particular features (Macrae et al., 1997), evaluating specific features (Livingston & Brewer, 2002), forming an impression (Hastie & Kumar, 1979), remembering them (Hamilton et al., 1980), being colour-blind (Richeson & Nussbaum, 2004), and considering alternatives and having an open mind (Gollwitzer, 1990; Kruglanski, 1990). Such goals determine the operations that are performed when encountering a target. Some of these goals implicate categories and stereotypes. Others do not. As such, lower-order goals that implicate stereotyping are incompatible with higher-order goals that denounce or reject stereotyping.

Figures 1A, 1B, and 1C illustrate this type of a goal system relating to an African American man. The person (stimulus target) is typically perceived in the context of a high-order goal to categorise that person using categories such as race, gender, and age. A category once activated is going to lead to heightened accessibility of category-relevant information, with the retrieval of that information also under the direction of goals. In Figure 1A high-order goals, such as the goal to understand the person's behaviour (epistemic goals) trigger lower-order goals, such as to understand behaviour by using the least effort possible, or the goal to stereotype others to

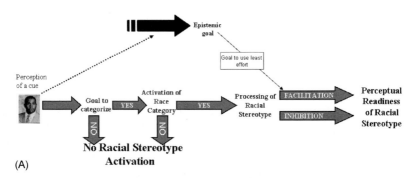

(A)

Figure 1A. Implicit epistemic goals and control of stereotype activation. The epistemic goal's activation, and its effects, depicted here represent pre-conscious processing—control steps exerted without conscious control yet being invoked. The dotted line from the face to the solid black arrow represents the possibility that encountering a person can trigger the goal to understand that person (and the cause of that person's actions). The solid black arrow represents the fact that this goal can be implicitly adopted prior to the face having been perceived. The arrow emerging from the epistemic goal indicates that the goal can impact the processing of a stereotype, in this instance facilitating the accessibility of the stereotype. The impact of an epistemic goal on stereotype processing may be mediated by the sub-goal to form a sufficiently good judgement using as little processing effort as possible, as indicated by the box through which the arrow passes. This ultimately yields stereotype accessibility (increased perceptual readiness).

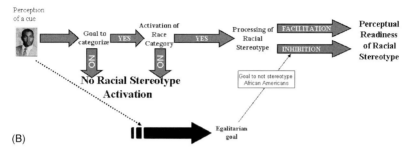

(B)

Figure 1B. Implicit egalitarian goals and control of stereotype activation. The egalitarian goal's activation, and its effects, depicted here represent pre-conscious processing—control steps exerted without conscious control yet being invoked. The dotted line from the face to the solid black arrow represents the possibility that encountering a person can trigger the goal to be egalitarian to members of that category. The solid black arrow represents the fact that this goal can be implicitly adopted prior to the face having been perceived. The arrow emerging from the egalitarian goal indicates that the goal can impact the processing of a stereotype, in this instance inhibiting the stereotype. The impact of an egalitarian goal on stereotype processing may be mediated by the sub-goal to not stereotype a specific group, as indicated by the box through which the arrow passes. This ultimately yields stereotype inhibition (decreased perceptual readiness).

understand and predict their behaviour. These goals are met by processing that determines which knowledge, from among many possible types of category-relevant knowledge, is retrieved and activated. It facilitates the retrieval and use of social stereotypes associated with the group. Similarly, the lower-order goal to use stereotypes can be facilitated if a higher-order goal such as self-esteem restoration is in place (see Figure 1C). This too would lead to the processing of specific types of category-relevant information—the stereotype.

However, the processing of these same social stereotypes can be inhibited if higher-order goals that are *incompatible* with the use of stereotypes (such as egalitarian goals) are also in place. Thus, if a category activates an egalitarian goal, the nature of the spreading activation from the category is altered relative to when the category is not associated with such a goal. Without an egalitarian goal we might expect a process that yields stereotype activation—a category triggers a goal to understand behaviour and make predictions about a target person; this is accomplished via a lower-order goal to retrieve and use category-relevant stereotypes. In contrast, and as depicted in Figure 1B, if the target activates an egalitarian goal as its more dominant association to the category, the egalitarian goal will inhibit the retrieval and use of social stereotypes that are incompatible with the egalitarian standard. This may be accomplished through the activation of lower-order goals that are incompatible with the goal of retrieving stereotypes, such as the goal to suppress stereotypes. Thus, an African

American man would trigger the goal to be egalitarian in dealings with African Americans, which in turn would trigger the inhibition, rather than retrieval, of social stereotypes associated with African Americans.

Goals and the control of categorisation.   As seen in Figures 1A and 1B, the process of stereotype activation involves the intermediary step of categorising the person as "a person" and as a member of a group to which the stereotype is associated. Categorisation itself is a multi-step process in which pre-attentive processes locate features, and those features then get matched against existing categories. It has been argued (Livingston & Brewer, 2002) that not even the categorisation of people into relevant "person groups" must occur automatically, but requires that one has the goal of categorising. Further, people are complex, multi-faceted targets (e.g., Dijksterhuis & van Knippenberg, 1996; Macrae, Bodenhausen, & Milne, 1995). Even if one has the goal of categorising, the way one categorises (which category is selected) is goal-based.

Macrae et al. (1995) found that once a person is categorised according to one group, from among the many to which a person belongs, inhibitory processes are triggered that shield that category from competing categories. Dijksterhuis and van Knippenberg (1996) also found that once a stereotypic category was activated, incompatible content was inhibited. What such work suggests is that asking a perceiver to react to a person in terms of race may inhibit categories such as gender and occupation. Goals may promote category use, but in so doing can implicitly inhibit the activation of competing categories and stereotypes. Goals that promote categorising to occupational groups may promote lawyer, professor, and fireman stereotypes, but inhibit racial stereotypes that may also be associated with, for example, Black firemen (see also Taylor, 1981).

The main point of this review is not merely "goals specify which of our many categories are triggered and inhibited". Livingston and Brewer (2002) have suggested this already in showing that goals disrupt the use of categories (see Figures 1A and 1B). The main point of this review is that given a specific category *is* activated, people may be perceived in a fashion that does not implicate stereotypes at all if goals interfere with such processing. Stereotype control can be accomplished when categorisation has occurred, yet goals direct processing such that stereotypes associated with the category are inhibited and other knowledge associated with the category is retrieved instead. Goals can direct the cognitive system to inhibit stereotypes *despite categorisation*, much as competing goals are inhibited when a focal goal is triggered and as semantic concepts are inhibited when an incompatible concept is primed (e.g., Glucksberg, Kreuz, & Rho, 1986). Figure 1C illustrates this process through a focus on two goals discussed in the coming pages—egalitarian and creativity goals—although a host of

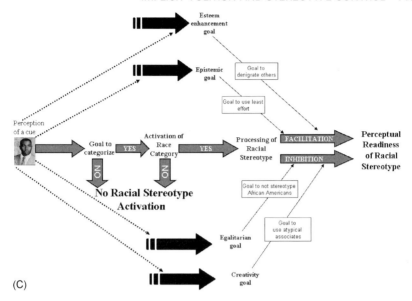

(C)

Figure 1C. Implicit volition and control of stereotype activation. The model depicted here represents pre-conscious processing—control steps exerted without conscious control yet being invoked. Dotted lines from the face to the solid black arrows represent the possibility that the processing of the face can trigger the goal pointed to by a given solid arrow. The solid black arrows represent the fact that the goals they point to could have been triggered prior to the face having been perceived, and thus that goal serves as a context in which face perception and subsequent processing occurs. Arrows emerging from a given goal indicate that the goal can impact the type of processing of a stereotype—a goal may inhibit stereotypes, it may facilitate stereotypes, it may be irrelevant to stereotypes. The impact of such goals on stereotype processing may be mediated by sub-goals, as indicated by the boxes through which these arrows pass. Ultimately, whether one's stereotypes are inhibited or facilitated (perceptual readiness) is dependent on the cumulative effect of one's various goals on the processing of the stereotype. The goals listed here are just a small subset of possible goals that can impact stereotype activation.

other goals could lead to such control as well. Figure 1C also illustrates that another way to conceive of implicit control over stereotyping is to focus not on its disruption, but on its facilitation due to the implicit goals that are triggered. Once again, the figure focuses on two such goals—esteem enhancement and need for structure—but a host of other goals could have similar effects on stereotype promotion.

The implicit inhibition of stereotypes following categorisation.   People, as social targets, are associated with both lower-order and higher-order goals. The particular higher-order goal activated (implicitly or not) is capable of triggering implicit operations that inhibit incompatible lower-order goals. Our research illustrates such activation and inhibition of lower-order goals, and the means associated with those goals, to the extent they are incompatible with higher-order goals. When a woman or an African American (the groups used in our research, but we do not limit the theoretical argument to these groups) is encountered and categorised, a person with egalitarian goals towards those groups (although the argument extends to other goals incompatible with stereotyping) is prepared to see such people as opportunities to move towards their goal. They have a heightened readiness to detect such people since they are goal relevant. They have heightened associations between their goal and the group such that the person triggers the goal. They shield the goal so that incompatible goals— those that activate stereotypes—are inhibited.

In our experimental approach we illustrate the cognitive system is wired in a way that allows us to "not stereotype" as part of the implicit operations that accompany goal pursuit (see Figure 1C). This review of the research evidencing intended, yet implicit, control over stereotype activation is organised according to the categories described in principle six (above). We will look at goals controlling stereotype activation by examining, in turn, research on implicitly activated goals that are implicitly pursued, turning next to research on implicitly activated goals that are explicitly pursued, and ending with explicitly activated goals that are implicitly pursued.

Implicitly activated goals with implicit goal operations

Moskowitz, Gollwitzer, Wasel, and Schaal (1999a) performed the first test of whether implicit goals direct cognitive operations so as to prevent stereotype activation. They focused on people who chronically pursue egalitarian goals: people who through practice, repetition, and frequency of pursuit, develop an implicit association between a particular group and egalitarian goals. Such people have a chronic state of implicit accessibility of this goal. For such people the process of stereotyping, and goals that promote stereotyping, are incompatible with their goal. Thus, the more dominant association to a given group for whom such a goal has formed would be the egalitarian goal, not the stereotype (and these two are incompatible). Men with chronic goals to be egalitarian to women were identified in a first session, one preceding the stereotype activation phase of each experiment by at least 2 weeks. This was accomplished by having participants take a multiple-choice test in which all possible answers forced one to endorse stereotypes of women. Prior to and after this test the participants completed a measure of gender stereotyping by filling out a series of semantic differential items assessing beliefs about various groups (including women). Decreases in the endorsement of stereotypic items on the semantic differential from time one to time two, which were due to the bias "expressed" on the test, were taken to indicate that the participant had a chronic goal. In essence, altered responses were a manifestation of the person's having held the goal to be not biased to a strong enough degree to (a) experience tension from the multiple choice test, and (b) necessitate compensating for the tension on the semantic differential.

Moskowitz et al. (1999a, Experiment 3) examined whether men with a chronic goal to be egalitarian to women would not have stereotypes of women activated when stimuli relevant to women were presented (whereas men without chronic goals would). Men were recruited for a session involving a reaction time task that, unbeknown to participants, assessed stereotype activation. The participants included individuals labelled as non-chronics along with the chronic egalitarians. The non-chronics were not high-prejudice people; they were people who value the goal of being egalitarian, but not chronically pursuing such goals (do not alter their semantic differential scores after expressing gender bias). Stereotype activation was assessed using a pronunciation task—words appearing on a monitor were to be read aloud into a microphone. On all trials, words were preceded by photographs of women and men (ostensibly as part of a test of whether images of famous people influence reading speed). On all trials the time between the prime (the face) and the pronunciation task was 200 milliseconds, not enough time for conscious control over the response to be initiated even if one were aware such control was relevant to this task (Bargh & Chartrand, 2000). On critical trials, words to be pronounced were either stereotype-relevant or control words. If stereotypes are activated, a priming effect would be found where stereotype-relevant words (but not control words) are responded to more quickly, but only following stereotype-relevant primes (following faces of women, but not men).

The results revealed a pattern of stereotype activation for non-chronics, but control over stereotype activation for chronics. Non-chronics had facilitated response times when pronouncing stereotype-relevant attributes after stereotype-relevant primes relative to their speed of pronouncing the same words following stereotype-irrelevant primes. They also exhibited facilitated response times when pronouncing stereotype-relevant words relative to stereotype-irrelevant (control) words following stereotype-relevant primes. However, participants with chronic egalitarian goals did not differ in their responses to target words as a function of the type of prime or type of word (see Table 1). When participants held a chronic goal to be egalitarian to women, there was no indication that stereotypes of women receive preferential/facilitated treatment in one's response after one had encountered the image of a woman. This occurred despite participants lacking conscious awareness of having a goal while performing the task or awareness of their stereotype control (since they lacked awareness the task assessed stereotypes).

TABLE 1
Response times, from Moskowitz et al. (1999a) Experiment 3

	Chronic egalitarian goal Prime type		No chronic egalitarian goal Prime type	
Word type	White female	White male	White female	White male
Stereotype-relevant	554	556	504	530
Stereotype-irrelevant	542	543	526	526

Response times (in ms) to stereotype-relevant and control words as a function of chronic egalitarian goals and prime type (from Moskowitz et al., 1999a, Experiment 3).

Moskowitz, Salomon, and Taylor (2000) replicated the finding of chronic goals leading to control of stereotype activation by examining White American participants and stereotypes of African Americans. White participants with chronic egalitarian goals towards Blacks and non-chronics were identified in this experiment by asking people to describe their hopes and goals for the future, their ideals. Participants who spontaneously mentioned working towards a world where African Americans were treated equally, or who described wanting to promote civil rights, were coded as having a chronic egalitarian goal towards African Americans. A minimum of 2 weeks later participants performed a memory task (used for presenting primes) that was followed (after 200 ms) by a pronunciation task. On critical trials the primes were either Black or White men and the words were either relevant to or irrelevant to the stereotype of Blacks.

The results replicated Moskowitz et al. (1999a). Non-chronics had facilitated response times when pronouncing stereotype-relevant words after African American faces relative to the same words following White faces (and relative to stereotype-irrelevant words following African American faces). People with chronic egalitarian goals did not differ in their responses to target words as a function of the type of prime or the type of word (see Table 2). Chronic egalitarians did not have stereotypes of African Americans activated upon exposure to a face of a Black man.

The proposed mechanism for control is that participants with chronic egalitarian goals have a more dominant association to the group than the stereotype – the egalitarian goal (even though the stereotype is known by all participants). The triggered egalitarian goal then inhibits the incompatible stereotype as part of the "goal-shielding" process. Next we review experiments illustrating this operating process—inhibition of stereotypes (Moskowitz et al., 1999a, Experiment 4) from a highly accessible egalitarian goal (Moskowitz et al., 2000, Experiment 2).

Moskowitz et al. (1999a, Experiment 4) used a negative priming task (reviewed earlier, e.g., Tipper, 1985) in which stereotype-relevant primes

TABLE 2
Response times, from Moskowitz et al. (2000) Experiment 1

Word type	Chronic egalitarian goal Prime type		No chronic egalitarian goal Prime type	
	Black male	White male	Black male	White male
Stereotype-relevant	498	489	427	485
Stereotype-irrelevant	480	477	465	482

Response times (in ms) to stereotype-relevant and control words as a function of chronic egalitarian goals and prime type (from Moskowitz et al., 2000, Experiment 1).

were to be ignored rather than attended to. Men with chronic goals of being egalitarian to women and non-chronics performed a pronunciation task. Each trial began with two words appearing, one of which was to be ignored. The to-be-ignored items were manipulated so that they were female names on half of the critical trials and gender-neutral on the rest. The word pairs were followed by a 200-ms interval ending with the appearance of a target word to be pronounced. Critical trials contained either words relevant to the female stereotype or control words. This procedure thus exposed participants to stereotype-relevant and control primes in a negative priming task, and then assessed reaction times to stereotype-relevant and control words. The data show that chronics implicitly *inhibited* the female stereotype if a stereotype-relevant prime had been ignored. This was evidenced by slower responses to stereotype-relevant words relative to control words (and relative to when stereotypic words were preceded by control primes). The accessible goal led to inhibition of responses incompatible with that goal when relevant cues were encountered. In contrast, non-chronics had stereotypes activated. Reaction times to stereotype-relevant words after female faces were faster relative to the same words following male faces. They also pronounced stereotype-relevant words faster than control words following female faces (see Table 3).

TABLE 3
Response times, from Moskowitz et al. (1999a) Experiment 4

Word type	Chronic egalitarian goal Prime type		No chronic egalitarian goal Prime type	
	White female	White male	White female	White male
Stereotype-relevant	770	748	747	783
Stereotype-irrelevant	757	768	773	765

Response times (in ms) to stereotype-relevant and control words as a function of chronic egalitarian goals and prime type (from Moskowitz et al., 1999a, Experiment 4).

The model not only predicts inhibition of stereotypes when a person with egalitarian goals encounters a member of a stereotyped group, it also suggests the presence of the target person boosts accessibility of the egalitarian goal. The person represents an opportunity to pursue the goal, and as such has forged over time a dominant association to the goal. Similar to a temptation triggering the focal goal incompatible with the temptation (Fishbach et al., 2003), the presence of stereotype-relevant cues (faces of people from a stereotyped group) should increase accessibility of egalitarian goals rather than the incompatible response (stereotype activation). To illustrate this, Moskowitz et al. (2000, Experiment 2) exposed White participants to faces of African American and White men (ostensibly as part of a memory task). After a 200-ms interval a lexical decision task was performed, where participants responded if a set of letters formed an English word. On critical trials words were presented that were able to assess goal activation—they were either related to the goal of being egalitarian or control words.

The results revealed that when words were relevant to egalitarianism, chronics had facilitated response times if those words were preceded by faces of African American men relative to White men. Faces of African American men did not lead to facilitated reaction times to control words. Non-chronics did not exhibit any differences in their responses to the target words, regardless of word type or type of prime preceding the word (see Table 4). The results show that in addition to stereotypes being inhibited, chronics have the goal to be egalitarian triggered by Black faces, faces that non-chronics associate more dominantly with a stereotype.

Chronic goals and implicit prejudice.   Plant and Devine (1998) note that chronic goals to control prejudice are determined not merely by the amount of motivation one has, but different sources of motivation. Just as conscious goals can be internally selected or presented to an individual by an external

TABLE 4
Response times, from Moskowitz et al. (2000) Experiment 2

Word type	Chronic egalitarian goal Prime type		No chronic egalitarian goal Prime type	
	Black male	White male	Black male	White male
Relevant to egalitarian goal	565	654	669	636
Irrelevant to egalitarian goal	619	649	623	651

Response times (in ms) to stereotype-relevant and control words as a function of chronic egalitarian goals and prime type (from Moskowitz et al., 2000, Experiment 2).

source, implicit goals can be differentiated according to whether their source is an internal or external motivation. Plant and Devine created two scales: one measures internal, the other external, motivation to respond without prejudice (IMS and EMS). The IMS consists of items such as "I attempt to act in non-prejudiced ways towards Black people because it is personally important to me" and "Because of my personal values, I believe that using stereotypes about Black people is wrong". The EMS consists of items such as "Because of today's PC (politically correct) standards I try to appear non-prejudiced towards Black people" and "I attempt to appear non-prejudiced towards Black people in order to avoid disapproval from others".

How do these implicit goals impact implicit bias? Though not concerned with stereotype activation, Devine, Plant, Amodio, Harmon-Jones, and Vance (2002) examined the impact of implicit goals on implicit prejudice. They predicted that people motivated to control prejudice for solely internal reasons (high IMS/low EMS) will demonstrate efficient self-regulation abilities, even when prejudice is hard to control. In Study 1 participants had to respond by indicating if stimuli were good or bad after being primed with faces. Overall, participants in the priming task revealed a race bias such that responses to negative words were faster when primed with Black faces. However, internally motivated participants (high IMS/low EMS) did not respond as quickly to negative words after being primed with Black faces relative to other groups (high IMS/high EMS, low IMS/high EMS, low IMS/low EMS). Study 2 used a different implicit measure, the implicit association test (IAT; e.g., Greenwald, McGhee, & Schwartz, 1998), to further support the idea that high IMS/low EMS individuals are more effective self-regulators. The IAT scores were consistent with the previous findings: Lower IAT scores were found for high IMS/low EMS participants as compared to the other three groups.

Implicitly primed goals and stereotype activation.   Chronic pursuit of a goal is not the only way a goal can attain a heightened state of accessibility. Subtle priming has been used in the literature to trigger goals in people who do not chronically pursue those goals. These procedures include: (a) asking participants to think about, or look at pictures of, people associated with goals of the perceiver, (b) exposing people to goals through subliminal presentation, (c) exposing people to goals through supraliminal presentation (in a task they do not recognise as being about goals), and (d) implicitly inferring goals in others and adopting those goals, implicitly, oneself through goal contagion. Our research on implicit control of stereotype activation has turned to such procedures. This shift is important to demonstrate that the effects just described are not limited to specific types of people. Although we started quite deliberately with chronics, assuming they would provide the strongest starting point to test of our model, we do not mean to imply the processes are limited to chronics. If implicit operations incompatible with stereotype activation are triggered by a goal, any person with the goal triggered would control stereotype activation.

Sassenberg and Moskowitz (2005) illustrated the generality of the goal systems logic in stereotype control by (a) shifting the focus off people with chronic goals, and (b) shifting the focus off egalitarian goals. In one experiment, unrelated to stereotyping, Sassenberg and Moskowitz primed participants with creativity goals. Their experiment illustrated that the goal of creativity involves implicit operations that lead to inhibition of typical associations to a stimulus. For example, participants primed with "doctor" were not faster to respond to "nurse" than to a control target. Typical associates to a target are disrupted if creativity goals are primed. A subsequent experiment extended this logic to the domain of stereotyping. If stereotypes are the typical association to a target (given default processing goals), creativity goals should disrupt these typical associations and implicitly control stereotyping. This should occur even when the goal is implicitly triggered and one is not aware one is trying to be creative.

Participants first performed a task in which they were exposed to goals relating to either creativity or thoughtfulness. Participants next performed a supposedly unrelated priming task. Attributes relevant to the stereotype of Blacks and control attributes were presented in a minority of the trials of a lexical decision experiment. On all trials faces of Black and White men were presented for 80 milliseconds prior to the lexical decision component of the trial. On critical trials the faces and targets are paired such that half of the faces are of Black and half of White men; half the faces are paired with stereotype-relevant attributes (the rest with control words).

The predicted pattern of inhibition and facilitation as a function of one's goals was revealed. Critically, participants primed with creativity goals had slower reaction times to attributes associated with Black stereotypes when those attributes were preceded by Black faces relative to White faces. Such an effect does not emerge for control words. Conversely, a priming effect is found for people not primed with creativity. These individuals are faster to stereotype-relevant words following Black (versus White) faces, with no effect for control words (see Table 5). When goal operations are incompatible with stereotype activation, the stereotype is not activated, despite one being unaware the goal was primed or that the task afforded control.

This section has reviewed experiments with both chronic and temporary goals that provide evidence for a category of goal pursuit called "implicitly activated goals with implicit operations". More importantly, these experiments illustrate automatic goal shielding in the domain of stereotype control. Goals to be egalitarian are not overturning or correcting for the activation of a stereotype. Goals are triggering operations that, though implicit, prevent stereotype activation. This control is due to the implicit

TABLE 5
Response times, from Sassenberg and Moskowitz (2005) Experiment 1

	Creativity goal Prime type		Thoughtfulness goal Prime type	
Word type	Black male	White male	Black male	White male
Stereotype-relevant	599	563	549	567
Stereotype-irrelevant	588	574	579	562

Response times (in ms) to stereotype-relevant and control words as a function of temporary creativity goals and prime type (from Sassenberg & Moskowitz, 2005, Experiment 1).

engagement of operations that proactively shield the goal. In this case, this operation is the inhibition of the stereotype given the presence of a goal-relevant person. A stereotype actually has a decreased likelihood of being triggered when the appropriate higher-order goals are in place (thus shielding the goal pursuit by decreasing the opportunities for its competitors to be triggered).

Implicitly activated goals with explicit goal operations

This category of control describes people who are aware that their responses are relevant to stereotyping, yet are not aware that a goal that exerts control over stereotyping has been triggered. This is a particularly important category of control because it characterises the way in which people often interact in day-to-day life: a manager may know she is evaluating an employee, explicitly doing so, yet she may not realise the role goals play in shaping that evaluation. An individual may be making a decision to avoid another individual, yet not realise the role of goals in shaping this decision. This category of control is relatively underexplored in the stereotyping literature. Perhaps only one experiment provides evidence of stereotype activation being controlled by implicit goals to be non-prejudiced in an explicit task, and even this work is not a precise illustration since it measures explicit attitudes, not chronic (implicit) goals. We assume a correlation between low prejudice attitudes and egalitarian goals, although these are not the same.

Lepore and Brown (1997) had participants make explicit ratings of a person whose behaviour was described. Participants low and high in prejudice attitudes were selected for the experiment. To test whether the stereotype associated with a category was controlled, participants were first subliminally exposed to the category label "Black" (Blacks, Afro-Caribbean, West Indians, coloured, afro, dreadlocks). If the stereotype was activated, stereotype-relevant qualities such as "aggressive" would be interpreted as being present in greater degrees when evaluating the behaviour of the person being described. If activation of the stereotype had been controlled, ratings of the target would not reflect heightened levels of stereotype-relevant traits. They found that the relationship between categories and stereotypes is dependent on one's attitudes. High-prejudice people showed increased use of the negative stereotype of Blacks in their judgements of the target relative to both low-prejudiced people and to high-prejudice people who had not been primed with the category "Black". Low-prejudiced people used negative qualities in their ratings in ways similar to people who had not been primed with the category "Black". Negative stereotypes of Blacks were not triggered even when the category "Black" had been. A caveat to this finding is that low-prejudiced people did not control activation or use of positive stereotypes. When primed with the category "Black" they used qualities such as "athletic" to a greater degree than low-prejudiced people who had not been primed. Such findings highlight the implicit flexibility of control. Given category activation, specific aspects of a stereotype (e.g., positive traits) are activated yet others (e.g., negative traits) are not.

Implicit goals that reduce stereotype activation are not the only goals that can shape how much stereotyping is evidenced in one's explicit responding. Implicit goals that promote stereotype activation are also examples of implicit control. Sassenberg, Moskowitz, Jacoby, and Hansen (2007) primed *competition* goals and then explicitly asked people to rate an outgroup on stereotypical qualities and homogeneity. Competition between groups is known to heighten intergroup hostility by increasing ingroup preference and outgroup derogation. When people have competition goals they categorise their competitors more rigidly than when competition does not exist and they focus on schema-consistent information. When feeling threatened by a competitor people make more homogeneous ratings of the outgroup (Corneille, Yzerbyt, Rogier, & Buidin, 2001; Ruscher, Fiske, Miki, & Van Manen, 1991) and have higher levels of stereotype activation (Spencer, Fein, Wolfe, Fong, & Dunn, 1998). Similar effects should emerge from competition goals that are implicitly primed.

In fact, Sassenberg et al. argue that implicit priming of the goal should not even require one be in direct competition with the outgroup one is evaluating. If competition goals are primed while the conscious task of evaluating the outgroup is being performed, stereotype activation should be increased. Heightened activation would be reflected in the outgroup being stereotyped more, seen as more homogeneous, and evaluated in a rigid and schema-consistent manner. In a first experiment competition goals were manipulated by asking participants to remember a situation where they either competed or cooperated with someone. Half did this with a Black partner in mind, and half were given no instructions regarding race.

Stereotype activation was subsequently assessed using a semantic differential. Stereotyping of African Americans was higher in the competition than the cooperation condition, independent of the race of the partner.

These findings were replicated in a second experiment that further examined perceptions of group homogeneity. East German participants worked on a test in dyads and were told they could earn an extra € 5 if their performance reached certain criteria. In the competition goals condition the extra money was awarded to the person in each dyad who performed best. In the control condition one had to give 20 correct answers to get the extra money. In the cooperation goals condition each participant got the money for correct answers to 20 or more questions in the responses of both participants. Measures of homogeneity of the ingroup and outgroup were created from ratings participants made of East and West German people described to them in profiles. The findings revealed that the West German outgroup was perceived as more homogeneous in the competition condition than in the cooperation or control conditions.

Implicit goals and stereotype use.   Despite a dearth of experiments in this category examining control of stereotype activation, quite a few experiments illustrate control over stereotype use. One example has already been reviewed (Plant & Devine, 1998). Another is provided by examining the impact of implicit goals on control over the speed with which one chooses to shoot a person. The firing of a weapon (in this case a video game weapon) is clearly an explicit choice, but is impacted both by implicit stereotypes and implicit goals. Glaser and Knowles (2008) along with Park, Glaser, and Knowles (2008) examined the implicit motivation to control prejudice (IMCP) – defined as an internalised and implicit goal to be egalitarian. IMCP was measured via two related constructs: an implicit *negative attitude towards prejudice* (NAP) and an implicit *belief that oneself is prejudiced* (BOP). Individuals high in NAP or high in BOP should not be motivated to avoid prejudice because they do not think they are susceptible to bias or because they do not think avoiding bias is an important or necessary aim. The Implicit Association Test (IAT; Greenwald et al., 1998) was used to assess both NAP and BOP. For NAP, IAT pairs included "prejudice" and "tolerance" along with "bad" and "good". For IAT pairs included "prejudiced" and "tolerant" along with "me" and "not me".

Across several experiments Glaser and Knowles find an impact of this motivation on the amount of cognitive resources needed to control the expression of bias against Black men. Prior research has revealed a "Shooter Bias" whereby participants are more likely to shoot unarmed Blacks than unarmed Whites. Glaser and Knowles found that (a) the strength of shooter bias is determined by whether people associate Blacks with weapons (as determined by an IAT for these categories and the control categories of

Whites and tools), and (b) for participants high in ICMP a strong association between Blacks and weapons did not relate to the degree of Shooter Bias. Implicit goals determined the manner in which this discriminatory behaviour was expressed. Park et al. (2008) further posited that although self-control often results in resource depletion, those high in IMCP should need fewer attentional resources to control stereotypic responses. They found that the effect of cognitive resource depletion on Shooter Bias is greater for those low in IMCP. One can behave in an egalitarian way and reduce biased actions even under conditions of minimal consciousness or effort. Implicit goals direct not only what is activated, but also how efficiently we pursue goals that require inhibiting a biased response after stereotypes are activated.

Peruche and Plant (2006) also examined how implicit goals impact the explicit reduction of bias in one's responding on a task conceptually similar to the shooter task. The experiment examined stereotypes relating Blacks to athleticism. The task showed pictures of sports-related equipment or neutral objects superimposed onto pictures of Black or White male faces. Race information was non-diagnostic in that an equal number of Black and White faces were associated with sports-related items. Participants had to respond quickly on the computer, indicating whether the object was sports related or not. Participants also completed the Plant and Devine (1998) IMS and EMS measures of motivation. Participants exhibited racial bias in the early trials (e.g. more mistakes were made when a Black face was presented with a neutral object) than in the later trials. Over time (later versus early trials) this bias was controlled across all participants. However, greater reduction in bias was associated with those high in IMS. The implicit goal allowed one to reduce stereotype-related errors in responding.

Consciously activated goals with implicit goal operations

The previous two sections have explored the effects of the implicit activation of a goal on the implicit control over stereotype activation. However, goals need not be implicitly primed to have implicit effects (as reviewed earlier in the third and sixth principles of implicit volition). Goals temporarily adopted in one context—that are explicit to the individual in that context—can lead to implicit processes of regulation that lead to control over stereotype activation. Such control can even extend to subsequent contexts, when the individual is no longer aware of the goals' increased accessibility or its relevance to the task at hand. It is important to examine the pursuit of (egalitarian) goals in individuals who are not implicitly primed with such goals for both practical and theoretical reasons. At the practical level this suggests stereotype control is not limited either to types of people, or to the presence of environmental cues that will trigger the goal. It suggests control is strategic in the traditional sense—capable of being consciously willed by any person (although one may not be conscious of the implementation of one's will). At the theoretical level it suggests that people can be proactive in their control of stereotyping through the same processes used by chronics— inhibition of stereotype activation, heightened accessibility of the goal in the presence of goal-relevant targets, and heightened sensitivity to goal-relevant opportunities that are present in the environment. As Chartrand and Bargh (1996) asserted (see also Bargh & Huang, 2009), explicitly selected goals and implicitly primed goals often have identical effects on cognitive operations. We thus posited that being conscious of the goal to be egalitarian would trigger the same operations as having an egalitarian goal primed.

Egalitarian goals and compensatory cognition. One way in which people become conscious of their goals is when processes of discrepancy detection reveal to the individual a shortcoming, failure, or incompleteness in one's goal pursuit (as reviewed above in the third principle of implicit volition). Once a discrepancy is detected, and a psychological tension state arises, the individual is impelled to reduce this deficit. That is, one engages in compensatory activity that moves one closer to goal attainment (for a review, see Martin & Tesser, 2009). This activity is referred to as *compensatory* because it is meant to offset the detected deficit that the goal represents. Much of the research examining goals that are triggered by discrepancy detection shares a methodological approach: one's short-comings (discrepancies) are typically made salient to the individual and they are then placed in a situation that clearly affords an opportunity for overt behaviour to address those shortcomings. In such situations explicit goals trigger explicit *compensatory behaviour*—compensatory in that it is behaviour aimed at counteracting and addressing the state of failure/ incompleteness. This process is described as explicit because of the similarity between the discrepancy-arousing task and the discrepancy-reducing task. The goal is still the focus of conscious attention when the compensatory response is made, and one knows the response can address the sense of incompleteness (e.g., Wicklund & Gollwitzer, 1981).

For example, in the research of Monteith and colleagues (Monteith, Ashburn-Nardo, Voils, & Czopp, 2002; Monteith & Mark, 2005; Montheith & Voils, 1998) people are explicitly reminded of a discrepancy between how they *would* act in a non-egalitarian way in situations where they *should* act in an egalitarian way.[5] Monteith (1993) found that such a discrepancy triggers

---

[5]Discrepancies are also consciously detected in experimental settings such as that created in research on hypocrisy (Stone, Weigand, Cooper, & Aronson, 1997) where participants are led to choose freely to publicly advocate for a position that opposes their personal opinion/behaviour (and then have that opposition brought to mind). A third example includes settings in which a

compensatory responses in the domain of prejudice. Participants experiencing a discrepancy had greater numbers of thoughts about their discrepant behaviour and took longer to read an essay about the causes of discrepant behaviour compared to participants whose discrepancies were not made salient. The variety of explicit compensatory responses that people engage to address discrepancies in their sense-of-self as egalitarian also include behavioural inhibition, retrospective reflection about one's shortcomings and goals, and greater reported liking for things related to the group one had been biased towards (e.g., Monteith et al., 2002).

Compensatory responding is not limited to behaviour or to conscious cognition. It also includes implicit responding—what Moskowitz (2001) called *compensatory cognition*. For example, Moskowitz (2002) found that participants compensate for an explicit failure in the domain of egalitarianism through an implicit response—selectively attending to environmental stimuli relevant to egalitarian goals. After explicitly reflecting on a failure in their life regarding being egalitarian (a discrepancy), participants next performed a seemingly irrelevant task where they identified the direction of stimulus movement while ignoring the movement of a distracting stimulus. Responses to the stimuli were made too quickly for conscious control to intervene, and additionally the stimuli themselves could not be consciously identified as being relevant to egalitarian goals. The stimuli were words, yet participants were not even able to identify them as words, let alone as being relevant to one's goals. However, responses were facilitated when target items contained egalitarian words, and slowed when the distracting items contained egalitarian words—explicitly triggered goals displaced implicit attention.

How does compensatory cognition impact stereotype activation? In some cases it may increase stereotype activation, in other cases the implicit response initiated by the control process may decrease activation. Spencer et al. (1998) had participants receive failure feedback on a test said to measure intelligence and likelihood for future success. They then demonstrated that this discrepancy detection led to the automatic activation of stereotypes. They posited that when self-esteem is threatened, a goal to attain a positive sense of self is triggered, and with it are triggered compensatory operations aimed at achieving the goal and ameliorating the tension state produced by the discrepancy. This includes explicit processes that enhance esteem, like derogating others. The compensatory operations also include implicit processes of heightened stereotype activation. The implicit stereotype accessibility observed was limited to derogatory,

person is given explicit failure feedback, such as poor performance being recorded in a domain of importance to the individual (e.g., Gollwitzer, Wicklund, & Hilton, 1982; Koole et al., 1999; Spencer et al., 1998).

stereotype-relevant words, suggesting that only a negative stereotype was activated as a strategic, yet implicit, means to compensate for self-esteem threat. Fein and Spencer (1997) similarly illustrated heightened stereotyping following a discrepancy, yet it is less clear if this is due to implicit activation or explicit stereotype use. The measurement of interest was explicit trait ratings. They found that participants with self-esteem goals rated a target as possessing more stereotypic characteristics than a control target. This effect did not emerge for people who did not have self-esteem goals triggered. This may be due to increased implicit accessibility of the stereotype, but it may also be due to increased explicit use of stereotyping as a way of compensating for the goal.

Moskowitz and Li (2009a) returned the focus to the more intuitive definition of control—preventing an unwanted response. Rather than examining compensatory responses that increase implicit stereotype accessibility, they focused on the inhibition of a stereotype as a compensatory response to a discrepancy. The goal domain in which discrepancies were detected was the goal to be egalitarian to Blacks. The implicit measure of stereotype activation and inhibition was a lexical decision task. Moskowitz and Li (2009a, Experiment 1) recruited participants who valued the goal of being egalitarian, but who were not in chronic pursuit of such goals. The discrepancy between one's goal of being egalitarian and one's actual egalitarian behaviour was manipulated by having half of the participants contemplate a personal failure at being egalitarian towards African Americans at some point in their recent life history. The remaining participants contemplated failure as well, to keep valence constant, but a failure irrelevant to egalitarianism—respecting traditions. Thus, all participants detected a discrepancy, but only half had a discrepancy that could be compensated for by pursuing the goal of being egalitarian and its associated operations.

Participants next performed an ostensibly unrelated computer-based task. Each trial began with a face, serving as a prime, paired with two words. The faces were said to be distractors to the main task of identifying whether the two words were identical or different. The next phase of the trial contained a lexical decision task. On critical trials the primes were either faces of Black or White men and the attributes in the lexical decision task were either relevant or irrelevant to the stereotype of Blacks. The question of interest was whether stereotype activation would be exhibited in the control group, and whether control of stereotype activation would be exhibited by participants experiencing a discrepancy in regard to their egalitarian goals.

The results revealed that participants who had experienced a discrepancy relating to tradition goals had facilitated reaction times to stereotypic words after Black faces relative to the reaction times to the same words presented after White faces. Additionally, reaction times to stereotype-relevant words following Black faces were faster than reaction times to stereotype-irrelevant words following Black faces. Most importantly, people with discrepancies relating to their egalitarian goals showed a *slow-down* in their responses to stereotype-relevant words after faces of Black men relative to the same words following faces of White men (see Table 6). To compensate for the discrepancy, goal-relevant process of stereotype inhibition had been initiated.

It is important to note that while the groups in this experiment spent different amounts of time thinking about African Americans while writing about a failure, it was the group who spent less time contemplating this group who showed greater stereotype activation, and the group that spent more time who inhibited stereotypes. This addresses a possible concern that differences in activation are not due to goals, but to semantic construct activation. A defining characteristic of goal pursuit is the way in which accessibility of the goal returns to baseline levels relative to other constructs. If the goal is attained the tension is lowered, and with it comes a cessation of goal-relevant responding (Bargh et al., 2001; Kawada, Oettingen, Gollwitzer, & Bargh, 2004; Koole et al., 1999; Liberman & Förster, 2000; Martin & Tesser, 2009). Unlike semantic construct accessibility, which merely fades with time and increases with increased use of the concept, use of a goal concept will lower accessibility if the tension state is addressed. Thus, semantic and goal activation yield opposing predictions for the Moskowitz and Li (2009a) experiment, and the results are consistent with the goal-shielding hypothesis (less stereotype activation for the group spending more time contemplating the category, when the time is spent addressing the goal that is implicitly being pursued).

Moskowitz and Li (2009a, Experiment 2) performed a conceptually similar experiment, except that the manner in which stereotype activation was assessed was altered. A procedure was used in which a slow-down in response time (e.g., Stroop, 1935), instead of facilitated reaction times,

TABLE 6
Response times, from Moskowitz and Li (2009a) Experiment 1

Word type	Egalitarian goal Prime type		Control goal Prime type	
	Black male	*White male*	*Black male*	*White male*
Stereotype-relevant	746	660	646	689
Stereotype-irrelevant	702	720	720	709

Response times (in ms) to stereotype-relevant and control words as a function of temporary egalitarian goals and prime type (from Moskowitz & Li, 2009a, Experiment 1).

would illustrate stereotype activation. Faster reaction times would instead be evidence of stereotype inhibition. This change was made to indicate that the process is not the mere operation of a behavioural inhibition system when a goal-relevant target person is encountered. Experiment 1 revealed a very specific "slow-down" pattern in which only responses to stereotypic words were slowed (rather than to any stimulus that followed a Black face). This finding argues against a generalised behavioural inhibition explanation for the findings. Nevertheless an experiment aimed at addressing this potential alternative mechanism more explicitly was conducted in which inhibition is exhibited by faster behaviour (facilitated reaction times) rather than slowed.

In this experiment a stereotype activation/inhibition assessment task was used that required participants to identify whether two words on a screen had the same colour font. On critical trials the words were always in different coloured fonts and were either attributes related to the stereotype of African Americans or control attributes. All trials were preceded by faces, either of African American or White men. If stereotypes are being activated by the primes, then people should be faster to detect and have attention directed towards words consistent with the stereotype. With focused attention being displaced from the colour-naming task to reading the words, responses to the colour-matching task will be slowed. Stereotype control is evidenced by this effect disappearing so that stereotype-relevant words no longer displace attention. And if semantic meaning is inhibited the participant could respond even faster to the colour-naming task.

The results showed that participants with tradition goals had slower reaction times to stereotype-relevant words after Black faces relative to the same words following White faces (and relative to stereotype-irrelevant words following Black faces). People with egalitarian goals showed facilitated response times to naming the font colour of stereotype-relevant words after faces of Black men relative to the same words following faces of White men. Once again, implicit stereotype inhibition followed having an egalitarian goal explicitly triggered.

An experiment from Moskowitz and Li (2009b, Experiment 3) helps to establish that these are indeed goals being activated. It was earlier reviewed that one characteristic of the tension-states that characterise goals is that attaining or affirming the goal releases the tension-state and eliminates goal striving. Thus, if one has greater exposure to a goal in the context of attaining it, the accessibility of the goal will actually decrease from this increased exposure (unlike semantic construct activation, which would increase; e.g., Higgins, 1996). In this experiment participants in the control condition contemplated success at being egalitarian. Thus the two groups of participants each had equal amounts of semantic activation of the concept "egalitarian". They differed in that one group should experience a state of completion from having affirmed their sense of self in this domain. However, the people who contemplated failure at being egalitarian should have a goal accessible. Participants next completed an ostensibly separate experiment utilising a serial priming procedure. Faces were presented as part of a memory test (identical to that used by Moskowitz et al., 2000), followed immediately on critical trials by stereotypic or control attributes presented as part of a lexical decision task.

The results revealed a similar pattern to those reported by Moskowitz and Li (2009a). Participants who had contemplated success at being egalitarian (thus attaining the goal) had facilitated reaction times to stereotype-relevant words after Black faces relative to the reaction times to the same words following White faces. Additionally, reaction times to stereotype-relevant words following Black faces were faster than reaction times to control words following Black faces. Most importantly, people with discrepancies relating to their egalitarian goals showed a slow-down in their responses to stereotype-relevant words after faces of Black men relative to the same words following faces of White men (see Table 7). Success at the goal released the "tension state" and thus led to the elimination of goal-shielding operations. Stereotypes were no longer being inhibited, and instead were activated upon detecting a category member. Failure at the goal led to inhibition of stereotypes upon detecting a category member. This pattern of inhibition of stereotypes to a stereotype-relevant target was, across three experiments, identical to that seen among participants with chronic goals. However, in these studies the goals were temporary, primed in the situation by people contemplating a failure.

Moskowitz and Li (2009b) further explored the question of whether these are in fact goals that are being primed by thinking of the people being presented in these experiments not simply as primes, but as means to the goal. Past research has shown that an association exists between a goal and opportunities to pursue that goal (e.g., Shah, 2005). If such an association exists, then we should see in participants an increased ability

TABLE 7
Response times, from Moskowitz and Li (2009b) Experiment 3

Word type	Egalitarian goal affirmation Prime type		Egalitarian goal failure Prime type	
	Black male	White male	Black male	White male
Stereotype-relevant	640	689	680	687
Stereotype-irrelevant	694	689	678	675

Response times (in ms) to stereotype-relevant and control words as a function of affirmation type and prime type (from Moskowitz & Li, 2009b, Experiment 3).

to detect goal-relevant stimuli in their environment when the goal is primed (as they represent opportunities or a means to pursue the goal). With egalitarian goals primed, members of groups that are the recipient of one's bias would be such a means. With tradition goals the same people would not afford an opportunity to move towards the goal and would not, therefore, receive preferential attention. In the experiment participants were shown photos of men four at a time, with the task of detecting the man wearing a bow tie. On some trials one African American was in the array at the same time as the focal stimulus (a White man in a bow tie). In other trials only White men were in the array. Did the face of a Black man, as an opportunity to start pursuing egalitarian goals, disrupt attention?

Results revealed a facilitated ability to detect goal-relevant means in the environment. This is manifested by slowed responding to the focal task (identifying the man in a bow tie). This does not occur when only White men exist in the stimulus array. And it does not occur for participants with tradition goals who are exposed to a Black man in the stimulus array. Only people with egalitarian goals are distracted and only by an African American face. This same pattern of results was replicated in an experiment using participants who contemplated success at being egalitarian towards African Americans as a control group. Thus, a tension-state needs to be present for the effect to emerge, not merely the heightened accessibility of concepts relating to African Americans or egalitarianism. The effect is the result of operations specific to unique goals.[6]

Affirmation and stereotype activation.   A subset of the experiments just reviewed affirmed people's sense-of-self-as-egalitarian and showed no evidence of egalitarian goal activation under those conditions. Following the discrepancy detection logic it was argued that affirming the goal eliminates the discrepancy, removing the goal (and hence goal-relevant operations). Such findings beg a related question—What type of success "shuts down" compensatory responding? Self-completion theory

---

[6]It could be argued that across all of the experiments of Moskowitz and colleagues, in which people contemplate failure at an egalitarian goal, the goal was implicit. Although the goal was initially explicit (writing about a failure), it could be argued that at the time of responding the goal was implicitly accessible. Implicit goal accessibility requires either that the individual is not aware the discrepancy increased the accessibility of a goal, or that the individual is not aware that the goal is activated at the time of the compensatory response. The tasks are performed in a separate room and have no overt resemblance that would allow participants to assume the reaction time task on the computer can in any way address the goals they had previously been contemplating. Thus the initial explicit goal may have receded from consciousness at the time the implicit response was made, and the response in no way calls the goal back to mind. In either case, an explicitly triggered goal is directing implicit responding. Our focus here is on the implicit response, not on whether it is initiated by an explicit or implicit goal. Each is possible.

(Wicklund & Gollwitzer, 1982) suggests the affirmation must occur in the specific domain in which a discrepancy was detected. However, self-affirmation theory (Steele, 1988) says that any restoration of the self system, an increase in self esteem, should resolve the tension, which is portrayed instead as a threat to the global self-system.

How do such issues relate to stereotype activation? We argue that the relationship of the affirmation to the specific goal (and its goal-specific operations) will determine whether goal operations (including stereotype inhibition or activation) will cease or continue. The exact same implicit process of stereotype activation may be affected by affirmation in different ways dependent on the goal being pursued. For example, Moskowitz and Li (2009a, 2009b) found that failure in one goal domain, egalitarianism, triggers implicit operations that reduce stereotype activation, whereas Spencer et al. (1998) found that failure in another goal domain, maintaining a positive global sense of self, triggers implicit operations that result in heightened stereotype activation. Affirmation should (and did) impact these processes differently—decreasing stereotype activation in the latter, increasing it in the former. However, a question remains as to how generalised the affirmation need be in order to satisfy the tension. A global affirmation satisfied the tension in the research of Spencer et al., implying any increase in self-esteem can shut down tension-states, including those that promote stereotype control. A specific affirmation (success at being egalitarian) satisfied the tension in the research of Moskowitz and Li (2009b), but this does not eliminate the possibility that a global affirmation would have a similar effect.

Moskowitz and Ignarri (in press) assert that in order for a tension state to be satisfied, and goal operations brought to a halt, the affirmation must be *specific to the goal domain*, as posited by the theory of symbolic self-completion (Wicklund & Gollwitzer, 1982). Why did a *global* affirmation satisfy the tension in the research of Spencer et al. (1998)? Moskowitz and Ignarri reason that it is for precisely the same reason a specific affirmation shuts down goal operations in their own work—because the goal undermined in the research of Spencer et al. is well matched to the affirmation. Recall that participants in the research of Spencer et al. are not merely given failure feedback in the domain of intelligence, but additionally told that the test indicates they have a poor likelihood for future success, thus undercutting global self-esteem. For this reason a global affirmation *is* *specific* to the goal the individuals in those experiments are pursuing. In sum, Moskowitz and Ignarri argue that it is not that a global affirmation is always successful at satisfying the tensions associated with goals. It is that when one is pursuing the goal of affirming the global sense of self, global affirmation is precisely able to address the goal and its associated tension. Specific tensions, such as the tension associated with being non-egalitarian to Blacks, would not be satisfied by global affirmation, but only by affirming the self-as-egalitarian.

To illustrate the specific nature of the relationship between goals, their associated implicit operations, and affirmation, Moskowitz and Ignarri (in press) had participants describe a failure in the domain of being egalitarian to Blacks. They then manipulated whether the affirmation that followed was one that promoted a positive global sense of self or one that was specific to the goal that had been threatened—egalitarianism. Participants next performed an ostensibly unrelated computer-based task in the next room. Each trial began with a face and a pair of words. The faces, actually primes, were described as distractors to the main task of identifying whether the words in each pair were identical. The next phase of the trial was a lexical decision task. On critical trials the primes were either faces of African American or White men and the attributes in the lexical decision task were either relevant or irrelevant to the stereotype of Blacks. The question of interest was whether stereotype inhibition would be found only among the people who had performed a global affirmation. For these people the affirmation should not "shut off" the goal striving, and inhibition, as seen in previous research, should emerge. However, participants who had the opportunity to affirm in the domain of egalitarianism should have a cessation of goal-relevant operations, thus eliminating inhibition and actually having an ironic increase in stereotype activation following their affirmation of self-as-egalitarian.

The results revealed a conceptually similar pattern to those reported by Moskowitz and Li (2009b). Participants who, after a failure, affirmed their sense of self as "egalitarian" had facilitated reaction times to stereotype-relevant attributes after Black faces relative to reaction times to the same words presented after White faces. Additionally, reaction times to stereotype-relevant words following Black faces were faster than reaction times to stereotype-irrelevant words following Black faces. Most importantly, people who had affirmed the global sense of self continued to show control over stereotype activation—there was no facilitation in their responses to stereotype-relevant words after faces of Black men relative to the same words following faces of White men. This pattern reveals that the goal to be egalitarian had not in fact been satisfied by the global affirmation and that the implicit operations of stereotype control were still running. However, satisfying the specific goal of being egalitarian led to these implicit inhibitory processes to stop, resulting in a return of stereotype activation.

This research highlights the point that affirmation per se does not lead to stereotype inhibition or activation. Inhibition or activation depends on the goal being pursued. This allows us to reconcile the seemingly incongruous fact that failure feedback sometimes increases stereotype activation, yet in other instances decreases (inhibits) it. Rather than concluding affirmation and failure must have a specific relationship to stereotyping, we instead argue that the specific goals triggered by failure will initiate appropriate compensatory cognitive operations. For some goals these operations include using stereotypes, for other goals the operations may involve counteractive control, such that the compensatory responses involve inhibiting stereotypes. Further, stereotype activation and inhibition depends on the type of affirmation that occurs. Does the affirmation address the particular goal in question?

CONCLUSION

Wilson and Brekke (1994) described a wide array of implicit biases—unconscious or uncontrollable cognition—that shape judgement, emotion, and behaviour, despite the individual not wanting to be influenced. They called this unwanted influence from undetected sources *mental contamination*. Sitting among this class of contaminants, perhaps at the head of the class, is the accessible stereotype. The question has been posed as to whether stereotypes, as silent, efficient, implicitly operating cognitive tools, are additionally "automatic". While this may seem a mere semantic distinction, this distinction is not trivial. If stereotypes are automatic their activation *cannot* be inhibited. If activated, they serve as a pervasive and hard-to-detect source of bias. If stereotypes are automatically made accessible, the only route to controlling the effects of stereotypes is to prevent stereotype use after the stereotype has been activated.

Regarding the possibility for successful control, Wilson and Brekke (1994) offer predictions of doom: "we are rather pessimistic about people's ability to avoid or correct for mental contamination. We suggest that the nature of human cognition, as well as the nature of lay theories about the mind, makes it difficult to satisfy all the conditions necessary to avoid contaminated responses" (p. 120). Although we agree with Wilson and Brekke's analysis of the difficulty of conscious control, let us reinstate optimism by suggesting that control need not be equated with correction. Rather than overturning contamination, it can be prevented.

We describe a different route to controlling stereotypes—inhibiting the stereotype from being activated after categorisation. This is accomplished through the workings of an implicit goal system. Stereotype activation is an implicit cognitive operation performed in the service of a goal. Given certain processing goals, individuals categorise people according to groups. Groups are associated with many concepts, attitudes, goals, and beliefs. Allport (1954, p. 21) stated: "a person with dark brown skin will activate whatever concept of Negro is dominant in our mind". However, the specification of the associations most "dominant in our mind" depends on the goals of the perceiver in relation to the context they are in and the person whom they have just categorised. It is not necessarily a stereotype. Thus, implicit processes of association lie at the heart of stereotyping, but they also lie at the heart of stereotype control and stereotype inhibition. Goals specify what associations are triggered versus inhibited once a person is categorised.

This proactive approach to stereotype control is nested within a much larger framework describing the implicit nature of the regulatory system. Thus, in some sense our focus is on implicit volition, with stereotyping as one small domain that illustrates implicit processes of self-regulation and how they interact with cognition. Yet in a different sense this work is the first to establish that goals can allow one to control stereotype activation, and this has implications for how we address an important social problem. In this way the "small domain" may actually be a bigger part of the story than the questions of consciousness and control in which it is nested.

The last five decades have seen increased societal concern with reducing stereotyping. With increased societal concern with fairness and control over bias in its many forms has been a parallel interest in social psychological laboratories—an increased experimental concern with the processes involved in the control of stereotyping. We suggest a novel approach—the implicit use of goals to prevent stereotype activation. At its heart, our argument for stereotype control is based on a simple associative principle—stereotypes and goals, like other knowledge structures, are associated, with some degree of strength, to other categories. This association can rise above some threshold for activation by the spreading of activation across an associative network when an appropriate stimulus has been encountered. We argue that activation can also be inhibited through processes of spreading inhibition. The question of interest is whether people are automatically responded to with a sufficiently strong associative response to a cue such that the stereotype must be activated whenever the cue (stimulus target) is encountered. We argue "no" and suggest the association to a goal may be dominant. A variety of contextual and motivational variables determine which associative links are activated versus inhibited after categorisation.

A particular person may be a woman, Black, a Kurd, a Muslim, or one's mother (or all of the above). Such a person is not encountered in a vacuum, but rather encountered in contexts where perceivers have goals that the person could potentially address. These goals may be explicit or implicit. The cognitive operations that are triggered will be determined by the goals one has pertaining to that target in that context. And these operations may be implicit or explicit. Neither stereotype use nor activation is thus automatic, but is a function of the explicit versus implicit goals triggered, and their accompanying implicit versus explicit cognitive operations.

REFERENCES

Aarts, H., Custers, R., & Holland, R. W. (2007). The nonconscious cessation of goal pursuit: When goals and negative affect are coactivated. *Journal of Personality and Social Psychology, 92*, 165–178.

Aarts, H., Gollwitzer, P. M., & Hassin, R. R. (2004). Goal contagion: Perceiving is for pursuing. *Journal of Personality and Social Psychology, 87*, 23–37.

Allport, G. W. (1954). The nature of prejudice. Reading, MA: Addison-Wesley.

Banaji, M. R., Hardin, C., & Rothman, A. J. (1993). Implicit stereotyping in person judgement. *Journal of Personality and Social Psychology, 65*, 272–281.

Bargh, J. A. (1990). Auto-motives: Preconscious determinants of thought and behaviour. Multiple affects from multiple stages. In E. T. Higgins & R. M. Sorrentino (Eds.), *Handbook of motivation and cognition: Foundations of social behaviour* (Vol. 2, pp. 93–130). New York: The Guilford Press.

Bargh, J. A. (1999). The cognitive monster: The case against controllability of automatic stereotype effects. In S. Chaiken & Y. Trope (Eds.), *Dual process theories in social psychology*. New York: The Guilford Press.

Bargh, J. A., & Chartrand, T. L., (2000). The mind in the middle: A practical guide to priming and automaticity research. In H. T. Reis & C. M. Judd (Eds.), *Handbook of research methods in social and personality psychology* (pp. 253–285). New York: Cambridge University Press.

Bargh, J. A., Gollwitzer, P. M., Lee-Chai, A., Barndollar, K., & Trötschel, R. (2001). The automated will: Nonconscious activation and pursuit of behavioural goals. *Journal of Personality and Social Psychology, 81*, 1014–1027.

Bargh, J. A., & Huang, J. Y. (2009). The selfish goal. In G. B. Moskowitz & H. Grant Halvorson (Eds.), *The psychology of goals* (pp. 127–150). New York: The Guilford Press.

Barron, K. E., & Harackiewicz, J. M. (2001). Achievement goals and optimal motivation: Testing multiple goal models. *Journal of Personality and Social Psychology, 80*, 706–722.

Baumeister, R. F., Bratslavsky, E., Muraven, M. B., & Tice, D. M. (1998). Ego-depletion: Is the active self a limited resource? *Journal of Personality and Social Psychology, 74*, 1252–1265.

Beauregard, K. S., & Dunning, D. (1998). Turning up the contrast: Self-enhancement motives prompt egocentric contrast effects in social judgement. *Journal of Personality and Social Psychology, 74*, 606–621.

Biernat, M. (2003). Toward a broader view of social stereotyping. *American Psychologist, 58*, 1019–1027.

Blair, I. (2001). Implicit stereotypes and prejudice. In G. B. Moskowitz (Ed.), *Cognitive social psychology: The Princeton symposium on the legacy and future of social cognition* (pp. 359–374). Hillsdale, NJ: Lawrence Erlbaum Associates Inc.

Blair, I. V., & Banaji, M. R. (1996). Automatic and controlled processes in stereotype priming. *Journal of Personality and Social Psychology, 70*, 1142–1163.

Brewer, M. B. (1988). A dual process model of impression formation. In T. K. Srull & R. S. Wyer (Eds.), *Advances in social cognition* (Vol. 1, pp. 1–36). Hillsdale, NJ: Lawrence Erlbaum Associates Inc.

Bruner, J. S. (1957). On perceptual readiness. *Psychological Review, 64*, 123–152.

Carver, C. S., & Scheier, M. F. (1981). *Attention and self-regulation: A control theory approach to human behaviour*. New York: Springer.

Carver, C. S., & Scheier, M. F. (1998). *On the self-regulation of behaviour*. New York: Cambridge University Press.

Carver, C. S., & Scheier, M. F. (1999). Stress, coping, and self-regulatory processes. In L. A. Pervin & O. P. John (Eds.), *Handbook of personality* (2nd ed., pp. 553–575). New York: The Guilford Press.

Chaiken, S., Liberman, A., & Eagly, A. H. (1989). Heuristic and systematic information processing within and beyond the persuasion context. In J. S. Uleman & J. A. Bargh (Eds.), *Unintended thought* (pp. 212–252). New York: The Guilford Press.

Chaiken, S., & Trope, Y. (Eds.). (1999). *Dual process theories in social psychology*. New York: The Guilford Press.

Chartrand, T. L., & Bargh, J. A. (1996). Automatic activation of impression formation goals: Nonconscious goal priming reproduces effects of explicit task instructions. *Journal of Personality and Social Psychology, 71*, 464–478.

Corneille, O., Yzerbyt, V., Rogier, A., & Buidin, G. (2001), Threat and the group attribution error: When threat elicits judgements of extremity and homogeneity. *Personality and Social Psychology Bulletin, 27*, 437–496.

Correll, J., Park, B., Wittenbrink, B., & Judd, C. M. (2002). The police officer's dilemma: Using ethnicity to disambiguate potentially threatening individuals. *Journal of Personality and Social Psychology, 83*, 1314–1329.

Custers, R. (2006). *On the underlying mechanisms of unconscious goal pursuit*. Unpublished doctoral dissertation, University of Utrecht.

Custers, R. (2009). How does our unconscious know what we want? The role of affect in goal representations. In G. B. Moskowitz & H. Grant (Eds.), *The psychology of goals* (pp. 179–202). New York: The Guilford Press.

Custers, R., & Aarts, H. (2005a). Beyond priming effects: The role of positive affect and discrepancies in implicit processes of motivation and goal pursuit. In W. Stroebe & M. Hewstone (Eds.), *European review of social psychology* (Vol. 16, pp. 257–300). Hove, UK: Psychology Press.

Custers, R., & Aarts, H. (2005b). Positive affect as implicit motivator: On the nonconscious operation of behavioural goals. *Journal of Personality and Social Psychology, 89*, 129–142.

Custers, R., & Aarts, H. (2007). Goal-discrepant situations prime goal-directed actions if goals are temporarily or chronically accessible. *Personality and Social Psychology Bulletin, 33*, 623–633.

Czopp, A. M., Monteith, M. J., & Mark, A. Y. (2006). Standing up for a change: Reducing bias through interpersonal confrontation. *Journal of Personality and Social Psychology, 90*, 784–803.

Devine, P. G. (1989). Stereotypes and prejudice: Their automatic and controlled components. *Journal of Personality and Social Psychology, 56*, 5–18.

Devine, P. G., Plant, E. A., Amodio, D. M., Harmon-Jones, E., & Vance, S. L. (2002). The regulations of explicit and implicit race bias: The role of motivations to respond without prejudice. *Journal of Personality and Social Psychology, 82*(5), 835–848.

Dijksterhuis, A., Aarts, H., & Chartrand, T. L. (2007). Automatic behaviour. In J. A. Bargh (Ed.), *Social psychology and the unconscious: The automaticity of higher mental processes*. Philadelphia: Psychology Press.

Dijksterhuis, A., Bos, M., Nordgren, L., & Van Baaren, R. B. (2006). On making the right choice: The deliberation-without-attention effect. *Science, 311*, 1005–1007.

Dijksterhuis, A., & van Knippenberg, A. (1996). The knife that cuts both ways: Facilitated and inhibited access to traits as a result of stereotype activation. *Journal of Experimental Social Psychology, 32*, 271–288.

Dovidio, J. F., Evans, N., & Tyler, R. B. (1986). Racial stereotypes: The contents of their cognitive representations. *Journal of Experimental Social Psychology, 22*, 22–37.

Elliott, E. S., & Dweck, C. S. (1988). Goals: An approach to motivation and achievement. *Journal of Personality and Social Psychology, 54*, 5–12.

Fein, S., & Spencer, S. J. (1997). Prejudice as self-image maintenance: Affirming the self through negative evaluations of others. *Journal of Personality and Social Psychology, 73*, 31–44.

Ferguson, M. J., & Porter, S. C. (2009). Goals and (implicit) attitudes: A social-cognitive perspective. In G. B. Moskowitz & H. Grant (Eds.), *The psychology of goals* (pp. 447–479). New York: The Guilford Press.

Fishbach, A., Friedman, R. S., & Kruglanski, A. W. (2003). Leading us not unto temptation: Momentary allurements elicit overriding goal activation. *Journal of Personality and Social Psychology, 84*, 296–309.

Fishbach, A., & Trope, Y. (2008). Implicit and explicit counteractive self control. In J. Y. Shah & W. L. Gardner (Eds.), *Handbook of motivation science*. New York: The Guilford Press.

Fiske, S. T., & Neuberg, S. L. (1990). A continuum of impression formation, from category-based to individuating processes: Influences of information and motivation on attention and interpretation. In M. P. Zanna (Ed.), *Advances in experimental social psychology* (Vol. 23, pp. 1–74). New York: Academic Press.

Fitzsimons, G. M., & Bargh, J. A. (2003). Thinking of you: Nonconscious pursuit of interpersonal goals associated with relationship partners. *Journal of Personality and Social Psychology, 84*, 148–164.

Förster, J., Liberman, N., & Friedman, R. S. (2007). Seven principles of goal activation: A systematic approach to distinguishing goal priming From priming of non-goal constructs. *Personality and Social Psychology Review, 11*(3), 211–233.

Förster, J., Liberman, N., & Higgins, E. T. (2005). Accessibility from active and fulfilled goals. *Journal of Experimental Social Psychology, 41*, 220–239.

Fox, E. (1995). Negative priming from ignored distractors in visual selection: A review. *Psychonomic Bulletin & Review, 2*(2), 145–173.

Galinsky, A. D., & Moskowitz, G. B. (2007). Further ironies of suppression: Stereotype and counter-stereotype accessibility. *Journal of Experimental Social Psychology, 42*, 833–841.

Gilbert, D. T., & Hixon, J. G. (1991). The trouble of thinking: Activation and application of stereotypic beliefs. *Journal of Personality and Social Psychology, 60*, 509–517.

Glaser, J., & Knowles, E. D. (2008). Implicit motivation to control prejudice. *Journal of Experimental Social Psychology, 44*(1), 164–172.

Glucksberg, S., Kreuz, R. J., & Rho, S. H. (1986). Context can constrain lexical access: Implications for models of language comprehension. *Journal of Experimental Psychology: Learning, Memory, and Cognition, 12*, 323–335.

Gollwitzer, P. M. (1990). Action phases and mind-sets. In E. T. Higgins & R. M. Sorrentino (Eds.), *Handbook of motivation and cognition* (Vol. 2, pp. 53–92). New York: The Guilford Press.

Gollwitzer, P. M. (1999). Implementation intentions: Strong effects of simple plans. *American Psychologist, 54*, 493–503.

Gollwitzer, P. M., Wicklund, R. A., & Hilton, J. L. (1982). Admission of failure and symbolic self-completion: Extending Lewinian theory. *Journal of Personality and Social Psychology, 43*, 358–371.

Grant, H., & Gelety, L. (2009). Goal content theories: Why differences in *what* we are striving for matter. In G. B. Moskowitz & H. Grant (Eds.), *The psychology of goals* (pp. 77–97). New York: The Guilford Press.

Greenwald, A. G., McGhee, D. E., & Schwartz, J. L. K. (1998). Measuring individual differences in implicit cognition: The implicit association test. *Journal of Personality and Social Psychology, 74*, 1464–1480.

Hamilton, D. L., Katz, L. B., & Leirer, V. O. (1980). Organisational processes in impression formation. In R. Hastie, T. M. Ostrom, E. B. Ebbesen, R. S. Wyer Jr., D. L. Hamilton, & D. E. Carlston (Eds.), *Person memory: The cognitive basis of social perception* (pp. 121–153). Hillsdale, NJ: Lawrence Erlbaum Associates Inc.

Hamilton, D. L., & Sherman, J. W. (1994). Stereotypes. In R. S. Wyer Jr., & T. K. Srull (Eds.), *Handbook of social cognition* (2nd ed., Vol. 2, pp. 1–68). Hillsdale, NJ: Lawrence Erlbaum Associates Inc.

Hamilton, D. L., & Trolier, T. K. (1986). Stereotypes and stereotyping: An overview of the cognitive approach. In J. F. Dovidio & S. L. Gaertner (Eds.), *Prejudice, discrimination, and racism* (pp. 127–163). Orlando, FL: Academic Press.

Hastie, R., & Kumar, P. A. (1979). Person memory: Personality traits as organising principles in memory for behaviour. *Journal of Personality and Social Psychology, 37*, 25–38.

Heider, F. (1944). Social perception and phenomenal causality. *Psychological Review, 51*, 358–374.

Higgins, E. T. (1989). Self-discrepancy theory: What patterns of self-beliefs cause people to suffer? In L. Berkowitz (Ed.), *Advances in experimental social psychology* (Vol. 22, pp. 93–136). New York: Academic Press.

Higgins, E. T. (1996). Knowledge activation: Accessibility, applicability, and salience. In E. T. Higgins & A. W. Kruglanski (Eds.), *Social psychology: Handbook of basic principles* (pp. 133–168). New York: The Guilford Press.

Holland, R. W., Hendriks, M., & Aarts, H. (2005). Smells like clean spirit: Nonconscious effects of scent on cognition and behaviour. *Psychological Science, 16*, 689–693.

Kawada, C. L. K., Oettingen, G., Gollwitzer, P. M., & Bargh, J. A. (2004). The projection of implicit and explicit goals. *Journal of Personality and Social Psychology, 86*, 545–559.

Kawakami, K., Dovidio, J., Moll, J., Hermsen, S., & Russin, A. (2000). Just say no (to stereotyping): Effects of training in the negation of stereotype associations on stereotype activation. *Journal of Personality and Social Psychology, 78*, 871–888.

Kay, A. C., Wheeler, C. S., Bargh, J. A., & Ross, L. D. (2004). Material priming: The influence of mundane physical objects on situational construal and competitive behavioural choice. *Organisational Behaviour and Human Decision Processes, 95*, 83–96.

Koole, S. L., Smeets, K., van Knippenberg, A., & Dijksterhuis, A. (1999). The cessation of rumination through self-affirmation. *Journal of Personality & Social Psychology, 77*, 111–125.

Kruglanski, A. W. (1990). Motivations for judging and knowing: Implications for causal attribution. In E. T. Higgins & R. M. Sorrentino (Eds.), *Handbook of motivation and cognition* (Vol. 2, pp. 333–368). New York: Guilford Press.

Kruglanski, A. W. (1996). Motivated social cognition: Principles of the interface. In E. T. Higgins & A. W. Kruglanski (Eds.), *Social psychology: Handbook of basic principles* (pp. 493–521). New York: The Guilford Press.

Kruglanski A.W., & Freund, T. (1983). The freezing and unfreezing of lay inferences: Effects on impressional primacy, ethnic stereotyping, and numerical anchoring. *Journal of Experimental Social Psychology, 19*, 448–468.

Kruglanski, A. W., Shah, J. Y., Fishbach, A., Friedman, R., Chun, W. Y., & Sleeth-Keppler, D. (2002). A theory of goal systems. In M. P. Zanna (Ed.), *Advances in experimental social psychology* (Vol. 34, pp. 331–378). San Diego, CA: Academic Press.

Kunda, Z., & Spencer, S. J. (2003). When do stereotypes come to mind and when do they color judgement? A goal-based theory of stereotype activation and application. *Psychological Bulletin, 129*, 522–544.

Lepore, L., & Brown, R. (1997). Category and stereotype activation: Is prejudice inevitable? *Journal of Personality and Social Psychology, 72*, 275–287.

Lewin, K. (1936). *Principles of topological psychology.* New York: McGraw-Hill.

Li, P., & Moskowitz, G. B. (2007). *Imitation and perspective taking in person perception.* Unpublished manuscript.

Liberman, N., & Förster, J. (2000). Expression after suppression: A motivational explanation of postsuppressional rebound. *Journal of Personality and Social Psychology, 79*, 190–203.

Lissner, K. (1933). Die Entspannung von Bedürfnissen durch Ersatzhandlungen [The relaxation of needs through substitutive acts]. *Psychologische Forschung, 18,* 218–250.

Livingston, R. W., & Brewer, M. B. (2002). What are we really priming? Cue-based versus category-based processing of facial stimuli. *Journal of Personality & Social Psychology, 82*(1), 5–18.

Logan, G. D. (1980). Short-term memory demands of reaction-time tasks that differ in complexity. *Journal of Experimental Psychology: Human Perception and Performance, 6,* 375–389.

Macrae, C. N., Bodenhausen, G. V., & Milne, A. B. (1995). The dissection of selection in person perception: Inhibitory processes in social stereotyping. *Journal of Personality and Social Psychology, 69,* 397–407.

Macrae, C. N., Bodenhausen, G. V., Milne, A. B., & Jetten, J. (1994). Out of mind but back in sight: Stereotypes on the rebound. *Journal of Personality and Social Psychology, 67,* 808–817.

Macrae, C. N., Bodenhausen, G. V., Milne, A. B., Thorn, T. M. J., & Castelli, L. (1997). On the activation of social stereotypes: The moderating role of processing objectives. *Journal of Experimental Social Psychology, 33,* 471–489.

Martin, L. L., & Tesser, A. (2009). Five markers of motivated behaviour. In G. B. Moskowitz & H. Grant (Eds.), *The psychology of goals* (pp. 257–276). New York: The Guilford Press.

Monteith, M. J. (1993). Self-regulation of prejudiced responses: Implications for progress in prejudice reduction efforts. *Journal of Personality and Social Psychology, 65,* 469–485.

Monteith, M. J., Ashburn-Nardo, L., Voils, C. I., & Czopp, A. M. (2002). Putting the brakes on prejudice: On the development and operation of cues for control. *Journal of Personality and Social Psychology, 83,* 1029–1050.

Monteith, M. J., & Mark, A. (2005). Changing one's prejudiced ways: Awareness, affect, and self-regulation. *European Review of Social Psychology, 16*(4), 113–154.

Monteith, M. J., & Voils, C. I. (1998). Proneness to prejudiced responses: Toward understanding the authenticity of self-reported discrepancies. *Journal of Personality and Social Psychology, 75*(4), 901–915.

Moskowitz, G. B. (1993). Individual differences in social categorisation: The effects of personal need for structure on spontaneous trait inferences. *Journal of Personality and Social Psychology, 65,* 132–142.

Moskowitz, G. B. (2001). Preconscious control and compensatory cognition. In G. B. Moskowitz (Ed.), *Cognitive social psychology: The Princeton symposium on the legacy and future of social cognition* (pp. 333–358). Hillsdale, NJ: Lawrence Erlbaum Associates Inc.

Moskowitz, G. B. (2002). Preconscious effects of temporary goals on attention. *Journal of Experimental Social Psychology, 38,* 397–404.

Moskowitz, G. B., & Gesundheit, Y. (2009). Goal priming. In G. B. Moskowitz & H. Grant (Eds.), *The psychology of goals* (pp. 203–233). New York: The Guilford Press.

Moskowitz, G. B., Gollwitzer, P. M., Wasel, W., & Schaal, B. (1999a). Preconscious control of stereotype activation through chronic egalitarian goals. *Journal of Personality and Social Psychology, 77,* 167–184.

Moskowitz, G. B., & Ignarri, C. (in press). Implicit goals and a proactive strategy of stereotype control. *Social and Personality Psychology Compass.*

Moskowitz, G. B., & Li, P. (2009a). *Stereotype inhibition from implicit goal shielding: A proactive strategy of stereotype control.* Manuscript submitted for publication.

Moskowitz, G. B., & Li, P. (2009b). *Compensatory cognition, implicit goal regulation, and the control of stereotype activation.* Manuscript submitted for publication.

Moskowitz, G. B., Li, P., & Kirk, E. (2004). The implicit volition model: On the preconscious regulation of temporarily adopted goals. In M. Zanna (Ed.), *Advances in experimental social psychology* (Vol. 36, pp. 317–413). San Diego, CA: Academic Press.

Moskowitz, G. B., Salomon, A. R., & Taylor, C. M. (2000). Implicit control of stereotype activation through the preconscious operation of egalitarian goals. *Social Cognition, 18,* 151–177.

Moskowitz, G. B., Skurnik, I., & Galinsky, A. D. (1999b). The history of dual-process notions, and the future of preconscious control. In S. Chaiken & Y. Trope (Eds.), *Dual-process theories in social psychology* (pp. 12–36). New York: The Guilford Press.

Neuberg, S. L. (1989). The goal of forming accurate impressions during social interactions: Attenuating impact of negative expectancies. *Journal of Personality and Social Psychology, 56,* 374–386.

Neuberg, S. L., & Newsom, J. T. (1993). Personal need for structure: Individual differences in the desire for simple structure. *Journal of Personality and Social Psychology, 65,* 113–131.

Park, S. H., Glaser, J., & Knowles, E. D. (2008). Implicit motivation to control prejudice moderates the effect of cognitive depletion on unintended discrimination. *Social Cognition, 26,* 379–398.

Peruche, B. M., & Plant, E. A. (2006). Racial bias in perceptions of athleticism: The role of motivation in the elimination of bias. *Social Cognition, 24*(4), 438–452.

Petty, R. E., & Wegener, D. T. (1999). The elaboration likelihood model: Current status and controversies. In S. Chaiken & Y. Trope (Eds.), *Dual-process theories in social psychology* (pp. 41–72). New York: The Guilford Press.

Plant, E. A., & Devine, P. G. (1998). Internal and external motivation to respond without prejudice. *Journal of Personality and Social Psychology, 75*(3), 811–832.

Posner, M. I., & Snyder, C. R. R. (1975). Attention and cognitive control. In R. L. Solso (Ed.), *Information processing and cognition: The Loyola symposium* (pp. 55–85). Hillsdale, NJ: Lawrence Erlbaum Associates Inc.

Powers, W. T. (1973). Feedback: Beyond behaviourism. *Science, 179,* 351–356.

Richeson, J. A., & Nussbaum, R. J. (2004). The impact of multiculturalism versus color-blindness on racial bias. *Journal of Experimental Social Psychology, 40,* 417–423.

Ruscher, J. B., Fiske, S. T., Miki, H., & Van Manen, S. (1991). Individuating processes in competition: Interpersonal versus intergroup. *Personality and Social Psychology Bulletin, 17,* 595–605.

Sassenberg, K., & Moskowitz, G. B. (2005). Don't stereotype, think different! Overcoming automatic stereotype activation by mindset priming. *Journal of Experimental Social Psychology, 41,* 506–514.

Sassenberg, K., Moskowitz, G. B., Jacoby, J., & Hansen, N. (2007). The carry-over effect of competition: The impact of competition on prejudice towards uninvolved outgroups. *Journal of Experimental Social Psychology, 43,* 529–538.

Shah, J. Y. (2003). Automatic for the people: How representations of significant others implicitly affect goal pursuit. *Journal of Personality & Social Psychology, 84,* 661–681.

Shah, J. Y. (2005). The automatic pursuit and management of goals. *Current Directions in Psychological Science, 14,* 10–13.

Shah, J. Y., Friedman, R., & Kruglanski, A. (2002). Forgetting all else: On the antecedents and consequences of goal shielding. *Journal of Personality & Social Psychology, 83,* 1261–1280.

Shah, J. Y., & Gardner, W. L. (2007). *Handbook of motivation science.* New York: The Guilford Press.

Shah, J. Y., Hall, D., & Leander, N. P. (2009). Moments of motivation: Towards a model of regulatory rotation. In G. B. Moskowitz & H. Grant (Eds.), *The psychology of goals* (pp. 234–254). New York: The Guilford Press.

Shah, J. Y., & Kruglanski, A. W. (2002). Priming against your will: How accessible alternatives affect goal pursuit. *Journal of Experimental Social Psychology, 38,* 368–383.

Spencer, S. J., Fein, S., Wolfe, C. T., Fong, C., & Dunn, M. A. (1998). Automatic activation of stereotypes: The role of self-image threat. *Personality and Social Psychology Bulletin, 24,* 1139–1152.

Srull, T. K. (1983). Organisational and retrieval processes in person memory: An examination of processing objectives, presentation format, and the possible role of self-generated retrieval cues. *Journal of Personality and Social Psychology, 44,* 1157–1170.

Srull, T. K., & Wyer, R. S. (1986). The role of chronic and temporary goals in social information processing. In R. M. Sorrentino & E. T. Higgins (Eds.), *Handbook of motivation and cognition* (pp. 503–547). New York: The Guilford Press.

Stangor, C., & Lange, J. E. (1994). Mental representations of social groups: Advances in understanding stereotypes and stereotyping. In M. P. Zanna (Ed.), *Advances in experimental social psychology* (Vol. 26). San Diego, CA: Academic Press.

Stapel, D. A., & Koomen, W. (2001). Let's not Forget the past when we go to the future: On our knowledge of knowledge accessibility. In G. B. Moskowitz (Ed.), *Cognitive social psychology: The Princeton symposium on the legacy and future of social cognition* (pp. 229–246). Hillsdale, NJ: Lawrence Erlbaum Associates Inc.

Steele, C. M. (1988). The psychology of self-affirmation: Sustaining the integrity of the self. In L. Berkowitz (Ed.), *Advances in experimental social psychology* (Vol. 21, pp. 261–302). New York: Academic Press.

Stone, J., Wiegand, A. W., Cooper, J., & Aronson, E. (1997). When exemplification fails: Hypocrisy and the motive for self-integrity. *Journal of Personality and Social Psychology, 72*(1), 54–65.

Stroop, J. R. (1935). Studies of interference in serial verbal reactions. *Journal of Experimental Psychology, 18,* 643–662.

Taylor, S. E. (1981). The interface of cognitive and social psychology. In J. H. Harvey (Ed.), *Cognition, social behaviour, and the environment* (pp. 189–212). Hillsdale, NJ: Lawrence Erlbaum Associates Inc.

Tetlock, P. E. (1985). Accountability: The neglected social context of judgement and choice. *Research in Organisational Behaviour, 7,* 297–332.

Thompson, E. P., Roman, R. J., Moskowitz, G. B., Chaiken, S., & Bargh, J. A. (1994). Accuracy motivation attenuates covert priming effects: The systematic reprocessing of social information. *Journal of Personality and Social Psychology, 66,* 259–288.

Tipper, S. P. (1985). The negative priming effect: Inhibitory priming by ignored objects. *Quarterly Journal of Experimental Psychology, 37,* 571–590.

Tolman, E. C. (1932). *Purposive behaviour in animals and men.* Oxford, UK: Appleton-Century.

Turner, M. L., & Engle, R. W. (1989). Is working memory capacity task dependent? *Journal of Memory and Language, 28,* 127–154.

Uleman, J. S., & Moskowitz, G. B. (1994). Unintended effects of goals on unintended inferences. *Journal of Personality and Social Psychology, 66,* 490–501.

Whitehead, J., Schmader, T., & Stone, J. (2008). *Investigating stigmatized targets' desire and ability to address prejudice in an outgroup member.* Manuscript submitted for publication.

Vohs, K. D., Kaikati, A. M, Kerkhof, P., & Schmeichel, B. J., (2009). Self-regulatory resource depletion: A model for understanding the limited nature of goal pursuit. In G. B. Moskowitz & H. Grant (Eds.), *The psychology of goals* (pp. 423–446). New York: The Guilford Press.

von Hippel, W., Sekaquaptewa, D., & Vargas, P. (1995). On the role of encoding processes in stereotype maintenance. *Advances in Experimental Social Psychology, 27,* 177–254.

Wegener, D. T., Dunn, M., & Tokusato, D. (2001). The flexible correction model: Phenomenology and the use of naive theories in avoiding or removing bias. In G. B. Moskowitz (Ed.), *Cognitive social psychology: The Princeton Symposium on the Legacy and Future of Social Cognition* (pp. 277–291). Mahwah, NJ: Lawrence Erlbaum Associates Inc.

Wegner, D. M. (1994). Ironic processes of mental control. *Psychological Review, 101*, 34–52.

Wegner, D. M., & Erber, R. (1992). The hyperaccessibility of suppressed thoughts. *Journal of Personality and Social Psychology, 63*, 903–912.

Wicklund, R. A., & Gollwitzer, P. M. (1981). Symbolic self-completion, attempted influence, and self-deprecation. *Basic and Applied Social Psychology, 2*, 89–114.

Wicklund, R. A., & Gollwitzer, P. M. (1982). *Symbolic self-completion*. Hillsdale, NJ: Lawrence Erlbaum Associates Inc.

Wilson, T. D., & Brekke, N. (1994). Mental contamination and mental correction: Unwanted influences on judgements and evaluations. *Psychological Bulletin, 116*, 117–142.

Zeigarnik, B. (1927). Das Behalten erledigter und unerledigter Handlungen [The retention of completed and uncompleted actions]. *Psychologische Forschung, 9*, 1–85.

EUROPEAN REVIEW OF SOCIAL PSYCHOLOGY
2009, 20, 146–191

Psychology Press
Taylor & Francis Group

Three decades of lay epistemics: The why, how, and who of knowledge formation

Arie W. Kruglanski, Mark Dechesne and Edward Orehek

University of Maryland, College Park, MD, USA

Antonio Pierro

University of Rome "La Sapienza", Rome, Italy

A conceptual integration and review are presented of three separate research programmes informed by the theory of lay epistemics (Kruglanski, 1989). They respectively address the "why", "how", and "who" questions about human knowledge formation. The "why" question is treated in work on the *need for cognitive closure* that propels epistemic behaviour and affects individual, interpersonal, and group phenomena. The "how" question is addressed in work on the *unimodel* (Kruglanski, Pierro, Mannetti, Erb, & Chun, 2007) depicting the process of drawing conclusions from the "information given". The "who" question is addressed in work on "epistemic authority" highlighting the centrality of source effects (including oneself as a source) in human epistemic behaviour. These separate research paradigms explore facets of epistemic behaviour that jointly produce human knowledge, of essential significance to people's' individual and social functioning.

Keywords: Need for closure; Unimodel; Epistemic authority; Rule following; Seizing.

The label *homo sapiens* by which the humankind is designated translates into "the knowing person", hinting at the essential importance for human affairs of knowledge and its construction. As individuals we form new knowledge constantly and continually. To carry out even the most mundane activities we need to *know* a variety of things. Before embarking on a bit of intelligible behaviour, no matter how small, we need to orientate ourselves in time and space, decide what our implementation intentions are for that particular instant, divine their feasibility under the circumstances, and so on. All these are types of knowledge that individuals need to formulate on a moment-to-moment basis.

Correspondence should be addressed to Arie W. Kruglanski, Department of Psychology, University of Maryland, College Park, MD 20742, USA. E-mail: arie@psyc.umd.edu

http://www.psypress.com/ersp   DOI: 10.1080/10463280902860037

Our social interactions are also suffused with prior knowledge. We quickly form a preliminary impression about our partners' identity (e.g., as regards their age, gender, nationality, or social status). We figure out what language they speak, what they know about a topic at hand, and what their attitudes and opinions are, so that we tailor our communications accordingly. In addition, our lives as group members and participants in larger collectivities (societies or cultures) are fundamentally guided by our shared knowledge of concepts, norms, and world views.

Given the ubiquity of knowledge formation concerns, and their essential psychological relevance to human thought, feeling, and action, understanding how knowledge is formed and changed defines a task of considerable importance for psychological science. Indeed, psychological researchers and theorists have examined epistemic processes in a variety of paradigms including those concerned with attitude formation and change (e.g., Maio & Haddock, 2007; Petty & Wegener, 1999), impression formation (Brewer, 1988; Fiske & Neuberg, 1990), judgement under uncertainty (Kahneman, 2003), and attribution (Hilton, 2007). Typically too, such endeavours, though insightful and useful, have addressed localised issues *specific* to a given content domain of knowledge (for a review see Kruglanski & Orehek, 2007).

More than 20 years ago, a paper published in the *Psychological Review* (Kruglanski, 1980) became the first in what was to become a long string of research reports and essays on the psychological factors involved in a *general* knowledge formation process. A more elaborate theory on this topic was featured in a volume *Lay Epistemics and Human Knowledge* published nearly a decade later (Kruglanski, 1989). Whereas the initial theoretical effort centred on a generalised, lay epistemic interpretation of attribution theory, subsequent work extended the approach to further topics, including cognitive consistency theories, attitudes and attitude change, cognitive therapy, social comparison processes, and the social psychology of science.

Subsequent to this early publication, extensive empirical and conceptual developments in lay epistemics took place under the aegis of three fairly separate research programmes, namely those on *closed mindedness* (see Kruglanski, 2004), the *unimodel* (see Kruglanski et al., 2007), and *epistemic authority* (see Kruglanski et al., 2005). The purpose of the present chapter is to offer an integrative, up-to-date synopsis of this work, affording a bird's eye perspective on knowledge formation processes and their ramifications for a broad variety of social psychological phenomena.

In what follows we first briefly recapitulate the theory of lay epistemics and describe the three separate research programmes it inspired, including the description of substantial novel data not covered in prior reviews. We conclude with a conceptual integration of these research programmes and indicate how the processes that they address form an integral part and parcel of the knowledge formation enterprise of potentially considerable real-world relevance.

THE THEORY OF LAY EPISTEMICS

The theory of lay epistemics concerns the process of knowledge formation. It outlines a general framework designed to pertain to all kinds of knowledge, scientific and lay, including personal knowledge of people and the world, religious knowledge, political knowledge, etc. Its point of departure has been Karl Popper's (1959) famous assertion that scientific knowledge is formed in the same general manner as lay knowledge, and hence that science is "common sense writ large". Popper and other philosophers of science (e.g., Paul Feyerabend, or Imre Lakatos) have noted that whereas knowledge formation is guided by the ideal of Truth, one can be never certain that this ideal has been realised. This implies that the concept of "knowledge" is best understood in its subjective sense, as a *belief*. This hardly implies that knowledge must be solipsistic or idiosyncratic. All to the contrary, knowledge typically is socially shared, and knowledge construction (whereas scientific or lay) is accomplished via a communal process (Hardin & Higgins, 1996).

According to our theory that regards knowledge as tantamount to belief, to have *knowledge* in which one does not *believe* is a contradiction in terms. However, some authors (e.g., Gawronski & Bodenhausen, 2006) have affirmed such possibility, so let us examine it carefully. For instance, consider an individual who *knows* the contents of some stereotype (e.g., that all professors are absent-minded) yet does not believe in it. Does that represent an inconsistency with our claim that subjective knowledge represents a belief? It does not! The confusion here is one between "believing that" and "believing in". Knowing the contents of a stereotype means that one *believes that* such a stereotype exists. For instance, one may believe very strongly *that* the stereotype of women states that women are relational, conflict avoidant, and nurturing, yet one might not personally subscribe to such a stereotype or *believe in it*. Similarly, one may know or *believe* very strongly *that* the ancient Egyptians believed the Earth to be flat, without oneself believing this to be true, etc.

Evidence

A major assumption of the lay epistemic theory is that knowledge is derived from evidence. In other words the individual is assumed to depart from an inference rule of an "if E then C" type in which the antecedent term represents the evidence (E), and the consequent term the conclusion C. Such conclusion can also be thought of as a hypothesis (H) that is supported by the evidence.[1] More formally speaking, the reasoning from evidence to conclusions is syllogistic. It includes a *major premise*, the "if E then C" inference rule, and a *minor premise*, which instantiates the antecedent of the rule E affirming that the evidence in question has been obtained, jointly yielding the conclusion C. For instance, a person might subscribe to the stereotype "if university professor then smart" (constituting a major premise), and infer that an encountered individual Dr Smith, known to be a university professor (minor premise) is, therefore, smart (the conclusion). A special category of evidence concerns other people's opinions. In particular, if these are revered by an individual—hence constituting "epistemic authorities" for that person—their views may carry particular weight for her or him and occasionally override other types of evidence. This lends the epistemic process a distinctly social flavour and highlights the centrality of social reality concerns (Hardin & Higgins, 1996) to human epistemic endeavours.

Terminating the epistemic sequence

It is generally agreed among philosophers of knowledge that the sequence of hypothesis generation and testing (whether in science or in common sense) has no unique or objective point of termination. In principle, one could continue constructing further and further hypotheses and proceed to test them interminably without ever crystallising firm knowledge on any topic. Of course, such epistemic "obsession" would be highly dysfunctional and paralysing. Indeed, most of the time people are quite capable of forming judgements based on available evidence and of self-regulating adaptively on the basis of those judgements. An important mechanism allowing this to happen has to do with a motivational variable referred to as the need for cognitive closure (Kruglanski, 2004). Two types of the need for closure have been distinguished, referred to respectively as the needs for nonspecific and specific closure.

---

[1]For Popper (1959) the process of hypothesis testing is represented by the premise If H then E, which implies that one can only falsify a hypothesis via a logical modus tollens (if E is false then we can conclude that H must be false), but not verify it as we are suggesting. According to our analysis, however, the knower may depart from the assumption that *if and only if* hypothesis H were true evidence E would be observed. The *if and only if* framing implies that not only if H then E is true, but also if E then H is true. This way one could logically derive the hypothesis from the evidence in a modus ponens fashion, whereby E (the evidence is observed) therefore H (the hypothesis is supported). Of course, the *if and only if* assumption may need to be modified on the basis of subsequent information which would cast doubt on the originally derived conclusion that H was proven or supported. For instance, if an alternative hypothesis H_1 were posed and the need to distinguish it from the original H arose, one would formulate an inference rule whereby *if and only if* H but not H_1 were true then E_1 would obtain, etc.

The need for nonspecific closure denotes a desire for a firm answer to a question; any firm answer as compared to confusion and ambiguity. The need for a specific closure denotes a specific, desirable, answer to a question, e.g., an esteem-enhancing answer, an optimistic answer, and so on. Each of these needs is assumed to vary in degree and to lie on a continuum ranging from a low to a high motivational magnitude. Thus, one may desire nonspecific closure strongly, mildly, or not at all, actually craving to avoid it. Similarly, one may desire to reach a particular conclusion (or specific closure) with varying degrees of strength. Finally, both types of need determine the length of the epistemic sequence of hypothesis generation and testing. The higher the need for nonspecific closure the shorter the sequence and the stronger the tendency to "seize and freeze" on accessible, closure-affording, evidence. The higher the need for a specific closure, the stronger the tendency to terminate the sequence when the available evidence appears to yield the desired conclusion, or to keep the sequence going until such conclusion seems implied by the evidence.

EXPLORATIONS IN LAY EPISTEMICS

Over the last three decades, research in the lay epistemic framework has taken place within three separate paradigms, centred respectively on (1) the *need for cognitive closure*, (2) the *unimodel* of social judgement, and (3) the concept of *epistemic authority*. We describe these in turn and show how they interface in addressing functionally interdependent facets of human epistemic behaviour.

Need for closure research: The "why" of epistemic behaviour

The intrapersonal level

The most extensive research programme to date inspired by the lay epistemic framework concerned the need for nonspecific cognitive closure. It addresses the underlying motivation of knowledge formation, addressing the "why" aspect of human epistemics. The magnitude of the need for closure was assumed to be determined by the perceived benefits of closure, and by the costs of lacking closure. For instance, the need for closure was assumed to be elevated where action was required because the launching of intelligible action requires prior closure. Additionally, the need for closure was assumed to be elevated in circumstances where the possession of closure would obviate costly or laborious information processing, as may occur under time pressure, in the presence of ambient noise, or when a person is fatigued or intoxicated (see Kruglanski, 2004, for a review). When the need for closure is elevated, the absence of closure is aversive and stressful.

In a recent pair of studies Roets and van Hiel (2008) found that in a decision-making context (i.e., where closure was required) high (but not low) NFCC scoring individuals had increased systolic blood pressure and heart rate as well as a rise in self-reported feelings of distress (Study 1). Moreover, as long as no conclusive solution was obtained, high (but not low) NFCC individuals showed a progressive increase of arousal assessed via a galvanic skin response. In addition to the transient situational determinants of the need for closure, this motivation was also assumed to represent a dimension of individual differences and a scale was constructed to assess it (Webster & Kruglanski, 1994). By now this scale has been translated into numerous languages and has been shown to converge in its results with situational manipulations of the need for closure;[2] an improved version of the scale was recently published by Roets and van Hiel (2007). These results pertained to phenomena on intrapersonal, interpersonal, group, and intergroup levels of analysis. In the present chapter we address them briefly. More extensive recent reviews are given in Kruglanski and Webster (1996), Kruglanski (2004), and in Kruglanski, Pierro, Mannetti, and DeGrada (2006c).

Seizing and freezing phenomena. As noted earlier, a heightened need for cognitive closure induces in individuals the tendency to "seize" on early, closure-affording evidence and "freeze" on the judgements (beliefs) it suggests. These tendencies were studied in reference to several classic phenomena in social cognition and perception.

For instance, Kruglanski and Freund (1983) presented participants with information about a target person's past behaviours in a work context. Participants were then asked to make a judgement about how successful the target would be at a new job. The information about the target included both positive and negative information, with the order of this information varied such that some participants saw the negative information first while others saw the positive information first. Need for closure was manipulated via time pressure by giving some participants a 3-minute limit to make their judgements (after listening to the information), with a stopwatch in sight reminding them of the time constraint. In the low time pressure condition, participants were told they would have an unlimited time to complete the judgements.

It was predicted that need for closure would exert a stronger primacy effect when participants were in a high (vs low) accountability conditions. To manipulate accountability, some participants were told that they would have

---

[2]In a recent paper, Roets, van Hiel, Cornelis, and Soetens (2008) argued that in addition to exerting a direct motivational effect similar to that of dispositional NFCC, situational manipulations of need for closure (via time pressure or noise) exert an effect on cognitive capacity as well manifesting in deteriorated task performance.

to explain their predictions to others and that their judgement would be compared to objective standards. In the low accountability condition participants were told that they would not be able to find out how other people judge the target or how the target actually performed at the new job.

As predicted, participants' judgements of the target person were based more on the early appearing information when under time pressure (vs no time pressure). As shown in Figure 1, the difference between the high as compared to the low time pressure conditions was significantly greater when accountability was high (vs low). These results demonstrate the ability of need for closure to induce the tendency to "seize" and freeze" on early information. The primacy effect of need for closure was subsequently replicated in a number of further studies, (Ford & Kruglanski, 1995; Freund, Kruglanski, & Shpitzazjzen, 1985; Richter & Kruglanski, 1998; Webster, Richter, & Kruglanski, 1996).

In an intriguing demonstration of need for closure's impact on the use of contextually activated information, Pierro and Kruglanski (in press) conducted a study on the influence of need for closure on the *transference effect* in social judgement. The Freudian concept of transference refers to the process by which a psychotherapeutic patient superimposes onto the therapist her or his childhood fantasies with regard to a significant childhood figure (typically a parent). However, Andersen and her colleagues (e.g., Anderson & Cole, 1990, Andersen, Glassman, Chen, & Cole, 1995) showed that the transference effect could be part and parcel of normal sociocognitive functioning in which a significant other's schema is mistakenly applied to a new target that resembles the significant other in some respects. In a first session of Pierro and Kruglanski's (in press) experiment participants completed the revised 14-item need for closure scale (Pierro & Kruglanski, 2005) and were asked to visualise and describe a

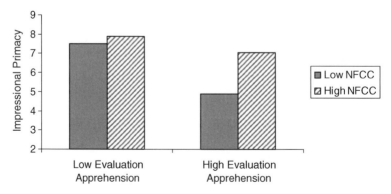

Figure 1. The effect of need for closure (NFCC, operationalised in this study via time pressure) and evaluation apprehension on impressional primacy (Kruglanski & Freund, 1983).

significant other. In a second session participants were presented with information about a target person with whom they expected to interact. The target person was either described in similar terms as their significant other, or was depicted as dissimilar from that person. After having studied this information, participants were presented with a recognition test of their memory for the target. Items about the target person that were not presented in the description were included in the recognition test. The degree of transference was operationally defined as the proportion of statements falsely recognised as having been included in the description of the target person that were consistent with the representation of the significant other provided in the first session. As shown in Figure 2, the results indicated that participants high on the need for closure exhibited a more pronounced transference effect, as indicated by higher false alarm rates, in the similar (vs dissimilar) condition than did participants low on the need for closure.

Other studies found evidence that need for closure, whether induced situationally or measured via a trait scale, augments the effects of prevalent stereotypes on judgements about persons (Dijksterhuis, Van Knippenberg, Kruglanski, & Schaper, 1996; Jamieson & Zanna, 1989; Kruglanski & Freund, 1983). A stereotype represents a knowledge structure affording quick judgements about members of a stereotyped "category." That need for closure augments the tendency to utilise stereotype-based evidence in impression formation therefore supports the notion that this need induces the "seizing" and freezing" tendencies assumed by the lay epistemic theory.

The interpersonal level

Beyond its effects on intrapersonal phenomena in the domain of social judgement, need for closure was shown to exert a variety of interpersonal

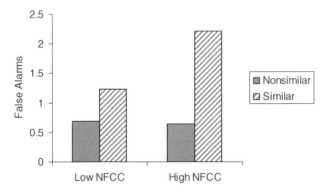

Figure 2. The effect of target similarity and need for closure (NFCC) on false alarm rate (Pierro & Kruglanski, in press).

phenomena in realms of linguistic expression, communication and persuasion, empathy, and negotiation behaviour.

Linguistic expression.   Several studies looked at need for closure effects on language abstractness in interpersonal communications. Abstract language indicates a *permanence* of judgements across situations, and hence a greater stability of closure. For instance, characterising an individual's behaviour in a given situation as reflecting this person's aggressiveness (an abstract depiction) implies that he or she may be expected to behave aggressively in other contexts as well. By contrast, depicting the same behaviour as a "push" (that is, concretely) carries fewer trans-situational implications. Accordingly, it is possible to predict that individuals under high (vs low) need for closure would generally tend to employ abstract terms in their communications. Consistent with this prediction, Boudreau, Baron, and Oliver (1992) found that participants, when communicating their impressions to a knowledgeable and potentially critical other (assumed to induce a fear of invalidity and lower the need for closure), tended less to describe a target in abstract trait terms than did participants communicating their impressions to a recipient assumed to have little knowledge on the communication topic.

Using Semin and Fiedler's (1991) linguistic category paradigm, Rubini and Kruglanski (1997) found that participants under high (vs low) need for closure (manipulated via noise *or* measured via the need for closure scale) tended to frame their questions in more abstract terms, inviting reciprocal abstractness from the respondents. That, in turn, contributed to the creation of greater interpersonal distance between the interlocutors, lessening their liking for each other. Webster, Kruglanski, and Pattison (1997) explored need for closure effects on the "linguistic intergroup bias (LIB)". The LIB reflects the tendency to describe negative ingroup behaviours in concrete terms and positive outgroup behaviours in concrete terms (suggesting their specificity), and to describe positive ingroup behaviours and negative outgroup behaviours in abstract terms (suggesting their generality). Consider how need for closure may impact these phenomena. On the one hand, need for closure should induce a general tendency towards abstraction because of the desire of high need for closure individuals for stable knowledge that transcends the specific situation. However, abstract judgements about positive outgroup and negative ingroup behaviours should run counter to the tendency for individuals with high need for closure to display ingroup favouritism (in so far as the in group is typically the provider of stable knowledge). These two tendencies work *in concert* as far as judgement of positive ingroup and negative outgroup behaviours are concerned, and are *in conflict* (hence possibly cancelling each other out) as far as negative ingroup and positive outgroup behaviours are concerned.

As shown in Figure 3, Webster et al. (1997) found that high (vs low) need for closure participants exposed to positive ingroup or negative outgroup behaviours described such behaviours more abstractly. However, high and low need for closure participants did not differ on the abstractness of their descriptions of negative ingroup or positive outgroup behaviours.

Persuasion. Research by Kruglanski, Webster, and Klem (1993) explored the conditions under which need for closure may increase or decrease the susceptibility to persuasion. To do this, participants were presented with information about a legal case, and allowed time to process the information and then to talk with a partner (fellow "juror") in order to reach a verdict in the case. When participants were given complete information about the case, including legal analysis suggesting the appropriate verdict, individuals high (vs low) on the need for closure were less likely to be persuaded by their fellow juror (who argued for the opposite verdict). However, when high need for closure individuals were given incomplete information lacking the legal analysis, they were more likely to be persuaded by their fellow juror than their low need for closure counterparts. In short, individuals high (vs low) on the need for closure tend to resist persuasion attempts when they have formed a crystallised opinion about a topic, but tend to change their attitudes when presented with persuasive appeals when they lack an opinion about the topic.

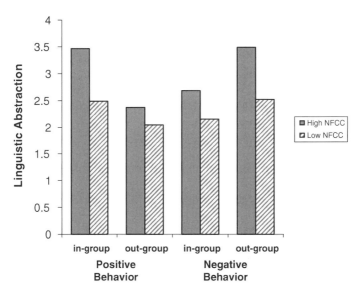

Figure 3. The effect of need for closure (NFCC), ingroup versus outgroup status, and type of behaviour on abstractness of description (Webster et al., 1997).

Empathy. Webster-Nelson, Klein and Irvin (2003) found that, because high need for closure individuals' tend to "freeze" on their own perspective, they are less able to empathise with their interaction partners, especially when those are dissimilar from themselves. In their study the need for closure was manipulated via an induction of mental fatigue. Using a dispositional measure of the need for closure, Schteynberg, Gelfand, Imai, Mayer, and Bell (2008) found that high (vs low) scorers were less sensitive to injustice done to their team-mate by the experimenter (perceived the experimenter as less unfair). In a referential task paradigm, Richter and Kruglanski (1999) found that individuals with high (vs low) dispositional need for closure tended less to implement an effective "audience design". They tended less to "tune" their messages to their interlocutors' unique attributes; as a consequence their communications were less effectively decoded by their recipients.

Negotiation behaviour. To test the effect of need for closure in the domain of negotiation behaviour, DeDreu, Koole, and Oldersma (1999) measured participants' dispositional need for closure and then (after a 30-minute delay) had them engage in a task in which they operated as sellers and interacted with presumed buyers (actually simulated by computer-programmed responses). The participant's (seller's) task was to negotiate the terms of the sale, including delivery time, price, and form of payment. Each of these was associated with rewards for the participant in the form of chances in a lottery such that greater profit for the seller was associated with higher chances of winning. Participants engaged in six rounds of negotiations, beginning with the buyer. The buyers' responses were pre-programmed to remain at a moderate level, while conceding slightly at each round. To manipulate the focal point to which participants might adjust their negotiations, they were either told that previous participants had received 11,000 points (high focal point), 3000 points (low focal point), or simply that the range of possible points was from 0 to 14,000 points (no focal point).

Three dependent measures were assessed. First, prior to the start of the negotiations participants were asked to indicate the minimum amount they would be willing to accept in the negotiation. Second, participants' concessions in the task were determined by the decrease in the amount of points participants demanded from the first to the last rounds of negotiation (with greater numbers indicating a larger concession). After the six trials (in which most participants did not reach an agreement), participants completed a self-report measure of the extent to which they thought systematically during the task.

As shown in Figure 4, individuals with high (vs low) dispositional need for closure tended more to adhere to anchor values. That is, they determined

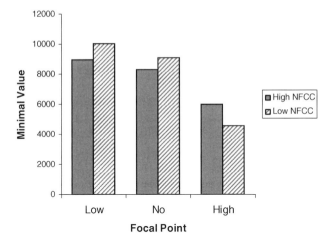

Figure 4. The effect of need for closure (NFCC) and focal point on the minimal value found acceptable in a negotiation (de Dreu et al., 1999).

the minimal profits they themselves would accept according to the alleged profits attained by others in the task. When no focal point was provided, high versus low need for closure participants did not differ in the minimal value they expressed the willingness to accept. In addition, high (vs low) need for closure participants made smaller concessions to their negotiation partners and engaged in less systematic information processing.

In another study on negotiation, De Dreu and Koole (1997) lowered participants' need for closure via accountability instructions (Tetlock, 1992) or by increasing the costs of invalid judgements (Kruglanski & Freund, 1983). These manipulations lowered participants' tendency to use the "*consensus implies correctness*" heuristic, as well as their tendency to behave competitively and to reach an impasse when a majority suggested a competitive strategy.

The foregoing findings exemplify need for closure effects on a variety of intrapersonal and interpersonal variables (for an extensive review see Kruglanski, 2004). Extensive research also examined the effects of the closure motivation on groups, resulting in a phenomenon of *group centrism* described next.

Group centrism.   Some people are more group oriented than others, and most people are more group oriented in some situations than in other situations. Kruglanski et al. (2006c) defined the concept of "group centrism" by the degree to which individuals strive to enhance the "groupness" of their collectivity. Groupness, in turn, has been defined by a firm, consensually supported, "shared reality" (Hardin & Higgins, 1996) unperturbed by dissents and disagreements. While reality sharing has been regarded as the defining essence of groupness (e.g., Bar-Tal, 1990, 2000), its attainment may be facilitated by several aspects of group interaction enhanced by the need for closure. At the initial phases of group formation, this can involve members' attempts to arrive at a speedy consensus, by exerting uniformity pressures on each other (DeGrada, Kruglanski, Mannetti, & Pierro, 1999).

To further test the influence of need for closure on the group decision-making process, Pierro, Mannetti, DeGrada, Livi, and Kruglanski (2003) engaged participants in a group task 2 months after participants' need for closure had been assessed. Participants were divided into groups based on their need for closure scores, with some groups containing high need for closure individuals and others individuals low on need for closure. Each group was composed of four individuals, each role-playing a manager in a corporation. The group's goal was to determine which of the company's employees should be given a cash award for their work performance. Each "manager" represented a candidate nominated by this "manager's" department. The dependent measures included the asymmetry of speaking time (seizing and holding the floor), perceptions of each participant's influence over the group, and each member's style assessed on the laissez faire/autocratic dimension.

The results indicated that groups composed of high (but not of low) need for closure members displayed the emergence of an autocratic group structure wherein influence emanates from a centralised authority, enhancing the likelihood of commonly shared opinions. As shown in Figure 5, in groups composed of high need for closure persons, some members more than others disproportionately controlled the group discussion by "seizing" the discussion floor and continuing to talk when others attempted to interrupt. Furthermore, in high (but not low) need for closure groups, members' level of autocratic style (as assessed by independent judges) was positively correlated with their control of the discussion floor. Finally, individuals' floor control was positively correlated with their influence on the group (as indexed by self-report and by assessment of independent observers). This research supports the notion that groups composed of high need for closure members are more likely to form autocratic structures, in which a single person or a restricted number of individuals serve as foci of influence, that shape the groups' commonly shared realities.

The laboratory findings just described are consistent with Gelfand's (2008) cross-cultural research carried out in 35 countries across the globe in which she finds a significant relationship between the country's degree of autocracy and situational constraint, in turn related to inhabitants' need for closure. Although these results may reflect the notion that high need for closure individuals tend to construct autocratic societies, they may also mean that life in tight, autocratic, societies tends to engender members with

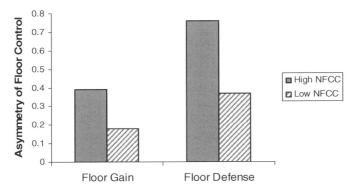

Figure 5. The effect of need for closure (NFCC) on asymmetry of floor control during group decision making (Pierro et al., 2003).

a high need for closure. These two possible tendencies are not necessarily incompatible. Their existence and interrelation could be profitably probed in further research.

In addition to influencing group structure, intensified quest for uniformity under heightened need for closure tends to lead to an intolerance of diversity (Kruglanski, Shah, Pierro, & Mannetti, 2002; Shah, Kruglanski, & Thompson, 1998). Diversity is a feature that may impede the arrival at consensus, thereby reducing the group's ability to reach closure. In this vein, heightened need for closure, through the implementation of time pressure and ambient noise, has been shown to lead to a rejection of opinion deviates in a working group (Kruglanski & Webster, 1991). Elevated need for closure was also found to foster favouritism towards one's ingroup, in direct proportion to its degree of homogeneity and opinion uniformity. Finally, need for closure was found to foster outgroup derogation (Kruglanski et al., 2002; Shah et al., 1998), which degree was *inversely* related to the outgroup's homogeneity and opinion uniformity (Kruglanski et al., 2002). These findings are consistent with the notion that high need for closure individuals are attracted to groups (whether ingroups or outgroups) that promise to offer firm shared realities to their members, affording stable cognitive closure.

The quest for stable shared reality on part of individuals with high need for closure should express itself in conservatism and the upholding of group norms and traditions. Indeed, both political conservatism (Jost, Glaser, Kruglanski, & Sulloway, 2003a, 2003b) and the tendency to maintain stable group norms across generational cycles (Livi, 2003) were found to be related to a heightened need for closure. Chirumbolo (2002), and Van Hiel, Pandelaere, and Duriez (2004) found that the relation between need for closure and conservatism was mediated by general political attitudes, notably Right Wing Authoritarianism, and Social Dominance Orientation.

Roets and van Hiel (2006) found additionally that these relationships reflected both the "freezing" and the "seizing" tendencies induced by the NFCC, the latter being specifically assessed via the Decisiveness facet of the NFCC scale. Chirumbolo and Leone (2008) also found in two election studies (the 2004 European elections and the 2005 Italian Regional elections) that need for closure was linearly (and positively) related to voting along the left right continuum. Finally, Chirumbolo, Areni, and Sensales (2004) found that Italian students high (vs low) on the need for closure were more nationalistic, religious, exhibited a preference for right-wing political parties, reported anti-immigrant attitudes, scored lower on pluralism and multiculturalism, and preferred autocratic leadership and a centralised form of political power.

Kosic, Kruglanski, Pierro, and Mannetti (2004) found evidence that need for closure augments loyalty to one's ingroup and instils a reluctance to abandon it and "defect" to alternative collectivities. Such loyalty persists to the extent that one's ingroup is salient in the individuals' social environment. If, however, an alternative group's views became overridingly salient, high need for closure may in fact prompt members to switch groups. In this vein, Croat and Polish immigrants to Italy who were high (vs low) on need for closure tended to assimilate less to the Italian culture (i.e., they maintained loyalty to their culture of origin) if their social environment at entry consisted of their co-ethnics. However, if it consisted of members of the host culture (i.e., of Italians), high (vs low) need for closure immigrants tended more to "defect" and assimilate to the Italian culture.

Need for closure may also influence the attitudes of members of existing groups towards potential newcomers into their midst. We have already reported Chirumbolo et al.'s (2004) finding as to the anti-immigration attitudes of high (vs low) need for closure Italians. More recently, Dechesne, Schultz, Kruglanski, Orehek, and Fishman (2008) investigated whether individuals high on the need for closure would prefer groups with impermeable (vs permeable) boundaries. Dutch undergraduate students first completed the need for closure scale, and subsequently read a news article highlighting either the permeability or the impermeability of their college's boundaries. Participants in the impermeable condition read a passage stating that "the choice of one's university is virtually irreversible" whereas participants in the permeable condition read a passage depicting the choice of one's university as reversible. As shown in Figure 6, participants high (vs low) on the need for closure expressed greater identification with impermeable (vs) permeable group boundaries that do not allow much traffic in and out of the group. The same pattern of results was found for liking of the group. Dechesne et al. (2008) also found that American students with high (vs low) need for closure had more negative attitudes toward immigration into the US.

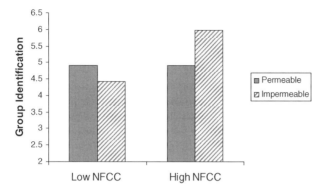

Figure 6. The effect of group permeability and need for closure (NFCC) on ingroup identification (Dechesne et al., 2008).

Conclusions. In summary, a great deal of research attests to the considerable role that the need for cognitive closure plays in intrapersonal, interpersonal, and group phenomena. Basically these have to do with the importance of knowledge construction processes in human affairs: At the individual level these processes affect the formation of social judgements, attitudes, and impressions. At the interpersonal level they enter into communication and persuasion, empathy, and negotiation behaviour, and at the group level into the formation of consensus and the forging of stable social realities for the members. In all these domains, and on all these levels of analysis, the need for closure has been shown to constitute a variable with implications for major classes of social psychological phenomena.

Essentially, the need for closure paradigm addresses the *motivational* underpinnings of knowledge formation, the "why" of epistemic behaviour, affecting the extent of information processing en route to a judgement, and the tendency to "seize and freeze" on judgement affording information. By contrast, the unimodel paradigm considered next "zooms in" on the *informational* aspect of the epistemic process and investigates the "how" of the epistemic process, illuminating the way in which given information exerts impact on individuals' judgements (Erb et al., 2003; Kruglanski & Thompson, 1999a, 1999b; Kruglanski et al., 2006b, 2007).

The unimodel of human judgement: The "how" of epistemic behaviour

The function of rule following in lay epistemics

A basic aspect of the lay epistemic theory concerns the role of evidence in knowledge formation. As noted earlier, the lay epistemic theory assumes that all knowledge derives from evidence, broadly conceived. In other words, to construct new knowledge, or to form a new judgement the individual is assumed to use an inference rule of an "if ... then" type, whereby if a given evidence E obtains, the conclusion C follows (or the hypothesis H is supported).

Although the foregoing depiction of inference as a case of syllogistic reasoning may seem deliberative, conscious, and explicit, it need be none of these. An identical mechanism may underlie processes typically considered as associative or "mechanistic". Consider the phenomenon of classical conditioning. Although it has been viewed as prototypic of associative learning, compelling evidence exists (Holyoak, Koh, & Nisbett, 1989; Rescorla, 1985; Rescorla & Holland, 1982; Rescorla & Wagner, 1972) that it is fundamentally rule based.

Thus, based on an extensive review of pertinent conditioning studies, Holyoak and colleagues (1989, p. 320) concluded that:

> representations of the environment take the form of ... [if then] rules that compose mental models ... the rat's knowledge about the relation between tones and shocks might be informally represented by a rule such as "if a tone sounds in the chamber then a shock will occur, so stop other activities and crouch."

From this perspective (Holyoak et al., 1989, p. 320):

> Rules drive the system's behaviour by means of a recognize–act cycle. On each cycle the conditions of rules are matched against representations of active declarative information, which we ... term *messages*; rules with conditions that are satisfied by current messages become candidates for execution. For example, if a message representing the recent occurrence of a tone is active, the conditions of the above rule will be matched and the actions it specifies may be taken.

Note the affinity of this conception to the basic syllogistic sequence: The "rule" assumed by Holyoak and colleagues (1989) is analogous to the major premise, and the "message" that "matches the rule" is analogous to the minor premise, i.e., instantiation of the antecedent term in the major premise, warranting the inference of the consequent term.

Whereas the work reviewed by Holyoak et al. (1989) concerned the phenomena of classical conditioning, a recent integration of evaluative conditioning phenomena attests that it too is "propositional"; that is, rule-following (Mitchell, De Houwer, & Lovibond, in press). In evaluative conditioning a neutral CS (e.g., a book) is presented concomitantly with an affectively laden UCS (e.g., a smiling, or a pouting face); subsequently, it is found that the CS acquired the affective valence of the UCS. Although evaluative conditioning differs in a number of important respect from classical conditioning (Baeyens, Crombez, Van den Bergh, & Eelen, 1988; Walther, Nagengast, & Trasselli, 2005) the rule following nature of the conditioning process appears common to both. As Mitchell et al. (in press) put it in reference to evaluative conditioning "... associative learning results, ... in humans ... not from the automatic formation of links, but from the operation of controlled reasoning processes" (p. 6) in which "The process of reasoning about the relationship between events produces ... declarative, propositional knowledge about those events ..." (p. 14), hence "[conditional, if-then] ... links that specify how the two events are related" (p. 15, parentheses added).

It is noteworthy that the rules involved in conditioning may be applied in given informational contexts with considerable ease and alacrity. The notion that "automatic" phenomena in the domain of (motor or cognitive) skill acquisition involve a routinisation of "if ... then" sequences has been central to Anderson's (1983) ACT* model that Smith (1984, 1989; Smith & Branscombe, 1988; Smith, Branscombe, & Bormann, 1988) extended to the realm of social judgement. That research has demonstrated that social judgements represent a special case of procedural learning based on practice that strengthens the "if ... then" components resulting in increased efficiency (or "automaticity").

Awareness

Efficiency implies, in turn, a lowered need to commit attentional resources to the carrying out of social judgements. In William James' (1890, p. 496) felicitous phrasing "consciousness deserts all processes when it can no longer be of use". According to his parsimony principle of consciousness, routinisation removes the need for conscious control of the process, rendering awareness of the process superfluous. In a related vein, Logan (1992) suggested that automatisation of certain skills effects a shift of attention to higher organisational levels.

It is in this sense, then, that some judgemental phenomena, mediated by well-routinised "if ... then" rules, may take place outside conscious awareness. Helmholtz (1910/2000) discussed the notion of unconscious *inference* in the realm of perception. More recently, social cognitive work on spontaneous trait inferences (Newman & Uleman, 1989; Uleman, 1987) suggests that lawful (i.e., rule-following) inferences presumably can occur without explicit inferential intentions, and without conscious awareness of making an inference. "The spontaneous trait inference that John is 'clumsy' on basis of the information that he stepped on Stephanie's foot while dancing" (Newman & Uleman, 1989, p. 156), surely requires the inference rule "if stepping on a dancing partner's foot, then clumsy" or some variant thereof: A person who did not subscribe to that premise would be unlikely to reach that particular conclusion.

Unconscious inferences are also exemplified by Schwarz and Clore's (1996) "feelings as information" model. A mood state may be mistakenly attributed to a given cause. For instance, a positive mood engendered by pleasant weather may be treated as a basis for an inference of a general life satisfaction (Schwarz & Clore, 1983, Schwarz, Servay, & Kumpf, 1985) based on an "if ... then" rule linking one's feeling state with general satisfaction. As Schwarz and Clore (1996, p. 437) summarised it "... reliance on ... experiences [for various inferences] generally does not involve conscious attribution".

Thus a variety of evidence and theoretical considerations converge on the notion that judgements (whether assessed directly or through their behavioural manifestations) are rule based and, in this sense, derived from "evidence". To make a judgement is to go beyond the "information given" (Bartlett, 1932; Bruner, 1973), by using it as testimony for a conclusion in accordance with an "if ... then" statement to which the individual subscribes. Such implicational structure appears to characterise explicit human inferences (Anderson, 1983), implicit conclusion drawing (Schwarz & Clore, 1996), conditioning responses in animal learning studies (Holyoak et al., 1989; Rescorla & Wagner, 1972), and perceptual judgements of everyday objects (Gregory, 1997; Pizlo, 2001; Rock, 1983). The elementary "if ... then" form appears essential to all such inferences, whether conscious or nonconscious, instantaneous or delayed, innate or learned. It is a fundamental building block from which all epistemic edifices are constructed.[3]

In describing the knowledge (or judgement) formation process as syllogistic, we do not mean to suggest that individuals necessarily engage in explicit syllogistic reasoning (e.g., Newell & Simon, 1972). Nor do we mean to imply that individuals are familiar with the intricacies of formal logic—a proposition belied by over 30 years of work on the Wason (1966) problem among others. For instance, people might incorrectly treat an *implicational* "If A then B" relation as an *equivalence* relation, "Only if A

---

[3]That the general implicational IF-THEN structure represents the gist of inference is a mainstay of most major depictions of this process in the philosophy of science and of knowledge literatures. Consider the venerated Hempel–Openheim (1948) scheme of scientific explanation, known as the deductive nomological (D-N) framework. According to this model, a scientific explanation contains two major elements: an *explanandum*, a sentence "describing the phenomenon to be explained" and an *explanans*, "the class of sentences that account for the phenomenon" (Hempel & Oppenheim, 1948, reprinted in Hempel, 1965, p. 247). For the explanans to successfully explain the explanandum, "the explanandum must be a logical consequence of the explanans" and "the sentences constituting the explanans must be true". (Hempel, 1965, p. 248). That is, any proper explanation takes the form of a sound deductive argument in which the explanandum follows as a conclusion from the premises in the explanans. For instance, the sentence "All gases expand when heated under constant pressure", or "If something is a gas, then it expands when heated under constant pressure", constitutes a major premise that in conjunction with the appropriate minor premise—that is, information that "some particular substance is a gas that has been heated under constant pressure"—affords the inference that this substance will expand, or an explanation of why it did expand.

then B", suggesting that also "if B then A" (which was not originally intended). We also accept that often people may be better able to recognise the "correct" implicational properties of concrete statements in familiar domains rather than those of abstract, unfamiliar statements (Evans, 1989). None of it is inconsistent with the notion that persons generally reason from subjectively relevant rules of implicational "if ... then" format (see also Abelson, 1968; Mischel & Shoda, 1995).

Parametric determinants of informational impact

Given the syllogistic structure of knowledge formation from evidence to conclusion, it is possible now to analyse the conditions under which the information given in a specific context would affect the individual's judgements. As noted earlier, a syllogism includes a major premise and a minor premise that jointly yield a conclusion. In this sense, the "information given" is the minor premise, which affirms the antecedent condition of a pre-existing inference rule serving as a major premise and mediating the road from evidence to conclusion. Accordingly, in order that a given piece of information exerted judgemental impact the individual should subscribe to the major premise linking a given antecedent condition and a given consequent in an "if X then Y" fashion. Subscribing to an inference rule is a matter of degree reflecting the strength of belief in the conditional association linking a given X with a given Y. The continuum of belief strength defines the *parameter of subjective relevance* of information X to conclusion Y.

However, a general subscription to an inference rule merely defines an *availability* of such rule in a person's memory (Higgins, 1996). In addition, the rule needs to be momentarily *accessible* to a person, or to be activated from memory. In turn, rule activation may be more or less difficult depending on its prior history of activation, i.e., its frequency and recency of activation (Higgins, 1996). The difficulty issue also arises in reference to an individual's ability to recognise that a given, situationally present, piece of information *matches* an inference rule and in this sense constitutes a minor premise that jointly with a major premise is capable of yielding a conclusion. Specifically, the information may be less or more salient in a given context, constituting a weaker or stronger signal against the background of irrelevant noise. In addition, the information may be presented in a more or less lengthy format and to be less or more difficult to decipher. All these may determine the difficulty of recognising that the information given is relevant to a requisite judgement, or represents a minor premise in the appropriate syllogism. The *difficulty of the inference task* (including the activation of the major premise from memory, and recognition that the information given represents the minor premise), defines another parameter that affects the degree to which the information given would impact the judgement rendered. Specifically, the greater the difficulty of the inference task, the greater should be the amount of *cognitive* and *motivational* resources needed to perform it.

As the foregoing discussion suggests, it is useful to distinguish conceptually between *potential relevance* of X to Y reflecting the degree to which the "If X then Y" inferential rule has been generally learned and believed in, and *contextual* or *perceived relevance* reflecting the degree to which X is recognised as relevant to Y in a given situation. Beyond degree of belief, perceived relevance is affected by accessibility of the rule, difficulty of identifying the X and individual's motivational and cognitive resources available for overcoming the difficulty.

Resource availability as a determinant of informational impact. The relationship between the availability of processing resources and the ability to handle demanding inferential tasks has implications for the kinds of information that would affect judgements in different circumstances: Under conditions of limited processing resources, the easier-to-process information is likely to be utilised and to affect judgements to a greater extent than the difficult-to-process information. However, under conditions of ample processing resources, the difficult-to-process information would be utilised more *if* it appears to be more relevant to the judgemental task than the easy-to-process information. The foregoing assumptions afforded a reconceptua-lisation of considerable body of research findings formerly interpreted from a dual mode perspective on social judgement (see Chaiken & Trope, 1999).

It is important to disavow here any implication that the presence or absence of cognitive resources is systematically related to the quality of cognitive inference performance. Thus we assume that highly routinised and accessible rules (major premises) can be processed with minimal resources when matched with the appropriate situational information (minor premises). Furthermore, we intend no implication that the presence of resources would lead individuals to rely on objectively "better" rules or even on subjectively "better" (more relevant) rules. All we are asserting is that, in the absence of resources, individuals would rely more on easy-to-process information, whereas in the presence of ample resources they would also entertain the use of more difficult information. These notions are illustrated in research reviewed below.

Persuasion research. A pervasive finding in persuasion research has been that "peripheral" or "heuristic" cues exert judgemental impact (i.e., effect change in recipients' attitudes or opinions) under conditions of low processing resources (e.g., where recipients' interest in the task is low, when they are cognitively busy or distracted, when their need for cognition is low, etc.). By contrast, "message arguments" typically exerted their effects under high processing resources (e.g., high interest in the task, or ample cognitive capacity). However, in reviews of these studies (Erb et al., 2003; Kruglanski, Pierro, Mannetti, Erb, & Chun, 2007; Kruglanski & Thompson, 1999a, 1999b; Kruglanski, Thompson, & Spiegel, 1999; Pierro, Mannetti, Erb, Spiegel, & Kruglanski, 2005) it became apparent that often in persuasion research the type of the information (i.e., "peripheral" or "heuristic" cues versus message arguments) was confounded with task demands. Because the message arguments were typically lengthier, more complex, and placed later in the informational sequence, their processing may have imposed higher processing demands than the processing of "cues" that were invariably brief, simple, and presented upfront. When these confoundings were experimentally removed, the previously found differences between conditions under which the "cues" versus the "message arguments" (or vice versa) exerted their persuasive effects were eliminated (Erb et al., 2003; Kruglanski et al., 2007; Kruglanski & Thompson, 1999a; Pierro et al., 2005).

One of the most important contributions of the dual-process models was the finding that when persuasion occurred as the result of "central" or "systematic" information processing, defined as *message* or *issue processing*, the resulting attitude change was more persistent over time and was more strongly related to subsequent behaviours. However this research always presented source information *briefly and upfront*, with message arguments coming later and being presented in a *lengthier and more complex* format. This research design led to the conclusion that persuasion as a result of "central" or "systematic" processing of message arguments led to greater attitude persistence and a stronger attitude–behaviour link. According to the unimodel framework, however, source information and message arguments serve the same role as evidence in forming judgements. Therefore any persuasion as a result of extensive processing of information, including source information, should lead to attitude persistence and behaviour consistent with the attitude.

To test this notion, Pierro, Mannetti, Orehek, and Kruglanski (2008) presented participants with either brief (50 words) or lengthy (full-page) source information. The source, an education consultant, was described as either expert (a full professor of cognitive psychology at a prestigious university specialising in curriculum development) or inexpert (a professor at a low-prestige technical institute studying the psychology of tourism). Participants then read a passage written by the source arguing for the adoption of a new policy that would require participation in psychology experiments for students. Student participants were told either that this policy would be implemented soon (high involvement) or that it would be implemented following their graduation (low involvement). Immediately after reading the persuasive message, only when the source information was lengthy (but not brief) were participants in the high-involvement condition more in favour of the policy when it was presented by an expert (vs inexpert) source. However, only when the source information was short (but not lengthy) were participants in the low-involvement condition more in favour of the policy when it was presented by an expert (vs inexpert) source. This result replicates prior findings by Kruglanski and colleagues (for recent review, see Kruglanski et al., 2007).

Despite the fact that the short source information did have immediate persuasive effect under low involvement, this effect did not persist as much as did the effect of lengthy source information under high involvement. Specifically, participants in the high involvement condition who received lengthy (vs short) source information displayed greater attitude persistence and intentions to participate in experiments 3 weeks later. Finally, Figure 7 shows that participants in the high-involvement condition and who received lengthy (vs brief) source information were more likely to engage in attitude-consistent behaviours by participating in an experiment they had been invited to attend in the expert (but not an inexpert) source condition. No such differences were found for participants in the low-involvement condition with an expert source, or the high-involvement condition with an inexpert source. This behaviour occurred a full month after participants had received the persuasive appeal, suggesting that attitude change as a result of extensively processed *source information* (often considered peripheral and heuristic) can result in persistent attitudes and a strong attitude–behaviour link.

The persistence of attitude change following extensive processing of source information suggests that it is the extent of information processing rather than the type of information (source vs message argument) that

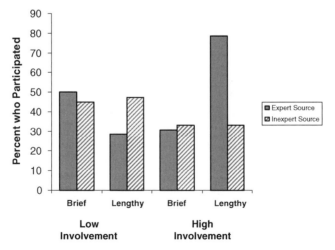

Figure 7. The effect of issue involvement, source expertise, and length of source information on participation behaviour (Pierro et al., 2008).

determines the stability of attitude change. Presumably, extensive processing of evidence warranting the adoption of a given attitude (i.e., source information or message argument) creates many linkages between the attitude concept and information stored in memory. These linkages may later facilitate retrieval of the attitude, rendering it readily activated and highly accessible, hence increasing its potential to guide behaviour (Fazio, 1990).

Dispositional attributions. A major question posed by attribution researchers concerned the process whereby a given behaviour performed by an actor is causally ascribed to the situational context, or to the actor's disposition. In this vein, Trope and Alfieri (1997) found that ambiguous behaviour tends to be disambiguated by assimilation to the context in which it is taking place. For instance, an ambiguous facial expression is likely to be perceived as sad if the context was sad as well (e.g., a funeral), and as happy if the context was happy (e.g., a party). However, once the behaviour had been identified, and the question of its causal origin was pondered, the context plays a subtractive (rather an assimilative) role in determining the behaviour's attribution. Specifically, the role of the context is subtracted to determine the role of the actor's disposition in producing the behaviour. For instance, if the context was sad, an individual's sad expression would not be attributed to the actor's dispositional sadness because other persons in the same situation would probably be sad as well.

Of present interest, Trope and Alfieri (1997) found that the assimilative process of behaviour identification was independent of cognitive load, whereas the subtractive process of dispositional attribution was undermined by load. These investigators also found that invalidating the information on which the behaviour identification process was based, by stating that the actor was unaware of the potential situational demands on their behaviour, did not alter these identifications, whereas invalidating that same information did alter the dispositional judgements. Two alternative explanations may account for these results: (1) that the two processes are qualitatively distinct, (2) that for some reason the behaviour identification task in Trope and Alfieri's (1997) work was less demanding than the dispositional attribution task.

Consistent with the latter interpretation, Trope and Gaunt (2000) discovered that when demands associated with the dispositional attribution task were lowered (e.g., by increasing the salience of the information given), the subtraction of context from dispositional attributions was no longer affected by load. Furthermore, Chun, Spiegel, and Kruglanski (2002) found that when the behaviour identification task was made more difficult (e.g., by decreasing the salience of the information given) it was also undermined by load. Under those conditions, too, invalidating the information on which the behavioural identifications were based did alter these identifications.

These findings are consistent with the present notion that, when a given inferential task (e.g., of "behaviour identification" or of "dispositional attribution") is sufficiently demanding, it is exigent of cognitive resources and can be undermined by load.

Base-rate neglect.   Earlier, we suggested that the judgemental impact of information depends on individuals appreciating its (subjective) relevance to the question at stake, and that such appreciation, in turn, depends on the relation between inferential task demands and processing resources. Jointly, these notions are capable of casting a new light on the problem of base-rate neglect, and on conditions under which statistical versus "heuristic" information may impact individuals' judgements.

In the original demonstrations of base-rate neglect (Kahneman & Tversky, 1973) the base-rate information was typically presented briefly, via a single sentence, and upfront. By contrast, the individuating ("representativeness") information was presented subsequently via a relatively lengthy vignette. If one assumes that participants in such studies had sufficient motivation and cognitive capacity to process the entire informational "package" with which they were presented, they might have been challenged to fully process the later, lengthier, and hence more demanding vignette information and to have given it considerable weight in the ultimate judgement. This is analogous to the finding in persuasion studies that the lengthier, later-appearing, message argument information but not the brief, upfront-appearing, "cue" information, has impact under ample processing resources (e.g., of high processing motivation and cognitive capacity). If the above is true, we should be able to "move" base-rate neglect around by reversing the relative length and ordinal position in the informational sequence of the base-rate and the individuating ("representativeness") information. A series of studies by Chun and Kruglanski (2006) attempted just that.

In our first study we replicated the typical lawyer–engineer paradigm (Kahneman & Tversky, 1973) in one condition by presenting brief and upfront base-rate information followed by lengthier individuating informa-tion. In another condition we reversed these relations by presenting brief individuating information first followed by lengthier and more complex base-rate information. To make the information complex and lengthy, the overall base-rate of lawyers was decomposed into base-rates of various sub-categories. For example, rather than being told that engineers made up 70% of the population and lawyers made up 30% of the population, participants were told that the population consisted of 14% electrical engineers, 6% chemical engineers, 9% divorce lawyers, 4% nuclear engineers, 10% civil engineers, 11% criminal lawyers, 12% sound engineers, 8% genetic engineers, 10% trade lawyers, and 16% mechanical engineers. As predicted, the former condition replicated the typical finding of base-rate neglect, whereas the latter condition revealed considerable base-rate utilisation.

A subsequent study added a manipulation of cognitive load in which participants rehearsed a nine-digit number while reading the information. As shown in Figure 8, the former results were now replicated in the low load condition, but were reversed in the high load condition. Under high cognitive load, when the base-rate information was presently briefly upfront, participants judged the likelihood of Dan being an engineer to be greater in the 70% engineer condition as compared to the 30% engineer condition. However, there was no significant difference between the two engineer conditions in the low cognitive load condition. This shows a use of the base-rate information while under load if the base-rates are easy to process. In contrast, when the base-rate information was lengthy and presented at the end, participants under load did not judge the likelihood of Dan being an engineer differently in the 70% as compared to the 30% condition. However, participants not under load did judge the likelihood of Dan being an engineer as significantly higher in the 70% condition as compared to the 30% condition. This demonstrates the use of base-rates when participants are not under load when the base-rates are difficult to process. Regardless of information type, under load the brief upfront information was utilised more than the lengthy subsequent information, whereas in the absence of load, the lengthy and subsequent information was utilised more.

To summarise then, evidence across domains (i.e., of persuasion, attribution, and judgement under uncertainty) supports the hypothesis that the higher the demands imposed by the inferential task at hand, the greater

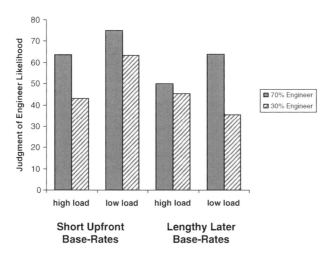

Figure 8. The effect of cognitive load, base-rate information, and difficulty of base-rate processing on likelihood estimation judgements (Chun & Kruglanski, 2006).

must be the processing resources if the information given is to exert judgemental impact commensurate with its potential relevance.

Relative relevance, task demands, and processing resources. Often the different types of information presented to research participants have (inadvertently) differed in their subjective relevance to these persons. For instance, in the domain of persuasion Pierro, Mannetti, Kruglanski, and Sleeth-Keppler (2004) carried out an extensive content analysis of experimental materials in persuasion studies to conclude that, typically, the "cues" presented to participants were judged as less relevant to the judgemental (attitudinal) topic than were the "message arguments". Recall that in much persuasion research the "cues" but not the "message arguments" exerted judgemental impact under low processing resources, whereas the "message arguments" did so under high processing resources. From the present perspective, it is possible to generalise these findings in terms of the following derivations:

(a) Given ample processing resources, the *more relevant* information (e.g., the "message arguments" in much persuasion research) would have a greater judgemental impact than the *less relevant* information; however (b) given limited processing resources (relative to the task demands) the *easier to process* information (of above threshold relevance) would have a greater judgemental impact than the *more difficult to process* information.

Pierro and colleagues (2004) tested these notions in three experimental studies based on the same research design in which (1) the relevance sequence (early information less relevant than subsequent information, or vice versa) and (2) processing motivation (high, low) were manipulated orthogonally. However, the studies differed in contents of the information given. In the first study, both the early and the later information consisted of message arguments; in the second study both consisted of heuristic information (namely, pertinent to the "consensus heuristic") and in the third study, contrary to the typical sequence in persuasion research, the early information consisted of message arguments and the later information, of heuristic cues (again regarding consensus).

All three experiments yielded the same general result: When the later, and hence the more difficult to process, information was more subjectively relevant to the judgemental topic than the early information, it exerted judgemental (persuasive impact) only under high motivation conditions but not under low motivation conditions. By contrast, the early, less relevant information exerted its effect only under low motivation but not under high motivation. A very different pattern obtained where the early information was more relevant than the latter information. Here the impact of the early information invariably overrode that of the later information: Under low processing motivation this may have been so because the earlier information was easier to process than the later information, and under high processing motivation—because the early information was in fact more relevant than the later information.

Metacognitive inferences: Ease versus content of retrieval.   In recent years social psychologists became increasingly interested in the problem of metacognitive inferences (for reviews see Jost, Kruglanski, & Nelson, 1998; Petty, Brinol, Tormala, & Wegener, 2007). One of the most researched metacognitive phenomena of social psychological interest has been the "ease of retrieval" effect in self-perception. The fascination with this phenomenon goes back to Tversky and Kahneman's (1973) classic work on the availability heuristic pertaining to the "ease with which instances or associations come to mind" (p. 208). In a well-known follow-up on Tversky and Kahneman's work, Schwarz et al. (1991) attempted to disentangle the experience of "ease" from the number of instances recovered because of the felt ease. For instance, in one of the Schwarz et al. (1991) studies participants were asked to retrieve either 6 or 12 instances of behaving assertively. Presumably it is easier to retrieve a few instances of a given behaviour than many instances. Hence, if ease of retrieval is responsible for the availability effect, participants should perceive themselves as more assertive after recalling 6 instances of assertive behaviour than after recalling 12 such instances. That is precisely what Schwarz et al. (1991) found, suggesting that the metacognitive experience of ease or fluency can serve as an important determinant of social judgements.

Following this seminal research, a variety of further studies sought to identify the boundary conditions for the ease of retrieval effect and to pinpoint the circumstances under which alternative sources of information (such as the content versus amount of retrieved information) would have a stronger judgemental effect than ease of retrieval (for reviews see Petty et al., 2007; Schwarz, 2004). Although a number of such boundary conditions were empirically identified, work on this topic stopped short of providing general theoretical understanding of circumstances under which a given information source (rather than its alternatives) would affect judgements. The unimodel affords such understanding. From its perspective, any contextually given information may affect judgements if it fits (as a minor premise) an inference rule (a major premise) to which an individual subscribes.

Support for this possibility was recently obtained in several experimental studies by Igou, Fishbach, and Kruglanski (2008). Specifically, this work demonstrated that the degree to which ease of retrieval versus the amount of instances retrieved affect social judgements depends on (1) the perceived validity of the inference rule linking *ease* of retrieval or the amount of instances retrieved to the corresponding trait, (2) saliency of the information concerning ease or amount of instances, and (3) accessibility of the ease = trait, and the amount = trait rules. For example, participants in one study were asked to rate the friendliness of targets based on the information provided. They were told that three people had been asked to recall instances in which they had been friendly. The information regarding the ease of retrieving relevant information, the amount of information retrieved, and the content of the retrieved information was manipulated. One target person ostensibly found recalling friendly behaviours to be either "easy" or "difficult", another either listed "many" or "only a few" behaviours, and the third recalled behaviours that were either "very friendly" or "only somewhat friendly". Participants rated the target person as friendlier in cases in which the target found it easy to recall behaviours, recalled many behaviours, or were very friendly. However, these differences were more pronounced (and were statistically significant only) when the critical pieces of information were underlined in the text, making the relevant piece of information salient.

Conclusions. Growing evidence from a variety of domains (persuasion, attribution, judgement under uncertainty, person perception) supports the unimodel's derivations that the subjective relevance of information determines its impact on judgements, that the appreciation of subjective relevance depends on the relation between task demands and (cognitive and motivational) resources, and that as a function of resources information may affect judgements either in accordance with its relative relevance or with its relative ease of processing.

Focusing on the concept of "evidence" highlighted by lay epistemic theory affords an integration of a large set of dual-process models of social judgements that assumed binary, qualitatively distinct, modes of processing. Such integration is achieved by highlighting the critical importance of several judgemental parameters in determining the impact of the information given on individuals' judgements and impressions, and by separating (both conceptually and empirically) the values of such parameters (e.g., information's degree of subjective relevance, or experienced difficulty of processing) from informational contents with which they were often confounded in prior research (for a more extensive discussion see Kruglanski et al., 2007).

Epistemic authority: The "who" of epistemic behaviour

According to lay epistemic theory the construct of evidence functions in the same way (i.e., syllogistically) irrespective of the specific contents of evidence. This doesn't mean, however, that all types of evidence have equal status. Different individuals may hold different assumptions about the conditional (if … then) relations between conceptual categories; hence they may differ in what to them constitutes compelling evidence for a given proposition. For an expert car mechanic an unusual noise emanating from the engine may compellingly signal a problem with the carburettor, whereas for a mechanically inexperienced individual this particular noise may have little informative value. In general, people's "evidential" assumptions in specific domains may vary widely depending on their background knowledge. Because people's concerns typically extend beyond their domains of expertise they may often rely on other people as knowledge providers. Thus a broad category of evidence refers to other people's opinions and is denoted by lay epistemic theory's construct of *epistemic authority* (Kruglanski, 1989; Kruglanski et al., 2005), that is, to a source on whom an individual turns to obtain knowledge on various topics (Kruglanski, 1989). In other words, individuals may subscribe to general "if X then Y" rules in which the antecedent X denotes a given epistemic authority, e.g., of an expert ("If Expert says so then it is Correct"), the group ("If the Group believes so, then it is Correct"), or the self ("If I believe so, then it is Correct").

The concept of "epistemic authority" is akin to the notion of *source credibility* (encompassing a combination of perceived expertise and trustworthiness) and it addresses the extent to which an individual is prepared to rely on a source's information and to accept it as evidence for the veracity of the source's pronouncements. The ascribed epistemic authority of various sources in the individuals' social environments may vary and the authority of a given source may vary across domains as well as across individuals' life-span developmental phases.

The features that identify a source as an epistemic authority can be *general*, having to do with seniority (for example, of an elder), a role (for example, of a priest, a leader or a teacher), level of education (for example, a PhD), appearance in print (for example, in a book or a newspaper), or *specific*, as in assigning epistemic authority to a particular person, or a particular newspaper (say, the *New York Times*).

Furthermore, a source may exert influence in numerous life domains, serving as a *generalized epistemic authority*; alternatively, it may influence only a specific area (for example, cardiology, statistics, or auto mechanics) where it is thought to possess valid knowledge. In the former role we may find priests, therapists, or parents, whereas in the latter role we may find specialists in certain well-defined fields. Individuals may differ widely in their reliance on various epistemic authorities and in their extent of such reliance across domains. Some people may accept the judgement of a source (a rabbi, a priest, a psychiatrist, or a teacher) in any life domain; others may consult a source with regard to matters related to its specific domain of competence, and to consult other sources in alternative life domains.

Source characteristics (such as expertise) were often implied to offer somewhat inferior counsel as to correct judgements, and were treated as suboptimal heuristics used only when one's processing resources were depleted and when one's "sufficiency threshold" of required confidence was low (Chaiken, Liberman, & Eagly, 1989). In contrast, according to the present theory epistemic authority of some sources (e.g., a religious prophet, a parent, a political leader, or the printed word) might be extremely powerful, often to the point of overriding other types of information and exerting a determinative influence on individuals' judgements and corresponding behaviours. Furthermore, whereas in prior treatments of source credibility effects, the discussion centred on sources *external* to the self (cf. Chaiken et al., 1989; Hovland, Janis, & Kelley, 1953; Kruglanski & Thompson, 1999a, 1999b; Petty & Cacioppo, 1986), the present theory considers the *self* as a particularly important target of epistemic authority assignments.

Research summarised in the paper by Kruglanski et al. (2005) has revealed (1) developmental trends involving a decline in authority assigned to the primary caregivers, coupled with an increase in epistemic authority attributed to the *self*, and involving an increase in differentiation and specificity of epistemic authorities across domains; (2) stable individual differences in epistemic authority effects; (3) a hierarchical structure and operation of epistemic authorities; (4) the relative role of the self and external sources as perceived epistemic authorities.

Developmental trends

Raviv, Bar-Tal, Raviv, and Houminer (1990) assessed children's attribution of epistemic authority to their *mothers, fathers, teachers,* and *friends.* They investigated kindergarten children (4–5-year-olds), first graders (6–7 years old), and third graders (8–9 years old). Several significant trends appeared in these data, yielding the following pattern of interest: during childhood (i.e., during the ages 4–10), (a) the perception of parents as epistemic authorities remains relatively stable, with decreases in a few knowledge areas, (b) the perception of the teacher as an epistemic authority remains stable with an increase in the area of science, (c) the perceived epistemic authority of friends increases in the social domain.

Raviv et al. (1990) also found that across age groups the perception of teachers and friends varied more as a function of knowledge areas than the perception of parents. The children selected teachers and friends as epistemic authorities in certain knowledge areas only, whereas the parents tended to be perceived as overall authorities across domains, possibly as a function of continued material dependence on the parents inducing a motivation to view them as all powerful and knowledgeable.

Individual differences in the distribution of epistemic authority assignments across sources

Individuals differ systematically in their distributional profiles of epistemic authority across sources: these differences, in turn, affect individuals' search for, and use of, information. Bar (1983) devised a Hierarchy of Epistemic Authorities Test designed to investigate the epistemic authority assigned by Israeli college students to various sources. This test revealed intriguing gender differences in epistemic authority assignments. In domains prototypically classified as masculine (such as work and finances) women viewed their *peer group* as a more dominant epistemic authority than did men, whereas in domains prototypically classified as feminine (social life, interpersonal relations, children's education) men endowed their *peer group* with greater epistemic authority than did women. Possibly then, where one's own epistemic authority is low (as may be the case for men in the feminine domains, and for women in masculine domains) one's reference group gains in epistemic authoritativeness as compared with domains where one's self ascribed epistemic authority is high.

The hierarchical organization of epistemic authorities. In Bar's (1983) research individuals' epistemic authorities predicted these people's behaviour in an "information-purchasing" task: Participants were willing to pay greater amounts of (hypothetical) money for information from their highest (domain-specific) authority than for information from lower epistemic authorities. This and other findings suggest the hierarchic organisation of epistemic authorities. Bar (1983, 1999) found that individuals turn first to information provided by sources whom they regard as highest in epistemic authority, that they process such information more extensively, that they derive from it greater confidence, and that they tend more to act in accordance with its perceived implications.

Bar (1999, Study 2) also inquired whether epistemic authority effects might not represent the workings of heuristic cues relied upon only in the absence of sufficient processing resources. To that end, Bar superimposed on her product choice procedure orthogonal manipulations of time pressure (high versus low) and evaluation apprehension (high versus low). Contrary to the suboptimal heuristics hypothesis the foregoing effects held across variations in time pressure and evaluation apprehension: Regardless of the presence/absence of time pressure and/or of evaluation apprehension participants (1) tended to first open the window on a PC pertaining to their dominant (versus non-dominant) epistemic authority, (2) were more confident in their decisions if those were based on the recommendations of a dominant (vs a non-dominant) epistemic authority, and (3) tended to spend more time on information contained in a "window" belonging to their dominant (vs non-dominant) epistemic authority. These results argue against the notion that epistemic authority functions merely as a "peripheral" or "heuristic" cue that affords low confidence and is used only when individuals' processing resources or motivational engagement are low.

Effects of self-ascribed epistemic authority: External information search under need for closure.   A unique aspect of the epistemic authority construct is that it treats identically the *self* and *external sources* of information. Indeed, several recent studies looked at informational effects as a function of the self-ascribed epistemic authority. In one such study, Pierro and Mannetti (2004, cited in Kruglanski et al., 2005) measured the strength of individuals' self-ascribed epistemic authority in the highly specialised domain of cell phones. To that end, they constructed a 13-item scale including questions such as "I truly have considerable knowledge about different types of cell phones", "I can say a great many things about technical specs of different cell phones", "I can offer people useful advice regarding the purchase of a cell phone". Pierro and Mannetti (2004) also assessed their participants' dispositional need for cognitive closure. The main dependent variable of interest was participants' readiness to search for information from external sources in case they entertained the purchase of a cell phone. It was found that the higher the individuals' *self-ascribed epistemic authority* in a domain, the less external information they purported to seek.

Of greater interest, the tendency to seek external information was moderated by the need for cognitive closure. For individuals with low self-ascribed epistemic authority, the higher their need for closure, the stronger their tendency to engage in an external information search. For individuals with high self-ascribed epistemic authority, the higher their need for closure, the lower their tendency to engage in an external search, and presumably the higher their tendency to rely on their own experience and experts. In other words, under the pressure for cognitive closure individuals are forced to choose, and to discriminate more acutely between their various epistemic authorities in selecting the source they trust the most.

Self-ascribed epistemic authority and learning from experience.   Among the most interesting implications of the epistemic authority construct are those concerning *learning from experience*. The concept of "experience" has long been privileged in psychological theory. The use of experiential learning in training and education has been inspired by John Dewey's (1916, 1958) instructional philosophy, Carl Rogers' (1951, 1967) person-centred approach to therapy, and humanistic psychology more generally (e.g., Shafer, 1978). In social psychology, Fazio and Zanna (1981) suggested that attitudes acquired via direct experience with the attitude object are the strongest, and most tightly related to behaviour. Yet these authors also hinted at the possibility of *moderators* that qualify the power of experience in shaping attitudes. As they put it (Fazio & Zanna, 1981, p. 184):

> An attitude formed by indirect means could conceivably also be held with extreme confidence, and, hence, be more predictive of behaviour than a direct experience attitude. For example, a child's attitude towards members of a given ethnic or racial group may be held with great confidence, even though formed indirectly because of his or her parents' extreme credibility.

This quote suggests that experience *may not* constitute a superior base of knowledge under all conditions. Yet Fazio and Zanna (1981) stop short of identifying the conditions under which direct experience will be less capable of shaping attitudes. The concept of self-ascribed epistemic authority may be helpful in this regard.

From this perspective, whether or not an individual would treat her or his personal experience as a reliable knowledge base may depend on this person's self-ascribed capability to draw reliable conclusions from the experience, or on her or his self-ascribed epistemic authority in a domain. In absence of such authority a person may fail to draw confident knowledge from the experience. An individual may speak English all her life without deriving the principles of English grammar from this experience; she may drink a wide range of wines over the years without forming notions about the different varietals or vintages; or play tennis on a weekly basis without forming notions about the proper strokes, strategies, and tactics of this game.

Our analysis suggests that the extent to which individuals tend to draw confident conclusions from any type of information is related to their assignment of authority to the information source. When the information consists of one's own experience, the source simply is oneself. In these circumstances, the higher one's self-ascribed epistemic authority, the more readily one may trust one's own interpretation of information, and the more one might be able to "benefit" from the experience. However, when the information is interpreted by an external communicator (e.g., a teacher or a parent), the individual's tendency to accept the interpretation may partially depend on the perceived gap in epistemic authority between the source and the self. When the authority imputed to the source is considerably higher than that imputed to the self, the source's pronouncements are likely to be attended closely and/or be assigned considerable weight. However, when the assigned authorities are more nearly equal, the source's statements might not be taken as seriously because of a sense that there is little the source could contribute over and above one's own ability to process the information.

In other words, a "reverence effect" may be expected whereby pronouncements by an external source will have greater impact on persons whose perceived *authority gap* between themselves and the source is large rather than small. In a study designed to investigate these notions, Ellis and

Kruglanski (1992) assessed their participants' self-ascribed epistemic authority in mathematics via a questionnaire specifically designed for this purpose. Participants also responded to the numerical aptitude test (Cattell & Epstein, 1975) to serve as a control measure for their actual maths ability, and they filled out a post-experimental questionnaire designed to assess their perceptions of their own and the instructor's epistemic authority in mathematics.

The mathematical learning task employed in this research consisted of multiplication problems in which some numbers were replaced by letters. The participants' task was to substitute the numbers for the letters. These substitutions were carried out in accordance with five arithmetic rules that participants needed to learn in the course of the experiment. Participants were randomly assigned to one of three experimental conditions: In the *experiential* condition they were given self-instruction booklets with exercises related to the five arithmetic rules. In the *instructional-principles* condition the experimenter was introduced as a PhD in mathematics, and he explicitly articulated the relevant mathematical principles. In the intermediate, *instructional-examples*, condition the instructor solved the problems on the board *and* stated the arithmetic principle underlying each solution.

Following these procedures, participants took a performance test on the principles they had just been taught. Participants in the two instructional conditions were additionally asked to estimate the gap in ability between themselves and the instructor. The results of this research indicated that method of instruction significantly interacted with participants' self ascribed epistemic authority (SAEA). The results are shown in Figure 9. Controlling for participants' actual mathematical ability, in the *experiential* condition participants with a high SAEA did significantly better than participants with a low SAEA. In the *instructional principles* condition the low SAEA

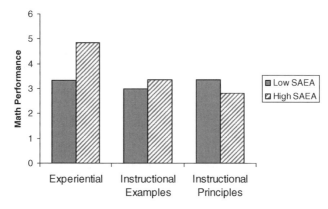

Figure 9. The effect of self-ascribed epistemic authority (SAEA) and instructional condition on maths performance (Ellis & Kruglanski, 1992).

participants tended to do better than their high SAEA counterparts, and in the intermediate, *instructional-examples* condition the high and low SAEA participants did not differ in their performance.

In the two instructional conditions participants with a high SAEA perceived the gap between their own and the instructor's ability as significantly lower than did participants with a low SAEA. Of greater interest, in both instructional conditions participants who perceived a large gap between themselves and the instructor did better in both instructional conditions than participants who perceived a smaller gap. A large gap indicates that the source's relative epistemic authority (compared to one's own) is considerable. This may turn the recipient into a "true believer", enhancing her or his readiness to accept the source's conclusions.

These findings identify an important boundary condition on the efficacy of experience as a mediator of learning. It appears that in order to be able to learn from experience individuals need to believe in their ability to draw inferences from the experience; that is, possess high self-ascribed epistemic authority in a domain. It is of particular interest that self-ascribed epistemic authority is empirically distinct from actual ability in a domain. In the study described here the correlation between the two, though significant, was relatively low ($r = .36$), and the interaction between SAEA and method of instruction remained significant, even after controlling for actual mathematical ability. Finally, it is of interest that in the instructional learning conditions participants whose perceived gap between own and instructor's ability was large (vs small) did significantly better at the mathematical learning task, attesting to a "reverence effect" whereby the impact of an external source is greater if its authority is high relative to one's own perceived authority.

Summary. Although according to lay epistemic theory all evidence functions in the same (syllogistic) manner, the evidence category subsumed under the notion of epistemic authority is special in a number of respects. It represents the fundamental notion that human knowledge is socially constructed and that it is heavily influenced by the opinions of significant others whose judgements one holds in high regard. It also touches on the *developmental aspect* of knowledge construction, the liberation of one's knowledge formation processes from reliance on a limited number of primary care givers, the evolution of epistemic self-reliance, and the diversification of one's array of information sources in accordance with their perceived domains of expertise. The concept of epistemic authority also acknowledges that individuals (as well as groups) may exhibit relatively stable differences in their hierarchy of epistemic authorities, which determines who they will turn to for information and advice, and on whose recommendations they will act. Finally, this concept suggests that individuals' tendency to independently process domain-specific information on a topic may be a function of a *gap* between their own self-ascribed epistemic authority and the perceived authority of a given communication source.

INTEGRATING THE WHY, HOW, AND WHO
OF LAY EPISTEMICS

The three research programmes inspired by the lay epistemic theory illuminate distinct aspects of knowledge formation. The need for closure programme focused on the *motivational underpinnings* of the process. The unimodel programme addressed the mechanism of justifying (or "proving") one's judgements and conclusions via the appropriate *evidence* and the psychological process that permits the information given to become such evidence. Finally, the epistemic authority programme addressed the essential *meta-cognitive*, *developmental*, and *differential* aspects of knowledge formation that determine how individuals function in their informational ecologies to form their opinions and attitudes.

It is of interest to consider how the three categories of process embodied by the foregoing research programmes interface, and what implications follow from their possible interrelations. The need for closure (representing the "why" of epistemic behaviour) represents a desire for firm knowledge. In turn, firm knowledge requires a firm inferential basis; that is, availability in memory of firmly believed-in rules or major premises to which situationally present information may be fitted, functioning as minor premises (representing the "how" of epistemic behaviour). It follows that, under high need for closure, individuals may be more likely *to form* such rules, as well as have a chronically accessible variety of general, "all-purpose" rules (or "heuristics") that they can use across a broad spectrum of situations.

Consistent with this logic, Dechesne and Wigboldus (2008) recently discovered that individuals high in need for closure are especially prone to form rules or notice systematic patterns even when not explicitly instructed to do so. Participants in the experiment were instructed to use designated keys on the keyboard to indicate as quickly and accurately as possible whether an A or a B appeared on a computer screen. The experiment consisted of 280 trials. Importantly, the As and the Bs appeared in a fixed order of ABBABAB. Awareness of this pattern, and its use as a rule, facilitates responding to upcoming stimuli. A reduction in response latencies over time can thus be interpreted as a manifestation of a stronger tendency to form and use inferential rules to respond to situational demands. To the extent that high (vs low) need for closure fosters the motivation to form and use rules, a more pronounced reduction of response latencies over time was expected to occur among high (vs low) need for closure participants. That is precisely what was found. As shown in Figure 10, downward trends in response latencies significantly covaried with the need for closure, such that higher need for closure was associated with a more pronounced trend in the

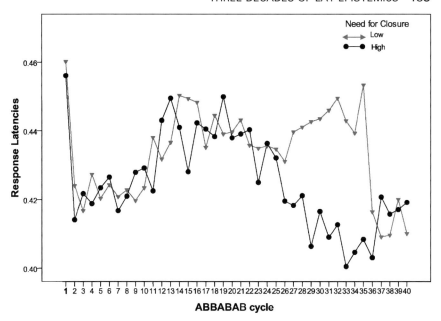

Figure 10. The effect of ABBABAB cycle and need for closure on response latencies (Dechesne & Wigboldus, 2008).

downward direction. Admittedly, the Dechesne and Wigboldus (2008) results could be due to motivated attention to the stimuli, rather than the tendency to form rules as such. Further studies (currently under way) are needed to explore in a more comprehensive manner the hypothesised rule-forming proclivity of high need for closure individuals.

It also seems plausible that high (vs low) need for closure individuals should subscribe to beliefs about general, all-purpose, epistemic authorities. A unique such authority is one's own self. Consistent with this notion, high (vs low) need for closure individuals have been consistently reporting higher confidence in their judgements, possibly reflecting a high self-ascribed epistemic authority, attesting to reliance on the "I am generally right" or "If it is my judgement, then it is correct" heuristic (Kruglanski, 2004). Moreover, considerable evidence reviewed earlier attests to group-centric tendencies under heightened need for closure (Kruglanski et al., 2006). A major aspect of group-centrism is the quest for consensus, or the "group is right" heuristic; that is, "if my group believes it, then it is correct" heuristic. There is also evidence that individuals under high need for closure prefer an autocratic or hierarchical decision-making structure, possibly reflecting the bestowal of epistemic authority on anointed experts, or operation of the "experts are correct" heuristic ("if expert, then correct"). In this sense the heightened confidence, the group-centric tendencies, and the autocratic orientations observed under high need for closure may all represent a reliance on broad, "all-purpose" rules affording a general inferential base for knowledge formation. Finally, as findings of Pierro and Mannetti (2004) suggest, under a heightened need for closure individuals may sharpen their discrimination between various epistemic authorities and come to rely more fully on their *dominant* epistemic authority, occupying the top of their epistemic hierarchy.

In short, the three research programmes based on the lay epistemic theory interlock in significant ways. Because knowledge is based on evidence, and evidence reflects an operation of "If Then" inferential rules, individuals who are particularly motivated to have stable knowledge (i.e., those with an elevated need for closure) may quickly construct such rules from contingency information. Because general inferential heuristics may afford quick formation of knowledge across diverse content domains, individuals with a high need for closure may be particularly prone to bestow domain-general epistemic authority on various agents including themselves.

Understanding these interrelated epistemic processes and their representation in real-world circumstances where knowledge formation may assume heightened psychological importance promises to offer new insights into a variety of social problems besetting contemporary societies. For instance, it would be of considerable interest to consider how uncertainty promoted by economic and political turmoil may elevate whole populations' need for cognitive closure, and how such need, in turn, might lead to group-centrism and derogation of (and readiness to engage in violence against) outgroups, as well as fostering the readiness to embrace fundamentalist, closure-affording, ideologies and epistemic authorities. In our own work we have found that exposure of participants to an uncertainty-evoking event, recall of the 9/11 attack on the Twin Towers in New York, elevated individuals need for cognitive closure, and that need for closure increased participants' tendencies toward ingroup favouritism, and outgroup derogation, as well as the positive evaluation of decisive and consistent ("staying on course") leaders and negative evaluation of open-minded and flexible ("flip flopper") ones (Orehek et al., 2007). Applying the theory of lay epistemics to major real-world phenomena constitutes an exciting challenge for future generations of research on knowledge formation processes, with significant contribution potential to policy in broad domains of endeavour.

REFERENCES

Abelson, R. P. (1968). Psychological implication. In R. P. Abelson, E. Aronson, W. J. McGuire, T. M. Newcomb, M. J. Rosenberg, & R. H. Tannenbaum (Eds.), *Theories of cognitive consistency: A sourcebook* (pp. 112–139). Chicago: Rand McNally.

Andersen, S. M., & Cole, S. W. (1990). "Do I know you?" The role of significant others in general social perception. *Journal of Personality and Social Psychology, 59,* 384–399.

Andersen, S. M., Glassman, N. S., Chen, S., & Cole, S. W. (1995). Transference in social perception: The role of chronic accessibility in significant-other representations. *Journal of Personality and Social Psychology, 69,* 41–57.

Anderson, J. R. (1983). *The structure of cognition.* Cambridge, MA: Harvard University Press.

Baeyens, F., Crombez, G., Van den Bergh, O., & Eelen, P. (1988). Once in contact always in contact: Evaluative conditioning is resistant to extinction. *Advances in Behaviour Research and Therapy, 10,* 179–199.

Bar, R. (1983). *Hierarchy of Epistemic Authority Test.* Unpublished Master's thesis, Tel-Aviv University.

Bar, R. (1999). *The impact of epistemic needs and authorities on judgement and decision making.* Unpublished doctoral dissertation, Tel Aviv University.

Bar-Tal, D. (1990). *Group beliefs: A conception for analyzing group structure, processes, and behaviour.* New York: Springer-Verlag.

Bar-Tal, D. (2000). *Shared beliefs in a society: A social psychological analysis.* Thousand Oaks, CA: Sage Publications, Inc.

Bartlett, F. C. (1932). *Remembering: A study in experimental and social psychology.* New York: Cambridge University Press.

Boudreau, L. A., Baron, R. M., & Oliver, P. V. (1992). Effects of expected communication target expertise and timing of set on trait use in person description. *Journal of Personality and Social Psychology, 18,* 447–451.

Brewer, M. B. (1988). A dual process model of impression formation. In T. K. Srull & R. S. Wyer (Eds.), *Advances in social cognition* (Vol. 1, pp. 1–36). Hillsdale, NJ: Lawrence Erlbaum Associates Inc.

Bruner, J. S. (1973). *Beyond the information given: Studies in the psychology of knowing.* Oxford, UK: Norton.

Cattell, R. B., & Epstein, A. R. (1975). *Comprehensive ability battery.* Champaign, IL: Institute for Personality and Ability Testing.

Chaiken, S., Liberman, A., & Eagly, A. H. (1989). Heuristic and systematic information processing within and beyond the persuasion context. In J. S. Uleman & J. A. Bargh (Eds.), *Unintended thought.* New York: Guilford Press.

Chaiken, S., & Trope, Y. (1999). *Dual process theories in social psychology.* New York: Guilford Press.

Chirumbolo, A. (2002). The relationship between need for cognitive closure and political orientation: The mediating role of authoritarianism. *Personality and Individual Differences, 32,* 603–610.

Chirumbolo, A., Areni, A., & Sensales, G. (2004). Need for closure and politics: Voting, political attitudes and attributional style. *International Journal of Psychology, 39,* 245–253.

Chirumbolo, A., & Leone, L. (2008). Individual differences in need for closure and voting behaviour. *Personality and Individual Differences, 44,* 1279–1288.

Chun W. Y., & Kruglanski, A. W. (2006). The role of task demands and processing resources in the use of base-rate and individuating information. *Journal of Personality and Social Psychology, 91,* 205–217.

Chun, W. Y., Spiegel, S., & Kruglanski, A. W. (2002). Assimilative behaviour identification can also be resource dependent: A unimodel perspective on personal-attribution phases. *Journal of Personality and Social Psychology, 83,* 542–555.

Dechesne, M., Schultz, J. M., Kruglanski, A. W., Orehek, E., & Fishman, S. (2008). *A psychology of borders: Need for closure and the allure of group impermeability.* Unpublished Manuscript, University of Maryland, MD, USA.

Dechesne, M., & Wigboldus, D. (2008). Unpublished data. University of Nijmegen, The Netherlands.

DeDreu, C. K. V., & Koole, S. L. (1997). *Motivated use of heuristics in negotiation.* Unpublished raw data.

DeDreu, C. K. W., Koole, S. L., & Oldersma, F. L. (1999). On the seizing and freezing of negotiator inferences: Need for cognitive closure moderates the use of heuristics in negotiation. *Personality and Social Psychology Bulletin, 25,* 348–362.

De Grada, E., Kruglanski, A. W., Mannetti, L., & Pierro, A. (1999). Motivated cognition and group interaction: Need for closure affects the contents and processes of collective negotiations. *Journal of Experimental Social Psychology, 35,* 346–365.

Dewey, J. (1916). *Democracy and education.* New York: Free Press.

Dewey, J. (1958). *Experience and nature.* New York: Collier Macmillan.

Dijksterhuis, A. P., Van Knippenberg, A. D., Kruglanski, A. W., & Schaper, C. (1996). Motivated social cognition: Need for closure effects on memory and judgement. *Journal of Experimental Social Psychology, 32,* 254–270.

Ellis, S., & Kruglanski, A. W. (1992). Self as epistemic authority: Effects on experiential and instructional learning. *Social Cognition, 10,* 357–375.

Erb, H. P., Kruglanski, A. W., Chun, W. Y., Pierro, A., Mannetti, L., & Spiegel, S. (2003). Searching for commonalities in human judgement: The parametric unimodel and its dual mode alternatives. In W. Stroebe & M. Hewstone (Eds.), *European review of social psychology* (Vol. 14, pp. 1–47). Hove, UK: Psychology Press.

Evans, J. St. B. T. (1989). *Bias in human reasoning: Causes and consequences.* Hove, UK: Lawrence Erlbaum Associates Ltd.

Fazio, R. H. (1990). Multiple processes by which attitudes guide behavior: The MODE model as an integrative framework. In M. P. Zanna (Ed.), *Advances in experimental social psychology* (Vol. 23, pp. 75–109). New York: Academic Press.

Fazio, R. H., & Zanna, M. P. (1981). Direct experience and attitude–behaviour consistency. In L. Berkowitz (Ed.), *Advances in experimental social psychology.* (Vol. 14, pp. 161–203). New York: Academic Press.

Fiske, S. T., & Neuberg, S. L. (1990). A continuum model of impression formation, from category-based to individuating processes: Influences of information and motivation on attention and interpretation. In M. P. Zanna (Ed.), *Advances in experimental social psychology* (Vol. 23, pp. 1–74). New York: Academic Press.

Ford, T. E., & Kruglanski, A. W. (1995). Effects of epistemic motivations on the use of accessible constructs in social judgements. *Personality and Social Psychology Bulletin, 21,* 950–962.

Freud, A. (1965). *Normality and pathology in childhood: Assessments of development.* New York: International Universities Press.

Freund, T., Kruglanski, A., & Schpitzajzen, A. (1985). The freezing and unfreezing of impressional primacy: Effects of the need for structure and the fear of invalidity. *Personality and Social Psychology Bulletin, 11,* 479–487.

Gawronski, B., & Bodenhausen, G. V. (2006). Associative and propositional processes in evaluation: An integrative review of implicit and explicit attitude change. *Psychological Bulletin, 132,* 692–731.

Gelfand, M. (2008). *Situated culture: A multilevel analysis of situational constraint across 35 nations.* Paper presented at the Social Psychology Winter Conference, Park City, Utah.

Gregory, R. L. (1997). *Eye and brain: The psychology of seeing* (5th ed.). Princeton, NJ: Princeton University Press.

Hardin, C. D., & Higgins, E. T. (1996). Shared reality: How social verification makes the subjective objective. In R. M. Sorrentino & E. T. Higgins (Eds.), *Handbook of motivation and cognition* (Vol. 3, pp. 28–84). New York: Guilford Press.

Helmholtz, H. v. (1910/2000). *Helmholtz's treatise on physiological optics*. Bristol, UK: Themmes Press.

Hempel, C. (1965). *Aspects of scientific explanation and other essays in the philosophy of science*. New York: Free Press.

Hempel, C., & Oppenheim, P. (1948). Studies in the logic of explanation. *Philosophy of Science*, *15*, 135–175. [Reprinted in Hempel (1965), pp. 245–290.].

Higgins, E. T. (1996). Knowledge activation: Accessibility, applicability and salience. In E. T. Higgins & A. W. Kruglanski (Eds.), *Social psychology: Handbook of basic principles*. (pp. 133–168). New York: Guilford Press.

Hilton, D. (2007). Causal explanation: From social perception to knowledge-based causal attribution. In A. W. Kruglanski & E. T. Higgins (Eds.), *Social psychology: A handbook of basic principles* (Vol. 2). New York: Guilford Press.

Holyoak, K. J., Kohl, K., & Nisbett, R. E. (1989). A theory of conditioned reasoning: Inductive learning within rule-based hierarchies. *Psychological Review*, *96*, 315–340.

Hovland, C. I., Janis, I. L., & Kelley, H. H. (1953). *Communication and persuasion*. Newhaven, CT: Yale University Press.

Igou, E. R., Fishbach, A., & Kruglanski, A. W. (20080. *An epistemic analysis of retrieval effects on judgement*. Unpublished manuscript, Tilburg University.

James, W. (1890). *The principles of psychology*. New York: Henry Colt & Co.

Jamieson, D. W., & Zanna, M. P. (1989). Need for structure in attitude formation and expression. In A. R. Pratkanis, S. J. Breckler, & A. G. Greenwald (Eds.), *Attitude structure and function*. Hillsdale, NJ: Lawrence Erlbaum Associates Inc.

Jost, J. T., Glaser, J., Kruglanski, A. W., & Sullaway, F. J. (2003a). Political conservatism as motivated social cognition. *Psychological Bulletin*, *129*, 339–375.

Jost, J. T., Glaser, J., Kruglanski, A. W., & Sullaway, F. J. (2003b). Exceptions that prove the rule: Using a theory of motivated social cognition to account for ideological incongruities and political anomalies. *Psychological Bulletin*, *129*, 383–393.

Jost, J. T., Kruglanski, A. W., & Nelson, T. T. O. (1998). Social metacognition: An expansionist review. *Personality and Social Psychology Review*, *2*, 137–154.

Kahneman, D. (2003). A perspective on judgement and choice: Mapping bounded rationality. *American Psychologist*, *58*, 697–720.

Kahneman, D., & Tversky, A. (1973). On the psychology of prediction. *Psychological Review*, *80*, 237–251.

Kosic, A., Kruglanski, A. W., Pierro, A., & Mannetti, L. (2004). Social cognition of immigrants' acculturation: Effects of the need for closure and the reference group at entry. *Journal of Personality and Social Psychology*, *86*, 796–813.

Kruglanski, A. (1980). Lay epistemologic process and contents: Another look at attribution theory. *Psychological Review*, *87*, 70–87.

Kruglanski, A., & Freund, T. (1983). The freezing and un-freezing of lay-inferences: Effects on impressional primacy, ethnic stereotyping and numerical anchoring. *Journal of Experimental Social Psychology*, *19*, 448–468.

Kruglanski, A. W. (1989). *Lay epistemics and human knowledge: Cognitive and motivational bases*. New York: Plenum.

Kruglanski, A. W. (2004). *The psychology of closed mindedness*. New York: Psychology Press.

Kruglanski, A. W., Erb, H. P., Pierro, A., Mannetti, L., & Chun. W. Y. (2006a). On parametric continuities in the world of binary either ors [target article]. *Psychological Inquiry*, *17*, 153–165.

Kruglanski, A. W., & Orehek, E. (2007). Partitioning the domain of social inference: Dual mode and systems models and their alternatives. *Annual Review of Psychology*, *58*, 291–316.

Kruglanski, A. W., Pierro, A., Mannetti, L., & DeGrada, E. (2006b). Groups as epistemic providers: Need for closure and the unfolding of group-centrism. *Psychological Review*, *113*, 84–100.

Kruglanski, A. W., Pierro, A., Mannetti, L., Erb, H. P., & Chun, W. Y. (2007). On the parameters of social judgement. In M. P. Zanna (Ed.), *Advances in experimental social psychology* (Vol. 39, pp. 255–296). New York: Academic Press.

Kruglanski, A. W., Raviv, A., Bar-Tal, D., Raviv, A., Sharvit, K., Ellis, S., et al. (2005). Says who? Epistemic authority effects in social judgement. In M. P. Zanna (Ed.), *Advances in experimental social psychology* (Vol. 37, pp. 345–392). New York: Academic Press.

Kruglanski, A. W., Shah, J. Y., Pierro, A., & Mannetti, L. (2002). When similarity breeds content: Need for closure and the allure of homogeneous and self-resembling groups. *Journal of Personality and Social Psychology, 83,* 648–662.

Kruglanski, A. W., & Thomson, E. P. (1999a). Persuasion by a single route: A view from the unimodel. *Psychological Inquiry, 10,* 83–109.

Kruglanski, A. W., & Thomson, E. P. (1999b). The illusory second mode or, the cue is the message. *Psychological Inquiry, 10,* 182–193.

Kruglanski, A. W., Thomson, E. P., & Spiegel, S. (1999). Separate or equal?: Bimodal notions of persuasion and a single process "unimodel". In S. Chaiken & Y. Trope (Eds.), *Dual-process theories in social psychology* (pp. 293–313). New York: Guilford Press.

Kruglanski, A. W., & Webster, D. M. (1991). Group members' reactions to opinion deviates and conformists at varying degrees of proximity to decision deadline and of environmental noise. *Journal of Personality and Social Psychology, 61,* 212–225.

Kruglanski, A. W., & Webster, D. M. (1996). Motivated closing of the mind: "Seizing" and "freezing". *Psychological Review, 103,* 263–283.

Kruglanski, A. W., Webster, D. M., & Klem, A. (1993). Motivated resistance and openness to persuasion in the presence or absence of prior information. *Journal of Personality and Social Psychology, 65,* 861–876.

Livi, S. (2003). *Il bisogno di chiusura cognitiva e la transmissione delle norme nei piccoli gruppi.* [The need for cognitive closure and normtransmission in small groups]. Unpublished doctoral dissertation, University of Rome "La Sapienza", Italy.

Logan, G. D. (1992). Attention and preattention in theories of automaticity. *American Journal of Psychology, 105,* 317–339.

Maio, G. R., & Haddock, G. G. (2007). Attitude change. In A. W. Kruglanski & E. T. Higgins (Eds.), *Social psychology: Handbook of basic principles* (2nd ed., pp. 565–586). New York: Guilford Press.

Mischel, W., & Shoda, Y. (1995). A cognitive-affective system theory of personality: Reconceptualizing situations, dispositions, dynamics, and invariance in personality structure. *Psychological Review, 102,* 246–268.

Mitchell, C. J., De Houwer, J., & Lovibond, P. F. (in press). The propositional nature of human associative learning. *Behavioural and Brain Sciences.*

Newell, A., & Simon, H. A. (1972). *Human problem solving.* Englewood Cliffs, NJ: Prentice Hall.

Newman, L. S., & Uleman, J. S. (1989). Spontaneous trait inference. In J. S. Uleman & J. A. Bargh (Eds.), *Unintended thought.* New York: Guilford Press.

Orehek, E., Fishman, S., Dechesne, M., Doosje, B., Kruglanski, A. W., Cole, A. P., et al. (2007). *Certainty quest and the social response to terrorism.* Unpublished manuscript. University of Maryland.

Petty, R. E., & Cacioppo, J. T. (1986). The elaboration likelihood model of persuasion. In L. Berkowitz (Ed.), *Advances in experimental social psychology* (Vol. 19, pp. 123–205). San Diego, CA: Academic Press.

Petty, R. E., Brinol, P., Tormala, Z. L., & Wegener, D. T. (2007). The role of metacognition in social judgement. In A. Kruglanski & E. T. Higgins (Eds.), *Social psychology: A handbook of basic principles.* New York: Guilford Press.

Petty, R. E., & Wegener, D. T. (1999). The elaboration likelihood model: Current status and controversies. In S. Chaiken & Y. Trope (Eds.), *Dual-process models in social psychology*. New York: Guilford Press.

Pierro, A., & Kruglanski, A. W. (2005). *Revised Need for Cognitive Closure Scale*. Unpublished manuscript. Università di Roma, "La Sapienza", Italy.

Pierro, A. & Kruglanski, A. W. (in press). "Seizing and freezing" on a significant-person schema: Need for closure and the transference effect in social judgement. *Personality and Social Psychology Bulletin*.

Pierro, A., & Mannetti, L. (2004). *Motivated consumer search behaviour: The effects of epistemic authority*. Unpublished manuscript. University of Rome "La Sapienza", Italy.

Pierro, A., Mannetti, L., DeGrada, E., Livi, S., & Kruglanski A. W. (2003). Autocracy bias in groups under need for closure. *Personality and Social Psychology Bulletin, 29*, 405–417.

Pierro, A., Mannetti, L., Erb, H. P., Spiegel, S., & Kruglanski, A. W. (2005). Informational length and order of presentation as determinants of persuasion. *Journal of Experimental Social Psychology, 41*, 458–469.

Pierro, A., Mannetti, L., Kruglanski, A. W., & Sleeth-Keppler, D. (2004). Relevance override: On the reduced impact of "cues" under high motivation conditions of persuasion studies. *Journal of Personality and Social Psychology, 86*, 251–264.

Pierro, A., Mannetti, L., Orehek, E., & Kruglanski, A. W. (2008). *Persistence of attitude change and attitude–behaviour correspondence based on extensive processing of source information*. Unpublished manuscript. University of Rome, "La Sapienza", Italy.

Pizlo, Z. (2001). Perception viewed as an inverse problem. *Vision Research, 41*, 3145–3161.

Popper, K. R. (1959). *The logic of scientific discovery*. New York: Basic Books.

Raviv, A., Bar-Tal, D., Raviv, A., & Houminer, D (1990). Development in children's perception of epistemic authorities. *British Journal of Developmental Psychology, 8*, 157–169.

Rescorla, R. A. (1985). Conditioned inhibition and facilitation. In R. R. Miller & N. E. Spear (Eds.), *Information processing in animals: Conditioned inhibition* (pp. 299–326). Hillsdale, NJ: Lawrence Erlbaum Associates Inc.

Rescorla, R. A., & Holland, P. C. (1982). Behavioural studies of social learning in animals. *Annual Review of Psychology, 33*, 265–308.

Rescorla, R. A., & Wagner, A. R. (1972). A theory of Pavlovian conditioning: Variations in the effectiveness of reinforcement and nonreinforcement. In A. H. Black & W. F. Prokasy (Eds.), *Classical conditioning II: Current research and theory* (pp. 64–99). New York: Appleton-Century-Crofts.

Richter, L., & Kruglanski, A. W. (1998). Seizing on the latest: Motivationally driven recency effects in impression formation. *Journal of Experimental Social Psychology, 13*, 279–301.

Richter, L., & Kruglanski, A. W. (1999). Motivated search for common ground: Need for closure effects on audience design in interpersonal communication. *Personality and Social Psychology Bulletin, 25*, 1101–1114.

Rock, I. (1983). *The logic of perception*. Cambridge, MA: MIT Press.

Roets, A., & van Hiel, A. (2006). Need for closure relations with authoritarianism, conservative beliefs and racism: The impact of urgency and permanence tendencies. *Psychologica Belgica, 46*, 235–252.

Roets, A., & van Hiel, A. (2007). Separating ability from need: Clarifying the dimensional structure of the Need for Closure Scale. *Personality and Social Psychology Bulletin, 33*, 266–280.

Roets, A., & van Hiel, A. (2008). Why some hate to dilly-dally and others do not: The arousal-invoking capacity of decision-making for low and high scoring need for closure individuals. *Social Cognition, 26*, 259–272.

Roets, A., van Hiel, A., Cornelis, I., & Soetens, B. (2008). Determinants of task performance and invested effort: A need for closure by relative cognitive capacity interaction analysis. *Personality and Social Psychology Bulletin, 34*, 779–792.

Rogers, C. R. (1951). *Client-centred therapy: Its current practice, implications, and theory.* Oxford, UK: Houghton Mifflin.

Rogers, C. R. (1967). *The therapeutic relationship and its impact: A study of psychotherapy with schizophrenics.* Oxford, UK: Wisconsin Press.

Rubini, M., & Kruglanski, A. W. (1997). Brief encounters ending in estrangement: Motivated language-use and interpersonal rapport. *Journal of Personality and Social Psychology, 12*, 1047–1060.

Schteynberg, G., Gelfand, M., Imai, L., Mayer, D., & Bell, C. (2008). [*Unpublished data.*] University of Maryland, College Park, USA.

Schwarz, N. (2004). Metacognitive experiences in consumer judgement and decision making. *Journal of Consumer Psychology, 14*, 332–348.

Schwarz, N., Bless, H., Strack, F., Klumpp, G., Rittenauer-Schatka, H., & Simons, A. (1991). Ease of retrieval as information: Another look at the availability heuristic. *Journal of Personality and Social Psychology, 61*, 195–202.

Schwarz, N., & Clore, G. L. (1983). Mood, misattribution, and judgements of well-being: Informative and directive functions of affective states. *Journal of Personality and Social Psychology, 45*, 513–523.

Schwarz, N., & Clore, G. L. (1996). Feelings and phenomenal experiences. In E. T. Higgins & A. W. Kruglanski (Eds.), *Social psychology: Handbook of basic principles* (pp. 433–465). New York: Guilford Press.

Schwarz, N., Servay, W., & Kumpf, M. (1985). Attribution of arousal as a mediator of the effectiveness of fear-arousing communications. *Journal of Applied Social Psychology, 15*, 178–188.

Semin, G. R., & Fiedler, K. (1991). The linguistic category model, its bases, applications and range. In W. Stroebe & M. Hewstone (Eds.), *European review of social psychology* (Vol. 2, pp. 1–30). London: Wiley.

Shafer, J. B. P. (1978). *Humanistic psychology.* Englewood Cliffs, NJ: Prentice Hall.

Shah, J. Y., Kruglanski, A. W., & Thompson, E. P. (1998). Membership has its (epistemic) rewards: Need for closure effects on ingroup bias. *Journal of Personality and Social Psychology, 75*, 383–393.

Smith, E. R. (1984). Model of social inference processes. *Psychological Review, 91*, 392–413.

Smith, E. R. (1989). Procedural efficiency: General and specific components and effects on social judgement. *Journal of Experimental Social Psychology, 25*, 500–523.

Smith, E. R., & Branscombe, N. R. (1988). Category accessibility as implicit memory. *Journal of Experimental Social Psychology, 24*, 490–504.

Smith, E. R., Branscombe, N. R., & Bormann, C. (1988). Generality of the effects of practice on social judgement tasks. *Journal of Personality and Social Psychology, 54*, 385–395.

Tetlock, P. E. (1992). The impact of accountability on judgement and choice: Toward a social contingency model. In M. P. Zanna (Ed.), *Advances in experimental social psychology* (Vol. 25, pp. 331–376). San Diego, CA: Academic Press.

Trope, Y., & Alfieri, T. (1997). Effortfulness and flexibility of dispositional judgement processes. *Journal of Personality and Social Psychology, 73*, 662–674.

Trope, Y., & Gaunt, R. (2000). Processing alternative explanations of behaviour: Correction of integration? *Journal of Personality and Social Psychology, 79*, 344–354.

Tversky, A., & Kahneman, D. (1973). Availability: A heuristic for judging frequency and probability. *Cognitive Psychology, 5*(2), 207–232.

Uleman, J. S. (1987). Consciousness and control: The case of spontaneous trait inferences. *Personality and Social Psychology Bulletin, 13*, 337–354.

Van Hiel, A., Pandelaere, M., & Duriez, B. (2004). The impact of need for closure on conservative beliefs and racism: Differential mediation by authoritarian submission and authoritarian dominance. *Personality and Social Psychology Bulletin, 30*, 824–837.

Walther, E., Nagengast, B., & Trasselli, C. (2005). Evaluative conditioning in social psychology: Facts and speculations. *Cognition and Emotion, 19*, 175–196.

Wason, P. C. (1966). Reasoning. In B. M. Foss (Ed.), *New horizons in psychology* (pp. 113–135). Harmondsworth, UK: Penguin.

Webster, D. M., & Kruglanski, A. W. (1994). Individual Differences in need for cognitive closure. *Journal of Personality and Social Psychology, 67*, 1049–1062.

Webster, D. M., Kruglanski, A. W., & Pattison, D. A. (1997). Motivated language use in intergroup contexts: Need for closure effects on the linguistic intergroup bias. *Journal of Personality and Social Psychology, 72*, 1122–1131.

Webster, D. M., Richter, L., & Kruglanski, A. W. (1996). On leaping to conclusions when feeling tired: Mental fatigue effects on impressional primacy. *Journal of Experimental Social Psychology, 32*, 181–195.

Webster-Nelson, D., Klein, C. T., & Irvin, J. E. (2003). Motivational antecedents of empathy: Inhibiting effects of fatigue. *Basic and Applied Social Psychology, 25*, 37–50.

EUROPEAN REVIEW OF SOCIAL PSYCHOLOGY
2009, 20, 192–231

Social neuroscience evidence for dehumanised perception

Lasana T. Harris
New York University, NY, USA

Susan T. Fiske
Princeton University, NJ, USA

Dehumanisation describes perceiving a person as nonhuman in some ways, such as lacking a mind. Social psychology is beginning to understand cognitive and affective causes and mechanisms—the psychological how and why of dehumanisation. Social neuroscience research also can inform these questions. After background on social neural networks and on past dehumanisation research, the article contrasts (a) research on *fully humanised* person perception, reviewing studies on affective and cognitive factors, specifically mentalising (considering another's mind), with (b) *dehumanised perception,* proposing neural systems potentially involved. Finally, the conclusion suggests limitations of social neuroscience, future research directions, and real-world consequences of this all-too-human phenomenon.

Keywords: Dehumanisation; Social neuroscience; Stereotype content model (SCM); Disgust; Morality.

Our perception makes category errors. People sometimes perceive other people as if they are animals or objects, and objects or animals as if they are people. Evolutionary advantages can accrue from anthropomorphism— perceiving animals or objects like people—given the memory benefits of social cognition (Johansson, Mecklinger, & Treese, 2004; Mason, Hood, & Macrae, 2004; Mason & Macrae, 2004; Meiser, 2003; Phelps, 2006a, 2006b; Phelps & LaBar, 2006; Plaks, Grant, & Dweck, 2005; Somerville, Wig, Whalen, & Kelley, 2006; Todd, Lewis, Meusel, & Zelazo, 2008; Todorov,

---

Correspondence should be addressed to Dr Lasana Harris, Department of Psychology, New York University, New York, USA. E-mail: lasana@nyu.edu

We thank Phil Goff and Jennifer Eberhardt for sharing their stimuli, and Rafael Escobedo and Jack Gelfand for their assistance and instruction in gathering the EEG data.

http://www.psypress.com/ersp   DOI: 10.1080/10463280902954988

Gobbini, Evans, & Haxby, 2007; van Knippenberg, van Twuyver, & Pepels, 1994; von Hecker & Dutke, 2004). However, what possible evolutionary argument supports discarding those advantages and viewing a person like an object? Social psychological evidence suggests that all-too-human mechanisms may underlie these misperceptions (Fiske, Harris, & Cuddy, 2004), perhaps facilitating harm normally limited to non-human objects, destructive behaviour otherwise not permissible towards humans. Social neuroscience provides converging evidence for these mechanisms.

Violent, demeaning behaviours directed towards people certainly indicate dehumanisation.[1] This chapter aims to address this important topic by providing a framework that incorporates cognitive-affective neuroscience methodologies. After giving some background on social neural networks and on past dehumanisation research, this article contrasts research on (a) humanised person perception, reviewing studies on affective and cognitive factors, specifically mentalising (considering another's mind) with (b) *dehumanised perception,* proposing neural systems potentially involved. Finally, the conclusion suggests limitations of social neuroscience, future research directions, and real-world consequences of this all-too-human phenomenon.

A NOTE ON SOCIAL NEUROSCIENCE

Before continuing, a word about the social neuroscience approach this chapter employs: For social psychologists also fluent in cognitive-affective neuroscience, social neuroscience allows investigation of behavioural phenomena that are difficult to measure using traditional experimental social-psychological methods and measures. Social neuroscience—an interdisciplinary approach to social psychological questions (Lieberman, 2007; Ochsner, 2007; Ochsner & Lieberman, 2001; Todorov, Harris, & Fiske, 2006)—can incorporate social psychological theory, along with other philosophical, economic, legal, and political sources, then test these unique predictions using human neuroscience methods. As a premise for hypotheses, this chapter uses the folk psychological answer to the philosophical question "What is human?": that is, viewing human beings as entities with internal lives or minds (Adolphs, 2004). Although this approach is susceptible to the problems inherent to folk psychology, the social neuroscience approach adds physiological data, providing converging evidence for self-report.

Social neuroscience, as an emerging field, defines the intersection of social psychology, cognitive-affective psychology, and human neuroscience

---

[1]We follow an inter-group bias model, so we discuss dehumanisation, a form of extreme intergroup bias, distinguishing among cognition, affect, and behaviour. We use the term *dehumanisation* to describe behaviour, *dehumanising prejudice* to describe affect, and *dehumanised perception* to describe cognitions throughout this article.

(Lieberman, 2007; Ochsner, 2007; Ochsner & Lieberman, 2001; Todorov et al., 2006). It depends on social psychological theories and methods, and measures commonly used in cognitive-affective neuroscience. Considering social psychology alone may not be sufficient to identify all the nuances of a complex phenomenon such as dehumanisation. That being said, the social neuroscience here is much closer to social psychology than other areas of social neuroscience, partially because of its use of traditional social psychological designs. Thus, neuroscience is just one more tool to understand social psychological questions.

BACKGROUND ON SOCIAL NEURAL NETWORKS

To frame the reports of brain activation patterns relevant to social responses, this background section first describes possible social functions of some relevant brain regions. The most common approach employed to study human beings in neuroscience is physiological measurement, particularly neuro-imaging. Functional magnetic resonance imaging (fMRI) measures a correlate of neural activity, cerebral blood flow. This flow occurs at a 4–6-second lag after neural activity, and is not a direct measure of neural activity but of oxygenated blood rushing to clusters of neurons after firing. The spatial resolution, though not nearly as good as electrophysiology in animals, is currently the best available for unobtrusive human brains, but the haemodynamic lag makes it difficult to specify precise timing because it occurs after neural activity. Therefore this measure is approximate at best. However, neuro-imaging studies allow the correlation of questionnaire or behavioural measures with a correlate of neural activation. Thus, several converging strategies can be used to make claims about brain function.

Electroencephalography (EEG) and magneto-encephalography (MEG) more directly measure neural activity in time but not in location. When clusters of neurons fire, an electrical current is conducted to the scalp through tissue, cerebrospinal fluid, and skull. This current is measured at the scalp, giving good temporal resolution about psychological process, but poor spatial resolution of neural structure—it cannot specify the exact location of clusters of neurons. However, reliable event-related potentials (ERPs) do fire to psychological processes, including face perception, cognitive conflict, and cognitive errors, making it a more direct measure of neural firing than fMRI. Neuro-imaging and EEG are the two methods we adopt from neuroscience in this chapter. However, all the other tools of cognitive-affective neuroscience are available to the social neuroscientist to provide converging evidence for the occurrence of psychological phenomena, including facial electromyography, galvanic skin responses, heart rate monitoring, neuropharmacology, and lesion studies.

Neural systems of person perception and social cognition

Several neural regions figure prominently in person perception and social cognition. For social psychologists, one of the most important insights is that the neuroscience literature understands one of the medial prefrontal cortex's (MPFC) functions as serving a person perception network (e.g., Haxby, Gobbini, & Montgomery, 2004). Various aspects of this network activate in forming impressions, understanding another's false beliefs ("Theory of Mind"), attributing dispositions, perceiving close others, and various social cognition tasks (for reviews see Amodio & Frith, 2006; Olsson & Ochsner, 2008).

The subsequent sections will describe relevant neural systems. Person perception involves the pregenual anterior cingulate cortex (pACC) specifically, a sub-region of MPFC, which activates during face perception, along with other neural areas such as the amygdala, insula, superior temporal sulcus (STS), fusiform gyrus of temporal cortex, precuneus, and posterior cingulate (Haxby et al., 2004; see Figure 1). The next subsections summarise relevant research on other aspects of person perception, specifically mental state inference (mentalising), familiarity, and the self.

Mentalising.   Mental state inference studies address people's ability to consider someone else's thoughts (see Frith & Frith, 2001). Paradigms often probe this mentalising ability with false belief tasks using cartoons or vignettes describing behaviour. These theory of mind (ToM) studies, along with studies of dispositional attribution (Harris, Todorov, & Fiske, 2005), reliably include the same brain regions, namely the MPFC, superior temporal sulci (STS), and right temporal-parietal junction (RTPJ). These areas implicated in person perception may behave differently in object and animal perception, as well as in dehumanised perception.

Familiarity.   Familiarity breeds liking, which links rewards to habituated and fluent social perception. Imaging studies of familiarity in particular and positive social affect more generally illustrate that MPFC activates to both familiar and positive social stimuli. Significantly greater MPFC activity occurs when mothers look at faces of their own child rather than other familiar children, and for familiar children more than unfamiliar children (Leibenluft, Gobbini, Harrison, & Haxby, 2004).

As social psychology shows, familiarity itself links to positivity. Mere exposure demonstrates that simply repeated conscious (Zajonc, 1968) or unconscious (Monahan, Murphy, & Zajonc, 2000) exposure to a neutral stimulus enhances both subsequent liking and subjective familiarity of the

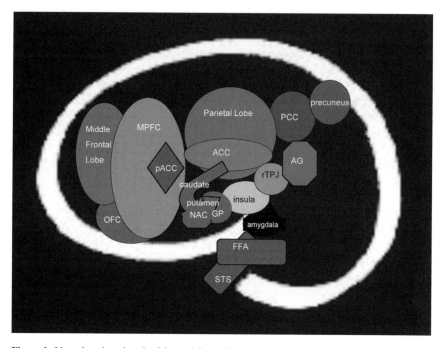

Figure 1. Neural regions involved in social cognition (see online for colour version). Many of these areas are implicated in more than one kind of social cognition, so the colour coding described below is a rough guide. Areas in blue tend to underlie person perception, specifically *medial prefrontal cortex* (MPFC) and *pregenual cingulate* (pACC) *amygdala, insula, superior temporal sulcus* (STS), *fusiform gyrus of temporal cortex* (FFA), *precuneus, posterior cingulate,* and occasionally *right temporal-parietal junction* (rTPJ). Areas in green tend to underlie social learning, including *orbital* (OFC) and *medial frontal regions* (MPFC), *amygdala, insula,* and *striatum, including nucleus accumbens* (NAC), *caudate, putamen,* and *globus pallidum* (GP). Areas in brown tend to underlie moral judgements, *MPFC, posterior cingulate, bilateral angular gyri* (AG), *middle frontal gyrus, bilateral parietal lobes,* and *insula.* Areas in pink and grey tend to underlie empathy, *amygdala, MPFC, STS, precuneus, anterior cingulate cortex* (ACC), and *insula.* This map shows their relative saggital and axial position in the brain, and structures are not drawn to scale and ignore their coronal positions.

stimulus. Familiar names are more popular, and people prefer the familiar letters associated with their own initials, suggesting that familiarity may plausibly explain this name-letter and other implicit egotism effects (Pelham, Mirenberg, & Jones, 2002). Familiar social targets generate positive affect that links in part to the self. Finally, friends have an easier time inferring each other's thoughts and feelings than strangers do (Stinson & Ickes, 1992), illustrating how familiarity moderates mental state inferences. Later sections return to the roles of MPFC and familiarity in dehumanised perception.

Self.   Social neuroscience also links the MPFC, particularly more ventral (lower) areas of MPFC, to thinking about the self. MPFC activates in paradigms where participants reflect on themselves, access self-knowledge, or compare the self to another (Johnson, Baxter, Wilder, Pipe, Heiserman, & Prigatano, 2002; Kelley, Macrae, Wyland, Caglar, Inati, & Heatherton, 2002; Lieberman, Jarcho, & Satpute, 2004). Self-regulation of affect also activates the MPFC (Ochsner, Knierim, Ludlow, Hanelin, Ramachandran, Glover, et al., 2004). Self-reflection allows people to infer the minds of others (Mitchell, Banaji, & Macrae, 2005), and it does activate the MPFC (along with the posterior cingulate and precuneus).

Research within social psychology on similarity to the self, such as self–other biases, self-referential effect, and self-esteem, has illustrated that the self serves as a positive attitude-object. In essence, things similar to the self become associated with positive affect, and denial of this association leads to less positive affect to self. The endowment effect suggests that people perceive objects belonging to the self as more valuable (Thaler, 1980).

Overall, MPFC activity is implicated in a number of networks involved in fundamental social cognitive processes, including inferring others' minds, preference for familiar others, and links to the most familiar and preferred social target, the self.

Neural systems of (social) reward

Social perception overlaps social reward, as supported by findings that social interaction tends to be intrinsically rewarding. Most people perceive themselves and others positively by default (Fiske, 2004, pp. 23–24; Kwan, John, Kenny, Bond, & Robins, 2004; Sears, 1983; Taylor & Brown, 1988; Taylor & Gollwitzer, 1995). The person-positivity bias is one of the most robust effects in interpersonal ratings; for example, people most often use the top half of rating scales to evaluate others. Of course, not everyone is perceived positively, but positive expectations are clearly the default for social targets.

In converging evidence, neural regions engaged in tracking reward and punishment value especially activate to social stimuli as well (Harris, 2007); these regions include orbital and medial frontal regions, amygdala, insula, and striatum, including nucleus accumbens, caudate, putamen, and globus pallidum (Delgado, 2007, see Figure 1). The MPFC also has a broader role here, primarily as an affective responsive area of the brain especially tuned to social rewards (Harris, McClure, Van den Bos, Cohen, & Fiske, 2007; Van den Bos, McClure, Harris, Fiske, & Cohen, 2007). Although the MPFC may be especially tuned for social perception, its broader function includes reward processing. Participants given an immediate reward for performance exhibit MPFC activity, but especially when a person rather than a computer administers the reward (McClure,

Laibson, Loewenstein, & Cohen, 2004). Thus social neuroscience and neuroeconomic evidence indirectly supports the person-positivity effect, which will prove relevant when comparing person perception to dehumanised perception.

Neural systems of moral judgement

Another aspect of dehumanised perception is moral, as we will argue that dehumanised others allegedly lie beyond normal human moral boundaries. Moral violators elicit disgust (Haidt, Rozin, McCauley, & Imada, 1997) and are often viewed as sub-human (Opotow, 1990). A moral module is viewed as necessary for human behaviour (Hauser, 2006). Moral judgements activate either a more cognitive or a more affective system (Greene, Sommerville, Nystrom, Darley, & Cohen, 2001). The more affective system includes MPFC, posterior cingulate, and bilateral angular gyri. The more cognitive system includes the middle frontal gyrus and bilateral parietal lobes. However, because of the role of disgust in marking moral violation, we also include the insula and strial regions in this network (see Figure 1).

Neural systems of empathy

Finally, we will invoke the role of empathy in contrasting person perception and dehumanised perception. Empathy appeared early in helping research (for review, see Batson, 1998), facilitating altruism (Batson, 1991), a process requiring thought about another's internal state. Subsequent work on perspective taking further suggests that empathy reduces prejudice (Galinsky & Moskowitz, 2000). Like social psychology, some neuroscience theory also considers empathy an outcome of emotional contagion (e.g., Levenson, 1996).

Other theories of empathy describe empathy as embodying another's experience (Singer & Fehr, 2005). Embodied social cognition (Niedenthal, Krauth-Gruber, & Ric, 2006) explains emotional reactions by arguing that emotional experiences mentally re-create patterns of neural activity similar to the patterns that occurred during the original experience of the event. Empathy can occur across separate sensory modalities such as pain and touch. Therefore, perceivers may re-create the experienced neural affective pattern of the target. This neural system includes the anterior cingulate cortex (ACC) and the anterior insula during empathy for pain (Singer & Fehr, 2005). The social neuroscience literature shows greater amygdala activity (also implicated in fear conditioning) when participants merely read third-person fearful versus neutral stories about other people (Ruby & Decety, 2004). The MPFC along with STS and precuneus also reliably activates in tasks requiring empathy (Decety & Jackson, 2004, 2006, see

Figure 1). Again, empathy would appear in humanised perception more than dehumanised perception.

One common theme: Medial prefrontal cortex in social cognition

Which neural structures activate most commonly across such complex processes? The relevant neural system must integrate both affective and cognitive information. One candidate focal structure is the MPFC. As previous sections indicate, this neural region activates in detecting valence and value, as well as in mentalising, with reciprocal connection to sub-cortical neural regions implicated in the immediate processing of information for moral decisions and empathy. Therefore our framework takes MPFC activation as an index of humanised perception in the context of our dehumanised perception tasks. This is not the definitive function of the MPFC, but given the literature, activation of the MPFC is one reliable index of humanised perception because of its ubiquity in social cognition, as just described. The next section describes dehumanised perception and its primary mechanism, mentalising, and begins by asking an old but useful philosophical question.

DEHUMANISATION: OUTCASTS, ANIMALS, AND OBJECTS HAVE (HARDLY ANY) MINDS

Before turning to dehumanised perception, let us define *humanised perception*: perceiving a target as possessing an internal life. An internal life is defined as active mental states; that is, thoughts and feelings. These thoughts and feelings presumably cause the target's behaviour, so they have a function and are not epiphenomenal. This definition holds when people perceive most other people. When humanised perception does not occur, and a person is viewed as a non-human target, we consider this phenomenon *dehumanised perception.*

Considering what is human fascinates philosophers, who use thought exercises to argue that the adoption of an "intentional stance" allows a folk psychology of the mind (Dennett, 1987). The *intentional stance* captures the idea that perceivers assume others are agents with plans, goals, and predispositions. When people think about others, they often think about their minds. Inferring what is in someone else's mind—i.e., *mentalising*—helps create one's mental representation of another person as a truly social target. After framing the philosophy of mind approach, other sub-sections will describe the intentional stance as applied or denied to outgroups, animals, and objects.

Philosophy of minds: Intentional and personal (moral) agents

First, entertain the following thought experiment demonstrating the intentional stance. What if, unbeknown to all, someone replaced your immediate family with robots? Consider these no ordinary robots, but robots that resemble and respond just as your family members. How would you distinguish your family from these robots? When lay people consider a similar question, the folk psychological answer is often that these robots will not have the minds or "inner lives" of a person; that is, the robots would not have the thoughts, feelings, and experiences that make up the rich mental lives of people (Appiah, 2003). They may have computer chips and circuits, but they lack the phenomenological experience of what it feels to be human. Similarly, when asked what makes humans unique, people cite intelligence, language, and complex emotions (Leyens et al., 2003), all of which require agency and mind.

To determine that others are human may not be as obvious as simply knowing in theory that they have a mind. The only mind that we know exists is our own because we have phenomenological experience only of our own mental lives. Therefore we infer whether other agents have minds like ours by assuming that a mind underlies their similar behaviour. Perhaps, therefore, strange (dissimilar or unfamiliar) behaviour suggests that the agent is not like us because our minds do not underlie such behaviour. The agent must not be quite human like I am quite human. Thus philosophy of mind plays a vital role in thinking about dehumanising a dissimilar other.

In summary, dehumanisation may result from inference driven by the other's alleged behaviour. This fits social psychology theory on dehumanisation. If behaviour is so heinous that we could not imagine ourselves performing it, then the actors may be dehumanised. Therefore moral judgement elevates or demotes people's human status. The philosophical theories certainly suggest as much—the intentional stance includes the higher-order stance called the *personal stance,* which identifies a person as a moral agent comparable to self (Dennett, 1987).

Assessing intention is not reserved simply for people, suggesting that this additional, personal-moral variable helps differentiate people from objects and animals. Consider another thought experiment: Is it permissible to dismember a computer with which one plays chess? Now consider dismembering a friend with whom one plays chess. Dennett's examples suggest that intentionality is not sufficient to differentiate people and objects because some behaviours are perceived as "right" and others as "wrong" towards the two kinds of intentional agents. The personal stance captures a separate inference reserved for people, a kind of moral filter on behaviour towards intentional agents. Dehumanisation may result from a failure of a person to activate the personal stance, a failure to indicate to the perceiver that the social target is not only an intentional but also a moral agent similar to self.

Dehumanising prejudice may deny intentional and personal agency

Social psychologists have long pondered the mechanisms of dehumanisation. Indeed social psychology itself expanded with the exodus of European Jewish researchers in the wake of the Nazi Holocaust, during which dehumanisation was the daily norm. Early work on prejudice provides a useful point of departure.

Social psychology has described dehumanisation as the worst kind of prejudice (Allport, 1954). Since Allport, the field has theorised about which groups get dehumanised: Outgroups perceived to act outside the prescribed boundaries of moral rules and values (Opotow, 1990; Staub, 1989), as well as social groups considered beyond societal norms (Bar-Tal, 1990), both lead to moral exclusion.

Dehumanisation theory also acknowledges differing forms, distinguishing *uniquely* human characteristics (e.g., language) from *typically* human characteristics (e.g., agency). Lacking either uniquely or typically human characteristics dehumanises one to the equivalent of, respectively, animals or objects (Haslam, 2006; Haslam, Bain, Loughnan, & Kashima, 2008; Loughnan & Haslam, 2007). A model of dehumanisation separates exclusion from unique humanity and typical human nature (Haslam, 2006). The model revisits the idea of essences, once proposed as an account of how people know the difference between computers and people (the answer: computers lacked the "human essence"; Turkle, 2005).

Denying *uniquely human* characteristics disallows aspects that humans share, compared with other species, such as courtesy, culture, intelligence, language, and so on, that elevate humans above animals. Hence, denying uniquely human characteristics reduces people to functional equivalents of animals. Denying *typically human-nature* characteristics disallows aspects central to people's folk definition of what it fundamentally means to be a good example of a human; for example, having complex emotions. Refuting these characteristics makes another appear more like a machine or automaton than a person. These unique and typical characteristics represent two distinct ways of dehumanising people (Loughnan & Haslam, 2007).

The field has researched one related mechanism to date: Outgroups allegedly do not feel complex emotions to the same extent as the ingroup (Leyens et al., 2001, 2003). *Infrahumanisation* theory of dehumanisation thus directly involves affect, drawing on the distinction between primary, basic emotions (sadness) and secondary, social, complex emotions (remorse). Infrahumanisation states that we attribute complex secondary emotions less to outgroups than ingroups (Leyens et al., 2001, 2003).

In infrahumanisation paradigms, participants attribute positive and negative primary and secondary emotions to ingroup and outgroup members (Leyens et al., 2001, 2003). The distinction between primary and secondary emotions is inherent in romance languages that distinguish between *émotion* and *sentiment*. The *émotions* are the affective reactions that people and animals both can feel, such as sadness or joy, whereas *sentiments* are complex affective reactions that only people can feel, such as regret or pride. *Émotions* in this sense are basic or primary emotions, whereas *sentiments* are higher-order or secondary emotions, most often social. Participants attribute equal numbers of positive and negative primary *émotions* to both ingroups and outgroups, but fewer positive and negative secondary *sentiments* to outgroups than ingroups. This phenomenon demonstrably occurs both explicitly and implicitly (Demoulin et al., 2005), suggesting that emotional infrahumanisation may result from immediate categorisation (Rodriguez-Torres, Leyens, Rodríguez Pérez, Betancor Rodriguez, Quiles del Castillo, Demoulin, et al., 2005).

People attribute greater humanness to themselves than to others (Haslam, Bain, Douge, Lee, & Bastian, 2005), and a possible mechanism is similarity (Vaes, Paladino, Castelli, Leyens, & Giovanazzi, 2003), but not familiarity (Cortes, Demoulin, Rodriquez, Rodriguez, & Leyens, 2005). Infrahumanisation reduced intergroup helping after a natural disaster (Cuddy, Rock, & Norton, 2007b) and decreased forgiveness following conflict (Tam et al., 2007). Further, when made aware of mass killings, ingroup members infrahumanise outgroup victims (Castano & Giner-Sorolla, 2006); if the ingroup is victim and the perpetrator ambiguous, increased empathy with ingroup victims increases outgroup infrahumanisation (Rodriguez, Coello, Betancor, Rodriguez, & Delgado, 2006), all this suggesting that negative outcomes and uncertainty may moderate infrahumanisation. Children as young as 6 show the infrahumanisation bias (Martin, Bennett, & Murray, 2008).

Relatedly, people associate outgroups and animals, specifically Blacks and apes (Goff, Eberhardt, Williams, & Jackson, 2008; see Figure 2). Across several studies these non-conscious associations appear in early perception and attention. Further, this association increases implicit endorsement of violence against Blacks, activates spontaneously from newspaper articles covering death-eligible Black defendants, and more strongly activates for Black targets ultimately sentenced to death.

Dehumanisation as inter-group cognitive bias and emotional prejudice

Dehumanisation, like other forms of inter-group bias, has both cognitive and affective components. Because group categorisation underlies all forms of dehumanisation, and social norms prescribe which categories get

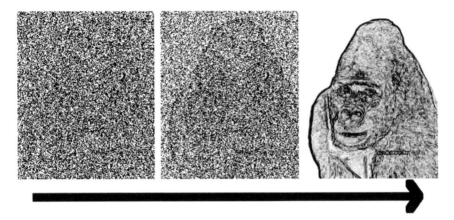

Figure 2. Illustration of the kinds of stimuli used in studies showing faster latent responses in White subjects to associations of Black people and apes. Participants were asked in one paradigm to watch a movie of a picture of an animal slowly clear from noise to image. White participants identified the image much sooner after being primed with Black (first image) than White (second image) faces.

dehumanised, dehumanisation results from an intergroup cognitive phenomenon. As an extreme emotional prejudice, dehumanisation may be motivated by the emotions involved.

Of most relevance here, social targets who elicit disgust are often linked to moral violations and suffer aggression from the perceiver (Haidt et al., 1997). Additionally, as we will see, they activate the disgust-related insula more and the mentalising MPFC much less than other social targets (Harris & Fiske, 2006); in questionnaire studies they are spontaneously mentalised less than other social targets (Harris, 2007). Thus, disgusting social targets both suffer the cognitive bias of dehumanised perception and fail to elicit complex, even slightly positive emotions. Because the cognitive process of mentalising helps detect dehumanised perception of disgusting outgroups, our work on dehumanisation involves both cognitive and affective processes.

Cognition and affect are not mutually exclusive processes, and infrahumanisation like dehumanised perception has elements of both components (an attributional process, even for emotions, must also be cognitive). We differentiate dehumanisation from infrahumanisation processes based on the dominant process involved—attribution of emotions versus attribution of mind—but because both phenomena involve affective as well as cognitive processes, we do not differentiate them based on relative emphases towards cognition or affect. Also, we consider dehumanised perception a denial of typical humanity, not unique humanity, since the phenomenon is concerned with mental state inference, a typically human quality; infrahumanisation theory seems to accommodate both denials.

In contrast: Object perception, animal perception, and anthropomorphism

So far we have seen that outcast humans may allegedly have hardly any mind; now we turn to the opposite case of objects and animals that may apparently have too much mind. People can infer mental states for targets that lack actual minds. People anthropomorphise machines and animals, suspending the belief that they do not have human consciousness (although the debate still contests animals' consciousness, see Gosling, Kwan, & John, 2003).

Perceiving and attributing human-like qualities to non-human targets (i.e., anthropomorphism), is not necessarily the opposite of dehumanised perception. Clearly, specific non-human targets are perceived like people. The most common cases are domestic animals, or pets; many pet owners attribute personalities to their pets (Gosling et al., 2003). This is not surprising, considering the great social services these animals provide, particularly companionship; studies show that after a traumatic life event, depressed elderly people with pets fare better than depressed elderly people without (NIH, 1987). Regardless of the extent to which animals have consciousness, along the dimension of humanised perception these animals may be perceived as more human than actual human beings who happen to be at the bottom of the social hierarchy. For this reason we consider dehumanised perception a cognitive error, and suggest that perceiving other people is also a mental, not strictly visual phenomenon. We will elaborate on object perception and anthropomorphism below.

As an everyday example, children commonly create imaginary people (imaginary friends) and effortlessly interact with them as if they exist. Even adults may hold or suspend their beliefs about whether a target possesses a mind, allowing either dehumanisation or anthropomorphism (for relevant articles, see Kwan & Fiske, 2008). Comparing object perception to person perception, and exploring the cognitive and neural mechanisms that underlie anthropomorphism provides subsequent hypotheses that address how people decide which targets have mental lives and which do not. The next two sections elaborate some psychological and neural mechanisms.

Object versus person perception.   Studies that contrast person and object perception (Harris et al., 2007; Mitchell, Heatherton, & Macrae, 2004) clearly implicate the MPFC in social perception. In one study participants saw pictures of positive and negative people and objects while fMRI recorded their neural responses (Harris et al., 2007). Pictures of people came from our Stereotype Content Model (SCM) social-groups database (Harris , 2007, Fig. 3), and pictures of objects came from the International Affective Picture System (IAPS; Lang, Bradley, & Cuthbert, 1996). "Positive"

High

Low

Warmth

Low   High

Competence

Figure 3. Stereotype content model (see online for colour version). The interaction of perceived trait warmth and competence predicts the type of emotion that different social groups elicit. Groups perceived as low on both dimensions are dehumanised groups who elicit *disgust* (blue) and include drug addicts and homeless people. Groups high on both dimensions elicit *pride* (red) and include college students and American heroes. Groups high on warmth, but low on competence elicit *pity* (yellow) and include elderly and disabled people. Groups low on warmth and high on competence elicit *envy* (green) and include business and rich people. All social groups come from US samples.

pictures of people (defined as pictures that activated MPFC) had pretested as eliciting pity, envy, or pride (all emotions that entail at least some positive valence); examples included, respectively, older and disabled people, rich and business people, and ingroup heroes. Wholly negative pictures were dehumanised people who elicit disgust (homeless people, drug addicts). Positive pictures of objects (e.g., flowers) pretested high (6 or more) on a 1–7 Likert scale of valence, while negative pictures of objects (e.g., a collapsed building) pretested low on the valence measure (2 or less). The objects data came directly from published ratings of the IAPS (see Lang et al., 1996). In the scanner, participants simply viewed each picture for 500 milliseconds while indicating either that the picture was positive or negative, or depicted a person or object.

Although no area of the MPFC activated more to people than objects overall, the neuroimaging results reveal an area of MPFC recruited exclusively for *valence differences among people*, but not for valence differences among objects. Also, a different area of MPFC activated more to positive than to negative stimuli in general. This combination of results suggests that positive and negative valence differentiates in a unique region for people, not objects, in the MPFC.

Valence extends to social and nonsocial feedback in critical learning experiences that guide future behaviour. Is receiving reward or punishment from a person the same experience as receiving reward or punishment from a computer program? Again contrasting person and object perception, we addressed this question with the following experiment. Participants in another imaging study performed a time-estimation task in which they had to guess how long different time-periods took to elapse (Van den Bos, McClure, Harris, Fiske, & Cohen, 2007). On each trial, participants first saw how much time they had to estimate (e.g., 9.5. seconds) before they then pressed a button to start the estimation, and another to signal when the specified time had elapsed. These participants received either a reward (juice) or a punishment (quinine, a bitter liquid), allegedly from either an experimenter or a computer program. In fact, a computer program randomly determined both types of feedback.

These data also show a region of MPFC (similar to the one identified in the above experiment) that differentiates reward and punishment for social stimuli (the experimenter), but not non-social targets (the computer program). Consistent with the Harris et al. (2007) data, but using a completely different paradigm, this study demonstrates neural differences between person and object perception; areas of MPFC integrate information and represent value that differentiates good and bad feedback from people, but not objects. These data hint at the possibility that receiving reward and punishment (learning cues for future behaviour) may be a separable psychological process for people and objects; a part of the brain distinguishes the source as person or object.

Similar evidence is provided by another imaging study where participants played an Ultimatum Game with either another person or a computer (Sanfey, Rilling, Aronson, Nystrom, & Cohen, 2003). Unfair offers from people activated regions of the insula, dorsal lateral prefrontal cortex, and MPFC extending into the ACC. These areas responded more when receiving unfair offers from people than when unfair offers were received from the computer, suggesting that simply perceiving intention (communicated by fair and unfair offers) is not sufficient for humanised perception.

This latter study illustrates another psychological process separable for people and objects. However, this study suggests separable intentions from people and objects, a trait unique to targets with mental lives. It also implies that people can infer intentions (or something like them) from objects, hinting that separable neural processes may underlie intentional inference from human and non-human agents. Possibly, people must suspend their belief that the object does not have a mental life, even if ever so temporarily, to imbue that object with a quality of mental life: intention. Are there cases beyond the context of economic games where people imbue non-human targets with mental life?

Anthropomorphism. Given that people infer fairness from objects, a trait implying mental life, but the neural processes underlying this inference are separable, it suggests that separable neural structures may underlie other mental inference processes for people and objects. We tested this hypothesis with a series of neuroimaging studies that extended previous work in social psychology on another form of mental life inference: dispositional attribution.

Social psychology has established that given the right combination of information about a social target's past behaviour and other people's behaviour, a perceiver will make a dispositional attribution to that social target. For instance, being told Jane shops in a health-food store, and then given additional low consensus information (Hardly anyone shops in that health-food store), low distinctiveness information (Jane shops in every other kind of health-food store), and high consistency information (In the past, Jane has always shopped in that health-food store), perceivers are likely to infer that there is something about Jane that caused her behaviour (Jane likes to shop in health-food stores). This covariance model of dispositional attribution (Kelley, 1972) has been well established in the field and predicts when people are likely to attribute the cause of behaviour to a social target, as apart from circumstances, particular entities, or ambiguous causes (McArthur, 1972).

Participants read high and low consensus, consistency, and distinctiveness information in a direct replication of the McArthur (1972) attribution paradigm, while we collected neural data using fMRI (Harris et al., 2005). Their task was to indicate who caused the behaviour, whether the human subject of the sentence, the entity, circumstance, or some combination. We replicated previous behavioural results of more dispositional attributions, given low consensus, low distinctiveness, and high consistency information. Activation in the superior temporal sulcus (STS; a region that tracks motion that appears to be made by a biological agent, implying intentions) exactly mimicked this pattern, namely activating in only one out of eight combinations. In addition, participants also showed increased MPFC activity to low distinctiveness and high consistency information, paired with either low consensus or high consensus information (in line with the literature using questionnaire data, showing that people neglect consensus information, relative to consistency and distinctiveness; Fiske & Taylor, 2008). Thus the MPFC activated in attributions to a specific person or to people in general.

To compare person and object perception, we then replicated this paradigm using objects as the targets performing behaviour. Because we did not want to demand anthropomorphism, we chose action sentences instead of emotion, accomplishment, and opinion sentences. As just described, participants first saw the action (The pen fell off the table) before information combinations that suggested a causal property residing in the pen (Hardly any other pen falls off the table; the pen falls off almost every other table; in the past the pen almost always fell off the table). Neural activity for these "dispositional" attributions for objects overlapped with the STS activity previously engaged for people, but also activated bilateral amygdala instead of MPFC. This suggests separable neural systems encoding dispositional inferences for objects, a phenomenon close to anthropomorphism, but distinct from (de)humanised perception.

Summary

After the previous section providing background on social neural networks, this section has focused on dehumanisation in various forms, starting with people normally understanding other people as having intents and agency; dehumanisation denies them an agentic mind. Dehumanised groups are extreme outgroups viewed as disgusting. In contrast, overly humanised objects and animals may acquire agency, but the neural mechanisms evidently differ.

PUTTING TOGETHER DEHUMANISATION AND SOCIAL NEUROSCIENCE

Previous sections have introduced first the social neuroscience of person perception and social cognition, social rewards, moral judgement, and empathy—and second, dehumanisation as a general form of prejudice and intergroup bias, noting its relevance to anthropomorphism and object perception. This section pulls together affect and cognition in social cognition, citing social psychology and social neuroscience evidence.

Affect in person perception: The stereotype content model

The social psychological literature provides a number of models that describe the affective process during person perception. This section begins with a review of a model predicting intergroup emotion, the stereotype content model (SCM; Fiske, Cuddy, & Glick, 2007; Fiske, Cuddy, Glick, & Xu, 2002), which we use as a framework to test dehumanisation linked to reported disgust. Then the section will discuss broader social-group approach–avoidance reactions, linked to amygdala activation, an area implicated in emotional vigilance.

The inter-group emotions literature suggests that affective reactions to social targets emerge from their perceived social categories and associated stereotypes (Alexander, Brewer, & Hermann, 1999; Fiske et al., 2002; Mackie & Smith, 2002; Neuberg & Cottrell, 2002; Stephan & Stephan, 2000). The stereotype content model (see Figure 3) begins with two basic dimensions of person perception: warmth and competence (Fiske et al., 2002, 2007; Peeters, 1983; Rosenberg, Nelson, & Vivekananthan, 1968; Tausch, Kenworthy, & Hewstone, 2007; Wojciszke, Bazinska, & Jaworski, 1998). People rapidly assess a social target's intention (good or ill) towards them. The warmth trait dimension captures the social target's assessed benevolent or malevolent intention, while the competence dimension captures the target's perceived ability to enact those intentions (Cuddy, Fiske, & Glick, 2007a; Fiske et al., 2002; Harris & Fiske, 2006). The resulting two-dimensional space predicts characteristic affective responses to distinct social categories, based on the interaction of perceived warmth and competence. Location of different social categories on the trait dimensions comes from their perceived status and competition, social structure variables associated with the inferred social category. Then, specific emotions are elicited by the social category (see also Eagly & Mladinic, 1989; Hamilton, 1981; Jackson et al., 1996; Stangor, Sullivan, & Ford, 1991; Zanna & Rempel, 1988).

The SCM rests on general social psychological principles and is well supported (Fiske et al., 2007). SCM data have come from US representative surveys (Cuddy et al., 2007a), US college samples (Fiske et al., 2002), as well as Asian and European samples (Cuddy et al., 2009). In these studies an initial sample within the population first lists the most relevant social categories in that context. The social categories with some consensus (above 15%) are then rated by a separate sample on the trait dimensions warmth and competence, and in some studies on the four predicted emotions (pride, envy, pity, disgust), four predicted behavioural intentions (active or passive harm or help), as well as the social structural predictors of warmth and competence (respectively, competition and status). A cluster analysis on the categories' scores on the warmth and competence trait ratings then generally results in the four quadrants towards the corners of the 2 × 2 space.

Social categories perceived as high on both warmth and competence elicit the ingroup, complex, positive, social emotion *pride*; in US samples these cultural prototype groups include middle-class people, American heroes (firefighters, police officers, astronauts), and college students (in college samples). These social targets are admired and respected. The high-high groups receive both active and passive help.

Social categories perceived as low in warmth but high on competence elicit the complex, ambivalent, social emotion *envy*: business people and rich people in all samples. These groups are perceived as not nice, but well respected; high-status outgroups in all samples tend to fall into this space. These groups receive the volatile combination of passive help (go-along-to-get-along) but also active attack, under social breakdown.

Social categories perceived as high on warmth but low on competence elicit the complex, ambivalent, social emotion *pity*: older people in all samples and disabled people in US samples. These likable social targets are perceived as inept and needing active help, being cared for, but often neglected (passive harm).

Finally, social categories perceived as low on both warmth and competence elicit the negative, basic emotion *disgust*. These extreme outgroups include homeless people and drug addicts in US samples (and poor people in all samples). These groups tend to be dehumanised targets (Harris & Fiske, 2006), a point that forms the basis of this chapter. As discussed previously, social targets who elicit disgust are often linked to moral violations and suffer aggression from the perceiver (Haidt et al., 1997). They receive both active and passive harm (neglect). We will come back to these groups in particular.

Cognition in person perception

Background on mentalising. Mentalising is a cognitive process that involves inferring a target's intention (Frith & Frith, 2001). Attributing intention is not simply reserved for people who presumably do have minds; perceivers also attribute intentions to objects that objectively do not have cognitions and emotions. Participants likewise infer the intentions of dots in biological motion (Heberlein, Adolphs, Tranel, & Damasio, 2004) and of shapes in non-random motion (Heider & Simmel, 1944). Inferring intention in these instances may rely on the assumption that the targets have goals that reside in their minds. Although obviously people realise that these targets are not human and do not have internal lives of any kind, nevertheless people continue to talk to cars and computers (though always knowing that no answer is forthcoming). Therefore, as discussed above, mentalising is a higher-order cognitive process that people quickly recruit even to non-human targets, and it *seems* to require the belief, if only temporarily, that the target has "an internal life," or conscious cognitive and emotional experiences.

However, mentalising with human targets has certain additional trademarks. Consider mentalising as a cognitive process with affective correlates; that is, it may often involve certain kinds of emotion. For instance, we can easily report how trustworthy a face seems, in fact, reliably after 100ms of face presentation (Willis & Todorov, 2006). A judgement of trustworthiness assesses the social target's good or ill intentions, which represent an immediate primitive affective (or at least evaluative) appraisal. This appraisal relies on the same neural architecture, the amygdala, as other immediate approach–avoid affective judgements such as fear (Engell, Haxby, & Todorov, 2007; Winston, Strange, O'Doherty, & Dolan, 2002). Yet this complex evaluation of intention occurs so quickly that it is difficult to make a case for the role of higher-order cognitive processes in this judgement. In fact, the amygdala often responds before information has even reached neo-cortical structures (LeDoux, 1998). Therefore, perhaps thinking about the mind of a person relies on both higher-order cognitive processes and sub-cortical affective structures that appraise intention and process basic emotion. Mentalising thus may be a cognitive response with affective correlates.

Mentalising as a cognitive process.   Social psychology has addressed two major aspects of mentalising: thinking about a target's mind by perspective taking and thinking about a target's mind by making dispositional inferences. In both cases, the *target*'s external features (e.g., facial appearance; see Todorov, Mandisodza, Goren, & Hall, 2005; Zebrowitz, 1999) perhaps most influence initial thoughts about that other's mind. These external features convey clues about the social target's internal state, but also activate stereotypes about the perceived social category (Fiske, 1998). Stereotypes guide inferences about the target's mind and assist in predicting the target's behaviour. Sometimes, however, perspective taking and considering the target's mind can short-circuit these default stereotyping processes.

First, perspective taking de-biases social thought on both the conscious and unconscious levels (Galinsky & Moskowitz, 2000). For example, perspective taking deactivates stereotypes by increasing cognitive overlap between the self and the other, allowing the other to be perceived as similar (Galinsky, Ku, & Wang, 2005). These effects occur both in real and minimal groups (Galinsky & Moskowitz, 2000). Prior to this work, social psychology had a long history of implicating perspective taking in elevating moral reasoning (Kohlberg & Hersh, 1977), encouraging altruism (Batson, 1991, 1998), and lowering aggression (Richardson, Hammock, Smith, & Gardner, 1994).

Second, people may consider another's mind and use those imagined mental contents as a marker of a stable attribute about that person. Because of their ability to deduce personality, people have famously been considered naïve scientists (Heider, 1958). Inferring a social target's disposition is a type of mentalising that makes a stable attribution to the target traits, goals, preferences, and the like, often in the service of predicting behaviour. Activating a disposition is similar to activating a stereotype because it includes a mental script of that social target's expected behavioural repertoire, as well as the perceiver's potential behaviour towards the social target. A friendly person who is reserved versus a friendly person who is outgoing each have different behavioural tendencies towards greeting with either a shy glance or a fierce hug. People may make "behavioural" predictions even about non-human agents, and anthropomorphising animals and objects may reflect the disposition-to-behaviour feature of mentalising processes (Gosling et al., 2003).

Attribution theory in social psychology has focused almost exclusively on the process of making dispositional attributions to others (Jones, 1979), including the dimensions that predict these attributions (Kelley, 1972; McArthur, 1972). Dispositional attributions are so crucial to social perception that people automatically infer dispositions from even thin slices of behaviour (Ambady & Rosenthal, 1993; Dunning, Meyerowitz, & Holzberg, 1989). In addition, these first impressions often influence global judgements of the individual (see Asch, 1946). This judgement anticipates affectively based good or bad evaluations of the social target, even when only the face, not detailed information itself is available (Todorov & Uleman, 2002). As noted, dispositional attribution activates the neural structures associated with mentalising. This suggests that implicit information about the social target, possibly correlated with affect, is relevant to thinking about their minds. We next explore social psychological data that provide converging evidence for the social neuroscience data on dehumanised perception.

Social psychological data on dehumanised perception

The neuroscience studies mentioned above generated a cognitive hypothesis testable with experimental social psychological paradigms: Perceivers less often infer the mental state of dehumanised people. This hypothesis is tested with a social cognitive paradigm that examines whether perceivers report mentalising dehumanised targets, and how they rate these targets on a number of dimensions drawn from the MPFC literature.

Cognitive responses to dehumanised people.   Because social targets who elicit disgust may not be perceived as human to the same extent as other social targets, the number of thoughts about the mental contents of dehumanised targets may differ from other social targets.

As one indicator, people describe other people using verbs that differentially abstract behaviour. *Mental state* verbs describe behaviour by implying the mental content of the agent, whereas *descriptive action* verbs and *interpretive action* verbs do not require inferring mental content (Semin & Fiedler, 1988). Therefore, the amount of mental state verbs participants generate in response to different social targets may help reveal the amount of mentalising to dehumanised targets. These targets should generate fewer mental state verbs when participants describe a day in that social target's life.

To demonstrate this effect, Princeton University undergraduates saw one of eight pictured social targets and were asked to image what their day is like. Pictures came from our larger picture database pretested on warmth and competence. Two pictures represented each SCM quadrant as follows: female college student and male American firefighter (pride), business woman and rich man (envy), elderly man and disabled woman (pity), and female homeless person and male drug addict (disgust). No ratings differentiated the social targets within each SCM quadrant, so the average ratings for each pair generated the measure for that part of the space.

Participants first described a day in the life of one pictured social target, using up to 15 lines. We used a coding scheme (Semin & Fiedler, 1988) to test the hypothesis. Specifically: while adjectives represent the most abstract level (e.g., thirsty), verbs are more concrete but, as noted earlier, can differentiate levels of abstractness. To review, the most abstract are *mental state verbs* that describe actions in terms of the target's internal state (e.g., quench). These are followed by *interpretive action verbs* that interpret the target's action (e.g., guzzle), and finally by *descriptive action verbs* (e.g., drink) that simply describe the action. Note what the examples in parentheses suggest about the cognition behind the use of each type of descriptive term: Adjectives describe the person, mental state verbs describe the mind of the person, interpretive action verbs interpret the behaviour of the person, while descriptive action verbs describe the behaviour in terms of the object being acted upon. This suggests that people will use fewer mental state verbs to describe a day in the life of dehumanised targets, if perceivers fail to think about the contents of the target's mind.

A pair of independent raters jointly classified verbs into the mental state, interpretive action, and descriptive action categories. The number of extracted verbs in each category and adjectives in the descriptions were averaged across the two raters, creating a single, reliable score per participant on each type of verb and adjective. No significant differences distinguished the total number of words used to describe the different social targets. Also, no significant differences appeared in adjectives, interpretive action verbs, or descriptive actions verbs used in the descriptions of any type of social target. However, as hypothesised, participants did use significantly fewer mental state verbs to describe a day in the life of dehumanised targets, compared with all the other social targets, suggesting that participants were spontaneously inferring the contents of the dehumanised targets' minds *less* than other social targets (Harris, 2007). These results suggest that perceivers do not infer the contents of dehumanised targets' minds or take their perspective to the same extent as they do for other social targets.

What processes could be associated with describing all the social targets? Participants, when instructed to imagine a day in the life of a social target, could have engaged in a variety of processes. For example, participants may use thoughts about their own social life in an attempt to imagine what another person's might be. Participants may also have thought about the social life of people familiar to them, people who might be similar to the social target. Participants may have attempted to empathise with the social targets, perhaps remembering experiences in their own life that correlate with the possible daily experiences of the social target. These plausible explanations may describe the strategy employed by participants when mentalising.

We next asked participants to rate the pictured social target on a number of dimensions, including their own subjective experience regarding the social target. These dimensions included ones chosen to assess potential mentalising: warmth, competence, similarity, familiarity, perceiver's ability to mentalise the target, perceiver's ability to infer target dispositions, and perceiver's empathy for the target. Other rating dimensions derived from the social psychological literature on dehumanisation: responsibility of target for own situation, control of target over own situation, being articulate, being intelligent, having complex emotionality, target being self-aware, ups and downs in target's life, and target's typical humanity.

A three-factor solution described the rating dimensions: a *competence-autonomy* dimension consisted of competent, articulate, intelligent, similar, responsible for situation, and control over situation; a *warmth-mentalising* dimension consisted of warm, mentalise, infer dispositions, and familiar; and an *emotional-connection* dimension consisted of typically human, empathise, complex emotions, and self-awareness. Significantly *less* competence-control and warmth-mentalising were reported for the dehumanised targets, consistent with the SCM. Dehumanised targets were rated significantly lower on rating dimensions derived from tasks that activate the MPFC. Participants think less about the contents of dehumanised targets' minds. They also rated these targets lower on personality and subjective-experience dimensions. No differences emerged on the emotional-connection dimension, except on the item typically human, on which the dehumanised targets were rated significantly lower than the other three (Harris, 2007).

Affective responses to dehumanised people.   Clearly, people have affective reactions when perceiving others. According to our research these reactions are more than simple positive or negative valence, and they depend on the perceived social group of the target. Consistent with complex affect responses to people is the notion that a person can evoke more than one affective response. Indeed, if asked, participants will report a variety of emotions in response to any one person. We documented this complexity by asking Princeton University students to rate pictured people on the four emotions predicted by the SCM.

All pictures came from our social groups database. All people represented one of eight pretested SCM groups. Two social categories depicted each quadrant as follows:

(a) *High warmth, high competence*—American heroes (e.g., firefighters, police officers, astronauts), college students;
(b) *Low warmth, high competence*—business people, rich people;
(c) *High warmth, low competence*—disabled people, elderly people;
(d) *Low warmth, low competence (dehumanised people)*—homeless people, drug addicts.

Demographic variables (race and gender) varied evenly across all social targets, and age varied evenly across all except the elderly people and college students.

Nearly 300 standardised pictures appeared in roughly numerically equivalent subsets, each presented as a separate sample, so participants rated only one individual subset in an online study. Each social target was rated on the following: *emotions* (pride, envy, pity, disgust), *warmth* (warm, trustworthy, friendly), *competence* (competent, capable, skilled), *social interaction* (similarity, familiarity, likelihood of interacting), and how *typically human* they appeared. The first two scales resulted from synonyms used in previous SCM studies to measure warmth and competence (see Fiske et al., 2002). Each scale had a Cronbach's alpha of at least .89.

Each type of social target elicited some degree of each emotion (Harris, 2007). Also, for the dehumanised people, 92% of their pictures elicited more disgust that the other three emotions. As would be expected, based on status and competence, the social interaction measure correlated positively with pride and envy, but negatively with pity and disgust (the low-competence half of the space). This pattern shows the most likelihood of interaction, similarity, and familiarity when the social target elicits pride, and the least when the target elicits disgust. The two ambivalent emotions, although the effect sizes are smaller, suggest closer social interaction ties to envy than to pity. These findings suggest that the emotion disgust may drive the dehumanised perception.

Social neuroscience data on dehumanised perception

Building on social psychology, the reciprocal nature of social neuroscience appears in a series of studies aimed at demonstrating dehumanised perception. The social psychological theory described thus far makes predictions about the neuroscience data, as discussed next.

Neural indicator of dehumanised perception.   To this point, we have not presented direct neuroimaging evidence of dehumanised perception. We have spent a significant part of the article describing a possible neural indicator of the phenomenon, reduced MPFC activation. We tested the hypothesis that MPFC activation to social groups that elicit disgust may be reduced, compared to other social groups that elicit a more ambivalent social emotion, and to a fixation baseline. In several studies, participants reported how they felt about pictures of social targets representing each quadrant of SCM space, while recording neural activity (Harris & Fiske, 2006, 2007; Harris et al., 2007). For instance, in one study (Harris & Fiske, 2006), participants saw pictures of social targets, faces expressing neutral emotion, landscapes, and carnival/Venetian-styled face-masks. Participants were asked to indicate via button press while viewing the images in the scanner which of four emotions (pride, envy, pity, and disgust) they felt towards each picture.

Behavioural data indicated that the social targets each elicited the predicted emotion above chance level. Accordingly, social targets that elicited pride, envy and pity, all activated MPFC above fixation and landscape baselines, and were more active in three versus one deviant cell contrast analyses. But not all targets activated this mentalising region: No significant MPFC activity emerged above fixation baseline or in the deviant cell contrast analysis in response to pictures of social targets who elicited disgust. Instead, these targets activated the amygdala and insula, areas associated with vigilance and visceral disgust. Moreover, a prior study showed a similar pattern of neural activity for disgusting objects. There was not a complete lack of MPFC activity to disgust-inducing social targets; a subsequent more focused region of interest (ROI) analysis within the overlapping area of MPFC that had activated in response to the other social targets above fixation baseline did reveal a much smaller effect size (roughly half) for the dehumanised targets, compared with the other three. We take these results as a neural indicator of dehumanised perception because a brain region involved in social cognition, including mentalising and person perception as discussed above, is less active to these social targets.

Background on the amygdala and insula.   Dehumanised perception describes a failure to infer the contents of a social target's mind. If participants in our studies are not thinking about the mind of homeless people and drug addicts, are they simply avoiding thoughts about the target, suppressing inferences about the social target's mind? Or are they just very unfamiliar with the social target, and therefore have no relevant mental substance for spontaneous mentalising? What other brain areas activate while the MPFC deactivates to dehumanised targets? The amygdala and the insula both are active in our studies, and both are affective neural regions of the person perception neural network.

Perhaps an over-simplified analogy of a security alarm approximately describes the function of the amygdala; it becomes active whenever emotionally significant stimuli are present (Whalen, 1998). This vigilance idea expands on its role in fear conditioning (Phelps, 2006a, 2006b); its specific function in approach–avoid affect will continually refine as the field advances. At a minimum, the amygdala receives direct input from the thalamus (a relay station in the brain), and from its seat in temporal cortex, projects to almost all of the brain directly or indirectly, and tracks trustworthiness judgements (Engell et al., 2007; Winston et al., 1998) and implicit bias (Phelps et al., 2000), for example. Untrustworthy and outgroup people both require vigilance.

The amygdala allows social interaction and perhaps triggers mentalising. Patients with amygdala lesions show ToM impairments (Fine, Lumsden, & Blair, 2001; Stone, Baron-Cohen, Calder, Keane, & Young, 2003), cannot attribute social meaning to animated geometrical shapes (Heberlein et al., 1998), cannot reason about social exchange (Stone, Cosmides, Tooby, Kroll, & Knight, 2002), and cannot process emotion from faces (Young et al., 1995). Similarly, primates decrease social functioning following amygdala lesions (Brothers, Ring, & Kling, 1990; Dicks, Myers, & Kling, 1969; Emery et al., 2001; Kling, Lancaster, & Benitone, 1970; Kling & Steklis, 1976). This suggests that the amygdala plays a key role in mental state inference and general social information processing.

The insula, like the amygdala, is a primary affective area, but the insula reliably attunes to disgust (Phan, Wager, Taylor, & Liberzon, 2002). It also activates to a range of affective stimuli and sometimes links to the basic negative emotion anger (Phan et al., 2002). Moreover, patients with damage to insula and striatal regions do not recognise disgust facial expressions, and do not report experiencing disgust, suggesting that this region is necessary for disgust (Calder, Keane, Manes, Antoun, & Young, 2000). More recently, the insula has been considered a key region for interoception as part of a punishment neural network (see Seymour, Singer, & Dolan, 2007). As a summary, the insula reliably indicates (negative) arousal. Unlike the amygdala, this brain region is not a bundle of sub-cortical nuclei, but is housed in the cortex, although close to sub-cortical structures.

The insula also allows empathising, as described above. Research has demonstrated that the insula is more active when participants witness a close other experience a negative event, specifically a mild shock (Singer et al., 2006). Although psychologists have considered empathy akin to mentalis-ing, neuroscientists view mentalising as the more cognitive component of the more affective empathy system, which involves a number of areas in addition to the insula (Singer, 2006).

In racial prejudice, these areas of the brain associate with approach–avoidance affect, and are both more active when White participants look at unfamiliar Black than White male faces (Hart et al., 2000; Lieberman, Hariri, Jarcho, Eisenberger, & Bookheimer, 2005; Phelps et al., 2000; Wheeler & Fiske, 2005). Moreover, these activations correlate with implicit measures of bias and fear such as the implicit association test (IAT) and startle-eye blink response (Phelps et al., 2000). Notably, the race-amygdala effect attenuates for familiar faces (Phelps et al., 2000), repeated faces (Hart et al., 2000), and individuated faces (Wheeler & Fiske, 2005). Therefore these affective areas of the person perception neural network may be crucial indicators of dehumanised perception.

Neural malleability in dehumanised perception. Previous social neuroscience shows that neural activation during intergroup bias, specifically racial bias paradigms, is malleable (Hart et al., 2000; Phelps et al., 2000; Wheeler & Fiske, 2005). Moreover, the neural areas that changed their activation patterns were areas more active to our dehumanised targets, further evidence that this dehumanisation bias could be influenced. One such paradigm (Wheeler & Fiske, 2005; for replication, see Harris & Fiske, unpublished; see Figure 4) shows that target-race difference in the amygdala and insula depends on the task: It reduces when participants individuate the social target by inferring the vegetable preference of pictured Black people (Harris & Fiske, unpublished; Wheeler & Fiske, 2005). This paradigm also successfully changed neural responses to dehumanised targets. Participants made vegetable-preference judgements or categorical judgements about dehumanised and other targets. A picture of a vegetable flashed before each pictured target. In the preference condition, participants indicated with a button press whether the targets would like the vegetable. To make this judgement, participants had to infer the target's preference without using the information conveyed by the social category (the vegetables were not associated with stereotypes). In the categorical condition, participants indicated whether the pictured social target was over or under middle age. To make this judgement, participants had to rely on external features of the target without getting into their minds, so this more superficial judgement should simply activate the social category.

Comparing neural responses to the dehumanised targets in the preference condition to activation in the categorical condition resulted in an area of MPFC being activated more for the preference judgements (Harris & Fiske, 2007). At least temporarily, perceivers could mentalise the dehumanised targets. In this instance participants often report using either their own preferences, or those of familiar others who resemble the targets, to make their response. The activated MPFC area was similar to the same contrast for the other social targets (Harris & Fiske, 2007).

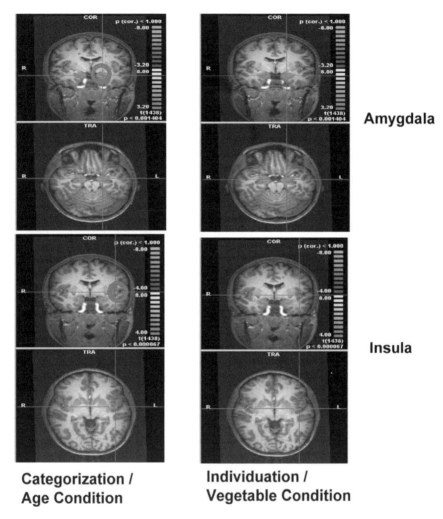

Figure 4. Manipulating amygdala and insula (see online for colour version). These contrast maps are the result of comparing black to white faces, with areas in orange showing more activation to black than white faces. The areas in the crosshairs show amygdala and insula activity change resulting from having participant categorise or individuate black and white faces. Participants made categorical over/under high school age judgements and individuated like/dislike vegetables judgements. There is significantly more activation in both brain regions to black faces than white faces after categorical versus individuated judgements. Each image also shows the *p*-value.

Electroencephalography (EEG)

Participants reported how they felt about pictures of social targets representing each quadrant of SCM space, while recording neural activity

220

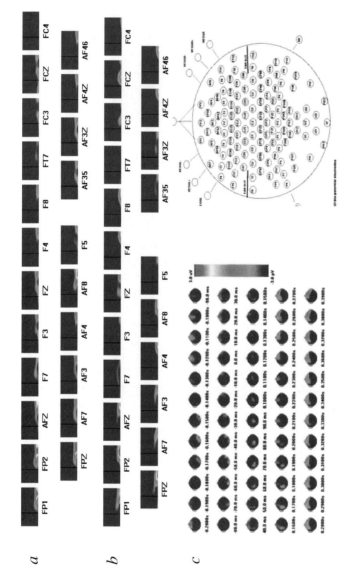

Figure 5. EEG activity to dehumanised groups (see online for colour version). Participants in the EEG study simply looked at pictures of social targets and reported the evoked emotion. (a) Average α waves in response to pride, pity, and envy targets, recorded from the frontal regions identified on the map in the bottom right corner. (b) Average α waves in response to disgust targets, recorded from the frontal regions identified on the map in the bottom right corner. (c) Heat maps showing areas of recorded signal 2000 milliseconds before through 3900 milliseconds after stimulus presentation. In all maps, brighter colours indicate more activity: a and b show less activity to dehumanised targets recorded in electrodes over frontal cortex, notably FPZ, FP1, and FP2; c shows more activity to social targets that are not dehumanised. Activity to all targets begins around 80 ms, over visual cortex, c shows differential activity to dehumanised targets beginning around 1600 ms over temporal cortex, then around 2400 ms over frontal cortex. Yellow electrodes in the array were not operationable.

with EEG (Harris, Gelfand, Escobedo, & Fiske, unpublished). The EEG data showed essentially compatible results with the previously described fMRI studies, and demonstrate a rapid time-frame for these responses. There is a differentiation in electrodes over frontal cortex approximately 100 ms after presentation of the social target. A first negative component responded maximally to those who elicited the complex social emotions of pride, envy, and pity, followed by a second negative component at 300 ms spread over most of the scalp. This latter component responded maximally to the dehumanised targets who elicited the simple basic negative emotion of disgust (see Figure 5 for scalp maps and intensity graphs). But does this evidence together with all the other evidence we described really indicate that these social targets are perceived as less human? Perhaps.

CONCLUSIONS

Thus far we have presented arguments and data supporting the claim that some social targets are not perceived as typically human to the same extent as other social targets. Specifically, people do not imagine the mental states of these dehumanised targets. This phenomenon, dehumanised perception, responds to social targets belonging to social groups perceived as low on trait warmth and competence that elicit the basic emotion disgust. Participants use fewer mental state verbs when describing these targets, and rate them lower on humanising dimensions. Furthermore, there is reduced activation in the MPFC, an area of the brain necessary for social cognition, when people look at these dehumanised targets, compared to other social targets and resting baselines. This difference occurs about 150 milliseconds after stimulus presentation. However, the MPFC can be reactivated to these dehumanised targets if perceivers spontaneously mentalise the targets by inferring their preference. This suggests that the phenomenon is not "hard-wired", and provides converging evidence for mentalising as a mediating mechanism necessary for perception of typical humans.

But why would a perceiver not infer the mental state of a target with mental states, given the predictive benefits of doing so? Recent research suggests that dehumanised perception may be a spontaneous regulation strategy. When participants are not able to escape looking at these dehumanised targets, as is the case in all the experiments in this line of research described thus far, participants show neural indicators of dehumanised perception. However, if participants are given the opportunity to escape looking at these targets, participants do not show neural activation patterns indicative of dehumanised perception. Also, physiological markers of disgust tend to be lower when participants engage in dehumanised perception compared to escape, providing further evidence that not perceiving another as human may be a regulation strategy, perhaps aimed at avoiding empathy exhaution (see Batson, 1991).

Limitations of social neuroscience approaches

Reverse inferences—inferring psychological function from brain data—plague any cognitive neuroscience correlational approach (see Poldrack, 2006). This problem can be more severe if the researcher treats the neuroscience data as the sole dependent variable, providing support for the occurrence of a mental process, because these data may mistakenly be viewed as sufficient evidence of the occurrence of that process. There are two ways around this problem. The first is to show via different statistical methods (for example modelling) that the neural region is indeed correlated with the specific variance of the underlying mechanism, satisfying multiple axioms. The other method is to provide converging evidence, and view the neural data as only part of the evidence, but not the whole. Because the brain region may compute additional functions, then researchers can test these alternatives using traditional behavioural methods, and a reciprocal research program is generated. Dissociations within the same paradigm provide strong support for one process over another. The latter has been our preferred strategy.

Having said this, we do not consider social neuroscience a sufficient social psychology, but it does address social psychological theory. Therefore, social psychologists can utilise this technique. It is becoming a theoretically distinct field because the reciprocal nature of the approach generates new theory, theory unique enough to the social neuroscience perspective that it is becoming distinct. The question remains whether social neuroscience in its infancy has developed enough theory to have an identifiably distinct body of work. That question will be answered as the field continues to generate research.

Another interesting aspect of social neuroscience is the parallel emergence of neuroeconomics (see Glimcher, Camerer, Poldrack, & Fehr, 2008, for review of the field). This field addresses questions specific to judgement and decision making, a perspective adjacent to social psychology, although focused on economic theory. Therefore, the technique differs, relying more on regressing economic models on brain data, and holding different requirements for behaviour (if the behaviour has no real-life economic consequences, then it is not a valid reflection of a phenomenon). Is social neuroscience distinct from other emergent techniques such as neuroeconomics? This question remains open.

Societal consequences of dehumanisation

If some affective experience correlates with failure to mentalise, while other affective experiences correlate with mentalising, then affect may be able to adjust dehumanised perception. Disgust as an emotion is associated among other things with the unfamiliar, and a social interaction measure has been inversely associated with disgust, suggesting that increasing familiarity with these targets may change how they are perceived. This relationship also suggests that affective responses to social targets are learned.

An investigation of social learning may reveal how these associations are learned (possibly from the media, socialisation processes, associations in culture), and how they may be extinguished. A possible societal consequence of this dehumanisation may be reduced helping and neglect of dehumanised groups. Disgust predicts both passive and active harm (Cuddy et al., 2008), and people report less willingness to help dehumanised groups (Cuddy et al., 2007). This suggests that problems like homelessness represent a challenge because people are not ordinarily motivated to help when thinking about members of this category.

To return to a variant of our earlier robot example, imagine a computer that plays chess and has an occasional conversation with its human competitor. Would it be egregious to dismember the computer? Imagine a friend with whom the competitor engages in the same activities; now consider dismembering the friend. The second consideration seems unpleasant because the friend is a person, and the computer is not. But what separates the two? A human essence is arguably the distinguishing factor, but what exactly is a human essence? Consider that the computer has intentions, just as the friend. But also consider that the computer cannot suffer, as the friend can suffer. Because people are aware of phenomenological states such as anger, pain, sadness, pleasure, and so on, they can identify when another person experiences these states. Furthermore, if the perceiver has experienced these phenomenological states resulting in a kind of spontaneous empathy, then people enjoy witnessing others' appetitive states such as pleasure, except for instances of schadenfreude triggered by envy from social comparison where these preferences are reversed, but dislike witnessing others' aversive states such as pain. Spontaneous vicarious reactions suggest empathy that distinguishes between immediate "hot", affective reactions that occur without intent, and intentional cognitions that can be "cold" and devoid of affect (Frith, 2003). Because people have hot empathic reactions to phenomenal states, perhaps this underlies their moral intuitions—their sense of right and wrong—a sense of morality (Haidt, 2007).

Final thoughts

The nature of perceived humanity is a fundamental question in a number of fields of scientific investigation, but often lies dormant and partially ignored because of the magnitude of the question. A social neuroscience approach, because of its reciprocal interdisciplinary nature, begins to strip away some of the mystique from large questions like this, making it possible to ask subsequent research questions. Therefore we also demonstrate a method that can tackle this difficult question concerning people. Emotions, intentionality, moral psychology, prejudice and inter-group relations, person perception, economic value, all relate to this research and require consideration in the research process. This makes social neuroscience a valuable technique for exploring social psychological questions because it generates new data and theory due to its interdisciplinary nature. By using philosophy as a mediator between social psychology and neuroscience, future generations of scientists may continue to unlock the fields' most complicated and important questions.

REFERENCES

Adolphs, R. (2004). Emotion, social cognition, and the human brain. In J. Cacioppo & G. Berntson (Eds.), *Essays in social neuroscience* (pp. 121–132). Cambridge, MA: MIT Press.

Alexander, M. G., Brewer, M. B., & Hermann, R. K. (1999). Images and affect: A functional analysis of out-group stereotypes. *Journal of Personality and Social Psychology, 77*, 78–93.

Allport, G. W. (1954). *The nature of prejudice*. Reading, MA: Addison-Wesley.

Ambady, N., & Rosenthal, R. (1993). Half a minute: Predicting teacher evaluations from thin slices of nonverbal behaviour and physical attractiveness. *Journal of Personality and Social Psychology, 64*, 431–441.

Amodio, D. M., & Frith, C. D. (2006). Meeting of minds: The medial frontal cortex and social cognition. *Nature Reviews, Neuroscience, 7*, 268–277.

Appiah, K. A. (2003). *Thinking it through: An introduction to contemporary philosophy*. New York: Oxford University Press.

Asch, S. E. (1946). Forming impressions of personality. *Journal of Abnormal and Social Psychology, 41*, 258–290.

Bar-Tal, D. (1990). Delegitimization: The extreme case of stereotyping and prejudice. In D. Bar-Tal, C. Graumann, A. Kruglanski & W. Stroebe (Eds.), *Stereotyping and prejudice: Changing conceptions*. New York: Spinger-Verlag.

Batson, C. D. (1991). *The altruism question: Towards a social-psychological answer*. Hillsdale, NJ: Lawrence Erlbaum Associates Inc.

Batson, C. D. (1998). Altruism and prosocial behaviour. In D. Gilbert, S. Fiske, & G. Lindzey (Eds.) *The handbook of social psychology* (Vol. 2, pp. 282–316). New York: McGraw-Hill.

Brothers, L. A., Ring, B., & Kling, A. S. (1990). Response of neurons in the macaque amygdala to complex social stimuli. *Behavioural Brain Research, 41*, 199–213.

Calder, A. J., Keane, J., Manes, F., Antoun, N., & Young, A. W. (2000). Impaired recognition and experience of disgust following brain injury. *Nature Neuroscience, 3*, 1077–1078.

Castano, E., & Giner-Sorolla, R. (2006). Not Quite Human: Infrahumanisation in response to collective responsibility for intergroup killing. *Journal of Personality and Social Psychology, 90*, 804–818.

Cortes, B. P., Demoulin, S., Rodriguez, R. T., Rodriguez, A. P., & Leyens, J. P. (2005). Infra-humanisation or familiarity? Attribution of uniquely human emotions to the self, the ingroup, and the outgroup. *Personality and Social Psychology Bulletin, 31*, 243–253.

Cuddy, A. J., Fiske, S. T., Glick, P. (2007a). The BIAS Map: Behaviours from intergroup affect and stereotypes. *Journal of Personality and Social Psychology, 92*, 631–648.

Cuddy, A. J., Fiske, S. T., Kwan V. S., Glick, P., Demoulin, S., Leyens, J. P., et al. (2009). Stereotype content model holds across cultures: Universal similarities and some differences. *British Journal of Social Psychology, 48*, 1–33.

Cuddy, A. J. C., Rock, M. S., & Norton, M. I. (2007b). Aid in the aftermath of Hurricane Katrina: Inferences of secondary emotions and intergroup Helping. *Group Processes and Intergroup Relations, 10,* 107–118.

Decety, J., & Jackson, P. L. (2004). The functional architecture of human empathy. *Behavioural and Cognitive Neuroscience Reviews, 3,* 406–412.

Decety, L., & Jackson, P. L. (2006). A social-neuroscience perspective on empathy. *Current Directions in Psychological Science, 15,* 54–58.

Delgado, M. R. (2007). Reward-related responses in the human striatum. *Annals of the New York Academy of Science, 1104,* 70–88.

Demoulin, S., Torres, R. R., Perez, A. R., Vaes, J., Paladino, M. P., Gaunt, R., et al. (2005). Emotional prejudice can lead to infrahumanisation. *European Review of Social Psychology, 15,* 259–296.

Dennett, D. (1987). *The intentional stance.* Cambridge, MA: MIT Press.

Dicks, D., Myers, R., & Kling, A. S. (1969). Uncus and amygdala lesions: Effects on social behaviour in the free-ranging rhesus monkey. *Science, 165,* 69–71.

Dunning, D., Meyerowitz, J. A., & Holzberg, A. D. (1989). Ambiguity and self-evaluation: The role of idiosyncratic trait definitions in self-serving assessments of ability. *Journal of Personality and Social Psychology, 57,* 1082–1090.

Eagly, A. H., & Mladinic, A. (1989). Gender stereotypes and attitudes towards women and men. *Personality and Social Psychology Bulletin, 15,* 543–558.

Emery, N. J., Capitanio, J. P., Mason, W. A., Machado, C. J., Mendoza, S. P., & Amaral, D. G. (2001). The effects of bilateral lesions of the amygdala on dyadic social interactions in rhesus monkeys (*Macaca mulatta*). *Behavioural Neuroscience, 115,* 515–544.

Engell, A. D., Haxby, J. V., & Todorov, A. (2007). Implicit trustworthiness decisions: Automatic coding of face properties in the human amygdala. *Journal of Cognitive Neuroscience, 19,* 1508–1519.

Fine, C., Lumsden, J., & Blair, R. J. (2001). Dissociation between 'theory of mind' and executive functions in a patient with early left amygdala damage. *Brain, 124,* 287–298.

Fiske, S. T. (2004). *Social beings: A core motives approach to social psychology.* New York: Wiley.

Fiske, S. T., Cuddy, A. J., & Glick, P. (2007). Universal dimensions of social cognition: Warmth and competence. *Trends in Cognitive Science, 11,* 77–83.

Fiske, S. T., Cuddy, A. J., Glick, P., & Xu, J. (2002). A model of (often mixed) stereotype content: Competence and warmth respectively follow from perceived status and competition. *Journal of Personality and Social Psychology, 82,* 878–902.

Fiske, S. T., Harris, L. T., & Cuddy, A. J. (2004). Why ordinary people torture enemy prisoners. *Science, 306,* 1421–1632.

Fiske, S. T., & Taylor, S. E. (2008). *Social cognition: From brains to culture.* Boston: McGraw-Hill.

Frith, C. (2003). The scientific study of consciousness. In M. A. Ron & T. W. Robbins (Eds.), *Disorders of brain and mind* (2nd ed., pp. 197–222). Cambridge, UK: Cambridge University Press.

Frith, U., & Frith, C. (2001). The biological basis of social interaction. *Current Directions in Psychological Science, 10,* 151–155.

Galinsky, A. D., Ku, G., Wang, C. S. (2005). Perspective-taking and the self–other overlap: Fostering social bonds and facilitation social coordination. *Group Processes and Intergroup Relations, 8,* 109–124.

Galinsky, A. D., & Moskowitz, G. B. (2000). Perspective-taking: Decreasing stereotype expression, stereotype accessibility, and in-group favoritism. *Journal of Personality and Social Psychology, 78,* 708–724.

Glimcher, P., Camerer, C., Poldrack, R., & Fehr, E. (2008). *Neuroeconomics: Decision making and the brain.* Oxford, UK: Elsevier.

Goff, P. A., Eberhardt, J. L., Williams, M., & Jackson, M. C. (2008). Not yet human: Implicit knowledge, historical dehumanisation, and contemporary consequences. *Journal of Personality and Social Psychology, 94*, 292–306.

Gosling, S. D., Kwan, V. S., & John, O. P. (2003). A dog's got personality: A cross-species comparative approach to personality judgements in dogs and humans. *Journal of Personality and Social Psychology, 85*, 1161–1169.

Greene, J. D., Sommerville, R. B., Nystrom, L. E., Darley, J. M., & Cohen, J. D. (2001). An fMRI investigation of emotional engagement in moral judgment. *Science, 293*(14), 2105–2108.

Haidt, J. (2007). The new synthesis in moral psychology. *Science, 316*, 998–1002.

Haidt, J., Rozin, P., McCauley, C., & Imada, S. (1997). Body, psyche, and culture: The relationship between disgust and morality. *Psychology and Developing Societies, 9*, 107–131.

Hamilton, D. L. (1981). *Cognitive processes in stereotyping and intergroup behaviour*. Hillsdale, NJ: Lawrence Erlbaum Associates Inc.

Harris, L. T. (2007). *Dehumanized perception fails to represent the contents of a social target's mind*. Dissertation thesis, Princeton University, NJ, USA.

Harris, L. T., & Fiske, L. T. (2006). Dehumanising the lowest of the low: Neuroimaging responses to extreme outgroups. *Psychological Science, 17*, 847–853.

Harris, L. T., & Fiske, S. T. (2007). Social groups that elicit disgust are differentially processed in mPFC. *Social Cognitive and Affective Neuroscience, 2*, 45–51.

Harris, L. T., McClure, S., Van den Bos, W., Cohen, J. D., & Fiske, S. T. (2007). Regions of MPFC differentially tuned to social and nonsocial affective stimuli. *Cognitive and Behavioural Neuroscience, 7*, 309–316.

Harris, L. T., Todorov, A., & Fiske, S. T. (2005). Attributions on the brain: Neuro-imaging dispositional inferences beyond theory of mind. *NeuroImage, 28*, 763–769.

Hart, A. J., Whalen, P. J., Shin, L. M., McInerney, S. C., Fischer, H., & Rauch, S. L. (2000). Differential response in the human amygdala to racial outgroup vs. ingroup face stimuli. *Brain Imaging, 11*, 2351–2355.

Haslam, N. (2006). Dehumanisation: An integrative review. *Personality and Social Psychology Review, 10*, 252–264.

Haslam, N., Bain, P., Douge, L., Lee, M., & Bastian, B. (2005). More human than you: Attributing humanness to self and others. *Journal of Personality and Social Psychology, 89*, 937–950.

Haslam, N., Bain, P., Loughnan, S., & Kashima, Y. (2008). Attributing and denying humanness to others. *European Review of Social Psychology, 19*, 55–85.

Hauser, M. D. (2006). The liver and the moral organ. *Social Cognitive and Affective Neuroscience, 1*, 214–220.

Haxby, J. V., Gobbini, M. I., & Montgomery, K. (2004). Spatial and temporal distribution of face and object representations in the human brain. In M. Gazzaniga (Ed.), *The cognitive neurosciences* (pp. 889–904). Cambridge, MA: MIT Press.

Heberlein, A. S., Adolphs, R., Tranel, D., & Damasio, H. (2004). Cortical regions for judgements of emotions and personality traits from point-light walkers. *Journal of Cognitive Neuroscience, 16*, 1143–1158.

Heberlein, S. A., Adolphs, R., Tranel, D., Kemmerer, D., Anderson, S., & Damasio, A. R. (1998). Impaired attribution of social meanings to abstract dynamic geometric patterns following damage to the amygdala. *Society for Neuroscience Abstracts, 24*, 1176.

Heider, F. (1958). *The psychology of interpersonal relations*. Wiley, New York.

Heider, F., & Simmel, M. (1944). An experimental study of apparent behaviour. *American Journal of Psychology, 57*, 243–259.

Jackson, L. A., Hodge, C. N., Gerard, D. A., Ingram, J. M., Ervin, K. S., & Sheppard, L. A. (1996). Cognition, affect, and behaviour in the prediction of group attitudes. *Personality and Social Psychology Bulletin, 22*, 306–316.

Johansson, M., Mecklinger, A., & Treese, A. (2004). Recognition memory for emotional and neutral faces: An event-related potential study. *Journal of Cognitive Neuroscience*, *16*, 1840–1853.

Johnson, S. C., Baxter, L. C., Wilder, L. S., Pipe, J. G., Heiserman, J. E., & Prigatano, G. P. (2002). Neural correlates of self-reflection. *Brain*, *125*, 1808–1814.

Jones, E. E. (1979). The rocky road from acts to dispositions. *American Psychologist*, *34*, 107–117.

Kelley, H. H. (1972). Attribution in social interaction. In E. E. Jones, D. E. Kanouse, H. H. Kelley, R. E. Nisbett, S. Valins, & B. Weiner (Eds.), *Attribution: Perceiving the cause of behaviour* (pp. 1–26). Hillsdale, NJ: Lawrence Erlbaum & Associates Inc.

Kelley, W. M., Macrae, C. N., Wyland, C. L., Caglar, S., Inati, S., & Heatherton, T. F. (2002). Finding the self? An event-related fMRI study. *Journal of Cognitive Neuroscience*, *14*, 785–794.

Kling, A. S., Lancaster, J., & Benitone, J. (1970). Amygdalectomy in the free-ranging vervet. *Journal of Psychiatric Research*, *7*, 191–199.

Kling, A. S., & Steklis, H. D. (1976). A neural substrate for affiliative behaviour in non-human primates. *Brain Behaviour and Evolution*, *13*, 216–238.

Kohlberg, L., & Hersh, R. H. (1977). Moral development: A review of the theory. *Theory Into Practice*, *16*, 53–59.

Kwan, V. S. Y., & Fiske, S. T. (2008). Missing links in social cognition: The continuum from nonhuman agents to dehumanised humans. *Social Cognition*, *26*, 125–128.

Kwan, V. S. Y., John, O. P., Kenny, D. A., Bond, M. H., Robins, R. W. (2004). Reconceptualizing individual differences in self-enhancement bias: An interpersonal approach. *Psychological Review*, *111*, 94–110.

Lang, P. J., Bradley, M. M., & Cuthbert, B. N. (2005). *International affective picture system (IAPS): Affective ratings of pictures and instruction manual. Technical Report A-6.* Gainesville, FL: University of Florida.

LeDoux, J. (1998). Fear and the brain: Where have we been, and where are we going? *Biological Psychiatry*, *44*, 1229–1238.

Leibenluft, E., Gobbini, M. I., Harrison, T., & Haxby, J. V. (2004). Mothers' neural activation in response to pictures of their children and other children. *Biological Psychiatry*, *56*, 225–232.

Levenson, R. W. (1996). Biological substrates of empathy and facial modulation of emotion: Two facets of the scientific legacy of John Lanzetta. *Motivation and Emotion*, *20*, 185–204.

Leyens, J. P., Cortes, B. P., Demoulin, S., Dovidio, J., Fiske, S. T., Gaunt, R., et al. (2003). Emotional prejudice, essentialism, and nationalism. *European Journal of Social Psychology*, *33*, 703–718.

Leyens, J. P., Rodriguez-Perez, A., Rodriguez-Torres, R., Gaunt, R., Paladino, M. P., Vaes, J., et al. (2001). Psychological essentialism and the differential attribution of uniquely human emotions to ingroups and outgroups. *European Journal of Social Psychology*, *31*, 395–411.

Lieberman, M. D. (2007). Social cognitive neuroscience: A review of core processes. *Annual Review of Psychology*, *58*, 259–289.

Lieberman, M. D., Hariri, A., Jarcho, J. M., Eisenberger, N. I., & Bookheimer, S. Y. (2005). An fMRI investigation of race-related amygdala activity in African-American and Caucasian-American individuals. *Nature Neuroscience*, *8*, 720–722.

Lieberman, M. D., Jarcho, J. M., & Satpute, A. B. (2004). Evidence-based and intuition-based self-knowledge: An fMRI study. *Journal of Personality and Social Psychology*, *87*, 421–435.

Loughnan, S., & Haslam, N. (2007). Animals and androids: Implicit associations between social categories and nonhumans. *Psychological Science*, *18*, 116–121.

Mackie, D. M., & Smith, E. R. (2002). Intergroup emotions: Prejudice reconceptualized as differentiated reactions to out-groups. In J. P. Forgas & K. D. Williams (Eds.), *The social self: Cognitive, interpersonal, and intergroup perspectives* (pp. 309–326). Philadelphia: Psychology Press.

Martin, J., Bennett, M., & Murray, W. S. (2008). A developmental study of the infrahumanisation hypothesis. *British Journal of Developmental Psychology, 26*, 153–161.

Mason, M. F., Hood, B. M., & Macrae, C. N. (2004). Look into my eyes: Gaze direction and person memory. *Memory, 12*, 637–643.

Mason, M. F., & Macrae, C. N. (2004). Categorising and individuating others: The neural substrates of person perception. *Journal of Cognitive Neuroscience, 16*, 1785–1795.

McArthur, L. A. (1972). The how and what of why: Some determinants and consequences of causal attribution. *Journal of Personality and Social Psychology, 72*, 171–193.

McClure, S. M., Laibson D. I., Loewenstein, G., & Cohen, J. D. (2004). Separate neural systems value immediate & delayed monetary rewards. *Science, 306*(5695), 503–507.

Meiser, T. (2003). Effects of processing strategy on episodic memory and contingency learning in group stereotype formation. *Social Cognition, 21*, 121–156.

Mitchell, J. P., Banaji, M. R., & Macrae, C. N. (2005). The link between social cognition and self-referential thought in the medial prefrontal cortex. *Journal of Cognitive Neuroscience, 17*, 1306–1315.

Mitchell, J. P., Heatherton, T. F., & Macrae, C. N. (2004). Distinct neural systems subserve person and object knowledge. In J. Cacioppo & G. Berntson (Eds.), *Essays in social neuroscience*. Cambridge, MA: MIT Press.

Monahan, J. L., Murphy, S. T., & Zajonc, R. B. (2000). Subliminal mere exposure: Specific, general, and diffuse effects. *Psychological Science, 11*, 462–466.

Neuberg, S. L., & Cottrell, C. A. (2002). Intergroup emotions: A socio-functional approach. In D. M. Mackie & E. R. Smith (Eds.), *From prejudice to intergroup relations: Differentiated reactions to social groups* (pp. 265–283). New York: Psychology Press.

Niedenthal, P., Krauth-Gruber, S., & Ric, F. (2006). *Psychology of emotion: Interpersonal, experiential and cognitive approaches*. New York: Psychology Press.

NIH. (1987). *The health benefits of pets. Workshop summary; September 10–11*. Bethesda, MD: National Institutes of Health, Office of Medical Applications of Research.

Ochsner, K. N. (2007). Social cognitive neuroscience: Historical development, core principles, and future promise. In A. Kruglanksi, & E. T. Higgins (Eds.), *Social psychology: A handbook of basic principles* (2nd ed., pp. 39–66). New York: Guilford Press.

Ochsner, K. N., Knierim, K., Ludlow, D. H., Hanelin, J., Ramachandran, T., Glover, G. et al. (2004). Reflecting upon feelings: An fMRI study of neural systems supporting the attribution of emotion to self and other. *Journal of Cognitive Neuroscience, 16*, 1746–1772.

Ochsner, K. N., & Lieberman, M. D. (2001). The emergence of social cognitive neuroscience. *American Psychologist, 56*, 717–734.

Olsson, A., & Ochsner, K. N. (2008). The role of social cognition in emotion. *Trends in Cognitive Sciences, 12*, 65–71.

Opotow, S. (1990). Moral exclusion and injustice: An introduction. *Journal of Social Issues, 46*, 1–20.

Peeters, G. (1983). Relational and informational patterns in social cognition. In W. Doise & S. Moscovici (Eds.), *Current issues in European social psychology* (Vol. 1, pp. 201–237). Cambridge, UK: Cambridge University Press.

Pelham, B. W., Mirenberg, M. C., & Jones, J. T. (2002). Why Susie sells seashells by the seashore: Implicit egotism and major life decisions. *Journal of Personality and Social Psychology, 82*, 469–487.

Phan, K. L., Wager, T., Taylor, S. F., & Liberzon, I. (2002). Functional neuroanatomy of emotion: A meta-analysis of emotion activation studies in PET and fMRI. *NeuroImage, 16*, 331–348.

Phelps, E. A. (2006a). Emotion and cognition: Insights from studies of the human amygdala. *Annual Review of Psychology, 57*, 27–53.

Phelps, E. A. (2006b). Emotion, learning, and the brain: From classical conditioning to cultural bias. In P. Baltes, P. Reuter-Lorenz, & F. Rosler (Eds.), *Lifespan development and the brain: The perspective of biocultural co-constructivism* (pp. 200–216). New York: Cambridge University Press.

Phelps, E. A., & LaBar, K. S. (2006). Functional neuroimaging of emotion and social cognition. In R. Cabeza & A. Kingstone (Eds.), *Handbook of functional neuroimaging of cognition* (pp. 421–453). Cambridge, MA: MIT Press.

Phelps, E. A., O'Connor, K. J., Cunningham, W. A., Funayama, E. S., Gatenby, J. C., Gore, J. C., et al. (2000). Performance on indirect measures of race evaluation predicts amygdala activation. *Journal of Cognitive Neuroscience, 12*, 729–738.

Plaks, J. E., Grant, H., & Dweck, C. S. (2005). Violations of implicit theories and the sense of prediction and control: Implications for motivated person perception. *Journal of Personality and Social Psychology, 88*, 245–262.

Poldrack, R.A. (2006). Can cognitive processes be inferred from neuroimaging data? *Trends in Cognitive Sciences, 10*, 59–63.

Richardson, D. R., Hammock, G. S., Smith, S. M., & Gardner, W. (1994). Empathy as a cognitive inhibitor of interpersonal aggression. *Aggressive Behaviour, 20*, 275–289.

Rodríguez, A., Coello, E., Betancor, V., Rodríguez, R., & Delgado, N. (2006). When is the infrahumanisation to a threatening outgroup higher? Effects of the ambiguity of situation and the empathy with ingroup. *Psicothema, 18*, 73–77.

Rodríguez-Torres, R., Leyens, J. P., Rodríguez Pérez, A., Betancor Rodriguez, V., Quiles del Castillo, M., Demoulin, S. et al. (2005). The lay distinction between primary and secondary emotions: A spontaneous categorization. *International Journal of Psychology, 40*(2), 100–107.

Rosenberg, S., Nelson, C., & Vivekananthan, P. S. (1968). A multidimensional approach to the structure of personality impressions. *Journal of Personality and Social Psychology, 9*, 283–294.

Ruby, P., & Decety, J. (2004). How would you feel versus how do you think she would feel? A neuroimaging study of perspective-taking with social emotions. *Journal of Cognitive Neuroscience, 16*, 988–999.

Sanfey, A. G., Rilling, J. K., Aronson, J. A., Nystrom, L. E., & Cohen, J. D. (2003). The neural basis of economic decision making in the ultimatum game. *Science, 300*, 1755–1757.

Sears, D. O. (1983). The person-positivity bias. *Journal of Personality and Social Psychology, 44*, 233–250.

Semin, G. R., & Fiedler, K. (1988). The cognitive functions of linguistic categories in describing persons: Social cognition and language. *Journal of Personality and Social Psychology, 54*, 558–568.

Seymour, B., Singer, T., & Dolan, R. (2007). The neurobiology of punishment. *Nature Reviews Neuroscience, 8*, 300–311.

Singer, T. (2006). The neural basis and ontogeny of empathy and mind reading: Review of literature and implication for future research. *Neuroscience and Biobehavioral Reviews, 30*, 855–863.

Singer, T., & Fehr, E. (2005). The neuroeconomics of mind reading and empathy. *American Economic Review, 95*, 340–345.

Singer, T., Seymour, B., O'Doherty, J., Klaas, E. S., Dolan, J. D., Frith, C. (2006). Empathic neural responses are modulated by the perceived fairness of others. *Nature, 439*, 466–469.

Somerville, L. H., Wig, G. S., Whalen, P. J., & Kelley, W. M. (2006). Dissociable medial temporal lobe contributions to social memory. *Journal of Cognitive Neuroscience, 18*, 1253–1265.

Stangor, C., Sullivan, L. A., & Ford, T. E. (1991). Affective and cognitive determinants of prejudice. *Social Cognition, 9*, 359–380.

Staub, E. (1989). *The roots of evil: The origins of genocide and other group violence*. New York: Cambridge University Press.

Stephan, W. G., & Stephan, C. W. (2000). An integrated theory of prejudice. In S. Oskamp (Ed.), *Reducing prejudice and discrimination* (pp. 23–45). Mahwah, NJ: Lawrence Erlbaum Associates Inc.

Stinson, L., & Ickes, W. (1992). Empathic accuracy in the interactions of male friends versus male strangers. *Journal of Personality and Social Psychology, 62,* 787–797.

Stone, V. E., Baron-Cohen, S., Calder, A., Keane, J., &Young, A. (2003). Acquired theory of mind impairments in individuals with bilateral amygdala lesions. *Neuropsychologia, 41,* 209–220.

Stone, V. E., Cosmides, L., Tooby, J., Kroll, N., & Knight, R. T. (2002). Selective impairment of reasoning about social exchange in a patient with bilateral limbic system damage. *Proceedings of the National Academy of Sciences, 99,* 17, 11531–11536.

Talairach, J., & Tournoux, P. (1988). *Co-planar stereotaxic atlas of the human brain*. New York: Thieme.

Tam, T., Hewstone, M., Cairns, E., Tausch, N., Maio, G., & Kenworthy, J. (2007). The impact of intergroup emotions on forgiveness in Northern Ireland. *Group Processes and Intergroup Relations, 10,* 119–136.

Tausch, N., Kenworthy, J., & Hewstone, M. (2007). The confirmability and disconfirmability of trait concepts revisited: Does content matter? *Journal of Personality and Social Psychology, 92,* 554–556.

Taylor, S. E., & Brown, J. D. (1988). Illusion and well-being: A social psychological perspective on mental health. *Psychological Bulletin, 103,* 193–210.

Taylor, S. E., & Gollwitzer, P. M. (1995). Effects of mindset on positive illusions. *Journal of Personality and Social Psychology, 69,* 213–226.

Thaler, R. (1980). Towards a positive theory of consumer choice. *Journal of Economic Behaviour and Organization, 1,* 39–60.

Todd, R. M., Lewis, M. D., Meusel, L., & Zelazo, P. D. (2008). The time course of social-emotional processing in early childhood: ERP responses to facial affect and personal familiarity in a go-nogo task. *Neuropsychologia, 46,* 595–613.

Todorov, A., Gobbini, M. I., Evans, K. K., & Haxby, J. V. (2007). Spontaneous retrieval of affective person knowledge in face perception. *Neuropsychologia, 45,* 163–173.

Todorov, A., Harris, L. T., & Fiske, S. T. (2006). Towards behaviourally inspired social neuroscience. *Brain Research, 1079,* 76–85.

Todorov, A., Mandisodza, A. N., Goren, A., & Hall, C. C. (2005). Inferences of competence from faces predict election outcomes. *Science, 308,* 1623–1626.

Todorov, A., & Uleman, J. (2002). Spontaneous trait inferences are bound to actors' faces: Evidence from a false recognition paradigm. *Journal of Personality and Social Psychology, 83,* 1051–1065.

Turkle, S. (2005). *The second self: Computers and the human spirit*. Cambridge, MA: MIT Press.

Vaes, J., Paladino, M. P., Castelli, L., Leyens, J. Ph., Giovanazzi, A. (2003). On the behavioural consequences of infra-humanisation: The implicit role of uniquely human emotions in intergroup relations. *Journal of Personality and Social Psychology, 85,* 1016–1034.

Van den Bos, W., McClure, S., Harris, L T., Fiske, S. T., Nystrom, L., & Cohen, J. D. (2007). Dissociating affective evaluation and social cognitive processes in ventral medial prefrontal cortex. *Cognitive and Behavioral Neuroscience, 7,* 337–346.

van Knippenberg, A., van Twuyver, M., & Pepels, J. (1994). Factors affecting social categorisation processes in memory. *British Journal of Social Psychology, 33,* 419–431.

von Hecker, U., & Dutke, S. (2004). Integrative social perception: Individuals in low working memory benefit from external representations. *Social Cognition, 22,* 336–365.

Whalen, P. J. (1998). Fear, vigilance, and ambiguity: Initial neuroimaging studies of the human amygdala. *Current Direction in Psychological Science, 7*, 177–188.

Wheeler, M. E., & Fiske, S. T. (2005). Controlling racial prejudice: Social-cognitive goals affect amygdala and stereotype activation. *Psychological Science, 16*(1), 56–63.

Willis, J., & Todorov, A. (2006). First impressions: Making up your mind after a 100-ms exposure to a face. *Psychological Science, 17*, 592–598.

Winston, J. S., Strange, B. A., O'Doherty, J., & Dolan, R. J. (2002). Automatic and intentional brain responses during evaluation of trustworthiness of faces. *Nature Neuroscience, 5*, 277–283.

Wojciszke, B., Bazinska, R., & Jaworski, M. (1998). On the dominance of moral categories in impression formation. *Personality and Social Psychology Bulletin, 24*, 1245–1257.

Young, A. W., Aggleton, J. P., Hellawell, D. J., Johnson, M., Broks, P., & Hanley, J. R. (1995). Face processing impairments after amygdalotomy. *Brain, 118*, 15–24.

Zanna, M. P., & Rempel, J. K. (1988). Attitudes: A new look at an old concept. In D. Bar-Tal & A. W. Kruglanski (Eds.), *The social psychology of knowledge* (pp. 315–334). Cambridge, UK: Cambridge University Press.

Zajonc, R. B. (1968). Attitudinal effects of mere exposure. *Journal of Personality and Social Psychology, 9*, 1–27.

Zebrowitz, L. A. (1999). *Reading faces: Window to the soul?* Boulder, CO: Westview Press.

EUROPEAN REVIEW OF SOCIAL PSYCHOLOGY
2009, 20, 232–271

Psychology Press
Taylor & Francis Group

The unconscious unfolding of emotions

Kirsten I. Ruys
Utrecht University, The Netherlands

Diederik A. Stapel
Tilburg University, The Netherlands

How do emotional reactions arise? We argue that emotional information processing and the resulting responses unfold from being *global* to *specific*: Initial emotional responses are typically based on general, positive–negative evaluations, whereas later emotional responses are based on more specific, fine-grained information processing. Global, positive–negative reactions may influence people's mood states, whereas detailed, fine-grained emotional reactions may cause specific emotions such as fear, disgust, or happiness to arise. Our view also entails that global and specific processing may both occur *unconsciously*. In this chapter we briefly discuss theories of emotion that inspired us, we provide empirical evidence for our global-to-specific unfolding view, and we explain consequences of our view for research on facial emotional expressions, imitation, and general mood states.

Keywords: Emotion; Mood; Information processing; Unconscious.

Emotions such as anger, fear, sadness, disgust, happiness, and surprise are essential for human functioning (Cacioppo & Gardner, 1999; Ekman, 1984; Frijda, 1988; Keltner & Gross, 1999; Öhman, 1992; Plutchick, 1994; Scherer, 1984). People have a better chance of staying alive when they experience fear when approaching a steep cliff, and of staying healthy when they experience disgust when seeing or smelling rotten food. However, the emotional reactions to emotional stimuli are not always the same, not even for one individual. A picture of your child taking his first few steps may sometimes elicit general positive feelings and at other times may elicit the more specific emotion of pride.

Correspondence should be addressed to Kirsten I. Ruys, Utrecht University, Department of Psychology, PO Box 80140, 3508 TC Utrecht, The Netherlands. E-mail: k.i.ruys@uu.nl

This research was supported by a "PIONIER" grant from the Netherlands Organization for Scientific Research awarded to Diederik A. Stapel.

DOI: 10.1080/10463280903119060

In this chapter we present a global-to-specific unfolding view of emotional responding that explains why and how an emotional stimulus may elicit different responses. We argue that emotional information processing and the resulting responses (be they physiological, behavioural, cognitive, or feeling responses) unfold from being *global* to becoming *specific*. This means that initial emotional responses to an emotional stimulus are based on general, overall, positive–negative evaluations, whereas later emotional responses are based on more specific, detailed, and fine-grained information processing (see Figure 1). These global, positive–negative reactions may influence people's mood states, whereas detailed, fine-grained emotional reactions may cause specific emotions to arise. Importantly, we assume that both global and specific emotional responses may occur without the need for conscious awareness.

Before we explain our global-to-specific unfolding view of emotional responding in more detail, we start with a discussion of existing emotion theories that inspired us while developing our view. Then, we will elaborate on and provide evidence for each of four elements of our global-to-specific-unfolding view of emotional responding. In the third part of this chapter we lay out the consequences of our global-to-specific unfolding view of emotional responding for research on the functions of facial emotional expressions, imitation, and general mood states. An interesting implication of our global-to-specific unfolding view of emotional responding that we discuss, for example, is that it explores people's responses to facial emotional expressions as emotional stimuli and as emotion communicators.

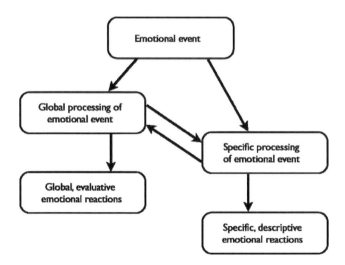

Figure 1. A global-to-specific unfolding view of emotional responding.

Last but not least, we discuss general implications of our global-to-specific unfolding view of emotional responding and talk about its limitations.

EXISTING THEORIES OF EMOTION

Our global-to-specific unfolding view focuses on the emotional responses that emotional events may elicit and incorporates several assumptions that underlie existing theories of emotion. All existing theories of emotion have been crucial in advancing our understanding in the field of emotions. Indeed, we think for example that appraisal theories and basic emotions theory should not be regarded as alternative emotion theories, but rather as complementary theories, in that appraisal theories focus on "the patterns of cognition that trigger an emotional response" (Barrett, Ochsner, & Gross, 2007, p. 179), whereas basic emotions theory focuses on the physical changes that automatically accompany the offset of an emotion. In this section we discuss appraisal theory, basic emotions theory, and theories of arousal and core affect, and explain which assumptions of these theories we incorporated in our global-to-specific unfolding view of emotional responding.

Appraisal theories

Appraisal theories of emotion can be distinguished from other theories of emotion by their emphasis on cognition. The central assumption is that estimates of the person-environment relationship (i.e., appraisals) are responsible both for the elicitation of emotions and for a differentiation between specific emotions (e.g., Frijda & Zeelenberg, 2001). Based on the pioneering work of Arnold (1960) and Lazarus (1968), most appraisal theorists now agree that a detailed set of appraisal criteria is necessary to predict which specific configuration of appraisals will produce a specific emotion in an individual (Frijda, 1988; Lazarus, 1991; Manstead & Fischer, 2001; Scherer, 1984; Smith & Ellsworth, 1985; Zeelenberg, van den Bos, van Dijk, & Pieters, 2002).

However, there is much debate in the modern emotion literature as to the specifics of the emotion appraisal process. What specific appraisals are needed to distinguish different emotions? For example, Lazarus (1991) argues that emotions are mainly the product of assessments of the personal significance of events (is it good for me? is it bad for me?; primary appraisals) and judgements concerning one's ability to cope with the situation (secondary appraisals). Similarly but more specifically, Weiner (1985) claims that emotions emerge from assessments of the valence of a particular outcome (is it good–bad?) and classifications of the cause of this outcome along the dimensions of locus, stability, and control. Others have claimed, however, that emotions need to be differentiated along a relatively larger number of appraisal dimensions to make some sense of our emotional lives (e.g., Evers, Fischer, Mosquera, & Manstead, 2005; Manstead & Fischer, 2001; Parkinson & Manstead, 1992; Scherer, 1984, 1999).

Even though the ultimate appraisal dimensions are still unknown, a critical assumption of appraisal theories is that specific processing plays an essential role in the production of emotions (Scherer, 1999). We argue that specific processing is particularly important for emotional responding. For example, being surprised by either a mouse or a tiger may both trigger the emotion of fear. Still, people's emotional responses to mice and tigers are quite different. In line with appraisal theories, we propose that which specific emotion and which emotional responses are produced after exposure to an emotion-eliciting stimulus depends on the information that is cognitively activated during such exposure (see also Neumann, 2000).

Basic emotions theory

In contrast to appraisal theories of emotion, the focus of basic emotions theory is on the innate and physical aspects of emotion, for example the assumed universality of emotional expressions. The roots of the basic emotions view can be traced back to Darwin (1872) who was interested in the similarities between humans and non-humans in the expression of emotions. This relates to the central tenet of basic emotions theory that an emotion is elicited by a specific, neural "affect program" that activates an automatic syndrome of hormonal, muscular, and autonomic effects that constitute the distinctive signature of a specific emotion (Ekman, 1992; Panksepp, 1998). The assumption that each specific emotion is represented by a specific affect program means that only a restricted number of basic emotions can exist (e.g., happiness, surprise, fear, disgust, sadness, and anger).

An essential part of basic emotions theory is that specific emotions are triggered automatically, without the need for conscious awareness. Ample evidence exists that global positive–negative classifications of stimuli occur quickly and unconsciously (Bargh, Litt, Pratto, & Spielman, 1989; Murphy & Zajonc, 1993; Stapel, Koomen, & Ruys, 2002; Winkielman & Berridge, 2004; Zajonc, 1980). However, the hypothesis that the specific, fine-grained processing necessary to trigger specific affect programs may occur unconsciously has often been denied (e.g., Bargh, 1997; Zajonc, 1980). In spite of this controversy, we argue in line with the basic emotions view and recent empirical evidence (Ruys & Stapel, 2008a) that processing of specific emotional content can occur unconsciously, and thus that affect programs may indeed be triggered automatically, without the need for controlled processing.

Theories of arousal and core affect

Whereas basic emotions theory assumes autonomic specificity of physiological emotional responses, other theories of emotion assume that the physical origin of all emotions is basically the same. The two-factor theory of Schacter and Singer (1962) for example claims that emotions consist of undifferentiated physiological arousal and situationally appropriate cognition. Schacter and Singer (1962) assume that cognitive interpretations of consciously experienced physiological arousal determine which particular emotion people experience. When people become aware of physiological changes in their bodies in response to an emotional event, they start searching for an explanation of these physiological changes. The conscious identification of a probable cause of their physiological arousal may result in the experience of the emotion associated with that cause. An essential aspect of the two-factor theory of emotion is thus that the experience of specific emotions relies on a conscious attribution process (Cornelius, 1996).

A modern variant of the two-factor theory of emotion is the theory of *core affect* (Barrett, 2005, 2007; Russell, 2003). The basic idea behind this theory is that emotional states arise from core affect in combination with the attribution of core affect to an object. Core affect, in turn, can be elicited both by internal and external stimuli. A major difference with the two-factor theory of emotion is that positive or negative valence accompanies the undifferentiated state of arousal. According to Russell (2003), core affect is "a neurophysiologic state that is consciously accessible as a simple, non-reflective feeling that is an integral blend of hedonic (pleasure–displeasure) and arousal (sleepy–activated) values" (p. 147). The experience of an emotion is the result of a categorisation process based on core affect and the outputs of other emotion components, such as appraisals about the emotional event and the physiological changes resulting from core affect and instrumental actions. Thus, knowledge about emotions is regarded as the main determinant of people's specific emotional perceptions and feelings (Barrett, 2005, 2007; Russell, 2003).

To us, the most interesting aspect of core affect theory is the idea that emotions develop from a global, positive–negative state to a more specific emotional state such as anger or fear, through the activation of emotion knowledge. In line with the theory of core affect, we argue that emotional reactions unfold from global, positive–negative reactions to more specific emotional reactions, and start occurring *before* most of the emotional event has been processed. The changing and developing nature of emotions and the importance of looking at the emotion *process* instead of looking at emotions as static states has also been emphasised by Scherer: "... we need to focus on emotion episodes that are characterized by constant changes in the underlying appraisal and reaction processes" (Scherer, 1999, p. 764).

Summary

Our global-to-specific unfolding view of emotional responding is heavily inspired by existing theories of emotion. We borrowed from appraisal theory the idea that specific processing is necessary for the occurrence of specific emotions like anger, fear, happiness, disgust, and surprise. In line with basic emotions theory we assume that these specific emotions can be induced automatically and unconsciously, thus without knowing what caused these specific emotions. Arousal and core affect theories of emotion brought us the developing and unfolding nature of emotional reactions. Our global-to-specific unfolding view complements these existing theories by focusing on the unfolding of emotional reactions that occur in response to emotional events.

FOUR ELEMENTS OF GLOBAL-TO-SPECIFIC UNFOLDING OF EMOTIONS

We propose that when one encounters an emotional stimulus, the first piece of information that becomes activated in one's mind is the positivity or negativity of this emotional stimulus (i.e., its valence). Imagine, for example, that you are confronted with your favourite dessert, a chocolate pie prepared by the best bakery in town. We argue that, in this case, the first thing to be activated in your mind will be an immediate global, *positive* reaction to the chocolate pie. Over time, more specific, fine-grained emotional stimulus information may become activated, like *food, brown, excellent taste, chocolate, fat, diet*. The activation of more specific information may elicit specific emotions like *joy* or *guilt*. Similarly, when you suddenly see a dangerous, poisonous snake crossing the trail while you are hiking in the woods, the first thing that is activated in your mind will be a global, *negative* reaction. The activation of more specific information, namely that the negative stimulus is a dangerous, poisonous snake you should not step on, and the elicitation of feelings of fear take more time. In a nutshell, what we propose is that people's responses to an emotional stimulus typically unfold from global, positive–negative reactions to specific emotional reactions like joy, guilt, or fear.

More formally, we define our global-to-specific unfolding view of emotional responding by four interrelated elements: (1) Processing of emotional information may on the one hand result in global, positive–negative responses and on the other hand lead to more specific, fine-grained responses. (2) Global positive–negative responses typically occur prior to more specific emotional responses. (3) Emotional reactions unfold over time from being global to becoming specific. (4) Both global and specific information processing may occur without conscious awareness.

These four elements of our global-to-specific unfolding view of emotional responding recently received direct empirical support from two studies that examined emotional reactions to subliminally presented emotional stimuli (Ruys & Stapel, 2008a). In this research we varied the *length of subliminal exposure* to a stimulus to manipulate whether global or more specific emotional responses would be triggered (see also, Ruys & Stapel, 2008b, 2008c; Stapel & Koomen, 2005, 2006; Stapel et al., 2002). The hypothesis was that *super quick* subliminal exposure to emotional stimuli would merely allow for global processing of the emotional stimuli and therefore that super quick exposures to these emotional stimuli would trigger global, emotional reactions. Thus, participants who were super-quickly exposed to fearful or disgusting pictures would show a general, negative emotional response compared to participants who were exposed to neutral pictures. A second hypothesis was that *quick* subliminal exposure to these emotional stimuli would allow for more specific processing of the emotional stimuli and therefore that quick exposures to these stimuli would trigger specific emotional reactions. Participants who were quickly exposed to fearful or disgusting pictures would thus show a fear or disgust response, respectively, compared to participants who were exposed to neutral pictures. This pattern of findings would not only reveal that stimulus events may sometimes elicit global, positive–negative responses and at other times elicit more specific, fine-grained responses. It would also demonstrate that global, positive–negative responses typically emerge prior to specific, fine-grained responses.

The distinction between quick (120 ms) and super quick subliminal exposures (40 ms) was established with a parafoveal vigilance task (see also, Bargh & Pietromonaco, 1982; Erdley & D'Agostino, 1988). In a parafoveal vigilance task, target stimuli are typically presented on the outer edges of the screen and not in the centre of the screen. When stimuli are presented in the periphery, it takes time to localise these stimuli. Therefore, a masked stimulus can be presented for a relatively long duration (e.g., 120 ms), without participants becoming aware of the content of the stimulus. This provides the opportunity to vary exposure time while stimulus presentation remains subliminal. In priming tasks where stimuli are presented in the centre of the screen, it is difficult to realise varying subliminal exposure times because then participants become more readily aware of the stimulus content, even with so-called "super quick" exposures (e.g., 40 ms).

In the research by Ruys and Stapel (2008a), participants were either quickly or super-quickly exposed to neutral (e.g., a horse) or emotional pictures. The emotional pictures were either fearful (e.g., a growling, mad dog) or disgusting (e.g., a dirty, non-flushed toilet). After the priming phase, participants' global and specific emotional reactions were measured with a cognitive, feeling, and behavioural measure following a multi-component perspective on emotion (Frijda, 1988; Scherer, 1984). In the word completion task that served as cognitive measure in Study 1, participants could complete fragments as disgust words (e.g., "si.." could be completed as "sick" or as "sing"), fear words (e.g., "sca ..." could be completed as "scared" or as "scarce"), and general negative words (e.g., "b.." could completed as "bad" or as "bid"). The occurrence of a specific emotion was expected to increase the tendency to complete word fragments as words related to that emotion (e.g., disgusted participants should be more likely than others to complete fragments as disgust words), whereas experiencing a global, negative mood was expected to increase the tendency to complete more fragments as general negative words. The scenario measure that served as cognitive measure in Study 2 consisted of (emotion-specific) fear and disgust scenarios. In one of the fear scenarios, participants imagined walking on the street at night and noticing that a suspicious person was moving towards them. They then indicated the likelihood that they would cross the street. We expected that scared participants would be more likely than participants who did not feel scared to interpret the situation as fearful and therefore to indicate that they would cross the street. The feeling measure consisted of a general mood question and eight specific emotion scales (i.e., fearful, disgusted, satisfied, relieved, proud, angry, shameful, and joyful). As a measure of behaviour, participants were asked to choose between participating in a scary-movies test or a strange-food test. We expected that fearful participants would choose the strange-food test to avoid more fear-eliciting materials, whereas disgusted participants would choose the scary-movie test to avoid exposure to exotic, potentially disgusting food.

As expected, the results showed that *quick* exposures to disgusting pictures increased the cognitive accessibility of disgust words and feelings of disgust. Similarly, fearful pictures increased the cognitive accessibility of fear words and feelings of fear. As depicted in Figure 2, participants completed more disgust words after quick exposures to disgusting pictures than after quick exposures to fearful or neutral pictures, and participants completed more fear words after quick exposures to fearful pictures than after quick exposures to disgusting or neutral pictures. Quick exposures to emotion-eliciting pictures also produced behavioural effects: Quick exposures to fearful pictures led participants to choose the strange-food test, whereas quick exposures to disgusting pictures led participants to choose scary movies. However, *super quick* exposures to these fearful or disgusting stimuli elicited global, negative feelings rather than a specific emotion: Super quick exposures to emotion-eliciting pictures increased the cognitive accessibility of general negative words and general negative feelings. As depicted in Figure 3, participants completed more general negative words after super quick exposures to disgusting or fearful pictures than after super quick exposures to neutral pictures. These findings were replicated in Study 2.

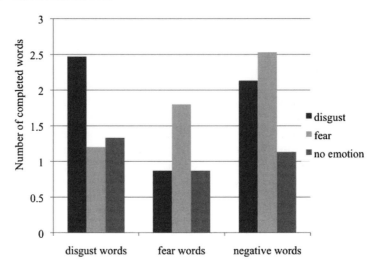

Figure 2. Mean number of words completed after quick exposure durations (120ms) as a function of prime (Study 1, Ruys & Stapel, 2008a).

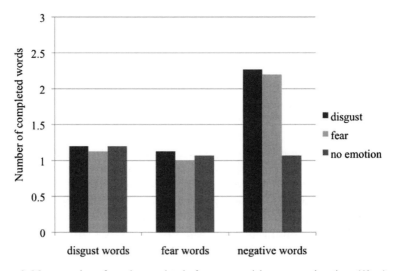

Figure 3. Mean number of words completed after super quick exposure durations (40ms) as a function of prime (Study 1, Ruys & Stapel, 2008a).

Thus, with little time available to process the emotional pictures, only global, evaluative information was activated, resulting in a global negative mood and the activation of general negative cognitions. However, with relatively plentiful time available to process the emotional pictures, specific fine-grained information was activated, leading to specific emotions (Ruys & Stapel, 2008a). These findings support the four elements of our global-to-specific unfolding view of emotional responding, namely that processing of emotional information may result in global, positive–negative responses and more specific, fine-grained responses; that global positive–negative responses typically occur prior to more specific emotional responses; that an emotional response unfolds over time from a global mood to a specific, meaning-based emotion like fear or disgust; and that both global and specific information processing may occur without conscious awareness. In the next four sections of this chapter we discuss additional theoretical and empirical support for each of the separate elements.

Distinguishing global and specific processing

People can focus on the forest or they can focus on the trees (see Navon, 1977). What once started out as a literal example to illustrate the principles of global and specific processing in visual perception has recently become an often-used metaphor to illustrate global and specific processing at the conceptual level. In the mean time, the distinction between processing at the global or holistic level and processing at the local or specific level has been well established (Derryberry & Tucker, 1994; Kimchi, 1992; Navon, 1977). Global processing occurs to get the gist or the essence of a visual scene, in this case the forest. Specific processing occurs to fill in the details of a visual scene, in this case the trees. Another way to look at the distinction is to say that global processing occurs from a relatively distant perspective and primarily activates the "big picture", whereas specific processing occurs from a nearby, zoomed-in perspective (see Avramova & Stapel, 2008).

Neuroscientific research indicates that global and specific processing depend on different systems in the brain (Adolphs, 2003; Derryberry & Tucker, 1994; Fink et al., 1996; LeDoux, 1989; Tucker & Williamson, 1984; Zajonc, 2000). Some researchers have assumed hemispheric specialisation, suggesting that specific, analytic processing takes place in the left hemisphere and global, holistic processing in the right hemisphere (for a review see Tucker & Williamson, 1984). Adolphs (2003) also suggests that inter-related but independent neural systems operate for coarse and detailed perceptual processing. In his view, however, coarse perceptual processing is initiated at the superior colliculus and feeds into the amygdala, striatum, and orbitofrontal cortex, whereas detailed perceptual processing takes place at the higher-order sensory cortices, including the fusiform gyrus and the superior temporal gyrus. Thus, different neuroscientific viewpoints support the existence of separate (but intertwined) global and specific processing systems.

Experimental studies have also shown the importance of global and specific processing, both at the perceptual level (Kimchi, 1992; Navon, 1977) and at the conceptual level (Förster, Friedman, & Liberman, 2004; Förster, Liberman, & Kuschel, 2008; Fujita, Henderson, Eng, Trope, & Liberman, 2006; Gasper & Clore, 2002; Smith & Trope, 2006; Stapel & Semin, 2007; Trope & Liberman, 2003; Vallacher & Wegner, 1987). An interesting finding by Fujita and colleagues (2006) is for example that spatial distance of an event (whether the event takes place in a city 3000 miles away, or a few blocks away) may determine to what extent people represent the event in a global or specific way. Specifically, when an event was believed to occur in a spatially near location, people were more likely to describe this event in concrete, specific terms than when the event was believed to take place in a spatially far location (Fujita et al., 2006). This research supports the idea that perceptual distance may influence the representation on a conceptual level.

More generally, the research referred to above demonstrates that the distinction between global and specific processing is essential in seeing and thinking. Our unfolding view of emotional responding entails that global and specific processing not only influence what people see and think, but also influence what people feel. The distinction between global and specific processing has interesting implications for the kind of emotional reactions that occur in response to an emotion-eliciting event. Global processing of an emotional event typically elicits positive–negative emotional reactions because a global way to represent an emotional event is in terms of its positive or negative valence. Specific processing of an emotional event elicits more fine-grained emotional reactions because specific processing is focused on features and details. As the research of Ruys and Stapel (2008a) showed: Some participants who were exposed to disgusting or fearful pictures reported more general negative feelings and showed an increased accessibility of general negative concepts (e.g., *bad*, *stupid*), whereas other participants reported specific feelings of disgust or fear, showed an increased accessibility of specific disgust-related or fear-related semantic concepts (e.g., *sick*, *scary*), and a decreased or increased inclination to avoid scary movies than participants who were subliminally exposed to neutral pictures.

Our distinction between global and specific emotional reactions may (and perhaps should) also remind one of Zajonc's (1980, 2000) notion of two independent systems for affective and non-affective processing. That is because we assume that global processing typically elicits positive–negative responses, whereas specific processing typically elicits more specific, detailed responses. However, an essential difference between our view and Zajonc's theory is that we do not think the processing itself is either affective or non-affective. We simply assert that people's emotional reactions can be general, positive–negative reactions (because global processing comprises the entire emotional event), and more specific, detailed reactions (because specific processing focuses on specific features of the emotional event). Both global and specific reactions can be affective: Global processing of emotional stimuli may, for example, produce a global, positive or negative mood, whereas specific processing may produce a specific emotion like happiness or disgust. However, global and specific reactions in response to an emotional event can also be non-affective: Global and specific processing may activate general positive or negative concepts (e.g., *good, bad*) and more specific emotional concepts (e.g., *frightening, delicious*) respectively.

A second difference between our view and Zajonc's theory is that we regard the global and specific processing systems as highly interrelated and interactive, whereas Zajonc (1980, 2000) regards the systems responsible for affective and non-affective processing as independent. Because global, positive–negative reactions typically occur prior to more specific, detailed emotional reactions, it seems highly plausible that global reactions may indeed influence the content of more specific reactions. Previous research examining the influence of automatic evaluations on more specific social categorisation processes supports this idea (Niedenthal & Cantor, 1986; Ruys, Dijksterhuis, & Corneille, 2008). Future research needs to determine whether global positive–negative emotional reactions, positive or negative mood states for example, also influence specific processing of emotional events.

In this section we have argued that global and specific emotional reactions result from global and specific processing respectively. However, we have to note that, besides evidence regarding the outcomes of global and specific processing systems (Ruys & Stapel, 2008a, 2008b), there is no direct experimental evidence showing that early, global emotional reactions result from global processing and that later, more specific emotional reactions result from specific processing. However, there is initial, indirect evidence for our hypothesis that global and specific processing produce global and specific emotional reactions. In this research, De Liver, van der Pligt, and Wigboldus (2007) explored the relation between construal level of an emotional event and to what degree people experience conflicting positive and negative feelings (i.e., ambivalence) towards the emotional event. They expected that global processing of an emotional event (e.g., blood donation) would lead to less experienced ambivalence than specific processing of the event. Thus, global processing was expected to generate either positive or negative feelings, whereas specific processing was expected to activate positive and negative feelings simultaneously. Importantly, both global and more specific feelings were expected to be equally intense.

In their Study 1, De Liver and colleagues (2007) showed that when blood donation or a short vacation was described to take place in the distant as opposed to the near future, participants experienced less ambivalence towards these events. A similar effect was obtained in Studies 3 and 4, where participants with a global processing mindset (e.g., induced by answering "why" questions) experienced less ambivalence towards 15 different objects and events (e.g., aeroplane, blind date) than participants with a specific processing mindset (e.g., induced by answering "how" questions). These findings indicate that global processing led to a relatively univalent and thus more global emotional response, whereas specific processing led to an ambivalent and thus more specific, complex emotional response.

In sum, both behavioural and neuroscience research supports the existence of separate systems responsible for global and specific processing, and thus the first and most important element of our global-to-specific unfolding view of emotional responding, namely that a given emotional event may elicit both a global, positive–negative reaction and a more specific, fine-grained response.

Priority of global processing

A second element of our global-to-specific unfolding view of emotional responding entails that global, evaluative responses typically occur prior to relatively more specific emotional responses. Thus, a global, evaluative reaction to a dangerous, poisonous snake crossing your path (i.e., *negative*) may unfold more rapidly than a specific, emotional reaction (i.e., *fear*). The assumed precedence of global over specific processing is in line with the concept of *micro-genesis* (Rosenthal, 2004; Werner, 1956). Micro-genesis refers to the idea that the fine-grained processing of stimuli around us involves a *global-to-specific* course of development. This means that people initially process a visual scene in a global, holistic way, followed by more specific, detailed processing of the visual scene (Navon, 1977).

Navon (1977) investigated whether global processing precedes specific processing by examining how quickly participants could identify, from a picture that consisted of a large character made out of small characters (now referred to as a Navon letter), the identity of the large character compared to the identity of the small characters. Navon demonstrated, for example, that the identity of the small characters did not influence recognition of the large character, while the identity of the large character did influence recognition of the small characters. These findings and the results of his other experiments strongly suggest that global processing occurs prior to more specific processing, or in Navon's words: "the perceptual system treats every scene as if it were in a process of being focused or zoomed in on, where at first it is relatively indistinct and then it gets clearer and sharper" (p. 354).

The precedence of global processing over specific processing is important for our global-to-specific unfolding view of emotional responding because we assume that global, positive–negative reactions occur prior to specific, fine-grained emotional reactions. The "automatic evaluation" effect (see Fazio, 2001) may easily be interpreted as providing evidence in favour of our claim that the priority of global processing may cause early, positive–negative reactions. This effect represents the idea that people automatically evaluate the stimuli in their environment on a positive–negative dimension (e.g., Bargh, Chaiken, Raymond, & Hymes, 1996; Fazio, 2001; Fazio, Sanbonmatsu, Powell, & Kardes, 1986). In a world that overwhelms us with all sorts of information, automatic evaluation seems a useful tool for guiding our attention.

The automatic evaluation effect is usually demonstrated in a sequential priming paradigm where participants respond to targets with a positive or negative valence, which are preceded by primes of the same valence (i.e., congruent primes) or the opposite valence (i.e., incongruent primes). The often-observed finding that participants respond more quickly to congruently primed targets than to incongruently primed targets indicates that the primes are evaluated automatically. Obviously, the existence of automatic evaluation effects is in line with early global processing, especially for new stimuli that one has not encountered before (Duckworth, Bargh, Garcia, & Chaiken, 2002).

Early global processing seems a clearly established phenomenon. Other studies support the idea that specific processing needs relatively more time to occur. In Study 4 of Stapel et al. (2002) participants were either quickly or super-quickly subliminally primed with black-and-white line drawings of either happy or sad female faces in a parafoveal vigilance task. After this priming task, participants rated a neutral face on a general positivity–negativity dimension and on a masculinity–femininity dimension. The results of this study showed that *super quick* exposures to happy female faces led to more positive judgements of a neutral face than super quick exposures to sad female faces, without having an effect on the more specific, masculinity–femininity dimension. Thus, when little time was available to process the subliminal primes, only global, evaluative information was activated. However, there was an effect on the masculinity–femininity dimension when exposure time was prolonged: *Quick* exposures to either happy or sad female faces led to more feminine judgements of a neutral face than *super quick* exposures to happy or sad female faces. Thus, when more time was available to process the subliminal primes, more specific fine-grained information was also activated (Stapel et al., 2002; see also Ruys & Stapel, 2008a, 2008b, 2008c; Stapel & Koomen, 2005, 2006). These results indicate that perceivers use the first moments of exposure to a stimulus to get a general idea of the kind of stimulus they are dealing with. Only when more time is available (e.g., with quick rather than super quick exposures), did specific, fine-grained processing occur—leading to specific, detailed responses.

The view that global processing of an emotional event precedes specific processing is also corroborated by research on experienced conflict as a function of construal level (De Liver et al., 2007). In Study 4 of the earlier-mentioned De Liver et al. studies, participants were asked to evaluate potentially ambivalent attitude objects as quickly as possible. Before the evaluation task, participants performed a Navon task in which they were instructed to focus either on the large characters of Navon letters (to induce a global processing mindset) or on the small characters of Navon letters (to induce a specific processing mindset). The results showed that participants were able to indicate their evaluation of the potentially ambivalent attitude objects more quickly when a global processing mindset was induced than when a specific processing mindset was induced. This finding strongly suggests that, compared to global processing, specific processing takes more time to complete.

Interestingly, our proposal that there is an early onset of global, positive–negative responses is also corroborated by research on people's responses to facial emotional expressions, measured with event related brain potentials (ERPs; Pizzagalli, Regard, & Lehmann, 1999; Smith, Cacioppo, Larsen, & Chartrand, 2003) and MEG recordings (Halgren, Raij, Marinkovic, Jousmäki, & Hari, 2000). These ERP and MEG recordings reveal, according to Palermo and Rhodes (2007), that crude positive–negative categorisations often occur rapidly (i.e., from 100 ms post-stimulus onset), whereas fine-grained processes necessary to recognise the identity of a face or to discriminate between basic emotional expressions typically need more time (i.e., an additional 70 ms). Thus, global reactions generally set off before more specific responses because global processing may start prior to specific, fine-grained processing. An additional explanation might be that global processing needs less time and resources to complete than specific processing (De Liver et al., 2007).

Our global-to-specific unfolding view of emotional responding argues that global positive–negative responses occur prior to more specific emotional responses. However, there is also empirical evidence showing that specific reactions in some cases precede global positive–negative responses (e.g., Stapel & Koomen, 2006; Storbeck & Robinson, 2004). Recently, Stapel and Koomen (2006) demonstrated that specific processing of detailed, descriptive features does not always take more time than global, evaluative processing. In a first study, Stapel and Koomen (2006) exposed participants either super-quickly or quickly subliminally to a smiling or a sad Asian male face. Next, participants were presented with a picture of a neutral male face that was either Asian or White and were asked to rate this face on a sad–happy dimension. Their first results were in line with our global-to-specific unfolding view of emotional responding: When the target was White, Asian emotion faces evoked an assimilation effect, such that happy faces led to more positive target judgements than sad faces. However, when the target was Asian, Asian faces evoked an assimilation effect with super quick exposure conditions and contrast with quick exposure conditions. Thus, contrast occurred when subliminal priming was long enough to activate a distinct representation of the primed information and when the prime was similar to the target stimulus in terms of category membership.

Their next aim was to show that people can be flexible in the way they process information (Stapel & Koomen, 2006). To illustrate, sometimes it makes sense to see immediately whether an animal is cute or threatening (by extracting global, positive–negative information), whereas at other times it is more functional to immediately see whether an animal is a snake or a spider (by extracting detailed information). In this follow-up study the target stimulus was always Asian, and participants were instructed that the priming task was an assessment of "Cultural differences in vigilance" or an assessment of "Individual differences in vigilance". The expectation was that participants who received the "cultural differences" instruction would be more sensitive to information on cultural differences and thus would be more likely to process ethnicity related information, even in super quick exposure conditions. The results showed that in the cultural instruction conditions, as expected, Asian emotion faces elicited a contrast effect, such that happy faces led to less positive target judgements of an Asian neutral face than sad faces. This finding indicates that even with super quick exposures, detailed information on the ethnicity of the prime face was activated. Thus, the increased sensitivity for ethnicity information activated both global and specific information and made the perceived information distinct. However, in the individual instruction conditions the results were similar to the first study and in keeping with global-to-specific unfolding: Asian emotion faces elicited assimilation when prime exposure was super quick and contrast when prime exposure was quick.

The results of Stapel and Koomen (2006) demonstrate that people can be flexible in how they process information. When a specific feature is important for a current task, perceivers may extract this feature even after super quick exposures to the stimulus event. However, what is important to note is that immediate specific processing only occurs when the emotional event is processed *top-down*. This means that people are already attuned to a specific kind of information, for instance due to the activation of a particular goal or when specific features are diagnostic for a task (Corbetta & Shulman, 2002; Storbeck & Robinson, 2004). However, when information processing is stimulus-driven or *bottom-up*, we assume in line with arousal and core affect theories that a global-to-specific unfolding of emotional responding occurs. Thus, when people are confronted with an unexpected emotion elicitor (e.g., a favourite dessert, a poisonous snake, a smiling face) global, positive–negative reactions typically occur prior to specific, detailed emotional reactions.

Another important implication of the finding that specific processing can occur immediately (Stapel & Koomen, 2006) is that global and specific processing do not seem to occur sequentially as argued by the component process model of Scherer (1999) and core affect theory of Russell (2003), but operate in parallel. The assumption that global and specific processing operate in parallel would explain how global and specific emotional responses can be opposite with respect to their valence. For example, one may initially experience a *positive* reaction towards a piece of chocolate pie that is followed by more specific, *negative* feelings of guilt.

Unfolding of emotional reactions

A third and crucial element of our global-to-specific view of emotional responding is that emotions are seen as dynamic processes that unfold and develop over time (Cacioppo & Gardner, 1999; Scherer, 1984). We assume that emotional reactions start *before* information processing is complete. Initial information processing may trigger global, positive–negative responses based on few information cues (e.g., *favourite dessert*), whereas later information processing may trigger specific, fine-grained emotional responses that are based on more elaborate information cues (e.g., *excellent taste*, *high on calories*). It makes sense to start your responses as quickly as possible because emotions often serve as warning signals that ask for immediate action. For example, when you encounter a dangerous, life-threatening snake, it is crucial to respond as quickly and as adequately as possible.

Scherer (1984, 1999) also emphasises the importance of looking at the emotion *process* instead of looking at emotions as static states. Scherer's component process model of emotions assumes that emotions result from relatively global and more specific processing of emotional events (Scherer, 1984, 1999). This model assumes a fixed number of predefined stimulus evaluation checks (i.e., appraisals of novelty, intrinsic pleasantness, goal/need conduciveness, coping potential, and compatibility with standards) that determine *whether* people experience an emotion and *what kind* of emotion people experience. We think that the postulated *novelty* and *intrinsic pleasantness* checks can be seen as instances of global processing, whereas the *goal/need conduciveness*, *coping potential*, and *compatibility with standards* checks can be seen as examples of more specific processing (for a similar divide see Grandjean & Scherer, 2008).

Thus, according to Scherer's component process model both global and more specific processing take place in response to an emotional event, and global processing occurs prior to specific emotional processing. In line with Scherer's model, our global-to-specific unfolding view of emotional responding distinguishes between global and specific emotional reactions. However, a crucial difference between Scherer's component process model and our view is the assumed need of conscious awareness for more specific processing. Grandjean and Scherer (2008, p. 350) recently suggested "that early appraisal checks, including novelty and intrinsic pleasantness detection, are likely to occur in an automatic, unconscious mode of processing, whereas later checks, specifically goal conduciveness, require more extensive, effortful, and controlled processing." As we explain in the next section, we argue that specific emotional reactions can occur without the need for conscious, controlled processing.

Unconscious elicitation

One might infer from our global-to-specific unfolding view of emotional responding that global processing occurs *without* conscious awareness and that specific processing occurs *with* conscious awareness. The likelihood that perceivers become aware of an emotional stimulus during specific, fine-grained processing may be greater than during global, positive–negative processing because specific processing starts later and takes more time than global processing. However, the fourth element of our global-to-specific unfolding view of emotional responding holds that *both* global and specific processing may occur *without conscious awareness*. This means that it is possible to experience a specific emotion like fear or disgust without knowing why you feel scared or disgusted. According to clinical therapists, the experience of fear, anger, or sadness without knowing the cause of these feelings occurs quite often. We assume that both global and specific emotional information processing do not need awareness to be instigated, for important theoretical and empirical reasons.

Theoretically, it makes perfect sense that specific emotions, like fear and disgust, may develop unconsciously. That is because emotions are highly functional for survival (Cacioppo & Gardner, 1999; Ekman, 1984; Frijda, 1994; Keltner & Gross, 1999; Öhman, 1992; Scherer, 1984). As Frijda (1994) noted: "The function of specific emotions is to signal events that are relevant to the individual's concerns, and to motivate behavior to deal with those events" (p. 121). The goal-directed and universal nature of emotions strongly suggests that our emotional system is designed to respond quickly and unconsciously to incoming emotional stimuli. This means that people may experience a specific emotion (e.g., fear, anger, joy, disgust), without being aware of what caused this specific emotion. Even though our intuition suggests that we cannot experience a specific emotion like fear without knowing why, it makes sense to respond as quickly as possible—thus before we are consciously aware of a threatening stimulus.

In order for specific emotions to be elicited without conscious awareness, quick unconscious detection of specific emotional information is a necessary prerequisite. Valence detection or a global positive–negative reaction is not enough to induce a specific emotion. To ensure our species' continued existence, our emotional system should be able to do more than make quick but crude positive–negative discriminations. For example, the perception of specific body posture cues may determine whether an assailant evokes not simply negativity, but anger or fear (Parkinson & Manstead, 1992). To quickly and properly respond to a stimulus, it is important to be able to automatically detect the valence of the stimulus as well as its specific meaning. For adequate responding it is crucial to know that something is "disgusting" and not "scary". Knowing that something is "negative" does not suffice. This is consistent with the assertion of an evolved fear module that can be triggered without the need for conscious cognition (Öhman & Mineka, 2003).

Also empirically, there is evidence that specific emotions may develop unconsciously. Neuroimaging and physiological studies strongly suggest that our brain is capable of discriminating between specific, unconsciously presented emotional stimuli. Neuroimaging techniques have revealed that specific neural patterns are activated in the brain in response to unconscious exposure to disgusted, fearful, sad, angry, and happy facial emotional expressions (Morris, De Gelder, Weiskrantz, & Dolan, 2001; Phillips et al., 2004), whereas physiological techniques have revealed that unconscious exposures to happy and angry facial emotional expressions evoke distinctive facial electromyographic (EMG) reactions in emotion-relevant facial muscles (Dimberg, Thunberg, & Elmehed, 2000).

Interestingly, our own experimental work shows that people may actually *experience* specific emotional feelings and show emotional *behaviour* after being unconsciously exposed to emotion-eliciting stimuli (Ruys & Stapel, 2008a). These experimental studies are also important for another reason. Specifically, in our studies we used *emotion-eliciting stimuli* (e.g., mad, growling dogs or dirty, non-flushed toilets) rather than *facial emotional expressions* (e.g., emotion faces showing fear or disgust) to unconsciously induce specific emotions. To our knowledge, previous research always used facial emotional expressions to study the unconscious nature of specific emotions.[1] However, facial emotional expressions are special kinds of emotional stimuli (Hariri, Tessitore, Mattay, Fera, & Weinberger, 2002; Kimura, Yoshinoa, Takahashi, & Nomura, 2004) with different (social) functions (Hess, Philippot, & Blairy, 1998; Keltner & Gross, 1999; Keltner & Haidt, 1999; Ruys & Stapel, 2008b). First, facial emotional expressions are not only emotional stimuli, they are also (and perhaps foremost) *reactions* to

---

[1]Although previous researchers have used emotion-eliciting pictures instead of facial emotional expressions as subliminal primes (e.g., Giner-Sorolla, Garcia, & Bargh, 1999; Krosnick, Betz, Jussim, & Lynn, 1992; Spruyt, Hermans, de Houwer, & Eelen, 2002), these studies investigated affective priming phenomena and did not examine specific emotional reactions like feelings of disgust or fear.

emotional stimuli. Moreover, people seem especially efficient in the perception of faces (Farah, Wilson, Drain, & Tanaka, 1998). For these reasons, it was important to show the unconscious elicitation of specific emotions like fear and disgust by subliminally exposing people to regular emotional stimuli like growling, mad dogs and dirty, non-flushed toilets.

Summary of the four elements

In the second part of this chapter we have argued and provided evidence for four elements of our global-to-specific unfolding view of emotional responding. The first element of this view entails that emotion elicitors may evoke global, positive–negative reactions and relatively specific, fine-grained reactions to these elicitors. As we have explained, empirical evidence strongly supports this view: Different neuroscientific views seem to support the existence of separate systems for global and specific processing.

A second element of our global-to-specific view entails that global processing typically occurs prior to specific processing of emotional information. The research that we have discussed indicates that when motivation and opportunity (due to time pressure or to information that competes for attention) are insufficient, only global, holistic processing may proceed. This is in line with the idea that the onset of global processing starts off before the emergence of fine-grained, specific processing.

The third element of our view of emotional responding emphasises the unfolding aspect of emotions. We assume that emotional reactions immediately start to occur. The timing difference between global and specific information processing systems causes emotional responses to develop over time. Thus, initial reactions to an emotional event will be global, positive–negative responses based on the entire emotional event, whereas later responses will be relatively specific and based on detailed features of the emotional event.

We also provided support for the fourth element of our global-to-specific unfolding view, namely that both global and specific processing may occur without conscious awareness. Research shows that the experience of specific feelings of fear or disgust, the activation of specific emotion knowledge, and emotion specific behaviour can all be triggered without knowing what caused these emotional reactions (see Ruys & Stapel, 2008a).

CONSEQUENCES OF GLOBAL-TO-SPECIFIC UNFOLDING

In the first two parts of this chapter we discussed the notion of global-to-specific unfolding of emotional responding in relatively general ways. We explained how people's emotional reactions to emotional events unfold from global, evaluative responses to specific, fine-grained emotional responses.

A confrontation with a dangerous, life-threatening snake may first elicit a negative emotional reaction based on global processing, followed by a fear response that is based on more specific, detailed processing of the emotional event. In the next sections of this chapter we will elaborate on the consequences of our global-to-specific unfolding view of emotional responding for research areas that are related to emotions. First, we will consider the way global-to-specific unfolding operates when people perceive facial emotional expressions, followed by a discussion of the consequences of global-to-specific unfolding for research on automatic imitation of facial emotional expressions. Then we discuss how global and specific processing of emotional information may influence the occurrence of general positive or negative mood states.

Functions of facial emotional expressions

Facial emotional expressions are important for the study of emotions not only because they are often part of people's emotional responses. Facial emotional expressions are also important because they may in turn elicit emotional reactions in perceivers of these expressions (Russell & Fernandez-Dols, 1997). However, a crucial difference between facial emotional expressions and other emotion elicitors is that facial expressions are essential for adaptive social behaviour and emotional development (Dunn, 1994; Hariri et al., 2002). In addition, humans are specialised in the perception of faces compared to other types of stimuli (Farah et al., 1998). For these reasons, the implications of global-to-specific unfolding on the perception and processing of facial emotional expressions need to be investigated separately.

It is clear that facial emotional expressions can evoke different kinds of reactions in perceivers. For example, when someone looks at you with an angry face, this face may elicit feelings of anger, fear, or perhaps even feelings of joy because the person is your enemy (Ruys, Spears, Gordijn, & de Vries, 2007). In other words, how you respond to an angry-looking person may depend on your knowledge of this person and the reasons for his or her anger. Without this knowledge, however, an angry facial expression may elicit negative feelings because in that case, an angry face is simply a negative emotional stimulus.

In general, at least two types of emotional reactions to facial emotional expressions can be distinguished (see also Ruys & Stapel, 2008b). On the one hand, facial emotional expressions may elicit *emotion elicitor reactions* (e.g., Murphy & Zajonc, 1993; Ruys et al., 2007; Stapel et al., 2002; Winkielman, Berridge, & Wilbarger, 2005). These emotional reactions are like reactions to any other pleasant or unpleasant emotion-eliciting stimulus. Thus, an emotion elicitor response to a smiling face is probably similar to an emotional response elicited by a picture of a sunny beach. On the other hand, facial emotional expressions may elicit *emotion messenger reactions* (see Ekman, 1992; Fridlund, 1994; Izard, 1994; Jakobs, Fischer, & Manstead, 1997; Keltner & Haidt, 1999; Russell, 1994; Van der Velde, Stapel, & Gordijn, 2008). These emotional reactions are responses to the communicative message that a face reveals. An essential aspect of emotion messenger reactions is that the expressed emotion is linked to the sender of the expression (Adolphs, 2006; Dimberg & Öhman, 1996). For example, an emotion messenger reaction to your smiling partner entails a response to the knowledge that your partner is happy.

Emotion elicitor reactions and emotion messenger reactions differ in their specificity. Emotion elicitor reactions are global, positive–negative responses to the facial emotional expression, whereas emotion messenger reactions are relatively specific because they are based on knowledge about the expression and its sender. An emotion elicitor reaction to, for example, an angry face corresponds to an initial, global, negative reaction, whereas an emotion messenger reaction to this angry face corresponds to a later, specific, fine-grained emotional reaction that is based on the knowledge that someone is angry.

Two experimental studies provide evidence for our hypothesis that facial emotional expressions evoke both emotion elicitor reactions and emotion messenger reactions (Ruys & Stapel, 2008b). In these studies participants were either super-quickly or quickly subliminally exposed to disgusted, fearful, angry, or neutral faces in a parafoveal vigilance task. After participants were exposed to these negative facial emotional expressions, they completed both global and specific measures of feeling and cognition, similar to the ones used in Ruys and Stapel (2008a). As shown in Figure 4, super quick exposures to these negative facial expressions primarily activated a global, negative evaluative response that was reflected in participants' moods. Accessibility of general negative cognitions increased in the same way. The activation of a global, evaluative response is in line with the idea that facial emotional expressions initially evoke an emotion elicitor reaction.

However, our studies also show that quick (instead of super quick) subliminal exposures to disgusted, fearful, or angry faces resulted in the activation of specific emotion knowledge, without influencing people's global and specific feelings. The results on the word completion task depicted in Figure 5 show that participants completed more disgust, fear, or anger words respectively after quick exposures to disgusting, fearful, or angry expressions than after quick exposures to the other facial expressions. Participants also completed more general negative words after quick expo-sures to disgusting, fearful, or angry expressions than after quick exposures to neutral expressions. The activation of specific emotion knowledge supports the idea that facial emotional expressions also evoke an emotion messenger reaction.

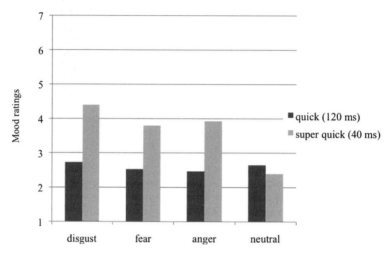

Figure 4. Mean general mood ratings as a function of prime expression and exposure duration (Study 1, Ruys & Stapel, 2008b).

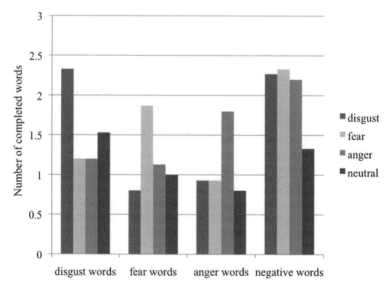

Figure 5. Mean number of words completed after quick exposure durations (120ms) as a function of prime expression (Study 1, Ruys & Stapel, 2008b).

In line with previous findings (Hariri et al., 2002), these results indicate that people's responses to facial emotional expressions are different from responses to other, more direct emotion elicitors (Ruys & Stapel, 2008a, 200b). People's initial, global, positive–negative responses to facial emotional expressions and other emotion elicitors like poisonous snakes or favourite desserts are similar. Interestingly, however, people's specific, fine-grained responses to these two types of emotional stimuli differ: Quick, subliminal exposures to disgusting or fearful pictures (e.g., a dirty, non-flushed toilet, a growling, mad dog) resulted in emotion specific effects on cognitive, feeling, and behavioural measures (Ruys & Stapel, 2008a). Specifically, participants who were exposed to either disgusting or fearful pictures were more likely to use disgust-related or fear-related words, reported they felt more disgusted or fearful, and were more likely to act as if they were disgusted or scared than participants who were exposed to neutral pictures. The response pattern to these more direct emotion elicitors differs from the pattern of responses to facial emotional expressions, such that more direct emotion elicitors elicited the specific emotion (e.g., disgust or fear), whereas facial emotional expressions merely activated emotion knowledge (e.g., increased accessibility of emotion-related words).

At first sight, the observation that emotional responses to facial emotional expressions differ from emotional responses to emotion eliciting pictures seems to contrast with the findings of Wicker and colleagues (2003). They showed that exposure to a disgusted facial expression activates the same neural representation as the inhalation of disgusting odorants. This suggests that perceptions of facial emotional expressions activate a neural structure that is also involved in the production of the associated emotion. Wicker and colleagues (2003) conclude from these findings that facial emotional expressions and more direct emotion elicitors evoke a similar emotional experience. However, we think this conclusion is unwarranted for several reasons. First, no evidence was obtained regarding participants' emotional experiences in response to the disgusted facial expressions. Therefore it is unclear whether both types of stimuli evoked similar levels of disgust. Second, it is possible that the neural substrate that was activated in response to both types of stimuli is involved in the recognition of disgusting situations, rather than the experience of feelings of disgust.

In sum, investigating people's responses to facial emotional expressions with a global-to-specific unfolding view of emotional responding has clarified essential differences between facial emotional expressions and other emotion elicitors (e.g., disgusted facial expressions versus dirty, non-flushed toilets). More specifically, global-to-specific unfolding has allowed us to identify emotion elicitor and emotion messenger reactions to facial emotional expressions and to reveal how both types of responses unfold over time.

Consequences for imitation research

An interesting result that emerges from our studies on emotion elicitor and emotion messenger reactions to facial emotional expressions is that facial emotional expressions do not necessarily elicit the corresponding emotional feelings in the perceivers (Ruys & Stapel, 2008b). This finding is in line with our hypothesis that facial emotional expressions activate the link between the emotion and the sender of the emotional expression (i.e., the emotion messenger function), but conflicts with an intriguing hypothesis that has emerged suggesting that emotion *imitation* leads to emotion *elicitation*.

Specifically, researchers have argued that exposure to a facial emotional expression activates the corresponding emotion in the perceiver by automatic imitation of the expression (Adelmann & Zajonc, 1989; Hatfield, Cacioppo, & Rapson, 1992; Niedenthal, 2007). Niedenthal (2007), for example, recently claimed in support of her embodiment theory of emotion that "... behavioral studies demonstrate that emotional expressions and gestures are visibly imitated by observers and that this imitation is accompanied by self-reports of the associated emotional state" (p. 1004). Thus, being confronted with an angry face should make you feel angry too. However, this kind of reaction—taking over the emotion or emotional expression of your opponent—is not always functional or sensible (Atkinson & Adolphs, 2005; Neumann & Strack, 2000; Van der Velde et al., 2008). Especially in the case of anger, a more effective response is to remain calm and keep a friendly posture than to immediately respond with aggression. What seems essential when confronted with an emotional person is to activate the most adequate response. Therefore, people need to quickly recognise the emotion that other people are experiencing.

In line with this reasoning, one purpose of imitation might be to facilitate emotion recognition. Researchers have proposed that perceivers automatically imitate the facial emotional expression they are exposed to and, as a consequence of the activation of the muscles in the face, experience the emotion associated with the facial expression, which in turn facilitates recognition of the emotion (Enticott, Johnston, Herring, Hoy, & Fitzgerald, 2008; Gallese, 2006; Goldman & Sripada, 2005; Hess & Blairy, 2001; Niedenthal, Brauer, Halberstad, & Innes-Ker, 2001; Oberman, Winkielman, & Ramachandran, 2007; Wicker et al., 2003). More specifically, Enticott and colleagues (2008) have suggested that mirror neurons simulate motoric behaviour that is observed, and that this simulation evokes a similar emotional experience that facilitates emotion recognition.

Several parts of the emotion imitation-elicitation-recognition hypothesis have received empirical support. Physiological research demonstrated that people imitate other people's facial emotional expressions (Dimberg, 1997; Dimberg & Öhman, 1996; Hess & Blairy, 2001), even when these facial emotional expressions are subliminally presented (Dimberg et al., 2000). Wicker and colleagues (2003) showed that after exposure to a disgusted facial expression and after inhalation of a disgusting odorant, the same neural substrates were activated in the brain. This suggests that perception of facial emotional expressions and production of the associated emotion rely on similar neural structures. Furthermore, Enticott and colleagues (2008) showed that mirror neuron activity strongly correlated with recognition accuracy of facial emotional expressions. This indicates that imitation of facial emotional expressions is associated with the recognition of these facial expressions.

Niedenthal and colleagues (2001) demonstrated that emotional experience is also associated with the recognition of facial emotional expressions. After the induction of happiness or sadness Niedenthal et al. (2001) asked participants to indicate the offset of a happy (or sad) facial expression that changed into a sad (or happy) facial expression. The results showed that participants more quickly detected the offset of a congruent facial emotional expression than the offset of an incongruent facial emotional expression. The experience of happiness or sadness thus seemed to facilitate recognition of the corresponding facial emotional expression.

Importantly, Hess and Blairy (2001) investigated the emotion imitation-elicitation-recognition hypothesis more directly. They exposed participants to angry, sad, disgusted, and happy facial expressions, and measured facial EMG. After exposure to each face, participants first indicated whether and to what extent the face reflected *happiness*, *sadness*, *fear*, *anger*, *disgust*, *surprise*, and *contempt*, and then indicated to what extent they themselves felt *irritated*, *sad*, *cheerful*, and *repulsed* (four sensations that corresponded to the emotions displayed by the facial emotional expressions). The facial EMG data showed imitation effects following angry, sad, and happy facial expressions. The rating data showed emotional contagion effects in response to happy and sad facial emotional expressions. Thus, participants indicated feeling cheerful or sad after exposure to a happy or sad facial expression respectively. However, despite this (limited) evidence for imitation and contagion effects, mediational analyses did not provide any support for the hypothesised link between imitation and emotional contagion. In addition, no evidence was obtained for the hypothesis that imitation facilitated emotion recognition through emotional contagion. Thus, even though exposure to facial emotional expressions led to imitation of the facial emotional expressions and resulted in emotional contagion, imitation clearly did *not* cause the emotional experience (Hess & Blairy, 2001).

Although the perception of facial emotional expressions, imitation of these facial emotional expressions, the experience of emotions, and emotion recognition seem to rely on similar processes, their exact causal relationships remain unclear. We conclude from the research referred to above that automatic imitation of facial emotional expressions facilitates the recognition of other people's emotions. However, the link between the imitation of facial emotional expressions and the experience of the specific corresponding emotional feelings is not substantiated. This suggests that emotional experience is unnecessary for the occurrence of facilitation effects in emotion recognition (Goldman & Sripada, 2005).

The notion we would like to put forward here—that imitation of facial emotion expressions does not necessarily evoke the feeling of the corresponding emotions—is in line with the idea that empathy is the main driver behind imitation of other people's gestures and facial expressions (e.g., Chartrand & Bargh, 1999). Imitating someone's facial emotional expression *and* having identical feelings is not always the best way to show your empathy (see for example Van der Velde et al., 2008), considering that empathy means to *recognise* the feelings of others and to appropriately *respond* to these feelings.

The observation that facial emotional expressions are likely to elicit global positive–negative emotional reactions and are less likely to elicit more specific corresponding emotions like anger, fear, and disgust (Hess & Blairy, 2001; Niedenthal et al., 2001) is consistent with our global-to-specific unfolding view. The notion that facial emotional expressions do not automatically elicit corresponding emotions is in line with our hypothesis that facial emotional expressions activate the link between the emotion and the sender of the emotional expression (Ruys & Stapel, 2008b). Our unfolding view predicts that global processing reveals the positivity or negativity of the stimulus, whereas specific processing reveals the knowledge that another person feels angry, sad, afraid, disgusted, or happy. The initial activation of negativity may produce general negative feelings and an increased accessibility of general negative cognitions (i.e., an emotion elicitor reaction), whereas the activation of the knowledge that the face is angry means an increase in the accessibility of anger-related concepts and information about the person (i.e., an emotion messenger reaction). Because the emotion is linked to another person, perceivers are less likely to automatically experience the emotion themselves.

Thus, global-to-specific unfolding does not predict the occurrence of specific emotions as a *primary* consequence of exposure to facial emotional expressions. In keeping with our emphasis on the *unfolding* nature of emotions, it seems very likely, however, that specific emotions do occur as a *secondary* emotional reaction in response to knowledge about the link between the emotional expression and the sender of the expression. For example, the angry facial expression of your daughter, who is angry with you for forgetting her birthday, might elicit feelings of guilt.

Consequences for mood research

Besides providing an innovative perspective on how emotions unfold, our global-to-specific unfolding view also has interesting implications for research on general mood effects. Typically, moods are described as different from emotions in that they are less specific, less intense, less likely to be triggered by a particular stimulus or event, and relatively longer lasting (Ekman, 1994; Frijda, 1993; Isen, 1984), although some researchers have argued that mood states can be more specific (e.g., Lazarus, 1994; Polivy, 1981). In this chapter we assume that moods are general positive or negative affective states, which may arise from specific emotions that have lost the link with an object and their intensity, but may also precede the occurrence of emotions. Interestingly, our global-to-specific unfolding view of emotional responding predicts and explains how moods originate in the latter case, when moods are elicited *prior to* the emergence of specific emotions.

Specifically, mood states are characterised by a global, positive or negative charge and result from the activation of diffuse and cognitively unbounded, evaluative information. These characteristics make it highly likely that initial, global positive–negative reactions that—according to our global-to-specific unfolding view—occur in response to emotional or affect-laden stimuli can be the origin of people's moods. Because global positive–negative reactions are mainly evaluative and thus diffuse and cognitively unbounded, they are likely to spill over to people's moods (Zajonc, 1980, 2000). A similar idea was put forward by Clore and Colcombe (2003) who suggested that "objectless, evaluative meaning" may become attached to a person's mood (p. 343). On a broader level, research indicates that the cognitive activation of semantic concepts (e.g., "aggressive", "old") is likely to simultaneously impact perception, motivation, behaviour, and evaluation systems (Bargh, 1997, 2006). We propose that the cognitive activation of evaluatively toned information may affect and colour a person's mood state by interactions between these psychological systems (see e.g., Treisman, 1996).

This reasoning is in line with Chartrand, van Baaren, and Bargh (2006) who argued that moods can occur as a result of automatic evaluations of stimuli in the environment. They hypothesised that automatic evaluations may influence mood in the case where repeated automatic evaluations have the same valence. When people are in a bad situation or environment, the continuous automatic activation of a negative valence may result in a negative mood and may therefore affect people's processing styles (e.g., Mackie & Worth, 1989; Schwarz & Clore, 1996). This negative mood signals that appropriate action is necessary and therefore activates a systematic, analytic processing style. When people are surrounded by positive things in a pleasant environment, the continuous activation of positive valence results in a positive mood. A positive mood signals that everything is fine and thus promotes an effortless, heuristic processing style.

Chartrand and colleagues (2006) tested their hypotheses by subliminally priming participants with either positive, negative, or neutral stimulus words (e.g., music, war, plant) in a parafoveal vigilance task. After this task, participants completed a mood questionnaire (Exp. 1), an impression formation task (Exp. 2), or a stereotyping task (Exps. 3 and 4). The results showed that participants reported a more positive mood and were more likely to use heuristic processing in the impression formation and stereotyping tasks after subliminal priming with positive words than after subliminal priming with negative words. Thus, multiple automatic evaluations of stimuli of the same valence influenced mood.

The results of Chartrand and colleagues are in keeping with our own findings that repeated positive–negative reactions resulting from global processing of valenced stimuli produce positive or negative moods (Ruys & Stapel, 2008a, 2008b; Stapel et al., 2002). Specifically, this research showed that super quick subliminal exposures to emotion eliciting pictures, facial emotional expressions, and even schematic faces, evoked diffuse positive–negative responses that spilled over onto the mood of the participants. For example, participants who were exposed super-quickly to smiling faces reported more positive affective experiences than participants who were exposed super-quickly to sad-looking faces (see Stapel et al., 2002).

These findings raise the question of what the boundary conditions are for the occurrence of mood effects after subliminal priming. Global-to-specific unfolding suggests that these mood effects depend on the stimuli people are exposed to and on how people process these stimuli. "Hot", emotional stimuli like dirty, non-flushed toilets or growling, mad dogs are always likely to elicit general positive or negative reactions and thus influence mood, independent of whether perceivers process these stimuli in a global or specific way. However, "cold", non-emotional stimuli, like personality traits or nouns (with a positive or negative connotation) are only likely to elicit positive or negative reactions when mainly their evaluative meaning is activated; that is, when processed in a global way. Detailed, specific processing of cold stimuli activates their descriptive meaning and cognitively constrains the initial diffuse, positive–negative reaction to these stimuli, making mood effects less likely.

We designed several studies to investigate these boundary conditions, as a conservative test of our global-to-specific unfolding view of emotional responding (Ruys & Stapel, 2008c). The first two studies investigated whether participants' explicit mood ratings would be affected by quick or super quick subliminal exposures to positive (e.g., *confident, persistent*) or negative (e.g., *arrogant, stubborn*) trait concepts. In line with global-to-specific unfolding, the results showed that super quick subliminal exposure conditions led to more positive mood judgements after exposures to positive trait concepts than after exposures to negative trait concepts, whereas quick subliminal exposure conditions did not cause any effects on mood judgements (see Figure 6). Thus, mood changes only occurred when prime exposures were sufficiently quick to activate evaluative reactions without any descriptive content. These findings support the idea that exposure to

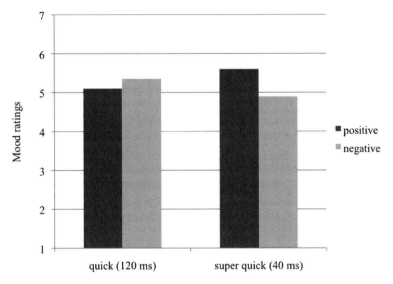

Figure 6. Mean general mood ratings as a function of prime valence and exposure duration (Study 1, Ruys & Stapel, 2008c).

cold concepts may elicit a corresponding mood state when the positive or negative evaluative tone of these concepts dominates the descriptive meaning.

In further studies (Ruys & Stapel, 2008c), we took our test of the boundary conditions of mood effects one step further and used more indirect ways to measure mood, namely by using a *need for cognition* scale[2] (Cacioppo & Petty, 1982; Cacioppo, Petty, Feinstein, & Jarvis, 1996) and a measure of *processing style* (Fiedler, 1990; Forgas, 1995; Gasper & Clore, 2002). We assessed processing style by looking at the impact of argument quality on persuasion, assuming that, as a consequence of their processing styles, participants in a positive mood are likely to be persuaded by both weak and strong arguments, whereas participants in a negative mood are more likely to be persuaded by strong than by weak arguments. These studies replicated our previous findings and again demonstrated that subliminal exposure to positive or negative trait concepts was most likely to

---

[2]Analogous to the effect of mood on people's information-processing styles (i.e., more systematic information processing in a negative mood and more heuristic processing in a positive mood), we proposed that people may experience a higher need for cognition when they feel bad than when they feel good. Thus, need for cognition may indirectly reflect people's mood states. A pretest demonstrated that a well-known, conscious mood induction technique (recalling positive or negative life events) indeed affected individuals' need for cognition (Ruys & Stapel, 2008c).

affect mood when prime exposures are sufficiently quick to activate evaluative reactions that have no specific descriptive content (Ruys & Stapel, 2008c). Importantly, by showing mood effects on these indirect mood measures, we could exclude a semantic priming account and increase the generalisability of our findings.

Together, our studies provide evidence for the hypothesis that exposure to cold concepts may affect people's explicit mood judgements, motivational states, and processing styles, and indicate that the bare essentials for mood induction consist of the activation of a positive or negative, dominating evaluative tone (Ruys & Stapel, 2008c). However, one could argue that changes in processing styles observed in our studies (Ruys & Stapel, 2008) were not due to changes in mood. Based on a cognitive tuning account, Ottati and colleagues proposed that affective cues like happy or angry facial expressions can serve as signals that directly promote heuristic or systematic processing styles (Ottati, Terkildsen, & Hubbard, 1997). Research has indeed shown that participants' processing styles were affected in response to certain affective cues, without affecting mood (Friedman & Förster, 2000; Ottati et al., 1997; Soldat & Sinclair, 2001). These findings suggest that changes in processing style do not always reflect changes in mood. We agree that situational demands may indeed alter people's processing strategies. However, we have theoretical and empirical reasons to conclude that mood was affected in our particular paradigm. A cognitive tuning account, for example, cannot explain the finding that no changes in processing style occurred when participants were quickly exposed to the priming stimuli. However, this finding can be explained by our mood-based account because it assumes specific processing and thus no mood effects under quick exposure conditions (Ruys & Stapel, 2008c). Also, considering that effects on reported mood paralleled processing style effects under both global and specific processing conditions, we conclude that moods indeed resulted from global, positive–negative reactions to our valenced priming stimuli.

In sum, research based on our global-to-specific unfolding view of emotional responding also provides insight into the development of mood states. First, this research has shown that moods merely require global, evaluative processing to arise, whereas emotions need additional, specific, fine-grained processing to unfold (Ruys & Stapel, 2008a, 2008b). This suggests that moods instigate prior to emotions and that moods are not only a by-product of emotions that have lost their urgency. Second, a common assumption that is contradicted by our global-to-specific unfolding view is that only "hot" stimulus materials, like music and movies, can produce mood effects (Clore & Colcombe, 2003; Innes-Ker & Niedenthal, 2002; Niedenthal, Rohman, & Dalle, 2003). As predicted by global-to-specific unfolding, and demonstrated by subliminal priming studies, moods can in fact be induced by exposure to cold concepts (Chartrand et al., 2006; Ruys & Stapel, 2008c). These findings challenge the idea that we need hot materials to induce mood.

CONCLUDING REMARKS

Our global-to-specific unfolding view of emotional responding unites work on affective priming, emotions, and moods. The central tenet of this view is that people's feelings, cognitions, and behaviours in response to an emotional stimulus are determined by the way they process this emotional information. The picture of a loved-one typically first elicits diffuse, positive feelings that are the result of global processing, and then specific feelings of happiness that are the result of more detailed processing of the picture. Theoretically, we have argued and shown that global, evaluative processing typically occurs prior to specific, more fine-grained processing. As a consequence of this timing difference, people's reactions to emotional stimuli unfold from diffuse, positive–negative reactions that determine mood, to detailed, fine-grained reactions that cause specific emotions to arise. In contrast to previous theorising we have argued and shown that both global, positive–negative processing and specific, fine-grained processing can unfold without the need for conscious awareness. This means that people can experience specific emotions like fear and disgust, without knowing what caused these emotional feelings, cognitions, and behaviours.

Our global-to-specific unfolding view of emotional responding comple-ments existing theories of emotion by focusing exclusively on the processes involved in the occurrence of emotions. Our unfolding view emphasises the emotional responses that emotional events may elicit and makes specific predictions regarding the emotional responses that are elicited: Research strongly supports the hypothesis that both global and specific emotional responses occur quickly and unconsciously, with the limitation that global emotional responses typically unfold before specific emotional responses are elicited.

Applying global-to-specific unfolding to the occurrence of emotional reactions has advanced our knowledge in a number of different ways. Comparing perceivers' global and specific reactions to facial emotional expressions and to more direct emotional stimuli such as dirty, non-flushed toilets and mad, growling dogs has revealed important differences between these two types of stimuli. Moreover, the comparison of these reactions casts doubt on the common assumption in the imitation literature that exposures to facial emotional expressions elicit the corresponding emotion in perceivers. Our global-to-specific unfolding perspective on emotional responding has also revealed that moods arise as a result of global, evaluative processing, whereas specific emotions need specific, fine-grained processing to occur. Furthermore, inspired by our global-to-specific theorising, we have argued and shown that moods can be evoked after exposures to "cold" semantic concepts, as long as these concepts are primarily processed in a global, evaluative way and result in the activation of a dominantly evaluative tone.

A limitation of this chapter might be that our global-to-specific unfolding view of emotional responding rests to a large extent on studies that used the parafoveal priming paradigm to support our claims. However, the parafoveal priming paradigm is recognised as a valid research tool in social and personality psychology (Bargh & Chartrand, 2000). What is important in using subliminal priming techniques is to make sure that participants are exposed to the primes for very brief durations, that the primes are properly masked, and that appropriate awareness checks are conducted. For the parafoveal priming paradigm in particular, it is essential to keep constant the distance between the eyes of the participant and the computer screen, to make sure that the participant is continually focused on the fixation point in the centre of the screen (by varying prime onset and prime location), and to present the primes in the parafoveal area, just outside the foveal region of attention (Bargh & Chartrand, 2000). In our studies that relied on a parafoveal priming paradigm, we followed these recommendations as closely as possible (Ruys & Stapel, 2008a, 2008b, 2008c; Stapel & Koomen, 2005, 2006; Stapel et al., 2002).

In our studies, participants were either super-quickly (i.e., 40 ms) or quickly (i.e., 120 ms) exposed to the emotion-eliciting stimuli. We chose these exposure durations because they represent the boundary durations in parafoveal priming (Bargh & Chartrand, 2000). We assumed that exposures of 40 ms only allow for the earliest stages of stimulus processing (i.e., global processing) and that exposures of 120 ms give more time for specific processing of the stimulus. Chartrand and colleagues (2006) used exposure durations of 60 ms in their parafoveal priming task that also resulted in global, positive–negative reactions (i.e., positive or negative mood), suggesting that 60 ms was too quick for specific processing of the primes. This is compatible with the fact that subliminal priming does not depend on fixed thresholds. Multiple characteristics of the situation (e.g., the intensity of the stimulus, the familiarity of the stimulus, lighting in the room, motivation of the perceiver, presence of other stimuli) determine when exposure durations are subliminal. Remember, for example, the classic basketball experiment of Simons and Chabris (1999), where participants watched a video clip of a group of people playing basketball and were asked to count the number of passes made by one of the teams. Approximately half of these participants failed to notice a person dressed in a hairy gorilla suit, who walked slowly across the scene for 9 seconds. Thus, even obvious stimuli can be present for seconds without perceivers becoming aware of the stimulus.

Another issue awaiting discussion is the well-known, indirect consequence of moods on people's processing styles: when people feel good they are more likely to rely on heuristic, easy, and global processing strategies, whereas when people feel bad they tend to use more demanding, systematic, and local processing strategies (Fiedler, 1990; Forgas, 1995; Gasper & Clore, 2002). What are the consequences of this influence of mood on processing style for people's emotional responses? Our global-to-specific unfolding view suggests that positive events are less likely to be processed specifically than are negative events, because positive events initially evoke positive moods. This is consistent with the fact that there is one positive basic emotion (i.e., happiness) versus four negative basic emotions (i.e., anger, sadness, disgust, and fear). Thus, in line with our global-to-specific unfolding view of emotional responding, positive emotions seem less specific than negative emotions.

In sum, then, we hope that we have presented our global-to-specific unfolding view of emotional responding as clearly and convincingly as possible. We feel that we have demonstrated that our view strongly contributes to the understanding of several important psychological phenomena, such as the induction and the occurrence of emotions and moods, the perception and interpretation of facial emotional expressions, and imitation. We hope that we will not be alone in concluding that global-to-specific unfolding cannot and should not be neglected in future psychological research, especially when it concerns studies of people's feelings and emotions.

REFERENCES

Adelmann, P. K., & Zajonc, R. B. (1989). Facial efference and the experience of emotion. *Annual Review of Psychology*, *40*, 249–280.

Adolphs, R. (2003). Cognitive neuroscience of human social behavior. *Nature Reviews Neuroscience*, *4*, 165–178.

Adolphs, R. (2006). Perception and emotion. *Current Directions in Psychological Science*, *15*, 222–226.

Arnold, M. B. (1960). *Emotion and personality*. New York: Columbia University Press.

Atkinson, A. P., & Adolphs, R. (2005). Nonconscious emotions. Visual emotion perception. Mechanisms and processes. In L. F. Barrett, P. M. Niedenthal, & P. Winkielman (Eds.), *Emotion and consciousness* (pp. 150–182). New York: The Guilford Press.

Avramova, Y. R., & Stapel, D. A. (2008). Moods as spotlights: The influence of mood on accessibility effects *Journal of Personality and Social Psychology*, *95*, 542–554.

Bargh, J. A. (1997). The automaticity of everyday life. In R. S. Wyer (Ed.), *Advances in social cognition* (Vol. 10, pp. 1–61). Mahwah, NJ: Lawrence Erlbaum Associates Inc.

Bargh, J. A. (2006). What have we been priming all these years? On the development, mechanisms, and ecology of nonconscious social behaviour. *European Journal of Social Psychology*, *36*, 147–168.

Bargh, J. A., Chaiken, S., Raymond, P., & Hymes, C. (1996). The automatic evaluation effect: Unconditional automatic attitude activation with a pronunciation task. *Journal of Experimental Social Psychology*, *32*, 104–128.

Bargh, J. A., & Chartrand, T. L. (2000). The mind in the middle. A practical guide to priming and automaticity research. In H. T. Reis & C. M. Judd (Eds.), *Handbook of research methods in social and personality psychology* (pp. 253–285). New York: Cambridge University Press.

Bargh, J. A., Litt, J., Pratto, F., & Spielman, L. A. (1989). On the preconscious evaluation of social stimuli. In A. F. Bennett & K. M. McConkey (Eds.), *Cognition in individual and social contexts* (pp. 357–370). Amsterdam: Elsevier Science Publishers BV.

Bargh, J. A., & Pietromonaco, P. (1982). Automatic information processing and social perception: The influence of trait information presented outside of conscious awareness on impression formation. *Journal of Personality and Social Psychology, 43,* 437–449.

Barrett, L. F. (2005). Feeling is perceiving: Core affect and conceptualization in the experience of emotion. In L. F. Barrett, P. M. Niedenthal, & P. Winkielman (Eds.), *Emotion and consciousness* (pp. 255–284). New York: The Guilford Press.

Barrett, L. F. (2007). The experience of emotion. *Annual Review of Psychology, 58,* 373–403.

Barrett, L. F., Ochsner, K. N., & Gross, J. J. (2007). On the automaticity of emotion. In J. Bargh (Ed.), *Social psychology and the unconscious: The automaticity of higher mental processes* (pp. 173–217). New York: Psychology Press.

Cacioppo, J. T., & Gardner, W. L. (1999). Emotion. *Annual Review of Psychology, 50,* 191–214.

Cacioppo, J. T., & Petty, R. E. (1982). The need for cognition. *Journal of Personality and Social Psychology, 42,* 116–131.

Cacioppo, J. T., Petty, R. E., Feinstein, J. A., & Jarvis, W. B. G. (1996). Dispositional differences in cognitive motivation: The life and times of individuals varying in need for cognition. *Psychological Bulletin, 119,* 197–253.

Chartrand, T. L., & Bargh, J. A. (1999). The Chameleon effect: The perception–behavior link and social interaction. *Journal of Personality and Social Psychology, 76,* 893–910.

Chartrand, T. L., van Baaren, R. B., & Bargh, J. A. (2006). Linking automatic evaluation to mood and information processing style: Consequences for experienced affect, impression formation, and stereotyping. *Journal of Experimental Psychology: General, 135,* 70–77.

Clore, G., & Colcombe, S. (2003). The parallel worlds of affective concepts and feelings. In J. Musch & K. C. Klauer (Eds.), *The psychology of evaluation* (pp. 169–188). Mahwah, NJ: Lawrence Erlbaum Associates Inc.

Corbetta, M., & Shulman, G. L. (2002). Control of goal-directed and stimulus-driven attention in the brain. *Nature Reviews Neuroscience, 31,* 201–215.

Cornelius, R. R. (1996). *The science of emotion: Research and tradition in the psychology of emotion.* Upper Saddle River, NJ: Prentice-Hall.

Darwin, C. (1872). *The expression of the emotions in man and animals.* London: John Murray.

De Liver, Y., van der Pligt, J., & Wigboldus, D. (2007). *Seeing the big picture: Influence of construal level on the experience of attitudinal conflict.* Unpublished manuscript.

Derryberry, D., & Tucker, D. M. (1994). Motivating the focus of attention. In P. M. Niedenthal & S. Kitayama (Eds.), *The heart's eye: Emotional influences in perception and attention* (pp. 167–196). San Diego, CA: Academic Press.

Dimberg, U. (1997). Facial reactions: Rapidly evoked emotional responses. *Journal of Psychophysiology, 11,* 115–123.

Dimberg, U., & Öhman, A. (1996). Behold the wrath: Psychophysiological responses to facial stimuli. *Motivation and Emotion, 20,* 149–181.

Dimberg, U., Thunberg, M., & Elmehed, K. (2000). Unconscious facial reactions to emotional facial expressions. *Psychological Science, 11,* 86–89.

Duckworth, K. L., Bargh, J. A., Garcia, M., & Chaiken, S. (2002). The automatic evaluation of novel stimuli. *Psychological Science, 13,* 513–519.

Dunn, J. (1994). Experience and understanding of emotions, relationships, and membership in a particular culture. In P. Ekman & R. J. Davidson (Eds.), *The nature of emotion. Fundamental questions.* New York: Oxford University Press.

Ekman, P. (1984). Expression and the nature of emotion. In K. R. Scherer & P. Ekman (Eds.), *Approaches to emotion* (pp. 319–343). Hillsdale, NJ: Lawrence Erlbaum Associates Inc.

Ekman, P. (1992). Are there basic emotions? *Psychological Review, 99*, 550–553.

Ekman, P. (1994). Moods, emotions, and traits. In P. Ekman & R. J. Davidson (Eds.), *The nature of emotion. Fundamental questions*. New York: Oxford University Press.

Enticott, P. G., Johnston, P. J., Herring, S., Hoy, K. E., & Fitzgerald, P. B. (2008). Mirror neuron activation is associated with facial emotion processing. *Neuropsychologia, 46*, 2851–2854.

Erdley, C. A., & D'Agostino, P. R. (1988). Cognitive and affective components of automatic priming effects. *Journal of Personality and Social Psychology, 54*, 741–747.

Evers, C., Fischer, A. H., Mosquera, P. M. R., & Manstead, A. S. R. (2005). Anger and social appraisal: A "spicy" sex difference? *Emotion, 5*, 258–266.

Farah, M. J., Wilson, K. D., Drain, M., & Tanaka, J. N. (1998). What is "special" about face perception? *Psychological Review, 105*, 482–498.

Fazio, R. H. (2001). On the automatic activation of associated evaluations: An overview. *Cognition and Emotion, 15*, 115–141.

Fazio, R. H., Sanbonmatsu, D. M., Powell, M. C., & Kardes, F. R. (1986). On the automatic activation of attitudes. *Journal of Personality and Social Psychology, 50*, 229–238.

Fiedler, K. (1990). Mood-dependent selectivity in social cognition. In W. Stroebe & M. Hewstone (Eds.), *European review of social psychology*, (Vol. 1, pp. 1–32). New York: Wiley.

Fink, G. R., Halligan, P. W., Marshall, J. C., Frith, C. D., Frackowiack, R. S. J., & Dolan, R. J. (1996). Where in the brain does visual attention select the forest and the trees? *Nature, 382*, 626–628.

Forgas, J. P. (1995). Mood and judgement: The Affect Infusion Model (AIM). *Psychological Bulletin, 117*, 39–66.

Förster, J., Friedman, R. S., & Liberman, N. (2004). Temporal construal effects on abstract and concrete thinking: Consequences for insight and creative cognition. *Journal of Personality and Social Psychology, 87*, 177–189.

Förster, J., Liberman, N., & Kuschel, S. (2008). The effect of global versus local processing styles on assimilation versus contrast in social judgement. *Journal of Personality and Social Psychology, 94*, 579–599.

Fridlund, A. J. (1994). *Human facial expression: An evolutionary view*. San Diego, CA: Academic Press.

Friedman, R. S., & Förster, J. (2000). The effects of approach and avoidance motor actions on the elements of creative insight. *Journal of Personality and Social Psychology, 79*, 477–492.

Frijda, N. H. (1988). The laws of emotion. *American Psychologist, 43*, 349–358.

Frijda, N. H. (1993). Mood, emotion episodes, and emotions. In M. Lewis & J. M. Haviland (Ed.), *Handbook of emotions* (pp. 381–403). New York: Guilford Press.

Frijda, N. H. (1994). Emotions are functional, most of the time. In P. Ekman & R. J. Davidson (Eds.), *The nature of emotion. Fundamental questions*. New York: Oxford University Press.

Frijda, N. H., & Zeelenberg, M. (2001). Appraisal. What is the dependent? In K. R. Scherer, A. Schorr, & T. Johnstone (Eds.), *Appraisal processes in emotion: Theory, methods, research* (pp. 141–155). New York: Oxford University Press.

Fujita, K., Henderson, M. D., Eng, J., Trope, Y., & Liberman, N. (2006). Spatial distance and mental construal of social events. *Psychological Science, 17*, 278–282.

Gallese, V. (2006). Intentional attunement: A neurophysiological perspective on social cognition and its disruption in autism. *Brain Research, 1079*, 15–24.

Gasper, K., & Clore, G. L. (2002). Attending to the big picture: Mood and global versus local processing of visual information. *Psychological Science, 13*, 34–40.

Giner-Sorolla, R., Garcia, M. T., & Bargh, J. A. (1999). The automatic evaluation of pictures. *Social Cognition, 17,* 76–96.

Goldman, A. I., & Sripada, C. S. (2005). Simulationist models of face-based emotion recognition. *Cognition, 94,* 193–213.

Grandjean, D., & Scherer, K. R. (2008). Unpacking the cognitive architecture of emotion processes. *Emotion, 8,* 341–351.

Halgren, E., Raij, T., Marinkovic, K., Jousmäki, V., & Hari, R. (2000). Cognitive response profile of the human fusiform face area as determined by MEG. *Cerebral Cortex, 10,* 69–81.

Hariri, A. R., Tessitore, A., Mattay, V. S., Fera, F., & Weinberger, D. R. (2002). The amygdala response to emotional stimuli: A comparison of faces and scenes. *NeuroImage, 17,* 317–323.

Hatfield, E., Cacioppo, J. T., & Rapson, R. L. (1992). Primitive emotional contagion. In M. S. Clark (Ed.), *Emotion and social behavior* (pp. 151–177). Newbury Park, CA: Sage.

Hess, U., & Blairy, S. (2001). Facial mimicry and emotional contagion to dynamic emotional facial expressions and their influence on decoding accuracy. *International Journal of Psychophysiology, 40,* 129–141.

Hess, U., Philippot, P., & Blairy, S. (1998). Facial reactions to emotional facial expressions: Affect or cognition. *Cognition and Emotion, 12,* 509–531.

Innes-Ker, A., & Niedenthal, P. M. (2002). Emotion concepts and emotion states in social judgement and categorisation. *Journal of Personality and Social Psychology, 83,* 804–816.

Isen, A. M. (1984). Toward understanding the role of affect in cognition. In R. S. Wyer & T. K. Srull (Eds.), *Handbook of social cognition* (Vol. 3, pp. 179–236), Hillsdale, NJ: Lawrence Erlbaum Associates Inc.

Izard, C. E. (1994). Innate and universal facial expressions: Evidence from developmental cross-cultural research. *Psychological Bulletin, 115,* 288–299.

Jakobs, E., Fischer, A. H., & Manstead, A. S. R. (1997). Emotional experience as a function of social context: The role of the other. *Journal of Nonverbal Behavior, 21,* 103–130.

Kimchi, R. (1992). Primacy of wholistic processing and global/local paradigm: A critical review. *Psychological Bulletin, 112,* 24–38.

Kimura, Y., Yoshinoa, A., Takahashi, Y., & Nomura, S. (2004). Interhemispheric difference in emotional response without awareness. *Physiology & Behavior, 82,* 727–731.

Keltner, D., & Gross, J. J. (1999). Functional accounts of emotions. *Cognition and Emotion, 13,* 467–480.

Keltner, D., & Haidt, J. (1999). Social functions of emotions at four levels of analysis. *Cognition and Emotion, 13,* 505–521.

Krosnick, J. A., Betz, A. L., Jussim, L. J., & Lynn, A. R. (1992). Subliminal conditioning of attitudes. *Personality and Social Psychology Bulletin, 18,* 152–162.

Lazarus, R. S. (1968). Emotions and adaptation. In W. J. Arnold (Ed.), *Nebraska symposium on motivation* (pp. 175–266). Lincoln, NE: University of Nebraska Press.

Lazarus, R. S. (1991). Progress on a cognitive-motivational-relational theory of emotion. *American Psychologist, 46,* 819–834.

Lazarus, R. (1994). The stable and the unstable in emotion. In P. Ekman & R. J. Davidson (Eds.), *The nature of emotion. Fundamental questions* (pp. 79–85). New York: Oxford University Press.

LeDoux, J. E. (1989). Cognitive-emotional interactions of the brain. *Cognition and Emotion, 3,* 267–289.

Mackie, D. M., & Worth, L. T. (1989). Processing deficit and the mediation of positive affect in persuasion. *Journal of Personality and Social Psychology, 57,* 27–40.

Manstead, A. S. R., & Fischer, A. H. (2001). Social appraisal: The social world as object of and influence on appraisal processes. In K. R. Scherer, A. Schorr, & T. Johnstone (Eds.), *Appraisal processes in emotion* (pp. 221–232). New York: Oxford University Press.

Morris, J. S., de Gelder, B., Weiskrantz, L., & Dolan, R. J. (2001). Differential extrageniculostriate and amygdala responses to presentation of emotional faces in a cortically blind field. *Brain, 124*, 1241–1252.

Murphy, S. T., & Zajonc, R. B. (1993). Affect, cognition and awareness: Affective priming with optimal and suboptimal stimulus exposures. *Journal of Personality and Social Psychology, 64*, 723–739.

Navon, D. (1977). Forest before trees: The precedence of global features in visual perception. *Cognitive Psychology, 9*, 353–383.

Neumann, R. (2000). The causal influences of attributions on emotions: A procedural priming approach. *Psychological Science, 11*, 179–182.

Neumann, R., & Strack, F. (2000). "Mood contagion": The automatic transfer of mood between persons. *Journal of Personality and Social Psychology, 79*, 211–223.

Niedenthal, P. M. (2007). Embodying emotion. *Science, 316*, 1002–1005.

Niedenthal, P. M., Brauer, M., Halberstadt, J. B., & Innes-Ker, A. H. (2001). When did her smile drop? Facial mimicry and the influences of emotional state on the detection of change in emotional expression. *Cognition and Emotion, 15*, 853–864.

Niedenthal, P. M., & Cantor, N. (1986). Affective responses as guides to category-based inferences. *Motivation and Emotion, 10*, 217–232.

Niedenthal, P. M., Rohman, A., & Dalle, N. (2003). What is primed by emotion concepts and emotion words? In J. Musch & K. C. Klauer (Eds.), *The psychology of evaluation* (pp. 307–333). Mahwah, NJ: Lawrence Erlbaum Associates Inc.

Oberman, L., Winkielman, P., & Ramachandran, V. S. (2007). Face to face: Blocking facial mimicry can selectively impair recognition of emotional expressions. *Social Neuroscience, 2*, 167–178.

Öhman, A. (1992). The psychophysiology of emotion: Evolutionary and non-conscious origins. In G. d'Ydewalle, P. Eelen, & P. Bertelson (Eds.), *International perspectives on psychological science: Vol. 2. The state of the art* (pp. 197–227). Hillsdale, NJ: Lawrence Erlbaum Associates Inc.

Öhman, A., & Mineka, S. (2003). The malicious serpent: Snakes as a prototypical stimulus for an evolved module of fear. *Current Directions in Psychological Science, 12*, 5–9.

Ottati, V., Terkildsen, N., & Hubbard, C. (1997). Happy faces elicit heuristic processing in a televised impression formation task: A cognitive tuning account. *Personality and Social Psychology Bulletin, 23*, 1144–1156.

Palermo, R., & Rhodes, G. (2007). Are you always on my mind? A review of how face perception and attention interact. *Neuropsychologia, 45*, 75–92.

Panksepp, J. (1998). *Affective neuroscience: The foundations of human and animal emotions.* London: Oxford University Press.

Parkinson, B., & Manstead, A. S. R. (1992). Appraisal as a cause of emotion. In M. S. Clark (Ed.), *Emotion, review of personality and social psychology.* Newbury Park, CA: Sage Publishers.

Phillips, M. L., Williams, L. M., Heining, M., Herba, C. M., Russell, T., Andrew, C., et al. (2004). Differential neural responses to overt and covert presentations of facial expressions of fear and disgust. *NeuroImage, 21*, 1484–1496.

Pizzagalli, D., Regard, M., & Lehmann, D. (1999). Rapid emotional face processing in the human right and left brain hemispheres: An ERP study. *Neuroreport, 10*, 2691–2698.

Plutchik, R. (1994). *The psychology and biology of emotion.* New York: HarperCollins.

Polivy, J. (1981). On the induction of emotion in the laboratory: Discrete moods or multiple affect states? *Journal of Personality and Social Psychology, 41*, 803–817.

Rosenthal, V. (2004). Microgenesis, immediate experience and visual processes in reading. In A. Carsetti (Ed.), *Seeing, thinking and knowing: Meaning and self-organisation in visual cognition and thought* (pp. 221–243). Dordrecht: Kluwer Academic Publishers.

Russell, J. A. (1994). Is there universal recognition of emotion from facial expression? *Psychological Bulletin, 115*, 102–141.

Russell, J. A. (2003). Core affect and the psychological construction of emotion. *Psychological Review, 110*, 145–172.

Russell, J. A., & Fernandez-Dols, J. M. (1997). What does a facial expression mean? In J. A. Russell & J. M. Fernandez-Dols (Eds.), *The psychology of facial expression* (pp. 3–30). Cambridge, UK: Cambridge University Press.

Ruys, K. I., Dijksterhuis, A., & Corneille, O. (2008). On the (mis)categorisation of unattractive brides and attractive prostitutes: Extending evaluative congruency effects to social category activation. *Experimental Psychology, 55*, 182–188.

Ruys, K. I., Spears, R., Gordijn, E. H., De Vries, N. K (2007). Automatic contrast: Evidence that automatic comparison with the social self affects evaluative responses. *British Journal of Psychology, 98*, 361–374.

Ruys, K. I., & Stapel, D. A. (2008a). The secret life of emotions. *Psychological Science, 19*, 385–391.

Ruys, K. I., & Stapel, D. A. (2008b). Emotion elicitor or emotion messenger?: Subliminal exposure to two faces of facial expressions. *Psychological Science, 19*, 593–600.

Ruys, K. I., & Stapel, D. A. (2008c). How to heat up from the cold: Examining the preconditions for unconscious mood effects. *Journal of Personality and Social Psychology, 94*, 777–791.

Schachter, S. & Singer, J. E. (1962). Cognitive, social, and psychological determinants of emotional states. *Psychological Review, 69*, 379–399.

Scherer, K. R. (1984). On the nature and function of emotion: A component process approach. In K. R. Scherer & P. Ekman (Eds.), *Approaches to emotion* (pp. 293–318). Hillsdale, NJ: Lawrence Erlbaum Associates Inc.

Scherer, K. R. (1999). On the sequential nature of appraisal processes: Indirect evidence from a recognition task. *Cognition and Emotion, 13*, 763–793.

Schwarz, N., & Clore, G. L. (1996). Feelings and phenomenal experiences. In E. T. Higgins & A. W. Kruglanski (Eds.), *Social psychology: Handbook of basic principles* (pp. 433–465). New York: Guilford Press.

Simons, D. J., & Chabris, C. F. (1999). Gorillas in our midst: Sustained inattentional blindness for dynamic events. *Perception, 28*, 1059–1074.

Smith, C. A., & Ellsworth, P. C. (1985). Patterns of cognitive appraisal in emotion. *Journal of Personality and Social Psychology, 52*, 475–488.

Smith, N. K., Cacioppo, J. T., Larsen, J. T., & Chartrand, T. L. (2003). May I have your attention, please: Electrocortical responses to positive and negative stimuli. *Neuropsychologia, 41*, 171–183.

Smith, P. K., & Trope, Y. (2006). You focus on the forest when you're in charge of the trees: Power priming and abstract information processing. *Journal of Personality and Social Psychology, 90*, 578–596.

Soldat, A. S., & Sinclair, R. C. (2001). Colors, smiles, and frowns: External affective cues can directly affect responses to persuasive communications in a mood-like manner without affecting mood. *Social Cognition, 19*, 469–490.

Spruyt, A., Hermans, D., de Houwer, J., & Eelen, P. (2002). On the nature of the affective priming effect: Affective priming of naming responses. *Social Cognition, 3*, 227–256.

Stapel, D. A., & Koomen, W. (2005). When less is more: The consequences of affective primacy for subliminal priming effects. *Personality and Social Psychology Bulletin, 31*, 1286–1295.

Stapel, D. A., & Koomen, W. (2006). The flexible unconscious: Investigating the judgemental impact of varieties of unaware perception. *Journal of Experimental Social Psychology, 42*, 112–119.

Stapel, D. A., Koomen, W., & Ruys, K. I. (2002). The effects of diffuse and distinct affect. *Journal of Personality and Social Psychology, 83*, 60–74.

Stapel, D. A., & Semin, G. R. (2007). The magic spell of language: Linguistic categories and their perceptual consequences. *Journal of Personality and Social Psychology, 93*, 23–33.

Storbeck, J., & Robinson, M. D. (2004). Preferences and inferences in encoding visual objects: A semantic comparison of semantic and affective priming. *Personality and Social Psychology Bulletin, 30*, 81–93.

Treisman, A. (1996). The binding problem. *Current Opinion in Neurobiology, 6*, 171–178.

Trope, Y., & Liberman, N. (2003). Temporal construal. *Journal of Personality and Social Psychology, 110*, 403–421.

Tucker, D. M., & Williamson, P. A. (1984). Asymmetric neural control systems in human self-regulation. *Psychological Review, 91*, 185–215.

Vallacher, R. R., & Wegner, D. M. (1987). What do people think they're doing? Action identification and human behavior. *Psychological Review, 94*, 3–15.

Van der Velde, S. W., Stapel, D. A., & Gordijn, E. H. (2008). *Imitation of emotion: When meaning leads to aversion.* Unpublished manuscript.

Weiner, B. (1985). An attributional theory of achievement motivation and emotion. *Psychological Review, 92*, 548–573.

Werner, H. (1956). Microgenesis and aphasia. *Journal of Abnormal Social Psychology, 52*, 347–353.

Wicker, B., Keysers, C., Plailly, J., Royet, J., Gallese, V., & Rizzolatti, G. (2003). Both of us disgusted in my insula: The common neural basis of seeing and feeling disgust. *Neuron, 40*, 655–664.

Winkielman, P., & Berridge, K. C. (2004). Unconscious emotion. *Current Directions in Psychological Science, 13*, 120–123.

Winkielman, P., Berridge, K. C., & Wilbarger, J. L. (2005). Unconscious affective reactions to masked happy versus angry faces influence consumption behavior and judgements of value. *Personality and Social Psychology Bulletin, 31*, 121–135.

Zajonc, R. B. (1980). Feeling and thinking: Preferences need no inferences. *American Psychologist, 35*, 151–175.

Zajonc, R. B. (2000). Feeling and thinking. Closing the debate over the independence of affect. In J. Forgas (Ed.), *Feeling and thinking: The role of affect in social cognition* (pp. 31–58). Cambridge, UK: Cambridge University Press.

Zeelenberg, M., van den Bos, K., van Dijk, E., & Pieters, R. (2002). The inaction effect in the psychology of regret. *Journal of Personality and Social Psychology, 82*, 314–327.

EUROPEAN REVIEW OF SOCIAL PSYCHOLOGY
2009, 20, 272–314

An integrative review of process dissociation and related models in social cognition

B. Keith Payne

University of North Carolina, Chapel Hill, NC, USA

Anthony J. Bishara

College of Charleston, Charleston, SC, USA

This chapter reviews the use of formal dual process models in social psychology, with a focus on the process dissociation model and related multinomial models. The utility of the models is illustrated using studies of social and affective influences on memory, judgement and decision making, and social attitudes and stereotypes. We then compare and contrast the process dissociation model with other approaches, including implicit and explicit tests, signal detection theory, and multinomial models. Finally we show how several recently proposed multinomial models can be integrated into a single family of models, of which process dissociation is a specific instance. We describe how these process models can be used as both theoretical and measurement tools to answer questions about the role of automatic and controlled processes in social behaviour.

Keywords: Automatic; Control; Implicit; Process dissociation; Social cognition.

One of the first things people want to know about behaviour is whether it was intended. Did that driver intend to cut me off? Did she brush his knee by mistake or on purpose? Psychologists want to understand the differences between volitional behaviours and those that are unintended or unconscious for much the same reason. The question of how much control people have over their actions is important for fundamental questions about free will, self-control, and consciousness.

Correspondence should be addressed to Keith Payne, Department of Psychology, Campus Box 3270, University of North Carolina, Chapel Hill, Chapel Hill, NC 27599, USA. E-mail: payne@unc.edu

The first author acknowledges support from National Science Foundation Grant 0615478. We thank Jazmin Brown for assisting with references.

http://www.psypress.com/ersp   DOI: 10.1080/10463280903162177

Theories about how automatic and controlled processes operate and interact have been developed in the form of dual process models in social psychology (Chaiken & Trope, 1999). Dual process models have typically been formulated as verbal descriptions of automatic and controlled processes or systems. But recently, attempts have been made to formalise these ideas into quantitative models of how automatic and controlled processes drive behaviour. These formal models allow researchers to test theories about exactly how automatic and controlled processes relate to each other and how they interact. This chapter reviews models rooted in the process dissociation procedure (Jacoby, 1991), a model developed to separate automatic and controlled uses of memory, which has been applied widely in recent years.

Several related models have been proposed, some of which assume different relationships between automatic and controlled processes. By comparing how well these models account for experimental data, researchers can accomplish two simultaneous goals. First, they can test hypotheses about the nature and relationships between automatic and controlled processes. Second, the models can provide quantitative estimates of the underlying processes. The models can thus serve as both theoretical and measurement tools, allowing researchers to test quantitative hypotheses about underlying processes that are not directly observable.

In this chapter we review research in which process dissociation and related models have been applied, to survey the kinds of insights they can generate. We then examine the assumptions of the model, and compare the process dissociation approach to the use of implicit tests and to alternative quantitative models. But first we begin by discussing how process dissociation and related models can shed light on the relative impact of automatic and controlled processes, and their influence on behaviour.

THE DOMINANCE OF AUTOMATICITY?

The automatic–controlled distinction has its roots in cognitive psychology research, primarily on attention (e.g., Posner & Snyder, 1975; Shiffrin & Schneider, 1977). This research identified information processing as automatic, based on several criteria. First, automatic processing is triggered passively by stimuli in the environment. Second, it cannot be interrupted once started. Third, automatic processing is efficient, in the sense that it is fast and effortless. And finally, automatic processing does not interfere with other processes, but runs in parallel with them. Controlled processes were defined as having the opposite qualities, namely being flexible, interruptible, effortful, and sequential. In a related vein, Bargh (1994) identified the "four horsemen": the lack of intentionality, efficiency, controllability, and awareness in automatic processes. Such lists of distinguishing features of automatic and controlled processes have been applied in various degrees and combinations to many social psychology questions. As we shall see in later sections, process dissociation in some ways challenges this taxonomic approach. But even within this framework of features of automaticity, opinions differ about the relative importance of automatic and controlled influences.

Early research by Langer and colleagues suggested that ordinary behaviour was "mindless" to a surprising extent (Langer, Blank, & Chanowitz, 1978). In field studies most participants complied with a request to let the experimenter jump in front of them in the queue at the copying machine, so long as the experimenter gave a reason. Any reason would do, apparently. Participants were about as likely to let the experimenter cut in when she gave a good reason ("May I use the Xerox machine, because I'm in a rush") as when she gave a silly reason ("May I use the Xerox machine, because I need to make copies"). The only case in which the experimenter did not find overwhelming compliance was when she gave no reason at all ("May I use the Xerox machine?"). Langer and colleagues interpreted these findings as evidence that in most of daily life people respond without thinking much about what they are doing. This conclusion was a reaction to theories such as cognitive dissonance (Festinger, 1957) and attribution theory (Heider, 1958), which assumed that people normally process incoming information in a thoughtful and elaborate way.

The emphasis on the prominence of automatic processing has continued in more recent writings. Bargh (1999) described automaticity as a "cognitive monster" whose influence is too powerful to chain with conscious, deliberate thought. Bargh and colleagues have argued that most ordinary behaviour is driven by automatic processes, and that the more we learn about automaticity the less room there is for conscious control processes to explain behaviour (Bargh, 1997, 2005; Bargh & Chartrand, 1999; Bargh & Ferguson, 2000). Wegner and colleagues have gone further, arguing that the experience of conscious control is an illusion and that the real causes of behaviour are never conscious (Wegner, 2002).

This expansive view of automaticity has been criticised by Kihlstrom, who dubbed it the "automaticity juggernaut" (Kihlstrom, 2006, 2007). In Kihlstrom's view the empirical literature does not support the claims that automatic processes dominate social life. He notes that studies portraying automatic processes as ubiquitous often rely on a watered-down definition of automaticity. Rather than requiring all of the features of automatic processing, they tend to establish only one or two (see also Moors & DeHouwer, 2006). And, following Bargh (1989, 1994), automaticity is treated as continuous in practice, rather than all or none. So if a process is "relatively automatic" it is hard to argue that only automatic processes are important or that controlled processes are irrelevant. Kihlstrom's critique argues that this almost exclusive emphasis on automaticity amounts to ignoring the advances of the cognitive revolution in favour of a return to a thinly veiled Skinnerian behaviourism.

If Kihlstrom is right, however, we still do not have a metric to gauge exactly how much conscious control should be emphasised. There is probably no generally applicable formula for answering such a question. That is why theories dealing with the interplay between automatic and controlled processes have generally stated their claims in terms of the moderating conditions that favour one process or the other. Dual process theories have been developed to account for the automatic–controlled distinction across a wide range of topics (Chaiken & Trope, 1999). The models vary in their scope, with some aimed at explaining relatively specific phenomena, such as attitude change (Gawronski & Bodenhausen, 2006; Petty & Briñol, 2006) or prejudice (Devine, 1989; Bodenhausen & Macrae, 1998). Others aim to explain the operation of automatic and controlled processing more broadly. For example, Strack and Deutsch (2004) distinguish between reflective and impulsive bases for social behaviour in general. Sloman's (1996) model addresses two systems of reasoning that support all thinking and decision making, and Smith and DeCoster's (2000) model links social psychology research on automatic and controlled processing with separable memory systems that may underpin implicit and explicit forms of memory.

Although these models (and many others not reviewed here) highlight different features of mental life, they all share an emphasis on the automatic–controlled distinction. They all differentiate the conditions when automatic versus controlled processes are most likely to come into play. These conditions are tied tightly to the definitions of automatic and controlled processes. Once we understand that automatic processes are efficient and effortless, whereas controlled processes are slow and effortful, it becomes clear when each kind of process is likely to matter. When conditions allow people to think slowly and carefully, controlled processes are likely to dictate behaviour. But when they are disinclined or unable to think carefully, automatic responses will be important.

The distinctions in these models are important and useful in understanding the relative roles of automaticity and control in social life. They allow researchers to predict, for example, that when people are tired or distracted or rushed they are more likely to respond based on automatic impulses than when they are energetic, focused, and unhurried. Such predictions have in fact been supported again and again. To name just a few examples, White American participants are more likely to mistake a harmless object for a weapon when it is paired with a Black person than a White person, and this bias becomes stronger as participants respond more quickly (Correll, Park, Judd, & Wittenbrink, 2002; Greenwald, Oakes, &

Hoffman, 2002; Payne, 2001); people are more likely to choose junk food over fruit when they are distracted by mentally rehearsing a number, as compared to paying full attention (Shiv & Fedorkhin, 1999); smokers tend to smoke more cigarettes when they are distracted than when they are not (Westling, Mann, & Ward, 2006). Dual process theories predict these findings because each reflects a conflict between automatic inclinations and controlled efforts to regulate responses. The contribution of automatic influences, relative to controlled influences, increases in each case when cognitive resources are taxed.

The fact that many dual process theories predict these results is both a strength and a weakness for the theories. On the one hand, predictive power is vital for a theory's value. On the other hand, these findings might be just as easily predicted by one dual process theory as another. Whether the phenomena are explained in terms of two systems of reasoning (Sloman, 1996), fast-learning and slow-learning memory systems (Smith & DeCoster, 2000), or reflective and impulsive systems (Strack & Deutsch, 2004), the predictions are often the same. So now that we know about some of the conditions that encourage automatic and controlled responding, we are still left with many unanswered questions.

One question is about the dominance of automaticity versus control, as debated in the writings of Bargh, Wegner, Langer, and Kihlstrom. If relative influence of automatic processing increases when cognitive resources are depleted, it does not follow that automatic influences are dominating controlled influences, or the other way around. We can only observe relative differences in impact across experimental conditions, but we cannot examine either kind of process in isolation. So the questions about which processes dominate, and under what conditions, are left unanswered.

More generally, dual process models do not usually specify exactly how automatic and controlled processes relate to each other. But in understanding conflicts between automatic and controlled influences, it is often essential to know how they are related. For example, when choosing snacks do participants select sweets by default, and only reconsider their choice if their impulses are suppressed? Or do their automatic impulses only drive their choices when controlled efforts fall apart? Or do automatic and controlled influences have equal and opposite effects, with each kind of process contributing additive force in a tug-of-war for control of action?

Most dual process theories do not distinguish between such process accounts at this level of detail. Moreover, it would be difficult to test them because increases in one process cannot usually be disentangled from decreases in the other. For instance, when participants smoke more under cognitive load, is it because controlled self-restraint processes are reduced, leaving automatic impulses untouched? Or when self-restraint declines, do automatic impulses flare up in their absence?

To answer these questions we need to pose a more formal model that makes assumptions about the relations between processes, and then test those assumptions. A benefit of this approach is that it can provide quantitative estimates of automatic and controlled influences separately. With these in hand, researchers are in a much better position to explain the chain of mechanisms leading from external conditions (e.g., a distracting environment) through cognitive processes (e.g., automatic impulses and controlled restraint) to behaviour (e.g., smoking). The process dissociation procedure provides a means for doing so.

THE PROCESS DISSOCIATION PROCEDURE

The process dissociation procedure is a family of models for estimating controlled and automatic contributions to behaviour. Jacoby (1991) developed the procedure as a means of separating controlled and automatic influences of memory, particularly in regard to the distinction between intended and unintended influences. But before reviewing how the procedure is applied in memory research, we will first illustrate it using everyday behaviour. Suppose that a half-hearted dieter has decided to enjoy sweets on weekends but not on weekdays. So each weekday morning he resolves to eat no sweets. On some weekdays he succeeds, and on others he does not. We can assume that there is an automatic attraction to sweets on both weekdays and weekends. But on weekdays that attraction is opposed by the intention to diet, whereas on weekends it is complimented by the intention to indulge.

We can gauge the dieter's self-control by comparing how much junk food he eats on weekends (when both automatic impulse and intent favour eating) versus weekdays (when impulse favours eating but self-control opposes it). If, for example, he eats sweets on weekends with a probability of .90, but he also eats sweets on weekdays with probability .20, then his probability of exerting self-control is .70.

Once we have an estimate of self-control, we need to make an assumption about how automatic and controlled influences are related. One plausible relationship is that automatic impulses drive behaviour whenever self-control fails. (We will examine alternative relationships later.) On this assumption, we can estimate the strength of the dieter's attraction to sweets. We do so by taking the likelihood that he eats despite an intention to the contrary (i.e., the .20 probability of indulging on weekdays), which represents not only the strength of the impulse but also failures of control (impulse * self-control failure). Because we know the likelihood of control failures $(1 - .70 = .30)$ we can disentangle the two by dividing by the rate of self-control failure $(.20/.30 = .67)$. We find, then, that our dieter's behaviours are driven by self-control with a probability of .70, and by automatic impulse with a probability of .67.

With this model in hand we can examine how behaviour changes as a function of various factors, and draw specific conclusions about the contributions of automatic and controlled mechanisms. In the study described above by Shiv and Fedorkhin (1999), for instance, participants were more likely to eat sweets when they were distracted than when they were not. If we examined our dieter's behaviour when he is distracted and when he is not, we could estimate the effect of distraction on automatic and controlled processes separately. We might find, for instance, that he eats more when distracted because self-control is reduced under distraction, leaving automatic appetites unaffected. Alternatively, we might find that he eats more when distracted because the distraction directly increases automatic appetites (for example, if the distraction involves food-related information).

The dieting case provides an intuitive example of how the procedure can be applied, but we can state it more precisely using its formal application in a memory experiment. Research on implicit memory has shown that past experience sometimes influences later performance even in the absence of conscious memory for the experience. Implicit memory has often been tested by comparing direct tests of memory—such as recall or recognition tasks— with indirect tests of memory. Indirect tests do not ask participants to refer back to a past experience; instead they measure facilitation in task performance resulting from prior experience. A commonly used example of an implicit memory test is word fragment completion (Tulving, Schacter, & Stark, 1982). Participants might be more likely to complete the fragment *Fre _ d* with Freud, as opposed to Freed, if they have recently read the psychoanalyst's name. This could happen even in the absence of conscious memory for reading it.

Indirect and direct memory tests are often affected differently by the same variables. For example, delay strongly affects direct tests, but affects indirect tests much less severely (Tulving et al., 1982). Such dissociations between indirect and direct tests have been used to argue for a theoretical distinction between implicit memory and explicit memory, based on either different anatomical systems (Schacter, 1987) or different cognitive operations (Roediger, 1990).

However, Jacoby (1991) noted that these important theoretical distinctions relied on an unspoken assumption that indirect tests reflected only automatic or unconscious processes, whereas direct tests reflected only consciously controlled processes. This "process pure" assumption is generally not justified, because conscious memory can affect implicit test performance, and automatic influences can affect explicit memory tests. For example, when asked to complete a word fragment with the first word that comes to mind, participants might think back to the study phase of an experiment to help generate a response. And when asked to respond with a word they remember studying, participants might use the first item that comes to mind, a strategy influenced by implicit memory.

If implicit memory processes affect explicit memory tests, and explicit memory processes affect implicit tests, then relying on these tests can be misleading. Jacoby's (1991) solution was to compare conditions in which implicit and explicit processes worked in concert to conditions in which they worked in opposition. For instance, in one experiment, participants studied a list of words while either paying full attention or dividing their attention between studying the words and a distracting auditory task (Jacoby, Toth, & Yonelinas, 1993). This distracting task was used to interfere with explicit memory for the words, but it was not expected to interfere with automatic influences of memory.

At test, participants completed word stems under two sets of conditions. In the *inclusion* condition they were instructed to complete the stems with studied words. If they could not recall studying an item they were told to complete the stem with the first word that came to mind. In this condition automatic and consciously controlled uses of memory work in concert. Responding based on conscious memory for a studied word, or responding based on items that came automatically to mind would lead to the same response. In the *exclusion* condition participants were told to complete the stem with a word that was *not* presented earlier in the experiment. This condition placed automatic and controlled uses of memory in opposition. If participants remembered studying a word, they could successfully exclude it. But if it came automatically to mind and they did not remember studying the word, they could be expected to complete the stem with it.

The process dissociation procedure formalises these relationships by positing that, in the in-concert condition, participants could complete the stem with a studied word either because they consciously remembered it (with probability C) or because it came automatically to mind (with probability A) in the absence of consciously controlled memory $(1-C)$:

$$P(\text{Studied item} \mid \text{Inclusion}) = C + A(1 - C). \qquad (1)$$

In the exclusion condition participants can be expected to use a studied item despite instructions to the contrary whenever the item comes automatically to mind but consciously controlled memory for the item fails:

$$P(\text{Studied item} \mid \text{Exclusion}) = A(1 - C). \qquad (2)$$

Because the experiment provides the empirical probabilities of responses in the inclusion and exclusion conditions, estimates of C and A processes can be solved. Conscious memory is estimated as the difference between performance on inclusion and exclusions conditions:

$$C = P(\text{Studied item} \mid \text{Inclusion}) - P(\text{Studied item} \mid \text{Exclusion}). \quad (3)$$

With C estimated, the automatic memory influence can also be derived by dividing performance in the exclusion condition by the rate of control failures:

$$A = P(\text{Studied item} \mid \text{Exclusion})/(1 - C). \quad (4)$$

Jacoby and colleagues (1993) found that the divided attention task reduced the rate of responses with studied words in the inclusion condition, but increased the use of studied words in the exclusion condition. By applying these above equations they found that this effect was due solely to the C parameter. Divided attention reduced C estimates from .25 to .00, but left A estimates unchanged (.47 and .46 in full attention and divided attention conditions).

This approach has been used to separate conscious recollection and automatic memory in many memory studies. But the basic logic can be applied to understand automatic and controlled contributions in any number of contexts. The critical aspect of the procedure is that researchers arrange an experiment such that automatic and controlled processes are placed in opposition in some conditions, and in concert in other conditions. If this is done, then a straightforward set of equations such as the ones above can be used to estimate automatic and controlled contributions. In the following section we review the diversity of topics that have been studied using process dissociation or closely related models to illustrate the kinds of insights that they provide. This review will not cover studies that are purely aimed at memory processes, as these have been reviewed elsewhere (Kelley & Jacoby, 2000; Yonelinas, 2002). Instead this review focuses on three topics in social psychology where the procedure has been applied most commonly. These include (1) social and affective influences on memory, (2) judgement and decision making, and (3) inter-group attitudes.

SOCIAL AND AFFECTIVE INFLUENCES ON MEMORY

Memory shapes social life in countless ways. Perhaps most fundamentally, memory processes determine how we mentally represent ourselves and other people. The psychology literature is full of evidence that we do not represent people objectively. Instead our representations are slanted with bias and filtered through selective attention. Biased memory representations are important to social interaction because they suggest a means by which biases are perpetuated. Each time a person revisits a biased memory, that bias is reinforced. What are the mechanisms that drive this cycle? Dual process theories stress that many social factors could influence behaviour either through automatic or controlled routes. But it is often difficult to localise such automatic or controlled pathways. Process dissociation has been useful in distinguishing these pathways in several studies of social and affective influences on memory.

Hense, Penner, and Nelson (1995) conducted one of the earliest studies using process dissociation to test the influence of social stereotypes on memory. They asked participants to study lists of traits related to stereotypes of the old and the young. The lists were said to describe a particular set of old and young individuals. After studying the traits, participants were asked to recall the traits that described the older and younger persons under two sets of instructions. In the inclusion condition participants were asked to respond with the trait they had studied or, if they could not remember the trait, to respond with the first word that came to mind. In the exclusion condition participants were asked to respond with a new trait that was not studied.

Results suggested that stereotypical traits had a selective influence on the automatic use of memory without affecting controlled recollection. Stereotype-consistent traits such as *slow* and *frail* came to mind automatically when thinking about an older target person. Controlled memory was reduced by a divided attention task, but this was independent of the stereotyping effect. Importantly, the bias in automatic memory was greater for participants who held negative attitudes towards the elderly.

Subsequent studies have generally supported these conclusions. In one study stereotype-based expectancies were found to lead to automatic memory biases most strongly when cognitive resources were limited by a distracting task (Sherman, Groom, Ehrenberg, & Klauer, 2003). Distraction also reduced controlled memory, resulting in a double threat to memory accuracy. The biases participants brought with them into these studies led to biases in their memory of their experience. After participants had left the study, those biased memories might continue to maintain participants' attitudes. After all, the participants could then easily recall many instances that confirmed the stereotype.

The fact that these biases were perpetuated via automatic processes suggests that they may be particularly deceptive when trying to sort out which memories are true and which are false. In support of this notion, one study asked participants to describe the phenomenology of their memories as "remembered", "known", or "guessed". Stereotype-consistent memory errors were described by participants primarily as "known" whereas accurate memories were mainly described as "remembered" (Macrae, Schloerscheidt, Bodenhausen, & Milne, 2002). The difference is that "known" memories feel true to participants, but lack vivid details such as the visual or aural experiences that accompanied them (Tulving, 1985). This difference is reasonable because, in the case of stereotypical errors, participants did not actually perceive the events at all; they inferred them based on their own expectations. Still, they did not label errors as guesses; they "just knew" them to be true.

Payne and colleagues explored this deceptive phenomenology in a study of the consequences for correcting memory biases (Payne, Jacoby, & Lambert, 2004). Participants studied lists of names typical of White Americans or Black Americans. Each name was described by an occupation that was stereotypically associated with Whites or Blacks (e.g., politician, basketball player). Later, at test, participants saw the names and were asked to remember whether each person was a basketball player or a politician. Following each response, participants rated their confidence from 50% (chance, or not at all confident) to 100% (absolute certainty). In this paradigm, automatic and controlled processes are placed in concert and in opposition, not through inclusion/exclusion instructions, but through congruence/incongruence between memory and stereotype bias. When a White name is described as a politician or a Black name as a basketball player, memory for the pairing and stereotypic biases both favour the same response. But when the pairings are stereotype incongruent, memory would lead to a correct answer whereas stereotype bias would lead to a stereotype-consistent error.

Replicating earlier studies, participants showed strong stereotypical memory distortions. Process dissociation analyses showed that the bias was entirely mediated through automatic influences rather than controlled memory. However, subjective experiences of confidence were not attuned to that automatic bias. As shown in Figure 1, automatic memory bias was equally prevalent when participants expressed 100% certainty as when they felt no confidence at all. Confidence was not completely uncalibrated, however. It was strongly related to estimates of controlled memory recollection.

Putting these findings together, we see that participants had a good sense of when they were responding based on controlled memory, and when controlled memory was poor. But when controlled memory failed they had no sense of when they were being biased by stereotypes. It has long been known that people do not necessarily have introspective access to the processes driving their behaviour (Nisbett & Wilson, 1977). But these findings suggest that they have better awareness of some processes than others. This implies that when participants try to avoid memory errors, they will succeed and fail in specific, predictable ways.

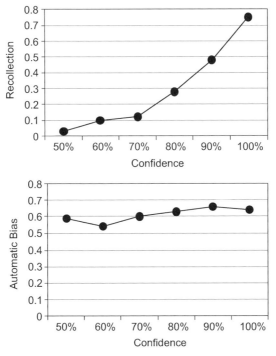

Figure 1. Relationships between subjective confidence and Recollection (top panel) and Automatic Bias (bottom panel). Confidence ranged from 50% (i.e., responding at chance) to 100% (i.e., complete confidence). Adapted from Payne et al. (2004).

In a second study some participants were given the opportunity to "pass" by not responding whenever they did not know the answer (Payne et al., 2004). Other participants were required to answer every item even if they had to guess. This arrangement allows participants to control their own accuracy rates based on their subjective feelings (Koriat & Goldsmith, 1996). As predicted on the basis of the confidence findings, participants in the "pass" condition made fewer errors because they adaptively refrained from responding when they were unsure. However, when they made errors they were just as likely to be stereotypically biased as participants in the control condition. Even when participants were deliberately trying to avoid errors, they failed to filter out stereotypical biases because they did not feel like biases.

The studies just reviewed suggest that information consistent with stereotypic expectations comes to mind automatically to bias memory. But in some cases information that violates expectations can have a greater impact on memory (Stangor & McMillan, 1992). According to much prior research and theory, the key difference is whether the inconsistent information violates expectancies strongly enough to attract attention and elicit effortful thought processes aimed at resolving the inconsistencies (Srull & Wyer, 1980; Stangor & McMillan, 1992). Because elaborate processing tends to benefit conscious recollection, we might expect expectancy-violating information to result in higher estimates of controlled memory.

A study of group favouritism supports the link between social expectancy violation and consciously controlled memory (Gaunt, Leyens, & Demoulin, 2002). People tend to perceive members of other social groups as well as their own social groups to experience "primary" emotions such as fear, anger, and surprise. These emotions are even perceived to be expressed by non-human animals. But people attribute more "secondary" emotions— those considered uniquely human, such as hope, sympathy, or guilt—more to in-group members than to out-group members (Leyens et al., 2001). Gaunt and colleagues (2002) used the process dissociation procedure to examine memory for primary and secondary emotions attributed to in-group and out-group members. During a study phase participants solved anagrams that paired the in-group (Belgians) or out-group (Arabs) with primary and secondary emotion words (e.g., *Belgians–sympathy*). Following the anagram task participants listened to an auditory list of similar group–emotion word pairs. At test, participants were presented with studied and new word pairs. They were asked to recognise studied items under exclusion instructions (accept only the word pairs from the anagrams) or inclusion pairs (accept pairs from either the anagram task or the auditory list). Based on Jacoby's (1991) prior work it was assumed that consciously controlled memory is necessary to distinguish between items from different sources.

Consistent with the notion that participants expected out-group members to have fewer uniquely human emotions and that violations of this expectation elicit effortful thought processes, estimates of controlled memory were higher for secondary emotions attributed to out-group members compared to in-group members. There was no group difference in memory for primary emotions, suggesting that "uniquely human" emotions attributed to out-group members were especially expectancy violating.

Summary of social memory research

These studies show how social groups can influence memory through either automatic or controlled processes. The process dissociation procedure was used in these studies to empirically separate those distinct routes. Although process dissociation was developed specifically to separate automatic and controlled contributions to memory, it has been broadened recently to investigate other phenomena, such as judgement and decision making.

JUDGEMENT AND DECISION MAKING

Extensions to decision making are very recent, but they offer an exciting way to reveal the processes underlying decisions. In one study Fitzsimons and Williams (2000) used a modification of the process dissociation procedure to investigate the *mere measurement effect*. The mere measurement effect is the finding that simply asking a person about how likely they are to perform a behaviour in the future actually increases the likelihood that they will perform that behaviour (Morwitz, Johnson, & Schmittlein, 1993; Sherman, 1980). Fitzsimons and Williams (2000, study 1) asked one group of participants how likely they would be to choose a new brand of candy bar, whereas the control group was not asked about the candy bar. The mere measurement effect suggests that the group that was asked would be more likely to choose the candy bar than the control group. In addition, participants were told that they were either more or less likely to actually receive the candy bar if they chose it. This manipulation was meant to manipulate the self-interest of participants. A rational (in the sense of self-interested) analysis would suggest that participants should be more likely to choose the candy bar when informed that they are likely to get the candy bar. By crossing the mere measurement with the self-interest information, this study created conditions in which the mere measurement effect was congruent with self-interest, and conditions in which it was incongruent with self-interest.

This study showed that, indeed, participants asked about their likely choice more often chose the candy bar. Using a modified model based on the logic of process dissociation, these researchers separated two components of the effect. One component reflected how strongly the intent question influenced choice regardless of self-interest (akin to the automatic component in the other studies discussed here). The other component reflected the extent to which choices were guided by the self-interest. This is related to the controlled component we have discussed, but because the procedure pitted self-interest against the mere measurement effect, this component reflected self-interested decision making. The mere measurement question influenced choices largely irrespective of whether it was consistent with self-interest or not, an effect driven by the automatic component (see also Kramer & Block, 2008, for evidence that superstitious beliefs influence consumer choices via automatic, but not controlled processes). Furthermore, results suggested that the controlled, self-interested process determined behaviour to a larger extent in a full attention condition than a divided attention condition.

Another interesting research effort has forged a connection between classic research on heuristics and biases (e.g., Tversky & Kahneman, 1974) with dual process theories of judgement using the process dissociation procedure. Several dual process theories have been proposed to account for the fact that people sometimes make decisions that appear rationally calculated, whereas other times they make decisions that are irrational, impulsive, biased, or based on simple heuristics (Kahneman & Frederick, 2002; Sloman, 1996; Stanovich & West, 2000). Ferreira and colleagues applied the process dissociation procedure to separate rule-based reasoning from heuristic reasoning (Ferreira, Garcia-Marques, Sherman, & Sherman, 2006). To do this they arranged decision problems in which the two types of reasoning could be placed in concert and in opposition.

For example, consider a problem posed by Ferreira and colleagues (2006). Imagine that there are two sets of envelopes, and some envelopes contain prizes. In the first set there are 10 envelopes, 2 of which contain a prize. In the second set there are 100 envelopes, 19 of which contain a prize. Which set of envelopes would you choose from? Although it is simple to calculate that there is a 20% chance for the first set and a 19% chance for the second set, many people feel compelled to choose from the second set because it has a larger absolute number of chances to win. This problem places rule-based reasoning (e.g., calculating the probabilities) and heuristic reasoning (e.g., preferring the larger absolute number) in opposition. Judgement research demonstrating heuristics or biases almost always relies on this kind of conflict, which in the process dissociation framework can be considered an opposition (or exclusion) condition. Ferreira and colleagues completed the conceptual possibilities by adding conditions in which rule-based and heuristic reasoning were also in concert. For example, consider the same problem described above except that the second set of envelopes now has 21 (instead of 19) chances to win out of 100. In this case, both rule-based reasoning and heuristic reasoning suggest choosing the second set, because the second set has both a larger probability of winning and a larger absolute number of chances to win. Using the combination of inclusion and exclusion conditions, Ferreira and colleagues examined several types of judgemental biases. First, ratio bias (as in the envelope problem) leads people to weight absolute numbers more heavily than proportional values (Kirkpatrick & Epstein, 1992). Second, in base-rate problems people tend to neglect base rates and form judgements based on salient but non-diagnostic information. Third, in conjunction problems people often mistakenly judge that the likelihood of a salient event is greater than the likelihood of a larger class of events that includes the event. For example, in the well-known Linda problem participants think that a bright, outspoken woman who is deeply concerned with social justice is more likely to be a feminist bank teller than to be a bank teller (Tversky & Kahneman, 1983).

By placing rule-based and heuristic reasoning in concert and in opposition, Ferreira and colleagues (2006) were able to measure these two reasoning components separately. They found that the two components were affected by different experimental manipulations, consistent with dual-process theories of reasoning. For example, instructions to complete the problems in a reflective, rational way as opposed to an intuitive way increased the rule-based reasoning parameter but did not affect heuristic reasoning parameter. In contrast, performing a distracting cognitive task while completing the problems reduced rule-based reasoning but did not affect heuristic reasoning. Finally, when participants were primed to respond heuristically by completing several practice problems in which heuristic responses led to the correct answers, estimates of heuristic reasoning increased.

A variation of the process dissociation procedure has been used to estimate processes involved in a classic judgemental bias, the anchoring effect. In typical anchoring experiments (e.g., Tversky & Kahneman, 1974) an initial question about a number influences a later number judgement. For example, a participant might be asked if there are more or fewer than 80 bowling lanes in the US (a low anchor), and then asked to estimate the exact number of bowling lanes in the country. Participants' estimates tend to be biased towards the anchor.

Several authors have suggested that anchoring effects may be the result of an accessibility bias (Chapman & Johnson, 1994, 1999; Strack & Mussweiler, 1997). Specifically, participants mentally test the anchor value in the initial question, and when they so, anchor-consistent information becomes more accessible. This heightened accessibility of anchor-consistent information contaminates the pool of accessible information used to later answer the number estimation question. Bishara (2005) expanded on this accessibility bias account with a dual-process model. In that model, anchoring effects result from automatic accessibility biases but only to the extent that more controlled processes fail. To examine controlled processes, participants were allowed to study the correct answers to some numerical questions in a separate study phase at the beginning of the experiment (e.g., studied "There are 130,000 bowling lanes in the US"). This knowledge would allow for the possibility of controlled recollection of the correct answer later on. Although participants intended to use this knowledge, to the extent that recollection failed, number judgements may be unintentionally biased by whether the anchor was high or low. Modelling results confirmed the predictions of the dual process account. The initial presentation of the answer did indeed selectively influence the controlled recollection parameter but not the accessibility parameter. In contrast, the direction of the anchor selectively influenced the accessibility parameter but not the controlled recollection parameter.

As a baseline comparison condition, some trials included an anchor unrelated to the number estimation question that followed. For example, prior to estimating the number of bowling lanes, a participant would answer a more/less question about the number of Coast Guard personnel in the country. Such unrelated anchors did not produce a significant anchoring effect (see Brewer & Chapman, 2002). Only related anchors led to significant changes in participants' number judgements.

Interestingly, whereas number judgements were strongly affected by the presence of a related anchor, participants' confidence in those judgements was not increased. Confidence was affected only by whether an item had been earlier studied or not. This pattern suggests that participants were able to accurately monitor the source of their number estimations: when they were estimating on the basis of recollection their confidence was high, but when they were forced to rely on whatever most easily came to mind their confidence was low. So, even though the anchoring effect was large in terms of number estimations, the anchoring effect was not a subjectively compelling illusion.

In a second experiment on the anchoring effect, participants were forced to make number estimations in one condition and were free to pass in another condition. To the extent that participants are able to monitor the failure of controlled processing, and thereby strategically withhold their responses, the option to pass should reduce the anchoring effect. In fact, not only did the option to pass reduce the anchoring effect, the anchoring effect was also reduced to nonsignificance. Further analyses suggested that participants were not passing at random; rather, participants strategically passed only when more controlled processing failed.

Overall, confidence and passing were related to anchoring biases (Bishara, 2005) in some of the same ways that they were related to stereotypical biases in memory (Payne et al., 2004). Just as stereotypical memory biases were unrelated to confidence, so was accessibility bias in the anchoring studies. Importantly, both studies (Bishara, 2005; Payne et al., 2004) highlight how the process dissociation approach can be used in conjunction with confidence and passing responses so as to better understand the level of awareness of psychological biases.

Summary of judgement and decision research

Studies applying process dissociation models to judgement and decision-making research have advanced thinking on several fronts. First, they have produced more direct evidence than previously available that decision making relies on both deliberative and heuristic processes. These distinct influences had been theoretically predicted on the basis of dual process models, but experiments had provided only indirect evidence for the underlying processes. Second, these studies are the first to provide estimates of both deliberative and heuristic processes individually. Based on previous studies, only the relative contribution of both processes could be inferred.

But if some variable (i.e., cognitive load) increased reliance of heuristics, it was impossible to tell whether that variable had its effects by increasing heuristic reasoning, decreasing rule-based reasoning, or some combination of both. Process dissociation estimates provided a means of resolving that ambiguity.

SOCIAL ATTITUDES AND STEREOTYPING

The study of heuristics and biases has been motivated by concern that they will reduce the quality of decisions and threaten the rationality of human decision makers. Stereotypes and group prejudices are often considered a type of heuristic thinking that not only reduces the quality of judgements for the decision maker, but also has unfair consequences for the person being judged. In this research the focus has been on separating automatically activated attitudes and stereotypes from consciously controlled responding. The distinction is important in studies of prejudice and stereotyping because consciously reported attitudes are often distorted by social desirability, self-presentation concerns, and other biases. And so it is vital to study automatic responses, which may differ from these strategic responses.

We have studied automatic and controlled components of prejudice and stereotyping by examining the influence of race in decisions about threat. For example, a study reported in Payne (2001) was conducted soon after the highly publicised death of Amadou Diallo, who was mistakenly shot by New York City police officers who mistook the wallet in his hand for a gun. Because Diallo was unarmed and Black, some critics alleged that the officers' use of force was biased by race. The question in our study was whether systematically mistaking a harmless object for a weapon can reveal unintended influences of racial attitudes and stereotypes.

Participants in the study attempted to distinguish between guns and harmless hand tools that were flashed briefly on a computer screen. Immediately preceding each gun or tool was a Black or White male face that served as a prime. This 2×2 design creates conditions in which intentional responding to the target items and automatic influences of racial stereotypes are in concert (analogous to an inclusion condition), and in opposition (analogous to an exclusion condition). For example, when the prime was Black and the target was a gun, participants could correctly respond "gun" either by intentionally controlled (C) detection of the gun, or by an automatic stereotypical response (A) when control failed $(1 - C)$: $C + A(1 - C)$. In contrast, when the prime was Black and the target was a tool, participants would incorrectly respond "gun" when controlled detection failed, but automatic stereotyping favoured the gun response: $A(1 - C)$. The degree of intentional control can be solved by the difference between "gun" responses in the inclusion and exclusion conditions. Given that estimate, the degree of automatic bias can be solved by dividing stereotypical false "gun" responses by failures of control $(1 - C)$.

This experiment controlled participants' intentions via the task requirements to distinguish guns from tools. For that reason, the Control estimate measures how well participants carried out their intentions by distinguishing between target objects. In contrast, participants do not intend to be influenced by the racial primes. The Automatic estimate measures how much their responses were biased by these unintended influences.

The results of the study showed that participants were indeed biased by the race primes, as participants were more likely to mistake a tool for a gun when it was primed with a Black face than a White face. This bias appears to be robust and widespread, as it has been demonstrated using several experimental paradigms and several participant populations, including college students, police officers, and civilian adult populations (Correll et al., 2002; Correll, Park, Judd, & Wittenbrink, 2007; Greenwald et al., 2002; Plant & Peruche, 2005). But more importantly for present concerns, the process dissociation estimates successfully separated automatic and controlled components of responses. Requiring participants to respond quickly sharply reduced the controlled component, a well-established characteristic of controlled processing. But the controlled component was unaffected by the race primes. In contrast, the race primes affected the automatic component, but response speed did not.

A key implication of the process dissociation model is that automatic biases drive responses whenever controlled processes fail. Control can fail for many reasons beyond making speedy judgements. For example, much research has shown that self-control can be seen as a limited-capacity resource. When self-control is exerted in one setting it can be temporarily depleted, leaving a person less likely to exert self-control in another setting (Muraven & Baumeister, 2000). Govorun and Payne (2006) tested whether the sort of controlled processing estimated in the weapons task is sensitive to this type of self-control depletion. Participants in one group completed hundreds of trials of an attention-demanding cognitive task (the Stroop colour naming task) whereas participants in the other group completed only a few trials. All participants then completed the weapons task to test whether exerting control in the initial task reduced subsequent control over responses. As expected, expending cognitive control in the initial task reduced the controlled component in the weapon bias, but not the automatic component (Govorun & Payne, 2006).

Although speeded responses and self-control depletion can enflame racial bias by reducing control, other factors can increase racial bias by increasing automatic stereotyping. For instance, in one study, Payne, Lambert, and Jacoby (2002) warned some participants that their responses could be biased by the race of the faces flashed before the objects. One group was given this warning and urged to avoid letting race bias their judgements. Another group was given the warning, but they were encouraged to use race to help them identify weapons, as if they were police engaged in racial profiling. Finally, a third group that served as a control were not warned about the impact of race at all.

Intuitively, we might expect warned participants to gain control over their responses. This is the idea behind insight-oriented therapies and educational efforts aimed at consciousness raising. Knowledge about a bias ought to confer a sort of power over it, according to this line of thinking. Yet research suggests that, in many cases, efforts at mental control have ironic consequences (Wegner, 1994). Trying not to think about race might leave people unable to think about anything but race, and trying not to make judgements based on stereotypes might leave those judgements hopelessly affected by stereotypes. This is precisely the pattern we observed. The group encouraged to use race stereotypes did indeed show greater bias than the control group in which race was not made salient. However, the group warned to avoid race stereotypes also showed heightened bias. In fact, they assumed that objects associated with Blacks were guns at rates indistinguishable from the group who intentionally used stereotypes. This pattern is striking because the group encouraged to use stereotypes and the group urged to avoid stereotyping had exactly opposing intentions, but their behaviours were the same. As expected, this difference was mediated by the automatic component in process dissociation analyses. Automatic influences of stereotypes were higher in both warned groups than in the control group.

The automatic and controlled influences estimated in the crucible of the weapons task have been linked to other meaningful behaviours. For instance in one study, after completing the weapons task, participants formed an impression of a new Black person from a vignette about a typical day in this person's life (Payne, 2005; see Higgins, Rholes, & Jones, 1977, Srull & Wyer, 1980). Although the facts and behaviours in the vignette were identical for all participants, the kinds of impressions they formed varied widely, and they depended on the kinds of automatic and controlled processes each participant displayed in the weapons task. Participants who showed the most stereotypical automatic biases in the weapons task liked the Black character less. This correlation is consistent with dozens of studies showing that automatic racial attitudes and stereotypes can colour social perception.

But the process dissociation analyses also revealed another pattern that is more striking. The impact of automatic bias depended on how much control participants exerted over their behaviours. Participants who were good at controlling their responses in the weapons task were also good at controlling the influence of automatic stereotyping in their social perceptions. For these participants, automatic stereotyping was not associated with more negative impressions. But for participants who were poor at controlling their responses in the weapons task the correlation between automatic bias and social impression was much stronger.

This pattern, in which the amount of intentional control determines whether automatic biases translate into overt behaviours, is consistent with verbally described dual process theories. One example is Strack and Deutsch's (2004) model which distinguishes between reflective and impulsive determinants of behaviour. Consistent with such models, several studies have shown that individual differences in cognitive control are important in moderating the relationship between implicit attitudes and behaviour. For example, Hofmann and colleagues (Hofmann, Gschwendner, Friese, Wiers, & Schmitt, 2008) examined behaviours that can be jointly driven by automatic impulses and self-control efforts, including eating sweets. They measured cognitive control using tests of working memory—the ability to mentally maintain and manipulate multiple pieces of information at the same time. Individuals with greater working memory are believed to have greater cognitive capacity to engage in controlled processing. Hofmann and colleagues measured automatic impulses towards sweets using the Implicit Association Test (Greenwald, McGhee, & Schwartz, 1998), and they measured explicit attitudes and beliefs about sweets using self-report measures. As predicted by dual process models, consciously reported attitudes and beliefs were better predictors of behaviour among participants with high working memory. In contrast, automatic impulses were better predictors among participants with low working memory (see also Hofmann, Friese, & Roefs, 2009). The same pattern was replicated for other tempting behaviours, including responding with anger to a provocation and time spent viewing erotic pictures. This relationship is similar to the pattern assumed by process dissociation: deliberate intentions drive behaviour when control is high, but automatic impulses drive behaviour when control is low.

These studies provide converging evidence, across several topics and several measures, for the systematic relationship between conscious intentions/beliefs, automatic impulses, and cognitive control abilities. Some of these studies relied on three different tests to measure intentions, automatic impulses, and control processes. But the process dissociation procedure provides an advantage by capturing all of these processes within the same task. Rather than equating automatic and controlled processes with different tasks, the components can then be modelled as they contribute to the same behaviour.

This ability to model different components within the same task provides the opportunity to study processes underlying varieties of prejudice well beyond the weapon bias. For example, many studies have shown that older adults tend to display greater prejudice than younger adults. There are competing explanations for why this happens. A common assumption is that older adults are more prejudiced because they grew up in an era where prejudice was more widespread and more acceptable. By this account, older adults simply have more prejudiced thought patterns that have stayed with them over the years. In contrast, older adults might display more prejudice because they are poorer at exerting control over their responses. By this account, older and younger adults may have similar levels of prejudice in their automatic responses, but younger adults are better able to control its expression (von Hippel, Silver, & Lynch, 2000).

Stewart, von Hippel, & Radvansky (2009) measured the racial attitudes of older and younger adults using the IAT and replicated the finding that older adults showed greater bias then their younger counterparts. Although the IAT is often considered a measure of solely implicit processes (i.e., the process-pure assumption) the process dissociation approach assumes instead that behaviour in any task reflect the joint operation of both automatic and controlled processes. The IAT includes "compatible" trials (e.g., *white–good*, *black–bad*) where automatic stereotypes and the correct task-appropriate response share a response key and "incompatible" trials (e.g., *white–bad*, *black–good*) where automatic stereotypes and the correct response are in conflict. Although response time is typically used to score the IAT, errors and correct responses can also be used, because respondents make more errors in incompatible conditions than compatible conditions. These compatible and incompatible trials are analogous to "inclusion" and "exclusion" conditions or "in concert" and "in opposition" conditions of the process dissociation procedure. Stewart and von Hippel thus applied the process dissociation procedure to examine whether the difference was driven by automatic or controlled aspects of responses. Consistent with the control-deficit hypothesis, older adults showed lower control estimates than younger adults, but the groups did not differ in their automatic biases.

Another common observation is that White Americans display greater anti-Black prejudice than Black Americans. This difference, too, could be explained by differences in either automatic responses or control over responses. Black Americans might be more favourable to Blacks in their automatic responses for the same reasons that most any other group shows in-group preferences (Hewstone, Rubin, & Willis, 2002). On the other hand, some theorists argue that Blacks internalise the prejudices and stereotypes that are dominant in society, and therefore they may have the same automatic associations as Whites do. If so, then Blacks may have to work harder to exert control over their responses. Stewart et al. (2009) also compared process dissociation components of IAT performance between White and Black respondents. Only the automatic component of responses distinguished the racial groups. So both race and age influenced the amount of bias displayed on the IAT, but they did so through different processes. White Americans showed more bias because they had more biased automatic impulses. Older adults showed more bias because they lacked control.

Many of the studies just described used process dissociation to understand how intentions fail, where goals break down, and why people act with more prejudice than they would like. To be sure, these are important aspects of contemporary prejudice, in which people often struggle to regulate automatic biases according to egalitarian ideals. Although trying not to be biased may be difficult in many contexts, there may be ways to proactively exert control over automatic responses before they influence behaviour. Stewart and Payne (2008) found that automatic race bias can be effectively reduced by committing to specific plans that activate counter-stereotypical thoughts. Implementation intentions are plans that link a behavioural opportunity to a specific response. They take the form of "if, then" guidelines that use cues in a person's environment to dictate specific goal-directed behaviour (Gollwitzer, 1999). In Stewart and Payne's study, participants completed the weapon identification task. In the critical condition they were instructed that every time they saw a Black face they should immediately think "safe" in order to counteract threat-related stereotypes. Participants in two control conditions were told to think either "quick" or "accurate" whenever a Black face appeared on the screen. These were used as "dummy" intentions because the task already required participants to respond quickly and accurately.

Results of the study are illustrated in Figure 2. Replicating previous findings, participants in the "think quick" and "think accurate" conditions showed race bias. But participants in the "think safe" condition did not. Critically, process dissociation analyses showed that this improvement was driven by reductions in the automatic component of responses. Even under conditions of fast and demanding responses, implementation intentions provided an effective means of reducing automatic bias.

Summary of attitudes and stereotyping research

Stereotypes and prejudice often have their effects automatically, leading many researchers to adopt implicit measurement strategies. Measures such as priming tasks (including the weapon identification task) and the IAT have been developed as methods of capturing automatic responses and avoiding intentional response strategies that might bias self-reports. But as the studies described here show, these tasks do not purely measure automatic processes. Instead, they reflect a mix of automatic responses and attempts to control responses. The process dissociation procedure reveals that prejudice in

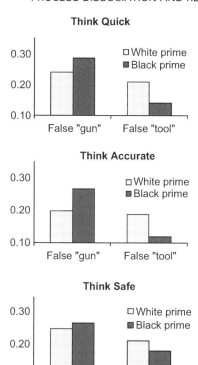

Figure 2. Patterns of bias in weapons task as a function of three implementation intentions. The y-axis represents the proportion of errors of each type. False gun errors refer to tools falsely called tools; false tool errors refer to tools falsely called guns. Adapted from Stewart and Payne (2008).

behaviour can be influenced by both automatic and controlled components of responses, and it provides a means for disentangling these. It also raises new questions about how automatic and controlled processes should be defined and measured, as we discuss next.

DEFINING AUTOMATICITY

The studies reviewed here illustrate that the automatic and controlled components estimated by process dissociation have different meanings when applied to different tasks or different contexts. Unlike approaches that define automaticity using lists of inherent features (such as intentionality, efficiency, controllability, and awareness), process dissociation requires that the researcher specify what it means to exert control in any given task. Automaticity is then defined as those influences that drive responses when control fails. As an example, in the weapons task, control is defined by respondents' task-relevant intentions to discriminate between guns and tools. This intention is what defines experimental conditions as "inclusion" or "exclusion"—that is, whether putative automatic influences such as stereotyping are congruent or incongruent with intended responses. To the extent that participants successfully carry out their task goal, they are considered to be controlling their responses. But to the extent that stereotypical reactions to Black faces influence responses independent of that goal, those stereotypes are driving behaviour automatically. It then becomes an empirical question how control and automatic influences, defined in terms of intent, relate to features such as efficiency, controllability, and awareness.

As the studies reviewed illustrate, there has been a good deal of convergence between process dissociation analyses and feature-based definitions of automatic and controlled processes. In the weapons task, C estimates were reduced under speeded responding (Payne, 2001) and self-control depletion (Govorun & Payne, 2006), providing evidence that controlled processes estimated by C were resource demanding. In contrast, A estimates were unaffected by these variables, suggesting efficiency.

Yet the two approaches will not always converge. Consider for example the study by Stewart and Payne (2008) in which implementation intentions to think counter-stereotypic thoughts reduced automatic bias, and did so under speeded responding. This effect has qualities of both automatic and controlled processes. Implementation intentions altered the (automatic) influence of racial stereotypes, but did so intentionally. An advantage of defining automatic and controlled influences in terms of specific task requirements or goals is that this approach can naturally accommodate cases that seem puzzling from a feature-based perspective. For instance, when an initially unconscious process becomes conscious through introspection, it gains some features of controlled processing (awareness) but may lack others (e.g., efficiency, controllability). And when an initially controlled process becomes automatised through practice it gains some "automatic" features such as efficiency, but may retain features such as intentionality and controllability. As in the case of implementation intentions, the process dissociation framework handles these cases by defining control and automaticity based on one set of criteria, and considering the others as empirical questions rather than defining assumptions.

In tasks such as the weapons task or the IAT, the criterion that defines control and automaticity is intent. Respondents intend to respond according to task instructions despite the presence of interfering information that may unintentionally influence responses. But in other tasks different criteria may be used. For example, in Jacoby's (1991; Jacoby et al., 1993) early memory studies it was conscious memory (recollection) that allowed participants to respond in a controlled way. To respond correctly in the exclusion condition respondents had to remember not simply that a word was familiar but also the context in which they experienced the word. Thus the C estimate can be used to measure conscious memory for the studied item, and the A estimate can measure unconscious memory—influences of past experience despite being unable to consciously recollect the experience.

In each case the researcher must think carefully about what control means in a given task or a given behaviour. Once the researcher has defined the criteria for control, automatic influences can be defined relative to those criteria. To do so, the process dissociation procedure makes some assumptions about the relationships between processes and performance. Violating these assumptions can distort process estimates, so it is important to consider whether the assumptions are warranted in a given research context. The next section discusses these assumptions and places them in the context of the assumptions made by alternative approaches.

ASSUMPTIONS OF PROCESS DISSOCIATION AND ALTERNATIVE MODELS

Mathematical models must make assumptions to relate actual data to formal equations. When applying the process dissociation procedure in a new context it is important to be clear about those assumptions. One assumption of process dissociation is that the controlled and automatic processes at work exert similar influences in inclusion and exclusion conditions. In other words, the two processes should exert as much influence together in the inclusion condition as they exert against each other in the exclusion condition.

The second assumption, which has been discussed more widely, is that automatic and controlled processes are independent of each other (for discussions of the independence assumption in memory research, see Curran & Hintzman, 1995, 1997; Jacoby, Begg, & Toth, 1997; Jacoby & Shrout, 1997; Rouder, Lu, Morey, Sun, & Speckman, 2008). Whether this assumption is met depends on the experimental paradigm that is being used. In some cases, automatic and controlled processes could be positively or negatively correlated with each other, which would violate the independence assumption. Because we cannot directly observe the processes we must indirectly test whether the processes are likely to be independent or dependent. One way to do this is to look for dissociations, or selective effects on one or both estimates. If automatic and controlled processes are independent, then it would be relatively easy to find variables that affect one but not the other. If the independence assumption is badly violated, then automatic and controlled processes would strongly covary with each other.

As a result, it would be difficult to find variables that affect one process without affecting the other.[1]

Much of the work reviewed here has been focused on examining selective effects on automatic and controlled components in the weapon identification procedure. For example, Payne (2001) found a double dissociation between the two processes. Prime pictures of Black and White faces affected the automatic component but not the controlled component. In contrast, speeded responding affected the controlled component but not the automatic component. These dissociations would not be expected if the independence assumption were violated in the weapon identification task.

However, for some tasks or under some conditions, it is always possible to violate the assumptions. Readers may be most familiar with these considerations in the context of common statistical tests. It is widely understood that different statistical tests make different assumptions. For example, analysis of variance (ANOVA) assumes (1) a dependent variable that is at least an interval scale, (2) a normally distributed dependent variable, and (3) homogeneity of variance across different conditions, among other things. If an assumption is violated slightly (e.g., a slightly skewed distribution) the resulting biases are usually small. If an assumption is violated badly (for example, distributions are heavily skewed) it is often a good idea to choose a different test that does not depend on the problematic assumption. Just as the failure of an assumption in a particular study does not invalidate the ANOVA technique in general, studies showing that an assumption of process dissociation has been violated do not invalidate the general method. Instead, other methods may be more appropriate in a particular context.

Consider some of the other methods that are sometimes used as alternatives to process dissociation. These include the task dissociation method (comparing explicit and implicit measures), signal detection theory, and multinomial models. Although they may not be explicitly stated, each of these approaches makes its assumptions that may be violated.

Consider first task dissociations. Although this method does not use a mathematical model, it still makes assumptions. By using an implicit task to measure automatic processes, and an explicit task to measure controlled or conscious processes, the task dissociation approach makes the tacit assumption that each measure is process pure. That is, one assumes that

---

[1]We use "independence" in the strong, stochastic definition of the word. That is, the independence assumption of interest is that control and automaticity are largely uncorrelated across participants and trials. This assumption is difficult to test directly because most analyses require aggregation across participants or trials. This stronger definition is not to be confused with weaker, theoretical independence, which refers merely to the fact that the theory allows parameters to vary on separate dimensions rather than forcing them onto a one-dimensional continuum.

the measures differ only on the dimension of interest to the researcher. If the two tasks differ in ways other than the explicit/implicit dimension, then any different results on explicit versus implicit tasks could be because of those other confounded features. The psychological processes behind implicit tasks (such as reaction times to classify words) and those behind explicit tasks (such as endorsing complex propositional statements) are very different. As a result, the assumption that implicit and explicit tasks differ only on the dimension of interest is not likely to be commonly met (Payne, Burkley, & Stokes, 2008).

Many of the studies reviewed here show empirically that the process-pure assumption is easily falsified. For example, studies demonstrating the role of controlled processing in implicit tests show that these tests do not purely measure automatic processes (e.g., Payne, 2001; Plant & Peruche, 2005; Stewart et al., 2009). And other studies have demonstrated the importance of automatic processing in "explicit" judgement tasks (Ferreira et al., 2006). Both process dissociation and task dissociation methods make assumptions to relate observed data to unobserved theoretical ideas. In the case of process dissociation those assumptions are made explicit, whereas in the task dissociation method they often remain unstated.

A second alternative approach is signal detection theory (SDT). Signal detection theory assumes that perceivers are natural statisticians who make decisions about events in the world the way that researchers decide whether to reject a null hypothesis (Tanner & Swets, 1954). A decision about what one is perceiving or how to respond is treated as a problem of detecting a signal in a noisy environment. Perceivers have a certain amount of evidence, and they select a criterion (similar to the conventional use of $p < .05$ in psychology research) that marks off how strong the evidence has to be before they will accept that a signal is present. Given a pattern of correct responses and errors, signal detection theory can separate sensitivity—the ability to discriminate when a signal is actually present or absent—from bias, a tendency to respond as if a signal is present whether it is or not. Signal detection theory is mute on issues of automatic versus intentionally controlled behaviour, and its development predated the current interest in automaticity.

Signal detection theory makes some of the same assumptions as process dissociation, and some that are different. For instance, SDT also makes an independence assumption. It assumes that sensitivity and bias are independent in the same way that process dissociation assumes that controlled and automatic components are independent (for discussion, see Rouder et al., 2007, 2008). In typical applications, signal detection also assumes normal distributions of evidence strength and equal variances. Beyond statistical assumptions, signal detection makes substantive assumptions about the way that humans process information. For instance, it assumes that decisions are made on the basis of a single continuum of evidence. Even if there are qualitatively different bases of information, signal detection models typically compress this information onto a single decision dimension. Process dissociation, in contrast, treats intentional control and automatic biases as qualitatively different bases for responding.

Finally, process dissociation can be considered to be a particular example of a multinomial model. A multinomial model posits a branching tree of unobserved cognitive processes, leading eventually to behavioural responses (Riefer & Batchelder, 1988). Process dissociation and various multinomial models can be seen as specific cases of a general family of models—although multinomial models do not necessarily have any connection to automatic and controlled processing; see Riefer, Hu, and Batchelder (1994) for a multinomial model of source memory that does not invoke the automatic/controlled distinction, and Klauer and Wegener (1998) for an application of a similar model to social memory. Process dissociation and multinomial models make similar assumptions. Both are aimed at separating unobservable psychological processes that give rise to observed behaviour. The relatedness of the models can be seen in the fact that the process dissociation model can be represented and estimated as a multinomial model with two process parameters (automatic and controlled components; Jacoby, 1998; Payne, Jacoby, & Lambert, 2005). In the next section we consider the relationship between process dissociation and related multinomial models that have been proposed.

INTEGRATION OF PROCESS DISSOCIATION AND OTHER MULTINOMIAL PROCESS MODELS

Several multinomial models have been developed as a means of separating automatic and controlled processing. These include the quadruple process model (Conrey, Sherman, Gawronski, Hugenberg, & Groom, 2005), which has been applied to several implicit tasks, and the ABC model (Stahl & Degner, 2007) which was developed to model performance on the Extrinsic Affective Simon Task (EAST; De Houwer, 2003). Comparing the process dissociation model to these may seem like comparing apples to oranges. However, we will show that many multinomial models of social cognition can be considered part of the same general family.

In order to understand how these various models relate to one another, it is important to consider which processes dominate in each model. In some dual process models, controlled processes play a dominant role. Controlled processes determine responses and choices, and only if controlled processes fail do automatic processes have influence. In other models, however, automatic processes are more dominant and trump controlled processes. In yet other models the relationship between control and automaticity is probabilistic. That is, one process dominates the other with a probability represented by a free parameter in the model (for discussion, see Bishara & Payne, 2009; Conrey et al., 2005; Jacoby, Kelley, & McElree, 1999).

The question of which processes dominate others is important for dual process theories. Different answers to the question of dominance would suggest different practical approaches to reducing automatic bias. For example, race biases in weapon identification could be reduced either by increasing the success of controlled processes or by decreasing automatic influences (or both). However, the relative usefulness of these two strategies will depend on which process dominates. If automaticity dominates responding, reducing automatic racial biases should be the most potent way of reducing the error. Thus, to reduce weapon identification errors, police officers might be trained to detect and correct race-biased thoughts. In contrast, if controlled processing dominates responding and stereotypes only have their effects when control fails, then preventing failures of control may be a more effective means of reducing the stereotypical error. As an example of an approach aimed at increasing controlled processing, criminologist James Fyfe (1988) has described interesting tactics that can prevent officers from having to make split-second decisions unless absolutely necessary, allowing officers to better focus their decision making on criterial aspects of the situation (i.e., those cues that make up the appropriate criterion for a decision, such as whether an object is actually a gun or not). Thus, understanding the dominance of processes may help guide research and practice towards methods of reducing bias.

The model that we have referred to throughout this chapter as the process dissociation model is a control-dominating model, shown at the top of Figure 3. In this model successful controlled processing (with probability C) leads to correct responses (+) in all conditions. Only when controlled processing fails $(1-C)$ do automatic influences hold sway. In those cases stereotypical responses are given with probability A, and counter-stereo-typical responses are given with probability $1-A$. To illustrate, consider how this model explains response patterns in the weapon identification task. When controlled processing succeeds, the tool or gun is correctly identified in all conditions. When controlled processing fails but automatic stereotypical associations drive responses, correct responses are only given in the congruent conditions; that is, conditions where the prime is associatively related to the target (e.g., black–gun). When controlled processing fails but automatic counter-stereotypical associations drive responses, correct responses are only given in the incongruent conditions (e.g., black–tool).

The bottom of Figure 3 shows the multinomial tree for an automaticity-dominating model. This model was originally developed for use in the

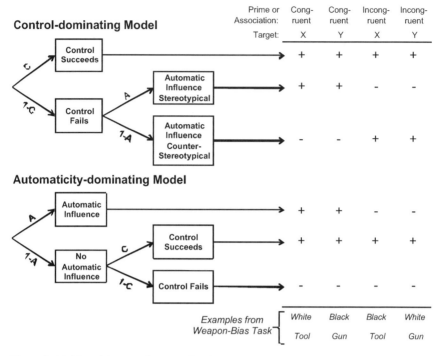

Figure 3. Multinomial processing trees for the C-dominant (Top) and A-dominant (Bottom) models. Branches lead to correct (+) and incorrect (−) responses.

Stroop Colour/Word task, where the automatic influence of word reading appears to dominate the controlled process of colour naming (Lindsay & Jacoby, 1994). In this model, automatic processes dominate performance; controlled processes only matter to the extent that automatic processes fail.

Figure 4 shows Conrey and colleagues' (2005) quad model, which includes four parameters. These include automatically activated bias (AC) and two controlled processes. One controlled parameter is discrimination (D), described in Conrey et al. (2005) as the likelihood that the correct response can be determined. The second controlled process is the overcoming of bias (OB), described as resolving conflicts between AC and D by inhibition (Conrey et al., 2005). If both AC and D are active, then OB determines which process drives the response. Finally, a guessing parameter (G) reflects general guessing tendencies when none of the other processes drive responses.

Figure 5 shows a model with a probabilistic relationship between controlled and automatic processes. One process dominates the other with a certain probability rather than all the time. It turns out that Figure 5 is algebraically equivalent to Conrey and colleagues' quad model, but with D

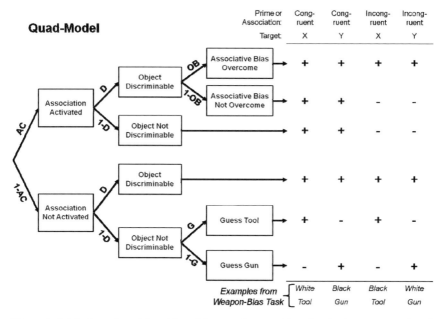

Figure 4. Original quad model multinomial processing tree. Branches lead to correct (+) and incorrect (−) responses.

relabelled as C, and AC relabelled as A (for proof, see Bishara & Payne, 2009). As revealed by Figure 5, the quad model acts like a control-dominating model with probability OB, and an automaticity-dominating model with probability 1–OB. As OB approaches 1, the quad model reduces to a version of the control-dominating model, with a parameter (G) at the final branch to account for general guessing biases for one target over another. We label this the C-dominant/G model (Buchner, Erdfelder, & Vaterrodt-Plünnecke, 1995).[2] As OB approaches 0, the quad model reduces to a version of the automaticity-dominating model that also has a guessing parameter (A-dominant/G). In other words, variants of the C-dominant and A-dominant models are nested within the quad model. Table 1 summarises the characteristics of the five models.

THEORETICAL COMPARISON OF MODELS

The integration of models shown in Figure 5 suggests new constraints on how model parameters can be interpreted. For example, in discussions of the

---

[2]Although the original process dissociation model lacks a guessing parameter, guessing biases are sometimes accommodated by the A parameter in that model.

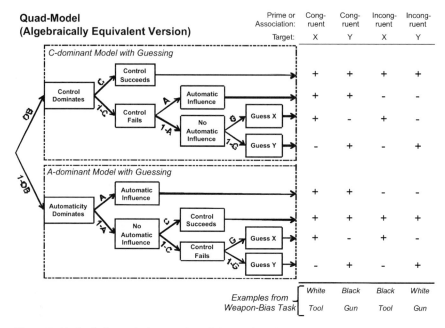

Figure 5. Algebraically equivalent version of the quad model. D has been relabelled as C, and AC has been relabelled as A. The organisation has been rearranged so as to highlight the quad model's relationship to other models. Branches lead to correct (+) and incorrect (−) responses. Adapted from Bishara and Payne (2009).

original quad model, strong claims have been about how the C parameter (originally labelled D) means detecting the correct response, whereas OB means implementing control operations to resolve the conflict (see Sherman et al., 2008). However, the integrated model in Figure 5 shows that a more general interpretation of parameters can be applied to all models. The C parameter can be interpreted simply as responding based on criterial information (e.g., the intended target objects), and the A parameter as responding based on primed or associative information.

The fact that the graphical order of parameters can be rearranged in mathematically equivalent ways (compare Figures 4 and 5) highlights the fact that multinomial models do not imply a temporal order. The lack of temporal order also poses important constraints on how the parameters can be interpreted. For example, the automatic component in the C-dominant model has been described as operating "in the wake of failed control" (Sherman et al., 2008, p. 328); it has also been argued that A operates "only when control has failed, and the model is not mathematically equipped to estimate early automatic processes" (p. 329). But the graphical "order" of the models only depicts which process is dominant when they conflict.

TABLE 1
Multinomial processing tree models in the process dissociation family

Model	Figure	Dominating process	Parameters	Guessing parameter?	Notes
C-dominant	3 (Top)	Controlled	2	No	Has accounted for weapon identification and judgement/decision-making task data
A-dominant	3 (Bottom)	Automatic	2	No	
Quad model	4 and 5	Probabilistic	4	Yes	OB parameter determines the probability of control processes dominating; has accounted for IAT data
C-dominant/G	5 (Top)	Controlled	3	Yes	Equivalent to quad model with $OB = 1$
A-dominant/G	5 (Bottom)	Automatic	3	Yes	Equivalent to quad model with $OB = 0$; equivalent to ABC model; has accounted for EAST data

OB = Overcoming Bias parameter, IAT = Implicit Association Test; EAST = Extrinsic Affect Simon Task.

(For examples of dual-process models that do specify temporal order, see Klauer & Voss, 2008.)

Our integration of models reveals similarities between process dissociation and quad models that have not been appreciated before. Past research has sometimes empirically compared how well C-dominant and A-dominant models account for empirical results by testing the fit of each model individually (e.g., Ferreira et al., 2006; Payne et al., 2005). Considering the integrated model shows how examining this overall model is functionally similar to comparing the simpler models nested within it. Rather than generating a goodness-of-fit statistic for each nested model, the OB parameter provides a probabilistic estimate of the likelihood that the C-dominant versus the A-dominant model best describes the data. At the extremes, when $OB = 1$ the model reduces to the C-dominant model. When $OB = 0$ it reduces the A-dominant model. Testing whether the OB parameter is significantly different from 0 and from 1, then, provides information about whether each of the simpler nested models can be rejected.

EMPIRICAL COMPARISON OF MODELS

The integration of models not only suggests other theoretical interpretations; the integration also allows empirical comparisons among models. In comparing models it is important to take into account the complexity of different models. Complex models (e.g., those with a large number of free parameters) can capitalise on chance, producing spuriously impressive fit statistics (see Pitt, Myung, & Zhang, 2002, for illustration). For example, the quad model will tend to produce smaller (i.e., better) G^2 values relative to the G^2 values of simpler models. Even if data were generated by the C-dominant/G or A-dominant/G model, the quad model would still produce at least as small a G^2 as would the correct model, thus giving the illusion that the quad model was well supported by the data. As a solution to complexity problems such as this, adjusted fit statistics are typically used, statistics such as the Akaike Information Criterion (AIC) and the Bayesian Information Criterion (BIC; see Burnham & Anderson, 2004; Kuha, 2004).

Using AIC and BIC, Bishara and Payne (2009) empirically compared multinomial process models of weapon identification data. Specifically, the C-dominant, C-dominant/G, A-dominant, A-dominant/G, and the quad model were compared. Across AIC and BIC, the C-dominant model accounted for the data better than any other model tested. Furthermore, the results were generally consistent across four different datasets and analyses of both group data and individual participant data. In the quad model the OB parameter was often significantly higher than 0, suggesting that automaticity-dominating models did not account for the data well. However, in no case was the OB parameter significantly lower than 1. In other words, even using parameter estimates of the quad model, the data were consistent with a control-dominating interpretation of weapon identification performance.

Others have compared control-dominating and automaticity-dominating models in different tasks. Ferreira and colleagues (2006) compared the C-dominant and A-dominant models in terms of their ability to account for performance across a variety of judgement and decision-making tasks. While both models provided an adequate fit to the data in most experiments, only the C-dominant model's parameters were influenced in predictable ways. For example, in the C-dominant model cognitive load selectively reduced the controlled parameter, as would be expected. In contrast, in the A-dominant model cognitive load had no significant effect on either the controlled or automatic parameter (although the manipulation did affect behavioural responses). Thus, the C-dominant model seemed consistent with performance on the judgement and decision-making tasks.

Sherman and colleagues (2008) briefly summarised a large-scale comparison between the C-dominant model and the quad model using the fit statistics AIC and BIC. They found that the C-dominant model tended to fit better for priming tasks (e.g., weapon identification), but that the quad model tended to fit better for the IAT. However, in datasets where the quad model fitted better than the C-dominant model, what was the reason? One possibility is that all the parameters of the quad model are needed to fit such data. However, it is also possible that simpler, untested models would also fit in some cases. It is possible that the Guessing parameter was the only necessary feature. Furthermore, it is unclear whether the OB parameter was significantly different from both 0 and 1. If the OB parameter was not significantly different from 1, then the simpler C-dominant/G model may account for the data well. Likewise, if the OB parameter was not significantly different from 0, then the simpler A-dominant/G model may account for the data well. In fact, many quad model analyses of the IAT often reveal at least one condition where OB is not significantly different from 0 (see Conrey et al., 2005). This pattern suggests that the A-dominant or A-dominant/G model may be viable in some circumstances, and it is worth investigating why.

CONTROL AND AUTOMATICITY DOMINANCE IN OTHER MODELS

The family of multinomial models shown in Figures 3–5 are not only useful for contrasting models but also for showing how models have unforeseen commonalities, even when models were designed for very different tasks. For example, Stahl and Degner (2007) developed a multinomial model for the Extrinsic Affective Simon Task (EAST). The EAST is a compatibility-based measure of implicit associations related to the IAT, but unlike the IAT it does not depend on relative evaluations of two items. In a multinomial model for the EAST, participants respond on the basis of automatically activated valence with probability A. In the absence of this influence (1–A) participants respond on the basis of controlled processing of the target information (C). If controlled processing fails (1−C) participants respond with a guessing bias (B) favouring one arbitrarily defined response key over the other. Stahl and Degner (2007) named this the ABC model after its parameter names.

The ABC model may seem familiar by now: the model is algebraically equivalent to the A-dominant/G model depicted at the bottom of Figure 5. This equivalency has at least two consequences. First, it highlights the fact that ABC is an automaticity-dominating model. The evidence garnered in favour of the ABC model of the EAST can be considered as evidence that automatic processes dominate in that task. Second, the equivalency shows that the ABC model has precise relationships to other models. For example, the ABC model is nested within the quad model. In particular, when OB is constrained to 0 the quad model becomes the ABC model. Likewise, data that is well fitted by the quad model may be well fitted by the ABC (i.e., A-dominant/G) model so long as OB is not significantly different from 0.

SUMMARY AND FUTURE DIRECTIONS FOR MODEL COMPARISONS

Multinomial models highlight what different theories have in common, such as controlled processes, automatic processes, and guessing biases. Multinomial models also highlight what is distinctive about each theory. One key distinction among different dual process theories is whether controlled or automatic processes dominate responding when they conflict. Model comparisons suggest that control-dominating models make good sense out of data from weapon bias experiments and decision-making tasks. However, automaticity-dominating models seem supported in other tasks, such as the EAST. Thus there may not be any one "correct" dual process multinomial model but, rather, different models may be more appropriate for different tasks and situations. Future research is needed to identify the task and situation features that encourage different processing routes.

Another avenue of future research has to do with temporal instantiations of models. Multinomial models in and of themselves are agnostic about the temporal order in which processes occur, and so they make no predictions about reaction time data. Building on the original process dissociation model, Klauer and Voss (2008) developed four time-based models. Each model made unique predictions about the qualitative pattern of results not only for errors (as do multinomial models), but also for reaction times. Results were consistent with a "default-interventionist" version of process dissociation, whereby controlled processing intervenes after automatic processes. For this reason, successful controlled processing is often associated with slower responses. Thus, results such as these suggest that process dissociation and related models can be refined and specified to address richer patterns of data, including temporal ordering of processes. More generally, the models reviewed here show that formal dual-process models are powerful tools for testing, elaborating, and unifying social cognitive theories.

CONCLUSION

Dual process theories acknowledge the importance of both automatic and controlled influences, but drawing conclusions is difficult without a means to quantify and compare their relative influence. Process dissociation provides a solution to this problem by allowing researchers to disentangle automatic and controlled components and compare them.

When cast in the form of multinomial process models, process dissociation allows tests of the relationships between processes, helping to answer questions about which process dominates the other. When process dissociation is considered in the context of other models such as the quad model or the ABC model, a striking set of interrelationships appears. Although these models were originally proposed as distinct models aimed at different purposes, they turn out to have a precise nested relationship. These models can therefore be seen as specific instances of a general family of models, varying in the relative dominance of automatic and controlled components. Empirical model-fitting procedures can test whether an automaticity-dominating or control-dominating model best explains a given set of data.

We end by returning to the question of whether social life is dominated by an "automaticity juggernaut" that leaves little room for consciously controlled action. Phrased this broadly, the question was probably always more of a philosophical than an empirical one. A virtue of formal models is that they force researchers to become more specific about their assumptions and their definitions, thereby rendering abstract questions more testable. An exciting contribution of the process dissociation family of models is the ability to test the dominance of automatic and controlled processes. But these process models encourage researchers to formulate the question more specifically. Rather than asking whether automatic or controlled influences are more powerful in general, researchers can empirically test the relative dominance of automatic and controlled influence on particular kinds of behaviour, particular tasks, for particular persons, or in particular situations. The question then becomes for what kinds of behaviours, what kinds of people, and in what kinds of situations do automatic or controlled processes dominate behaviour? The models integrated here set the stage for answering this next generation of questions.

REFERENCES

Bargh, J. A. (1989). Conditional automaticity: Varieties of automatic influence in social perception and cognition. In J. S. Uleman & J. A. Bargh (Eds.), *Unintended thought* (pp. 3–51). New York: Guilford Press.

Bargh, J. A. (1994). The four horsemen of automaticity: Awareness, intention, efficiency, and control in social cognition. In R. S. Wyer & T. K. Srull (Eds.), *Handbook of social cognition* (pp. 1–40). Hillsdale, NJ: Lawrence Erlbaum Associates Inc.

Bargh, J. A. (1997). The automaticity of everyday life. In R. S. Wyer (Ed.), *Advances in social cognition* (Vol. 10, pp. 1–61). Mahwah, NJ: Lawrence Erlbaum Associates Inc.

Bargh, J. A. (1999). The cognitive monster: The case against the controllability of automatic stereotype effects. In S. Chaiken & Y. Trope (Eds.), *Dual-process theories in social psychology* (pp. 361–382). New York: Guilford Press.

Bargh, J. A. (2005). Bypassing the will: Toward demystifying the nonconscious control of social behaviour. In R. R. Hassin, J. S. Uleman, & J. A. Bargh (Eds.), *The new unconscious* (pp. 37–58). New York: Oxford University Press.

Bargh, J. A., & Chartrand, T. L. (1999). The unbearable automaticity of being. *American Psychologist, 54*, 462–479.

Bargh, J. A., & Ferguson, M. J. (2000). Beyond behaviourism: On the automaticity of higher mental processes. *Psychological Bulletin, 126*, 925–945.

Bishara, A. J. (2005). *Control and accessibility bias in single and multiple anchoring effects.* Unpublished doctoral dissertation, Washington University.

Bishara, A. J., & Payne, B. K. (2009). Multinomial process tree models of control and automaticity in weapon misidentification. *Journal of Experimental Social Psychology, 45*, 524–534.

Bodenhausen, G., & Macrae, C. (1998). Stereotype activation and inhibition. Stereotype activation and inhibition. In *Advances in Social Cognition*, 11, 1–52. Mahwah, NJ: Lawrence Erlbaum Associates Inc.

Brewer, N., & Chapman, G. (2002). The fragile basic anchoring effect. *Journal of Behavioural Decision Making, 15*, 65–77.

Buchner, A., Erdfelder, E., & Vaterrodt-Plünnecke, B. (1995). Toward unbiased measurement of conscious and unconscious memory processes within the process dissociation framework. *Journal of Experimental Psychology: General, 124*, 137–160.

Burnham, K., & Anderson, D. (2004). Multimodel inference: Understanding AIC and BIC in model selection. *Sociological Methods & Research, 33*, 261–304.

Chaiken, S., & Trope, Y. (Eds.). (1999). *Dual-process theories in social psychology*. New York: Guilford Press.

Chapman, G., & Johnson, E. (1994). The limits of anchoring. *Journal of Behavioural Decision Making, 7*, 223–242.

Chapman, G., & Johnson, E. (1999). Anchoring, activation, and the construction of values. *Organizational Behaviour and Human Decision Processes, 79*, 115–153.

Conrey, F. R., Sherman, J. W., Gawronski, B., Hugenberg, K., & Groom, C. (2005). Separating multiple processes in implicit social cognition: The quad model of implicit task performance. *Journal of Personality and Social Psychology, 89*, 469–487.

Correll, J., Park, B., Judd, C. M., & Wittenbrink, B. (2002). The police officer's dilemma: Using ethnicity to disambiguate potentially threatening individuals. *Journal of Personality and Social Psychology, 83*, 1314–1329.

Correll, J., Park, B., Judd, C., & Wittenbrink, B. (2007). The influence of stereotypes on decisions to shoot. *European Journal of Social Psychology, 37*, 1102–1117.

Curran, T., & Hintzman, D. L. (1995). Violations of the independence assumption in process dissociation. *Journal of Experimental Psychology: Learning, Memory, and Cognition, 21*, 531–547.

Curran, T., & Hintzman, D. L. (1997). Causes and consequences of correlations in process dissociation. *Journal of Experimental Psychology: Learning, Memory, and Cognition, 23*, 496–504.

De Houwer, J. (2003). The extrinsic affective Simon task. *Experimental Psychology, 50*, 77–85.

Devine, P. G. (1989). Stereotypes and prejudice: Their automatic and controlled components. *Journal of Personality and Social Psychology, 56*, 5–18.

Ferreira, M. B., Garcia-Marques, L., Sherman, S. J., & Sherman, J. W. (2006). Automatic and controlled components of judgement and decision making. *Journal of Personality and Social Psychology, 91*, 797–813.

Festinger, L. (1957). *A theory of cognitive dissonance*. Evanston, IL: Row, Peterson.

Fitzsimons, G., & Williams, P. (2000). Asking questions can change choice behaviour: Does it do so automatically or effortfully? *Journal of Experimental Psychology: Applied, 6*, 195–206.

Fyfe, J. (1988). Police use of deadly force: Research and reform. *Justice Quarterly, 5*, 165–205.

Gaunt, R., Leyens, J., & Demoulin, S. (2002). Intergroup relations and the attribution of emotions: Control over memory for secondary emotions associated with the ingroup and outgroup. *Journal of Experimental Social Psychology, 38,* 508–514.

Gawronski, B., & Bodenhausen, G. V. (2006). Associative and propositional processes in evaluation: An integrative review of implicit and explicit attitude change. *Psychological Bulletin, 132,* 692–731.

Gollwitzer, P. M. (1999). Implementation intentions: Strong effects of simple plans. *American Psychologist, 54,* 493–503.

Govorun, O., & Payne, B. (2006). Ego-depletion and prejudice: Separating automatic and controlled components. *Social Cognition, 24,* 111–136.

Greenwald, A., McGhee, D., & Schwartz, J. (1998). Measuring individual differences in implicit cognition: The implicit association test. *Journal of Personality and Social Psychology, 74,* 1464–1480.

Greenwald, A. G., Oakes, M. A., & Hoffman, H. G. (2002). Targets of discrimination: Effects of race on responses to weapon holders. *Journal of Experimental Social Psychology, 39,* 399–405.

Heider, F. (1958). *The psychology of interpersonal relations.* New York: Wiley.

Hense, R. L., Penner, L. A., & Nelson, D. L. (1995). Implicit memory for age stereotypes. *Social Cognition, 13,* 399–415.

Hewstone, M., Rubin, M., & Willis, H. (2002). Intergroup bias. *Annual Review of Psychology, 53,* 575–604.

Higgins, E. T., Rholes, W. S., & Jones, C. R. (1977). Category accessibility and impression formation. *Journal of Experimental Social Psychology, 13,* 141–154.

Hofmann, W., Friese, M., & Roefs, A. (2009). Three ways to resist temptation: The independent contributions of executive attention, inhibitory control, and affect regulation to the impulse control of eating behaviour. *Journal of Experimental Social Psychology, 45,* 431–435.

Hofmann, W., Gschwendner, T., Friese, M., Wiers, R. W., & Schmitt, M. (2008). Working memory capacity and self-regulatory behaviour: Towards an individual differences perspective on behaviour determination by automatic versus controlled processes. *Journal of Personality and Social Psychology, 95,* 962–977.

Jacoby, L. L. (1991). A process dissociation framework: Separating automatic from intentional uses of memory. *Journal of Memory and Language, 30,* 513–541.

Jacoby, L. L. (1998). Invariance in automatic influences of memory: Toward a user's guide for the process-dissociation procedure. *Journal of Experimental Psychology: Learning, Memory, and Cognition, 24,* 3–26.

Jacoby, L. L., Begg, I. M., & Toth, J. P. (1997). In defense of functional independence: Violations of assumptions underlying the process-dissociation procedure? *Journal of Experimental Psychology: Learning, Memory, and Cognition, 23,* 484–495.

Jacoby, L., Kelley, C., & McElree, B. (1999). The role of cognitive control: Early selection versus late correction. *Dual-process theories in social psychology* (pp. 383–400). New York: Guilford Press.

Jacoby, L. L., & Shrout, P. E. (1997). Toward a psychometric analysis of violations of the independence assumption in process dissociation. *Journal of Experimental Psychology: Learning, Memory, and Cognition, 23,* 505–510.

Jacoby, L., Toth, J., & Yonelinas, A. (1993). Separating conscious and unconscious influences of memory: Measuring recollection. *Journal of Experimental Psychology: General, 122,* 139–154.

Kahneman, D., & Frederick, S. (2002). Representativeness revisited: Attribute substitution in intuitive judgement. In T. Gilovich, D. Griffin, & D. Kahneman (Eds.), *Heuristics and biases: The psychology of intuitive judgement* (pp. 49–81). New York: Cambridge University Press.

Kelley, C. M., & Jacoby, L. L. (2000). Recollection and familiarity: Process-dissociation. In E. E. Tulving, E. Fergus, & I. M. Craik (Eds.), *The Oxford handbook of memory* (pp. 215–228). New York: Oxford University Press.

Kihlstrom, J. F. (2006). The automaticity juggernaut. In J. Baer, J. C. Kaufman, & R. F. Baumeister (Eds.), *Psychology and free will*. New York: Oxford University Press.

Kihlstrom, J. F. (2007). The psychological unconscious. In O. John, R. Robins, & L. Pervin (Eds.), *Handbook of Personality: Theory and research*, 3rd ed. New York: Guilford Press.

Kirkpatrick, L. A., & Epstein, S. (1992). Cognitive-experiential self theory and subjective probability: Further evidence for two conceptual systems. *Journal of Personality and Social Psychology*, *63*, 534–544.

Klauer, K., & Voss, A. (2008). Effects of race on responses and response latencies in the weapon identification task: A test of six models. *Personality and Social Psychology Bulletin*, *34*, 1124–1140.

Klauer, K. C., & Wegener, I. (1998). Unraveling social categorization in the "Who said what?" paradigm. *Journal of Personality and Social Psychology*, *75*, 1155–1178.

Koriat, A., & Goldsmith, M. (1996). Monitoring and control processes in the strategic regulation of memory accuracy. *Psychological Review*, *103*, 490–517.

Kramer, T., & Block, L. (2008). Conscious and nonconscious components of superstitious beliefs in judgement and decision making. *Journal of Consumer Research*, *34*, 783–793.

Kuha, J. (2004). AIC and BIC: Comparisons of assumptions and performance. *Sociological Methods & Research*, *33*, 188–229.

Langer, E., Blank, A., & Chanowitz, B. (1978). The mindlessness of ostensibly thoughtful action: The role of "placebic" information in interpersonal interaction. *Journal of Personality and Social Psychology*, *36*, 635–642.

Leyens, J. P., Rodriguez, A. P., Rodriguez, R. T., Gaunt, R., Paladino, P. M., Vaes, J., et al. (2001). Psychological essentialism and the differential attribution of uniquely human emotions to ingroups and outgroups. *European Journal of Social Psychology*, *31*, 395–411.

Lindsay, D., & Jacoby, L. (1994). Stroop process dissociations: The relationship between facilitation and interference. *Journal of Experimental Psychology: Human Perception and Performance*, *20*, 219–234.

MacRae, C., Schloerscheidt, A., Bodenhausen, G., & Milne, A. (2002). Creating memory illusions: Expectancy-based processing and the generation of false memories. *Memory*, *10*, 63–80.

Moors, A., & DeHouwer, J. (2006). Automaticity: A theoretical and conceptual analysis. *Psychological Bulletin*, *132*, 297–326.

Morwitz, V., Johnson, E., & Schmittlein, D. (1993). Does measuring intent change behaviour? *Journal of Consumer Research*, *20*, 46–61.

Muraven, M., & Baumeister, R. F. (2000). Self-regulation and depletion of limited resources: Does self-control resemble a muscle? *Psychological Bulletin*, *126*, 247–259.

Nisbett, R., & Wilson, T. (1977). Telling more than we can know: Verbal reports on mental processes. *Psychological Review*, *84*, 231–259.

Payne, B., Lambert, A., & Jacoby, L. (2002). Best laid plans: Effects of goals on accessibility bias and cognitive control in race-based misperceptions of weapons. *Journal of Experimental Social Psychology*, *38*, 384–396.

Payne, B. K. (2001). Prejudice and perception: The role of automatic and controlled processes in misperceiving a weapon. *Journal of Personality and Social Psychology*, *81*, 181–192.

Payne, B. K. (2005). Conceptualizing control in social cognition: How executive control modulates the expression of automatic stereotyping. *Journal of Personality and Social Psychology*, *89*, 488–503.

Payne, B. K., Burkley, M., & Stokes, M. B. (2008). Why do implicit and explicit attitude tests diverge? The role of structural fit. *Journal of Personality and Social Psychology*, *94*, 16–31.

Payne, B. K., Jacoby, L. L., & Lambert, A. J. (2004). Memory monitoring and the control of stereotype distortion. *Journal of Experimental Social Psychology, 40*, 52–64.

Payne, B. K., Jacoby, L. L., & Lambert, A. J. (2005). Attitudes as accessibility bias: Dissociating automatic and controlled components. In R. Hassin, J. Bargh, & J. Uleman (Eds.), *The new unconscious.* Oxford, UK: Oxford University Press.

Petty, R., & Briñol, P. (2006). Understanding social judgement: Multiple systems and processes. *Psychological Inquiry, 17*, 217–223.

Pitt, M., Myung, I., & Zhang, S. (2002). Toward a method of selecting among computational models of cognition. *Psychological Review, 109*, 472–491.

Plant, E. A., & Peruche, B. M. (2005). The consequences of race for police officers' responses to criminal suspects. *Psychological Science, 16*, 180–183.

Posner, M. I., & Snyder, C. R. R. (1975). Attention and cognitive control. In R. L. Solso (Ed.), *Information processing and cognition: The Loyola Symposium* (pp. 55–85). New York: Wiley.

Riefer, D. M., & Batchelder, W. H. (1988). Multinomial modeling and the measurement of cognitive processes. *Psychological Review, 95*, 318–339.

Riefer, D. M., Hu, X., & Batchelder, W. H. (1994). Response strategies in source monitoring. *Journal of Experimental Psychology: Learning, Memory, and Cognition, 20*, 680–693.

Roediger, H. L. (1990). Implicit memory: Retention without remembering. *American Psychologist, 45*, 1043–1056.

Rouder, J., Lu, J., Morey, R., Sun, D., & Speckman, P. (2008). A hierarchical process-dissociation model. *Journal of Experimental Psychology: General, 137*, 370–389.

Rouder, J. N., Lu, J., Sun, D., Speckman, P. L., Morey, R. D., & Naveh-Benjamin, M. (2007). Signal detection models with random participant and item effects. *Psychometrika, 72*, 583–600.

Schacter, D. L. (1987). Implicit memory: History and current status. *Journal of Experimental Psychology: Learning, Memory, and Cognition, 13*, 501–518.

Sherman, J., Gawronski, B., Gonsalkorale, K., Hugenberg, K., Allen, T., & Groom, C. (2008). The self-regulation of automatic associations and behavioural impulses. *Psychological Review, 115*, 314–335.

Sherman, J., Groom, C., Ehrenberg, K., & Klauer, K. (2003). Bearing false witness under pressure: Implicit and explicit components of stereotype-driven memory distortions. *Social Cognition, 21*, 213–246.

Sherman, S. J. (1980). On the self-erasing nature of errors of prediction. *Journal of Personality and Social Psychology, 39*, 211–221.

Shiffrin, R. M., & Schneider, W. (1977). Controlled and automatic human information processing: II. Perceptual learning, automatic attending and a general theory. *Psychological Review, 84*, 127–190.

Shiv, B., & Fedorikhin, A. (1999). Heart and mind in conflict: The interplay of affect and cognition in consumer decision making. *The Journal of Consumer Research, 26*, 278–292.

Sloman, S. A. (1996). The empirical case for two systems of reasoning. *Psychological Bulletin, 119*, 3–22.

Smith, E. R., & DeCoster, J. (2000). Dual-process models in social and cognitive psychology: Conceptual integration and links to underlying memory systems. *Personality and Social Psychology Review, 4*, 108–131.

Srull, T. K., & Wyer, R. S. (1980). Category accessibility and social perception: Some implications for the study of person memory and interpersonal judgements. *Journal of Personality and Social Psychology, 38*, 841–856.

Stahl, C., & Degner, J. (2007). Assessing automatic activation of valence: A multinomial model of EAST performance. *Experimental Psychology, 54*, 99–112.

Stangor, C., & McMillan, D. (1992). Memory for expectancy-congruent and expectancy-incongruent information: A review of the social and social developmental literatures. *Psychological Bulletin, 111,* 42–61.

Stanovich, K. E., & West, R. F. (2000). Individual differences in reasoning: Implications for the rationality debate. *Behavioural and Brain Sciences, 23,* 645–665.

Stewart, B., & Payne, B. (2008). Bringing automatic stereotyping under control: Implementation intentions as efficient means of thought control. *Personality and Social Psychology Bulletin, 34,* 1332–1345.

Stewart, B., von Hippel, W., & Radvansky, G. (2009). Age, race, and implicit prejudice: Using process dissociation to separate the underlying components. *Psychological Science, 20,* 164–188.

Strack, F., & Deutsch, R. (2004). Reflective and impulsive determinants of social behaviour. *Personality and Social Psychology Review, 8,* 220–247.

Strack, F., & Mussweiler, T. (1997). Explaining the enigmatic anchoring effect: Mechanisms of selective accessibility. *Journal of Personality and Social Psychology, 73,* 437–446.

Tanner, W., & Swets, J. (1954). A decision-making theory of visual detection. *Psychological Review, 61,* 401–409.

Tulving, E. (1985). Memory and consciousness. *Canadian Psychology, 26,* 1–12.

Tulving, E., Schacter, D. L., & Stark, H. A. (1982). Priming effects in word-fragment completion are independent of recognition memory. *Journal of Experimental Psychology: Learning, Memory, and Cognition, 8,* 336–342.

Tversky, A., & Kahneman, D. (1974). Judgement under uncertainty: Heuristics and biases. *Science, 185,* 1124–1131.

Tversky, A., & Kahneman, D. (1983). Extension versus intuitive reasoning: The conjunction fallacy in probability judgement. *Psychological Review, 90,* 293–315.

von Hippel, W., Silver, L. A., & Lynch, M. E. (2000). Stereotyping against your will: The role of inhibitory ability in stereotyping and prejudice among the elderly. *Personality and Social Psychology Bulletin, 26,* 523–532.

Wegner, D. M. (1994). Ironic processes of mental control. *Psychological Review, 101,* 34–52.

Wegner, D. M. (2002). *The illusion of conscious will* Cambridge, MA: MIT Press.

Westling, E., Mann, T., & Ward, A. (2006). Self-control of smoking: When does narrowed attention help? *Journal of Applied Social Psychology, 36,* 2115–2133.

Yonelinas, A. P. (2002). The nature of recollection and familiarity: A review of 30 years of research. *Journal of Memory and Language, 46,* 441–517.

EUROPEAN REVIEW OF SOCIAL PSYCHOLOGY
2009, 20, 315–344

The dynamics of self-regulation

Ayelet Fishbach
University of Chicago, IL, USA

Ying Zhang
University of Texas, Austin, TX, USA

Minjung Koo
Sungkyunkwan University, Seoul, Korea

Research on the dynamics of self-regulation addresses situations in which people select goal-directed actions with respect to other existing or still missing actions towards accomplishing that goal. In such situations people can follow two possible patterns: they can highlight a goal by attending to it more if they have attended to it, or they can balance their goals by attending to a goal more if they have not attended to it. The choice of which pattern to follow depends on the representation of goal actions: when actions signal commitment, people highlight, and when actions signal progress, people balance. We identify several variables that determine whether people follow a dynamic of commitment-induced highlighting or progress-induced balancing. We then discuss the implications of this model for seeking, giving, and responding to feedback.

Keywords: Self-regulation; Goals; Motivation; Feedback.

Choice of actions follows the multiple goals that people hold. For example, people may simultaneously wish to stay fit, advance their careers, spend time with family, and develop new hobbies, and these goals, in turn, influence their decisions to exercise, go back to school, take a family vacation, and enrol in a tennis class. Retrieving a course of actions that will satisfy each of these goals separately is a relatively simple self-regulatory task. However, the challenge of self-regulation is to monitor the simultaneous pursuit of goals that compete for resources such as time (e.g., career and family) or that directly undermine each other's attainment (e.g., getting in shape and

Correspondence should be addressed to Ayelet Fishbach, The University of Chicago, Booth School of Business, 5807 S. Woodlawn Ave., Chicago IL 60637, USA.
E-mail: ayelet.fishbach@ChicagoBooth.edu

 DOI: 10.1080/10463280903275375

enjoying food). In this typical, multi-goal context, successful self-regulation requires prioritising goals and deciding at any moment which goal to attend to while compromising or postponing other goals.

Classic goal research addresses the criteria for adopting a goal (Atkinson, 1974; Lewin, Dembo, Festinger, & Sears, 1944; Tolman, 1932; Vroom, 1964), and an underlying assumption is that similar criteria influence the decision to adopt the goal and the subsequent decision to pursue it. For example, if a person prioritises staying healthy over enjoying tasty (yet high-calorie) food, the motivational priority of health should always be higher, such that the person chooses to eat healthily while compromising food enjoyment at each opportunity. In contrast with this view, research over the past decade has documented several variables that influence the motivational priority a goal receives, such as contextual cues or opportunities that activate the goal and trigger its pursuit (Aarts & Dijksterhuis, 2000; Chartrand & Bargh, 1996; Ferguson & Bargh, 2004; Kruglanski et al., 2002; Moskowitz, 2002; Shah & Kruglanski, 2003). For example, health-conscious individuals will at times eat fatty food because they encounter cues for this (otherwise less valuable) goal in an advertisement or perceive an opportunity to eat unhealthy foods. In addition, certain goal properties influence the motivational priority a goal receives. For example, people prefer to pursue goals that have a clear end state over those that are abstract and ongoing (e.g., meeting a particular performance standard vs. doing well more generally; Heath, Larrick, & Wu, 1999; Locke & Latham, 1990), and for those goals with a clear end state, the likelihood of attending the goal increases as individuals approach that end state (Förster, Higgins, & Idson, 1998; Hull, 1934; Kivetz, Urminsky, & Zheng, 2006; Losco & Epstein, 1977).

Attending to one goal in a multi-goal context inevitably implies the neglect of other, background goals. These background goals can subsequently receive greater priority and rebound; alternatively, their motivational priority declines further. To understand self-regulation, therefore, considering a sequence of actions that either balances between pursuing a focal and background goals or highlights the pursuit of the focal goal over a sequence of actions is useful (Dhar & Simonson, 1999). Accordingly our research explores patterns of self-regulation when a person considers completed as well as upcoming goal actions. For example, we consider the choices of a diner who wishes to eat fatty food as well as stay in shape and who selects both an entrée and a dessert. The diner can either balance between these goals (e.g., by selecting a tasty dessert after having a healthy entrée) or highlight one goal across these selections (e.g., selecting a healthy dessert after a healthy entrée). When the diner balances, the likelihood of selecting a healthy dessert decreases if a healthy entrée was previously selected. In contrast, when the diner highlights, the likelihood of selecting a healthy dessert increases if a healthy entrée was previously selected.

In this chapter we review our research programme on the dynamics of self-regulation (Fishbach & Dhar, 2005; Fishbach, Dhar, & Zhang, 2006; Fishbach & Zhang, 2008; Koo & Fishbach, 2008; Zhang, Fishbach, & Dhar, 2007). This research attests that the pattern of self-regulation individuals follow (highlighting vs. balancing) depends on how they represent their goal pursuits. We distinguish between two representations: expressing commitment towards a desirable state and making progress towards this state. We argue that, in a commitment representation, people wish to highlight the pursuit of a single, most important goal across a sequence of actions, whereas in a progress representation they wish to balance between pursuing this goal and attending to others. As a result, in a commitment frame, attending to a goal increases its motivational priority more than a failure to attend the goal. In a progress frame, not attending to a goal increases its motivational priority more than attending to it.

We organise this chapter into several parts. First, we describe the self-regulatory process in each of the two dynamics: *commitment-induced highlighting* versus *progress-induced balancing*. Second, we identify several variables that influence the representation of goal pursuits and the corresponding dynamics that people follow. Some of these variables concern the individuals' state—whether they wish to assess their goal commitment or the progress they made on a goal. Other variables concern the context of self-regulation (e.g., the arrangement of choice alternatives) and whether it signals commitment versus progress representation of goal pursuits. The third section explores the role of feedback in self-regulation. We use our framework to examine when positive feedback is more effective than negative feedback in motivating action and vice versa, and how people's response to feedback corresponds to whether they seek it for themselves and give another person positive versus negative feedback. We summarise the main predictions our model makes in Table 1.

PART I: THE DYNAMICS OF SELF-REGULATION

Actions consistent with goal pursuit may either express commitment to this goal or signal that progress was made. For example, after opting for the healthy meal option, individuals may conclude either that leading a healthy lifestyle is important for them or that they have made progress on their health goals. These inferences reflect people's self-observations and their desire to imbue meaning into actions. We define *commitment* as a sense that the goal is valuable and expectancy of attainment is high (Fishbein & Ajzen, 1974; Lewin et al., 1944; Liberman & Förster, 2008; Vroom, 1964). We further define *progress* as a sense of moving forward on a goal and reducing discrepancy to a desired state (Carver & Scheier, 1998). In this section we address the pattern of self-regulation under each of these goal frames.

TABLE 1
The dynamics of self-regulation: Predictions

Commitment-induced highlighting	*Progress-induced balancing*
Determining variables	
Questions on commitment	Questions on progress
Uncertain and low commitment	Certain and high commitment
Salient superordinate goal	Non-salient superordinate goal
Items presented apart	Items presented together
Feedback	
Seek more positive feedback	Seek more negative feedback
Give more positive feedback	Give more negative feedback
Positive feedback increases goal adherence	Negative feedback increases goal adherence

When people represent goal actions in terms of expressing commitment to a desirable end state, they observe their own behaviour in order to infer whether the underlying goal is valuable to them and whether they expect to successfully pursue it. They then follow an inferential process similar to how one learns about one's attitudes (Atkinson, 1964; Atkinson & Raynor, 1978; Bem, 1972; Cialdini, Trost, & Newsom, 1995; Feather, 1990). That is, congruent goal actions serve as a signal for personal commitment more than incongruent actions, and they increase the subsequent motivational priority of a goal. For example, individuals would experience greater commitment to their job if they look back and consider completed tasks at work, at which point they might even decide to stay in the office after hours to complete some additional tasks. If however, individuals focus on what they have not completed, they would infer lower commitment to the job and be more likely to leave early that day.

In contrast, when people represent goals in terms of making progress, they focus on the discrepancy between an existing state and a desirable one, and their self-regulation is oriented towards moving forward and reducing the discrepancy. In line with cybernetic models of self-regulation, progress towards the end state provides a sense of partial goal attainment, signalling that less effort is needed to accomplish the goal, whereas failure to progress signals that more effort is needed (Carver & Scheier, 1998; Higgins, 1987; Locke & Latham, 1990; Miller, Galanter, & Pribram, 1960; Powers, 1973). For example, focusing on completed tasks at work might lead to relaxing and leaving early, whereas considering uncompleted tasks might signal greater discrepancy and increase the motivation to stay after hours. As this example demonstrates, monitoring progress and reducing a discrepancy does not require the goal to have a concrete end state. The two goal frames (commitment and progress) are similarly applicable to goals that do not have a particular end state (e.g., study a new language, develop one's career) as well as those that do (complete a course, finish some tasks at work).

Commitment-induced highlighting versus progress-induced balancing

We argue that when goal actions express commitment they increase the motivation to choose congruent actions subsequently in a pattern of highlighting. Conversely, when goal actions express progress they decrease the motivation to choose congruent actions in a pattern of balancing. It follows that, after a person pursues a goal, inferences of commitment would increase interest in similar, complementary actions, whereas inferences of progress would decrease interest in such actions. Similarly, after an initial failure to pursue a goal, inferences of low commitment would undermine a person's motivation to choose congruent actions, but inferences of lack of progress would increase the motivation to take such actions because the person feels a need to compensate by increasing effort.

Two factors therefore increase individuals' motivation to work on a goal: (a) the presence of goal commitment, which they infer from pursuing a goal, and (b) the lack of goal progress, which they infer from not pursuing a goal. Conversely, low commitment, which individuals infer from not pursuing a goal, and sufficient progress, which they infer from pursuing a goal, both undermine the motivation to choose actions that further a goal. We assume goal commitment and progress are competing representations of goal pursuits, with opposite motivational consequences. That is, an action that signals commitment to a goal is less likely to signal progress towards the goal and vice versa (see also Kelley, 1972, for a similar assumption in attribution theory).

PART II: WHEN ACTIONS EXPRESS COMMITMENT VERSUS MAKING PROGRESS

Social organisations that promote self-regulation differ in the extent to which they advocate highlighting or balancing as their prevailing principle. For example, Alcoholics Anonymous recommends complete sobriety and, in this model, each day of sobriety signals an increase in commitment. In contrast, Weight Watchers advocates balancing by proposing a "point system" in which dieters can trade off eating and exercising. In this model, exercising signals progress towards the weight-loss goal and can justify consumption of high-calorie food.

Similar to social organisations that prescribe different dynamics of self-regulation, individual differences exist in the extent to which people construe their goal actions as a signal for commitment or progress, and such differences influence the pattern of self-regulation they follow. For example, people exercise in order to get in shape, and many also eat healthy as a means to achieve this same goal. In a study conducted with gym users

(Zhang et al., 2007) we found that some of them perceived their workouts as a signal of commitment to getting in shape, whereas others perceived their workouts as a signal that they were making progress towards getting in shape. In addition, these gym users varied by the extent to which they were optimistic that they would adhere to and even improve their exercising regime. These individual differences predicted their choice of healthy food, such that those who viewed exercising as commitment were more interested in healthy eating if they were optimistic that they would exercise in the future; hence, they were highlighting. Those who viewed exercising as progress, however, were more interested in healthy eating if they were not so optimistic that they would exercise much; hence, they were balancing.

Beyond these individual differences, in this section we identify several variables that influence whether people infer commitment or progress from their actions. Some of these variables influence the questions people ask when pursuing a goal ("Am I committed?" vs. "Have I made progress?"), whereas others refer to the presentation of the action alternatives and whether it activates a commitment versus a progress frame.

Asking about commitment versus progress

When people evaluate their level of commitment ("Do my actions indicate I am committed to this goal?") they follow a dynamic of highlighting, and when they evaluate their level of progress ("Do my actions indicate I am making sufficient progress?") they follow a dynamic of balancing. Then when do they ask about commitment versus progress? The questions people ask themselves often follow the questions they get from others. For example, when teachers encourage their students to consider whether academic success reflects commitment to academic goals, the students are more likely to infer their level of commitment than if the teachers ask them to consider whether they have made progress by succeeding. In addition, people's pre-existing commitment certainty may determine whether they ask themselves about goal commitment versus progress. If their commitment is low or uncertain, they are more likely to ask about commitment and represent their goal actions as expressing commitment than if they are certain their commitment is high. We next elaborate on these possibilities.

Responding to framing questions

A hard-working lawyer can explain the decision to stay late in the office as an expression of devotion (commitment) or as a reflection of the desire to complete some assignments at work (progress). Asking the lawyer to consider the validity of each of these inferences—commitment versus progress—can in turn influence how she views her actions. Asking framing questions thus influences the representation of goal pursuits because people ask themselves whether a particular inference should be made, and in order to address the question they need to at least temporarily adopt the representation that underlies the question.

To demonstrate the effect of framing questions, we (Fishbach & Dhar, 2005, Study 3) asked participants to recall pursuing academic, financial, or health goals. For each goal they listed, we asked half of the participants whether their action expressed their level of commitment to the goal while the other half were asked whether the action made progress towards the goal. Next participants indicated their interest in pursuing competing goals, which would balance for the initial action. We found that regardless of participants' agreement with the framing (commitment vs. progress) questions, those who answered questions on commitment expressed lower interest in pursuing competing goals than those answering questions on progress; hence, they were less likely to seek a balance between the focal goal and competing ones. For example, we asked participants who considered academic goals to indicate whether, whenever they study, they feel more committed to academics or feel they are making progress on their academic tasks. These participants then rated their interest in socialising with friends the night after studying. We found that those who answered questions on commitment were less interested in socialising after studying than those who answered questions on progress. Subtle cues in the form of framing questions appear to influence the framing of actions and what goals individuals subsequently attend to, even when they feel at liberty to reject the conclusions the questions imply (e.g., that they feel more committed).

Framing questions do more than alter the meaning of complete actions in the past; they also change the meaning of actions people plan to pursue in the future, and these effects on the meaning of future plans influence what a person chooses to do in the present. To demonstrate the effect of planned, future goal actions, we (Zhang et al., 2007) compared present actions among participants whom we asked to consider the meaning of future, planned actions towards their goal commitment versus progress. We found that when planned, future actions signalled commitment and competence (Bandura, 1997; Taylor & Brown, 1988; Weiner, 1979), they promoted similar goal-congruent actions in the present—a pattern of highlighting. When, however, future plans signalled progress towards a goal, they substituted for such actions in the present—a pattern of balancing (Oettingen & Mayer, 2002).

Moreover, the degree to which past and planned goal actions influence present ones is proportional to how much the past or planned actions achieve. If they achieve a lot, these actions will have greater impact on either engagement or disengagement in the present. Therefore, when people are optimistic and believe they will achieve more in the future than they did in the past (Buehler, Griffin, & Ross, 1994; Weinstein, 1989; Zauberman & Lynch, 2005), future plans may ironically exert a greater impact on immediate goal pursuit than retrospection of past actions in spite of the hypothetical nature of future plans. Specifically, thinking optimistically about future actions motivates similar present actions more than considering completed actions in the past when optimism signals goal commitment, and it would undermine this motivation when optimism signals goal progress.

In a study that examines these effects of optimism, we (Zhang et al., 2007, Study 1) approached gym members at the beginning of the year, when people tend to make New Year's resolutions, and asked them to think about their workout frequency in the coming year or the frequency of their actual workouts in the previous year. Not surprisingly, gym members planned to exercise more frequently in the upcoming year than they did in the past year; thus, they were optimistic. Half of these gym members further indicated whether workouts signal commitment to the health goal. For example, they rated their agreement with a statement such as "*having worked out* (or "*planning to work out*") *that much means I must really care about my health*". The rest of them indicated whether workouts signal progress towards the health goal. For example, they rated their agreement with "*having worked out* (or "*planning to work out*") *that much, I am* (or "*will be*") *closer to my workout objectives*". Next we measured whether gym members would complement exercising with healthy drinking. We offered them a choice of a beverage for immediate consumption, either healthy spring water or unhealthy sugared soda. As Figure 1 shows, under a commitment frame the share of healthy choice was higher among participants who envisioned a future (vs. past) workout regime, because they considered a greater amount of exercise and highlighted this expected goal pursuit by choosing a healthy drink. However, under a progress frame the share of unhealthy choice was higher for participants who envisioned a future (vs. past) workout regime, because they balanced for the greater amount of exercise by choosing an unhealthy drink. Future plans appear to have a greater impact on present choices than past actions when people believe they will do more in the future than in the past. The direction of the influence depends on the representation of actions in terms of commitment or progress.

Pre-existing commitment certainty

Pre-existing levels of commitment to a goal influence whether people interpret their actions as a signal of commitment or progress. People ask themselves about their goal commitment when they are still unsure about pursuing the goal and their commitment is uncertain or relatively low. When people are ambiguous about their level of goal commitment, they wish to

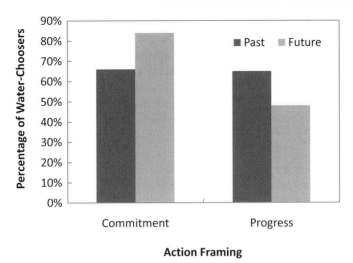

Figure 1. Choice of drinks (healthy spring water vs. unhealthy sugar soda) as a function of time focus and action framing.

determine whether a goal is important to them and worth pursuing further. However, once people are certain about their commitment to a goal, they ask about progress and represent goal actions as making progress. As a result, before commitment is certain, completed goal actions increase goal adherence more than lack of actions since completed actions signal higher commitment and promote self-regulation through highlighting. In contrast, once commitment is certain, a lack of goal actions increases goal adherence more than completed actions because missing actions signal greater discrepancy and need for progress, which promote self-regulation through balancing (see also Brunstein & Gollwitzer, 1996; Wicklund & Gollwitzer, 1982).

To investigate the effect of commitment certainty on the pattern self-regulation individuals follow, we (Koo & Fishbach, 2008) used goals with a clear end state to which we manipulated initial commitment (certain and high vs. uncertain and low) and participants' attention to what they had accomplished (to date) versus what remained for them to accomplish (to go). When goals have a clear end state, any accomplishment (e.g., 50% to date) can also be framed as a lack of accomplishment (e.g., 50% to go) without altering the objective information on the level of goal attainment. The question we addressed was which emphasis is more motivating: accomplished actions (to date) or unaccomplished actions (to go). We assume that if people highlight, accomplished actions should increase their motivation to adhere to a goal more than unaccomplished actions. However, if they balance, unaccomplished actions should have greater impact on their motivation than completed ones. We predicted that when commitment is uncertain, an emphasis on accomplished actions would increase goal adherence because accomplished actions signal greater commitment than missing ones. An emphasis on unaccomplished actions would, in contrast, increase the goal adherence when commitment is certain, because it signals a higher need for progress than completed actions.

In a study that supports these predictions (Koo & Fishbach, 2008, Study 1), student participants rated their motivation to study for either an elective-course exam, which had a pass/fail grade and for which the commitment to study was therefore uncertain and relatively low, or to a core-course exam, which had a letter grade and for which the commitment to study was therefore certain and relatively high. Before they rated the amount of time and effort they would devote to studying for one of the exams, the participants considered either the exam materials they had already covered or those they had yet to cover. We found that, for the elective-course exam (uncertain commitment), the focus on completed coursework increased students' motivation to study more than the focus on remaining coursework. However, for the core-course exam, the focus on remaining (vs. completed) coursework increased the motivation to study more (see Figure 2). This pattern reflects participants' distinct representations of goal pursuits. When commitment was uncertain they chose to study because they had completed some coursework before—they were highlighting the study goal. When commitment was certain they chose to study because they had remaining, uncompleted coursework—they were balancing between past and present efforts. Indeed, we found that the focus on completed (vs. remaining) work for the elective-course exam increased the value of studying, which in turn increased the motivation to study. We found no evidence for inferring value of studying for a core-course exam, which suggests that participants only inferred commitment from studying for an elective exam.

Research on self-regulation has traditionally focused on pursuit of personal goals, such as academic and health goals. However, many of the goals people strive to attain qualify as group goals. These are goals a collection of individuals works together to achieve (Weldon, Jehn, & Pradhan, 1991; Zander, 1980). Examples include goals such as engaging in social movements, pledging to charity, volunteering for community outreach programmes, generating ideas in team meetings, and accomplishing chores with housemates. When working on a group goal, others' accumulated contributions or lack of contributions are likely to influence an individual's motivation to invest resources in the goal. Specifically, if people ask about their level of commitment to the group goal, they are more likely to invest resources if they consider others' contributions versus lack of contributions, because existing contributions indicate the goal is important. That is,

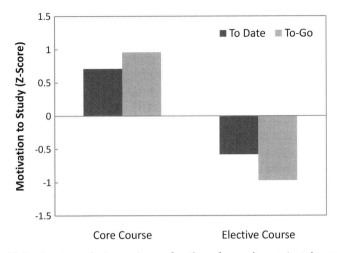

Figure 2. Motivation to study (*z*-score) as a function of commitment (certain: core course; uncertain: elective course) and focus on accomplished actions (to date) versus remaining actions (to go).

people's actions follow (or highlight) other group members' actions. In contrast, if people are already committed and therefore ask about the progress towards the group goal, they are more likely to invest their resources if they consider the lack of (vs. existing) contributions, because lack of contributions indicates more progress is required to achieve the goal. That is, people's actions compensate (or balance) for other group members' lack of actions.

In order to examine contributions to a group goal, we (Koo & Fishbach, 2008, Study 4) conducted a large-scale field study in collaboration with Compassion Korea, a charity organisation dedicated to helping children in developing countries. As part of the study we initiated a campaign to help AIDS orphans in Africa. The solicited population included regular donors who were making monthly donations to this charity ("hot list") and new donors who indicated their interest but had not yet made any contributions ("cold list"). The two groups varied by their commitment level, which was higher for those on the hot list than the cold list. The solicitation letter indicated that Compassion set a goal to raise 10 million won, and that approximately half of the money had already been raised through various channels. Depending on the experimental condition, the letter further emphasised either accumulated or remaining contributions to complete the campaign goal. We then measured the effectiveness of the charity appeal by the amount of donations we raised. As Figure 3 shows, among the cold-list donors an emphasis on accumulated contributions (50% to date) increased the average contribution more than an emphasis on remaining contributions

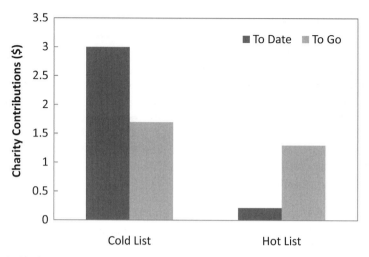

Figure 3. Charity contributions as a function of commitment certainty (low: cold list; high: hot list) and focus on accumulated contributions (to date) versus remaining contributions (to go). (Hot-list participants' regular monthly donations were not included in the analysis.)

(50% to go). This pattern reflects highlighting other group members' contributions by contributing more if others already have. In contrast, among the hot-list donors, an emphasis on remaining contributions (50% to go) increased the average contribution more than an emphasis on accumulated contributions (50% to date). This pattern reflects a dynamic of balancing by using one's own contributions to make up for others' lack of contributions.

The sources of motivation to contribute to group goals—expressing commitment versus making progress—appear similar to those characterising the pursuit of personal goals. However, rather than highlighting versus balancing one's own actions, group members either follow or compensate for others' contributions to the group goals.

Group identification

Despite the benefits group goals produce, individuals do not always work efficiently or effectively in collective settings. Although incongruence in values and demographic difference among members can explain much inefficiency of groups (Jehn, Chadwick, & Thatcher, 1997), group productivity or performance also tend to suffer because of motivational deficits that occur when people share a goal (e.g., social loafing, Kidwell & Bennett, 1993; Ringelmann, 1913; and free riding, Kerr & Bruun, 1983). For example, only 11.8% of the sample in the Koo and Fishbach study (2008, Study 4) contributed to our charity campaign. In the previous section we addressed one factor that influences the source of motivation when contributing to group goal striving: commitment to the group goal. In this section we explore a related construct—whether individuals identify with the group. We assume that, similar to commitment certainty, differences in the degree of identification will influence when and why people contribute to a group goal.

We define group identification as the degree to which individuals categorise other group members as part of themselves (Ashmore, Deaux, & McLaughlin-Volpe, 2004; Leonardelli & Brewer, 2001; Tajfel & Turner, 1986; Turner, 1987). The more individuals identify with a group, the more committed they feel and the more likely they are to experience the positive and negative outcomes of the group as their own (Ellemers, Spears, & Doosje, 1997; McCauley, 2001). We attest that group identification determines whether one's source of motivation is based on an evaluation of the merits of the group goal or the need for progress on that goal. Low group identifiers are posited to ask whether a group goal is worth pursuing. Therefore, an emphasis on other group members' prior effort expenditures should increase their own contribution. High group identifiers, on the other hand, are already committed to their group goal, and, consequently are posited to focus on the need for progress. Therefore, emphasising others' lack of effort expenditures should increase their own contribution.

We explored the impact of group identification on contribution to a group goal in a series of studies that manipulated group identification and the focus on accumulated versus remaining contributions by other group members. In one study (Fishbach, Henderson, & Koo, 2009, Study 1) we assessed contributions of ideas to a focus group. To measure each individual's contribution we used nominal groups in which participants work individually but assume their input will be collapsed with other group members (Jackson & Williams, 1985). The group goal was to generate 10 promotion ideas for a new cellular phone, and other group members had allegedly already generated 5 ideas before the participants joined the group. We manipulated identification by having participants purportedly work in conjunction with socially distant or close others. Specifically, they learned that other team members were either students affiliated with the participants' own university (high identification) or they were students at other (possibly rival) universities (low identification). We manipulated the framing of contributions by other group members (allegedly, 50%) by informing participants that other group members had contributed about half of the ideas to date or by informing them that half of the ideas were missing to meet the goal. Figure 4 displays the number of promotion ideas participants contributed to their group. As shown, the focus on accumulated contributions to date (vs. remaining contributions to go) increased idea generation for those affiliated with distant others (low identification) but decreased idea generation for those affiliated with close others

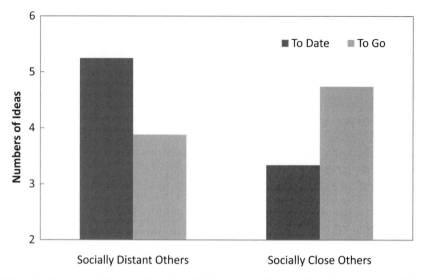

Figure 4. Idea generation as a function of identification (low: socially distant others; high: socially close others) and focus on accumulated contributions (to date) versus remaining contributions (to go).

(high identification). Interestingly, group identification did not increase overall contributions. Rather it influenced the source of the motivation to invest in the goal: either to participate if the cause appeared valuable (for low identifiers) or to promote progress if the valuable cause was not progressing at a sufficient pace (for high identifiers).

Another study (Fishbach et al., 2009, Study 3) explored how identification with a victimised group influences whether individuals contribute to a charity campaign more if they consider the fact that others have already contributed or if they consider the fact that others have not contributed. This study manipulated group identification by referring to the victimised group as part of the self (i.e., "we") versus separate from the self (i.e., "they"; Cialdini et al., 1976; Dovidio, Piliavin, Gaertner, Schroeder, & Clark, 1991). Specifically, shortly after the Kenyan riots in December 2007 we sent solicitation letters to potential charity donors. These letters either referred to "our Compassion children" suffering from the violence "in our world" (high identification) or to the children "in Africa" suffering from the violence "there" (low identification). Similar to our previous study (Koo & Fishbach, 2008, Study 4), the letter further emphasised that we had already raised approximately half of the money through various channels or that we still needed about half of the money to complete the campaign goal.

As Figure 5 shows, among low identifiers ("they"), an emphasis on accumulated contributions increased the average amount of donations more

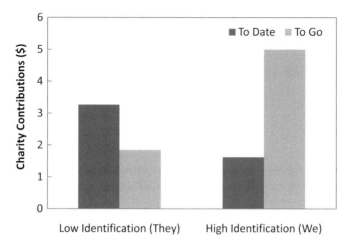

Figure 5. Charity contributions as a function of group identification and focus on accumulated contributions (to date) versus remaining contributions (to go).

than an emphasis on remaining contributions. This pattern reflects a dynamic of highlighting or following other group members' contributions. In contrast, among high identifiers ("we"), an emphasis on remaining contributions increased the average amount of donations more than an emphasis on accumulated contributions. This pattern reflects a dynamic of balancing or compensating for other group members' lack of contributions. Another study (Fishbach et al., 2009, Study 4) confirms that only low identifiers infer that a charity campaign is more valuable when they consider accumulated contributions to date (vs. contributions still to go). In addition, only high identifiers infer a higher need for progress when they consider remaining contributions to go (vs. to date).

In summary, the questions people ask influence their pattern of self-regulation. When they are unsure about their commitment they invest more in a goal if they focus on existing contributions (highlighting). But when they are sure about their commitment, and ask about their progress, they invest more in a goal if they focus on the absence of contributions (balancing). The questions people ask may depend on the questions someone asks them, as well as on their level of commitment to a goal, including their degree of identification with group members with whom they share a goal.

Contexts activate goal frames

The context in which a person contemplates pursuit of a goal can influence the frame of this goal—commitment or progress—and whether the person then follows a dynamic of highlighting or balancing. Specifically, we find that people are more likely to highlight (vs. balance) goals when a superordinate goal becomes salient in the course of self-regulation. In addition, people are more likely to highlight when choice alternatives that pertain to different goals are presented separately and appear to be in competition (e.g., healthy and unhealthy food in different bowls), and they are more likely to balance when choice alternatives are presented together and appear complementary (e.g., healthy and unhealthy food in a single bowl).

Salient superordinate goal

The degree to which individuals interpret goal actions in terms of expressing commitment or making progress partially depends on their attention to the specific action (or subgoal, e.g., a workout) as opposed to its superordinate goal (e.g., a health goal). If the superordinate goal is salient, successful attainment of an action can signal commitment to this goal more than it can provide a sense of progress, since the overall goal is far from reach. Therefore completing a single activity would increase a person's motivation to highlight the goal by pursuing consistent actions. If, however, the superordinate goal is not salient and a person focuses on the activity itself, successful attainment of an action signals goal progress and even fulfilment, and it motivates balancing by moving away from the goal.

In a study that tested the effect of superordinate goal accessibility, we (Fishbach et al., 2006, Study 2) explored whether gym users would choose to accompany their workout with another health-promoting activity—healthy eating. In order to increase the accessibility of the superordinate health goals, participants completed an experimental survey attached to either a "health and fitness" hardcover book or a phone directory (the control). Both books served as clipboards. To manipulate participants' perceived successful workouts, we had them evaluate their own workouts while (presumably unintentionally) seeing a fictitious participant's responses. That fictitious participant listed either a smaller or a larger amount of exercising time, which made participants believe their own workout was relatively successful or insufficient. We found that when the superordinate health goal was salient (the "health and fitness" clipboard), those who learned they exercised a lot expressed greater interest to eat healthy than those who learned they exercised a little—a pattern of highlighting. However, in the absence of the superordinate goal prime, those who learned they exercised a lot were less interested to eat healthy than those who learned they exercised a little—a pattern of balancing (see Figure 6).

Another study (Fishbach et al., 2006, Study 4) found that proximal actions signal goal progress whereas distant actions signal goal commitment, because individuals evaluate their distant actions by the superordinate goals

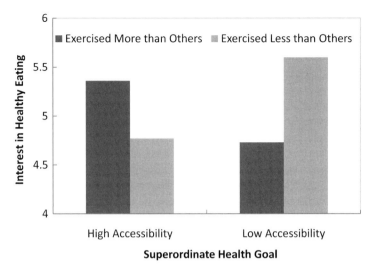

Figure 6. Interest in healthy eating as a function of superordinate health goal accessibility and the amount of exercising (high: participants believed they exercised more than others; low: they believed they exercised less than others).

they serve (Liberman & Trope, 1998; Trope & Liberman, 2003; Vallacher & Wegner, 1987). For example, exercising in the near future would likely mean "sweating", but in the distant future exercising more likely would mean "improving health". Similar to priming a superordinate goal, the focus on the distant future therefore makes people construe their actions more as a signal of commitment and less as an indication of progress. We further found that inferences of progress (vs. commitment) mediate the effect of goal pursuit in the proximal versus distant future on interest in pursuing complementary actions. We can therefore conclude that initial success increases goal adherence when individuals focus on the superordinate goal, because the action seems to signal commitment more than progress. Initial failure, however, increases motivation when individuals focus on the action itself, because the failure signals a lack of goal progress rather than a lack of commitment.

Presentation format

The arrangement of alternatives also influences the dynamic of self-regulation that individuals follow. Individuals often make selections from sets that include items serving multiple goals. For example, they browse through a television guide that includes educational shows and light sitcoms. They go through highbrow news magazines and lowbrow fashion magazines on a newsstand or select from menu courses that are either healthy or tasty.

In such situations, the presence of the different alternatives activates the corresponding goals (Shah & Kruglanski, 2003) and the arrangement of the alternatives influences people's perceptions of them as competing against versus complementing each other, which in turn influences the dynamics of self-regulation. For example, the presence of healthy fruits and unhealthy candies activates the health goal versus satisfying one's craving for sweets motives, and their arrangement in one versus two bowls influences the perception of these alternatives as competing versus complementary, which determines people's choice between them.

In a series of studies that tested for these possibilities, we (Fishbach & Zhang, 2008) found that separating items into two sets (e.g., two bowls), versus presenting them together in one set (e.g., one bowl), determines whether individuals perceive the items as conflicting versus complementary. When the items are presented apart they seem conflicting and promote a highlighting dynamic of choice; when the items are together they seem complementary and promote a balancing dynamic of choice.

These dynamics have unique consequences for situations in which the items in a set pose a self-control conflict; for example, when people contemplate between low- and high-calorie foods (Baumeister, Heatherton, & Tice, 1994; Kuhl & Beckmann, 1985; Loewenstein, 1996; Metcalfe & Mischel, 1999; Rachlin, 1997; Stroebe, Papies, & Aarts, 2008; Trope & Fishbach, 2000). When goal and temptation alternatives (e.g., healthy and unhealthy foods) are presented apart from each other, they seem to be in competition. As a result, people are more likely to resolve the conflict in favour of the goal alternatives in a dynamic of highlighting: they assign a greater value to goal alternatives (e.g., educational shows, news magazines) than to tempting alternatives, and consistently choose goal alternatives for both immediate and future consumption. In contrast, when choice alternatives appear together and seem to complement each other, thus promoting balancing, people tend to resolve the self-control conflict in favour of the immediately gratifying temptation option. As a result, they value the tempting alternatives (e.g., watching sitcoms, reading lowbrow fashion magazines) more than the goal alternatives and prefer these tempting alternatives for immediate consumption, thereby postponing the consumption of goal alternatives to a future occasion. The reason tempting alternatives are selected first in this presentation format is that their value is immediate, whereas the value of the goal alternatives, although larger, is delayed. Thus, in a self-control conflict, a balancing dynamic would most often take the form of "first temptation then goal" rather than "first goal then temptation".

To demonstrate these effects, we (Fishbach & Zhang, 2008, Study 1) presented healthy and unhealthy food items in one of three presentation formats: (a) together in one image to induce a sense of complementarity and a dynamic of balancing; (b) in two separate images next to each other to induce a sense of competition and a dynamic of highlighting; or (c) in two separate experimental trials as a control condition (see Figure 7). We purposely selected healthy and unhealthy food items that were similarly positive when evaluated independently (e.g., fresh tomatoes vs. cheeseburger). As Figure 8 shows, presenting these items together in one image increased liking for unhealthy foods, whereas presenting them apart in separate images increased liking for healthy foods. A follow-up study (Fishbach & Zhang, 2008, Study 4) found that when goal and temptation alternatives were presented together (vs. apart), they appeared to complement each other but did not appear more similar to each other: thus we can rule out the possibility that the presentation formats simply influence people's ability to mentally separate goal from tempting alternatives.

In another study (Fishbach & Zhang, 2008, Study 6), participants faced a choice between a healthy bag of carrots and an unhealthy chocolate bar. Presenting these items in sorted piles, one for each food type, increased the share of participants who chose carrots over chocolates, compared to presenting the options together in one pile. Importantly, we can conclude that a presentation format helps individuals to identify a self-control problem if it causes their actions to be more closely associated with the strength of their high-order goal (e.g., whether they would like to lose weight). Indeed, only when we presented the healthy and unhealthy options apart, thereby prompting highlighting, were participants' concerns with weight watching positively associated with the healthy choice of carrots over chocolates. Concern with weight watching did not predict choice when we presented the options together. When options are presented apart, people appear to more easily identify a self-control problem and make choices congruent with the motivational strength of the goal to watch their weight. Presenting options together eliminates the self-control conflict because those concerned with their weight feel they can eat unhealthily now and balance for their unhealthy choice later (Myrseth & Fishbach, 2009).

Together   **Apart**

Figure 7. Examples for presenting food images together or apart. [To view this figure in colour, please visit the online version of this paper.]

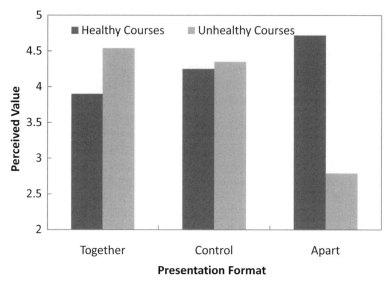

Figure 8. Perceived value of healthy and unhealthy menu courses as a function of presentation format.

Other studies assessed a sequence of actions that balances or highlights goals or temptations. We (Fishbach & Zhang, 2008, Study 5) found that presenting options together in one unified choice set induces the sequence of balancing, whereas presenting the same options apart in two separate choice sets induces the sequence of highlighting. Specifically, participants in this study selected courses from a menu that depicted healthy and unhealthy options either together on one menu or apart in two clearly separated menu sections. When the courses appeared together on a single menu, the majority of the participants (over 50%) preferred to order an unhealthy entrée and a healthy dessert. This choice sequence represents balancing: first temptation then goal. However, when the same food options appeared on two menus— one exclusively for healthy courses and the other exclusively for unhealthy courses—the majority of the participants preferred to order both a healthy entrée and a healthy dessert, thus choosing to highlight the more important health goal.

On the basis of these and similar findings, we propose that in a self-control dilemma, balancing may often result in giving in to temptation in the present. Then, to the extent that a person's choices for the future are not binding, the person may repeatedly choose tempting alternatives while postponing pursuit of a more important goal; for example, the dieter may keep promising himself to start the diet tomorrow. We conclude that when facing goals and temptations that are in conflict, following a pattern of highlighting the choice of goal items is beneficial.

In summary, the contexts of self-regulation influence the dynamic of self-regulation individuals follow. When a superordinate goal is salient, it prompts a commitment representation of goal pursuits and highlighting, whereas a progress representation and balancing are more likely in the absence of a salient superordinate goal. In addition, when action alternatives appear to compete with each other, they prompt a pattern of highlighting one type of alternatives, whereas when these options appear to complement each other, they promote balancing between the alternatives.

PART III: FEEDBACK ON SELF-REGULATION

Feedback is inherent to self-regulation; hence people associate specific social roles with providing feedback on successful versus unsuccessful goal pursuits. Thus educators, coaches, and bosses all provide feedback that helps individuals monitor their goal pursuits. In addition, people seek feedback from those around them, regardless of their social role, including friends, family members, colleagues, and neighbours. The feedback people seek can refer to mastery goals, such as how well they perform a new skill, but also to relationship goals, such as how well they maintain their marriage or friendships. Across these social agents and various goals, we examine how goal frames (commitment vs. progress) influence the feedback individuals seek, give, and respond to.

Responding to feedback

We draw a general distinction between positive feedback on accomplishments, strengths, correct responses versus negative feedback on lack of accomplishments, weaknesses, and incorrect responses. We propose that distinct motivational consequences exist for receiving positive and negative feedback. Positive feedback increases goal adherence when it signals greater commitment to the goal, but negative feedback increases the goal adherence when it signals lack of goal progress. For example, we find that feedback on completed actions promotes goal adherence more than feedback on required actions when individuals are unsure about their commitment, but the opposite pattern emerges when individuals wish to monitor their progress (Koo & Fishbach, 2008). Similarly, in another set of studies (Fishbach et al., 2006), feedback on successful (vs. failed) goal pursuit increased the motivation to select similar goal-congruent actions when the superordinate goal was salient, but the same feedback on success (vs. failure) diminished the motivation to work on the goal when the focus was on the action itself.

Feedback often includes direct information about the positive versus negative aspects of one's performance. Alternatively, feedback also comes in the form of affective information, and people rely on their emotions or moods as a source of feedback for self-regulation (Beer & Keltner, 2004; Carver & Scheier, 1998; Frijda, 1986; Higgins, 1987; Schwarz & Clore, 1983; Tangney, Miller, Flicker, & Barlow, 1996). In addition, we find that direct performance feedback also exerts its influence by inducing an emotional response. That is, the feedback induces positive or negative moods, which in turn inform people about their commitment to or progress towards their goals, thus influencing the strength of the motivation to adhere to a goal.

Whether mood then increases or decreases the motivational priority of a goal is often a matter of mood attribution to either a source unrelated to the goal or to the progress on this goal. If people attribute mood to a source unrelated to the goal (e.g., background music), a positive mood informs them to adopt this pursuit more than a negative mood does (Aspinwall, 1998; Fishbach & Labroo, 2007; Trope & Neter, 1994). If, however, people attribute the source of their mood to progress towards accomplishing a goal, a positive mood informs them more than a negative mood does that they have made adequate progress, and they subsequently relax their efforts in pursuing this goal (Carver & Scheier, 1998; Martin, Ward, Achee, & Wyer, 1993).

In support of this analysis, we (Eyal, Fishbach, & Labroo, 2009) found in a series of studies that positive mood decreases performance when one attributes it to progress towards a goal, but it improves performance when one attributes it to an unrelated source. Participants in one study completed a word association task that induced a positive or negative mood outside conscious awareness (e.g., they listed associations for positive-valence words such as "beautiful" vs. negative-valence words such as "ugly"; Isen, Johnson, Mertz, & Robinson, 1985). Those in the misattribution condition were then led to believe their mood indicated their level of progress on this presumed "creativity task", whereas the rest of the participants remained unaware of the source of their mood. Next we assessed participants' performance on an anagram task that presumably measured a similar creativity skill. As Figure 9 shows, among those who remained unaware of the source of their mood, positive mood improved performance on the anagram task more than negative mood did. However, among those who misattributed mood to performance, negative mood increased performance more than positive mood did. A follow-up study found that people infer greater commitment to the goal—but no greater progress—from a positive (vs. negative) mood unrelated to their performance. Correspondingly, people also infer greater goal progress—but no greater commitment—from a positive (vs. negative) mood related to performance on the goal. We can thus conclude that positive mood increases motivation when it signals commitment and negative mood increases motivation when it indicates lack of sufficient progress towards a goal.

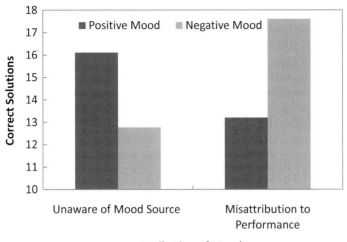

Figure 9. Number of correct solutions on an anagram task as a function of mood attribution.

Whereas in several studies we manipulated the attribution of performance-unrelated mood, in other studies we manipulated the attribution of performance-related mood to performance (correct attribution) versus an unrelated source (incorrect attribution). Participants in these studies received positive or negative feedback on their performance and were then led to believe their moods resulted from the feedback or an unrelated source. We found that mood attribution, rather than the true source of one's mood, determined the impact of mood on goal adherence. Specifically, positive moods increased goal adherence when participants attributed mood to a goal-unrelated source, whereas negative moods increased goal adherence when participants attributed mood to the lack of progress on the goal.

In addition to mood, people's representation of goal pursuits—expressing commitment versus making progress—influences how they respond to feedback on self-regulation. We reviewed several factors that influence the representations of goal actions, and on the basis of the previous analysis we assume these representations shift over time as people gain experience in a particular domain. In particular, as people move from a novice to an expert status they begin to think of a goal less in terms of evaluating commitment and more in terms of monitoring progress. For example, college freshmen might wish to decide whether enrolling in college was the right decision, whereas college seniors might be more likely to ask about the pace of their progress and whether it is sufficient to graduate on time. These changes in goal frames may determine the impact of feedback delivered at different points in time: The novice would increase effort in response to positive feedback (inferring commitment), whereas the experienced individual would increase effort in response to negative feedback (inferring lack of progress; see also Louro, Pieters, & Zeelenberg, 2007). Indeed, in our studies on relationship goals, we (Fishbach & Finkelstein, 2009) find that new friends wish to connect more after receiving positive (vs. negative) feedback from their friend, for example, about something nice they did for that person. In contrast, old friends express a greater desire to connect with each other after receiving negative (vs. positive) feedback from their friend, for example, about missing an important occasion.

Feedback seeking and giving

As individuals advance towards a goal, their frames shift from expressing commitment to making progress and the share of negative feedback increases. As a result, not only do they respond more to negative feedback, but they also seek less positive and more negative feedback. In addition, when providing the feedback, individuals increase the share of negative feedback and decrease the share of positive feedback as the recipient of the feedback advances towards the goal.

To demonstrate these shifts in feedback as a function of goal advancement, we (Finkelstein & Fishbach, 2009) manipulated the actual or perceived advancement on goals and tested feedback seeking and giving. For example, in a study that tested feedback seeking, participants learned a new task (typing in German for American students) and could choose between receiving feedback either on their mistakes or on their correct responses after each typing trial up to seven trials. As participants progressed on the typing task, a larger proportion of them sought the negative feedback. Thus, gaining experience resulted in more negative feedback seeking.

Similar shifts exist in feedback giving. We (Fishbach & Finkelstein, 2009) examined the feedback friends give to each other as a function of whether they feel their relationship is either relatively new or long standing. Participants listed a non-romantic friend and then answered either a set of questions that made them feel they had known this person for a long time or a set of questions that made them feel they had known this person for a short time. For example, participants perceived their relationship as relatively long standing when they indicated whether they had known their friend for more than a couple of years (most did), but they perceived their relationships as relatively new when they indicated whether they had known the friend for more than 20 years (few did). To assess feedback giving, participants then wrote a short toast for their partner for an upcoming event, such as a birthday party, in which they could express both their appreciation for, as well as criticism towards, that individual. As predicted, participants who were made to feel their relationship was long standing were more likely to give their partner negative feedback (i.e., to "roast" rather than toast), compared with those who felt their relationships were relatively new.

In summary, our research suggests that feedback influences self-regulation by either providing information on goal commitment or on the level of progress towards that goal. These effects of feedback often depend on how people interpret the mood the feedback elicited. If positive mood signals commitment to a goal, it increases goal adherence, but if positive mood signals sufficient goal progress, it decreases goal adherence. Importantly, individuals not only respond to feedback, they also actively seek and give feedback on goal performance. We find parallels in the emphasis on positive versus negative feedback across three modalities— giving, receiving, and responding—such that as people advance towards a goal, they shift towards more negative feedback.

SUMMARY AND CONCLUSIONS

The work on the dynamics of self-regulation aims to explore the problem of prioritising goals in a multiple goal context (Fishbach & Dhar, 2005; Fishbach et al., 2006; Fishbach & Zhang, 2008; Koo & Fishbach, 2008; Zhang et al., 2007). In particular, we ask when people follow a dynamic of highlighting a single goal over a sequence of actions and when they follow a dynamic of balancing between goals over this sequence. In this way we wish to identify when the initial pursuit of a goal increases the motivational priority of a goal more than failing to pursue it.

We propose that the pattern of self-regulation an individual follows depends on the representation of goal actions in terms of expressing commitment or making progress. When people interpret goal actions as a signal for goal commitment, they are more likely to take similar actions that highlight the goal. Likewise, when people interpret absence of actions as a signal for low commitment, they are less likely to follow the goal. Conversely, when people interpret goal actions as a signal that progress has been made and the discrepancy to goal attainment is now reduced, they balance by relaxing their efforts. Likewise, they are also more likely to follow the goal if they consider lack of actions and absence of progress. We therefore conclude that either acting on a goal or failing to do so can potentially increase the motivational priority of the goal, depending on the inference one makes and the resulting dynamics of self-regulation.

We reviewed research that supports the presence of different goal frames and their implications for the patterns of self-regulation that individuals follow. We find that when people interpret an action as indicative of commitment, they make similar choices that inhibit competing goals (Shah, Friedman, & Kruglanski, 2002; Stroebe, Mensink, Aarts, Schut, &

Kruglanski, 2008). When they interpret the same action as indicative of progress, however, they disengage from the goal and attend to other goals (Khan & Dhar, 2006; Monin & Miller, 2001). We further find that future goal plans function in a similar manner as past actions, since people infer commitment or progress on the basis of planned (hypothetical) actions.

Our program of research identifies several variables that influence the representation of goal actions, some of which affect the question individuals ask—commitment or progress—whereas others influence which representation the context activates. This research further has implications for feedback on self-regulation, including feedback individuals give, receive, and respond to.

Implications of our research go beyond personal goals to situations in which people join other group members in tasks such as generating ideas at team meetings or contributing to a charity. Practical implications of this framework abound: social agents, such as educators and managers, may benefit from considering the information people derive from their actions (commitment or progress) and the implications for what they decide to do next. For example, mandatory goal pursuits or imposed choices (e.g., banning unhealthy products) might signal to people that they have made progress towards a goal (e.g., of leading a healthier lifestyle) without them experiencing the corresponding boost in goal commitment, because they did not voluntarily select the goal (Brehm, 1966). In such situations, imposed choices may be effective in the short run but will promote balancing between the imposed goal and alternative goals and eventually might decrease the likelihood of making complementary, voluntary choices towards achieving the imposed goal (e.g., by promoting unhealthy behaviours). In addition, when people work on a goal without making any progress—for example, when they invest effort in a futile cause, as in sunk-cost situations (Arkes & Ayton, 1999; Arkes & Blumer, 1985)—they may experience commitment without progress. Such experience should be mostly effective in increasing commitment and motivating the voluntary choice of similar complementary actions that pursue the same goal.

REFERENCES

Aarts, H., & Dijksterhuis, A. (2000). Habits as knowledge structures: Automaticity in goal-directed behavior. *Journal of Personality and Social Psychology*, *78*, 53–63.

Arkes, H. R., & Ayton, P. (1999). The sunk cost and Concorde effects: Are humans less rational than lower animals? *Psychological Bulletin*, *125*, 591–600.

Arkes, H. R., & Blumer, C. (1985). The psychology of sunk cost. *Organisational Behavior and Human Decision Processes*, *35*, 124–140.

Ashmore, R. D., Deaux, K., & McLaughlin-Volpe, T. (2004). An organising framework for collective identity: Articulation and significance of multidimensionality. *Psychological Bulletin*, *130*, 80–114.

Aspinwall, L. G. (1998). Rethinking the role of positive affect in self-regulation. *Motivation & Emotion, 22*, 1–32.

Atkinson, J. W. (1964). *An introduction to motivation.* Oxford, UK: Van Nostrand.

Atkinson, J. W. (1974). Strength and motivation and efficiency of performance. In J. W. Atkinson & J. O. Raynor (Eds.), *Motivation and achievement* (pp. 193–218). New York: Wiley.

Atkinson, J. W., & Raynor, J. O. (1978). *Personality, motivation, and achievement.* New York: Halsted Press.

Bandura, A. (1997). *Self-efficacy: The exercise of control.* New York: W. H. Freeman/Times Books/Henry Holt & Co.

Baumeister, R. F., Heatherton, T. F., & Tice, D. M. (1994). *Losing control: How and why people fail at self-regulation.* San Diego, CA: Academic Press.

Beer, J. S., & Keltner, D. (2004). What is unique about self-conscious emotions? Comment on Tracy & Robins' "Putting the self into self-conscious emotions: A theoretical model". *Psychological Inquiry, 15*, 126–129.

Bem, D. J. (1972). Self-perception theory. In L. Berkowitz (Ed.), *Advances in experimental social psychology* (Vol. 6, pp. 1–62). New York: Academic Press.

Brehm, J. W. (1966). *Theory of psychological reactance.* Burlington, MA: Academic Press.

Brunstein, J. C., & Gollwitzer, P. M. (1996). Effects of failure on subsequent performance: The importance of self-defining goals. *Journal of Personality and Social Psychology, 70*, 395–407.

Buehler, R., Griffin, D., & Ross, M. (1994). Exploring the "planning fallacy": Why people underestimate their task completion times. *Journal of Personality and Social Psychology, 67*, 366–381.

Carver, C. S., & Scheier, M. F. (1998). *On the self-regulation of behavior.* New York: Cambridge University Press.

Chartrand, T. L., & Bargh, J. A. (1996). Automatic activation of impression formation and memorization goals: Nonconscious goal priming reproduces the effects of explicit task instructions. *Journal of Personality and Social Psychology, 71*, 464–478.

Cialdini, R. B., Borden, R. J., Thorne, A., Walker, M. R., Freeman, S., & Sloan, L. R. (1976). Basking in reflected glory: Three (football) field studies. *Journal of Personality and Social Psychology, 34*, 366–375.

Cialdini, R. B., Trost, M. R., & Newsom, J. T. (1995). Preference for consistency: The development of a valid measure and the discovery of surprising behavioral implications. *Journal of Personality and Social Psychology, 69*, 318–328.

Dhar, R., & Simonson, I. (1999). Making complementary choices in consumption episodes: Highlighting versus balancing. *Journal of Marketing Research, 36*, 29–44.

Dovidio, J. F., Piliavin, J. A., Gaertner, S., Schroeder, D. A., & Clark, R. D. (1991). The arousal: Cost–reward model and the process of intervention: A review of the evidence. In M. Clark (Ed.), *Prosocial behavior. Review of personality and social psychology* (Vol. 12, pp. 86–118). Newbury Park, CA: Sage.

Ellemers, N., Spears, R., & Doosje, B. (1997). Sticking together or falling apart: Ingroup identification as a psychological determinant of group commitment versus individual mobility. *Journal of Personality and Social Psychology, 72*, 617–26.

Eyal, T., Fishbach, A., & Labroo A. L. (2009). *When mood cues goal progress versus goal adoption: A matter of (mis)attribution.* Unpublished manuscript, University of Chicago.

Feather, N. T. (1990). Bridging the gap between values and actions: Recent applications of the expectancy-value model. In E. T. Higgins & R. M. Sorrentino (Eds.), *Handbook of motivation and cognition: Foundations of social behavior* (Vol. 2, pp. 151–192). New York: Guilford Press.

Ferguson, M. J., & Bargh, J. A. (2004). Liking is for doing: The effects of goal pursuit on automatic evaluation. *Journal of Personality and Social Psychology, 87*, 557–572.

Finkelstein, S. R., & Fishbach, A. (2009). *Seeking and giving negative feedback in self-regulation.* Unpublished manuscript, University of Chicago.

Fishbein, M., & Ajzen, I. (1974). Attitudes towards objects as predictors of single and multiple behavioral criteria. *Psychological Review, 81*, 29–74.

Fishbach, A., & Dhar, R. (2005). Goals as excuses or guides: The liberating effect of perceived goal progress on choice. *Journal of Consumer Research, 32*, 370–377.

Fishbach, A., Dhar, R., & Zhang, Y. (2006). Subgoals as substitutes or complements: The role of goal accessibility. *Journal of Personality and Social Psychology, 91*, 232–242.

Fishbach, A., & Finkelstein, S. R. (2009). *Seeking, giving and responding to feedback from relationship partners.* Unpublished manuscript, University of Chicago.

Fishbach, A., Henderson, M. D., & Koo, M., (2009). *Group goals and sources of motivation: When others don't get the job done, I (might) pick up the slack.* Unpublished manuscript, University of Chicago.

Fishbach, A., & Labroo, A. (2007). Be better or be merry: How mood affects self-control. *Journal of Personality and Social Psychology, 93*, 158–173.

Fishbach, A., & Zhang, Y. (2008). Together or apart: When goals and temptations complement versus compete. *Journal of Personality and Social Psychology, 94*, 547–559.

Förster, J., Higgins, E., & Idson, L. C. (1998). Approach and avoidance strength during goal attainment: Regulatory focus and the "goal looms larger" effect. *Journal of Personality and Social Psychology, 75*, 1115–1131.

Frijda, N. H. (1986). *The emotions.* Cambridge: Cambridge University Press.

Heath, C., Larrick, R., & Wu, G. (1999). Goals as reference points. *Cognitive Psychology, 38*, 129–166.

Higgins, E. T. (1987). Self-discrepancy: A theory relating self and affect. *Psychological Review, 94*, 319–340.

Hull, C. L. (1934). The rat's speed-of-locomotion gradient in the approach to food. *Journal of Comparative Psychology, 17*, 393–422.

Isen, A. M., Johnson, M. M., Mertz, E., & Robinson, G. F. (1985). The influence of positive affect on the unusualness of word associations. *Journal of Personality and Social Psychology, 48*, 1413–1426.

Jackson, J. M., & Williams, K. D. (1985). Social loafing on difficult tasks: Working collectively can improve performance. *Journal of Personality and Social Psychology, 49*, 937–942.

Jehn, K. A., Chadwick, C., & Thatcher, S. M. B. (1997). To agree or not to agree: The effects of value congruence, individual demographic dissimilarity, and conflict on workgroup outcomes. *International Journal of Conflict Management, 8*, 287–305.

Khan, U., & Dhar, R. (1996). Licensing effect in consumer choice. *Journal of Marketing Research, 43*, 259–266.

Kelley, H. H. (1972). Attribution in social interaction. In E. E. Jones, D. E. Kanouse, H. H. Kelley, R. E. Nisbett, S. Valins, & B. Weiner (Eds.), *Attribution: Perceiving the causes of behavior* (pp. 1–26), Morristown, NJ: General Learning Press.

Kerr, N. L., & Bruun, S. E. (1983). Dispensability of member effort and group motivation losses: Free-rider effects. *Journal of Personality and Social Psychology, 44*, 78–94.

Kidwell, R. E., & Bennett, N. (1993). Employee propensity to withhold effort: A conceptual model to intersect three avenues of research. *Academy of Management Review, 18*, 429–456.

Kivetz, R., Urminsky, O., & Zheng, Y. (2006). The goal-gradient hypothesis resurrected: Purchase acceleration, illusionary goal progress, and customer retention. *Journal of Marketing Research, 43*, 39–58.

Koo, M., & Fishbach, A. (2008). Dynamics of self-regulation: How (un)accomplished goal actions affect motivation. *Journal of Personality and Social Psychology, 94*, 183–195.

Kruglanski, A. W., Shah, J. Y., Fishbach, A., Friedman, R., Chun, W. Y., & Sleeth-Keppler, D. (2002). A theory of goal systems. In M. P. Zanna (Ed.), *Advances in experimental social psychology* (Vol. 34, pp. 331–378). San Diego, CA: Academic Press.

Kuhl, J., & Beckmann, J. (1985). *Action control from cognition to behavior*. New York: Springer-Verlag.

Leonardelli, G. J., & Brewer, M. B. (2001). Minority and majority discrimination: When and why. *Journal of Experimental Social Psychology, 37*, 468–485.

Lewin, K., Dembo, T., Festinger, L., & Sears, P. S. (1944). Level of aspiration. In J. M. Hunt (Ed.), *Personality and the behavioral disorders* (pp. 333–371). New York: Roland Press.

Liberman, N., & Förster, J. (2008). Expectancy, value and psychological distance: A new look at goal gradients. *Social Cognition, 26*, 515–533.

Liberman, N., & Trope, Y. (1998). The role of feasibility and desirability considerations in near and distant future decisions: A test of temporal construal theory. *Journal of Personality and Social Psychology, 75*, 5–18.

Locke, E. A., & Latham, G. P. (1990). *A theory of goal setting & task performance*. Upper Saddle River, NJ: Prentice-Hall.

Loewenstein, G. (1996). Out of control: Visceral influences on behavior. *Organisational Behavior and Human Decision Processes, 65*, 272–292.

Losco, J., & Epstein, S. (1977). Relative steepness of approach and avoidance gradients as a function of magnitude and valence of incentive. *Journal of Abnormal Psychology, 86*, 360–368.

Louro, M. S., Pieters, R., & Zeelenberg, M. (2007). Dynamics of multiple goal pursuit. *Journal of Personality and Social Psychology, 93*, 174–193.

Martin, L. L., Ward, D. W., Achee, J. W., & Wyer, R. S. (1993). Mood as input: People have to interpret the motivational implications of their moods. *Journal of Personality and Social Psychology, 64*, 317–326.

McCauley, C. (2001). The psychology of group identification and the power of ethnic nationalism. In D. Chirot & M. Seligman (Eds.), *Ethnopolitical warfare: Causes, consequences, and possible solutions* (pp. 343–362). Washington, DC: APA Books.

Metcalfe, J., & Mischel, W. (1999). A hot/cool-system analysis of delay of gratification: Dynamics of willpower. *Psychological Review, 106*, 3–19.

Miller, G. A., Galanter, E., & Pribram, K. H. (1960). *Plans and the structure of behavior*. New York: Henry Holt.

Monin, B., & Miller, D. T. (2001). Moral credentials and the expression of prejudice. *Journal of Personality and Social Psychology, 81*, 33–43.

Moskowitz, G. B. (2002). Preconscious effects of temporary goals on attention. *Journal of Experimental Social Psychology, 38*, 397–404.

Myrseth, K. O. R., & Fishbach, A. (2009). Self-control: A function of knowing when and how to exercise restraint. *Current Directions in Psychological Science, 18*, 247–252.

Oettingen, G., & Mayer, D. (2002). The motivating function of thinking about the future: Expectations versus fantasies. *Journal of Personality and Social Psychology, 83*, 1198–1212.

Powers, W. T. (1973). *Behavior: The control of perception*. Oxford, UK: Aldine.

Rachlin, H. (1997). Self and self-control. In J. G. Snodgrass & R. L. Thompson (Eds.), *The self across psychology: Self-recognition, self-awareness, and the self-concept. Annals of the New York Academy of Sciences* (Vol. 818, pp. 85–97). New York: New York Academy of Sciences.

Ringelmann, M. (1913b). Recherches sur les moteurs animés: Travail de l'homme [Research on animate sources of power: The work of man]. *Annales de l'Institut National Agronomique, 2e série–tome, 12*, 1–40.

Schwarz, N., & Clore, G. L. (1983), Mood, misattribution, and judgments of well-being: Informative and directive functions of affective states. *Journal of Personality and Social Psychology, 83*, 1261–1280.

Shah, J. Y., Friedman, R., & Kruglanski, A. W. (2002). Forgetting all else: On the antecedents and consequences of goal shielding. *Journal of Personality and Social Psychology, 83,* 1261–1280.

Shah, J. Y., & Kruglanski, A. W. (2003). When opportunity knocks: Bottom-up priming of goals by means and its effects on self-regulation. *Journal of Personality and Social Psychology, 84,* 1109–1122.

Stroebe, W., Mensink, W., Aarts, H., Schut, H., & Kruglanski, A. W. (2008). Why dieters fail: Testing the goal conflict model of eating. *Journal of Experimental Social Psychology, 44,* 26–36.

Stroebe, W., Papies, E. K., & Aarts, H. (2008). From homeostatic to hedonic theories of eating: Self-regulatory failure in food-rich environments. *Applied Psychology: An International Review, 57,* 172–193.

Tajfel, H. & Turner, J. C. (1986). The social identity theory of intergroup behavior. In S. Worchel & W. Austin (Eds.), *Psychology of intergroup relation.* Chicago: Nelson-Hall.

Tangney, J. P., Miller, R. S., Flicker, L., & Barlow, D. H. (1996). Are shame, guilt, and embarrassment distinct emotions? *Journal of Personality and Social Psychology, 70,* 1256–1269.

Taylor, S. E., & Brown, J. D. (1988). Illusion and well-being: A social psychological perspective on mental health. *Psychological Bulletin, 103,* 193–210.

Tolman, E. C. (1932). *Purposive behavior in animals and men.* New York: Appleton-Century-Crofts.

Trope, Y., & Fishbach, A. (2000). Counteractive self-control in overcoming temptation. *Journal of Personality and Social Psychology, 79,* 493–506.

Trope, Y., & Liberman, N. (2003). Temporal construal. *Psychological Review, 110,* 403–421.

Trope, Y., & Neter, E. (1994). Reconciling competing motives in self-evaluation: The role of self-control in feedback seeking. *Journal of Personality and Social Psychology, 66,* 646–657.

Turner, J. C. (1987). A self-categorisation theory. In M. Hogg, P. Oakes, S. Reicher, & M. S. Wetherell (Eds.), *Rediscovering the social groups: Studies in the social psychology of intergroup relations.* London: Academic Press.

Vallacher, R. R., & Wegner, D. M. (1987). What do people think they're doing? Action identification and human behavior. *Psychological Review, 94,* 3–15.

Vroom, V. H. (1964). *Work and motivation.* New York: Wiley.

Weiner, B. (1979). A theory of motivation for some classroom experiences. *Journal of Educational Psychology, 71,* 3–25.

Weinstein, N. D. (1989). Optimistic biases about personal risks. *Science, 246,* 1232–1233.

Weldon, E., Jehn, K. A., & Pradhan, P. (1991). Processes that mediate the relationship between a group goal and improved group performance. *Journal of Personality and Social Psychology, 61,* 555–569.

Wicklund, R. A., & Gollwitzer, P. M. (1982). *Symbolic self-completion.* Hillsdale, NJ: Lawrence Erlbaum Associates Inc.

Zander, A. (1980). The origins and consequences of group goals. In L. Festinger (Ed.), *Retrospections on social psychology* (pp. 205–235). New York: Oxford University Press.

Zauberman, G., & Lynch, J. G. Jr. (2005). Resource slack and propensity to discount delayed investments of time versus money. *Journal of Experimental Psychology: General, 134,* 23–37.

Zhang, Y., Fishbach, A., & Dhar, R. (2007). When thinking beats doing: The role of optimistic expectations in goal-based choice. *Journal of Consumer Research, 34,* 567–578.

EUROPEAN REVIEW OF SOCIAL PSYCHOLOGY
2009, 20, 345–381

Unravelling the motivational yarn: A framework for understanding the instigation of implicitly motivated behaviour resulting from deprivation and positive affect

Martijn Veltkamp
University of Twente, Enschede, The Netherlands

Henk Aarts and Ruud Custers
Utrecht University, The Netherlands

Research suggests that the motivation to perform specific behaviours can originate in the unconscious. This implicit motivation can generally be traced to two basic sources: Deprivation of essential resources and positive affect attached to the specific behaviour. Yet, whereas previous research has increased our understanding of the emergence of implicit motivation, there is little theoretical analysis and empirical research that addresses how these sources interact in producing motivation. This chapter presents a framework for the comprehension of implicitly motivated behaviour resulting from deprivation and positive affect. The framework consists of two essential components. First, it proposes that mental representations of behaviour direct and prepare individuals to engage in behaviour. Second, it suggests that a reward signal either emanating from deprivation or positive affect acts upon behaviour representations to produce motivated behaviour. We present several findings supporting the framework and discuss these findings in the context of non-conscious goal pursuit and needs.

Keywords: Deprivation; Motivation; Non-conscious goal pursuit; Needs; Positive affect.

Human beings often perform concrete actions in the pursuit of a specific goal. The most defining feature of such goal pursuit is that it not only requires the initiation of the proper actions, but also the motivation to see it

Correspondence should be addressed to Martijn Veltkamp, University of Twente, Department of Marketing Communication and Consumer Psychology, PO Box 217, 7500AE Enschede, the Netherlands. E-mail: m.veltkamp@utwente.nl

The preparation of this paper was supported by the Netherlands Organization for Scientific Research (VENI-VIDI-VICI scheme grants 451-06-014, 452-02-047, 453-06-002).

http://www.psypress.com/ersp   DOI: 10.1080/10463280903388665

through. In order to get a cup of coffee, one has to mentally select and prepare the necessary behaviour (walking to the machine), but the successful performance of that behaviour also requires that the effort it takes (walking the distance to the machine, taking a detour because of construction, finding another machine that *does* work) is matched by a motivation for the behaviour. In theories and models of goal-directed behaviour it is often assumed that whether one becomes motivated to perform a behaviour depends on conscious reflections and formed intentions (e.g., self-efficacy theory, Bandura, 1986; self-determination theory, Deci & Ryan, 1985; theory of reasoned action, Fishbein & Ajzen, 1975; goal-setting theory, Locke & Latham, 1990). However, recent research has revealed that motivated behaviour can also arise outside conscious awareness. Specifically, work on non-conscious goal pursuit (for overviews, see e.g., Custers & Aarts, 2005a; Dijksterhuis, Chartrand, & Aarts, 2007) shows that when a particular behaviour is desired (i.e., a behavioural goal; Fishbach & Ferguson, 2007; Gollwitzer & Moskowitz, 1996), merely rendering the mental representation of that behaviour accessible produces motivated behaviour without people necessarily being aware of this motivation and without them consciously forming an intention.

The observation that many motivated behaviours may develop non-consciously rather than originate from conscious intentions, raises the question of what motivates people to execute these behaviours. Theories that regard the motivation to attain a specific behaviour as originating from conscious reflection especially emphasise the role of expectancy and value (e.g., Ajzen, 1985; Atkinson, 1964; Bandura, 1986; Gollwitzer, 1990; Locke & Latham, 1990). For example, people's motivation for a behaviour increases with the expectancy of being able to successfully perform it (Ajzen, 1985; Bandura, 1986). Also, value-related factors such as attitudes (how would you feel about performing a behaviour) and social norms (how would others feel about you performing a behaviour) are thought to be taken into account when people form intentions that are assumed to subsequently motivate behaviour (Fishbein & Ajzen, 1975). However, because in these theories the factors that influence people's motivation to engage in a particular behaviour have to be combined into an intention by conscious deliberation, they do not explain how behaviour is motivated in the absence of such conscious processes. In the present chapter we will therefore focus on the sources of motivation that are able to instigate motivation for a specific behaviour outside conscious awareness.

Research addressing the issue of which sources may implicitly motivate behaviour suggests that positive affect is such a motivational source. Positive value or affect was already considered to be a vital input in the process of forming intentions (e.g., Fishbein & Ajzen, 1975; Locke & Latham, 1990), but there is no compelling reason to assume that positive affect can only motivate behaviour through such a conscious route. Indeed, recent work suggests that implicit affective processes are essential in decision making and goal pursuit (Bechara, Damasio, & Damasio, 2000; Ferguson & Bargh, 2004; Phelps, 2005; Winkielman & Berridge, 2004). Building on these insights, it has been proposed that priming can non-consciously motivate behaviour due to the positive affect that is mentally associated with behaviour representations (Aarts, Custers, & Veltkamp, 2008b; Custers & Aarts, 2005a), with affect being conceptualised as the valence assigned to an entity (Fazio, Sanbonmatsu, Powell, & Kardes, 1986; Zajonc, 1980) and not a feeling state or emotion that people experience (Isen & Diamond, 1989; Russell, 2003). For example, various positive experiences with partying may create an association between partying and positive affect. Consequently, rendering the behaviour representation of partying accessible could result in a motivation to party outside conscious awareness, because the positive affect associated with the behaviour (partying) signals that it is something that is desired.

Another source that has been shown to be a strong motivator, and that may be able to motivate behaviour without the need for conscious interventions, is deprivation of resources that are needed by people. Deprivation of crucial resources (e.g., fluid, food, or social contact) has long been considered an important motivator (e.g., Maslow, 1943; McDougall, 1908; Murray, 1938) and explains why the motivation for many behaviours fluctuates over time (e.g., one may be motivated to sleep when tired, but not after waking up), which is something that would not be expected from rather stable associations of behaviour representations with positive affect. Supporting the proposition that deprivation can motivate behaviour non-consciously, recent studies have shown that the effects of subliminal priming on motivation are conditional on the level of deprivation (e.g., Bermeitinger et al., 2009; Karremans, Stroebe, & Claus, 2006; Strahan, Spencer, & Zanna, 2002; Veltkamp, Aarts, & Custers, 2008a).

Although the observation that positive affect and deprivation can motivate behaviour may sound obvious, little work has systematically analysed how these sources can exactly result in implicit motivation. Also, it seems to be a complicated enterprise to grasp how the two sources of motivation are related and how they interact in motivating behaviour. Previous work on this matter mainly has examined both sources separately. Accordingly, the question of how these two sources interact in motivating concrete behaviour has hitherto received only little theoretical analysis and empirical attention.

The present chapter aims to fill this gap by presenting a framework that helps to comprehend and examine non-conscious motivation of human behaviour (see Figure 1). This framework consists of two essential components. First, it proposes that mental representations of behaviour

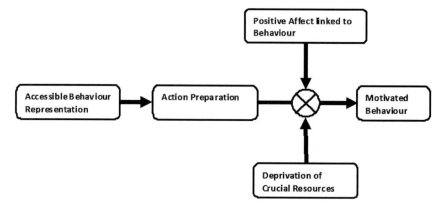

Figure 1. A framework of implicitly motivated behaviour. An accessible behaviour representation prepares action and results in overt motivated behaviour depending on deprivation or positive affect attached to the behaviour representation.

direct and prepare behaviour. However, whether the mental preparation of the behaviour results in overt motivational behaviour (i.e., results in allocating resources and spending effort to perform the behaviour) is thought to depend on motivational factors. That is, the framework suggests that deprivation of crucial resources and positive affect interact with the accessibility of these representations to bring about the actual motivation to engage in the behaviour. In particular, the framework puts forward that motivated behaviour requires the mental representation of that behaviour to be accessible, and that the rewarding value of the behaviour is modulated by either positive affect attached to the behaviour representation or deprivation. This way, people may become motivated to engage in a specific behaviour without being aware of the actual motivational sources behind that behaviour.

   To present and substantiate this framework in more detail we will discuss various findings—mainly presenting work from our own lab. We will elaborate on the role of mental representations in motivated behaviour and then turn to the role of deprivation to find out how deprivation may affect the motivational properties of these representations. Furthermore, whereas the role of positive affect as an implicit motivator of behaviour has been discussed in an earlier review (Custers & Aarts, 2005a), we will also provide an update of the research that has been conducted in the last 5 years on this issue for the sake of completeness and understanding. Finally, we will examine how deprivation and positive affect associated with a behaviour representation may work together to motivate behaviour, and discuss implications of this framework for the literature on motivation.

Before we move on, however, we want to be clear about how we conceptualise motivation. In line with other research that uses a process approach to study the intensity and persistence of behaviour (cf. Brehm & Self, 1989; Geen, 1995; Young, 1961), we consider motivation as the amount of energy a person mobilises to invest effort in the pursuit of a behaviour. Motivated behaviour can be discerned from non-motivated behaviour in a number of ways. For instance: it is more persistent over time, the pursuit of the behaviour continues in the face of obstacles, and the behaviour is preferred over attractive alternatives (Bargh, Gollwitzer, Lee Chai, Barndollar, & Trotschel, 2001). Motivation can be absent or range from low to high (i.e., the *motivational strength* can differ). It is important to note that for the present purposes we are mainly interested in sources that non-consciously *create* motivation (i.e., from absence to presence) and will therefore not discuss factors that may increase or decrease the motivational strength for behaviour that is already motivated (e.g., expectancies, regulatory fit; Higgins, 2000; Oettingen, 2000) or that may increase the likelihood that the motivated behaviour will actually be performed (e.g., implementation intentions; Gollwitzer, 1993).

THE ROLE OF BEHAVIOUR REPRESENTATIONS IN MOTIVATED BEHAVIOUR

To understand how people become motivated to perform specific behaviours without awareness of the origin of this motivation, it is important to first discuss how people can perform behaviours without conscious intent at all. Answers to this question date back to the nineteenth century, when the principle of ideomotor action was proposed. This principle holds that behaviours are mentally represented and that activating a "... [mental] representation of a movement awakens in some degree the actual movement which is its object" (James, 1890, p. 526; cf. Carpenter, 1874). Supporting this view, modern scientific accounts regard behaviour representations that are available in our repertoire as embedded in a connective network that encompasses perception, cognition, but also action (Prinz & Barsalou, 2000). Thus, perceiving words referring to a behaviour (such as painting) are expected to activate the semantic knowledge about that action, but also representations of objects or tools associated with the behaviour (e.g., Marsh, Hicks, & Bink, 1998; Tucker & Ellis, 1998), and of the movements required to perform the behaviour. Because activating behaviour representations also activates the corresponding motor programs in the pre-motor cortex (Glenberg & Kaschak, 2002; Pulvermüller, 2005; Zwaan & Taylor, 2006), subliminally priming a behaviour representation will automatically prepare this behaviour and increase the likelihood of its execution (e.g., Chartrand & Bargh, 1999; Greenwald, 1970; Prinz, 1997).

Although activating behaviour representations prepares the execution of those behaviours outside conscious awareness, an additional signal may be necessary to instigate actual motivation to perform the behaviour. That is, previous work on non-conscious goal pursuit suggests that for an activated behaviour representation to result in motivated behaviour, the behaviour has to be mentally represented as a desirable state (i.e., a goal; Fishbach & Ferguson, 2007; Gollwitzer & Moskowitz, 1996). Thus, activating a behaviour representation is thought to prepare the execution of the behaviour, but to only motivate behaviour if the behaviour is desirable (i.e., has motivational value to the organism, cf. Higgins, 2006).

In a recent attempt to experimentally differentiate between action preparation and motivation, Aarts, Custers, and Marien (2008a) compared the effects of priming the behaviour representation of exertion with those of attaching this representation subliminally to positively valenced stimuli. Specifically, the representation of exertion was primed by subliminally presented words such as *exert* or *vigorous*. Shortly (100 ms) after this prime either neutral (priming condition) or positive information (words such as *pleasant*; positive affect condition) appeared, consciously visible to participants. If positive affective information directly follows the primes that activate the behaviour representation, it is thought to be linked to this representation and to act as a reward signal indicating that performing the behaviour is desirable. In a control condition, the representation of exertion was not primed. Participants then allegedly had to test a new research instrument. They squeezed a handgrip after the word *squeeze* appeared on the computer screen and the force with which they squeezed was measured. In line with expectations, results showed that mere priming causes participants to (covertly) prepare the execution of the behaviour. That is, there was a faster development of force compared to the control condition. However, this force rapidly decreased again over time, indicating that the behaviour was not motivated (see Figure 2). Attaching positive affect to the representation of exertion, however, not only led to preparation, but also to motivation of the behaviour. This was demonstrated by an increased physical *persistence* in executing the behaviour (see Figure 2). Together, these results demonstrated that a behaviour representation has to be represented as rewarding to cause motivated behaviour.

By now, research has revealed several ways in which representations of behaviours that are already represented as desired can become activated and induce motivation without conscious intervention. The first and most commonly used way is through exposure to words that are semantically related to the representation itself (e.g., words such as "win", "strive", and "achieve" prime the representation of "achievement", see Bargh et al.,

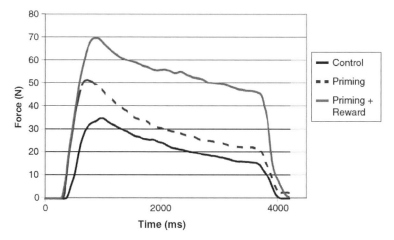

Figure 2. Development of force on the handgrip as a function of the experimental manipulations (adapted from Aarts et al., 2008b).

2001). However, recently it has been shown that goal representations can also be primed if one observes another person perform a specific behaviour that implies a given goal (e.g., Aarts, Gollwitzer, & Hassin, 2004; Dik & Aarts, 2007; Hassin, Aarts, & Ferguson, 2005; Loersch, Aarts, Payne, & Jefferis, 2008). Furthermore, thinking about a significant other (e.g., Fitzsimons & Bargh, 2003; Shah, 2003), smelling a particular scent (e.g., scent of cleaning fluid; Holland, Hendriks, & Aarts, 2005; Holland, Veling, & Aarts, 2008), and perceiving a member of a stereotyped group (e.g., nurses; see Aarts et al., 2005) that is associated with a specific goal (e.g., helping) are capable of priming a goal in the person's mind. Thus, in daily life there are many internal and external triggers (such as one's thoughts, or a movie on television) that can activate mental representations of behavioural goals and hence increase the motivation for that behaviour without conscious intervention.

Apart from examining the environmental cues that prime desirable behaviour representations and potentially induce non-conscious motivated behaviour, it is also important to understand how the enhanced accessibility of these representations acts on our mental and behavioural system in the absence of conscious awareness. The answer may already have been indicated by Kurt Lewin about 70 years ago: he stated that "a strongly accented goal so transforms the situation that practically all objects acquire a reference to this goal" (Lewin, 1935, p. 102). Indeed, the motivation to perform a behaviour seems to tune the mental system towards engaging in that behaviour. Research showed that (subliminal) priming of desirable behaviour representations (e.g., earning money) biases attention to objects (e.g., a wallet or coin) associated with the behaviour (e.g., Aarts, Dijksterhuis, & de Vries, 2001; Ferguson & Bargh, 2004), increases the likelihood that objects and tasks are seen as instrumental in attaining the opportunity to engage the behaviour (e.g., Balcetis & Dunning, 2006; Kay & Ross, 2003), and modulates conscious experiences of being motivated to perform it (e.g., Custers & Aarts, 2005b; Fitzsimons & Bargh, 2003; Veltkamp et al., 2008a). Thus, the motivation to perform a specific behaviour seems to bring the mental system in a state of readiness for goal pursuit, which facilitates goal attainment.

Whereas priming the representation of a behavioural goal has been shown to tune higher cognitive processes in the service of performing goal-directed behaviour, such priming effects may even occur on a more fundamental level. Specifically, a person's motivation to engage in a behaviour or to attain a goal has been proposed to affect basic perceptual processes. Perception has been conceptualised as a tool in the service of action. Therefore objects instrumental in performing an action are expected to be spontaneously perceived as being bigger (Bruner, 1957). Accordingly, several studies have provided evidence for this functional size perception account by showing that the perceived size of objects (e.g., coins) is positively related to their value (for an overview, see e.g., Bruner & Postman, 1949). Although intriguing and groundbreaking, the early studies reporting these findings were heavily criticised because of poor methodology and potential confounds between objective value and size (Eiser & Stroebe, 1972; Tajfel, 1957, 1959). However, recent neuroscientific findings do suggest that top-down processes that operate in the service of motivation affect perception in early visual processing areas (e.g., Bundesen, Habekost, & Kyllingsbaek, 2005; Desimone & Duncan, 1995; Serences & Yantis, 2006). This indicates that motivational states can modulate basic perceptual processes that are assumed to be outside the reach of conscious control.

In sum, representations of behaviour are crucial in preparing and motivating behaviour. Such representations can be triggered by a variety of cues. Once activated, these representations are capable of modulating low-level perception processes as well as higher cognitive processes that facilitate the performance of the behaviour and the attainment of goals. An important question emanating from this line of thought is how the human mental system is able to determine when a behaviour is desirable to attain and when not, in the absence of conscious awareness (see e.g., Aarts et al., 2008b; Bargh, 2006; Custers & Aarts, 2005a). It is proposed here that when a mental representation of a behaviour is activated, deprivation and positive affect motivate the execution of the respective behaviour by providing a reward signal that indicates that engaging in the behaviour is desirable.

FROM DEPRIVATION OF CRUCIAL RESOURCES TO MOTIVATED BEHAVIOUR

Deprivation of crucial resources is often considered an important motivational source for behaviour (e.g., Fiske, 2004; Mook, 1996; Murray, 1938; Pittman & Zeigler, 2007). Deprivation is an especially powerful motivator because some resources are essential to the well-being and optimal functioning of the organism. Failure to replenish deprived resources like fluid or food may eventually result in illness or even death. Indeed, conditions of extreme deprivation have been found to result in obsessive thoughts and fantasising about the lacking resources (e.g., Read, 1996; Wolf, 1958). Furthermore, deprivation may be a good candidate to motivate behaviour outside awareness, as it is a biologically based source of motivation, present in both humans and other animals. An important question, however, is how deprivation increases the motivation for behaviours that reduce deprivation.

By far the most influential theory that explains how deprivation results in motivated behaviour is that of homeostasis. Homeostasis refers to the process by which organisms keep the amount of essential resources at a fixed level under changing conditions (Cannon, 1932; see also Cooper, 2008). In order to maintain a fixed amount of resources, deprivation produces a compensatory increase in motivation for behaviours functional in replenishing the resources in question, which eventually restores the balance. Although the concept of homeostasis was originally used to explain how bodily states of deprivation (food, fluid, oxygen) affect behaviour, it was adopted in theorising on psychological needs (Murray, 1938). In recent definitions of needs, the idea that motivated behaviour is caused by a state of deprivation is still a central assumption (e.g., Baumeister & Leary, 1995; Deci & Ryan, 2000; Fiske, 2004), but especially in psychology needs have also been defined and operationalised differently. For example, the concepts of goals (Grouzet et al., 2005; Maslow, 1970), wants (Pittman & Zeigler, 2007), and desires (Maslow, 1970; Murray, 1938; Reiss, 2004) have all been used as synonyms for needs, although none of those concepts is directly related to deprivation. Furthermore, to test whether people have certain needs, researchers do not often measure the state of deprivation but instead ask individuals how much they need a resource (e.g., Aarts et al., 2004), how important certain events are for them (e.g., Reiss & Havercamp, 1998) or how satisfying it is to perform certain actions (e.g., Sheldon, Elliot, Kim, & Kasser, 2001). These inconsistencies make it rather unclear whether the concept of needs refers to resources regulated through homeostasis or something else altogether.

There seems to be consensus that the need to belong, referring to people's need for non-aversive interactions within already existing interpersonal relations, motivates behaviour according to the homeostatic principle (see e.g., Baumeister & Leary, 1995; Fiske, 2004; cf. the work on social contact and deprivation in the context of attachment, Bowlby, 1980; Harlow, 1958). That is, a deprivation of such interactions will increase people's motivation for such interactions. However, there is disagreement about other social needs. For many social needs (e.g., need for achievement, autonomy, closure, cognition, competence, control, and self-enhancement) it is unclear whether they motivate behaviour through deprivation or not. Such needs are supposed to differ in strength between individuals, in that some people do and others do not have a specific need (or have it to a lesser degree; see e.g., Pittman & Zeigler, 2007; Sheldon et al., 2001). For such needs, then, it is both tenable to propose that they depend on deprivation as well as that they depend on positive affect: deprivation may motivate behaviour for such needs depending on how important or desirable a resource is to an individual (McClelland, 1951; Reiss, 2004), or individual differences in needs such as a need for achievement may reflect differences in how desirable or positive the act of achieving is for an individual (see e.g., Senko, Durik, & Harackiewicz, 2008; Thompson & Schlehofer, 2008). However, as our present purpose is to understand how deprivation results in motivation, especially in a non-conscious fashion, we will confine our analysis to resources for which it is clear that they are crucial for one's well-being (such as fluid, food, or social contact).

Whereas the concept of needs is rather unclear and ambiguous in a host of research programmes, studies that conceptualised needs as deprivation of crucial resources (in line with the homeostatic principle) have been quite informative about the effects of deprivation on motivation. Specifically, by now, several studies have shown that increases in, for example, fluid or food deprivation result in increased attention for objects that are instrumental in reducing deprivation (e.g., Jones, Bruce, Livingstone, & Reed, 2006; Mogg, Bradley, Hyare, & Lee, 1998), approach reactions towards instrumental objects (e.g., Raynor & Epstein, 2003; Seibt, Häfner, & Deutsch, 2007), and increased consumption of resources such as food or fluid (see e.g., Fitzsimons, 1972; Le Magnen, 1985).

The research on homeostatic behaviour regulation referred to above suggests that deprivation directly leads to motivated behaviour. However, although a direct link between deprivation and behaviour may fit well with the behaviourists' approach towards stimulus–response habits (e.g., Watson, 1925), such a homeostatic model may be too rigid and simplistic to explain all circumstances that can induce deprivation-motivated behaviours in both animals and humans (e.g., Berridge, 2004; Pinel, Assanand, & Lehman, 2000). Rather, motivated behaviour seems to be based on the acquisition of knowledge about a link between a deprivation-reducing behaviour (e.g., drinking) and deprivation (e.g., of fluid).

Importantly, assuming that such knowledge usually derives from learning processes under conditions of deprivation, this suggests that deprivation motivates behaviour via the mental representations of that behaviour.

The central role of learning processes in the link between deprivation and motivated behaviour has a well-established theoretical and empirical tradition in psychological science. Early psychological theories suggested that an organism has to learn through reinforcement that certain responses are functional in reducing deprivation while other responses are not (e.g., Hull, 1931). For instance, animal research showed that when infant rats are only allowed to reduce fluid deprivation by means of eating lettuce (and hence never *drink* to reduce deprivation) this results in distorted drinking behaviour when given access to water later in life (Milgram, 1979; Milgram, Krames, & Thompson, 1974). Such findings support the idea that the link between fluid deprivation and the basic act of drinking as a deprivation-reducing behaviour has to be learnt.

According to incentive theory (Bindra, 1974; Bolles, 1972; Toates, 1986), animals as well as humans do not merely learn to associate deprivation (e.g., of fluid) with a particular behaviour (e.g., drinking), but rather that performing a specific behaviour is rewarding given that there is a state of deprivation. Thus, one may originally learn through trial-and-error that drinking water, for example, is only rewarding when one is deprived of fluids. Through reinforcement, then, the link between the rewarding properties of the specific behaviour under conditions of deprivation will eventually be stored in memory. In other words, what incentive theory suggests is that deprivation increases the motivation for deprivation-reducing behaviours by modulating the rewarding properties of the mental representations of these behaviours, which signal that the behaviour is worth pursuing. Supporting this idea, research has shown that the reward value of objects instrumental in reducing deprivation increases with increasing deprivation (e.g., Cabanac, 1979; Ferguson & Bargh, 2004; Seibt et al., 2007) and diminishes again when deprivation decreases (Berridge, 2004; Cabanac, 1979; Gottfried, O'Doherty, & Dolan, 2003).

The notion that deprivation acts on, and modulates, the rewarding value of the representation of a deprivation-reducing behaviour suggests that this representation has to be mentally accessible to influence overt motivated behaviour. However, there is actually little empirical work testing this idea. In fact, most studies on deprivation seem to support a direct link between deprivation and motivated behaviour (e.g., Drobes et al., 2001; McClelland & Atkinson, 1948; Mogg et al., 1998; Raynor & Epstein, 2003). It is important to note, however, that in studies suggesting a direct link participants are consciously aware of their state of deprivation, either because they are instructed to abstain from for example eating or drinking (e.g., Drobes et al., 2001; McClelland & Atkinson, 1948), or because they are asked questions about deprivation (e.g., Drobes & Tiffany, 1997; Raynor & Epstein, 2003). Thus, the behaviour of interest is rendered accessible to all participants, which confounds deprivation with accessibility of the representation of related deprivation-reducing behaviours.

In one of the few studies in which deprivation and accessibility were manipulated orthogonally, Strahan and colleagues (2002) obtained an interaction effect between subliminal priming of the representation of drinking and fluid deprivation on the amount of drinking: Deprived participants drank more during a taste test when primed with the concept of drinking, whereas non-deprived participants were not influenced by the primes. These priming effects emerged even though the representation of the behaviour was already rendered accessible by explicitly asking participants several times about their state of deprivation before the dependent variable was assessed. Whereas conscious and non-conscious priming effects in motivated behaviour have been demonstrated to occur independently (e.g., Bargh et al., 2001), participants' opportunity to explicitly reflect on their state of fluid deprivation before assessing drinking behaviour provides a challenge as to the meaning of the subliminal priming effects. In another recent study (Aarts et al., 2004), the interaction between deprivation (of income) and accessibility of a behaviour representation (earning money) was investigated without making any reference to the behaviour or the state of deprivation before the assessment of the dependent variable. Although the results of this study showed a similar interaction between deprivation and priming to the Strahan et al. (2002) study, deprivation was operationalised as the extent to which participants felt that they needed money, which could also be tapping into how positive they perceived the act of gaining money to be. Therefore, the findings may either represent an instance of deprivation-motivated behaviour or of positive affect-motivated behaviour.

To test the effects of accessibility of behaviour representations on the relation between deprivation and motivation, we (Veltkamp, Aarts, & Custers; 2008a, 2008b) therefore focused on a resource that is obviously regulated through deprivation: fluid. Furthermore, we made sure that the mental representation of drinking was not activated by anything other than a priming procedure in which the level of accessibility was unobtrusively manipulated. In one study (Veltkamp et al., 2008a, Study 2), students participated either before or after lunchtime. Pilot work had shown that people usually drink during lunch and are almost twice as deprived of fluids before than after their lunch (cf. Hulshof et al., 2004). Thus, by testing only before or after lunch we were able to test participants under different levels of fluid deprivation, without participants being aware of this. In the first stage of the experiment participants engaged in a priming task where the concept of drinking was rendered accessible for half of the participants by subliminally priming the words *thirst* and *drinking* (each word 20 times).

Finally, participants engaged in a taste test where they had to taste and evaluate soda, and their consumption (in grams) was measured as a dependent variable. It was found that relatively highly deprived individuals (participation before lunch) consumed more soda, but only if the mental representation of drinking had been primed before (see Figure 3).

We also examined the interplay of deprivation and accessibility on basic perception (Veltkamp et al., 2008b, Study 1). As mentioned earlier, there is suggestive, but not conclusive evidence that the motivation for a specific behaviour can spontaneously increase the perceived size of objects that are instrumental in performing the behaviour (e.g., Bruner & Goodman, 1947; Bundesen et al., 2005). Thus, by taking the functional size perception idea into the lab, we tested whether fluid deprivation and behaviour accessibility affected the perceived size of a glass of water. In this experiment participants first engaged in a task where the representation of drinking was subliminally primed. Subsequently they performed a size estimation task, where they had to estimate the size of a glass of water as it was presented on the computer screen. Finally, participants indicated their level of deprivation by indicating how long ago they last consumed fluids ($M = 2.1$ hours). To prevent the representation of drinking from becoming accessible by anything other than the priming procedure, participants indicated their deprivation level at the end of the experiment and no reference to the objects was made until they appeared on the screen and their size had to be estimated. Results showed that the glass was only perceived to be bigger for participants who were relatively deprived and for whom the representation of drinking was mentally accessible (see Figure 4), indicating that those participants were

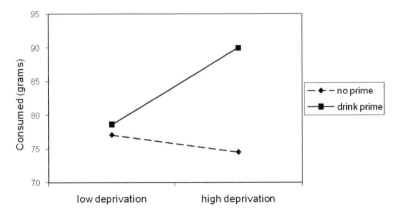

Figure 3. Quantity of drinking (in grams) as a function of deprivation and accessibility (adapted from Veltkamp et al., 2008a, Study 2).

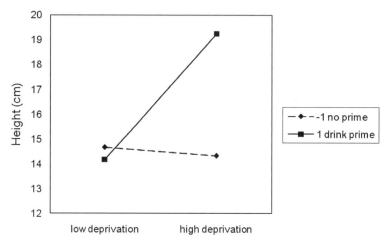

Figure 4. Perceived size of glass as a function of deprivation and accessibility (adapted from Veltkamp et al., 2008b, Study 1).

motivated to reduce their deprivation and ready to do so on a basic perceptual level.

Together these studies show that, when deprived (of, e.g., fluid or food), one will not become motivated to drink or eat until the representation of the drinking or eating behaviour itself has been primed by cues that have become associated with those behaviours (e.g., perceiving a McDonalds sign, a clock indicating lunchtime, or thinking about that plate you broke could all activate the mental representation of eating). Note, however, that the studies discussed above mainly focus on mild rather than severe deprivation. Under conditions of severe deprivation, bodily sensations themselves may activate the corresponding behaviour representation. Specifically, one may start to consciously experience a dry mouth when fluid-deprived and an empty stomach when food-deprived (Mook, 1996; Rolls et al., 1980), which renders the relevant behaviour representations accessible and thus motivates behaviour in the absence of further primes.

To recapitulate, deprivation motivates deprivation-reducing behaviour by modulating the rewarding properties of the mental representation of that behaviour. Specifically, people learn throughout life that specific behaviours are rewarding to perform given a state of deprivation. As a result, being in a deprived state will eventually automatically alter the rewarding properties of behaviours and objects that are instrumental in reducing the deprivation (e.g., Berridge, 2001; Cabanac, 1979; Ferguson & Bargh, 2004; Seibt et al., 2007). However, the actual emergence of deprivation-motivated behaviour requires the mental representation of the behaviour to be mentally accessible, whether we are aware of it or not (Veltkamp et al., 2008a, 2008b).

MOTIVATED BEHAVIOUR IN THE ABSENCE OF DEPRIVATION: THE CASE OF POSITIVE AFFECT

So far, we have examined the role of deprivation in motivating people to engage in behaviours to reduce the deprivation. However, there are also behaviours in an individual's repertoire that are perceived to be positive and, as such, can motivate the person to engage in them. For example, one may go for a stroll for no other reason than for the joy of it, or one may want to drink a soda because one simply likes it. In such cases the motivation to engage in a specific behaviour does not seem to be contingent on a state of deprivation, but instead is driven by the fact that the behaviour is positive in itself. Thus, apart from deprivation, positive affect can be considered another source of motivation. This affective-motivational signal can take different forms and arise from many events. For example, one may anticipate the enjoyment of going out with friends; develop a rapid appetite for a Sushi-King meal when one learns that this meal is ordered by a good friend; or become more eager to earn some additional cash when one observes someone else smiling upon making money by operating a slot machine. More generally, the motivation to engage in specific behaviours (e.g., socialising, eating sushi, earning money) can increase as a result of a link between the representation of the behaviour and positive affect.

The idea that positive affect is another important source of motivation to engage in behaviour is supported by an abundance of research in several areas. For example, in the literature on persuasion (for overviews, see e.g., Chen & Chaiken, 1999; Petty, Wegener, & Fabrigar, 1997) it has been shown that creating more positive attitudes towards specific behaviours can increase the motivation (or intention) for these behaviours (e.g., showing celebrities driving environmentally friendly cars may increase the willingness to buy such cars). The operation of such an attitude–behaviour link can occur quite spontaneously (e.g., Wilson, Lindsay, & Schooler, 2000), and can take place even in the absence of deprivation (e.g., Shimp, Stuart, & Engle, 1991). In a related vein, research on operant conditioning showed that the motivation to engage in behaviour can increase if that behaviour has been followed by positive feedback in the past (e.g., a child consistently praised when riding a bike may become more motivated to go cycling; see e.g., Krosnick, Betz, Jussim, Lynn, & Stephens, 1992; Kuykendall & Keating, 1990). Furthermore, in the literature on self-determination it is explicitly stated that when all human needs are met, people will still be motivated to perform certain behaviours because they derive intrinsic motivation from performing these actions (Deci & Ryan, 1985, 2000; cf. Berlyne, 1960). Although this intrinsic motivation may be expressed in different ways (in terms of e.g., pleasure, joy, interest, curiosity, or challenge), the common theme is that the behaviour is associated with positive affect. Findings from different research areas, then, provide strong support for the idea that the positivity of a behaviour can result in motivated behaviour that is not contingent on deprivation states.

Taking into account that people are motivated to perform a given behaviour non-consciously when they represent that behaviour in terms of a desired state or goal (e.g., Custers & Aarts, 2005a; Dijksterhuis et al., 2007), it seems that the mental system can process information about the positivity of a behaviour on an implicit level. Such implicit processing of affective information is indeed consistent with research showing that affective processes can moderate decision making and behaviour very quickly and without reaching conscious awareness (e.g., Damasio, 1994; Dijksterhuis & Aarts, 2003; LeDoux, 1996).

Building on these findings, it has recently been proposed that motivated behaviour results from associations between behaviour representations and positive affect (Aarts et al., 2008a; Custers & Aarts, 2005b). Such associations are thought to act as a reward signal that can indicate— without conscious awareness—whether a behaviour is worth engaging in and pursuing or not. An association between a behaviour representation and positive affect can arise when a person performs the behaviour in close temporal proximity to the activation of positive affective information. Furthermore, apart from directly performing the behaviour, the representation of behaviour may also be linked to positive affect by mere co-activation (e.g., when the perception of others performing the behaviour is followed by a smile). In essence, any event that activates the representation of a specific behaviour and positive affect at (nearly) the same time should lead to the development of an association between the two (e.g., Aarts et al., 2008a; Custers & Aarts, 2005b) and act as a reward signal that is not conditional on a state of deprivation.

Preliminary evidence for this "positive affect as implicit motivator" perspective comes from research suggesting that so-called "pleasure-centres" in the brain (mainly targeting the nucleus accumbens) are involved in the mechanism that turns positive affect into a motivator (see e.g., Shizgal, 1999). For example, rats performing an arbitrary behaviour such as pressing a lever that is followed by positive affect become highly motivated to perform that behaviour (as the behaviour activates the pleasure-centre; Olds & Milner, 1954). The motivational strength of a behaviour under such positive affective circumstances is demonstrated by research showing that animals run uphill and leap over hurdles (Edmonds & Gallistel, 1974) and cross electrified grids (Olds, 1958) in order to engage in the behaviour associated with positive affect. Importantly, such effects occur even in the absence of physiological deprivation states such as thirst or hunger (Shizgal, 1997). This research demonstrates that positive affect can work as a reward signal that motivates behaviour.

Recent research suggests that such reward signals can also motivate behaviour outside awareness. In a study by Pessiglione and colleagues (2007) participants engaged in a task in which they could win money on successive trials by squeezing a handgrip. The amount of money at stake (a pound versus a penny) was subliminally primed during each trial. This prime affected the force of handgrip, along with skin conductance and activation in the ventral palladium, an area known to be devoted to emotional and motivational output of the limbic system. Building on these findings, Bijleveld, Custers, and Aarts (in press) recently tested the effects of subliminal reward cues on pupil dilation, which has been shown to be an accurate measure of resource investment and effort mobilisation (Ahern & Beatty, 1979; Kahneman, 1973). The authors argued that a high reward should result in more motivation and hence in more resource recruitment to obtain a reward, thereby increasing the pupil size. However, this enhanced pupil dilation effect as a result of recruiting more mental resources would show up only if obtaining the reward required considerable mental effort. To test this idea, during several trials participants could earn money (low vs high reward; 1 or 50 eurocents) by recalling random digits (easy vs difficult; three or five digits). Rewards were presented subliminally (17 ms) in half of the trials, and supraliminally (300 ms) in the remaining trials. As expected, regardless of whether the reward was presented subliminally or supraliminally, people recruited more resources (larger pupil size) in response to high reward cues, but only when the reward required considerable mental effort to obtain it (see Figure 5). This research suggests that people use reward

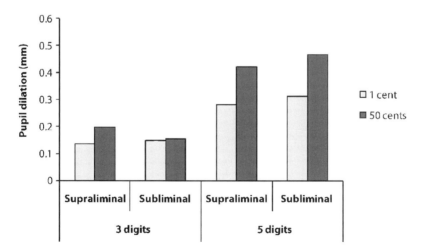

Figure 5. Maximum increase in pupil diameter as a function of reward, number of digits, and supraliminal versus subliminal coin presentation (adapted from Bijleveld et al., in press).

information in a strategic manner to recruit resources, without this information ever reaching conscious awareness.

Recently researchers have started to investigate how reward information attached to behaviour representations may motivate people to specifically engage in that behaviour. For example, in one study (Custers & Aarts, 2007) participants were either subliminally primed or not with words representing the behaviour of socialising. Next they performed a mouse-click task that, if sufficient time was left, was followed by a lottery in which they could win tickets for a popular student party. Thus working quickly on the task was instrumental in attaining the goal of socialising. Participants also took an implicit measure (EAST; De Houwer, 2003) that tapped their associative strength between socialising and positive affect. It was established that participants put more effort (were faster) into the instrumental (mouse-click) task when the behaviour representation of "socialising" was primed, and this effect was more pronounced for participants who more strongly associated the act of socialising with positive affect (see Figure 6). In a similar vein, Ferguson (2007) showed that priming the behaviour representation of "treating people equally" caused participants to vote against cutting Medicare (a federal programme that offers aid to specific minority groups) when they associated the concept of egalitarianism with positive affect. Obviously these studies adopted an individual difference approach towards the associative strength between behaviour and positive affect, and hence the findings are correlational in nature. However, they do show that priming effects on motivated behaviour are conditional on the positive valence of the behaviour.

If motivated behaviour can originate from positive affect associated with behaviour representations, then creating such links in a lab environment should also result in affect-motivated behaviour. This idea has recently been put to the test (Aarts et al., 2008a, 2008b; Custers & Aarts, 2005b; Holland, Wennekers, Bijlstra, Jongenelen, & van Knippenberg, 2009; Veltkamp et al.,

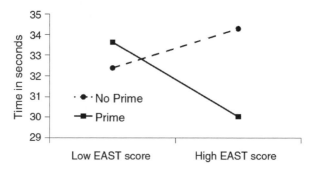

Figure 6. Time spent on mouse-click task as a function of valence (adapted from Custers & Aarts, 2007, Study 2).

2008b). These studies used an adaptation of an evaluative conditioning paradigm (De Houwer, Thomas, & Baeyens, 2001), enabling the researchers to co-activate behaviour representations with positive affective information.

For example, Aarts and colleagues (2008b) tested whether creating a link between a behaviour representation and positive affect outside awareness would motivate participants to engage in the behaviour, and hence perceive objects instrumental in performing the behaviour bigger in size (as would be predicted by the functional perception hypothesis; Bruner, 1957; see also Veltkamp et al., 2008b). In one study (Study 1) participants engaged in the conditioning task where the (for the research participants) originally neutral behaviour representation of doing puzzles was subliminally presented and immediately followed by consciously visible positively or neutrally valenced words. As an indication of motivation, participants then engaged in a size estimation task where they estimated the size of objects instrumental in performing the behaviour (e.g., a puzzle booklet). For half of the participants, a 3-minute delay was introduced prior to the size estimation task. The delay allowed the researchers to test whether the effects on size perception were motivational in nature, as motivational effects should remain constant or get stronger after delay, whereas memory or accessibility effects should weaken (e.g., Bargh et al., 2001; Chartrand, Huber, Shiv, & Tanner, 2008). Results showed that creating a link between the behaviour representation and positive affect increased the perceived size of puzzle objects, both immediately following the conditioning procedure and after a delay (see Figure 7). Thus these findings show that creating a link between behaviour representations and positive affect motivates people to engage in the behaviour.

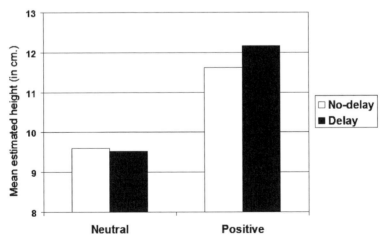

Figure 7. Perceived object size as a function of the experimental treatment (adapted from Aarts et al., 2008a, Study 1).

Whereas the findings discussed above support the positive affect as implicit motivator account, one may argue that linking positive affect to a behaviour representation renders the *evaluation* of that behaviour as more positive, thus reflecting an *evaluative* rather than a *motivational* process. If this line of reasoning is true, then linking negative affect to a behaviour representation should reduce the motivation to perform an originally neutral behaviour as a result of more negative evaluations. To address this issue, Custers and colleagues linked a neutral behaviour representation to positive, neutral, or negative affect. Participants were then asked to evaluate the behaviour. It was shown that conditioning rendered the positively conditioned behaviours more positive and the negatively conditioned behaviours more negative compared to neutrally conditioned behaviours (Custers & Aarts, 2005b, Study 2b). However, motivational measures such as the perceived size of objects instrumental in attaining a behaviour (Veltkamp et al., 2008b, Study 2) or self-reported motivation to perform a behaviour (Custers & Aarts, 2005b, Study 2c) showed an increased motivation for positive conditioning, but no difference between negative conditioning and neutral conditioning.

The observation that positive affect impinged on motivation while negative did not is in line with several models proposing that affect consists of two separate dimensions—a positive and a negative one—that independently contribute to motivation and behaviour in opposite directions (e.g., Cacioppo & Berntson 1999; Gray, 1987; Lang, 1995; Schneirla, 1959; Watson & Clark, 1992; Watt, 1998). Positive affect is associated with the preparation and motivation of action, whereas negative affect reduces the motivation and puts behaviour on hold. Consistent with this view, follow-up research showed that pairing negative affect to behavioural states dampens the motivation for pre-existing desirable behavioural states but not for behavioural states in which there is no motivation to engage to begin with (Aarts, Custers, & Holland, 2007; Veling & Aarts, 2009). Together, then, these findings suggest that positive affect, but not necessarily negative affect, creates the motivation to engage in behaviour outside conscious awareness.

It is important to note that behaviours capable of reducing deprivation (such as drinking) do not necessarily have rewarding value in the absence of deprivation (cf. Seibt et al., 2007). Hence, priming such behaviour representations does not increase the motivation to engage in the behaviour in the absence of deprivation (see Veltkamp et al., 2008a). However, based on the "positive affect as implicit motivator" research discussed above, this does not mean that creating a link between a deprivation-reducing behaviour and positive affect cannot motivate behaviour. That is, unobtrusively pairing the representation of drinking water with positive affect may increase the motivation to drink a glass of water in the absence of fluid deprivation. Whereas this idea can easily be tested (Veltkamp,

Custers, & Aarts, 2009), establishing such an effect raises the question of how deprivation and positive affect work together in motivating people to engage in a specific behaviour, such as drinking a glass of water. This is the issue that we will turn to now.

THE INTERPLAY BETWEEN DEPRIVATION AND POSITIVE AFFECT

Our framework and the studies reported so far suggest that the preparation and motivation of behaviour requires the mental representation of the behaviour to be active. Whether a behaviour representation that is rendered accessible results in actual motivation depends on deprivation or its association with positive affect. Thus, when deprivation is absent, people can still be motivated to engage in deprivation-reducing behaviour when the representation is attached to positive affect. An important issue that has been left untouched up to this point, however, is how the two sources of motivated behaviour work together. Do they have additive effects on motivation, in that the presence of both deprivation and positive affect results in stronger motivation than if only one of these sources is present? Or do they interact, such that the effects of one source of motivation depend on the absence or presence of the second one?

Recent research testing the effects of two different non-conscious inputs on motivation suggests that they may interact. Specifically, Aarts and van Honk (2009) compared the effects of a cognitive manipulation of motivation (linking behaviour representations with positive affect) with those of a hormonal manipulation: intake of testosterone. The hormone testosterone is thought to generate unconscious broad-spectrum motivations to act. That is, low levels of testosterone have been shown to result in apathy and lack of motivation in general (e.g., Tostain & Blanc, 2008), and increasing testosterone levels modulates the working of subcortical brain structures involved in unconscious aspects of motivated behaviour (e.g., Packard, Cornell, & Alexander, 1997). However, attaching positive affect to a behaviour representation differs, as it targets cortical and subcortical areas relevant for the non-conscious preparation and motivation for that *specific* behaviour.

To test the combined effects of testosterone and positive affect, healthy young female participants received testosterone or placebo treatment (Aarts & van Honk, 2009). Next, neutral behaviours were subliminally paired with positive or neutral affect in a conditioning paradigm and participants indicated how much they wanted to perform the primed activity (Custers & Aarts, 2005b). Results showed that attaching the behaviours to positive affect increased the motivation to perform them, but only in the placebo condition. In the testosterone condition the motivation was high for all behaviours, irrespective of the conditioning procedure (see Figure 8). The finding that testosterone and positive affect can, in the absence of a joint contribution, lead to similar motivational effects indicates that behaviour can be motivated by different sources that rely on the same motivation and reward processing system.

The idea of one underlying mechanism that turns behaviour representations into motivated behaviour suggests that if one source (e.g., deprivation) motivates behaviour, the second source (e.g., positive affect) may not add much to the motivational equation, as the presence of a single source already gives input or a signal that a behaviour is rewarding to perform and thus instigates motivated behaviour. In a sense, then, the organism might adaptively set a limit on its capacities when motivation is sufficient for an action to be performed, in order not to needlessly spoil its processing resources (Bishop, 2009). Thus, whereas deprivation may typically motivate behaviour by providing a rewarding signal to engage in the behaviour, positive affect will offer such a rewarding signal and motivate behaviour in the absence of deprivation.

Circumstantial evidence for this idea comes from animal research. For example, the amount of consumed fluid in non-deprived rats has been shown to be positively related to the strength of the rewarding property of the fluid (operationalised as the percentage of sucrose added to it), while overall fluid consumption is high when animals are deprived (Mook & Cseh, 1981; see Mook, 1996). In addition, research on preferential behaviour suggests that as food deprivation decreases and a state of satiation kicks in,

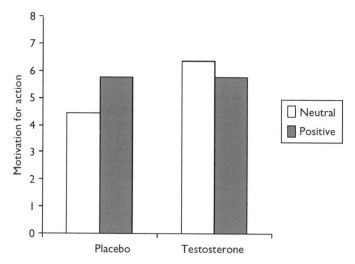

Figure 8. Motivation as a function of conditioning and the testosterone manipulation (adapted from Aarts & van Honk, 2009).

animals become more selective in the food they consume (Barbano & Cador, 2006; Rudski, Billington, & Levine, 1994). Assuming that preferences are based on affective processes, these studies suggest that deprivation and positive affect associated with behaviour can interact in their effects on the motivation to engage in behaviour.

In a recent set of studies we empirically examined the effects of deprivation and positive affect attached to behaviour representations more directly in a single research design (Veltkamp et al., 2009). Specifically, we tested how fluid deprivation and positive affect influenced the motivation to drink to reduce the deprivation. In a first study, fluid deprivation was manipulated by allowing half of the participants to drink water at the start of the experiment after they had consumed a set of dry biscuits in an alleged product-comparison task. Subsequently, the mental representation of drinking water was unobtrusively paired with either positive or neutral affective information in a computer task, using the same co-activation procedure as in earlier research (Aarts et al., 2008a, 2008b; Custers & Aarts, 2005b). Finally, participants engaged in another product-comparison test where they had to compare and drink from three differently shaped glasses filled with water. In actuality this test allowed us to unobtrusively measure the amount of consumed water as an indication of the motivation to drink. The results showed that deprivation and positive affect interacted, in that fluid deprivation increased the motivation to drink, but that pairing with positive affect motivated behaviour merely when deprivation was low or absent (see Figure 9).

This finding shows that the motivation to perform a behaviour can be caused by a state of deprivation but if such a deprivation is absent, motivated behaviour can result from an association between a behaviour and positive affect. These findings are consistent with earlier work proposing that the association between behaviour and positive affect creates a desired goal to engage in the behaviour (Aarts et al., 2008b; Custers & Aarts, 2005a). In other words, the association between drinking water and positive affect results in the specific goal of drinking water. As previous research suggests, however, the effects of fluid deprivation on the motivation to drink may be reduced by actions not typically associated with reducing fluid deprivation, yet capable of reducing the current state of deprivation (Milgram, 1979; Milgram et al., 1974). Accordingly, eating food with high fluid content may reduce the deprivation of fluid and the motivation to drink water as well. This very same act of eating should not reduce the motivation to drink arising from the established link between drinking and positive affect, as this positive affect-motivated source can encourage people to drink in the absence of deprivation. Indeed, it is known that people have a tendency to consume more than they need (Pinel et al., 2000; Rolls, Rolls, Rowe, & Sweeney, 1981), suggesting that, at least in the domain of drinking

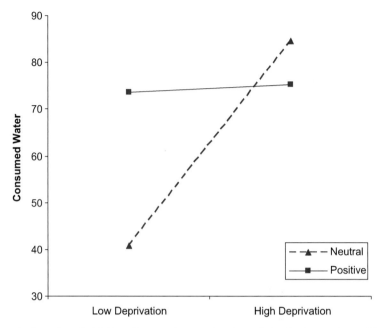

Figure 9. Quantity of drinking (in grams) as a function of deprivation and conditioning (adapted from Veltkamp et al., 2009, Study 1).

and eating, positive affect attached to behaviour can act as a motivator even when basic needs are satisfied and deprivation is absent.

To test this idea, we (Veltkamp et al., 2009, Study 2) asked participants to abstain from drinking fluid for 3 hours before participating in our experiment, thereby creating a relatively high level of fluid deprivation (for a similar procedure, see Ferguson & Bargh, 2004; Strahan et al., 2002). Next, drinking water was paired with positive or neutral affect. Accordingly, at this point participants may be motivated to drink because of either fluid deprivation or the non-conscious goal to drink water (due to its association with positive affect). The experiment then took a twist. Half of the participants were allowed to eat a certain amount of a food with a high fluid content—i.e., cucumber, which contains 96% water (Davidson, 1999)— whereas the other half were not. In the eating condition, then, participants were able to reduce their fluid deprivation through performing an action that is usually not considered to be instrumental in quenching thirst. Finally, participants were allowed to drink water ad libitum. It was found that eating cucumber reduced water intake when drinking was motivated only by deprivation, but cucumber consumption did not diminish water intake when drinking had been paired with positive affect (see Figure 10). Thus, the motivation to drink water ceases to exist without executing that specific

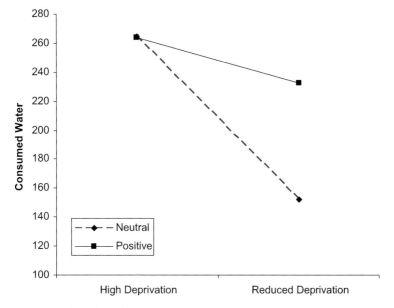

Figure 10. Quantity of drinking (in grams) as a function of deprivation-reduction and conditioning (adapted from Veltkamp et al., 2009, Study 2).

behaviour after fluid deprivation has been reduced by eating, but remains if there is link between drinking water and positive affect.

Taken together, then, these findings support the idea that the motivation to engage in a specific behaviour can emerge from two different sources (deprivation and positive affect), which modulate the reward value assigned to a behaviour. However, both motivational sources react differently to deprivation-reducing methods that do not refer to the behaviour at issue. That is, the motivation to drink may be reduced if fluid deprivation is resolved by eating. However, if the representation of drinking water is associated with positive affect, the representation may start to operate as a desired goal in itself, motivating us to engage in that specific behaviour even when deprivation is reduced by other means. Therefore deprivation and positive affect can lead to similar, but also to different, effects on motivated behaviour.

GENERAL DISCUSSION

In this chapter we have presented a framework for the comprehension and examination of non-consciously motivated human behaviour that arises from two basic sources: deprivation of crucial resources, and an association between behaviour representations and positive affect. Specifically, the framework holds that the accessibility of mental representations of behaviour is crucial in preparing the execution of behaviour. Importantly, the framework suggests that deprivation of crucial resources as part of a homeostatic principle modulates the reward value of the behaviour representation, and accordingly turns the preparation into actual motivation to engage in the behaviour. When deprivation is absent, however, an association of a behaviour representation with positive affect can act as a reward signal and thus motivate behaviour as well. We presented several findings that provided support for this framework of motivated behaviour. The present analysis thus clarifies the distinction between different sources of non-conscious motivation, by showing how deprivation and positive affect separately result in motivation for behaviour and how these two sources may interact in their effects on motivation.

In our framework a crucial role is allocated to the mental representations of behaviour. Activating behaviour representations prepares people to initiate the corresponding overt behaviour, even though these representations are activated outside awareness; i.e., through subliminal priming (e.g., Aarts et al., 2008a; Pulvermüller, 2005). In doing so, our framework takes into account the most proximal determinant of behaviour (e.g., Bargh, 1990), explaining non-conscious influences on behaviour such as the habitual activation of a behaviour in a familiar environment (Aarts & Dijksterhuis, 2000) or activation of normative behaviour in a particular social setting (Aarts & Dijksterhuis, 2003). Although a certain degree of motivation for the behaviour must exist to turn preparation into overt behaviour, the initial occurrence of those behaviours is thought to be driven by changes in accessibility, rather than desirability.

However, most contemporary models of motivated goal-directed behaviour do not explicitly explain the role of behaviour representations in determining people's motivation to engage in behaviour (e.g., Bandura, 1986; Deci & Ryan, 1985; Fishbein & Ajzen, 1975; Locke & Latham, 1990). Rather, these models mainly aim to specify the conditions that cause people to consciously assess the desirability of behaviours or to consciously set and adopt goals to engage in the behaviours. Focusing instead on mental representations of behaviour as the proximal determinant of motivated behaviour fits with recent developments in research on non-conscious processes in motivated behaviour, and as such may open new ways to understand and examine how deprivation and positive affect alter people's motivation to engage in behaviour. We will now briefly discuss how the framework may contribute to current research that examines the sources and processes of human motivated behaviour.

Sources of motivation in non-conscious goal pursuit

The idea that mere priming of behaviour representations influences motivated behaviour in the absence of awareness of the source of this influence is consistent with recent developments in research on non-conscious goal pursuit (for overviews, see Custers & Aarts, 2005a; Moskowitz, Li, & Kirk, 2004). Research in this area shows that (subliminally) priming a behaviour representation (e.g., of helping) can induce motivation for that behaviour outside conscious awareness, depending on whether that behaviour is represented as a desired state or not. The question of how people non-consciously "know" whether the behaviour is represented as a desired state, and hence worth engaging in, has led to intriguing speculation about the workings of the mind by introducing concepts such as automated will (Bargh et al., 2001), implicit volition (Moskowitz et al., 2004), or implicit intention (Wood, Quinn, & Kashy, 2002). However, such terms merely stretch the applicability of inherently conscious concepts to the unconscious level and do not explain how the unconscious can perform operations that until recently were assumed to require consciousness. The present framework takes a somewhat different stance on the matter. That is, the framework specifies two potential sources (deprivation and positive affect) that turn accessible representations of behaviour into a state of readiness for goal pursuit, and thus motivate people to engage in the behaviour in the absence of awareness of the sources of their motivation. As such, our framework offers insight into the boundary conditions of priming effects on motivated behaviour.

Furthermore, it is important to note that previous research on non-conscious goal pursuit suggests that priming a behaviour representation associated with positive affect may cause that representation to operate as a goal that people want to attain (Bargh & Huang, 2009; Custers & Aarts, 2005b; Fishbach & Ferguson, 2007). Conceptualising non-conscious goals in terms of an association between a behaviour representation and positive affect may have implications for the way people's motivation to engage in a behaviour ceases after they have been able to perform the behaviour. Specifically, one of the important characteristics of motivated goal-directed behaviour is that the cognitive processes supporting the goal remain active until that goal is attained (Aarts, 2007; Förster, Liberman, & Friedman, 2007; Goschke & Kuhl, 1993; Marsh et al., 1998). This suggests that the operation of deprivation-reducing behaviours (e.g., drinking water) associated with positive affect does not depend on deprivation under these circumstances, but rather should stop after that behaviour has been performed (e.g., Förster et al., 2007).

Deprivation and an association of behaviour representations with positive affect are important sources of non-conscious goal pursuit, but many behaviours that people perform are preceded by conscious reflection, so what is the role of the motivational sources in such situations? In fact, dual-process models in psychology (see Chaiken & Trope, 1999) focus exactly on how non-conscious processes versus conscious processes act on attitudes and motivation. Non-conscious and conscious processes in such models are expected to be able to operate at the same time, where non-conscious processes are often regarded to result in impulses (to perform the most desirable action), and where conscious processes allow other factors to be taken into account (e.g., social desirability of performing a behaviour, long-term goals) that may require a different path of action. However, several dual-process theories argue that implicit processes not only predict non-consciously motivated behaviour, but can also serve as input for conscious deliberation (e.g., Strack & Deutsch, 2004). Thus deprivation and positive affect may not only motivate behaviour non-consciously, but they may also indirectly motivate conscious goal pursuit, such as implied by recent models proposing a mediating role of construal (Kay & Ross, 2003) or an active self-concept (Wheeler, DeMarree, & Petty, 2007) in priming effects on motivated behaviour. The present framework may provide a valuable contribution to dual-process theories, then, in that it explains how on an implicit level two sources of motivation operate and work together to motivate behaviour outside conscious awareness.

The relation between deprivation, positive affect, and needs

The present chapter not only examined the crucial role of the accessibility of behaviour representations in preparing overt behaviour and the effects of deprivation and positive affect in motivating behaviour. It also sheds new light on how these two sources of motivation may interact in producing people's motivation to engage in a specific behaviour.

It is important to emphasise that most research on motivated behaviour tends to conceptualise the sources of motivated behaviour in terms of needs (e.g., Baumeister & Leary, 1995; Fiske, 2004; Maslow, 1943; McClelland, 1951; Murray, 1938; Sheldon et al., 2001). Although it is certainly a parsimonious strategy to use one concept for similar sources, the current framework suggests that it may be important to differentiate between deprivation and positive affect in understanding and examining the occurrence of motivated behaviour. Thus the motivation to engage in a specific behaviour that is thought to result from social needs (such as a need for achievement, affiliation, power, closure, cognition, or safety) can be explained in terms of being deprivation motivated (in which case motivation should depend on underlying states of deprivation; Deci & Ryan, 2000; McClelland, 1951) or positive affect motivated (in which case behaviours such as performing well on an anagram task or seeking power in a social situation are positive in itself; Kruglanski & Chun, 2008; Senko et al., 2008). Which of these two sources actually accounts for motivated behaviour may have important implications, as the effect of positive affect attached to behaviour representations on motivated behaviour seems to be dependent on the absence or presence of a state of deprivation (Veltkamp et al., 2009).

To further illustrate the importance of differentiating between deprivation and positive affect as non-conscious sources of motivation, consider for example a teenager who spends a fortune on visiting online chat-rooms. She may be motivated to do so either because she is deprived of social contact and has a need to belong (Baumeister & Leary, 1995), or because she enjoys visiting chat-rooms. In the first case, stimulating social contact (e.g., signing her up for soccer to interact with her peers) may reduce chat-room visits. However, this may not be true in the latter case. That is, our framework suggests that when a person is motivated to visit chat-rooms because that behaviour is associated with positive affect, offering the opportunity to engage in another deprivation(need to belong)-reducing behaviour (e.g., soccer) does not necessarily decrease the motivation to engage in visiting chat-rooms. However, the reverse may be true as well. Making chat-rooms less attractive may reduce chat-room visits but not the need for social contact, which may cause other detrimental behaviours to arise. In short, failing to correctly distinguish between deprivation and positive affect as sources of motivated behaviour may not only hamper theoretical research on motivation but may lead to bad parental decisions in daily life as well.

It should be noted that, although the present chapter examines the effects of deprivation and positive affect as motivational sources in general, the studies that directly tested the role of deprivation in our framework were limited to behaviours for which it was clear they could be motivated both by positive affect and deprivation; namely drinking behaviour. However, based on the assumption that the occurrence of many social behaviours relies on the activation of the representation of those behaviours, it seems likely that the proposed contribution of deprivation and positive affect also applies to a broader area of our behavioural repertoire. For example, if socially excluding members of a minority group as an act of discrimination can be motivated by deprivation of a positive self-image (Fein & Spencer, 1997), then the mental representation of that behaviour may be rewarding conditional on the state of deprivation. In theory, attaching this representation to positive affect would also motivate the behaviour in the absence of deprivation, which thus may explain people's motivation to discriminate minorities in terms of an interplay between positive affect associated with the behaviour and deprivation (Kunda & Spencer, 2003). In sum, we believe that the way deprivation motivates behaviour and interacts with positive affect depends on a general mechanism that should govern biological as well as social needs. However, testing these predictions of our framework in social settings would prove an interesting avenue for further research.

CONCLUDING REMARK

Kant once stated that "... we can never, even by the strictest examination, get completely behind the secret springs of action" (1785/2004, p. 17). Indeed, psychological research shows that people have troubles in determining the true causes of their behaviour (e.g., Nisbett & Wilson, 1977; Wegner, 2002). However, rendering it especially hard to assess the secret sources of action is the recent observation that the motivation for behaviour can develop outside people's conscious awareness (e.g., Dijksterhuis et al., 2007). In the present chapter we presented a framework that aimed to unravel the apparent motivational yarn that underlies such non-consciously motivated behaviour. Our approach allows us to differentiate between two basic sources of human motivation: deprivation of crucial resources and an association between behaviour representations and positive affect. We presented findings of several studies that provided support for the proposed role of deprivation and positive affect in motivating behaviour. By focusing on the operation of these two motivational sources and the way they interact in their effects on the motivation to perform behaviour, we hope the current framework may further our understanding of human motivation and will provide a good starting point for future research on this matter.

REFERENCES

Aarts, H. (2007). On the emergence of human goal pursuit: The non-conscious regulation and motivation of goals. *Social Psychology and Personality Compass, 1,* 183–201.

Aarts, H., Chartrand, T. L., Custers, R., Danner, U., Dik, G., Jefferis, V., et al. (2005). Social stereotypes and automatic goal pursuit. *Social Cognition, 23,* 464–489.

Aarts, H., Custers, R., & Holland, R. W. (2007). The non-conscious cessation of goal pursuit: When goals and negative affect are coactivated. *Journal of Personality and Social Psychology, 92,* 165–178.

Aarts, H., Custers, R., & Marien, H. (2008a). Preparing and motivating behavior outside of awareness. *Science, 319,* 1639.

Aarts, H., Custers, R., & Veltkamp, M. (2008b). Goal priming and the affective-motivational route to non-conscious goal pursuit. *Social Cognition, 26,* 497–519.

Aarts, H., & Dijksterhuis, A. (2000). Habits as knowledge structures: Automaticity in goal-directed behavior. *Journal of Personality and Social Psychology, 78,* 53–63.

Aarts, H., & Dijksterhuis, A. (2003). The silence of the library: Environment, situational norm, and social behavior. *Journal of Personality and Social Psychology, 84,* 18–28.

Aarts, H., Dijksterhuis, A., & de Vries, P. (2001). On the psychology of drinking: Being thirsty and perceptually ready. *British Journal of Psychology, 92,* 631–642.

Aarts, H., Gollwitzer, P. M., & Hassin, R. R. (2004). Goal contagion: Perceiving is for pursuing. *Journal of Personality and Social Psychology, 87,* 23–37.

Aarts, H., & Van Honk, J. (2009). Testosterone and unconscious positive priming increase human motivation separately. *NeuroReport, 20,* 1300–1303.

Ahern, S., & Beatty, J. (1979). Pupillary responses during information processing vary with Scholastic Aptitude Test scores. *Science, 205,* 1289–1292.

Ajzen, I. (1985). From intentions to actions: A theory of planned behaviour. In J. Kuhl & J. Beckmann (Eds.), *Action control: From cognition to behaviour* (pp. 11–37). Berlin: Springer.

Atkinson, J. W. (1964). *An introduction to motivation*. Oxford, UK: Van Nostrand.

Balcetis, E., & Dunning, D. (2006). See what you want to see: Motivational influences on visual perception. *Journal of Personality and Social Psychology, 91*, 612–625.

Bandura, A. (1986). *Social foundations of thought and action: A social cognitive theory.* Englewood Cliffs, NJ: Prentice-Hall.

Barbano, M. F., & Cador, M. (2006). Differential regulation of the consummatory, motivational and anticipatory aspects of feeding behavior by dopaminergic and opioidergic drugs. *Neuropsychopharmacology, 31*, 1371–1381.

Bargh, J. A. (1990). Auto-motives: Preconscious determinants of social interaction. In E. T. Higgins & R. M. Sorrentino (Eds.), *Handbook of motivation and cognition* (Vol. 2, pp. 93–130). New York: Guilford Press.

Bargh, J. A. (2006). What have we been priming all these years? On the development, mechanisms, and ecology of non-conscious social behavior. *European Journal of Social Psychology, 36*, 147–168.

Bargh, J. A., Gollwitzer, P. M., Lee Chai, A., Barndollar, K., & Trötschel, R. (2001). The automated will: Non-conscious activation and pursuit of behavioral goals. *Journal of Personality and Social Psychology, 81*, 1014–1027.

Bargh, J. A., & Huang, J. Y. (2009). The selfish goal. In G. Moskowitz & H. Grant (Eds.), *Goals.* New York: Guilford Press.

Baumeister, R. F., & Leary, M. R. (1995). The need to belong: Desire for interpersonal attachments as a fundamental human motivation. *Psychological Bulletin, 117*, 475–482.

Bechara, A., Damasio, H., & Damasio, A. R. (2000). Emotion, decision making and the orbitofrontal cortex. *Cerebral Cortex, 10*, 295–307.

Berlyne, D. E. (1960). *Conflict, arousal and curiosity* New York: McGraw-Hill.

Bermeitinger, C., Goelz, R., Johr, N., Neumann, M., Ecker, U. K. H., & Doerr, R. (2009). The hidden persuaders break into the tired brain. *Journal of Experimental Social Psychology, 45*, 320–326.

Berridge, K. C. (2001). Reward learning: Reinforcement, incentives, and expectations. In D. L. Medin (Ed.), *The psychology of learning and motivation* (Vol. 40, pp. 223–278). New York: Academic Press.

Berridge, K. C. (2004). Motivation concepts in behavioral neuroscience. *Physiology and Behavior, 81*, 179–209.

Bijleveld, E., Custers, R., & Aarts, H. (in press). The unconscious eye opener: Pupil dilation reveals strategic recruitment of mental resources upon subliminal reward cues. *Psychological Science.*

Bindra, D. (1974). A motivational view of learning, performance, and behavior modification. *Psychological Review, 81*, 199–213.

Bishop, S. J. (2009). Trait anxiety and impoverished prefrontal control of attention. *Nature Neuroscience, 12*, 92–98.

Bolles, R. C. (1972). Reinforcement, expectancy, and learning. *Psychological Review, 79*, 394–409.

Bowlby, J. (1980). *Attachment and loss: Vol. 3. Loss.* New York: Basic Books.

Brehm, J. W., & Self, E. A. (1989). The intensity of motivation. *Annual Review of Psychology, 40*, 109–131.

Bruner, J. S. (1957). On perceptual readiness. *Psychological Review, 64*, 123–152.

Bruner, J. S., & Goodman, C. C. (1947). Value and need as organizing factors in perception. *Journal of Abnormal and Social Psychology, 42*, 33–44.

Bruner, J. S., & Postman, L. (1949). Perception, cognition, and behavior. *Journal of Personality, 18*, 14–31.

Bundesen, C., Habekost, T., & Kyllingsbaek, S. (2005). A neural theory of visual attention: Bridging cognition and neurophysiology. *Psychological Review, 112*, 291–328.

Cabanac, M. (1979). Sensory pleasure. *The Quarterly Review of Biology, 54*(1), 1–29.

Cacioppo, J. T., & Berntson, G. G. (1999). The affect system: Architecture and operating characteristics. *Current Directions in Psychological Science, 8*, 133–137.

Cannon, W. B. (1932). *The wisdom of the body*. New York: WW Norton.

Carpenter, W. B. (1874). *Principles of mental physiology*. London: Henry S. King.

Chaiken, S., & Trope, Y. (1999). *Dual-process theories in social psychology*. New York: Guilford Press.

Chartrand, T. L., & Bargh, J. A. (1999). The chameleon effect: The perception–behavior link and social interaction. *Journal of Personality and Social Psychology, 76*, 893–910.

Chartrand, T. L., Huber, J., Shiv, B., & Tanner, R. J. (2008). Non-conscious goals and consumer choice. *Journal of Consumer Research, 35*, 189–201.

Chen, C., & Chaiken, S. (1999) The Heuristic-Systematic Model in its broader context. In S. Chaiken & Y. Trope (Eds.), *Dual-process theories in social psychology* (pp. 73–96). New York: Guilford Press.

Cooper, S. J. (2008). From Claude Bernard to Walter Cannon. Emergence of the concept of homeostasis. *Appetite, 51*, 419–427.

Custers, R., & Aarts, H. (2005a). Beyond priming effects: The role of positive affect and discrepancies in implicit processes of motivation and goal pursuit. In M. Hewstone & W. Stroebe (Eds.), *European review of social psychology* (Vol. 16, pp. 257–300). Hove, UK: Psychology Press.

Custers, R., & Aarts, H. (2005b). Positive affect as implicit motivator: On the non-conscious operation of behavioral goals. *Journal of Personality and Social Psychology, 89*, 129–142.

Custers, R., & Aarts, H. (2007). In search of the non-conscious sources of goal pursuit: Accessibility and positive affective valence of the goal state. *Journal of Experimental Social Psychology, 43*, 312–318.

Damasio, A. R. (1994). *Descartes' error: Emotion, reason, and the human brain*. New York: Putnam.

Davidson, A. (1999). *The Oxford companion to food*. Oxford, UK: Oxford University Press.

Deci, E. L., & Ryan, R. M. (1985). *Intrinsic motivation and self-determination in human behaviour*. New York: Plenum Press.

Deci, E. L., & Ryan, R. M. (2000). The "what" and "why" of goal pursuits: Human needs and the self-determination of behavior. *Psychological Inquiry, 11*, 227–268.

De Houwer, J. (2003). The extrinsic affective Simon task. *Experimental Psychology, 50*, 77–85.

De Houwer, J., Thomas, S., & Baeyens, F. (2001). Association learning of likes and dislikes: A review of 25 years of research on human evaluative conditioning. *Psychological Bulletin, 127*, 853–869.

Desimone, R., & Duncan, J. (1995). Neural mechanisms of selective visual attention. *Annual Review of Neuroscience, 18*, 193–222.

Dijksterhuis, A., & Aarts, H. (2003). On wildebeests and humans: The preferential detection of negative stimuli. *Psychological Science, 14*, 14–18.

Dijksterhuis, A., Chartrand, T. L., & Aarts, H. (2007). Effects of priming and perception on social behavior and goal pursuit. In J. A. Bargh (Ed.), *Social psychology and the unconscious: The automaticity of higher mental processes* (pp. 51–132). Philadelphia: Psychology Press.

Dik, G., & Aarts, H. (2007). Behavioral cues to others' motivation and goal pursuits: The perception of effort facilitates goal inference and contagion. *Journal of Experimental Social Psychology, 43*, 727–737.

Drobes, D. J., Miller, E. J., Hillman, C. H., Bradley, M. M., Cuthbert, B. N., & Lang, P. J. (2001). Food deprivation and emotional reactions to food cues: Implications for eating disorders. *Biological Psychology, 57*, 153–177.

Drobes, D. J., & Tiffany, S. T. (1997). Induction of smoking urge through imaginal and in vivo procedures: Physiological and self report manifestations. *Journal of Abnormal Psychology, 106,* 15–25.

Edmonds, D. E., & Gallistel, C. R. (1974). Parametric analysis of brain stimulation reward in the rat: III. Effect of performance variables on the reward summation function. *Journal of Comparative and Physiological Psychology, 87,* 876–883.

Eiser, J. R., & Stroebe, W. (1972). The effects of incidental stimulus variation on absolute judgments. In W. Stroebe (Ed.), *Categorization and social judgment* (Vol. 3, pp. 50–86). New York: Academic Press.

Fazio, R. H., Sanbonmatsu, D. M., Powell, M. C., & Kardes, F. R. (1986). On the automatic activation of attitudes. *Journal of Personality and Social Psychology, 50,* 229–238.

Fein, S., & Spencer, S. J. (1997). Prejudice as self-image maintenance: Affirming the self through derogating others. *Journal of Personality and Social Psychology, 73,* 31–44.

Ferguson, M. J. (2007). On the automatic evaluation of end-states. *Journal of Personality and Social Psychology, 92,* 596–611.

Ferguson, M. J., & Bargh, J. A. (2004). Liking is for doing: The effects of goal pursuit on non-conscious evaluation. *Journal of Personality and Social Psychology, 87,* 557–572.

Fishbach, A., & Ferguson, M. F. (2007). The goal construct in social psychology. In A. Kruglanski & E. T. Higgins (Eds.), *Social psychology: Handbook of basic principles* (pp. 490–515). New York: Guilford Press.

Fishbein, M., & Ajzen, I. (1975). *Belief, attitude, intention and behaviour: An introduction to theory and research.* Reading, MA: Addison-Wesley.

Fiske, S. T. (2004). *Social beings: A core motives approach to social psychology.* New York: Wiley.

Fitzsimons, J. T. (1972). Thirst. *Physiological Reviews, 52,* 468–529.

Fitzsimons, G. M., & Bargh, J. A. (2003). Thinking of you: Non-conscious pursuit of interpersonal goals associated with relationship partners. *Journal of Personality and Social Psychology, 84,* 148–163.

Förster, J., Liberman, N., & Friedman, R. S. (2007). Seven principles of goal activation: A systematic approach to distinguishing goal priming from priming of non-goal constructs. *Personality and Social Psychology Review, 11,* 211–233.

Geen, R. G. (1995). *Human motivation: A social psychological approach.* Pacific Grove, CA: Brooks/Cole Publishing Company.

Glenberg, A. M., & Kaschak, M. P. (2002). Grounding language in action. *Psychonomic Bulletin & Review, 9,* 558–565.

Gollwitzer, P. M. (1990). Action phases and mindsets. In R. M. Sorrentino & E. T. Higgins (Eds.), *Handbook of motivation and cognition.* New York: Guilford Press.

Gollwitzer, P. M. (1993). Goal achievement: The role of intentions. In W. Stroebe & M. Hewstone (Eds.), *European review of social psychology* (Vol. 4, pp. 141–185). Chichester, UK: Wiley.

Gollwitzer, P. M., & Moskowitz, G. B. (1996). Goal effects on action and cognition. In E. Higgins & A. W. Kruglanski (Eds.), *Social psychology: Handbook of basic principles* (pp. 361–399). New York: Guilford Press.

Goschke, T., & Kuhl, J. (1993). Representation of intentions: Persisting activation in memory. *Journal of Experimental Psychology: Learning, Memory, and Cognition, 19,* 1211–1226.

Gottfried, J., O'Doherty, J., & Dolan, R. J. (2003) Encoding predictive reward value in human amygdala and orbitofrontal cortex. *Science, 301,* 1104–1107.

Gray, J. A. (1987). *The psychology of fear and stress* (2nd ed.). New York: Cambridge University Press.

Greenwald, A. G. (1970). Sensory feedback mechanisms in performance control: With special reference to the ideo-motor mechanism. *Psychological Review, 77,* 73–99.

Grouzet, F. M., Kasser, T., Ahuvia, A., Dols, J. M. F., Kim, Y., et al. (2005). The structure of goal contents across 15 cultures. *Journal of Personality and Social Psychology, 89*, 800–816.

Harlow, H. (1958). The nature of love. *American Psychologist, 13*, 673–685.

Hassin, R., Aarts, H., & Ferguson, M. J. (2005). Automatic goal inferences. *Journal of Experimental Social Psychology, 41*, 129–140.

Higgins, E. T. (2000). Making a good decision: Value from fit. *American Psychologist, 55*, 1217–1230.

Higgins, E. T. (2006). Value from hedonic experience *and* engagement. *Psychological Review, 113*, 439–460.

Holland, R. W., Hendriks, M., & Aarts, H. (2005). Smells like clean spirit. Non-conscious effects of scent on cognition and behavior. *Psychological Science, 16*, 689–693.

Holland, R. W., Veling, H., & Aarts, H. (2008). *The smell of pursuit: The role of olfactory cues in the regulation and motivation of social behavior.* Manuscript submitted for publication.

Holland, R. W., Wennekers, A. M., Bijlstra, G., Jongenelen, M. M., & Van Knippenberg, A. (2009). Self-symbols as implicit motivators. *Social Cognition, 27*, 581–602.

Hull, C. L. (1931). Goal attraction and directing ideas conceived as habit phenomena. *Psychological Review, 38*, 487–506.

Hulshof, K. F. A. M., Ocke, M. C., van Rossum, C. T. M., Buurma-Rethans, E. J. M., Brants, H. A. M., Drijvers, J. J. M. M., et al. (2004). *Resultaten van de voedselconsumptie 2003* [Results of food consumption 2003]. Bilthoven: RIVM rapport 350030002.

Isen, A. M., & Diamond, G. A. (1989). Affect and automaticity. In J. S. Uleman & J. A. Bargh (Eds.), *Unintended thought* (pp. 124–152). New York: Guilford Press.

James, W. (1890). *The principles of psychology* (Vol. 1). New York: Holt.

Jones, B. T., Bruce, G., Livingstone, S., & Reed, E. (2006). Alcohol-related attentional bias in problem drinkers with the flicker change blindness paradigm. *Psychology of Addictive Behaviors, 20*, 171–177.

Kahneman, D. (1973). *Attention and effort*. Englewood Cliffs, NJ: Prentice-Hall.

Kant, I. (2004). *Fundamental principles of the metaphysics of morals* (Trans. T. K. Abbott). Whitefish, MT: Kessinger Publishing. [Original work published 1785.]

Karremans, J. C., Stroebe, W., & Claus, J. (2006). Beyond Vicary's fantasies: The impact of subliminal priming and brand choice. *Journal of Experimental Social Psychology, 42*, 792–798.

Kay, A. C., & Ross, L. (2003). The perceptual push: The interplay of implicit cues and explicit situational construals on behavioral intentions in the Prisoner's Dilemma. *Journal of Experimental Social Psychology, 39*, 634–643.

Krosnick, J. A., Betz, A. L., Jussim, L. J., Lynn, A. R., & Stephens, L. (1992). Subliminal conditioning of attitudes. *Personality and Social Psychology Bulletin, 18*, 152–162.

Kruglanski, A. W., & Chun, W. Y. (2008). Motivated closed-mindedness and its social consequences. In J. Y. Shah & W. L. Gardner, *Handbook of motivation science* (pp. 84–99). New York: Guilford Press.

Kunda, Z., & Spencer, S. J. (2003). When do stereotypes come to mind and when do they color judgment? *Psychological Bulletin, 129*, 522–544.

Kuykendall, D., & Keating, J. P. (1990). Altering thoughts and judgments through repeated association. *British Journal of Psychology, 29*, 79–86.

Lang, P. J. (1995). The emotion probe: Studies of motivation and attention. *American Psychologist, 50*, 372–385.

Le Doux, J. (1996). *The emotional brain*. New York: Simon & Schuster.

Le Magnen, J. (1985). *Hunger*. Cambridge, UK: Cambridge University Press.

Lewin, K. (1935). *A dynamic theory of personality: Selected papers*. New York: McGraw-Hill.

Locke, E. A., & Latham, G. P. (1990). *A theory of goal setting and task performance*. Englewood Cliffs, NJ: Prentice Hall.

Loersch, C., Aarts, H., Payne, B. K., & Jefferis, V. E. (2008). The influence of social groups on goal contagion. *Journal of Experimental Social Psychology, 44*, 1555–1558.

Marsh, R. L., Hicks, J. L., & Bink, M. L. (1998). Activation of completed, uncompleted, and partially completed intentions. *Journal of Experimental Psychology: Learning, Memory, and Cognition, 24*, 350–361.

Maslow, A. H. (1943). A theory of human motivation. *Psychological Review, 50*, 370–396.

Maslow, A. H. (1970). *Motivation and personality*. New York: Harper & Row.

McClelland, D. C. (1951). *Personality*. New York: Holt, Rinehart & Winston.

McClelland, D. C., & Atkinson, J. W. (1948). The projective expression of needs: 1. The effect of different intensities of the hunger drive on perception. *The Journal of Psychology, 25*, 205–222.

McDougall, W. (1908). *Introduction to social psychology*. London: Methuen.

Milgram, N. W. (1979). On the inadequacy of a homeostatic model: Where do we go from here? *Behavioral and Brain Sciences, 2*, 111–112.

Milgram, N. W., Krames, L., & Thompson, R. (1974). Influence of drinking history on food-deprived drinking in the rat. *Journal of Comparative and Physiological Psychology, 87*, 126–133.

Mogg, K., Bradley, B. P., Hyare, H., & Lee, S. (1998). Selective attention to food-related stimuli in hunger: Are attentional biases specific to emotional and psychopathological states, or are they also found in normal drive states? *Behavior Research and Therapy, 36*, 227–237.

Mook, D. G. (1996). *Motivation: The organization of action*. New York: WW Norton.

Mook, D. G., & Cseh, C. L. (1981). Release of feeding by the sweet taste in rats: The influence of body weight. *Appetite, 2*, 15–34.

Moskowitz, G. B., Li, P., & Kirk, E. R. (2004). The implicit volition model: On the preconscious regulation of temporarily adopted goals. In M. P. Zanna (Ed.), *Advances in experimental social psychology* (Vol. 36, pp. 317–404). New York: Academic Press.

Murray, H. A. (1938). *Explorations in personality*. New York: Oxford University Press.

Nisbett, R. E., & Wilson, T. D. (1977). Telling more than we know: Verbal reports on mental processes. *Psychological Review, 84*, 231–259.

Oettingen, G. (2000). Expectancy effects on behavior depend on self-regulatory thought. *Social Cognition, 18*, 101–129.

Olds, J. (1958). Self-stimulation of the brain. *Science, 127*, 315–324.

Olds, J., & Milner, P. (1954). Positive reinforcement produced by electrical stimulation of the septal area and other regions of rat brain. *Journal of Comparative and Physiological Psychology, 47*, 419–427.

Packard, M. G., Cornell, A. H., & Alexander, G. M. (1997). Rewarding affective properties of intra-accumbens injections of testosterone. *Behavioral Neuroscience, 111*, 219–224.

Pessiglione, M., Schmidt, L., Draganski, B., Kalisch, R., Lau, H., Dolan, R. J., et al. (2007). How the brain translates money into force: A neuroimaging study of subliminal motivation. *Science, 316*, 904–906.

Petty, R. E., Wegener, D. T., & Fabrigar, L. R. (1997). Attitudes and attitude change. *Annual Reviews in Psychology, 48*, 609–647.

Phelps, E. A. (2005). The interaction of emotion and cognition. In L. F. Barrett, P. M. Niedenthal, & P. Winkielman (Eds.), *Emotion and consciousness*. New York: Guilford Press.

Pinel, J. P. J., Assanand, S., & Lehman, D. R. (2000). Hunger, eating, and ill health. *American Psychologist, 55*, 1105–1116.

Pittman, T. S., & Zeigler, K. R. (2007). Basic human needs. In A. Kruglanski & E. T. Higgins (Eds.), *Social psychology: Handbook of basic principles* (pp. 473–489). New York: Guilford Press.

Prinz, J. J., & Barsalou, L. W. (2000). Steering a course for embodied representation. In E. Dietrich & A. Markman (Eds.), *Cognitive dynamics: Conceptual change in humans and machines* (pp. 51–77). Cambridge, MA: MIT Press.

Prinz, W. (1997). Perception and action planning. *European Journal of Cognitive Psychology, 9,* 129–154.

Pulvermüller, F. (2005). Brain mechanisms linking language and action. *Nature Reviews Neuroscience, 6,* 576–582.

Raynor, H. A., & Epstein, L. H. (2003). The relative-reinforcing value of food under differing levels of food deprivation and restriction. *Appetite, 40,* 15–24.

Read, P. P. (1996). *Alive: The story of survivors.* New York: Mass Market Paperback/J.B. Lippincott Co.

Reiss, S. (2004). Multifaceted nature of intrinsic motivation: The theory of 16 basic desires. *Review of General Psychology, 8,* 179–193.

Reiss, S., & Havercamp, S. M. (1998). Toward a comprehensive assessment of fundamental motivation: Factor structure of Reiss Profile. *Psychological Assessment, 10,* 97–106.

Rolls, B. J., Rolls, E. T., Rowe, E. A., & Sweeney, K. (1981). Sensory specific satiety in man. *Physiology and Behavior, 27,* 137–142.

Rolls, B. J., Wood, R. J., Rolls, E. T., Lind, H., Lind, W., & Ledingham, J. G. G. (1980). Thirst following water deprivation in humans. *American Journal of Physiology: Regulatory, Integrative and Comparative Physiology, 239,* 476–482.

Rudski, J. M., Billington, C. J., & Levine, A. S. (1994). Naloxone's effects on operant responding depend upon level of deprivation. *Pharmacology, Biochemistry and Behavior, 49,* 377–383.

Russell, J. A. (2003). Core affect and the psychological construction of emotion. *Psychological Review, 110,* 145–172.

Schneirla, T. C. (1959). An evolutionary and developmental theory of biphasic processes underlying approach and withdrawal. In M. R. Jones (Ed.), *Nebraska Symposium on Motivation* (pp. 1–42). Lincoln, NE: University of Nebraska Press.

Seibt, B., Häfner, M., & Deutsch, R. (2007). Prepared to eat: how immediate affective and motivational responses to food cues are influenced by food deprivation. *European Journal of Social Psychology, 37,* 359–379.

Senko, C., Durik, A. M., & Harackiewicz, J. M. (2008). Historical perspectives and new directions in achievement goal theory: Understanding the effects of mastery and performance-approach goals. In J. Y. Shah & W. L. Gardner, *Handbook of motivation science* (pp. 100–113). New York: Guilford Press.

Serences, J. T., & Yantis, S. (2006). Selective visual attention and perceptual coherence. *Trends in Cognitive Sciences, 10,* 38–45.

Shah, J. Y. (2003). Automatic for the people: How representations of significant others implicitly affect goal pursuit. *Journal of Personality and Social Psychology, 84,* 661–681.

Sheldon, K. M., Elliot, A. J., Kim, Y., & Kasser, T. (2001). What is satisfying about satisfying events? Testing 10 candidate psychological needs. *Journal of Personality and Social Psychology, 80,* 325–339.

Shimp, T. A., Stuart, E. W., & Engle, R. W. (1991). A program of classical conditioning: Experiments testing variations in the conditioned stimulus and context. *Journal of Consumer Research, 18,* 1–12.

Shizgal, P. (1997). Neural basis of utility estimation. *Current Opinion in Neurobiology, 7,* 198–208.

Shizgal, P. (1999). On the neural computation of utility: Implications from studies of brain stimulation reward. In D. Kahneman, E. Diener, & N. Schwarz (Eds.), *Well-being: The foundations of hedonic psychology* (pp. 502–526). New York: Russel Sage.

Strack, F., & Deutsch, R. (2004). Reflective and impulsive determinants of social behavior. *Personality and Social Psychology Review*, *8*, 220–247.

Strahan, E. J., Spencer, S. J., & Zanna, M. P. (2002). Subliminal priming and persuasion: Striking when the iron is hot. *Journal of Experimental Social Psychology*, *38*, 556–568.

Tajfel, H. (1957). Value and the perceptual judgment of magnitude. *Psychological Review*, *64*, 192–204.

Tajfel, H. (1959). The anchoring effects of value in a scale of judgments. *British Journal of Psychology*, *50*, 294–304.

Thompson, S. C., & Schlehofer, M. M. (2008). The many sides of control motivation: Motives for high, low, and illusory control. In J. Y. Shah & W. L. Gardner, *Handbook of motivation science* (pp. 41–56). New York: Guilford Press.

Toates, F. M. (1986). *Motivational systems*. Cambridge, UK: Cambridge University Press.

Tostain, J. L., & Blanc, F. (2008). Testosterone deficiency: A common, unrecognized syndrome. *Nature Clinical Practice Urology*, *5*, 388–396.

Tucker, M., & Ellis, R. (1998). On the relations of seen objects and components of potential actions. *Journal of Experimental Psychology: Human Perception and Performance*, *24*, 830–846.

Veling, H., & Aarts, H. (2009). Putting behavior on hold decreases reward value of need-instrumental objects outside of awareness. *Journal of Experimental Social Psychology*, *45*, 1020–1023.

Veltkamp, M., Aarts, H., & Custers, R. (2008a). On the emergence of deprivation-reducing behaviors: Subliminal priming of behavior representations turns deprivation into motivation. *Journal of Experimental Social Psychology*, *44*, 866–873.

Veltkamp, M., Aarts, H., & Custers, R. (2008b). Perception in the service of goal pursuit: Motivation to attain goals enhances the perceived size of goal-instrumental objects. *Social Cognition*, *26*, 720–736.

Veltkamp, M., Custers, R., & Aarts, H. (2009). *On subliminal persuasion: The role of needs and evaluative conditioning in motivating behaviour*. Manuscript submitted for publication.

Watson, D., & Clark, L. A. (1992). Affects separable and inseparable: On the hierarchical arrangement of the negative affects. *Journal of Personality and Social Psychology*, *62*, 489–505.

Watson, J. B. (1925). *Behaviorism*. New York: People's Institute.

Watt, D. F. (1998). Affect and the limbic system: Some hard problems [Commentary]. *Journal of Neuropsychiatry*, *10*, 113–116.

Wegner, D. M. (2002). *The illusion of conscious will*. Cambridge, MA: MIT Press.

Wheeler, S. C., DeMarree, K. G., & Petty, R. E. (2007). Understanding the role of the self in prime-to-behavior effects: The active-self account. *Personality and Social Psychology Review*, *11*, 234–261.

Wilson, T. D., Lindsey, S., & Schooler, T. (2000). A model of dual attitudes. *Psychological Review*, *107*, 101–126.

Winkielman, P., & Berridge, K. C. (2004). Unconscious emotion. *Current Directions in Psychological Science*, *13*, 120–123.

Wolf, A. V. (1958). *Thirst: Physiology of the urge to drink and problems of water lack*. Springfield, IL: Charles C. Thomas Publisher.

Wood, W., Quinn, J. M., & Kashy, D. A. (2002). Habits in everyday life: Thought, emotion, and action. *Journal of Personality and Social Psychology*, *83*, 1281–1297.

Young, P. T. (1961). *Motivation and emotion*. New York: John Wiley & Sons.

Zajonc, R. B. (1980). Feeling and thinking: Preferences need no inferences. *American Psychologist*, *35*, 151–175.

Zwaan, R. A., & Taylor, L. J. (2006). Seeing, acting, understanding: Motor resonance in language comprehension. *Journal of Experimental Psychology: General*, *135*, 1–11.

Author index

Aarts, H., 103, 104, 105, 106, 108, 110, 316, 332, 339, 346, 347, 348, 350, 351, 352, 353, 356, 357, 358, 360, 361, 362, 363, 364, 365, 366, 367, 368, 369, 370, 371, 373, 374
Abelson, R. P., 56, 165
Abramson, L. Y., 4, 16, 25, 35
Achee, J. W., 336
Adelmann, P. K., 256
Adolphs, R., 193, 210, 217, 241, 253, 256
Aggleton, J. P., 217
Ahern, S., 361
Ahuvia, A., 353
Ajzen, I., 317, 346, 370
Alexander, G. M., 365
Alexander, M. G., 209
Alfieri, T., 169
Alicke, M. D., 2, 11, 14, 15, 22, 27, 28, 30, 32, 33, 34
Allen, T., 304, 306
Allik, J., 25
Allport, G. W., 3, 97, 99, 136, 201
Amaral, D. G., 217
Ambady, N., 212
Amodio, D. M., 121, 195
Andersen, S. M., 152
Anderson, C. A., 26
Anderson, D., 306
Anderson, J. R., 163, 164
Anderson, S., 217
Andrew, C., 250
Ansay, C., 61
Ansell, E., 23
Antoun, N., 217
Appiah, K. A., 200
Areni, A., 160
Arkes, H. R., 340
Arndt, J., 16, 26, 27, 36
Arnold, M. B., 234
Aronson, E., 3, 35, 36, 56, 127
Aronson, J. A., 206
Asch, S. E., 212
Ashburn-Nardo, L., 127, 128
Ashmore, R. D., 327
Aspinwall, L. G., 336

Assanand, S., 354, 367
Asuncion, A. G., 55
Atkinson, A. P., 256
Atkinson, J. W., 2, 316, 318, 346, 355
Avramova, Y. R., 241
Ayton, P., 340

Baeyens, F., 162, 363
Bailenson, J., 85
Bailey, J., 56
Bain, P., 201, 202
Baker, S. M., 80, 81
Balcetis, E., 352
Banaji, M. R., 25, 98, 99, 108, 197
Bandura, A., 321, 346, 370
Bar, R., 177
Bar-Tal, D., 60, 147, 158, 175, 176, 178, 201
Barbano, M. F., 367
Barden, J., 65, 87, 90
Bargh, J. A. 85, 98, 99, 102, 103, 105, 106, 109, 110, 117, 127, 130, 235, 238, 245, 250, 258, 259, 263, 264, 273, 274, 316, 347, 349, 350, 351, 352, 355, 356, 358, 363, 368, 370, 371
Barlow, D. H., 336
Barndollar, K., 106, 130, 349, 350, 356, 363, 371
Baron, R. M., 154
Baron-Cohen, S., 217
Barrett, L. F., 234, 236
Barron, K. E., 109
Barsalou, L. W., 349
Bartlett, F. C., 164
Bastian, B., 202
Batchelder, W. H., 300
Batson, C. D., 22, 198, 211, 221
Batts, V., 57
Baumeister, R. F., 12, 15, 16, 17, 27, 36, 101, 290, 332, 353, 354, 372, 273
Baxter, L. C., 197
Bazinska, R., 209
Beatty, J., 361
Beauregard, K. S., 15, 28, 107
Becerra, A., 82, 83, 88

Subject index

Contents of Volumes 11–20

Volume 12, 2002

Volume 13, 2002*

Volume 14, 2003

*Two volumes published in 2002.

Volume 17, 2006

Volume 18, 2007

Volume 20, 2009